107

Contents

P9-CED-302

Introduction	4

Discover	6
Top 20	10
Itineraries	20
Berlin Today	30
Eating & Drinking	38
Shopping	50

Explore	58
Getting Started	60
Mitte	66
Tiergarten & Moabit	98
Prenzlauer Berg & Mitte North	114
Friedrichshain & Lichtenberg	130
Kreuzberg & Treptow	142
Neukölln	164
Charlottenburg & Schöneberg	176
West of the Centre	194

Experience	208
Events	210
Film	216
LGBT	224
Nightlife	236
Performing Arts	248

Understand	258
History	260
Architecture	280

Plan	292
Accommodation	294
Getting Around	302
Resources A-Z	305
Vocabulary	312
Further Reading	313
Index	315

Introduction

The German capital is home to approximately 3.6 million inhabitants and welcomes five million visitors per year; a number that is set to rise with Berlin's increasing popularity as a tourist destination. However, the city rarely feels cramped. Sprawling across nearly 900 square kilometres, Berlin is nine times larger than Paris, closer in size to New York, but, with half the population of the Big Apple and 12 times fewer annual visitors, it can sometimes feel more like a village... sometimes like a reclaimed, post-apocalyptic metropolis.

It's not just the lack of crowds that makes the city appear sparse; from the remaining symbols of Prussian greatness to the brutalist remnants of GDR town-planning, the style of Berlin's architecture and the weight of its history can seem to overshadow its citizens. Fortunately, the city's vast reach means there's plenty of room for green spaces too: Tiergarten, Tempelhofer Feld and countless neighbourhood parks offer respite from the concrete urban environment and from reminders of the city's fascinating but troubled past.

As in any other city, public transport is best avoided at rush hour, supermarket queues can be atrocious, finding a table for brunch, especially on a Saturday, is nigh-on impossible, and there's always something sticky on the steps leading down to the U-Bahn. But there's ample compensation to be found in Berlin's first-rate museums and cutting-edge galleries, its street food and flea markets, third-wave coffee and vegan doughnuts, kite-flying and roller-blading, impeccable orchestras and trail-blazing techno. Above all, it's the anything-goes attitude of this über-cool city that is sure to win you over.

Berlin

timeout.com / berlin

139

ONE WEEK WITH

187

Tiergarten *p103*

ABOUT THE GUIDE

This is one of a series of Time Out guidebooks to cities across the globe. Written by local experts, our guides are thoroughly researched and meticulously updated. They aim to be inspiring, irreverent, well-informed and trustworthy.

Time Out Berlin is divided into five sections: Discover, Explore, Experience, Understand and Plan.

Discover introduces the city and provides inspiration for your visit.

Explore is the main sightseeing section of the guide and includes detailed listings and reviews for sights and museums, restaurants & cafés ⑩, bars & pubs ⑩, and shops & services ⑩, all organised by area with a corresponding street map. To help navigation, each area of Berlin has been assigned its own colour.

Experience covers the cultural life of the city in depth, including festivals, film, LGBT, music, nightlife, theatre and more.

Understand provides in-depth background information that places Berlin in its historical and cultural context.

Plan offers practical visitor information, including accommodation options and details of public transport.

Hearts

We use hearts 💙 to pick out venues, sights and experiences in the city that we particularly recommend. The very best of these are featured in the Top 20 (*see p10*) and receive extended coverage in the guide.

Maps

A detachable fold-out map can be found on the inside back cover. There's also an overview map (*see p8*) and individual streets maps for each area of the city. The venues featured in the guide have been given a grid reference so that you can find them easily on the maps and on the ground.

Prices

All our **restaurant listings** are marked with a euro symbol category from budget to blow-out (€-€€€€), indicating the price you should expect to pay for an average main course: € = under €10; €€ = €11-€20; €€€ = €21-€30; €€€€ = over €30.

A similar system is used in our **Accommodation** chapter based on the hotel's standard prices for one night in a double room: **Budget** = under €70; **Moderate** = €70-€120; **Expensive** = €120-€190; **Luxury** = over €190.

Discover

Top 20	**10**
Itineraries	**20**
Berlin Today	**30**
Eating & Drinking	**38**
Shopping	**50**

Brandenburger Tor

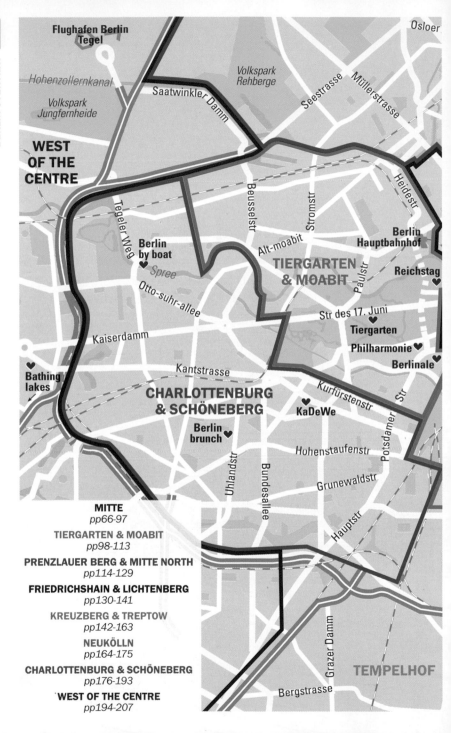

Flughafen Berlin Tegel

Hohenzollernkanal

Volkspark Rehberge

Volkspark Jungfernheide

Seestrasse

Müllerstrasse

Osloer

Saatwinkler Damm

WEST OF THE CENTRE

Beusselstr

Stromstr

Heidestr

Tegeler Weg

Berlin by boat ♥

Spree

Otto-suhr-allee

Alt-moabit

TIERGARTEN & MOABIT

Paulstr

Berlin Hauptbahnhof

Reichstag ♥

Str des 17. Juni ♥

Tiergarten

Kaiserdamm

Kantstrasse

Philharmonie ♥

Berlinale ♥

♥ Bathing lakes

CHARLOTTENBURG & SCHÖNEBERG

Berlin brunch ♥

KaDeWe

Kurfürstenstr

Str

Potsdamer

Uhlandstr

Bundesallee

Hohenstaufenstr

Grunewaldstr

Hauptstr

MITTE
pp66-97

TIERGARTEN & MOABIT
pp98-113

PRENZLAUER BERG & MITTE NORTH
pp114-129

FRIEDRICHSHAIN & LICHTENBERG
pp130-141

KREUZBERG & TREPTOW
pp142-163

NEUKÖLLN
pp164-175

CHARLOTTENBURG & SCHÖNEBERG
pp176-193

WEST OF THE CENTRE
pp194-207

Grazer Damm

TEMPELHOF

Bergstrasse

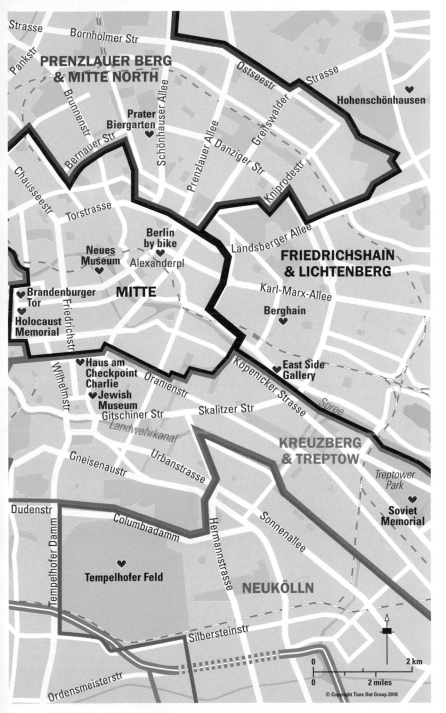

Strasse
Bornholmer Str
Pankstr

PRENZLAUER BERG & MITTE NORTH

Brunnenstr
Bernauer Str
Chausseestr

Ostseestr
Strasse

Schönhauser Allee

Prater Biergarten

Prenzlauer Allee

Danziger Str

Greifswalder

Kniprodestr

♥ Hohenschönhausen

Torstrasse

Berlin by bike

Neues Museum ♥

Alexanderpl

Landsberger Allee

FRIEDRICHSHAIN & LICHTENBERG

MITTE

Friedrichstr

Karl-Marx-Allee

♥ Brandenburger Tor

♥ Holocaust Memorial

Berghain ♥

Wilhelmstr

♥ Haus am Checkpoint Charlie

Oranienstr

Köpenicker Strasse

♥ East Side Gallery

Spree

♥ Jewish Museum

Gitschiner Str

Skalitzer Str

Landwehrkanal

Gneisenaustr

Urbanstrasse

KREUZBERG & TREPTOW

Treptower Park

Dudenstr

Columbiadamm

Sonnenallee

♥ Soviet Memorial

Tempelhofer Damm

Hermannstrasse

♥ Tempelhofer Feld

NEUKÖLLN

Silbersteinstr

Ordensmeisterstr

0   2 km
0   2 miles

© Copyright Time Out Group 2018

9

Top 20

*Berlin's best, from museums and
memorials to biking and bathing*

01 Reichstag

02 Brandenburger Tor

03 Neues Museum

04 Tiergarten

05 Soviet Memorial
     (Sowjetisches Ehrenmal am Treptower Park)

06 Holocaust Memorial
     (Denkmal für die ermordeten Juden Europas)

07 Haus am Checkpoint Charlie

08 Tempelhofer Feld

09 Gedenkstätte Berlin-Hohenschönhausen

10 East Side Gallery

11 Jüdisches Museum

12 Philharmonie

13 KaDeWe

14 Berlin by boat

15 Berlinale

16 Berlin's bathing lakes

17 Berghain

18 Berlin brunch

19 Berlin by bike

20 Prater Biergarten

01

Reichstag *p105*

This neo-Baroque edifice housing
the German Bundestag (Parliament)
survived wars, Nazis, fire, bombing
and the country's division, only to
return as a symbol of a new era in
German politics. A tour around the
iconic dome, designed by Sir Norman
Foster, is thoroughly recommended.

02

Brandenburger Tor *p71*

Berlin's long-suffering victory arch, the Brandenburg Gate, served as a visual flashpoint for much of the trauma to have beset Germany in the 20th century – standing alone in no-man's-land during the GDR era and providing the backdrop to the euphoria of 1989. Restored to its rightful place at the heart of the city, this monument to unity is a must-see on any Berlin itinerary.

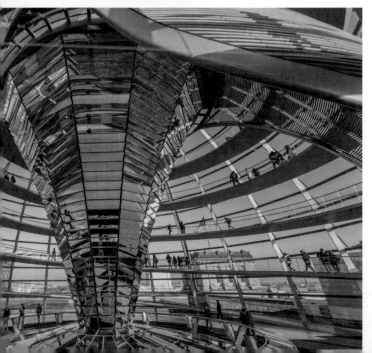

03

Neues Museum *p75*

It's hard to pick just one of the five museums on Berlin's UNESCO-listed Museumsinsel, but the Neues Museum is an unmissable highlight. David Chipperfield's award-winning rebuild is a suitably stunning home for a treasure trove of artefacts from pre-, early and ancient history, including the Ancient Egyptian bust of Queen Nefertiti.

04

Tiergarten *p103*

This vast park in the heart of the city comes into its own during spring and summer, when you can happily lose yourself amid its woodlands, lakes and miles of greenery.

05

Soviet Memorial *p162*

One of Berlin's most impressive public monuments, this memorial to Soviet soldiers killed in World War II is located in a peaceful riverside park. It's as bombastic and intimidating as you would expect.

06

Holocaust Memorial *p73*

Architect Peter Eisenman's Memorial to the Murdered Jews of Europe (Denkmal für die ermordeten Juden Europas) is intentionally disorienting; a striking sculptural statement that invites visitors in, only to create a feeling of unease. It is rightfully at the forefront of the city's attempts to come to terms with its past.

07

Haus am Checkpoint Charlie *p147*

Once the flashpoint between East and West, today the former Checkpoint Charlie border crossing offers tacky souvenir stalls, coachloads of trippers, and actors pretending to be US and Soviet guards. But it also features this intriguing little museum.

08

Tempelhofer Feld *p173*

The vast 1920s airport west of Neukölln now stands empty, but the surrounding airfields and runways have become a huge park for cycling, kite-flying and open-air festivals.

09

Gedenkstätte Berlin-Hohenschönhausen *p140*

Former inmates of this Stasi internment facility lead chilling tours through the depths of their former jail, describing the horrors inflicted on them by the GDR's notorious secret police.

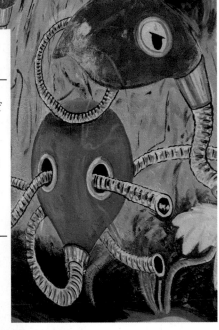

10

East Side Gallery *p135*

One of the few remaining strips of the Berlin Wall is still festooned with the murals that became iconic across the world after reunification. The riverside views are great, too.

11

Jüdisches Museum *p149*

Daniel Libeskind's beautiful, yet deliberately oppressive building houses a masterful museum devoted to the turbulent history of Judaism in Germany.

12

Philharmonie *p252*

Designed by architect Hans Scharoun and home to one of the best orchestras in the world, an evening spent in the Philharmonie is one of Berlin's most exquisite pleasures – if you can get a ticket.

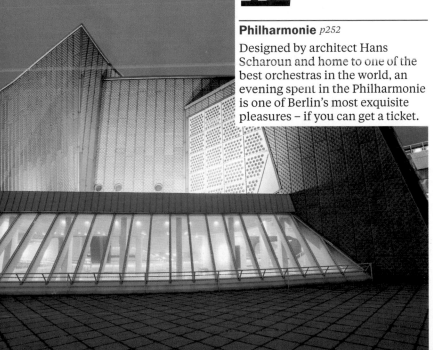

12

13

KaDeWe *p54*

The legendary department store is more than a century old and has stood at the heart of the city's shopping scene through thick and thin. Today it's as opulent as ever, especially the food hall on the sixth floor.

14

Berlin by boat *p186*

Winding through the centre of Berlin, the River Spree offers a different perspective on this once-divided city. There's no shortage of tour operators offering trips along the river, the Landwehrkanal or across the lakes, and some services are included on the city travelcard.

15

Berlinale *p218*

The Internationale Filmfestspiele (founded in 1951) is the world's most popular film festival, in terms of audience attendance figures. A major fixture on the global cultural calendar, it sees Potsdamer Platz transformed into a glittering stage of glamour, excitement and major movie stars each February.

16

Berlin's bathing lakes *p198*

It's the height of summer, the sun's beating down – where is everyone? They've packed a bike, a basket of beer and a towel and headed out on the S-Bahn to one of the dozens of lakes, large and small, that surround the city.

17

Berghain *p243*

Hour-long queues, intimidating bouncers and being told '*nicht heute*' ('not today') are all part and parcel of your initiation to this infamous temple to techno. If you run the gauntlet and get in, be prepared for a night, day and night again of dancing in a *Matrix*-esque, post-apocalyptic setting... with regular smoothie breaks, of course.

18

Berlin brunch *p192*

Brunch is the quintessential Berlin meal. Join the locals as they linger over top-notch coffee and all-day weekend menus that mix the best of a traditional German breakfast with flavours and influences from around the world.

19

Berlin by bike *p65*

'Berg' means mountain in German, but Prenzlauer Berg, Kreuzberg, Schöneberg et al have nothing more challenging than gentle inclines, plus kilometres of dedicated cycle paths, cyclist-wary drivers and countless bike-hire outlets, making this the ideal city in which to take to two wheels.

20

Prater Biergarten *p123*

Relaxing with friends, family, colleagues and fellow beer-drinkers in a huge, leafy garden is a fabulous way to while away a warm weekend. Pratergarten has one of the oldest and biggest beer gardens in the city and offers a congenial insight into German culture. Schnitzel, Wurst and Sauerkraut are optional but highly recommended.

COME
HERE YOU

Get to know the Berlin attractions
with pulling power, and book them
for less with Time Out.

Itineraries

Make the most of every Berlin moment with our tailored travel plans

ESSENTIAL WEEKEND

Budget €100-120 per day.
Getting around If you don't want to walk, either buy a day ticket for public transport (€7) or rent a bike (*see p65* Berlin by bike).

DAY 1

Morning

Sprawling **Tiergarten** park (*see p103*) is the green heart of Berlin. Strolling among the acres of grass, trees and lakes can easily swallow up a sunny day, but more dedicated sightseers should head to the **Siegessäule** (*see p104*) in the centre for magnificent views. From the monument, head down Lichtensteinallee for a hearty breakfast at the delightfully bucolic **Café am Neuen See** (*see p106*), then head east on Strasse des 17 Juni, past the Soviet Memorial, to the **Brandenburger Tor** (*see p71*) – one of the city's most recognisable icons. Just to the north is the equally famous **Reichstag** (*see p105*), seat of the German parliament; a visit to Norman Foster's dome is free, as long as you've booked online in advance. Return to the Brandenburg Gate and continue south on Ebertstrasse as far as the **Denkmal für die ermordeten Juden Europas** (*see p73*), a powerful memorial to victims of the Holocaust.

Siegessäule

Afternoon

Decent independent eateries are hard to find around here, so it's worth seeking out **Café Nö!** (*see p81*) for a spot of lunch before continuing down Ebertstrasse to **Potsdamer Platz** (*see p106*), home to an array of modern malls, cinemas and tower blocks. Get an express lift up to the **Panoramapunkt** observation decks (*see p110*) for another awesome view of the city. Then head east along the remains of the Wall at Niederkirchner Strasse to the infamous Checkpoint Charlie crossing point between East and West Berlin. Today, it's a tacky tourist mess of souvenir shops, kebab joints and coachloads of visitors, but it's still worth visiting the mini-museum at the **Haus am Checkpoint Charlie** (*see p147*). Heading down Friedrichstrasse, make a detour to the **Jüdisches Museum** (*see p149*) to experience Daniel Libeskind's striking and emotive architecture. To the south, boutiques and cafés are now mushrooming in Kreuzberg's Hallesches Tor district; check out **Hallesches Haus** (*see p152*) for a restorative coffee and some window-shopping, then a late-afternoon ramble along the **Landwehrkanal**.

Potsdamer Platz

Lode & Stijn

Evening

Now you're perfectly placed to sample the restaurants, cafés and bars of Kreuzkölln. Go high-end at **Eins44** (*see p169*) or **Lode & Stijn** (*see p157*), or get a Lebanese fast-food fix at **Azzam** (*see p166*). Once you're suitably fed, head for **Würgeengel** (*see p159*), an iconic cocktail bar which encapsulates the best of Berlin's nightlife: moody lighting, well-served cocktails and an ever-present haze of smoke. If you want to continue the party, check out the trendy **Prince Charles** club on Prinzenstrasse (*see p245*) or kitsch, queer and welcoming **Barbie Deinhoff**'s (*see p231*). Or, if you're feeling brave, taxi over to Friedrichshain to try your luck at **Berghain** (*see p243*).

DAY 2

Morning

There's no shortage of breakfast spots around Berlin and indulging in a long and lazy **brunch** is a Berlin experience not to be missed (*see p192*). After a hearty feed, you'll be ready for the **Museumsinsel** (Museum Island; *see p74*), Berlin's UNESCO-listed museum quarter. This is one of the city's most visited areas and it's easy to see why – the group of five major museums makes for an immersive cultural experience. You can't possibly visit them all in one morning, so make your choice between the Pergamonmuseum, with its examples of ancient architecture; the Altes Museum, brimming with antique treasures; the Alte Nationalgalerie for medieval art; the Bode-Museum for sculptures and Byzantine art, and the Neues Museum, with pieces from Ancient Egypt and early history.

Silo Coffee

Hackesche Höfe

Barcomi's

Afternoon

After the morning's cultural overload, wander a few steps north to the **Scheunenviertel** (*see p84*), a historic enclave of shops and cafés, many hidden in a maze-like warren of courtyards or *Höfe*; the most famous are the Jugendstil **Hackesche Höfe** (*see p85*). Refuel at **Moggs** (*see p92*), which serves up the hugest, juiciest salt-beef sandwiches this side of Lower Manhattan. Mitte's classy boutiques attract fashionistas to the area around Mulackstrasse and Alte Schönhauser Strasse; check out the likes of **Das Neue Schwarze** (*see p97*), **Lala Berlin** (*see p96*) and **DSTM** (*see p96*) for the definitive Berlin black, structured look. This district is also a gallery heartland; along **Auguststrasse** (*see p86*) are some of the coolest art spots in town. Enjoy coffee and cake at **Barcomi's** (*see p90*) before sauntering south to Alexanderplatz, the former hub of East Berlin during the GDR era. Remnants of the brutalist architecture of the day remain – most notably in the shape of the **Fernsehturm** (*see p88*), completed in 1969. It's worth braving the queues for a ride up to the observation deck and an early evening drink in the revolving café.

Fernsehturm

Evening

For dinner, head two stops north on the U8 to Rosenthaler Platz to check out the restaurants around Torstrasse: sample quality locavore dining at **Das Lokal** (*see p92*), Vietnamese *banh mí* at **Côcô** (*see p91*) or simple Middle Eastern fare at **Yarok** (*see p94*). There are plenty of bars here too, where you can round off the night in a blur of cocktails and dancing; for a selection, *see p94 and p239*. If you'd rather skip the bar hopping and hardcore partying (we don't blame you), you're well-placed to experience Berlin's rich cultural offering, with opera at the world-renowned **Komische Oper** (*see p251*), cutting-edge theatre at **Maxim Gorki Theater** (*see p255*) and the **Sophiensaale** (*see p256*), or circus acts and shimmying feather boas at **Chamäleon** (*see p256*).

Komische Oper

BUDGET BREAK

Budget €40-€50.
Getting around A day pass on public transport (€7) is the most cost-effective way of seeing the city. If you plan to visit several payable attractions, consider a discount card (*see p64*). Alternatively, hire a bike for around €10 per day. In general, summer is a better time to visit Berlin on a budget: street markets and strolls through the park are easier on the wallet than museum visits and shopping to escape the cold.

Morning

Brunch in Berlin won't break the bank and should keep you going for the rest of the day. **Silo Coffee** in Friedrichshain (*see p137*) serves hearty breakfasts for less than a tenner. From here, you can stroll through the street art and market stalls of the **RAW Gelände** (*see p134*) to **East Side Gallery** (*see p135*), where artists have decorated a stretch of the Berlin Wall. Enjoy views up and down the River Spree before crossing the picturesque Oberbaumbrücke into Kreuzberg. Continue east along the river, perhaps stopping in summer for a dip at the **Badeschiff** (*see p161*). Beyond the sculpture of the *Molecule Man* is **Treptower Park** (*see p161*), where you can stroll along the river and check out the impressive **Soviet War Memorial** (*see p162*) at the park's southern end.

Oberbaumbrücke

Badeschiff

Ankerklause

Türkischer Markt

Museumsinsel

Afternoon

A bike will come in handy for whizzing up to Neukölln for lunch. Don't miss the thriving Arabic food scene on Sonnenallee. At **Azzam** (*see p166*), a bowl of houmous the size of your head (plus pitta and veg) is under €4. If you're here on a Tuesday, Friday or Saturday, head for the Maybachufer to people-watch and nab a bargain at the **Türkischer Markt** (*see p171*). Time for some sightseeing? In Mitte, the **Deutscher Dom**, the **Französischer Dom**, the **Denkmal für die ermordeten Juden Europas** (*see p73*) and the **Brandenburger Tor** (*see p71*) are all free to visit. Alternatively, head north on the S-Bahn to Nordbahnhof to visit the **Gedenkstätte Berliner Mauer** (*see p125*) and learn about the political and physical division of the city.

Evening

In the warmer months, the best way to spend a summer evening is along one of Berlin's many waterways, sipping cold beer from a *Spätkauf*. On the Spree near Monbijou Park, you can watch the salsa dancing and go for a stroll across the **Museumsinsel** (*see p74*) at sunset. Or head to the **Landwehrkanal**, where the cobblestone Admiralbrücke draws street musicians and a vibrant crowd. From here, you have your pick of some cheap and cheerful restaurants – try pizza at **Il Casolare** or ramen at **Cocolo** (for both, *see p154*). There's plenty of unpretentious watering holes, too, such as the charming faux-nautical **Ankerklause** (*see p166*). In less clement weather, check *Index* (indexberlin.de) for listings of free gallery openings. And, if you want to go partying, head to cosy club **Süss war Gestern** (*see p243*): admission is free before 11pm and drinks are dangerously cheap.

FAMILY DAY OUT

Budget €200-€250 for a family of four.
Getting around Children under six
travel free on public transport. That's the
good news. The bad news is that many
stations still don't have lifts, so you'll
either need to carry buggies upstairs
yourself or rely on the kindness of
strangers. Buses, however, are designed
to tilt towards the pavement at each
stop, making it easy to get on with a
pushchair or pram, and all vehicles
have a designated parking area for
Kinderwagen. The M100 and M200 buses
are usually double-decker and run past
all the key tourist destinations. Kids
love sitting on the top deck and parents
love the price – just the cost of a normal
single ticket. Cycling is also an option.
There are cycle lanes all over town and
off-road paths weaving through the city's
parks. **Fat Tire Bikes** (Panoramastrasse
1A, Alexanderplatz, Mitte, 2404 7991,
www.berlinfahrradverleih.com) rents out
children's bikes, as well as bike trailers.

Deutsches Technikmuseum

Deutsches Technikmuseum Berlin

Morning

Finding somewhere child-friendly for
breakfast is never a problem in Berlin,
especially around Prenzlauer Berg,
and Kreuzberg. Seek out one of the
city's *Kindercafés*, which are especially
designed for families. **Kindercafe
Milchbart** (Paul-Robeson-Strasse
6, 6630 7755, www.milchbart.net) in
Prenzlauer Berg has its own climbing
area, sandbox and ball pond, plus
excellent coffee and healthy eats.
After breakfast, you could attempt
a museum. The **Bode Museum**
(*see p78*) is particularly good for
families as it houses an interactive
children's museum aimed at four- to
ten-year-olds. Nearby **Monbijou
Park** on Oranienburger Strasse – just
over the pedestrian bridge from the
Bode Museum – has playgrounds and,
in summer, a great paddling pool.
Alternatively, dinosaur fanatics will
enjoy the fossils and multimedia displays
at the **Museum für Naturkunde** (*see
p80*). Teens might prefer to head
to the **Computerspielemuseum** (*see
p136*) on Karl-Marx-Allee. Afterwards,
they can release some excess energy
at the **Raw Tempel** (Revaler Strasse
99, Friedrichshain), a sports and arts
complex housed in a dilapidated set of
old factories that includes **Der Kegel**
climbing centre (www.derkegel.de) and
the **Skatehalle** skateboarding centre
(www.skatehalle-berlin.de).

Afternoon

When you start feeling peckish, take the U7 to south-west Kreuzberg for a wide choice of food options. Try **Café Kreuzzwerg** (Hornstrasse 23, 9786 7609, www.cafe-kreuzzwerg.de) or **Café Blume** (Fontanestrasse 32, 6449 0778, www.blumeberlin.de) close to **Volkspark Hasenheide** (*see p151*). The park has an adventure playground, crazy golf course and small zoo. Also in this area is the huge supervised indoor playground **Jolo** (Am Tempelhofer Berg 7D, 6120 2796, www.jolo-berlin.de), where facilities include an inflatable mountain, mini bumper cars and a snack bar. And, to the south, is the vast expanse of **Tempelhofer Feld** (*see p173*), perfect for safe cycling, kite-flying and picnics. Once the kids have let off steam, make your way to the **Haus am Checkpoint Charlie** (*see p147*), which displays the old cars and balloons that people used to circumvent the Wall. There are fine views from the tethered balloon (*see p148*) nearby. Another option is to visit the **Deutsches Technikmuseum Berlin** (*see p148*) for vintage locomotives and cars, computers and gadgets, plus fantastic hands-on experiments. After that you're one stop on the U2 from Potsdamer Platz, where family-friendly attractions include the **aquarium** (*see p87*), **Legoland Discovery Centre** (*see p109*) and the **Panoramapunkt** observation deck (*see p110*).

Tempelhofer Feld

Museum für Naturkunde

Evening

Head back to Kreuzberg for dinner. Kids eat for free on Sundays at **Italian Osteria No.1** (*see p151*) and there's more family-friendly fare at **Tomasa Villa Kreuzberg** (*see p151*). For dessert, seek out some ice-cream at **Isabel's Eiscafé** (Böckstrasse 51, 6981 6832, www.eiscafe-isabel.berlin/) or **Fräulein Frost** (*see p169*). If you're ready for a child-free evening, there are a number of English-speaking babysitting agencies: **Babysitter-Express Berlin** (4000 3400, www.babysitter-express.de) operates a 24-hour hotline for all your childcare emergencies and **Kinderinsel** (4171 6928, www.kinderinsel.de/en) offers round-the-clock childcare for kids up to 14.

Museum für Naturkunde

When to Visit

Berlin by season

Spring

Even if the canals haven't totally thawed out yet, sun-starved Berliners come out in droves, determined to enjoy their coffee alfresco, coat or not. In April, the Japanese **Kirschblütenfest** (*see p212*) is a particular highlight. By May, Berlin is in full swing, with the riotous **May Day** (*see p212*) and, later, the buzzing **Karneval der Kulturen** (*see p213*) taking over the streets of Kreuzberg. All in all, late spring hits Berlin's sweet spot: not too hot, not too cold, not too crowded – local kids don't get out of school until July.

Summer

Summer is when Berlin really turns on the charm, though you won't have it all to yourself. Expect gorgeous days by the Spree and lots of company. However, the city is so spread out that the crowds are never overwhelming. The street festivals are a highlight, too: among the best are the **Fête de le Musique** *(see p213)*, **Christopher Street Day Parade** *(see p213)* and **Tanz im August** *(see p214)*. The huge number of free outdoor activities makes summer a great time for budget travellers, though accommodation prices are slightly higher from June to August. Don't forget your swimming costume to make the most of the lakes and outdoor pools.

Karneval der Kulturen

Berlin's lakes

Festival of Lights

Autumn

Summer weather can continue well into September and early October, with some lovely sunny days, peaking around the **Berlin Marathon** (*see p214*), but as November draws near, the climate becomes increasingly damp and cold – although the fog along the canals can be quite atmospheric. Skip Berlin's half-hearted attempt at Oktoberfest and enjoy, instead, a string of excellent cultural events, from **Berlin Art Week** (*see p214*) and the **International Literaturfest** (*see p214*) to the **Festival of Lights** (*see p215*). Hotel prices dip in autumn, before rising again towards Christmas.

Winter

There's plenty to admire about Berlin in winter. The cold weather, dark nights and frozen canals highlight Berlin's austere architecture and make the prospect of spending hours in the city's compelling museums all the more appealing. If loud noises and home-made fireworks aren't your thing, skip **Silvester** (New Year's Eve) and come earlier in December for **Christmas markets** (*see p215*), *Glühwein* and a lux day at the spa (see **Liquidrom** *p152*, **Vabali** *p113* and **Stadtbad Neukölln** *p175*). In February, the world-class **Berlinale** (*see p218*) brings international cinema and its attendant glamour to town.

Christmas market

Berlin Today

Growing pains in the German capital

The fifth of February 2018 marked the day the Berlin Wall had been down for longer than it was ever up. As the Wall becomes just another attraction for an increasing majority of tourists too young to remember 1989, and as the last traces of war and division are tidied away into museums, Berlin faces a new challenge. Can the city bring the same courage and imagination to bear on the challenges of the present, as it has shown in grappling with the trials of the past?

Reborn as a single entity in 1989 – with formal German reunification following a year later – Berlin has revelled in its role as the rebellious, anarchic teenager among major European cities for nearly three decades. Undoubtedly, it still retains a sense of rule-breaking freedom, vanishingly rare elsewhere on the continent. Clubs – with their wonderfully unpredictable door policies – never seem to close. You can still smoke in bars. You can still buy alcohol at any time of day or night. You can still sunbathe naked on a summer's day.

IM DIR WAS
BRAUCHST.

Saugut!

Why
Not?

feiern

LOVE IS POSSIBLE

M LIEGT
ALLES AUF
BODEN?"
ERKRAFT,
AMA"

I ♥
BERLIN

31

At the same time, however, the city's popularity as both a tourist destination and a place to live is driving significant change. The decades-long redevelopment of the Museumsinsel is slowly nearing completion; the nearby Staatsoper reopened in 2017, and the rebuilt Berliner Stadtschloss is due to open in 2019 (*see p33 Return of the Stadtschloss*), rounding off a breathtaking city-centre showcase of cultural institutions – though one, perhaps, that would be more familiar to residents of 19th-century Berlin than to anyone who grew up here in the 1980s or '90s.

Berlin is maturing into a world city, as most people would have it, and the evidence is visible everywhere: in the quantity and quality of the city's cultural offerings; in the number of languages heard on the streets (Berlin is home to half a million foreign nationals, hailing from 185 different countries); and in the sheer range of restaurants opening every week. Having confused *Currywurst* with gourmet cuisine for so many years, the city has now developed into a genuine 'foodie' destination, with fabulous restaurants that reflect an increased multiculturalism opening every week to sit alongside the perennially popular Vietnamese and Turkish establishments (*see p44*).

Smoking, graffiti and *Currywurst*: despite gentrification, some Berlin customs endure.

And that could be the end of the story. Indeed, visitors on a short trip may well conclude that, while remaining true to its progressive traditions, Berlin is nonetheless a serious international city. Returning visitors, however, might notice that things are not quite so rosy. For a start, they might wonder where all the space has gone. Ten years ago, Berlin was still a city of abandoned buildings and empty lots. No one talked about property the way they did in London or Paris. Everyone rented, and the people who lived in the coolest spaces, in the coolest locations, were there because they were the coolest people, not because they were the richest.

Return of the Stadtschloss

Recreating history

First built in the 15th century to establish the authority of the Margraves of Brandenburg over an uppity population, Berlin's *Stadtschloss* (City Palace) served as winter residence to various Electors of Brandenburg, then Kings of Prussia (1701–1871) and finally Emperors of Germany (1871–1918).

The *Schloss* changed dramatically over the centuries, developing from a fortified castle into a vast Protestant Baroque palace in the 18th century (following plans drawn up by the German architect Andreas Schlüter) and serving as the backdrop to several key moments in Prussian and German history. During the Revolution of 1848, huge crowds gathered outside to demand liberal reform; 70 years later, the Spartacus League leader, Karl Liebknecht, declared his German Socialist Republic from one of the balconies (see *p269*).

However, once the new Reichstag opened down the road in 1894, the palace lost its unofficial position as the symbolic centre of the German Empire and was largely side-lined for most of the 20th century. Between the wars, parts of the building were used as a museum; the National Socialists largely ignored the place, and the Allies reduced it to a burned-out shell during World War II.

In 1950, what remained of the palace was destroyed on the orders of the GDR government, who replaced it with the Palast der Republik (completed 1976). Of the original building, only the portal and balcony from which Karl Liebknecht had made his speech were preserved and later added to the façade of the new Council of State building. In 2003, the Palast der Republik was itself demolished, giving new impetus to already heated arguments over what should be done with the space. The final decision was to build a broadly faithful reconstruction of Schlüter's 18th-century palace to accommodate the newly formed Humboldt Forum. This cultural centre will rehouse the Ethnological and Asian Art museums from Dahlem (see *p203*) as well as a permanent exhibition on 'Berlin & the World' that includes an unflinching appraisal of German colonialism and modern-day issues around globalisation. The project has, of course, divided opinion. Cynics suggest that rebuilding the seat of Prussian Imperialism and then using it to house exhibitions on world cultures is a typical fudge, guaranteed to please no one, while idealists claim it will restore the unity and integrity of the historic centre of Berlin, at the same time as it continues the city's proud tradition of dealing courageously and openly with German history. The new/old City Palace is scheduled to open in late 2019; commentators and critics are already sharpening their pencils...

A Tale of Two Airports

Out with the old but 'when?' with the new

When the last commercial flight took off from Tempelhof Airport in 2008, the airfield quickly found a new lease of life as the world's largest inner-city park (*see p173*). Unsurprisingly, it wasn't long before the city government began to regret its generosity, attempting to sell large parts to developers in 2011. They would have gotten away with it, too, but for a petition organised by the 100% Tempelhofer Feld initiative, which gathered enough signatures to force the city into holding a referendum. When the votes were counted, over 64% had chosen to keep Tempelhof as it is, and this was a large enough majority to make the result legally binding. Politicians and investors threw up their hands in despair; Berliners threw up theirs in celebration.

But politicians, investors and residents are all joined in despair at the debacle that is Berlin Brandenburg Airport, a multi-billion-euro white elephant located 11 miles (18 kilometres) south of the city centre. Originally due to open in 2011 to replace both Berlin Tegel and Berlin Schönefeld airports, it is not now expected to start operation until 2020, or even 2021. A list of everything that has gone wrong – a faulty fire-safety system, a chief engineer who wasn't an engineer, lighting that couldn't be turned off, financial mismanagement, corruption, even controversy over the new airport's name – would fill a book longer than this, but, still, there's something oddly satisfying about the sheer scale of this balls-up: a characteristic Berlin subversion of the famously efficient German economic machine.

Now, with the fastest-rising property prices in the world (over 20% in 2017) and a population consistently growing by more than 50,000 people per year, Berlin has become a city of cranes, with every nook and cranny earmarked for development. The city's famous murals are disappearing: by the time you read this article, the triptych of political caricatures near Savigny Platz station will have vanished behind a block of 'micro-apartments', and the 'world tree' at Tiergarten will be obscured by a property developer's office. The pressure on space is starting to worry a city that prides itself on being different.

In its best image of itself, Berlin is a haven for people who feel excluded elsewhere. Since

With the property boom, Berlin has become a city of cranes, with every nook and cranny earmarked for development.

2015, and Angela Merkel's short-lived 'open door' policy, this has included thousands of refugees from the world's poorest and most war-ravaged countries. By and large, Berliners have offered a wonderfully generous welcome, though the integration and long-term future of Germany's newest residents remains a heated topic, particularly given the resurgence of far-right nationalist political parties. More generally, Berlin acts as a refuge for people who don't fit in to more conservative environments, and when the city lives up to its best image of itself, 'more conservative environments' basically describes the rest of the world. But what happens when Berlin becomes just another big city, where people come to fit in, not to stand out, to make money, not to make a difference? A significant number of people in the city are not willing to

Berlin acts as a refuge for people who don't fit in to more conservative environments

let this happen without a fight; Berliners have a long history of activism and, importantly, the means to make themselves heard, as proved by the Tempelhofer Feld referendum (*see p34* A Tale of Two Airports).

Following local elections in 2016, which returned a left-wing coalition of SDP, Greens and the Left Party, the city government has become significantly more energetic in responding to concerns about the pace of change. It has actively tried to prevent the city from being hollowed out by Airbnb, first by introducing a blanket ban on short-term visitor lets in 2016, which turned out to be unenforceable, then by overturning this in favour of strict conditions and penalties; the new rules came into operation on 1 May 2018. The city government is also taking a proactive approach to Uber: the app is permitted in the city, but drivers are not allowed to undercut the fares charged by regular cabbies. But perhaps the area in which the city authorities are doing most to make their presence felt – under considerable pressure from grass-roots movements – is with a raft of measures designed to take the heat out of the property market, including rent caps, development-free zones and increased social housing subsidies. Most effective so far are the *Milieuschutz* (social environment protection) laws, intended to stop landlords undertaking expensive renovations designed to price out existing tenants.

Since local elections in 2016, Berlin Mayor Michael Müller of the SPD has headed a firmly left-of-centre coalition with Die Linke (the Left Party) and the Greens.

Even so, since much of the property boom is fuelled by foreign investment capital, many Berliners worry that these efforts fall into the 'too little, too late' category. It's not just residential property; commercial rents are also sky-rocketing as countless start-ups compete for space with older NGOs, artist collectives, small magazines and social projects – a reflection of the way people's motives for coming to the city have changed in recent years.

The wave of immigration that began in the early 2000s led to some fairly crass examples of gentrification and high levels of resentment among born and bred Berliners, but, on the whole, incomers then were seeking to escape more rigid social and political mores elsewhere. They came with dreams of making the world a better place as writers, artists and campaigners. More recent arrivals tend to be avoiding high levels of unemployment and economic uncertainty elsewhere (particularly in southern Europe and South America), brought about in part by the financial crisis of 2008. Less utopian than their predecessors, they're often IT professionals or entrepreneurs attracted to Berlin's heavily promoted start-up scene. In Berlin, it's possible that these successive waves of immigration are simply indicators of an overall direction of travel towards conformity with neoliberal values. Or, perhaps, the shared love of an extraordinary city will forge unexpected alliances, leading to new solutions for old problems. One thing is certain: people here continue to feel a sense of agency; they certainly won't be sitting back and letting forces beyond their control spoil the place they love.

Berliners have a long history of activism and, importantly, the means to make themselves heard

By and large, Berliners have offered a wonderfully generous welcome to the waves of refugees that have arrived since 2015, but the resurgence of far-right nationalism makes their future far from secure.

Eating & Drinking

City of appetites

Dining out in Berlin, while easy on the wallet, was once an uninspiring experience. If you liked fatty pork, you were in luck: traditional restaurants served hearty, stick-to-your ribs fare and plenty of it. Turkish and Vietnamese eateries added some variety, but only in a standardised, blandified version of their national cuisines. And then there was *Currywurst*...

Now, three decades since the fall of the Wall, eating out in Berlin has undergone a sea change. Finally, the city's appetite for exciting gastronomy has caught up with its craving for every other pleasure in life. An influx of global expats, combined with the ambition of the city's chefs and entrepreneurs, is redefining the parameters of the Berliner palate, and new levels of diversity have driven up standards. Formerly drab districts, such as Mitte and Kreuzberg are emerging as foodie havens, while Neukölln's hipster population has invigorated a groundswell of pop-ups and street food. The only aspect of eating out that has remained wonderfully and reassuringly the same is Berlin's legendarily brusque service (*see p46* Service with a Smile).

WOCHEN
MARKT
DI 12-20
FR 12-20
SA 10-18

vielviel koffein

Street Food Thursday *p160*

At the upper reaches of the market, there are still a few trusty warhorses serving the great and good their allocation of upmarket meat and veg. Much-revered venues such as **Borchardt**, **Grill Royal**, **Lutter und Wegner** (Charlottenstrasse 56, Mitte, 2029 5415, www.l-w-berlin.de), and **Pauly Saal** (Auguststrasse 11-13, Mitte, 3300 6070, paulysaal.com) are sprinkled with Michelin stars and attract a plutocratic clientele. These have been joined by more contemporary ventures, such as **Cinco**, **Hugos** (*see p110*), **Nobelhart & Schmutzig** (*see p150*) and **Eins44**, which provide welcome culinary innovation. Chefs such as Sebastian Frank (**Horváth**), Dalad Kambhu (**Kin Dee**, *see p111*) and wunderkind Dylan Watson-Brawn (**Ernst**, Gerichtstrasse 54, Wedding, www.ernstberlin.de) have gained superstar status.

Meanwhile, at the other end of the scale, there has been a mini-revolution in the quality and diversity of the city's street food, with Berliners showing an unquenchable appetite for new experiences and flavours. The proliferation of eclectic pop-ups and foodie events demonstrates the dynamic new DIY ethic invigorating the city's eating-out scene, with intrepid young cooks creating anything from tapioca dumplings to ceviche, Nigerian *fufu* to

❤ Best fine dining

Borchardt *p81*
Feeding Berlin's VIPs since the Kaiser.

Cinco *p110*
Award-winning food by top chef Paco Perez.

Eins44 *p169*
Haute cuisine in a post-industrial atmosphere.

Grill Royal *p81*
Carnivores come out to play.

Horváth *p156*
Revolutionised Austrian cuisine.

Katz Orange *p92*
Stunning surroundings and an inventive seasonal menu.

In the know
Food blogs

Foodbloggers wield enormous power in Berlin. Pop-ups, collaborations and new ventures come and go with such speed that, for the very latest on this week's must-visit spot, you'd be wise to follow the sensitive tastebuds of the food bloggers at stilinberlin.de, berlinfoodstories.com and iheartberlin.de.

Katz Orange

Cinco

Korean buns. Plenty of new, promising spots close almost as soon as they've opened, but, if a stall or pop-up proves its chops, it may graduate to more permanent premises.

German cuisine

If you want a taste of old Berlin, there are a few places, such as Mitte's **Kellerrestaurant im Brecht-Haus** (Chausseestrasse 125, 282 3843, www.brechtkeller.de) and Prenzlauer Berg's **Prater** (*see p123*), that still bear some resemblance to their historic roots. Berlin's traditional cooking has always been of the meat-and-two-veg variety. *Eisbein* is the signature local dish, a leathery skinned and extremely fatty pig's trotter, sometimes marinated and usually served with puréed peas. You won't find it on the menu, however, in anything but the most doggedly old-school establishments. More appetising specialities come with the seasons: spring is *Spargelzeit* ('asparagus time'), usually the white stuff served with boiled potatoes and Hollandaise; in June, little strawberry huts pop up across the city; August is for forest-fresh mushrooms, particularly frilly *Pfifferlinge* (chanterelles);

♥ **Best German food**

Café Einstein *p110*
Wood-panelled haven that's redolent of another era.

Einstein Unter den Linden *p81*
Tradition and innovation on Berlin's most famous street.

Marjellchen *p183*
Atmospheric gem serving East-Prussian cuisine.

Spätzle & Knödel *p137*
Southern German dumplings and delights.

Schwarzwaldstuben *p93*
Hansel and Gretel meet Schwäbisch slow food.

> **In the know**
> **Price categories**
>
> We use the following price codes for restaurant listings throughout the guide; they represent the average cost of one main dish.
>
> **€** = under €10
>
> **€€** = €11-€20
>
> **€€€** = €21-€30
>
> **€€€€** = over €30

Einstein Unter den Linden *p81*

In the know
Veggie eats

Venture beyond the traditional restaurants and you'll find plenty of eateries serving innovative vegetarian and vegan food for every meal. For brunch and doughnuts, check out **Brammibal's Donuts** (Maybachufer 8, Neukölln, brammibalsdonuts.com); for lunch, try the burgers at **Let It Be** (Treptowerstrasse 90, Neukölln, letitbevegan.de) or the clean-eating options at **Daluma** (Weinbergsweg 3, Mitte, daluma.de). There's coffee and cake at **Café Vux** (see *p172*) and bowlfuls of goodness at **Holy Flat** (Lenaustrasse10, Neukölln, www.holy-flat. com). And finally, for dinner, try exquisite Chinese at **Tianfuzius** (Regensburger Strasse 1, Schöneberg, tianfu.de), or the cosmopolitan vegan nosh at **Lucky Leek** (*p121*).

then it's *Kürbiszeit* ('pumpkin time') from November. Proponents of *Neue Deutsche Küche* ('New German Cuisine') make the most of these seasonal offerings, with a focus on fresh, locally sourced produce. You can sample reinterpretations of German standards at **Volt** (Paul-Lincke-Ufer 21, Kreuzberg, 3384 02320, www.restaurant-volt.de) and **Restaurant Bierberbau** (Durlacher Strasse 15, Wilmersdorf, 853 2390, www.bieberbau-berlin.de). If you can get in and have money to spend, go to **Horváth** (*see p156*) where the award-winning chef Sebastian Frank combines German and Austrian cuisines with flair.

Regional cuisines from Germanic Europe are well represented in the city and probably superior to the strictly local offerings: try south German at **Schwarzwaldstuben** (*see p93*), Austrian at **Schneeweiss** (*see p137*), **Austria** (*see p151*) and **Café Einstein** (*see p110*),

Brammibal's Donuts

and Swiss at **Nola's am Weinberg** (*see p92*). In the decidedly traditional atmosphere of Charlottenburg's **Marjellchen** (*see p183*), you can even sample the cooking of East Prussia, Pomerania and Silesia.

Berlin's most famous contribution to postwar German cuisine, however, is *Currywurst,* a sliced pork sausage covered in an oleaginous gloop of tomato ketchup with curry powder. Berlin, for some reason, wears its curry-sauce-sausage heritage with pride, although there are rumours that the dish actually originates from Hamburg. (It's best not to bring this up.) Try the traditional version under the railway arches at Prenzlauer Berg's venerable **Konnopke's Imbiss**, or the upmarket organic version – and the city's best chips – at **Witty's** (*see p184*).

The shock of the new

Berliners – for many years deprived of novelty on the culinary front – are wild for every new food trend and hip eatery. Opening nights can see hundreds of people turn up, alerted by Facebook event pages. In recent years Berlin's food crazes have encompassed everything from artisanal ice-cream to ramen, houmous, pulled pork and Korean *bibimbap.* Whatever the latest foodie trend, Berliners want to try it.

Increasingly, tapas-style dining is being applied to other cuisines, including Thai at **Kin**

❤ **Snacktime superstars**

Azzam *p166*
Generous portions of Middle-Eastern delights.

Konnopke's Imbiss *p120*
A Prenzlauer Berg institution.

Imren Grill *p169*
The best doner kebab in town!

Markthalle Neun *p160*
Plenty to choose from at this hipster hot spot.

Vöner *p137*
Veggie and vegan fast food.

Currywurst

Street Food Thursday

Dee (*see p111*) and vegetable-centric small plates at gastropub **St Barts** in Kreuzberg (*see p157*). In 2018, artisanal doughnuts (matcha doughnut anyone?) and small-batch spirits were tipped as upcoming trends. To see what's next on the menu, visit the Street Food Thursday nights at **Markthalle Neun** (*see p160*), or **Bite Club**'s Friday night events on the Kreuzberg riverside (Hoppetosse by Badeschiff, Eichenstrasse 4, biteclub.de). One food trend that shows no sign of going out of fashion is Berliners' appetite for **brunch**. Lingering over a long, leisurely breakfast is the city's favourite way to start the weekend, and the best eateries go out of their way to offer something special (*see p192* Berlin brunch).

Global flavours

The brevity of Germany's colonial experience means no deep-rooted link with a foreign cuisine. However, reunification resulted in a better-travelled population and, in the beginning at least, lots of relatively cheap real estate where young restaurateurs could try out their ideas. With an increasingly cosmopolitan clientele to encourage ethnic variety at street level, Berlin dining has been getting steadily more international.

Turkish food, which arrived with post-war *Gastarbeiter* ('guest workers'), is deeply embedded in the western side of town. Kreuzberg claims to be the place where the doner kebab was invented in the early 1970s, forever associated with **Hasir** (Adalbertstrasse 10, Kreuzberg, 614 2373, www.hasir.de). Italian cuisine has also long been well represented (**Osteria No.1**, *see p151*; **Sale e Tabbachi**, *see p150*).

An influx of refugees from South Vietnam in the 1970s and contract workers from North Vietnam in the 1980s has given Berlin a significant Vietnamese population and a surfeit of Vietnamese food: from unappetizing, greasy boxes of noodles at seemingly every street corner to exquisite, freshly prepared *pho* and *bánh mì*. A pioneer of authentic modern Vietnamese cooking in the city, **Si An** (*see p122*) is still going strong. Korean food is likewise well represented at **Ixthys** (*see p191*) and **Yam Yam** (Alte Schönhauser Strasse 6, Mitte, 2463 2486, www.yamyam-berlin.de), where *bibimbap* is king – a bowl of steaming rice, meat, kimchi and a fresh fried egg, all waiting to be mashed into a droolworthy mass of comfort food, topped with lashings of spicy sauce.

Benedict *p189*

Service with a Smile
Berliner brusqueness at its best

While some cities bring panache to waiting tables (Rome), bonhomie (Madrid), or what seems to be a sincere desire to make you have that nice day (San Francisco), traditionally Berlin waiters have specialised in the kind of brusque insouciance that could leave a starving diner choking with rage, particularly on a Saturday at brunch-time when poor service reaches its apotheosis in Berlin. Times are changing, however, and you're now just as likely to be greeted with hospitality, an authoritative rundown of the locally sourced specials and a recommendation for some excellent wine pairings. This is, sort of, how things should be, but it has the unfortunate effect of making you feel that you could be anywhere in the world.

Fear not, old habits die hard; if you stay in Berlin for a few days and eat out a lot, you are more than likely to be barked at or cold-shouldered at least once. How to respond? Don't start looking anxious, wondering what you've done wrong, or getting irate. Maintain a stony expression; if you can, raise an eyebrow. Perhaps mutter loudly to your companion, '*Das Leben ist kein Ponyhof*' (Life's not a pony-stable – apparently a Berlin synonym for luxury). You're not intimidated; you're not impressed. Carry it off, and the waiting staff will soon warm up. If not, and if the service is truly unapologetically bad – don't tip. A Berliner wouldn't.

There's good-quality Japanese at **Sasaya** (*see p122*), Thai at **Thai Park** (*see p189*), Chinese at **Asia Deli** (Seestrasse 41, Wedding, 45084219) and Indonesian at **Mabuhay** (Köthener Strasse 28, Kreuzberg, 265 1867, mabuhay.juisyfood.com). Indian food, however, presents something of a problem. There are places all over town, but standards are dire. **Chutnify** (Sredzkistrasse 43, Prenzlauerberg, 4401 0795, www.chutnify.com), a British import serving up South Indian cuisine, including thalis, offers a glimmer of hope.

Other immigrants have also brought their own culinary traditions. You'll find fashionable Russian borscht and vodka on offer at **Gorki Park** (Weinbergsweg 25, Mitte, 448 7286, gorki-park.de) and **Pasternak** (*see p121*), and artisan burgers at a wave of fancy US-style burger joints, such as **The Bird** (Am Falkplatz 5, Prenzlauer Berg, 5105 3283, https://thebirdinberlin.com) and at the sporadic **Burgers & Hip Hop** open-air party (www.facebook.com/burgersandhiphop).

Edible works of art at Princess Cheesecake.

Market forces

Thanks to its increasingly global population, Berlin is teeming with open-air markets selling wholesome comestibles from around the world. Every Tuesday and Friday, you can join locals stocking up on delicious fresh produce, snacks and knick-knacks along the sprawling **Türkischer Markt** on Maybachufer (*see p171*). On Saturdays, in among the handicraft and gifts, look out for a Brazilian lady selling unbelievably good *feijoada* (black bean stew), *moqueca de peixe* (fish, coconut and dende oil stew) and *coxinhas* (fried dumplings). Over in Charlottenburg, meanwhile, Berlin's Thai community offers up all manner of delicacies alfresco at **Thai Park** (*see p189*), a giant picnic in the Preussenpark.

Kaffee und Kuchen

Pretty much every street in the city boasts a coffee shop or a bakery, and the tradition of taking a leisurely afternoon break for '*Kaffee und Kuchen*' (coffee and cake) is one of the most appealing aspects of Berlin life. For a quirky twist, try Mitte's **Princess Cheesecake** where the impossibly rich and decadent creations range from beetroot-flavoured chocolate cheesecake to home-made truffles with Earl Grey-flavoured ganache. If you're after something more old-school, then **Anna Blume** should fit the bill; of the gazillions of similarly quaint, charming and floral coffee shops that abound, this one seems to have the edge on the competition, thanks to its chocolate-box atmosphere, killer cakes and insanely addictive coffee. Fortunately, the watery filter coffee consumed by Berliners for decades has now been replaced by so-called 'third-wave coffee', introduced by US and Aussie immigrants. Small-scale roasteries have sprung up all over the city; **Bonanza** in Prenzlauer Berg was one of the first on the scene and is still hard to beat.

Drink up

Berliners do like a drink, and the city's reputation as an excellent drinking destination is well-deserved. Beer is the main tipple,

♥ Best coffee & cake

Anna Blume *p119*
Stylish surroundings and desserts to die for.

Barcomi's *p90*
Cynthia's baking revolution began here.

Bonanza *p120*
Third-wave coffee for connoisseurs.

Five Elephant *p156*
Home-roasted coffee and home-made cakes.

Konditorei Buchwald *p106*
160 years of German baking perfection.

Princess Cheesecake *p93*
Mouth-watering selection of beautifully presented cakes, including vegan options.

Bonanza

although local brews such as Berliner Kindl, a party staple, are poor compared to the best of Bavaria or Bohemia. Germans will often boast of the German beer purity laws, which ensure that beers brewed inside the country can only contain water, malted barley, hops and yeast. Still, craft beer – while viewed with some suspicion – is catching on. Check out the **BRLO Brauhaus** in Gleisdreieck Park (Schöneberger Strasse 16, 0151-7437 4235, www.brlo-brwhouse. de), **Vagabund Brauerei** (Antwerpener Strasse 3, Wedding, www.vagabundbrauerei.com) or the home brewery in the cellar bar of the **Circus Hostel** (*see p301*).

The capital's changing demographics mean that tiny, elite cocktail bars are also on the increase. Places such as **Buck and Breck**, **Becketts Kopf** and **Pauly Saal** (*see p40*) are setting the benchmark for avant-garde mixology, but cultured snorts can be found in every part of town at venues such as **Galander Kreuzberg**, **Tier** (*see p171*) and **Cordobar** (*see p94*), the latter being the cognoscenti's wine bar of choice.

Never fear, there are also still plenty of characterful dives and unpretentious *Kneipen* (traditional pubs) – almost one on every corner in some parts of town. Unreconstructed, untouched by changing fashions, with nicotine-stained walls and gruff locals hogging all the bar stools, they have a rough appeal that is the perfect antidote to an overdose of hipster hotspots. The beer is cheap and good too – although you'll have to pay with cash.

In summer, Berliners take their drinking outside: café tables spread out on to the pavements, beer gardens bustle and beach bars spring to life in waterside locations. In fact, enjoying a *Feierabend* (after-work) beer or Club Maté (a fizzy-soda based on the South America stimulant *maté*) on a wooden table outside a *Späti* (late shop) is a fine Berlin custom.

♥ Best dive bars

Ankerklause *p166*
A lively local institution.

Bar 3 *p94*
Nocturnal hang out of the art stars.

Barbie Deinhoff's *p231*
Queer, noisy, wonderful.

Bei Schlawinchen *p158*
Beware, it never closes!

Mama Bar *p170*
A living-room setting for enjoying great beer.

In the know
Smokers' paradise

Thirty per cent of Berliners smoke and, thanks to a local 2009 ruling protecting bar owners' right to make a living, smokers can continue to ruin their health in the warmth and comfort of most Berlin bars and clubs. Even bars that serve food either have separate smoking sections or pull out the ashtrays as soon as the kitchens close, and in *Kneipen* (traditional pubs) smoking is practically obligatory. If you're tempted yourself – or just want to break the ice with an attractive stranger – asking for '*eine Kippe*' is usually met with good grace and generosity.

Becketts Kopf

Tipping and etiquette

Popular venues in Berlin are versatile. Restaurants tend to be relaxed, roomy and delightfully cheap compared to other western European capitals, and they often have bars, where you're welcome to drink even if you have no intention of eating. Bars, in their turn, often serve food. Cafés are popular for a long breakfast, weekend brunch, light lunch and the traditional *Kaffee und Kuchen*, then turn into bars by night. Licensing laws are relaxed, so you can often get a beer or a glass of wine to go with your sandwich at any of time of day.

In restaurants, it's customary to tip around ten per cent. Tips are handed directly to the server rather than left on the table. Don't say *danke* ('thank you') as you hand over the cash, unless you want the server to keep the change. In bars, people tend to pay their own way and drink at their own pace – partly because, in many places, bills are only totted up as you leave – but ceremonial rounds of Jägermeister, tequila or vodka are a local nightlife feature. Hardly anywhere shuts before 1am and most bars stay open much later – some until the last customers leave.

❤ Cocktail kings

Becketts Kopf *p122*
Theatre meets art meets mixology.

Buck and Breck *p94*
Small is beautiful.

Green Door *p193*
Classic and classy, Berlin style.

Galander Kreuzberg *p152*
Skilful, friendly staff create serious cocktails.

Newton Bar *p83*
As glossy and glam as Helmut Newton's photos.

Rum Trader *p189*
Rum-lovers' paradise.

Würgeengel *p159*
Arty and louche, with a classic menu.

Shopping

Flea markets and vintage fashion meet high-end design and global brands

---

Shopping in Berlin can be a frustrating experience. There is no single pedestrian area, no truly instinctive centre of gravity that draws you in. Instead, there are several shopping neighbourhoods in various stages of development, gentrification and corresponding counter-culture.

The heavily trafficked Kurfürstendamm in the West is undoubtedly the most tightly packed with the biggest global players: it's home to the only Apple store in the city, for instance. However, wandering away from the main street in search of 'hidden gems' proves to be a disheartening experience. To find these in Berlin, you need to hop on the U-Bahn and head away from Ku'Damm. But where to go? Fashion-forward, well-paid, bright young things may try Weinmeisterstrasse in Mitte, where independent boutiques rub shoulders with expensive chain stores. Hippies and alternative folk could be well-served in Bergmannstrasse, Kreuzberg, where incense burners and boho prints reign supreme.

The bookshop at Urban Spree *p139*

A mixed bag

Even in the city's most more distinctive areas, Berlin has a way of pushing against the grain, as the lowbrow and highbrow, mainstream and avant-garde, designer chic and street style coexist in striking juxtapositions. A quirky independent art bookshop might thrive next to a global megastore, a cheeky sex shop can nestle comfortably among some of the city's most exclusive boutiques. Even the influx of big-name international brands over the past two decades hasn't dampened the impulse of Berlin's progressives to keep things interesting: they just move to one side and start a pop-up kiosk in a former cat sanctuary selling home-made *bibimbap*. Or something.

Although malls and international franchises are increasingly in evidence – a nod either to the broader smartening-up of the city or to soul-destroying commercialism, depending on your point of view – there is still plenty of colourful, home-grown talent and entrepreneurial spirit to discover, with fashion, food and 'lifestyle' leading the way.

♥ Only in Berlin

Ampelmann Shop *p95*
Get your own little red and green men.

Erich Hamann Bittere Schokoladen *p189*
Berlin's oldest chocolate factory.

Hard Wax *p159*
Berlin techno on vinyl.

Harry Lehmann *p188*
Marlene Dietrich's favourite perfumery.

KaDeWe *p54*
Still the city's finest luxury department store.

RSVP *p97*
A blissful oasis of old-school stationery.

Voo

Perhaps the best example of the contrasts in the city's shopping scene is the vast **Bikini Berlin** (Budapesterstrasse 38-50, Tiergarten, www.bikiniberlin.de), which could be described as a mega-mall for affluent arty hipsters. A minimal, stylish 'experience' featuring more esoteric brands than one would expect to find in the average identikit shopping centre, Bikini Berlin bills itself as a 'concept mall' aimed at the 'urban customer'. For a similar vibe, but in smaller premises, head across town to Mitte's **Soho House** (*see p299*) where **The Store Berlin** (www.thestores.com/berlin) sells luxury items, ranging from fashion, books, plants and cult cosmetics to cold-pressed juices, in an imaginative retail space; there's even a retro hair and beauty salon at the rear. Similarly curated homewares and chic accessories can be found at **Hallesches Haus** (*see p152*) in Kreuzberg.

Shopping by area

Charlottenburg remains the upmarket showpiece it always was. Major department stores and the flagship outlets of familiar international names march westwards from **KaDeWe** on Wittenbergplatz and along the Kurfürstendamm, west Berlin's major shopping avenue. Luxury brands cluster on Fasanenstrasse, while more discreet boutiques, interior design outlets and tasteful bookshops are scattered around the streets between the Ku'damm and Kantstrasse. Knesebeckstrasse, on either side of Savignyplatz, is good for bookshops: try the excellent English-language section at **Marga Schoeller Bücherstube** (*see p185*), which sold anti-Nazi pamphlets in the 1930s and is still going strong; or, for art and architecture, check out **Bücherbogen** (*see p184*).

Heading in the opposite direction, at Potsdamer Platz, there's the big **Arkaden** shopping mall (Alte Potsdamer Strasse 7, potsdamerplatz.de/shopping). Nearby in the

❤ Best for fashion

Andreas Murkudis *p112*
A glorious array of designer goodies.

Aura *p171*
Vintage silk kimonos.

DSTM *p96*
Slinky black leather from Canadian-born designer Jen Gilpin.

LaLa Berlin *p96*
Fashionistas worldwide covet Leyla Piedayesh's knitwear.

Mykita *p96*
Berlin's home-grown sunglasses brand is a global success story.

Overkill *p160*
A temple to the trainer.

Voo *p160*
Designer concept store.

Aura

❤ KaDeWe

Tauentzienstrasse 21-24 (21210, www. kadewe.com). U1, U2, U3 Wittenbergplatz. **Open** *10am-8pm Mon-Fri; 10am-9pm Sat.* **Map** *p178 H9 Department store*

The grand dame of them all, Kaufhaus des Westens (Department Store of the West) to give it its full title, is still the pick of Berlin's malls. Shopping here, or at least gazing at the wares, has been an essential Berliner experience for more than a century. Founded in 1907 by Adolf Jandorf, acquired by Herman Tietz in 1926 and later 'Aryanised' and expropriated by the Nazis, KaDeWe was the only one of Berlin's famous turn-of-the-last-century department stores to survive the war intact; it has been extensively modernised over the last two decades.

KaDeWe stocks an impressive range of high-end designers and has tried to shed its stuffy image by bringing in upbeat, younger labels such as Alice+Olivia and London shoe brand Buffalo. If you're in the market for a new designer handbag, evening gown or Rolex this is still the place to come, but what really distinguishes KaDeWe from your Harrods and Galeries Lafayette is the sixth floor. Here you'll find the quintessential luxury food-hall experience in a city otherwise teeming with budget supermarkets. With counter after counter of delicatessens, butchers, pâtisseries and grocers, and plenty of prepared foods to take away, the olfactory experience as you move between sections is an experience in itself. The oyster bar is a perfect mid-shop pit stop, and after a visit to the champagne bar, you may need to hand your credit cards over to a more responsible adult. There's something quintessentially 'Charlottenburg' about the KaDeWe: a bit stuffy and *bürgerlich* to be sure, but underneath it all, more than a little decadent. Head up another level to reach a cavernous glass-roofed restaurant with a fine view of Wittenbergplatz below.

Tagesspiegel building, the high-end 'concept' store **Andreas Murkudis** (*see p112*) showcases a tasteful spectrum of luxury goods, from Dries van Noten to beautifully crafted, insanely expensive trinkets, baubles and fripperies from home and abroad.

In Mitte, department stores and yet more international brands line Friedrichstrasse, including an elegant branch of **Galeries Lafayette** (*see p83*), but the area between Alexanderplatz and Rosenthalerplatz fizzles with adventurous and eccentric shops. Shady Mulackstrasse is where the fashion pack list their favourite stores: **Das Neue Schwarz** (*see p97*) for second-hand threads is well worth visiting, as are boutiques such as **Baerck** (no.12, 2404 8994, baerck.net) and Vivien Westwood haven **Worlds End** (no.26, 8561 0073), each offering up quirky and quality fashion. Local brands, such as **Starstyling** (no.4, 9700 5182, www.starstyling.net) and **Lala Berlin** (*see p96*), design and produce their own gear, much loved by locals in the know. Also in this area you'll find popular street labels (Urban Outfitters, Cos and Adidas), as well as Berlin vintage favourites **Made in Berlin** (*see p96*) and **Pick n Weight** (*see p153*). The graffitied, eastern end of Torstrasse has a proliferation of concept stores and big brands selling everything from high-end sneakers to covetable antiques, jewellery, and more minimal and tasteful fashion.

The gentrification of Mitte has been driving less affluent shoppers in the direction of Friedrichshain and Kreuzberg, where a more student (and 'perennial student') population dominates. The Bergmannstrasse neighbourhood in Kreuzberg is where you find second-hand shops, small designer outlets, music stores, bookshops and delis. One of the best bookshops in the city, **Another Country** has been catering to Kreuzbergers in German and English for decades, as

Another Country *p152*
Eccentric treasure trove of second-hand English books.

Bücherbogen *p184*
Enormous bookstore with a generous international selection.

do you read me?! *p96*
Books on fashion, design, architecture and beyond.

Marga Schoeller Bucherstube *p185*
Old-school charm in an historic space.

Modern Graphics *p160*
Packed with all your comic book faves.

Saint George's *p124*
A staple for the English literary community.

Modern Graphics

has the charming, little **Ebert und Weber** nearby (Falckensteinstrasse 44, 6956 5193, www.ebertundweber.de).

Neukölln's shopping scene is rather incoherent; however, the leafy area around Maybachufer conceals a few delights that are worth seeking out if you're in the area. Try **Sing Blackbird** (*see p170*) for chunky knit sweaters and floral dresses, along with a coffeeshop for post-rummage refuelling; **Aura** (*see p171*) for traditional silk kimonos, and **Vintage Galore** (*see p171*) for Scandinavian and mid-century furnishings, along with a tastefully curated rack of pre-loved clothing. New shops and cafés are popping up all the time, so this area rewards a wander on a pleasant day. You never know what you might stumble across.

Market analysis

Berlin hosts several interesting flea markets. Sunday's **Mauerpark Flohmarkt** has an eclectic selection but is regarded as somewhat touristy by locals and gets rammed quickly. The **Kunst und Trödel Markt** by Tiergarten station (*see p112*) is a great place for collectors, while the **Flohmarkt am Boxhagener Platz** mixes old furniture and bric-a-brac with work by local artists and T-shirt designers. Markets are also a great place to sample some of the city's foodie trends, from traditional covered produce markets, such as **Arminius Markthalle**, to Sunday's Street Food auf Achse at the **KulturBrauerei** (*see p118*), where hipsters

♥ Best for food & drink

Arminius Markthalle *p113*
Trad covered market serving foodie treats.

Dong Xuan Center *p141*
Epicentre of Vietnamese delights.

Hopfen & Malz *p129*
Craft beer paradise.

KaDeWe *p54*
The sixth floor is a gourmand's dream.

Kollwitzplatz farmers' market *p123*
Local, organic and fresh.

Markthalle Neun *p160*
Some of the city's best street food.

Thai Park am Preussen Park *p189*
Authentic Thai food in an informal setting.

Arminius Markthalle

snack on Indian *vada pav* and wild game burgers. At the biweekly **Türkischer Markt** on Maybachufer, you can find everything from freshly baked bread to organic cheese and Greek olives, while the **Kollwitzplatz farmers' market** sells a wide range of local artisan produce. And, during weekends in the summer, you will find a delicious Thai food market run by Berlin's Asian community in Wilmersdorf's **Preussenpark**.

Opening hours

Shops generally open at around 10am and are permitted to stay open until 10pm. However, small and traditional stores tend to close around 6pm; most bigger stores and more adventurous smaller retailers stick it out at least until 8pm. Most shops are open on Saturday afternoons, but nearly all are closed on Sunday (unless your trip happens to coincide with one of the city's elusive shopping weekends). Credit and debit cards, PIN machines and contactless payment are less widely used than elsewhere, with most transactions still made in cash.

💗 Best street markets

Arkonaplatz Flohmarkt *p95*
Arrive early to bag your retro Berlin bargain.

Flohmarkt am Boxhagener Platz *p138*
Home-made goodies, fresh produce and flea market finds.

Mauerpark Flohmarkt *p124*
Ever popular Sunday flea-market-cum-festival.

Türkischer Markt *p171*
Yummy Turkish snacks and supplies.

Winterfeldtplatz Markt *p193*
Brandenburg's farmers offer their wares to the denizens of Schöneberg.

Arkonaplatz Flohmarkt

Türkischer Markt

Explore

	Getting Started	60
	Mitte	66
	Tiergarten & Moabit	98
	Prenzlauer Berg & Mitte North	114
	Friedrichshain & Lichtenberg	130
	Kreuzberg & Treptow	142
	Neukölln	164
	Charlottenburg & Schöneberg	176
	West of the Centre	194

Schloss Charlottenburg *p187*

Getting Started

Berlin covers a vast 891 sq km, but the area inside the *Ringbahn* (the 37-km/23-mile overground railway that loops round the city centre) is where you'll find most of the sights, museums, restaurants, shops, bars and entertainment options. Only a few ever-more crumbling remnants of the Berlin Wall remain here (*see p63* Getting Over the Wall), but the infamous East–West divide is still perceptible in the two halves of the city, with Charlottenburg and the western suburbs home to far wealthier inhabitants than the eastern districts, which have larger populations of immigrants and cash-strapped artists. Although Mitte is the city's historic centre, Berlin remains relatively decentralised, with no single built-up area where the population congregates in commuter madness but several different *Kieze* (neighbourhoods) and suburbs (*see p62* In the know), each with its own distinct identity and appeal. For an overview of this fascinating city, stand on the observation platform of the Fernsehturm and see it all spread out before you.

❤ Best viewpoints

Elsenbrücke *Map p144 U10*
A view of the River Spree, the Oberbaumbrücke and *Molecule Man*.

Fernsehturm *p88*
Pricey but worth it – on a clear day.

Klunkerkranich *p174*
A laid-back summertime rooftop bar in Neukölln.

Reichstag Dome *p105*
Gain a free insight into the workings of the German Parliament.

Siegessäule *p104*
Climb to the top for sweeping views over Tiergarten.

Teufelsberg *p203*
Survey the entire city and surroundings from an abandoned US listening post.

Fernsehturm *p88*

Neighbourhoods and landmarks

In the days of division, **Mitte** (*see p66*) lay on the eastern side of the city, but today it is once again the centre in every respect – historically, culturally, politically and commercially. The Fernsehturm on Alexanderplatz is the unmissable landmark in the east and can be seen from all over the city. Mitte's main thoroughfare is Unter den Linden, a grand east–west avenue full of mighty neoclassical paeans to the imperial era, such as the recently renovated Staatsoper. At its eastern end is the Museuminsel (*see p74*), incorporating a cluster of major museums, the Berliner Dom and the rebuilt Stadtschloss. South of Unter den Linden, there are glitzy shops along Friedrichstrasse, and cathedrals and concert halls around the Gendarmenmarkt. Things get more bohemian to the north, particularly around the Scheunenviertel, Berlin's historic Jewish quarter. At the western end of Unter den Linden is the iconic Brandenburger Tor (*see p71*), once the ceremonial entrance to the city; the undulating concrete blocks of the Holocaust Memorial (*see p73*) lie just to the south.

The Brandenburg Gate marks the border between Mitte and **Tiergarten** (*see p98*), with the huge wooded park of the same name stretching away on the western side (*see p103*) as far as the Zoologischer Garten. This district also incorporates the Reichstag (*see p105*), complete with glass cupola, and other key buildings of the government quarter along the Spree. South of the park, the postmodern entertainment and commercial zone of Potsdamer Platz adjoins the Kulturforum, home to institutions such as the Neue Nationalgalerie (*see p109*), the Philharmonie (*see p252*) and a whole slew of embassies. To the north of Tiergarten is the relatively central but unassuming district of **Moabit** (*see p112*).

Kastanienallee leads north-east from Mitte into **Prenzlauer Berg** (*see p114*), easily Berlin's most picturesque residential neighbourhood and Mitte's fashionable adjunct in terms of nightlife and gastronomy; east Berlin's gay district is focused on the northern reaches of Schönhauser Allee. Just to the west, there's an evocative history lesson to be had at the Berlin Wall memorial on the edge of working-class **Gesundbrunnen** (*see p125*). East of Prenzlauer Berg is **Friedrichshain** (*see p132*), which has the most 'East Berlin' feel of the inner-city districts. Its spine is the broad GDR-era Karl-Marx-Allee; photographers gravitate to the East Side Gallery (*see p135*), while bohos, students and young tourists flock to the lively area around Simon-Dach-Strasse. Heading further east out of town, **Lichtenberg** (*see p139*) has a few reminders of Stasi oppression (*see p140*) and the East Berlin Zoo.

❤ Best for Ostalgie

Ampelmann Shop *p95*
East Berlin's most enduring and endearing mascot.

DDR Museum *p88*
Immerse yourself in East German living, complete with Lispy dancing and surveillance.

Karl-Marx-Allee *p134*
The GDR's grandest boulevard.

Marx-Engels Forum *p87*
Pay your respects to the founding fathers of communism.

Ständige Vertretung *p83*
Drink a beer surrounded by reminders of the old geopolitical divisions.

Trabi Museum *p147*
A museum devoted to the cult car.

❤ Best museums for families

Computerspiele Museum *p136*
Nostalgic for parents; fun for teens.

Domäne Dahlem *p203*
A historical working farm.

Haus am Checkpoint Charlie *p144*
Escape vehicles and getaway stories bring the Berlin Wall to life.

Labyrinth Kindermuseum *p127*
A must for budding DIY-ers.

Museum für Naturkunde *p80*
Dinosaur skeletons and multimedia displays.

Story of Berlin *p182*
An interactive intro to German history.

In the know
Berlin by area

Berlin is divided into 12 major *Bezirke*, or boroughs, which are then sub-divided into more manageable *Ortsteile* (districts). For example, the *Bezirk* of Mitte is made up of Moabit, Tiergarten, Wedding, Gesundbrunnen, Hansaviertel and, confusingly, Mitte, sometimes referred to as Mitte-Mitte. An *Ortsteil* may be broken down further into *Kieze* (neighbourhoods), but these are culturally and socially created areas, rather than official designations. In this guide, we have generally used the *Ortsteile* to organise our area chapters, as they are the most relevant for visitors when exploring the city.

Getting Over the Wall

Finding what's left

'Is there anything left of the Wall?' That's the first question asked by many visitors. The answer is, 'Not very much.' A short section has been preserved on the border between Mitte and Wedding at the **Gedenkstätte Berliner Mauer** (see p125). It's kept in pristine condition – any graffiti is removed straight away – and it is the only place where you can see what the various layers of defence looked like. A documentation centre provides background information.

Another section of the inner Wall, the side that faced East Berlin, stands on the Friedrichshain bank of the Spree along Mühlenstrasse. Known as the **East Side Gallery** (see p135), it was covered with paintings by international artists in the 1990s and is in a perpetual fight for survival against low-grade graffiti on the one hand and property developers on the other.

And on **Niederkirchnerstrasse** (see p146), along the border between Kreuzberg and Mitte, there's a stretch preserved with graffiti and pockmarks inflicted by the hammers and chisels of souvenir-chipping 'Wall tourists' in the winter of 1989-90.

For more on the history of the Wall, visit the **Haus am Checkpoint Charlie** (see p147) in Kreuzberg or the **Wall Museum** (see p135) in Friedrichshain.

Crossing the River Spree south from Friedrichshain (via the photogenic Oberbaumbrücke) takes you into the former West Berlin neighbourhood of **Kreuzberg** (see p142), once the city's main alternative-lifestyle nexus and the capital of Turkish Berlin. The northern part of Kreuzberg, bordering Mitte, contains some important museums, including the Jüdisches Museum (see p149), as well as Friedrichstrasse's Cold War landmark, Checkpoint Charlie (see p147). Bergmannstrasse is lively with cafés and retro shops, while bars and clubs line Oranienstrasse and the eastern area around Schlesisches Tor. South of Kreuzberg, hip and happening **Neukölln** (see p164) provides access to the vast expanse of Tempelhofer Feld (see p173), while large and leafy Treptower Park contains the imposing Soviet War Memorial (see p162). East again is **Köpenick** (see p163), famous for its medieval architecture and access to the Müggelsee (see p199).

West of Kreuzberg lies **Schöneberg** (see p190), a residential district centred around Winterfeldtplatz, with its popular market. Berlin's historic gay district stretches along and around Motzstrasse and Fuggerstrasse, while Wittenbergplatz, at Schöneberg's north-west corner, is the location of KaDeWe (see p54), continental Europe's biggest department store. It marks the beginning of the well-heeled district of **Charlottenburg** (see p176), Berlin's West End, whose main artery is the Kurfürstendamm, a typical high-end shopping drag. The palace that gives the district its name is to the north. **West of the Centre** (see p194) is the Olympiastadion, the biggest single example of Nazi-era architecture still extant. The forested Grunewald and a cluster of bathing lakes (see p198) entice residents out

of the city in warmer weather, while the sculptured gardens and royal residences of **Potsdam** (see p204), the capital of Brandenburg, make it a popular day trip for tourists.

Museums and collections

The **Museumsinsel** (see p74) is an island in the River Spree that was designated a World Heritage Site by UNESCO in 1999 thanks to its five world-class cultural institutions. The **Altes Museum, Neues Museum, Alte Nationalgalerie, Bode-Museum** and **Pergamonmuseum** (for all, see pp77-80) serve as a stunning repository of cultural artefacts and heritage from around the world. In 2019 they were joined by the **Humboldt Forum** (see p79) inside the rebuilt Stadtschloss, which will house the city's ethnographic and Asian art exhibits. To the north, the animal exhibits in the **Museum für Naturkunde** (see p80) are a draw for kids.

The city's fraught and remarkable 800-year history is brought to life at the interactive **Story of Berlin** (see p182), while the ambitious and sprawling **Deutsches Historisches Museum** (see p78) provides a broader and more serious overview of German history. The Cold War and life in the GDR are laid bare in the **Museum in der Kulturbrauerei** (see p119) and the chilling **Stasi Museum** (see p141). But for more on the history of the Wall, it's worth visiting the heavily touristed **Haus am Checkpoint Charlie** (see p147). Nearby, the **Jüdisches Museum** (see p149) in Kreuzberg is housed in a remarkable building by Daniel Libeskind and is the biggest museum in Europe dedicated to the lives of Jewish people.

Art lovers won't leave the city disappointed. The **Gemäldegalerie** (*see p108*) has a world-class collection of 13th to 18th-century European art, while the **Neue Nationalgalerie** (*see p109*) has pieces by the great modern artists of the early 20th century. Other notable art repositories include Dahlem's **Brücke Museum** (*see p203*), for German expressionism; **Museum Berggruen** (*see p187*), for work by the likes of Paul Cézanne, Alberto Giacometti and Henri Matisse; and the **Hamburger Bahnhof** (*see p112*) for art from the 1960s to the present day. To round it all off, the **Kunstgewerbe Museum** (Museum of Decorative Arts; *see p109*) is a trove of fine decorative treasures, encompassing art, fashion and design.

Other interests and specialisms are catered for by the **Museum für Film und Fernsehen** (*see p109*), an enormous German film archive, and the **Deutsches Technik Museum** (*see p148*), which has an array of German technology on show, from steam trains and ship simulators to mills and breweries. For family-friendly fun and games, visit the **Computerspiele Museum** (*see p136*) or explore the inimitable **Museum der Dinge** (*see p154*), a veritable *Wunderkammer* of 20th-century artefacts. Finally, the **Schwules Museum** (*see p110*) offers a unique and thought-provoking exploration of Berlin's LGBTIQ history.

Note that most museums are closed on Mondays but are open and free between 6pm and 10pm on Thursdays.

Discount cards and visitor passes

Most of the major museums and galleries are administered by the **Staatliche Museen zu Berlin** (SMB; www.smb.museum/home.html), including the Altes Museum, the Pergamonmuseum and the Gemäldegalerie. SMB offers a three-day card (€29; €14.50 reductions), available from any of its museums.

There are also two excellent-value discount cards aimed at tourists, which combine unlimited transport within designated zones, with a bundle of other discounts and deals at partnering tourist and cultural attractions, shops, bars and clubs. The **Berlin CityTourCard** (www.citytourcard.com) costs €16.90 for a 48-hour pass for zones A and B, €23.90 for 72 hours and €33.90 for five days; it is available from tourist offices, BVG and S-Bahn ticket machines and from the airports. The **Berlin WelcomeCard** (www.berlin-welcomecard.

de) costs €19.90 for 48 hours in zones A and B, €28.90 for 72 hours (€45 including access to museums at Museum Island) and €36.90 for five days.

Another option is the **Berlin Pass** (www.berlinpass.com, €89 for three days), which allows entry to over 50 attractions and free hop-on, hop-off bus tours around the city.

▶ *For information on visitor passes for Prussian palaces in Potsdam and elsewhere, including Schloss Charlottenburg, visit www.spsg.de. See p204 In the know.*

Getting around

Berlin's system of underground (U-Bahn), overground (S-Bahn), trams and buses is efficient and comprehensive but can often be confusing for newcomers. There are just not enough signs or information in the stations, so you'll have to keep your wits about you. For details, *see p303*. In addition to public transport, taxis and Uber rides are readily available (*see p304*). Renting bicycles is a particularly pleasant way to see the city (*see right* Berlin by bike), and walking is always an option, although you're likely to need public transport at some point to cover the large distances. For a unique perspective on the city, take a boat along the Spree or other waterways (*see p186* Berlin by boat).

Tours

There are heaps of tours to help you learn about the history, architecture, street art and culture of Berlin, by bike, boat, bus or on foot. **Insider Tours** (www.insidertour.com) are led by very well-informed English-speaking guides who reveal the history of the city in a series of themed tours, including a Cold War guided tour along the former death-strip and the Wall. **Alternative Berlin** (http://alternativeberlin.com/) offers a look at the counter-culture of the city, taking you through squats, street art and skateparks. If you'd rather see the city on two wheels, **Fat Tire Tours** (www.fattiretours.com/berlin) offers a few different routes, including the Third Reich and Nazi Berlin, the Berlin Wall, and the Gardens and Palaces of Potsdam. Segway tours are also available. **Berlin Pass** (*see p64*) offers sightseeing bus tours of the city, with stops at some of the city's most famous icons, such as Potsdamer Platz, Checkpoint Charlie and Museumsinsel (€19). For a full list of available tours, see www.visitberlin.de/en/sightseeing-tours-berlin.

💙 Berlin by bike

Cycling through Berlin with the wind in your hair is an experience not to be missed. Flat, with lots of cycle routes, parks and canal paths, the city is best seen by bike. That said, caution is required. Cobbles, tram lines, aimless pedestrians, other cyclists and careless drivers all pose hazards. Few locals wear helmets, but you'd be wise to get your hands on one, especially if you're used to riding on the left.

Bicycles can be carried on the U-Bahn (except during rush hour, 6-9am and 2-5pm) in designated carriages, up to two per carriage. More may be taken on the S-Bahn at any time of day. In each case an extra ticket (€1.90 for zones A and B) must be bought for each bike. This means you can train it back to the city after a cycle ride to the lakes, or if you get hopelessly lost. A good guide to cycle routes is the *ADFC Fahrradstadtplan* (€6.90), available in bike shops, but most bus shelters also have city maps which will help you regain your bearings.

These days, there's a surplus of bike-sharing apps in Berlin, such as **Mobike** (mobike.com), **Donkey Republic** (www.donkey.bike), **Lidl Bike** (www.lidl-bike.de) and **Deezer Nextbike** (www.deezernextbike.de). Typically, there's a small sign-up fee of around €10, and then rates are charged by the half hour (€1-

€1.50). Maximum full-day fees are around €15. Bikes can be picked up all over the city (you'll notice all sorts of colourfully branded cycles) and at designated docking stations. However, if you're planning an excursion or want to explore Berlin's streets more fully, you'd do well to pick up a bicycle from a hire shop. Not only are the bikes better quality, but you'll also get free servicing and advice; €8-15 euros a day is the going rate. Some of the best are **Berlin on Bike** (Knaackstrasse 97, Kulturbrauerei, Prenzlauer Berg, www.berlinonbike.de); **Fahrradstation** (Dorotheenstrasse 30, Mitte, www.fahrradstation.com) and **Wicked Wheels** (Grossbeerenstrasse 53, Kreuzberg, www.wicked-wheels.de).

Once you've got your chariot, it's time to hit the road. Cycling around Tempelhofer Feld (*see p173*), along the Landwehrkanal or through Treptower Park to the site of the Soviet Memorial (*see p162*) all make for unforgettable rides. If you're feeling more ambitious and you've a couple of days to spare, it's possible to cycle the whole 160-km route of the Berlin Wall.

▶ *If you're walking around the city, remember that bike lanes are taken very seriously in Berlin – don't wander into them without looking if you want to avoid a collision with an irate cyclist.*

Mitte

For decades, Mitte – meaning 'middle' or 'centre' – floundered in a no-man's-land between East and West. But now, as extensive construction continues apace, Mitte is right back in the swing of things. It contains many of Berlin's biggest sights: the Brandenburg Gate (Brandenburger Tor), the TV Tower (Fernsehturm) and the magnificent UNESCO World Heritage Site of Museum Island (Museumsinsel), which is in the midst of an epic overhaul, scheduled to be fully completed by 2025. But there's much more to this area than ticking off the sights – galleries abound, as do cool shops. As for nightlife, take your pick from fine dining at the likes of Borchardt and Grill Royal to the bar scene that stretches down Torstrasse, and the late-night kebab mecca of Rosenthalerplatz. While many bars have gone upmarket and the clubs have relocated further away from the centre, there's plenty of life in the old dog yet and still lots of reasons to stay up late.

♥ Don't miss

1 Brandenburger Tor *p71*
Berlin's long-suffering victory arch now back to its former glory.

2 Neues Museum *p75*
View Nefertiti's bust in this neoclassical museum restored by David Chipperfield.

3 Denkmal für die ermordeten Juden Europas *p73*
This sea of standing stones serves as a graphic memorial to the Holocaust.

4 Humboldt Forum *p79*
Many promises have been made about this cultural centre in the newly rebuilt Stadtschloss.

5 Museum für Naturkunde *p80*
Children love to roam among the dinosaur skeletons in this fascinating natural history museum.

6 Fernsehturm *p88*
Experience a bird's-eye view of the city.

7 Pergamonmuseum *p80*
Still world class despite the building work.

Alexanderplatz *p86*

MITTE
Restaurants & cafés

1 Barcomi's p90
2 Borchardt p81
3 Café Fleury p90
4 Café Nö! p81
5 Chicago-Williams p90
6 CôCô p91
7 Common Ground p91
8 District Mot p91
9 Einstein Unter den Linden p81
10 Grill Royal p81
11 House of Small Wonder p92
12 Ishin Mittelstrasse p81
13 Katz Orange p92
14 Lebensmittel in Mitte p92
15 Das Lokal p92
16 Mogg p92
17 Nola's am Weinberg p92
18 Noto p92
19 Princess Cheesecake p93
20 Schwarzwaldstuben p93
21 Store Kitchen p93
22 Tadshikische Teestube p93
23 The Tree p93
24 Trois Minutes sur Mer p93
25 Yarok Berlin p94

Bars & pubs

1 Altes Europa p94
2 Bar 3 p94
3 Buck and Breck p94
4 Cordobar p94
5 Kim Bar p94
6 Mein Haus am See p94
7 Newton Bar p83
8 Ständige Vertretung p83
9 Tausend p83

Shops & services

1 Acne Studios p95
2 Ampelmann Shop p95
3 Arkonaplatz Flohmarkt p95
4 Bonbon Macherei p95
5 Brille 54 p83
6 Buchhandlung Walther König p95
7 Civilist p96
8 The Corner Berlin p83
9 do you read me?! p96
10 DSTM p96
11 Dussmann das KulturKaufhaus p83
12 Fun Factory p96
13 Galeries Lafayette p83
14 LaLa Berlin p96
15 Made in Berlin p96
16 Mykita p96
17 Das Neue Schwarz p97
18 Oona p97
19 Pro QM p97
20 RSVP p97
21 Soto p97
22 Whisky & Cigars p97
23 Wood Wood p97
24 Zionskirchplatz Farmers' Market p97

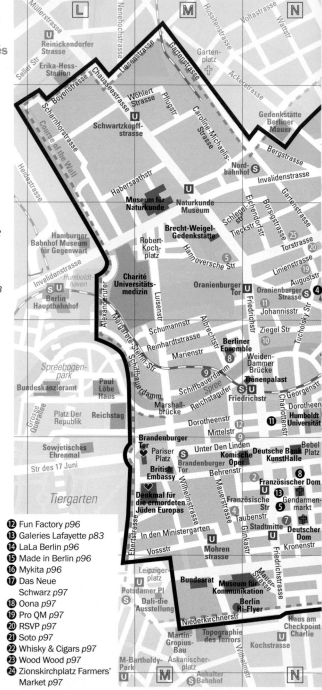

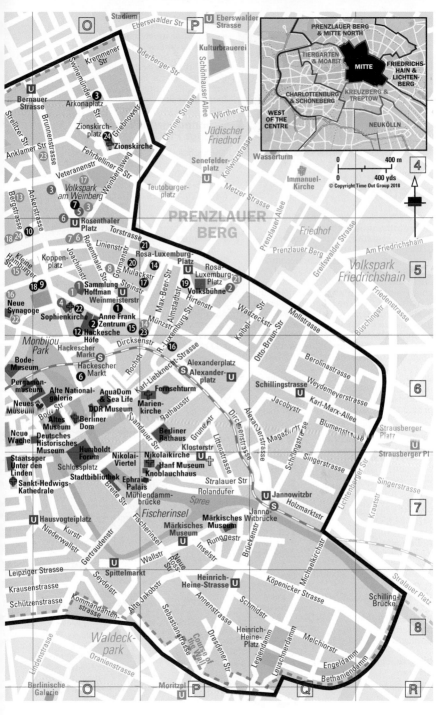

Stadium

P U Eberswalder Strasse

Kremmener Str
Eberswalder Str
Kulturbrauerei

Swinemünder Str
Oderberger Str
Schönhauser Allee

U
Bernauer Strasse
Arkonaplatz
Zionskirch-platz 24
Zionskirche
Griebnowstr

Chorner Strasse
Jüdischer Friedhof

Wörther Str
Wasserturm

Strelitzer Str
Brunnenstrasse
Anklamer Str
23
Fehrbelliner Str
Weinbergsweg
Veteranenstr
Senefelder-platz U
Immanuel-Kirche

0   400 m
0   400 yds
© Copyright Time Out Group 2018

4

Bergstrasse 13
3
17
Volkspark am Weinberg
Teutoburger-platz
Metzer Strasse

PRENZLAUER BERG

7 3
U Rosenthaler Platz 6
Torstrasse
Rosa-Luxemburg-Platz

Friedhof
Prenzlauer Berg Strasse
Am Friedrichshain

Volkspark Friedrichshain

5

Ackerstrasse
18 24 10
7 6
Linienstrasse
21

Koppen-platz
Joachimstr
Gormannstr
20
Mulackstr
14
Rosa Luxemburg Platz U
21
2

Kleine Hamburger Str 15
18 9
8
Steinstr
17
Volksbühne
19

Neue Synagoge 16
22
1
Sammlung Hoffman
Weinmeisterstr U
Max-Beer-Str
Almstadtstr
Hirtenstr

4
22
Sophienkirche 2 Anne Frank 1 Zentrum
12 Hackesche Höfe 15 23
Münzstr
Rosa-Luxemburg-Strasse

Monbijou Park
Hackescher Markt S
Dircksenstr
Rochstr
16

Bode-Museum
Hackescher Markt 6
Karl-Liebknecht-Strasse
Alexanderplatz
Berolinastrasse

Pergamon-museum
Alte National-galerie
6
AquaDom & Sea Life
Fernsehturm
U Alexander-platz
Schillingstrasse
Weydemeyerstrasse

Neues Museum
DDR Museum
Marien-kirche
Rathausstr
Jacobystr
Karl-Marx-Allee

Neue Wache
Altes Museum
Berliner Dom
Spandauer Str
Berliner Rathaus
Grunerstr
Magazinstrasse
Blumenstrasse
Strausberger Platz

Deutsches Historisches Museum
Humboldt Forum
Klosterstr
Dircksenstrasse
Schillingstr
U Strausberger Pl

Staatsoper Unter den Linden
Schlossplatz
Nikolai-Viertel
Nikolaikirche U
Hanf Museum
Singerstrasse
Lichtenberger Str
Singerstrasse

Sankt-Hedwigs-Kathedrale
Stadtbibliothek
Ephraim-Palais
Knoblauchhaus
Stralauer Str
Krautstr

Mühlendamm-brücke
Rolandufer
Spree
U Jannowitzbr
Holzmarktstr

U Hausvogteiplatz
Fischerinsel
Janno-witzbrücke S

7

Kurstr
Niederwallstr
Fischerinsel
Märkisches Museum
Märkisches Museum
Runggestr
Inselstr
Brückenstr
Michaelkirchstr

Leipziger Strasse
Gertraudenstr
Sevdelstr
U
Wallstr
Neue Roß Str
Schilling-Brücke

Krausenstrasse
Spittelmarkt
Alte Jakobstr
Heinrich-Heine-Strasse U
Köpenicker Strasse
Stralauer Platz

Schützenstrasse
Kommandanten-strasse
Sebastianstrasse
Annenstrasse
Schmidtstr
Leuschnerdamm

8

Lindenstrasse
Waldeck-park
Oranienstrasse
Dresdener Str
Heinrich-Heine-Platz
Course of the Wall
Heinrich-Heine-damm
Engeldamm
Bethaniendamm

Berlinische Galerie
O
Moritzpl P
Q
R

PRENZLAUER BERG & MITTE NORTH
TIERGARTEN & MOABIT
MITTE
FRIEDRICHS-HAIN & LICHTEN-BERG
CHARLOTTENBURG & SCHÖNEBERG
KREUZBERG & TREPTOW
WEST OF THE CENTRE
NEUKÖLLN

Pariser Platz

UNTER DEN LINDEN & AROUND

From before the domination of the Hohenzollerns through to the Weimar Republic, and from the Third Reich to the GDR, the entire history of Berlin can be found on or around the celebrated street of **Unter den Linden**. Originally laid out to connect the town centre with the king's hunting grounds of Tiergarten, and running east from the Brandenburger Tor to Museumsinsel, the street got its name from the *Linden* (lime trees) that shaded its central walkway. Hitler, concerned that the trees obscured the view of his parades, had them felled, but they were later replanted.

During the 18th and 19th centuries, the Hohenzollerns erected Baroque and neoclassical buildings along their capital's showcase street. The side streets were laid out in a grid by Great Elector Friedrich Wilhelm

for his Friedrichstadt district. It was primarily a residential street of nobles' palaces until German reunification in 1871, when it was transformed into a bustling commercial avenue befitting Berlin's new status as a *Weltstadt*. By the 1900s, contemporary commentators were already comparing it to Paris for its decadent nightlife scene.

Brandenburger Tor and Pariser Platz

The focal point of Unter den Linden's western end is the **Brandenburger Tor** (Brandenburg Gate; *see p71*). West of the gate stretches the vast expanse of the **Tiergarten** (*see p103*), Berlin's central park. Just to the north is the phoenix-like **Reichstag** (*see p105*), while ten minutes' walk south is the even more dramatically reconceived **Potsdamer Platz** complex.

Immediately east of the Brandenburger Tor is **Pariser Platz**, which was given its name in 1814 when Prussia and its allies conquered Paris. This square, enclosed by embassies and bank buildings, was once seen as Berlin's *Empfangssaal* – its reception room. Foreign dignitaries would ceremoniously pass through on their way to visit tyrants and dictators in their palaces, and today this remains the area where you'll still see enormous limos carting around politicians and diplomats. In 1993, it was decided the Tor looked a little exposed, so plans were drawn up to revive Pariser Platz, with new buildings on the same scale as the old ones, featuring conservative

❤ Time to eat & drink

Leisurely brunch
Common Ground *p91*, Café Fleury *p90*

Cheap lunch
Ishin Mittelstrasse *p81*, Yarok Berlin *p94*

Coffee and cake
Barcomi's *p90*, Princess Cheesecake *p93*

Taste of Vietnam
District Mot *p91*, Côcô *p91*

Blow-out dining
Borchardt *p81*, Grill Royal *p81*, Das Lokal *p92*

Drink among the art stars
Bar 3 *p94*, Kim Bar *p94*

❤ Time to shop

Designer glasses for that Berlin look
Brille 54 *p83*, Mykita *p96*

Books make you smarter
do you read me?! *p96*, Dussmann das KulturKaufhaus *p83*, Buchhandlung Walther König *p95*

Fashionista faves
DSTM *p96*, LaLa Berlin *p96*, Wood Wood *p97*, Das Neue Schwarz *p97*

Your piece of Berlin
Ampelmann Shop *p95*, RSVP *p97*, Arkonaplatz Flohmarkt *p95*

Indulge your vices
Fun Factory *p96*, Whisky & Cigars *p97*

**In the know
Getting around**

With five U-Bahn lines, one S-Bahn that bisects the district and a multitude of trams heading north, east and west from Alexanderplatz, you're spoilt for public transport options in Mitte. 'Der Alex' is the central hub and most visitors to Berlin will at least change connections here. Plenty of regional trains leave from Alexanderplatz too, heading to Potsdam, Spreewald and other popular day-trip destinations. For a picturesque walk, get off the S-Bahn at Hackescher Markt and walk over the beautifully restored Friedrichsbrücke for a stunning introduction to Museum Island.

❤ Brandenburger Tor

Pariser Platz. S-Bahn Brandenburger Tor.
***Map** p68 M7.*

Constructed in 1791 to a design by Carl Gotthard Langhans and modelled on the Propylaea gateway into ancient Athens, the Brandenburg Gate was built as a triumphal arch celebrating Prussia's capital city. It was initially called the Friedenstor (Gate of Peace) and is the only city gate remaining from Berlin's original 18. (Today, only a few U-Bahn station names recall the other city gates, such as Frankfurter Tor or Schlesisches Tor). The Quadriga statue, a four-horse chariot driven by Victory and designed by Johann Gottfried Schadow, sits on top of the gate. It has had an eventful life. When Napoleon conquered Berlin in 1806, he carted the Quadriga off to Paris and held it hostage until his defeat in 1814. The Tor was badly damaged during World War II and, during subsequent renovations, the GDR removed the Prussian Iron Cross and turned the Quadriga round so that the chariot faced west. The current Quadriga is actually a 1958 copy of the 18th-century original. The Brandenburg Gate was stranded in no-man's-land between East and West Berlin for 30 years, and from its vantage point on top of the gate, the statue had a front row seat for some of the most significant moments in reunification history. The Quadriga watched on when Ronald Reagan called on Mr Gorbachev to 'Tear down this wall!'. It was there too when, on 22 December 1989, the Brandenburger Tor border crossing was reopened, and Helmut Kohl, the West German chancellor, walked through to be greeted by Hans Modrow, the East German prime minister, just prior to Germany's reunification. Since then both gate and Quadriga have been given facelifts. The Iron Cross has been replaced, and the Quadriga turned back to face into Mitte once again.

exteriors and contemporary interiors. Some old faces are back on the historical sites they occupied before World War II: the reconstructed **Adlon** hotel (*see p298*) is now at its old address, as is the **British Embassy**, round the corner at Wilhelmstrasse 70-71. (Wilhelmstrasse is closed to traffic for a block south of the square because of security provisions for the Embassy.) On the south-west corner of the square – the last building to complete the Pariser Platz puzzle – is the underwhelming **US Embassy**.

While outwardly conforming to aesthetic restrictions, many of the straightforward exteriors front flights of fancy within. Frank Gehry's **DG Bank** at no.3 has a huge, biomorphic interior dome hidden behind its regular façade. The **Dresdner Bank** opposite is virtually hollow, thanks to another interior atrium. Next door, Christian de Portzamparc's **French Embassy** features a space-saving 'vertical garden' on the courtyard wall, and 'french windows' extending over two storeys.

Directly to the south of Pariser Platz is the vast **Denkmal für die ermordeten Juden Europas** (Memorial to the Murdered Jews of Europe, Holocaust Memorial; *see p73*). Designed by Peter Eisenman (from an original plan with sculptor Richard Serra), it's a city-block-size field of concrete slabs, arranged in rows but sloping in different directions on uneven ground. Conceived in 1993, the project became mired in controversy. The winning design of the initial competition was rejected by then Chancellor Kohl, and there was no end of argument over the second competition, including rows over location (the chosen site has no particular link to the Holocaust), function (should such a monument draw a line under history or seek to stimulate debate and discussion?), delivery (one of the companies involved in construction was subsequently removed due to links with Degesch, wartime Zyklon B producers) and content (many feel the memorial should honour all victims of the Holocaust, not only Jewish ones).

In the wake of this memorial, assorted other victim memorials have been built or are planned (*see p82* Remember, Remember). The first of these was erected on the other side of Ebertstrasse in 2008: Elmgreen and Dragset's **Denkmal für die im Nationalsozialismus verfolgten Homosexuellen** (Monument to the Homosexuals Persecuted During National Socialism). It looks like one of the slabs from the Jewish Denkmal but contains a video installation.

Between the Denkmal and the Leipziger Platz/Potsdamer Platz complex is an area filled with representations from Germany's various *Länder*. If you want to visit the

site of Hitler's World War II bunker, head to the car park on the corner of In den Ministergärten and Gertrud-Kolmar-Strasse. There is nothing to see, other than an information board detailing in English and German the history of the Führerbunker, but it's chilling nonetheless.

East along Unter den Linden

Heading east along Unter den Linden, passing the 1950s Stalinist wedding cake-style **Russian Embassy** on your right, and, on the next block, the box office of the **Komische Oper** (*see p251*), you'll reach the crossroads with Friedrichstrasse, once a café-strewn focus of Weimar Berlin, now a fairly characterless home to fancy shops.

On the other side of the junction, on the right, housed in the ground floor of a 1920s building that's now occupied by Deutsche Bank, is the **KunstHalle**, displaying items from the bank's massive collection. Facing the art gallery across Unter den Linden stands the **Staatsbibliotek** (open to all, and there's a small café), usually filled with students from the **Humboldt-Universität**. The university's grand old façade has been restored, as have the two statues of the Humboldts (founder Wilhelm and his brother Alexander), between which booksellers set up tables in good weather.

Across the street is **Bebelplatz**, site of the notorious Nazi book-burning, commemorated by Micha Ullmann's subterranean monument set into the Platz itself. The glass has become pretty scratched, unfortunately, and it can be hard to see through. Dominating the square's eastern side is the **Staatsoper** (*see p252*), built in neoclassical style by Georg Wenzeslaus von Knobelsdorff in 1741-43. Following extensive renovations, which included raising the ceiling to create better acoustics, the Staatsoper finally reopened two years behind schedule in 2017.

Just south of the Staatsoper (and also designed by Knobelsdorff, in 1747) is **Sankt-Hedwigs-Kathedrale**, a curious circular Roman Catholic church, inspired by the Pantheon in Rome. A minute's walk east of here is another church, **Friedrichswerdersche Kirche**. This imposing brick structure, which was designed by Karl Friedrich Schinkel, was completed in 1831. It was badly damaged in World War II but reopened in the late 1980s as a homage to its architect. Structural problems meant it closed again in 2012 – and remains shut. Across the Schinkelplatz lay the **Bauakademie**, the architect's proto-modernist School of Architecture. It was demolished to make room for a GDR ministry, but reconstruction is scheduled to begin in 2021.

♥ Holocaust Memorial (Denkmal für die ermordeten Juden Europas)

Cora-Berliner-Strasse 1 (2639 4336, www. holocaust-denkmal.de). U2, S1, S2, S25 Potsdamer Platz. **Open** *Memorial 24hrs daily. Information centre Apr-Sept 10am-8pm Tue-Sun. Oct-Mar 10am-7pm Tue-Sun.* **Admission** *free.* **Map** *p68 M7.*

No debate about the intersection of history, architecture and the form of Berlin's reunified cityscape lumbered on for so long or conjured so much controversy as the one that engendered this grid of concrete blocks. In the 1990s, Chancellor Kohl promised that a memorial to the victims of the Holocaust would be built in Berlin. The winning design of a 1995 competition was a concrete slab the size of two football fields, bearing the names of all 4.2 million identified Holocaust victims. But the cliché of equating the enormity of the crime with the size of the memorial was widely criticised, and Chancellor Kohl rejected the design. A second competition in 1998 produced a scheme by Peter Eisenman and Richard Serra (who pulled out for personal reasons) involving 4,000 columns.

The Memorial to the Murdered Jews of Europe, a scaled-down version of Eisenman's design, was eventually unveiled in 2005 and consists of a 'field' of 2,711 'stelae', arranged in undulating rows on 19,704sq m (212,000sq ft) of ground, with an attendant information centre. Each of the concrete slabs has its own foundation, and they tilt at differing angles. Ranging in height from 20 cm to 4.7 m, the slabs are as individual as headstones. The effect is (no doubt deliberately) reminiscent of the packed graves in Prague's Old Jewish Cemetery. There's no vantage point or overview; to fully engage with the structure you need to walk into it. It's haunting in places, especially on overcast days and near the middle of the monument, where it's easy to feel a sense of confinement as you lose sight of the outside world; other visitors to the monument are seen in glimpses as they pass between the stelae, only to quickly disappear. Early criticism often focused on the monument's lack of specificity – there are no stars of David here, no obvious symbolism or recognition of German culpability – but it has since won grudging recognition from many former critics. In 2012, concerns that the slabs were beginning to crack and crumble resulted in the addition of steel collars to reinforce the concrete.

The information centre is at the south-east corner of the site, mostly underground. It's like a secular crypt, containing a sombre presentation of facts and figures about the Holocaust's victims.

▶ *For details of other memorials around the city, see p82* Remember, Remember.

On the west side of Bebelplatz is Rocco Forte's **Hotel de Rome** (*see p298*), occupying what used to be the East German central bank, and the late 18th-century **Alte Bibliotek**. Alongside that, in the centre of Unter den Linden, stands a restored equestrian statue of Frederick the Great.

On the north side of Unter den Linden, the **Neue Wache** (New Guardhouse), constructed by Schinkel in 1816-18, originally served as a guardhouse for the royal residences in the area. Today, it is a hauntingly plain memorial to the 'victims of war and tyranny', with an enlarged reproduction of a Käthe Kollwitz sculpture, *Mother with Dead Son*, at its centre. Beneath this are the remains of an unknown soldier and an unknown concentration camp victim, surrounded by earth from World War II battlefields and concentration camps.

Next to it, to the east, is the Baroque **Zeughaus**, a former armoury with a deceptively peaceful pink façade. Following renovations that were completed in 2006, it once again houses the **Deutsches Historisches Museum**. The new wing by IM Pei hosts changing exhibitions and has a fine café.

This whole last eastern stretch of Unter den Linden is undergoing further heritage restoration. The rebuilding of the nearby **Stadtschloss**, a symbolic and hugely controversial project (*see p30* Berlin Today), has been heralded as the act that will make Berlin, once more, the 'Athens on the Spree'.

Museumsinsel

The eastern end of Unter den Linden abuts the island in the Spree where Berlin was 'born' and the site of the original town, Cölln. The northern part, with its magnificent collection of museums and galleries, is known as Museumsinsel (Museum Island) and has been on UNESCO's World Cultural Heritage list since 1999. The southern half (much enlarged by landfill), once a neighbourhood for the city's fishermen (known as Fischerinsel), is now dominated by a clutch of grim tower blocks.

The five Museumsinsel museums (the Pergamonmuseum, Altes Museum, Alte Nationalgalerie, Bode-Museum and Neues Museum) are all undergoing a massive restoration programme; beset with spiralling costs and frequent delays, the works are set to continue for some years yet. The projects include the James Simon Gallery, a €75 million visitor centre designed by the British architect David Chipperfield that is being built beside the Neues Museum. It will be linked to the Neues, Altes, Pergamon and Bode museums by an underground passageway decorated with archaeological objects.

The **Pergamonmuseum**, one of Berlin's main attractions, is a showcase for three huge and important examples of ancient architecture: the Hellenistic Pergamon Altar (part of a Greek temple complex from what is now western Turkey), the Babylonian Gate of Ishtar and the Roman Market Gate of Miletus. The museum also contains the Museum für Islamische Kunst (Museum of Islamic Art).

Schinkel's superb **Altes Museum**, from 1830, houses a permanent collection of antiquities, including sections on the Romans and Etruscans, and rotating temporary exhibitions, while the renovated **Alte Nationalgalerie** is home to a wide-ranging collection of 19th-century painting and sculpture.

Although the Pergamon is Berlin's most visited museum and the Altes is the most striking, it's the **Neues Museum** (*see p75*) that is arguably the one to visit if you're short of time. Reopened in 2009 after a rebuild overseen by British architect David Chipperfield, the museum is home to the famous bust of Queen Nefertiti, along with other treasures of Egypt, the Stone Age and pre- and early history.

Dominating the Museumsinsel skyline is the huge, bombastic **Berliner Dom**. It's worth climbing right up to the cathedral's dome for fine views over the city. In front of here, bounded on one side by the neoclassical colonnade of the Altes Museum, is the **Lustgarten**, an elegant green square.

Across the main road bisecting the island is where the GDR's parliament complex once stood. The original palace, the **Stadtschloss**, home to the Hollenzoherns since 1451, witnessed both the overthrow of the Kaisers and the failed 1918 Spartacist uprising. It was badly damaged in World War II. Instead of rebuilding this symbol of Prussian militarism, the GDR demolished the palace in 1950, and Erich Hoenecker

❤ Neues Museum

Bodestrasse 1 (266 424242, www.smb. museum/nm). U6, S1, S2, S5, S7, S25, S75 Friedrichstrasse, or S5, S7, S75 Hackescher Markt. **Open** *10am-6pm Tue, Wed, Fri-Sun; 10am-8pm Thur. Entry by timed ticket.* **Admission** *€12; €6 reductions, or Museumsinsel ticket (see p74).* **Map** *p68 O6.*

Designed by Friedrich August Stüler in the mid-19th century, the Neues Museum was left a vacant wreck for years, following bomb damage in World War II. Reconstruction began in the GDR in the late 1980s, only to be abandoned when Germany was reunified. The job of rebuilding the Neues Museum finally went to architect David Chipperfield, whose design was awarded the European Union Prize for Contemporary Architecture in 2011. It beautifully blends architectural elements of old and new by accentuating the original design with modern elements used to restore structural continuity.

The museum reopened in 2009 and houses the Egyptian Museum & Papyrus Collection, the Museum of Prehistory & Early History and artefacts from the Collection of Classical Antiquities. The most famous object is the bust of the Egyptian queen Nefertiti (which Germany refuses to return to Egypt despite repeated requests). The Prehistory and Early History galleries, which trace the evolution of *Homo sapiens*

from 1,000,000 BC to the Bronze Age, have the skull of a Neanderthal from Le Moustier and reproductions (and some originals) of Heinrich Schliemann's famous treasure from ancient Troy, including works in ceramic and gold, as well as weaponry. The famed 'Berlin Golden Hat' is the most notable piece in the room dedicated to the Bronze Age. Look out, too, for the sixth-century BC grave of a girl buried with a gold coin in her mouth. Information is available in English. Admission is within a half-hour ticketed time slot, so book online to skip the queues.

built his 1970s showpiece, Palast der Republik, there, which grew to be loved by East Berliners. After lengthy arguments and disagreements, the asbestos-ridden Palast was finally demolished in 2009, and the controversial decision was reached to rebuild the Stadtschloss. Scheduled to open at the end of 2019, the new building will house the **Humboldt Forum**, a centrepiece for the collection of Berlin's state museums, alongside exhibition and event spaces, restaurants and a cinema. In the mean time, webcams are tracking the construction process and a series of pop-up events are taking place (humboldtforum.com), including open days to allow visitors a peek at the work in progress.

▶ *A new metro station, U5 Museumsinsel, is due to open near the Stadtschloss in 2020. For more on the Stadtschloss redevelopment, see p33 Berlin Today.*

South of Unter den Linden

What the Kurfürstendamm was in postwar West Berlin, **Friedrichstrasse** had been and is trying to be again: the city's glitziest shopping street. As with Unter den Linden, the north–south street (starting at Mehringplatz in Kreuzberg and ending at Oranienburger Tor in Mitte) was laid out as part of the late 17th-century Baroque expansion of the city.

The liveliest, sleekest stretch of the street is that between **Checkpoint Charlie** (*see p147*) and Friedrichstrasse station. A huge amount of money has been poured into redevelopment here, with office buildings and upmarket shops and malls galore, although it's a pretty soulless place. Look out for the all-glass façade of the modernist-style **Galeries Lafayette** (no.75), the acute angles of the expressionist **Quartier 206** (nos.71-74) and the monolithic geometric mass of **Quartier 205** (nos.66-70). Otherwise, there are luxury-car showrooms, and boutiques for Mont Blanc, Cartier and countless other high-class concerns.

Just to the east of this stretch lies the square of **Gendarmenmarkt**, one of the high points of Frederick the Great's vision for the city. Here, two churches – the **Französischer Dom**, home to the **Hugenottenmuseum**; and the **Deutscher Dom** – frame the **Konzerthaus** (*see p251*), the home base of the Deutsches Symphonie-Orchester Berlin.

Just west of Friedrichstrasse, on Leipziger Strasse, is the **Museum für Kommunikation**.

▶ *Many other interesting sights are close by, over the Mitte border with Kreuzberg. For these, see pp142-163 Kreuzberg & Treptow.*

North of Unter den Linden

The continuation of Friedrichstrasse north of Unter den Linden is less appealing and lively than its southern stretch. Friedrichstrasse station once had an interior notable mostly for its ability to confuse. Its role as the only East–West border crossing point open for all categories of citizen involved a confusing warren of passageways and interior partitions. Today, it is open and full of shops.

Following the line of the train tracks east along Georgenstrasse, you'll come upon the **Berliner Antik & Flohmarkt** – a succession of antiques stores, bookshops and cafés in the *Bogen* ('arches'), underneath the railway.

The building just to the north of the railway station is known as the **Tränenpalast** (Palace of Tears). This was where departing visitors left their Eastern friends and relations who could not follow them through the border.

Across Friedrichstrasse stands the **Admiralspalast**, a landmark theatre from 1910 that survived wartime bombing. The building contains a 1,600-seat theatre used over the decades for everything from Broadway transfers to the Staatsoper. There are also two smaller performance spaces and a restored Roman-style bathhouse turned 21st-century spa.

Crossing the river on the wrought-iron Weidendammer Brücke, a left turn on Schiffbauerdamm brings you to the **Berliner Ensemble** (*see p255*), with its bronze statue of Bertolt Brecht, who directed the company from 1948 to 1956, surrounded by quotations from his works. *Die Dreigroschenoper* (*The Threepenny Opera*) was premiered here on 31 August 1928. The theatre's canteen, down some steps in the backyard, is open to the public, and is a great place to grab a cheap bite to eat. There are also various congenial bars and less touristy restaurants along the riverfront, beyond which this neighbourhood begins to merge into what is now the government quarter.

Back on Friedrichstrasse stands the **Friedrichstadtpalast** (*see p257*), a large variety venue that was an entertainment hotspot during the GDR days, since it took hard currency; it still pulls the crowds today, albeit mostly grannies from out of town. Further north is the **Brecht-Weigel-Gedenkstätte**, home to Bertolt Brecht (until his death in 1956) and his iconic actor wife Helene Weigel. Both are buried in the **Dorotheenstädtische Friedhof** (open 8am-dusk daily) next door, along with the architect Schinkel, the author Heinrich Mann and the philosopher Hegel.

Two worthwhile museums are five and ten minutes' walk from here: the **Museum**

Humboldt Forum and Berliner Dom

für Naturkunde (Natural History Museum) and the **Hamburger Bahnhof – Museum für Gegenwart** (Hamburg Station – Museum of Contemporary Art), which puts on excellent temporary exhibitions within the atmospheric confines of a former railway station (*see p77*).

Sights & museums

Alte Nationalgalerie
Bodestrasse 1-3 (266 424242, www.smb. museum/ang). U6, S1, S2, S5, S7, S25, S75 Friedrichstrasse, or S5, S7, S75 Hackescher Markt. Open 10am-6pm Tue, Wed, Fri-Sun; 10am-8pm Thur. Admission €8; €4 reductions, or Museumsinsel ticket (see p74). Map p68 O6.

With its ceiling and wall paintings, fabric wallpapers and marble staircase, the Old National Gallery is a sparkling home to one of the largest collections of 19th-century art and sculpture in Germany. Friedrich Stüler was commissioned to design the building to house the collection of wealthy industrialist JHW Wagener in 1861, who donated it to the Prussian state. The 440 paintings and 80 sculptures span the years from Goethe to the early modern period, with Romantic German artists such as Adolph Menzel, Caspar David Friedrich, Max Liebermann and Carl Spitzweg well represented. There are also some first-rate works from Manet, Monet and Rodin. Although the gallery is worth a visit, don't expect to see any kind of definitive German national collection.

Altes Museum
Am Lustgarten (266 424242, www.smb. museum/am). U6, S1, S2, S5, S7, S25, S75 Friedrichstrasse, or S5, S7, S75 Hackescher Markt. Open 10am-6pm Tue, Wed, Fri-Sun; 10am-8pm Thur. Admission €10; €5 reductions, or Museumsinsel ticket (see p74). Map p68 O6.

Opened as the Royal Museum in 1830, the Old Museum was originally the home for all the art treasures on Museumsinsel. It was designed by Schinkel and is considered one of his finest buildings, with a particularly magnificent entrance rotunda, where vast neon letters declare that 'All Art Has Been Contemporary'. The Egyptian galleries are now housed in the Neues Museum round the corner (*see p75*), but this building showcases other ancient civilisations, with an excellent look at the Etruscans and Romans on the top floor. The main floor exhibits the collection of classical antiquities, including a world-class selection of Greek art; pride of place goes to the superlative third-century bronze, *The Praying Boy*.

Berliner Dom
Am Lustgarten (2026 9136, guided tours 2026 9119, www.berliner-dom.de). U6, S1, S2, S5, S7, S25, S75 Friedrichstrasse, or S5, S7, S75 Hackescher Markt. Open Apr-Sept 9am-7pm daily. Oct-Mar 9am-7pm daily. Admission €7; €4 reductions; free under-18s. Map p68 O6.

The dramatic Berlin Cathedral celebrated its centenary in 2005. Built in Italian Renaissance style, it was destroyed during World War II and remained a ruin until 1973, when extensive restoration work began. It has always looked fine from the outside, but now that the internal work is complete, it is fully restored to its former glory. Crammed with detail and containing dozens of statues of eminent German Protestants, its lush 19th-century interior is hardly the perfect acoustic space for the frequent concerts that are held here (even on the colossal organ), but it's worth a visit to see the crypt containing around 90 sarcophagi of notables from the Hohenzollern dynasty, or to clamber up for splendid views from the cupola. Call to book a guided tour.

Bode-Museum

*Monbijoubrücke (266 424242, www.smb.
museum/bm). U6, S1, S2, S5, S7, S25, S75
Friedrichstrasse, or S5, S7, S75 Hackescher
Markt. **Open** 10am-6pm Tue, Wed, Fri-
Sun; 10am-8pm Thur. **Admission** €12; €6
reductions, or Museumsinsel ticket (see p74).
Map p68 N6.*

Built by Berlin architect Ernst Eberhard
von Ihne in 1904, the Bode-Museum was
originally intended by Wilhelm von Bode
to be a home for art from the beginnings of
Christendom; it now contains the Byzantine
Collection, Sculpture Collection and the
Numismatic Collection. The neo-Baroque
great dome, the basilica hall and the glorious
cupola were carefully restored in the early
years of the new millennium to keep up
with modern curatorial standards, but they
retain their magnificence. Most impressively,
despite having one of the world's largest
sculpture collections and more than half
a million pieces in the coin collection,
the museum somehow retains a totally
uncluttered feel, and the sculptures stand
free from off-putting glass cases. Highlights
include the wall-length Apse Mosaic from
AD 545 and the 14th-century Mannheim
High Altar.

Brecht-Weigel-Gedenkstätte

*Chausseestrasse 125 (200 571 844, www.
adk.de/de/archiv/gedenkstaetten). U6
Oranienburger Tor. **Open** Guided tours
(every 30 mins) 10-11.30am, 2-3.30pm Tue;
10-11.30am Wed; 10-11.30am, 5-6.30pm Thur;
10-11.30am Fri; 10am-3.30pm Sat; 11am-6pm
Sun; and by appointment. **Admission** €5;
€2.50 reductions. No cards. **Map** p68 M5.*

Brecht's home from 1948 until his death in
1956 has been preserved exactly as he left it.
Tours of the house (phone in advance for an
English tour) give interesting insights into the
life and reading habits of the playwright. The
window at which he worked overlooks the
grave of Hegel in the neighbouring cemetery.
Brecht's wife, actress Helene Weigel,
continued living here until her death in 1971.
The Brecht archives are kept upstairs.

Deutsche Bank KunstHalle

*Unter den Linden 13-15 (202 0930, www.
deutsche-bank-kunsthalle.de). U6
Französische Strasse. **Open** 10am-8pm daily
Admission €4; €3 reductions; free under-
12s. Free to all Mon. **Map** p68 N7.*

Deutsche Bank took over management of this
space from the Guggenheim in April 2013
and now holds four shows a year, with guest
curators invited to build exhibitions from the
banks's vast corporate art collection.

Deutscher Dom

*Gendarmenmarkt, entrance in
Markgrafenstrasse (2273 0431). U2, U6
Stadtmitte. **Open** May-Sept 10am-7pm
Tue-Sun. Oct-Apr 10am-6pm Tue-Sun.
Guided tours every half hour 11am-5pm; call
first for English- or French-speaking guide.
Admission free. **Map** p68 N7.*

The neoclassical domed tower of this church
– and the identical tower of the Französischer
Dom on the other side of the square – were
built in 1780-85 by Carl von Gontard for
Frederick the Great, in imitation of Santa
Maria in Montesanto and Santa Maria del
Miracoli in Rome. The Deutscher Dom was
intended for Berlin's Lutheran community.
The dome is topped by a 7-m (23-ft) gilded
statue representing Virtue. Badly damaged
by Allied bombing in the war, the church
and tower burned down in 1943, and were
restored in the 1980s and '90s.

Inside is a permanent exhibition on
the history of Germany's parliamentary
system, from the 1848 revolution through
the suspension of parliamentary politics by
the Nazis, up to the present day. Visitors
are encouraged to consider the role of
parliaments throughout the modern world,
but there are no translations, so to get
much out of this without a guided tour your
German must be up to scratch.

Deutsches Historisches Museum

*Zeughaus, Unter den Linden 2 (203 040,
www.dhm.de). U6 Französische Strasse.
Open 10am-6pm daily. **Admission** €8; €4
reductions; free under-18s. **Map** p68 O6.*

The permanent exhibition in the Zeughaus
provides an exhaustive blast through German
history from 100 BC to the present day,
divided chronologically into significant
eras. The museum originally had trouble
raising the funds to buy historical objects,
but there's enough here now for the exhibits
to work on their own, without the need for an
overarching narrative. German nationalism
becomes the focus once you enter the 19th
century, and, later on, more than one room
is dedicated to the Nazi era. The DHM has
succeeded admirably in looking the past
straight in the eye, although the attempt to be
impartial means that it's sometimes factual
to the extreme. Temporary exhibitions are
housed in the gorgeous IM Pei building.

Französischer Dom & Hugenottenmuseum

*Gendarmenmarkt (229 1760, www.
franzoesischer-dom.de). U2, U6 Stadtmitte.
Open see the website. **Admission** Church
free. Tower €3; €1 reductions. No cards.
Map p68 N7.*

Museum für Naturkunde *p80*

Built in the early 18th century for Berlin's 6,000-plus-strong French Protestant community, the church (known as the Französischen Friedrichstadtkirche) was later given a Baroque domed tower, as was the Deutscher Dom across the square. The tower, with its fine views over Mitte, is purely decorative and unconsecrated – and not part of the modest church, which has a separate entrance at the western end.

An exhibition on the history of the French Protestants in France and Berlin-Brandenburg is displayed within the building. The museum chronicles the religious persecution suffered by Calvinists (note the bust of Calvin on the outside of the church) and their subsequent immigration to Berlin after 1685, at the behest of the Hohenzollerns. The development of the Huguenot community is also detailed, with

paintings, documents and artefacts. One part of the museum is devoted to the church's history, particularly the effects of World War II – it was bombed during a Sunday service in 1944 and remained a ruin until the mid 1980s. The tower and museum were closed for extensive renovation work in 2017-18.

♥ Humboldt Forum

Stadtschloss, Unter den Linden 3 (265 9500, www.humboldtforum.com). U2 Hausvogteiplatz or U6 Französische Strasse. **Map** *p68 O7.*

Eagerly anticipated, the Humboldt Forum is the cultural centre that will sit like a jewel inside the new Berliner Stadtschloss. Opening in stages from late 2019, the forum promises to bring together diverse cultures and perspectives and to seek new insights into topical issues around globalisation.

The exhibition spaces will host the state's collection of artefacts from Oceania, Central America, Africa and the Far East, which were previously displayed at the ethnology and Asian art museums in Dahlem (see p203). Look out for masks and effigies from New Guinea, and a remarkable collection of original canoes and boats. There are also superb carvings from Benin and the Congo, beaded artefacts from Cameroon and a host of archaeological objects and fine artworks from India, Japan, China and Korea, dating from the early Stone Age to the present. In addition to the museum exhibits, a new exhibition entitled 'Berlin and the World' will explore the city's relationship to global issues of migration, war, religion and culture.

Museum für Kommunikation
Leipziger Strasse 16 (202 940, www.mfk-berlin.de). U2 Mohrenstrasse, U2, U6 Stadtmitte. **Open** *9am-8pm Tue; 9am-5pm Wed-Fri; 10am-6pm Sat, Sun.* **Admission** *€5; €3 reductions; free under-17s. No cards.* **Map** *p68 M8.*

A direct descendant of the world's first postal museum (founded in 1872), this collection covers a bit more than mere stamps. It traces the development of telecommunications up to the internet era, though philatelists might want to head straight to the basement and ogle the 'Blue Mauritius', one of the world's rarest stamps.

❤ Museum für Naturkunde
Invalidenstrasse 43 (8891 408591, www.museumfuernaturkunde.berlin). U6 Naturkundemuseum. **Open** *9.30am-6pm Tue-Fri; 10am-6pm Sat, Sun.* **Admission** *€8; €5 reductions.* **Map** *p68 M5.*

Berlin's renovated Natural History Museum is a real trove. The biggest (literally) draw is the skeleton of a Brachiosaurus dinosaur, which weighed 50 tons at death and is as high as a four-storey house. 'Oliver' – as the dinosaur is nicknamed – is one of the world's largest known land animals and was discovered in the early 1900s. Don't miss the creepy *Forschungssammlungen* (research collections), which show off some of the museum's store of over a million pickled animals suspended in jars of alcohol. Berlin's most famous polar bear, Knut, who died in 2011, is now stuffed and on display.

❤ Pergamonmuseum
Bodestrasse 1-3 (266 424242, www.smb.museum/pm). U6, S1, S2, S5, S7, S25, S75 Friedrichstrasse, or S5, S7, S75 Hackescher Markt. **Open** *10am-6pm Mon-Wed, Fri-Sun; 10am-8pm Thur.* **Admission** *€12; €6 reductions, or Museumsinsel ticket (see p74).* **Map** *p68 N6.*

One of the world's major archaeological museums, the Pergamon should not be missed, although protracted and ongoing renovations may affect the visitor experience until 2023. The museum comprises the Antikensammlung (Collection of Classical Antiquities) and the Vorderasiatisches Museum (Museum of Near Eastern Antiquities) and, among its many treasures, contains three unmissable exhibits. The star attraction is the Hellenistic Pergamon Altar, dating from 170-159 BC; huge as it is, the museum's partial reconstruction is only a third of the original's size. In an adjoining room, and even more architecturally impressive, is the towering Roman Market Gate of Miletus (29m/95ft wide and almost 17m/ 56ft high), erected in AD 120. This leads through to the third of the big attractions: the extraordinary blue- and ochre-tiled Gate of Ishtar and the Babylonian Processional Street, dating from the reign of King Nebuchadnezzar (605-562 BC). There are plenty of other astonishing things to see, including some stunning Assyrian reliefs. The Pergamon is also home to the Museum für Islamische Kunst (Museum of Islamic Art), which takes up some 14 rooms in the southern wing. This wide-ranging collection includes applied arts, crafts, books and architectural details from the eighth to the 19th centuries. Entrance to this museum is included in the overall admission price, as is an excellent audio guide.

▶ *The cost and timescale of the museum's renovation programme have both increased, meaning that the Pergamon Altar is now likely to remain closed until 2023.*

Sankt-Hedwigs-Kathedrale
Bebelplatz (203 4810, www.hedwigs-kathedrale.de). U2 Hausvogteiplatz, or U6 Französische Strasse. **Open** *10am-5pm Mon-Wed, Fri; 11am-5pm Thur; 1-5pm Sun.* **Admission** *free. Guided tours €1.50.* **Map** *p68 N7.*

Constructed in 1747 for Berlin's Catholic minority, this circular Knobelsdorff creation was bombed out during the war and only reconsecrated in 1963. Its modernised interior contains a split-level double altar with a ribbed dome. The crypt holds the remains of Bernhard Lichtenberg, who preached here against the Nazis, was arrested, and died while being transported to Dachau in 1943.

Schinkel Pavillon
Oberwallstrasse 1 (2088 6444, www.schinkelpavillon.de). U2 Hausvogteiplatz. **Open** *noon-6pm Thur-Sun.* **Admission** *€4; reductions €3.* **Map** *p68 N7.*

This gallery space is in the gardens of the Kronprinzenpalais, which itself claims to be the world's first contemporary art institution: the palace displayed work by Berlin's expressionists from 1918 until the Nazis closed it down for showing 'degenerate' art. Today, the octagonal pavilion with its wall-to-ceiling glass, designed to GDR specifications in 1969, happily shows all manner of installation, sculpture and performance art, cheerily degenerate or not. Philippe Parreno, Douglas Gordon and James Franco have all appeared.

Tränenpalast

Reichstagsufer 17 (4677 77911, www.hdg. de/traenenpalast). **Open** *9am-7pm Tue-Fri; 10am-6pm Sat, Sun.* **Admission** *free.* **Map** *p68 N6.*

Immediately after the construction of the Berlin Wall, the GDR erected a check-in hall at Friedrichstrasse railway station in 1962. On the border between east and west, the hall was soon renamed the *Tränenpalast*, or Palace of Tears, as it was here that families and friends on opposing sides of the wall were forced to separate. In autumn 2011, the building reopened as a museum commemorating the division of Berlin. Visit the restored inspection rooms to experience the oppressive atmosphere.

Restaurants & cafés

▶ *If you're after a cheap and filling lunch, join the jovial cast and crew at the Berliner Ensemble canteen (see p255).*

♥ Borchardt €€€-€€€€

Französische Strasse 47 (8188 6262). U6 Französische Strasse. **Open** *11.30am-late daily.* **Map** *p68 N7* ❷ *Brasserie*

The original Borchardt opened next door at no.48 in the late 19th century. It became the place for politicians and society folk, until it was destroyed in World War II. Now, Roland Mary and Marina Richter have reconstructed a highly fashionable, Maxim's-inspired bistro. People come not for the respectable French food, but for the clannish atmosphere, where you can often spot a film star or politico. Ideal if you fancy a dozen oysters and a fillet of pike-perch or beef after a cultural evening nearby.

Café Nö! €-€€

Glinkastrasse 23 (201 0871, www.cafe-noe. de). U6 Französische Strasse. **Open** *noon-1am Mon-Fri.* **Map** *p68 M7* ❹ *Wine bar*

This unassuming but right-on wine bar with simple and wholesome meals is owned by a former GDR rock musician now continuing

his family's gastronomy tradition. Given the mostly bland or overpriced restaurants in the neighbourhood, this is a genuine pearl. Snacks include the shaved Swiss cheese tête de moine and anchovy crostini; more substantial fare includes Alsatian *Flammkuchen*, and *Maultaschen* (ravioli) with spinach.

Einstein Unter den Linden €€-€€€

Unter den Linden (2043 632, einstein-udl. com). U6 Französische Strasse. **Open** *7am-late Mon-Fri; 8am-late Sat, Sun.* **Map** *p68 M7* ❾ *Austro-German*

Although it remains the quintessential Viennese coffeehouse, new management has breathed life into this wood-panelled classic. Known as the meeting place for politicians, Einstein has been open for breakfast, lunch and *Apfelstrudel* for the past 20 years. Now you can also expect a formidable wine and dinner menu, a testament to classic Austrian cuisine, with a nod and wink to a younger and more contemporary foodie crowd.

♥ Grill Royal €€€-€€€€

Friedrichstrasse 105B (2887 9288, www. grillroyal.com). U6, S1, S2, S5, S7, S25, S75 Friedrichstrasse. **Open** *6pm-1am daily.* **Map** *p68 N6* ❿ *Steakhouse*

One of the city's best-known venues, nestled on the riverside, Grill Royal is a stylish, friendly and profoundly meaty experience. Not for vegetarians or those on a diet or budget, Grill is as compelling for its people-watching potential as it is for its (stoutly priced) steaks, seafood and accoutrements. The meat is sourced from local suppliers as well as from Argentina, Ireland and Australia. The walls are adorned with rather striking soft-porn art from the owner's collection. Reservations essential.

♥ Ishin Mittelstrasse €-€€

Mittelstrasse 24 (2067 4829, www.ishin.de). U6, S1, S2, S5, S7, S25, S75 Friedrichstrasse. **Open** *11am-9.30pm Mon-Fri; noon-9.30pm Sat.* **Map** *p68 M6* ⓬ *Japanese*

This cheap and cheerful Japanese diner is popular with those in the know. Customers sit at long benches and chow down on sushi, soups and don bowls. Service is quick and, while there are better Japanese restaurants in the city, Ishin provides a welcome light and tasty alternative to the bakeries or heavy German fare more generally available in this part of the town.

Remember, Remember

There are many victims to memorialise

Nowhere is the vexed question of Germany's relationship to its past dramatised more intensely than in the startling proliferation of memorials at the heart of Berlin.

The centrepiece, of course, is the memorial to Jewish Holocaust victims – the **Denkmal für die ermordeten Juden Europas** (*see p73*), a hugely controversial project that took years to accomplish. The idea of some kind of central memorial had been around since the 1980s, when what is now the **Topographie des Terrors** (*see p148*) opened on the site of the former Gestapo headquarters. Then, in 1993, the **Neue Wache** (*see p74*), a memorial to the 'victims of fascism and militarism' under the Communists, was recast as one to the 'victims of war and violent rule'. This involved installing an enlarged replica of Käthe Kollwitz's statue, *Mother with Dead Son*. There were immediate protests that this put murdered victims on the same level as dead perpetrators and memorialised them in a form contrary to Jewish tradition. Chancellor Kohl then promised that a memorial would be erected solely for Jewish victims of the Holocaust.

Meanwhile, representatives of other persecuted groups – Gypsies, gays, the mentally or physically disabled, prisoners of war, political prisoners, forced labourers and blacks – all pointed to the inadequacy of a memorial for Jewish victims alone. Roma groups argued that the extermination of their people should not be separated from that of the Jews, but then refused to share a memorial with homosexuals. In 2008, a memorial to gay victims of the Nazis, **Denkmal für die im Nationalsozialismus verfolgten Homosexuellen**, designed by Michael Elmgreen and Ingar Dragset, was unveiled on the edge of the Tiergarten (*see p103*). It's a lone concrete slab and includes a small window through which a video of two men kissing can be viewed. After criticism by lesbian groups, this is now rotated every two years with a video of two women.

Since 2012, a memorial to Gypsy victims of the Nazis, in the shape of a fountain by Israeli memorial specialist Dani Karavan, has been situated on the corner of the Tiergarten closest to the Reichstag, just behind an impromptu memorial to people killed going over the Wall, and not far from the **Sowjetisches Ehrenmal** (Soviet War Memorial; *see p102*). And, on another corner of the Tiergarten, in the parking area behind the Philharmonie, is a memorial to the mentally and physically disabled victims of the Nazis' T4 euthanasia programme.

There's more to come. Currently under discussion are memorials for those who died during the expulsion of Germans from Poland and Czechoslovakia after World War II, for those who were persecuted for deserting the German army and for those who died while serving in the Bundeswehr. Memorials related to the Berlin Wall are planned at both Checkpoint Charlie and the East Side Gallery. And conservatives are now asking for a memorial plaque to the victims of 1970s terrorist group, the RAF (aka the Baader-Meinhof gang).

Keen for something positive to stand in this increasingly baleful landscape, the city commissioned a 'Monument to Germany's Liberty and Unity' to be placed in front of the new Stadtschloss (*see p33*). The winning design was a 55-metre (180-foot) dish-shaped see-saw called *Bürger in Bewegung* (Citizens in Motion). However, budgetary constraints mean its construction is on hold for the foreseeable future.

Mother with Dead Son

Bars & pubs

Newton Bar
Charlottenstrasse 57 (2029 5421, www. newton-bar.de). U6 Französische Strasse. **Open** *11am-late daily.* **Map** *p68 N7* ❼

Homage seems to be Berlin's preferred method for naming bars, and here iconoclastic fashion photographer Helmut Newton is immortalised. For those unfamiliar with his pictures of statuesque models, an entire wall of this large bar is dedicated to a series of his black and white nudes. Stick to the classics, martinis or a good single malt, settle into the cosy seating and watch the world go by from the heated terrace with a view on to Gendarmenmarkt.

Ständige Vertretung
Schiffbauerdamm 8 (282 3965, www. staev.de). U6, S1, S2, S5, S7, S25, S75 Friedrichstrasse. **Open** *10.30am-1am daily.* **Map** *p68 M6* ❽

The knick-knack-filled Ständige commemorates the still-controversial decision to move the German capital from Bonn to Berlin after reunification. Ständige Vertretung – 'permanent representation' – was the name West and East Germany used to describe the special consulates they kept in each other's countries, not wanting to legitimise the other by calling it an embassy. Due to the pub's proximity to the government quarter, you get the odd politician popping in for some draught Kölsch. There's a lovely terrace by the river in summer, and you can get a bite to eat too.

Tausend
Schiffbauerdamm 11 (2758 2070, www. tausendberlin.com). U6, S1, S2, S5, S7, S25, S75 Friedrichstrasse. **Open** *7.30pm-late Tue-Sat.* **Map** *p68 M6* ❾

With its unmarked entrance – look for the iron door under the train overpass – and strict entrance policy, this grown-up bar is as exclusive as Berlin gets. This is where the well-heeled come to be seen sipping innovative drinks in a stylish, steel-ceilinged interior lit by eerily eye-like 3D installations. Try a bracing wasabi cocktail in summer or a malt whisky served with local pine honey in winter. Go late, look sharp. Skip the Backroom Cantina restaurant and its fussy fusion menu.

Shops & services

❤ Brille 54
Friedrichstrasse 71 (2094 6060, www. brille54.de). U6 Französische Strasse. **Open** *10am-7pm Mon-Fri; 10am-6pm Sat.* **Map** *p68 N7* ❺ *Accessories*

This small, sleek space for specs in Quartier 206 was designed by hot young local architects Plajer & Franz. Lots of smart international eyewear brands are found here, including Lindberg, Thom Browne and Oliver Peoples. **Other location** Kurfürstendamm 50, Charlottenburg (882 6696).

The Corner Berlin
Französische Strasse 40 (2067 0940, www. thecornerberlin.de). U6 Französische Strasse. **Open** *10.30am-7.30pm Mon-Fri; 10am-7pm Sat.* **Map** *p68 N7* ❽ *Fashion/Homewares*

Typically plush surroundings for this luxury 'lifestyle' shop. There's designer nightclub clobber for both sexes: Rick Owens biker jackets and studded Christian Louboutin slippers for the boys; silken Lanvin tunics and Balenciaga handbags for the girls. Plus, there's an incongruous section of beautiful modernist antique furniture by the likes of Arne Jacobsen and Charles Eames. **Other locations** Markgrafenstrasse 45, Mitte (2061 3764); Wielandstrasse 29, Charlottenburg (8892 1261).

❤ Dussmann das KulturKaufhaus
Friedrichstrasse 90 (2025 1111, www. kulturkaufhaus.de). U6, S1, S2, S5, S7, S25, S75 Friedrichstrasse. **Open** *9am-midnight Mon-Fri; 9am-11.30pm Sat.* **Map** *p68 N6* ⓫ *Books & music*

Intended as a 'cultural department store', this spacious five-floor retailer has books, magazines, CDs and DVDs. You can borrow reading glasses (€10 deposit) or a portable CD player (€50 deposit) for the time you're in the store. The huge English-language section has an excellent selection of cookbooks and travel literature among novels and non-fiction. The well-hidden 'vertical garden,' designed by French botanist Patrick Blanc, houses thousands of tropical plants on a single 270sqm wall. There's also a café-restaurant serving afternoon tea, coffee and small plates.

Galeries Lafayette
Friedrichstrasse 76-78 (209 480, www. galerieslafayette.de). U6 Französische Strasse. **Open** *10am-8pm Mon-Sat.* **Map** *p68 N7* ⓭ *Department store*

The most famous of Paris's *grand magasins* built itself a Berlin outpost in the mid-1990s when the city underwent a post-reunification construction boom. Fashion-wise, it caters across the board, with sophisticated labels such as Ferragamo and Agnès B for genteel Charlottenburg mums, while French rock-chic from Sandro and The Kooples caters for a younger crowd. As expected, the food halls are excellent, if a little less spectacular than at KaDeWe (*see p54*), with a fine butcher selling Charolais beef and capons from Burgundy.

ALEXANDERPLATZ & THE SCHEUNENVIERTEL

The Scheunenviertel

If the area south of Friedrichstrasse station is the commercial face of Mitte, the Scheunenviertel (stretching around the north bank of the River Spree, running east from Friedrichstrasse to Hackescher Markt), is an area in its final throes of bohemian gentrification.

Today, this is one of Berlin's main nightlife districts and art quarters, littered with restaurants and galleries. Once far enough out of town that it was safe to build the highly flammable hay barns (*Scheunen*) here, this was also historically the centre of Berlin's immigrant community, including many Jews from Eastern Europe. During the 1990s, it again began to attract Jewish immigrants, including both young Americans and Orthodox Jews from the former Soviet Union; now, Berlin has the fastest-growing Jewish population in Europe.

Around the same time, following the fall of the Wall, the Scheunenviertel became a magnet for squatters with access to the list of buildings supposedly wrecked by lazy urban developers, who had ticked them off as 'gone' in order to meet quotas but had actually left them standing. With many other buildings in disrepair, rents were cheap, and the new residents soon learned how to take advantage of city subsidies for opening galleries and other cultural spaces. Result: the Scheunenviertel became Berlin's hottest cultural centre.

The first of these art-squats was **Tacheles**, on the western end of Oranienburger Strasse, the spine of the Scheunenviertel. Built in 1907, the building originally housed an early attempt at a shopping mall. It had stood vacant for years when squatted by artists after the Wall came down. It then became a rather arrogant arbiter of hip in the neighbourhood, with studios and performance spaces, a cinema and several edgy bars and discos, and eventually became one of Berlin's most popular tourist attractions. In 2012, the final group of artists left after much protest, following the occupants of the bars, restaurants and other art studios, who had previously agreed to take a €1m pay-off from developers.

These days, few of the original gentrifiers remain, with luxury flats forcing out even mainstream institutions: the photography museum **C/O Gallery** (*see p181*), which was housed in the magnificent red-brick Postführamt, was forced to move out to Charlottenburg in 2012. Still, plenty of galleries, boutiques and cafes remain, making this one of Berlin's most rewarding quarters for a ramble.

Across Tucholskystrasse, at Oranienburger Strasse 32, is an entrance to the **Heckmann Höfe** (the other is on Auguststrasse), a series of courtyards that have been delightfully restored to accommodate shops and restaurants. The

---

In the know
Stolpersteine

Walking around Berlin, you may stumble across a brass-plated cobblestone with writing engraved on it – this is a Stolpersteine (literally 'stumbling block'), set down to remember a victim of the Holocaust in front of their house.

Remarkably, these are the work of a private citizen: artist Gunter Hemnig, who casts and installs each one. Since 1992, he's put in over 40,000 of them across Europe, with close to 3,000 in Berlin alone, the majority commemorating Jewish victims, but also Roma, homosexuals and victims of euthanasia. Touchingly, the cost of each one is covered by private donation, usually from the current residents of the building, who do the research and add the name to a searchable database (www.stolpersteine. eu). The stone will usually tell you a person's name, date of birth and where they were murdered.

free-standing building, with the firm's coat of arms in the pavement in front of it, was once the stables.

A little further down the block stands the **Neue Synagoge**, with its gleaming golden Moorish-style dome. Turning into Grosse Hamburger Strasse, you'll find yourself surrounded by Jewish history. On the right, on the site of a former retirement home, there's a memorial to the thousands of Berlin Jews who were forced to congregate here before being shipped off to concentration camps. Behind the memorial is a park that was once Berlin's oldest Jewish cemetery; the only gravestone left is that of the father of the German Jewish renaissance, Moses Mendelssohn, founder of the city's first Jewish school, next door at no.27. A rash of post-reunification anti-Semitism by empowered East German skinheads led to all synagogues and Jewish institutions being put under 24-hour guard. That the school has such a heavy security presence, even today, only adds to the poignancy of this place.

Located across the street at nos.15-16 is the **Missing House**, a memorial by Christian Boltanski, in which the walls of a bombed-out house have the names and occupations of former residents inscribed on the site of their vanished apartments. A little further on, the **Sophienkirche** (from which nearby Sophienstrasse gets its name) is one of Berlin's few remaining Baroque churches. It is set back from the street behind wrought-iron fences, and, together with the surrounding ensemble, is one of the prettiest architectural sites in the city. The interior is a little disappointing, however.

At the end of Oranienburger Strasse, at the corner of Rosenthaler Strasse, is the famous **Hackesche Höfe**. Built in 1906-07, these form a complex of nine interlinking Jugendstil courtyards with elegant ceramic façades. The Höfe symbolise Berlin's new Mitte: having miraculously survived two wars, the forgotten, crumbling buildings were restored in the mid 1990s using the old plans. Today, they house an upmarket collection of shops, galleries, theatres, cafés, restaurants and cinemas, which get rammed with tourists.

A few doors up Rosenthaler Strasse is a tumbledown alley alongside the Central cinema, in which a workshop for the blind was located during World War II. Its owner managed to stock it fully with 'blind' Jews and helped them escape or avoid the camps. Now it houses alternative galleries, bars and shops. In the same complex is the **Anne Frank Zentrum**, home to a multimedia exhibition that tells the life story of the young Dutch diarist who was murdered in Bergen-Belsen. Across the street from the Hackesche Höfe, and under the S-Bahn arches, there are further bars, restaurants and shops.

There are still more fashionable shops along **Rosenthaler Strasse** and around the corner on **Neue Schönhauser Strasse**, as well as some good sandwich and coffee bars. This area has settled into being Berlin's

Hackesche Höfe p85

At nos.20-21 are the **Sophie-Gips Höfe**, which came into being when wealthy art patrons Erika and Rolf Hoffmann were denied permission to build a gallery in Dresden for their collection of contemporary art. Instead, they bought this complex between Sophienstrasse and Gipsstrasse, restored it, and installed the art here – in the **Sammlung Hoffman** – along with their spectacular private residence.

Running between the west end of Oranienburger Strasse and Rosenthaler Strasse, **Auguststrasse** was the original core of Berlin's eastern gallery district; it was here that the whole Mitte scene began almost two decades ago. Known as Mitte's 'Art Mile', the street makes for a good afternoon's stroll. Important venues include Thomas Olbricht's **Me Collectors Room** at no.68 (8600 8510, www.me-berlin.com) and the redeveloped **Jüdische Mädchenschule** complex (nos. 11-13), containing such art spaces as Michael Fuchs Galerie, CWC Gallery and the Eigen Art Lab. Across the road, the **KW Institute for Contemporary Art** at no.69 (243 4590, www.kw-berlin.de, closed Tue, €8) is a polarising bellwether of the Berlin art scene, but usually has something worth seeing. Also check out **Galerie Eigen Art** (no.26, 280 6605, www.eigen-art.com).

Alexanderplatz and around

Visitors who have read Alfred Döblin's raucous novel *Berlin Alexanderplatz* or seen Fassbinder's masterful television adaptation may arrive here and wonder what this dead space is. What happened was that, in the early 1970s, Erich Hönecker decided that this historic area should reflect the glories of socialism, and so he tore it all down. He replaced it with a masterpiece of Commie kitsch: wide boulevards; monotonous white buildings filled with cafés and shops (though to a degree these took their cue from modernist structures dating from the Weimar era, such as the block between the south-west side of the square and the station); and, of course, the impressive golf-ball-on-a-knitting-needle, the **Fernsehturm** (Television Tower). The goofy clock topped with the 1950s-style atom design signals the time in (mostly) former socialist lands; water cascades from the Brunnen der Völkerfreundschaft ('Fountain of the Friendship of Peoples').

The original 1990s plans to replace most of Alexanderplatz with a dozen or so skyscrapers based on New York's Rockefeller Center, among which the Fernsehturm would remain standing, met mass resistance due to surrounding GDR apartment buildings having to be demolished. These

hip centre, and is a great place to come if you're in the market for new clothes. Most of the original houses have now been renovated and the gaps left by wartime bombing have been filled in by slick new buildings or ergonomic playgrounds. Even the *Plattenbauten*, the East German prefabs, have been spruced up, although, in their higher-rise form, they continue to curse Berlin's suburbs.

Leading off Rosenthaler Strasse, **Sophienstrasse** is Mitte's most picturesque street. Built in the 18th century, it was restored in 1987 for the city's 750th anniversary, with craftworkers' ateliers that have replicas of old merchants' metal signs hanging outside them. This pseudo-historicism has now become part of a more interesting mix of handicraft shops. The brick façade of the **Handwerker Verein** at no.18 is particularly impressive. If you wander into the courtyard (as you can with most courtyards that aren't private), you'll find the **Sophiensaele** (*see p256*), an interesting performing-arts space in an old ballroom. The Sophiensaele was also the location of the first German Communist Party HQ.

plans are unlikely to come to fruition, with most Berliners expecting the redevelopment of Alexanderplatz to take place around the time their new airport opens – never, in other words. For now, though, the Kaufhaus department store on the north-west of the square has been expanded and has lost its 1970s façade, while the 22,000 square metres (237,000 square feet) of new shopping space on the north-east corner has ruined the square's communist-era sightlines and obscured the view across Grunerstrasse of the domed **Kongresshalle** and the **Haus des Lehrers** with its first-floor frieze – two of Berlin's finest examples of GDR architecture. Beyond them is Alexa, a giant new mall that no one likes.

One of the few survivors from pre-war Alexanderplatz sits in the shadow of the Fernsehturm: the **Marienkirche**, Berlin's oldest parish church, dating from the 13th century. Later 15th-century (the tower) and 18th-century (the upper section) additions enhance the building's harmonious simplicity.

Just south of here stands the extravagant **Neptunbrunnen**, an 1891 statue of the trident-wielding sea god, surrounded by four female figures representing the Elbe, Rhine, Oder and Vistula rivers. It was moved here from the Stadtschloss when the Communists demolished it in 1950. Overlooking Neptune from the south-east is the huge red-brick bulk of the **Berliner Rathaus** (Berlin Town Hall), known as the **Rotes Rathaus** due to its terracotta bricks and its role as the town hall for East Berlin during the GDR period. (For guided tours, call 9026 2411.) To the south-west is the open space of **Marx-Engels Forum**, one of the few remaining monuments to the old boys – the huge statue of Karl and Fred begs you to take a seat on Marx's lap. On Spandauer Strasse, behind the Radisson Hotel, is the entrance to the **AquaDom & Sea Life**, one of Mitte's more eccentric attractions, and round the corner on the river is the hardly more sensible **DDR Museum**.

For a vague impression of what this part of the city might have looked like before Allied bombers and the GDR did their work, take a stroll around the **Nikolaiviertel**, just south of Alexanderplatz. This is Berlin's oldest quarter, centred around the Nikolaikirche (dating from 1220). The GDR's reconstruction involved bringing the few undamaged buildings from this period together into what is essentially a fake assemblage of history. There are a couple of historic residences, including the **Knoblauchhaus** and the **Ephraim-Palais**. You'll also find Enlightenment big shot Gottfried Lessing's house, cafés (including a reconstruction of Zum Nussbaum, a

contender for the oldest bar in Berlin) and expensive shops. On the southern edge of the district is the **Hanf Museum** (Hemp Museum).

Long before the infamous Wall, Berlin had another one: the medieval **Stadtmauer** (City Wall) of the original 13th-century settlement. There's almost as much left of this wall (a couple of minutes' walk east of the Nikolaiviertel, on Littenstrasse/Waisenstrasse) as there is of the more recent one. Built along the wall by the junction with Parochialstrasse is the extremely old restaurant **Zur Letzten Instanz**, which takes its name from the neighbouring law courts. There has been a restaurant on this site since 1621, Napoleon supposedly having stopped off here for refreshment. Just over the Spree from here is the church-like red-brick **Märkisches Museum**, which houses a rambling collection tracing the history of the city, and the small neighbouring **Köllnischer Park**, once home to Schnute and Maxi, Berlin's two flesh-and-blood brown bears – and official symbols of the city. Schnute, the last city bear, passed away in 2015, and, much to the relief of animal lovers, there are no plans to find a replacement.

Sights & museums

Anne Frank Zentrum

*Rosenthaler Strasse 39 (288 865 610, www. annefrank.de). U8 Weinmeisterstrasse. **Open** 10am-6pm Tue-Sun. **Admission** €5; €3 reductions; €12 families; free under-10s. No cards. **Map** p68 O5.*

This permanent exhibition about the life and death of Anne Frank opened in 2006 and is a co-project with the Anne Frank House in Amsterdam. Pictures, collages, films and special objects describe the world of the diarist and her family in the context of National Socialism, the persecution of the Jews and World War II.

AquaDom & Sea Life

*Spandauer Strasse 3 (992 800, www. visitsealife.com/berlin). S5, S7, S75 Hackescher Markt. **Open** 10am-7pm daily. **Admission** €17.50; €12.50 reductions. **Map** p68 O6.*

Billed as two attractions in one, both involving lots of water and plenty of fish. Sea Life leads you through 13 themed aquaria offering fish in different habitats. The AquaDom is the world's largest free-standing aquarium – a space age tuboid that looks like it might have just landed from some alien planet. A lift takes you up through the middle of this giant cylindrical fishtank – a million litres of saltwater that is home to 2,500 colourful creatures and is enfolded by the atrium of the Radisson Blu hotel. Unfortunately, only the staff are allowed to scuba-dive through the tank to feed the fish.

DDR Museum

*Karl Liebknecht Strasse 1 (847 123 731, www. ddr-museum.de). S5, S7, S75 Hackescher Markt. **Open** 10am-8pm Mon-Fri, Sun; 10am-10pm Sat. **Admission** €9.80; €6 reductions; free under-6s. **Map** p68 O6.*

Bright blue neon signage and a Trabant in the window welcome you into 'one of Europe's most interactive museums!' This is *Ostalgie* in action. Touchscreens, sound effects and even the 'DDR Game' mean that the more distasteful aspects of East German life are cheerfully glossed over. The museum is essentially a collection of GDR memorabilia, from travel tickets to Palast der Republik serviettes. Climb inside the Trabi or sit on a GDR couch in a GDR living room where you can watch GDR TV. Even the much-feared Stasi get the interactive family treatment too – you can pretend to be a Stasi officer and listen in on a bugged flat. Take it all with a large pinch of salt.

Ephraim-Palais

*Poststrasse 16 (2400 2162, www. stadtmuseum.de/ephraim-palais). U2, U5, U8, S5, S7, S75 Alexanderplatz. **Open** 10am-6pm Tue, Thur-Sun; noon-8pm Wed. **Admission** €7; €5 reductions; free under-18s. Free 1st Wed of mth. No cards. **Map** p68 P7.*

Built in the 15th century as a lavish townhouse, remodelled in late Baroque style in the 18th century, demolished by the Communists, and then rebuilt by them close to its original location for the 750th anniversary of Berlin in 1987, the Ephraim-Palais is today home to temporary exhibitions about Berlin's history drawn from the city's collection. Soft chandelier lighting and parquet floors lend a refined air to the place. Be aware that in 2020 the palace will be closed for at least six months for renovation.

❤ Fernsehturm

*Panoramastrasse 1A (no phone, www.tv-turm. de). U2, U5, U8, S5, S7, S75 Alexanderplatz. **Open** Mar-Oct 9am-midnight daily. Nov-Feb 10am-midnight daily. **Admission** €15.50; €9.50 reductions; free under-4s. **Map** p68 P6.*

Built in the late 1960s at a time when relations between East and West Berlin were at their lowest ebb, the 365-m (1,198-ft) Television Tower – its ball-on-spike shape visible all over the city – was intended as an assertion of communist dynamism and modernity, while at the same time providing a transmission tower to compete with the powerful television signals emanating from the West. The design by Herbert Henselmann was inspired by the launch of Sputnik, the first artificial satellite, in October 1957. Henselmann's tower would have a tapering shaft, to represent a rocket soaring into the sky; and at the very top would be a bright, socialist-red sphere to represent a satellite.

Construction began in 1965, and the Fernsehturm finally opened on 7 October 1969 – the 20th anniversary of the founding of the GDR. It marked the very centre of the city in the manner of a medieval church tower, allowed the second GDR TV station to commence broadcasting, and advertised the thrusting triumph of socialism in a form visible for miles around, in particular all over West Berlin. Communist authorities were, however, displeased to note a particular phenomenon: when the sun shone on the tower, reflections on the ball formed the shape of a cross. Berliners dubbed this phenomenon 'the Pope's revenge'. Nevertheless, the authorities were proud enough of their tower to make it one of the central symbols of the East German capital, and today it is one of Berlin's most popular graphic images.

Take an ear-popping trip in the lift to the observation platform at 203m (668ft): a great way to orient yourself early on a visit to Berlin. When the weather is clear, the view is unbeatable by night or day – particularly looking westwards, where you can take in the whole of the Tiergarten and surrounding area. If heights make you hungry, take a twirl in the revolving restaurant, which offers an even better view. There are usually queues to get up there, however.

Hanf Museum

*Mühlendamm 5 (242 4827, www. hanfmuseum.de). U2, U5, U8, S5, S7, S75 Alexanderplatz. **Open** 10am-8pm Tue-Fri; noon-8pm Sat, Sun. **Admission** €4.50, €3 reductions; free under-10s. No cards. **Map** p68 P7.*

The world's largest hemp museum aims to teach the visitor about the uses of the plant throughout history, as well as touching on the controversy surrounding it. The café (doubling as a video and reading room) serves cakes made with hemp, as well as those without it.

Knoblauchhaus

*Poststrasse 23 (240 020 171, www. knoblauchhaus.de). U2, U5, U8, S5, S7, S75 Alexanderplatz. **Open** 10am-6pm Tue-Sun. **Admission** free. **Map** p68 O7.*

This neoclassical mid 18th-century townhouse was once home to the influential

Neue Synagoge

Knoblauch family and contains an exhibition about some of their more prominent members. However, the real draw is the house's striking interior. The first floor contains an exhibition about the increasingly sophisticated middle-class tastes of post-Napoleonic Germany, while the second floor hosts temporary exhibitions about 19th-century cultural history.

Marienkirche

*Karl-Liebknecht-Strasse 8 (2475 9510, www. marienkirche-berlin.de). U2, U5, U8, S5, S7, S75 Alexanderplatz. **Open** 10am-6pm daily. **Admission** free. **Map** p68 O6.*

Construction of the Marienkirche began in 1270, making it one of Berlin's few remaining medieval buildings. Just inside the door is a wonderful 'Dance of Death' fresco dating from 1485, and the 18th-century Walther organ here is considered his masterpiece. Marienkirche hit the headlines in 1989 when the East German civil rights movement chose it for one of their first sit-ins, since churches were among the few places where people could congregate without state permission.

Märkisches Museum

*Am Köllnischen Park 5 (240 020 171, www. stadtmuseum.de/maerkisches-museum). U2 Märkisches Museum. **Open** 10am-6pm Tue-Sun. **Admission** €5; €3 reductions. Free 1st Wed of mth. **Map** p68 P7.*

One of Berlin's state museums, the Märkisches Museum is the primary location of the 'Stiftung Stadtmuseum Berlin'. With new director Paul Spies at the helm, a far-reaching shake up of the state museums is already underway. Presenting a host of artefacts related to the culture and history of the city, different sections examine themes such as Berlin as a newspaper city, women in Berlin's history, city guilds, intellectual Berlin and the military. There are models of the city at different times, and some good paintings, including works by members of the Brücke group. Note that the museum will be closed for at least three years from 2020, with renovations also affecting the nearby Marinehaus. Upon reopening, the two buildings will be at the heart of a new museum and creative quarter centred on Köllnischen Park.

Neue Synagoge

*Centrum Judaicum, Oranienburger Strasse 28-30 (8802 8316, www.centrumjudaicum. de). S1, S2, S25 Oranienburger Strasse. **Open** see the website for details. **Admission** see the website for details. No cards. **Map** p68 N5.*

Built in 1857-66 as the Berlin Jewish community's showpiece, it was the New Synagogue that was attacked during Kristallnacht in 1938, but not too badly damaged – Allied bombs did far more harm in 1945. The façade remained intact and the Moorish dome has been rebuilt. Inside is a permanent exhibition about Jewish life in Berlin and a glassed-in area protecting the ruins of the sanctuary. Tours are available, both of the synagogue and the surrounding area, but book ahead.

Nikolaikirche
*Nikolaikirchplatz (240 020 171, www. stadtmuseum.de/nikolaikirche). U2, U5, U8, S5, S7, S75 Alexanderplatz. **Open** 10am-6pm daily. **Admission** €5; €3 reductions; free under-18s. Free 1st Wed of mth. **Map** p68 P7.*

Inside Berlin's oldest congregational church is an interesting collection chronicling the city's development until 1648. Old tiles, tapestries, and stone and wood carvings – even punishment devices – are on display. There are fascinating photos of wartime damage, plus examples of how the stones melted together in the heat of bombardment.

Sammlung Boros
*Reinhardtstrasse 20 (no phone, www. sammlung-boros.de). U6 Oranienburger Tor. **Open** by appointment. **Admission** €15; €9 reductions. No cards. **Map** p68 M5.*

More akin to a museum than an actual gallery, this concrete World War II bunker has been transformed into a 3,000sqm space containing the formidable collection of advertising mogul Christian Boros and his wife Karen. Works on view include contemporary greats such as Olafur Eliasson and Sarah Lucas, as well as a healthy selection of contemporary local and international names that have caught Boros's beady eye. Tours are on weekends by appointment only; book well in advance through the website.

Sammlung Hoffman
*Sophienstrasse 21 (2849 9121, www.sophie-gips.de). U8 Weinmeisterstrasse. **Open** (by appointment only) 11am-4pm Sat. **Admission** €8. No cards. **Map** p68 O5.*

Erika and Rolf Hoffmann's private collection of international contemporary art includes a charming floor installation by Swiss video artist Pipilotti Rist, a luxurious art library, and work by Lucio Fontana, Frank Stella, Douglas Gordon, Felix Gonzalez-Torres and AR Penck. Guided tours take place every Saturday by appointment – felt slippers supplied. Every summer, the entire display changes.

Restaurants & cafés

♥ Barcomi's €
*Sophie-Gips-Höfe, Sophienstrasse 21 (2859 8363, www.barcomis.de). U8 Weinmeisterstrasse. **Open** 9am-9pm Mon-Sat; 10am-9pm Sun. **Map** p68 O5 ❶ Café*

Berlin's very own domestic goddess, Cynthia Barcomi, opened her first café in Kreuzberg back in 1997 – a different age in reunified Berlin years. The American expat brought her nation's sweet treats to Berlin, doling out blueberry pancakes and whoopee pies

The Corner Berlin *p83*

as well as bagels. She now supplies baked goods all over town and has two bestselling cookbooks under her belt. The café is situated in a quiet courtyard near Hackescher Markt, and locals flock to the outdoor tables to escape the tourist hubbub. **Other location** Bergmannstrasse 21, Kreuzberg (694 8138).

♥ Café Fleury €
*Weinbergsweg 20 (4403 4144). U8 Rosenthaler Platz. **Open** 8am-8pm Mon-Sat; 9.30am-8pm Sun. **No cards**. **Map** p68 O4 ❸ Café*

This wildly popular French café at the bottom of the hill up to Prenzlauer Berg provides the perfect perch from which to people-watch over a buttery croissant and café au lait. A variety of cakes, tarts, salads and baguettes are offered for lunch.

Chicago-Williams €€
*Hannoverschestrasse 2 (2804 2422, www. chicagowilliamsbbq.com). U6 Oranienburger Tor. **Open** 5pm-midnight daily. **Map** p68 M5 ❺ Barbecue*

At Berlin's first real attempt at aping a Southern-style barbecue shack, platters of smoked meats come piled high on plastic

Commonground

trays. The unctuous ribs are a particular highlight, but pulled pork, pastrami, steak and other favourites are all available. There's an extensive menu of craft beers, IPAs, pale ales and dark beers surprisingly, all produced in small batches by German brewers, who are usually notoriously Pilsner-centric. The place gets rowdy as the night progresses, when the owner starts firing out complimentary Jäger shots.

❤ CôCô €
Rosenthalerstrasse 2 (5547 5188, www. banhmi-coco.de). U8 Rosenthaler Platz. Open 11am-10pm Mon-Thur; 11am-11pm Fri, Sat; noon-10pm Sun. No cards. Map p68 O5 ⑥ *Vietnamese*

There's been a *banh mi* explosion in Berlin. Contending for the title of Perfect Sandwich, this Vietnamese speciality combines fatty pâté and roast pork slices, offset by coriander and zingy pickled daikon and carrot, all in an airy-light baguette (rice flour is used to combat the humidity in Vietnam). CôCô's choice of sandwich fillings includes *banh mi thit nuong* (with lemongrass meatballs) and *banh mi chay* (with tofu), as well as the classic variety – all are made to order at the

bar. If the sun's out, take your sandwich to the nearby Weinbergpark and munch in peace on the hillside.

❤ Commonground €
Rosenthalerstrasse 1 (no phone, www. commongrnd.de). U8 Rosenthaler Platz. Open 7.30am-midnight Mon-Thur; 7.30am-2am Fri; 8.30am-2am Sat; 8.30am-midnight Sun. No cards. Map p68 O5 ⑦ *Café*

Run by the team behind Friedrichshain's immensely popular Silo Coffee, Commonground is situated inside the ground floor of the Circus Hotel. Bigger than it looks from the outside, the café features comfy armchairs, an outdoor terrace and the quality coffee, snacks and craft cocktails you'd expect. Step in for one of the best brunch menus in Berlin.

❤ District Mot €-€€
Rosenthaler Strasse 62 (2008 9284, www. districtmot.com) U8 Rosenthaler Platz. Open noon-midnight daily. Map p68 O5 ⑧ *Vietnamese*

Immensely fun, with a fabulous venue that makes you feel you're in downtown Saigon, District Mot serves up a street-food menu with aplomb. The bao burger has won Berlin's best burger award more than once, and, as long as you don't mind sitting on a plastic stool and using toilet paper as a napkin, there's more than enough on the menu to satisfy the hungriest visitor. If you're feeling a bit more grown up, the Chen Che in a courtyard just over the road, offers clay-pot Vietnamese kitchen in a calm tea-house style environment.

House of Small Wonder €-€€
Johannisstrasse 20 (2758 2877, www. houseofsmallwonder.de). U6 Oranienburger Tor. **Open** *9am-5pm daily.* **No cards.** **Map** *p68 N5* ⓫ *Japanese*

What happens when you take Japanese food, give it an American twist and bring it to the heart of Berlin? You get the House of Small Wonder. Opened by husband and wife team Shaul Margulies and Motoko Watanbe, the café is based on their successful Brooklyn joint, with a menu that offers unlikely juxtapositions of Eastern and Western flavours. All in a lovely, airy and suitably eccentric setting.

Katz Orange €€€
Bergstrasse 22 (983 208 430, www. katzorange.com). U8 Rosenthaler Platz. **Open** *6pm-late daily.* **Map** *p68 N4* ⓭ *Modern German*

Set off the street in a handsome 19th-century red-brick ex-brewery, Katz Orange is a grown-up restaurant for locavore dining with an excellent late-night cocktail bar attached. The restaurant takes pains to source local produce from trusted farmers and suppliers to create a short menu of seasonal dishes. A beautiful dining experience with a Berlin flavour.

Lebensmittel in Mitte €€
Rochstrasse 2 (2759 6130). U8 Weinmeisterstrasse. **Open** *noon-4pm, 5-11pm Mon-Sat.* **No cards.** **Map** *p68 P5* ⓮ *German/Austrian*

This deli/restaurant is a little journey into the joys of southern German and Austrian cuisine. The deli at the front offers fine cheeses, rustic bread, organic veg, sausages and even Austrian pumpkin-seed oil. But you can also settle on to long wooden benches beneath the antlers on the wall, and dine on high-fat, carb-loaded dishes such as *Leberkäse*, tongue, rösti and cheese *Spätzle* accompanied by a broad selection of southern German and Austrian wines or Bavarian beer. Laptops not allowed.

❤ Das Lokal €€-€€€
Linienstrasse 160 (2844 9500, www. lokal-berlin.blogspot.co.uk). S1, S2, S25 Oranienburger Strasse. **Open** *5pm-late daily.* **Map** *p68 N5* ⓯ *Modern German*

Das Lokal comes from fine heritage: it opened while the much-loved Kantine was being redesigned alongside David Chipperfield's studio. The weekly changing seasonal menu might feature starters of pigeon with chestnuts, mussels in broth or asparagus croquettes – all designed to demonstrate the superior flavour of well-sourced produce. It's also an oasis for offal dishes and for game, which is plentiful in Berlin's surrounding forests.

Mogg €-€€
Auguststrasse 11-13 (0176 6496 1344, www. moggmogg.com). U6 Oranienburger Tor. **Open** *11am-10pm Mon-Fri; 10am-10pm Sat, Sun.* **Map** *p68 N5* ⓰ *Deli*

This New York-style deli is a lunchtime hotspot for local galleristas, where all the necessaries are pitch-perfect: the pickles pack a hefty crunch; fresh coleslaw is just the right side of creamy-sour; and the toasted rye bread reveals a fluffy interior. Yet all play second fiddle to the thick wodge of smoky goodness that is their pastrami meat. The menu features classics such as the Reuben, topped with melted 'Swiss' cheese, sauerkraut and a special dressing, plus matzo ball soup and cream cheese bagels.

Nola's am Weinberg €€
Veteranenstrasse 9 (4404 0766, www.nola. de). U8 Rosenthaler Platz. **Open** *10am-1am daily.* **Map** *p68 O4* ⓱ *Swiss*

This former park pavilion has a fabulous terrace overlooking the park slope, as well as a bar and dining room. Expect artery-hardening Swiss fare, such as venison goulash with mushrooms and spinach noodles, or cheese and spinach rösti topped with a fried egg. On Sundays, they do a magnificently generous brunch buffet.

Noto €€-€€€
Torstrasse 173 (2009 5387, www.noto-berlin.com). U8 Rosenthaler Platz. **Open** *6pm-midnight daily.* **Map** *p68 N5* ⓲ *Haute cuisine*

Noto exemplifies contemporary Berlin dining: a laid-back setting, with the chef-owner cooking traditional German produce made modern through creative techniques. The succinct menu changes weekly, zipping from cocoa and pumpkin ravioli in a rabbit ragoût to the signature dish of veal spare ribs in an Asian-style sweet marinade.

Princess Cheesecake

and Western European kitchens, the menu is fresh, healthy and vibrant. Expect dishes like quinoa and celeriac salad, with chicory and blood orange or grilled aubergine with chickpeas. A fancy Italian, **Cecconi's**, is also part of the complex, should you fancy anything a little more substantial.

Tadshikische Teestube €
KunstHof, Oranienburger Strasse 27 (204 1112, www.tadshikische teestube.de). S1, S2, S25, Oranienburger Strasse, or U6 Oranienburger Tor. **Open** *4-11pm Mon-Fri; noon-11pm Sat, Sun.* **Map** *p68 N5* ㉒ *Café*

Originally the Soviet pavilion at the 1974 Leipzig Fair, this charming Tajik tearoom was lovingly preserved and for many years operated out of the grander Palais on the Moat. It's had to move – but a new owner has arrived to continue this Berlin oddity at a new location in an old art gallery. Remove your shoes, lounge around on the plushly carpeted floors and enjoy a full Russian tea service with sweet buckwheat pancakes on the side.

The Tree €
Brunnenstrasse 167 (6796 1848, www. facebook.com/thetree.berlin). U8 Rosenthaler Platz. **Open** *noon-3pm, 5.30-10pm Mon-Fri; 1-10pm Sat, Sun.* **No cards. Map** *p68 O4* ㉓ *Sichuan*

The passion project of a landscape architect and an engineer, this Chinese noodle house is beautifully designed and has an event space attached where you may see pop-up exhibitions. The reasonably priced menu features cold starters and noodle dishes. Expect traditional Sichuan with a fresh, modern twist. The handmade pressed noodles are a joy, whether served dan-dan style or in a hearty, meaty broth.

Trois Minutes sur Mer €€€
Torstrasse 166 (6730 2052, www.3minutessurmer.de). U8 Rosenthaler Platz. **Open** *6-11pm Tue-Sat; 10am-11pm Sun.* **Map** *p68 N5* ㉔ *French*

Here, the traditional Parisian bistro aesthetic (art deco bar stools, paper tablecloths) sits alongside nouveau Berlin touches (GDR light fittings and funky red bar stools). Excellent fish options, such as red mullet and bream, come impeccably cooked, all crisp skin and translucent flesh. There are also more gutsy dishes: a reduced coq au vin, and *escargots de bourgogne* dripping in garlic butter. Presentation is visually spare, any jus neatly daubed and portions squared off; the suckling pig dish is a geometric wonder. Start with some foie gras pâté (ethical stance dependent) and end with the tarte tatin. Booking advised.

❤ Princess Cheesecake €
Tucholskystrasse 37 (2809 2760, www. princess-cheesecake.de). U6 Oranienburger Tor. **Open** *10am-8pm daily.* **Map** *p68 N5* ⑲ *Café*

A perfect pit stop during a day's Auguststrasse gallery-hopping, Princess Cheesecake is where you can try the venerable 'Kaffee und Kuchen' tradition – Germany's equivalent of afternoon tea. Decor takes equally from minimalism as it does from the baroque, and the cakes are accordingly clean-lined but opulent in flavour. Try a classic baked cheesecake or one of the more adventurous numbers such as 'Mi Cariño Suave', laden with candied almonds and toffee and topped with quark cream. **Other location** Knesebeckerstrasse 32, Charlottenburg (8862 5870).

Schwarzwaldstuben €€
Tucholskystrasse 48 (2809 8084, www. schwarzwaldstuben-berlin.com). S1, S2, S25 Oranienburger Strasse. **Open** *9am-midnight daily.* **No cards. Map** *p68 N5* ⑳ *German*

Some of the best German cooking comes from Swabia, but Swabian restaurants tend to be filled with teddy bears and knick-knacks. This place, however, is casually chic, and wears its mounted deer head ironically. Food is excellent: the soups are hearty; stellar main courses include the *Schäufele* with sauerkraut and potatoes; and the *Flammkuchen* (a sort of German pizza) is good. Another plus is the popular Rothaus Tannenzapfle beer on tap.

The Store Kitchen €
Torstrasse 1 (4050 44550, www.thestores. com/berlin) U8 Rosenthaler Platz. **Open** *10am-7pm Mon-Sat.* **Map** *p68 P5* ㉑ *International*

Part of the Soho House concept store, The Store Kitchen is the brainchild of Berlin food culture mover and shaker Tommy Tanock. Fusing ingredients from Mediterranean

♥ Yarok Berlin €

Torstrasse 195 (9562 8703, www.yarok-restaurant.de). U6 Oranienburger Tor, U8 Rosenthaler Platz. **Open** *2-11pm daily.* **No cards.** **Map** *p68 N5* **㉕** *Middle Eastern*

This *Imbiss* sets the bar high. Serving some of the finest Middle-Easten *Tellers* (plates) in the city, Yarok – meaning 'green' in Hebrew – offers up yummy falafel, silky houmous, spectacular minced-beef kebab and zingy juices, all at great prices.

Bars & pubs

Altes Europa

Gipsstrasse 11 (2809 3840, www.alteseuropa.com). U8 Weinmeisterstrasse. **Open** *noon-1am Mon-Sat; 2pm-1am Sun.* **No cards.** **Map** *p68 O5* **①**

The gentle minimalism of the decor – big picture windows, basic furnishings and nothing but a few old maps and prints on the walls – is a relief in an increasingly touristy neighbourhood, and this inviting place is good for anything from a mid-afternoon drink to a rowdier night out with friends. The bar serves light meals, Ukrainian vodka and draught Krusovice in both dark and light varieties to a mixed, youngish crowd.

♥ Bar 3

Weydingerstrasse 20 (2804 6973). U2 Rosa-Luxemburg-Platz. **Open** *9pm-late Tue-Sat.* **No cards.** **Map** *p68 P5* **②**

Located in a backstreet off Torstrasse, this cosy bar is a favourite of Mitte media types and art stars. With a large horseshoe-shaped bar dominating the room, it's bar stools or standing only, as this place seriously packs out with a slick, bespectacled clientele and the occasional actor or celebrity. The house wine is very good. Or try the Kölsch beer from Cologne – tradition dictates that it's served in a tiny glass, constantly refilled by the barman until you abandon it half-full or lay a beer mat over the top.

Buck and Breck

Brunnenstrasse 177 (www.buckandbreck.com). U8 Rosenthaler Platz. **Open** *7pm-late winter; 8pm-late summer.* **Map** *p68 O4* **③**

A tiny little speakeasy hidden away behind a plain door, Buck and Breck is not such a well-kept secret these days, but still a very pleasant place to drink. Ring the doorbell to enter the one-room bar where mixologists will create astounding creations with the seriousness of scientists. With only room for 20 or so guests, this is an intimate experience and less hipstery than you might expect. Smoking is allowed inside, but cell phones aren't.

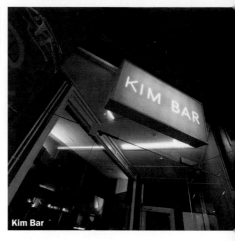

Kim Bar

Cordobar

Grosse Hamburger Strasse 32 (2758 1215, www.cordobar.net). S1, S2, S25 Oranienburger Strasse, U8 Rosenthaler Platz. **Open** *7pm-2am Tue-Sat.* **Map** *p68 O5* **④**

The Parisian-wine-bar-with-small-plates model has become extremely popular in recent years, and Mitte finally has an excellent example. The Cordobar is owned by Austrian sommelier Willi Shlögl and friends (including film director Jan-Ole Gerster), so the list focuses on southern German and Austrian wines, with many unsulphured 'natural' bottles. Hot and cold dishes, such as blood-sausage pizza or smoked eel with brussels sprouts, are also available.

♥ Kim Bar

Brunnenstrasse 10 (no phone, www.kim-bar.com). U8 Rosenthaler Platz. **Open** *8pm-late Tue-Sat.* **No cards.** **Map** *p68 O4* **⑤**

A veteran of the Mitte scene, Kim has been a favourite with twentysomething art-scenesters since it opened in 2007, although its ramshackle atmosphere and charm have received a bit of a sprucing up in recent years. The entrance is low-key: look for an all-glass façade and crowds of people sporting billowy monochrome clothing. Cheap drinks and a rotating roster of neighbourhood DJs add to the don't-give-a-damn aesthetic.

Mein Haus am See

Brunnenstrasse 197-198 (2759 0873, www.mein-haus-am-see.club). U8 Rosenthaler Platz. **Open** *9am-late daily.* **No cards.** **Map** *p68 O4* **⑥**

This hugely popular split-level joint is situated a stone's throw from busy Rosenthaler Platz and is a great alternative to the tired Sankt Oberholz. The owners' slightly vapid claim is that 'it's not a bar, it's not a club, it's something sexier in between', but it's certainly hard to categorise. There are exhibitions, readings, DJs and it almost never closes, so whether you want another beer, a sobering coffee or a panino at 4.30am, this is the place to come. Excellent breakfasts too.

Shops & services

Acne Studios
*Weinmeisterstrasse 2 (9700 5187, www. acnestudios.com). U8 Weinmeisterstrasse. **Open** 11am-8pm Mon-Sat.* **Map** *p68 O5* ❶ *Fashion*

Sweden's Acne just keeps going from strength to strength, having completed its transformation from cult jeans label to fully fledged global empire with its slinky draping and quality materials. The bulbous white Berlin flagship store, hidden behind a crumbling shopfront, features skin-tight jeans, fine knitwear and silken evening wear for both men and women.

❤ Ampelmann Shop
Rosenthaler Strasse 40-41 (4404 8801, www. ampelmann.de). S5, S7, S75 Hackescher Markt. **Open** *9.30am-9pm Mon-Thur; 9.30am-9pm Fri, Sat; 1-6pm Sun.* **Map** *p68 O5* ❷ *Gifts & souvenirs*

You'll find a huge variety of stuff emblazoned with the old East's enduring symbol, the jaunty red and green traffic-light men (*see below* In the know). As you can see from the number of shops dotted around the city, they've become unofficial city mascots and have even started colonising West Berlin road crossings too. **Other locations** DomAquarée, Karl-Liebknecht-Strasse 1, Mitte (2758 3238); Potsdamer Platz Arkaden, Alte

Potsdamer Strasse 7, Tiergarten (2592 5691); Markgrafenstrasse 37, Kreuzberg (4003 9095).

❤ Arkonaplatz Flohmarkt
Arkonaplatz (786 9764, www.troedelmarkt-arkonaplatz.de). U8 Bernauer Strasse. **Open** *10am-4pm Sun.* **Map** *p68 O4* ❸ *Market*

A broad array of retro gear – ranging from vinyl to clothing, books to trinkets, bikes to coffee tables – all available here at moderate prices. The golden rule of flea markets applies at Arkonaplatz: the best stuff gets snapped up early.

Bonbon Macherei
Oranienburger Strasse 32 (4405 5243, www.bonbonmacherei.de). S1, S2, S25 Oranienburger Strasse. **Open** *noon-7pm Wed-Sat.* **No cards.** **Map** *p68 N5* ❹ *Food & drink*

A nostalgic candy shop that offers sweet, sour and everything in between. You can watch Katja Kolbe and Hjalmar Stecher produce their boiled sweets in the on-site workshop using vintage equipment and traditional recipes. High quality at reasonable prices, but beware – the shop sometimes closes in July and August for a much-needed holiday.

❤ Buchhandlung Walther König
Burgstrasse 27 (2576 0980, www. buchhandlung-walther-koenig.de). S5, S7, S75 Hackescher Markt. **Open** *10am-8am Mon-Sat.* **Map** *p68 O6* ❻ *Books & music*

Cologne-based Walther König is Germany's top art publisher, with several branches dotted throughout Europe; it also stocks the bookshops at Berlin's museums. This flagship store by Museumsinsel heaves with beautifully reproduced catalogues and a comprehensive range of critical-theory literature. These books would make a handsome gift for the art-lover in your life.

In the know
Ampelmännchen

Wondering why the pedestrian traffic lights have much jauntier little red and green men than in other cities? Both are wearing hats, and the green man has a very purposeful stride. They are *Ampelmännchen*, a hangover from East Germany, which had different traffic lights from West Germany. In the euphoria following the collapse of Communism, the *Ampelmännchen* started to die out and be replaced by their more straight-laced western counterparts – until *Ostalgie* struck and a campaign was launched to bring them back. Due to their marketability as souvenirs, you can now see them on both sides of the reunified city.

Civilist

*Brunnenstrasse 13 (8561 0715, www. civilistberlin.com). U8 Rosenthaler Platz. **Open** noon-7pm Mon-Fri; 11am-6pm Sat. **Map** p68 O4*  *Accessories*

No self-respecting Berlin skater would be seen in anything other than a Civilist wool beanie. This neatly designed shop is run by the local *Lodown* magazine crew, focusing on limited-edition collaborations and mature skate labels including HUF and aNYthing. There's a special Nike SB shop a few doors down.

♥ do you read me?!

*Auguststrasse 28 (6954 9695, www. doyoureadme.de). U8 Rosenthaler Platz, or S1, S2, S25 Oranienburger Strasse. **Open** 10am-7.30pm Mon-Sat. **Map** p68 O5 ❾ Books & music*

On Mitte's main art drag, this small shop's shelves heave with glossy picks of global fashion, style, art and design print media. The magazines are attractively presented, and there's a small selection of books in the back.

♥ DSTM

*Torstrasse 161 (4920 3750, www.dstm.co). U8 Rosenthaler Platz. **Open** noon-8pm Mon-Fri; 1-8pm Sat. **Map** p68 N5 ❿ Fashion*

There's plenty of young Berlin designers cutting their teeth at boutiques around the city, but Canadian-born Jen Gilpin's label, Don't Shoot The Messenger, is the definitive city look. Local influences can be read from all over: shades of Marlene Dietrich's austere raunchiness and even the complex fastenings of fetish-ware are apparent in the billowy clothing, made mostly in fine black silk and leather. Angular cutouts offer glimpses of flesh, and sleek shapes are conjured by inventive draping that proves Gilpin's skilled technique.

♥ Fun Factory

*Oranienburger Strasse 92 (2804 6366, www. funfactory.com). S5, S7, S75 Hackescher Markt. **Open** noon-8pm Mon-Thur; 11am-9pm Fri, Sat. **Map** p68 O5 ⓬ Sex shop*

Berlin's temple to adult toys lies slap-bang in the middle of Hackescher Markt's central shopping area. With an interior designed by American futurist Karim Rashid, the two-floor shop caters to a mixed gay/straight crowd of all stripes. Staff are extremely helpful if advice is needed.

♥ LaLa Berlin

*Alte Schönhauser Strasse 3 (2009 5363, www. lalaberlin.com). U2 Rosa-Luxemburg-Platz. **Open** 11am-7pm Mon-Sat. **Map** p68 P5 ⓮ Fashion*

do you read me?!

Iranian-born Leyla Piedayesh knocks out stylish and cosy knitwear at her Mitte boutique. She's got a shop in Copenhagen too and has become well known across the Atlantic, not least due to famous fans such as Claudia Schiffer, Cameron Diaz and Jessica Alba.

Made in Berlin

*Neue Schönhauser Strasse 19 (2123 0601). U8 Weinmeisterstrasse. **Open** noon-8pm Mon-Sat. **Map** p68 O5 ⓯ Fashion*

Another branch of the Kleidermarkt clothes empire, where the 'better stuff' supposedly goes – vintage Barbour, Burberry and Lacoste, for example. It's still pretty cheap, though, and offers a ton of great no-name 1980s gear. Every Tuesday between noon and 3pm, you'll get a 20% discount. **Other location** Friedrichstrasse 114A, Mitte (2404 8900).

♥ Mykita

*Rosa-Luxemburg-Strasse 6 (6730 8715, www.mykita.com). U2, U5, U8, S5, S7, S75 Alexanderplatz. **Open** 11am-7pm Mon-Fri; 11am-6pm Sat. **Map** p68 P6 ⓰ Accessories*

This Berlin-based glasses label has been a mainstay for fashion-conscious locals since 2004, but the brand has hit the big time since some of its more experimental frames were picked up by the likes of Lady Gaga. The handmade prescription frames and sunglasses are presented on stark, industrial shelving in this beautifully lit, ultra-minimalist store.

❤ Das Neue Schwarz

Mulackstrasse 38 (2787 4467, www. dasneueschwarz.de). U2 Rosa-Luxemburg-Platz, U8 Weinmeisterstrasse. Open noon-8pm Mon-Sat. Map p68 P5 ❶ *Fashion*

Mulackstrasse is full of expensive designer boutiques, so Das Neue Schwarz ('the new black') is a great alternative for those looking for a (relative) bargain. The hand-selected stock offers almost-new designer pieces from past seasons, most still with tags. There's stuff for both boys and girls: chunky Céline handbags, flashy Bernard Willhelm bomber jackets, Chloé wedges and Dries Van Noten suits, to name just a few.

Oona

Auguststrasse 26 (2804 5905, www.oona-galerie.de). S1, S2, S25 Oranienburger Strasse, U8 Rosenthaler Platz. Open 2-6pm Tue-Fri; 1-6pm Sat. Map p68 O5 ❶ *Accessories*

In addition to its permanent collection, this 'gallery for contemporary jewellery' features work by young creatives from Japan, Australia and elsewhere in Europe. The gallery and artists choose a special theme and work with architects, photographers and interior designers to develop a concept. A mix of precious and non-precious materials means there's a corresponding mix of price tags.

Pro QM

Almstadtstrasse 48-50 (2472 8520, www. pro-qm.de). U2 Rosa-Luxemburg-Platz. Open 11am-8pm Mon-Sat. Map p68 P5 ❶ *Books & music*

This art bookshop has the rarified design of a white cube, but don't let that put you off – inside the ambience is extremely welcoming, with staff encouraging lengthy browsing. There's a particularly strong selection of urban and critical theory, in both German and English, as well as an active schedule of talks by artists, writers and architects.

❤ RSVP

Mulackstrasse 14 & 26 (3195 6410, www.rsvp-berlin.de). U8 Weinmeisterstrasse. Open 11am-7pm Mon-Sat. Map p68 O5 ❷ *Gifts & souvenirs*

This small but beautiful boutique is the perfect pit stop if you're looking for a gift or have a passion for some of the world's most beautiful notebooks. Expect stationery for the aesthete: art deco scissors, exotic erasers, weighty Rivoli writing paper, Polish notebooks and Koh-I-Noor mechanical pencils. It's just gorgeous.

Soto

Torstrasse 72 (2576 2070, www.sotostore. com). U2 Rosa-Luxemburg-Platz. Open 11am-7pm Mon-Fri; 11am-8pm Sat. Map p68 P5 ❷ *Fashion*

One for the boys, with a curated selection of cult labels on offer: limited-edition Flyknit Nikes, soft woollen slacks from Norse Projects or fine knitwear from Acne. Complete the look with a pair of tortoiseshell shades from Italy's Super 4 and something from their extensive accessories range, from spotty socks to chunky headphones.

❤ Whisky & Cigars

Sophienstrasse 8-9 (282 0376, www.whisky-cigars.de). S5, S7, S75 Hackescher Markt. Open 11am-7pm Mon-Fri; 11am-6pm Sat. Map p68 O5 ❷ *Food & drink*

Two friends with a love of single malts are behind this shop, which stocks 450 whiskies, plus cigars from Cuba, Jamaica and Honduras, among other sources. Regular tastings too.

❤ Wood Wood

Rochstrasse 4 (2804 7877, www.woodwood. dk). U8 Weinmeisterstrasse. Open noon-8pm Mon-Fri; noon-7pm Sat. Map p68 P5 ❷ *Fashion*

An avant-garde design collective from Copenhagen, Wood Wood offers beautiful, angular and sometimes outrageous street fashion, sneakers and accessories by Japanese (or co-opted by Japan) designers, such as Sonia Rykiel, Comme des Garçons and White Mountaineering. Almost half the stock is Wood Wood's own, an explosion of prints, stitching and bright colours tempered by clean, classic cuts.

Zionskirchplatz Farmers' Market

Zionskirchplatz. U2 Senefelderplatz, U8 Rosenthaler Platz. Open 11am-6.30pm Thur. Map p68 O4 ❷ *Market*

Regional growers sell fruit and vegetables, fresh fish, home-made jams, assorted breads, and organic cheese from Berliner Käsehandel. Farmers set up on the cobbled walkway surrounding one of Berlin's most beautiful churches, making this a truly picturesque market whatever the time of the year.

Tiergarten & Moabit

A slightly uncertain mish-mash of districts plus the grand green park that gives the area its name, Tiergarten straddles the centre of Berlin; it's home to dozens of embassies as well as the iconic Reichstag parliament building. Tiergarten was once hemmed in on the east by the Wall, but these days it's right at the heart of things again, stretching from the futuristic Hauptbahnhof in the north to the Zoo in the south-west.

South of the park is Potsdamer Platz, Berlin's rejuvenated commercial centre, as well as the museums and venues of the Kulturforum – including the spectacular modernist Philharmonie concert hall. Further south still, the rather unlovely former red-light drag of Potsdamer Strasse is experiencing something of a revival, as a score of galleries have relocated there in recent years, driven out of Mitte by sharply rising rents.

Since the fall of the Berlin Wall, Moabit, once a border district of West Berlin, has been trying to work out what to do with its new-found centrality. Despite a couple of star attractions and some encouraging additions to the line-up of places of eat, drink and shop, it's unlikely Moabit will become the next Neukölln anytime soon.

❤ Don't miss

1 Reichstag *p105*
Drenched in history, the rebuilt Reichstag inspires awe, but remember to book ahead.

2 Tiergarten *p103*
Stroll through this ex-royal hunting ground, and don't miss the gleaming Siegessäule.

3 Philharmonie *p252*
Find out why Germany is classical music's superpower at this world-class concert hall.

4 Gemäldegalerie *p108*
Immerse yourself in the world of the Flemish Renaissance.

5 Vabali Spa *p113*
Unwind in 20,000 square metres of gorgeous pools, saunas and gardens.

Reichstag

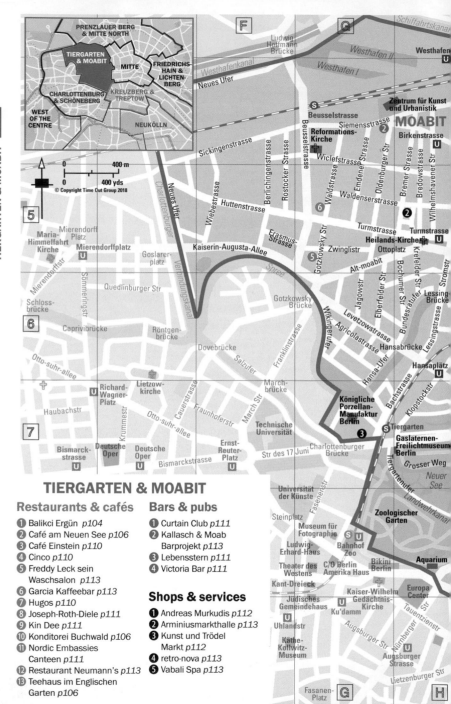

TIERGARTEN & MOABIT

Restaurants & cafés

1. Balikci Ergün *p104*
2. Café am Neuen See *p106*
3. Café Einstein *p110*
4. Cinco *p110*
5. Freddy Leck sein Waschsalon *p113*
6. Garcia Kaffeebar *p113*
7. Hugos *p110*
8. Joseph-Roth-Diele *p111*
9. Kin Dee *p111*
10. Konditorei Buchwald *p106*
11. Nordic Embassies Canteen *p111*
12. Restaurant Neumann's *p113*
13. Teehaus im Englischen Garten *p106*

Bars & pubs

1. Curtain Club *p111*
2. Kallasch & Moab Barprojekt *p113*
3. Lebensstern *p111*
4. Victoria Bar *p111*

Shops & services

1. Andreas Murkudis *p112*
2. Arminiusmarkthalle *p113*
3. Kunst und Trödel Markt *p112*
4. retro-nova *p113*
5. Vabali Spa *p113*

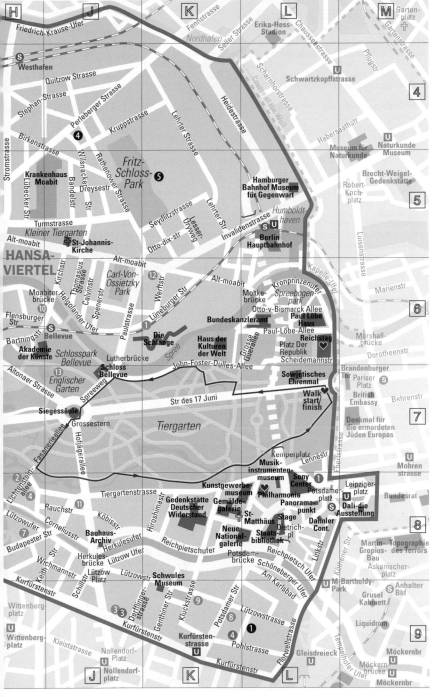

H J K L M

Friedrich-Krause-Ufer

Fennstrasse

Seller Strasse

Erika-Hess-
Stadion

Chausseestrasse

Garten-
platz

Nordhafen

Gartenstrasse

Westhafen

Quitzow Strasse

Heidestrasse

Scharnhorststrasse

Course of the Wall

Schwartzkopffstrasse

Pflugstr

4

Stephan-Strasse

Perleberger Strasse

Kruppstrasse

Lehrter Strasse

Habersaathstr

Museum für   Naturkunde
Naturkunde   Museum

Birkenstrasse

Wilsnacker Strasse

Rathenower Strasse

Fritz-
Schloss-
Park

Brecht-Weigel-
Gedenkstätte

Stromstrasse

Lübecker Str

Krankenhaus
Moabit

Bandelstr

Dreysestr

Lehrter Str

Hamburger
Bahnhof Museum
für Gegenwart

Robert-
Koch-
platz

5

Turmstrasse

Seydlitzstrasse

Otto-dix-str

Lesser-
Uryweg

Invalidenstrasse

Humboldt-
haven

Kleiner Tiergarten

Alt-moabit

St-Johannis-
Kirche

Alt-moabit

Berlin
Hauptbahnhof

Luisenstrasse

HANSA-
VIERTEL

Kirchstr

Thomasius

Calvinstr

Spenerstr

Carl-Von-
Ossietzky
Park

Werftstr

Lüneburger Str

Alt-moabit

Kapelle Ufer

Marienstr

Moabiter
brücke

Helgolander Ufer

Paulstrasse

Die
Schlange

Moltke-
brücke

Spreebogen-
park

Otto-v-Bismarck Allee

Bundeskanzleramt

Kronprinzenufer

Paul Löbe
Haus

6

Flensburger
Str

Bartningstr

Bellevue

Akademie
der Künste

Schlosspark
Bellevue

Lutherbrücke

Schloss
Bellevue

Spree

Haus der
Kulturen
der Welt

Grosse Querallee

Paul-Löbe-Allee

John-Foster-Dulles-Allee

Reichstag

Platz Der
Republik

Scheidemannstr

Marshall-
brücke

Dorotheenstr

Englischer
Garten

Spreeweg

Sowjetisches
Ehrenmal

Brandenburger
Tor   Pariser
Platz

British
Embassy

Behrenstr

Altonaer Strasse

Siegessäule

Grossestern

Str des 17 Juni

Tiergarten

Walk
start/
finish

Denkmal für
die ermordeten
Jüden Europas

7

Fasanenallee

Hofjägerallee

Kemperplatz

Lennéstr

Ebertstrasse

Mohren
strasse

Lichtenstein
allee

Musik-
instrumenten-
museum

Sony
Center

Leipziger-
platz

Rauchstr

Tiergartenstrasse

Kunstgewerbe-
museum

Gemälde-
galerie

Philharmonie

Potsdamer
platz

Dali-die
Ausstellung

Bundesrat

Lützowufer

Corneliusstr

Gedenkstätte
Deutscher
Widerstand

Hiroshimastr

St-
Matthäus

Panorama-
punkt

Stage

Damler
Cont.

Martin-   Topographie
Gropius-   des Terrors
Bau

8

Budapester Str

Bauhaus-
Archiv

Herkulesufer

Neue
National-
galerie

Dietrich-
pl

Staats-
bibliothek

Reichpietsch Ufer

Köthener Str

Linkstr

Askanischer-
platz

Wichmannstr

Keith Str

Herkules-
brücke

Lützow Ufer

Reichpietschufer

Potsdam-
brücke

Schöneberger Ufer

M-Bartholdy-
Park

Anhalter
Bhf

Schillstr

Lützow
Platz

Lützowstr

Schwules
Museum

Kluckstrasse

Am Karlsbad

Flottwellstrasse

Grusel
Kabinett

Wittenberg-
platz

Dörflinger
strasse

Genthiner Str

Potsdamer Str

Lützowstrasse

Liquidrom

9

Wittenberg-
platz

Kleiststrasse

Kurfürstenstr

Nollendorf-
Platz

Kurfürsten-
strasse

Pohlstrasse

Kurfürstenstr

Gleisdreieck

Möckernbr

Nollendorf-
platz

Temelhofer Ufer

Möckern
brücke

Möckernbr

THE PARK & THE REICHSTAG

A hunting ground for the Prussian electors since the 16th century, **Tiergarten** (*see right* A stroll through the Tiergarten) was opened to the public in the 18th century. It was badly damaged during World War II; in the desperate winter of 1945-46, almost all the surviving trees were cut down for firewood, and it wasn't until 1949 that Tiergarten started to recover. Today, though, joggers, nature lovers, gay cruisers and picnickers pour into the park in fair weather. There's no finer place from which to appreciate it all than the beer garden of the **Café am Neuen See** on Lichtensteinallee.

All roads entering the Tiergarten lead to the park's largest monument, the **Siegessäule** (Victory Column), which celebrates the last wars Germany managed to win. The park's main thoroughfare, **Strasse des 17 Juni** (the date of the East Berlin workers' strike of 1953), is one of the few pieces of Hitler's plan for 'Germania' that actually got built – a grand east–west axis, lined with Nazi lamp posts and linking Unter den Linden to Neu-Westend. The Siegessäule was moved here from its original position in front of the Reichstag.

Towards the eastern end of Strasse des 17 Juni, just west of the **Brandenburger Tor** (*see p71*), stands the **Sowjetisches Ehrenmal** (Soviet War Memorial). Once the only piece of Soviet property in West Berlin, it was built in 1945-46 out of granite and marble from the ruins of Hitler's Neue Reichskanzlei, but posed a political problem. Standing in the British Zone, it was surrounded by a British military enclosure, which was in turn guarded by Berlin police – all to protect the monument and the two Soviet soldiers who stood guard. The tanks flanking it are supposed to have been the first two Soviet tanks into Berlin.

At the north-eastern corner of the park stands the **Reichstag** (*see p105*). Described by Kaiser Wilhelm II as the 'Imperial Monkey House', it hasn't had a happy history. But, in 1999, Lord Norman Foster's brilliant refitting of the building was unveiled. His crowning achievement is the glass cupola: a trip to the top should be a must-do on any visitor's agenda.

When the decision was made in 1991 to make Berlin the German capital, the area north of the Reichstag was picked as the central location for new government buildings. Designed by Axel Schultes and Charlotte Frank, the immense **Spreebogen** complex, also known as the Band des Bundes, is built over a twist in the River Spree (*Bogen* means 'bend'). It crosses the river twice and the old East–West border once, symbolising the reunion of Berlin. The most notable building is Schultes and Frank's **Bundeskanzleramt** (Federal Chancellery).

South of the Bundeskanzleramt's western end is the **Haus der Kulturen der Welt** (House of World Cultures), an impressive piece of modern architecture with a reflecting pool that contains a Henry Moore sculpture. Formerly known as the Kongresshalle and nicknamed the 'pregnant oyster', the HdKdW opened in 1957 as a gift from the United States and today hosts exhibits from cultures around the world.

Also on the park's northern boundary stands **Schloss Bellevue**, a minor palace

---

♥ Time to eat, drink & shop

Coffee stop
Garcia Kaffeebar *p113*

Pretending you're a Weimar-era intellectual
Café Einstein *p110*, Joseph-Roth-Diele *p111*

Boating with a beer
Café am Neuen See *p106*

Blow-out dinner
Cinco *p110*, Hugos *p110*

Fine foods and beverages
Arminiusmarkthalle *p113*

Hip homewares
retro-nova *p113*, Andreas Murkudis *p112*

Siegessäule

In the know
Getting around

Once you're inside the Tiergarten, you're about as far as it gets from U-Bahn and S-Bahn lines in Berlin. Practically, this means at most a 20-minute walk, since the park is ringed with stations, including the famous Berlin Zoo station on its western edge. If you do get footsore, don't despair: there are often cycle rickshaws waiting by the Siegessäule. Potsdamer Platz is served by U2, S1, S2 and S25 lines. Berlin Hauptbahnhof is the main hub in Moabit.

❤ A stroll through the Tiergarten

U55, S1, S2, S25 Brandenburger Tor.
Map p100 L7.

Make like a Berliner and stretch your legs with a stroll, jog or cycle through Berlin's most famous park. Whether you're hunting famous monuments, a beer and a sausage, or a spot to sunbathe naked, you'll find what you're looking for. From Turkish families enjoying a grill-party to gay men cruising one another, all of life is here. This 5-km (3-mile) circuit will return you to your starting point ready for your next adventure within an hour or so. Don't worry if you get lost, the park is full of maps with 'You Are Here' markers.

Start with the **Brandenburger Tor** at your back. Cross the road, heading west, up the right-hand side of **Strasse des 17 Juni**. This wide thoroughfare is regularly pedestrianised for national holidays, important football games and concerts, but you should beware cyclists zooming down the cycle lanes. On your right, you'll see the **Sowjetisches Ehrenmal**, complete with tanks. 100 m further on, carefully cross the busy road then turn north-west into the park, following the paths but bearing right until you reach the banks of the River Spree. Follow the river, then, at the **Lutherbrücke** (Luther's bridge), turn left back into the park

following the Spreeweg until you reach the **Siegessäule**. Wave hello to 'Gold-Else' (as Berliners call the statue) and then cross over, entering the southern half of the Tiergarten for the first time. Continue south-west from the Siegessäule, following the broad path known as Fasanerieallee as far as a little bridge over a stream. On sunny days, you'll pass fields of sunbathers and happy picnickers. If you've worked up an appetite, cross the bridge and immediately turn right towards **Café am Neuen See**. If not, then follow the stream east. You'll soon meet a bigger path known as the Grosser Weg. Keep bearing right until you meet another bridge. Cross it and keep on going. Soon you'll hear the traffic on Tiergartenstrasse just ahead. Now take the turning left onto the **Luiseninsel**, a small island where you'll find a statue of Queen Luise, wife of Frederick William III of Prussia, among beautiful flowers in spring and summer. Leave the island via the **Ahornsteig** (maple path) and continue on without deviating. On your right, you'll see an open meadow full of the strange rocks of the **Global Stone Project**, a private and somewhat eccentric peace initiative. Finally, reaching the end of the Ahornsteig, turn left and then immediately right to find yourself back at the Brandenburger Tor.

TIERGARTEN & MOABIT

from 1785 that's now the official residence of the German President. Across the river, a serpentine 718-apartment residence for Federal employees, nicknamed '*Die Schlange*' (the snake), winds across land that was formerly used as a goods yard. West of Schloss Bellevue is the post-war **Englischer Garten**, landscaped in the style of Capability Brown and filled with plants donated by the English royal family and various horticultural societies.

Just north of here, the smaller branch of the **Akademie der Künste** (*see p253*) has a varied programme of arts events and classical concerts. The district between the Akademie and the loop of the Spree is known as the **Hansaviertel**, a post-war housing project designed by a who's who of architects as part of the 1957 Interbau Exhibition for the 'city of tomorrow'. It's of great interest to lovers of concrete modernism, if a little desolate.

Sights & museums

Gaslaternen-Freilichtmuseum Berlin

Strasse des 17 Juni (9025 4124, www. museumsportal-berlin.de/en/museums/ gaslaternen-freilichtmuseum-berlin). S5, S7, S75 Tiergarten. **Open** *24hrs daily.* **Admission** *free.* **Map** *p100 H7.*

A charming little oddity right by the Tiergarten S-Bahn station, this open-air gas-lamp museum has over 90 examples of historic streetlights, all lovingly restored. Take a turn through here at night and bask in their historic glow.

Haus der Kulturen der Welt

John-Foster-Dulles-Allee 10 (3978 7175, www. hkw.de). U55 Bundestag or S3, S5, S7, S75 Hauptbahnhof. **Open** *10am-7pm daily; event times vary.* **Admission** *varies.* **Map** *p100 K6.*

Set up in 1989 to promote the arts of developing countries, the 'House of World Cultures' features a lively programme of concerts, exhibitions and symposia centred around global cultural questions. Housed in Hugh Stubbins' oyster-like building, erected in 1957 as America's contribution to the Interbau Exhibition, this is a treasured Berlin cultural institution. There's a decent café on the premises.

Siegessäule

Strasse des 17 Juni (391 2961). S5, S7, S75 Bellevue. **Open** *Summer 9.30am-6.30pm Mon-Fri; 9.30am-7pm Sat, Sun. Winter 10am-5pm Mon-Fri; 10am-5.30pm Sat, Sun.* **Admission** *€3; €2.50 reductions; free under-5s. No cards.* **Map** *p100 J7.*

Tiergarten's biggest monument was built in 1871-73 during Berlin's original transformation into the German capital, to commemorate Prussian campaigns against Denmark (1864), Austria (1866) and France (1870-71). Originally positioned in front of the Reichstag, it was moved by Hitler to form a centrepiece for the east–west axis connecting western Berlin with the palaces and ministries of Mitte. On top of the column is a gilded goddess of victory by Friedrich Drake; captured French cannons and cannonballs, sawn in half and gilded, decorate the column itself. Contemporary wags joked about the glum-looking Victoria as 'being the only woman in town without a man.' It's an arduous 285 steps up to the viewing platform.

Restaurants & cafés

Balikci Ergün €€

Lüneburger Strasse 382 (397 5737). S5, S7, S75 Bellevue. **Open** *5pm-midnight daily.* **No cards.** **Map** *p100 K6* ❶ *Turkish*

Opened by a Turkish ex-football player, this is as close to an Anatolian fish shack as you'll find in Berlin. The formula is simple but effective: daily fresh fish charred on the grill, zingy side salads and plenty of cold beer. It's tucked away beneath a railway arch, and the ceiling is covered in notes from appreciative diners.

Haus der Kulturen der Welt

❤ Reichstag

Platz der Republik 1 (227 32152, www.
bundestag.de/en/). U55, S1, S2, S25
Brandenburger Tor. **Open** *8am-midnight*
daily (last entry 9.45pm). **Admission** *free.*
Map *p100 L6.*

The imposing Reichstag was controversial
from the beginning. Architect Paul
Wallot struggled to find a style that would
symbolise German national identity at a
time – 1884-94, shortly after unification
– when no such style or identity existed.
The scene of Weimar squabblings, it was
then badly damaged by fire on 17 February
1933; an incident for which the Nazis
blamed Dutchman Marius van der Lubbe,
a Communist, and which they used as an
excuse to begin their seizure of power. The
Reichstag remained a burnt-out ruin during
the Third Reich and was then stranded for
decades beside the Wall. But following its
celebrated renovation by Lord Foster in
the 1990s, the Reichstag finally became
a fitting home for the Bundestag (Federal
Parliament). Foster conceived of it as a
'dialogue between old and new': graffiti
scrawled by Russian soldiers in 1945 was left
on view, and there was no attempt to deny
the building's turbulent history.

No dome appeared on Foster's original
plans, but the German government insisted
upon one as a sop to conservatives. Foster, in
turn, demanded that unlike the structure's
original dome (damaged in the war and
demolished in the 1950s), the new dome
must be open to visitors as a symbol of
political transparency; due to the materials
used, it ended up costing even more than a
replica would have done. A lift whisks you
up to the roof; from here, ramps lead to the
top of the dome, from where there are fine
views of the city. At the centre is a funnel
of mirrors, angled so as to shed light on
the workings of democracy below, but also
lending an almost funhouse effect to the
dome. An excellent (free) audio guide points
out all the surrounding landmarks.

A trip to the top of this open, playful and
defiantly democratic space is a must, but
note that you can't just rock up any more:
following a series of terrorist threats in
2010, you must book in advance by filling in
an online form at visite.bundestag.de and
suggesting three possible time-slots at least
three working days in advance.

TIERGARTEN & MOABIT

Sony Center

❤ Café am Neuen See €-€€
Lichtensteinallee 2 (254 4930, www. cafeamneuensee.de). S5, S7, S75 Tiergarten. **Open** *9am-late daily.* **No cards.** *Map p100 H8* ② *Brasserie*

Hidden away by a small lake in the western part of the Tiergarten, this café, beer garden and brasserie rolled into one is among Berlin's most idyllic spots. In summer, there are rowing boats for hire, and it's a fun and buzzy place to while away an afternoon, eating excellent stone-baked pizza washed down with big jugs of Pilsner – or, unusually for Berlin, cider. With a warm welcome for children, this is the perfect spot for families to grab a bite during a ramble through the Tiergarten.

Konditorei Buchwald €
Bartningallee 29 (391 5931, www.konditorei-buchwald.de). S5, S7, S75 Bellevue. **Open** *9am-7pm daily.* **No cards.** *Map p100 J6* ⑩ *Café*

One Berlin institution (afternoon coffee and cake) celebrated by another: Buchwald, which has been pumping out the sugar and caffeine fix in style for over 160 years. The premises are charming and old-fashioned. The cakes, particularly the *Baumkuchen*, are legendary. Arrive early afternoon, grab a table and savour the history.

Teehaus im Englischen Garten €€
Altonaer Strasse 2 (3948 0400, www.teehaus-tiergarten.com). S5, S7, S75 Bellevue. **Open** *noon-11pm Tue-Sat; 10am-11pm Sun.* **No cards.** *Map p100 J7* ⑬ *German*

This 1950s garden in the north-west of the Tiergarten was designed to commemorate Anglo-German relations during the blockade of Berlin and is filled with trees donated by George VI. The charming thatched tea house serves seasonal specialities, such as venison stew or goose leg with dumplings.

POTSDAMER PLATZ & SOUTH OF THE PARK

At the south-east corner of the Tiergarten is the resurrected **Potsdamer Platz**, intended to be the reunified city's commercial centrepiece. In the 1920s, Potsdamer Platz was reckoned to be one of Europe's busiest intersections; the first-ever traffic lights stood here (a replica of which can be seen today on the south side of the square). Like much of Berlin, it was bombed flat in World War II. In the years that followed, the borders of the British, American and Soviet occupation zones met at this point, meaning that even among the late 1940s ruins it remained a centre of commerce – no matter which direction the police approached, black market traders were able to escape into another zone. The Wall snuffed out all activity in the area for several decades, and it became a grim no-man's-land, identifying with neither East or West.

After reunification, fierce debate ensued over whether the redevelopment of Potsdamer Platz should adopt the typical scale of a 'European' city or go for an 'American' high-rise approach. A group of internationally renowned super-architects locked horns with the city's traditionalist building commissioner, Hans Stimmann. The result was a compromise: medium-height development except on Potsdamer Platz itself, where high-rises up to 90 metres

(295 feet) were allowed but with a slightly more uniform look than the proposed experimental designs.

Opinions are mixed as to the success of the finished article; some architectural critics finding its non-nationalistic idiom too much like 'a nebulous international airport space'. Even so, this once-isolated island of redevelopment is now beginning to feel worn in, a natural part of a long-disjointed urban landscape, with the western side of the **Park am Gleisdreieck** providing a green link to Kreuzberg and Schöneberg.

Helmut Jahn's soaring **Sony Center**, surprisingly light in steel and glass, contains the **Forum**, an urban entertainment complex that in turn holds the **CineStar** multiplex (*see p221*), the more offbeat **Arsenal** cinema (*see p220*) and the **Museum für Film und Fernsehen**. (There's another multiplex over the road in the Daimler quarter, the CinemaxX.) Served also by a clutch of five-star hotels, including the **Ritz-Carlton** (*see p298*) and the **Grand Hyatt** (*see p298*), Potsdamer Platz is also now the main venue for the **Berlin International Film Festival** (*see p218*). But there's little to recommend in terms of eating, drinking or shopping. It's all franchise culture.

The **Kaisersaal Café** from the old Grand Hotel Esplanade, a listed building, was one of only two Potsdamer Platz buildings to survive World War II and the subsequent clear-out. It originally stood on the Sony site, but when plans for the area solidified, the café was found to be in a bad position, so the whole structure was moved 75 metres (246 feet) to its present location on the building's north side, where it's been integrated into the apartment complex on Bellevuestrasse.

The other major corporate presence at Potsdamer Platz is **Daimler** (formerly DaimlerChrysler), responsible for most of the development south of the Sony Center. One of the most admired of the area's buildings is Hans Kollhoff's triangular, brick-clad tower at **Potsdamer Platz 1**, which, together with the curved Deutsche Bahn tower over the road, forms the gateway to the area. It's the tallest building here; the **Panoramapunkt** platform up top offers fine views.

A few doors down the road at Alte Potsdamer Strasse 5 is **Haus Huth**, the only other building to survive from before World War II. For decades a lonely structure in the middle of overgrown wasteland, it now stands next to the three-storey Arkaden shopping mall. At the top is the **Daimler Contemporary** gallery, which exhibits works from the auto manufacturer's big-name art collection (*see also p109* In the know).

Immediately west of the Potsdamer Platz development is one of the city's major concentrations of museums, galleries and cultural institutions. Collectively known as the **Kulturforum** and built in anticipation of reunification, it was based on the designs of Hans Scharoun. Scharoun himself designed the **Staatsbibliotek** (State Library) and the gold **Philharmonie** (*see p252*), home to the Berlin Philharmonic; adjacent is the **Musikinstrumentenmuseum** (Musical Instrument Museum).

One block west is a low-rise museum complex. Its biggest draw is the **Gemäldegalerie** (Picture Gallery), but the **Kunstgewerbemuseum** (Museum of Decorative Arts) is also worth a peek. Here too is the **Kunstbibliotek** (Art Library), and a decent café and shop. Next door is the **Matthäuskirche** (Matthias Church) and, to the south, the bold glass cube of the **Neue Nationalgalerie** (New National Gallery).

Between the north flank of the Kulturforum and the south flank of Tiergarten runs **Tiergartenstrasse**, the main drag of Berlin's revived diplomatic quarter. Part of Albert Speer's plan for 'Germania', the street originally contained the embassy buildings (designed by German architects) of Hitler's Axis allies. Damaged by bombing, they were largely abandoned, and Tiergartenstrasse became an eerie walk past decaying grandeur. But with the land often still owned by the respective governments, embassies were reconstructed at their old addresses during the diplomatic relocation from Bonn, and this area became embassy row again.

The moving **Gedenkstätte Deutscher Widerstand** (Memorial to the German Resistance) lies south on Stauffenbergstrasse, a street named after the leader of the July 1944 plot to kill Hitler. At the corner of Stauffenbergstrasse and Reichpietschufer is **Shell House** (1932), a curvaceous expressionist masterpiece by Emil Fahrenkamp. Five minutes' walk west along the **Landwehrkanal** sits the gleaming white building of the **Bauhaus Archiv – Museum für Gestaltung** (Museum of Design); a further ten-minute walk leads to the less highbrow attractions of the **Zoologischer Garten & Aquarium** and the hub of West Berlin around **Bahnhof Zoo** and the Ku'damm (*see p180*).

Sights & museums

Bauhaus Archiv – Museum für Gestaltung

Klingelhöferstrasse 13-14 (254 0020, www. bauhaus.de). U1, U2, U3, U4 Nollendorfplatz. **Open** *see the website for details.* **Map** *p100 J8.*

Walter Gropius, founder of the Bauhaus school, designed this elegant white building that now houses this absorbing design museum. The permanent exhibition presents a selection of furniture, ceramics, prints, sculptures, photographs and sketches created in the Bauhaus workshop between 1919 and 1933, when the school was closed down by the Nazis. There are also first-rate temporary exhibitions from the extensive archive, such as a show about Kandinsky's tenure as a teacher. An interesting gift shop sells design icons, including the Bauhaus lamp by Wilhelm Wagenfeld. The museum was closed for renovations in 2018, ready for the Bauhaus centenary in 2019.

Daimler Contemporary
*Haus Huth, Alte Potsdamer Strasse 5 (2594 1420, www.art.daimler.com). U2, S1, S2, S25 Potsdamer Platz. **Open** 11am-6pm daily. **Admission** free. **Map** p100 L8.*

As you'd expect, Daimler's collection is serious stuff. It sticks to the 20th century, specifically abstract and geometric art; the collection numbers around 1,800 works from artists such as Josef Albers, Max Bill, Walter de Maria, Jeff Koons and Andy Warhol. The gallery rotates themed portions of the collection, typically 30-80 works at a time, and often stages joint shows with other private collections. Daimler hosts one (free) guided tour per month, delving deep into the themes of the current collection. The date depends on the exhibition schedule but is almost always on a Saturday afternoon; check the website for details. *See also below* In the know.

Dalí – Die Ausstellung
*Leipziger Platz 7 (0700 325 423 7546, www.daliberlin.de). U2, S1, S2, S25 Potsdamer Platz. **Open** Sept-Jun noon-8pm daily. Jul-Aug 10am-8pm daily (last entry 7pm). **Admission** €12.50; €9.50 reductions; free under-6s. **Map** p100 M8.*

There is no obvious reason why Berlin boasts a Salvador Dalí museum, let alone one as good as this. It was opened in 2009 to commemorate 20 years since both the fall of the Wall and the artist's death: the somewhat tenuous Berlin theme is that Dalí 'tore down walls in his art'. There are more than 400 Dalí originals on show – drawn from a pool of more than 2,000 works from private collections – including drawings, lithographs, etchings, woodcuts, illustrated books, documents and supporting works, original graphics and complete portfolios. As a purely commercial venture, the entrance fee is stiff.

Gedenkstätte Deutscher Widerstand
*Stauffenbergstrasse 13-14 (2699 5000, www.gdw-berlin.de). U2, S1, S2, S25 Potsdamer Platz. **Open** 9am-6pm Mon-Wed, Fri; 9am-8pm Thur; 10am-6pm Sat, Sun. Guided tours 3pm Sun. **Admission** free. **Map** p100 K8.*

The Memorial to the German Resistance chronicles the German resistance to National Socialism. The building is part of a complex known as the Bendlerblock, owned by the German military from its construction in 1911 until 1945. At the back is a memorial to the conspirators killed on this site during the attempt to assassinate Hitler on 20 July 1944. Regular guided tours are in German only, but you can book an English tour four weeks in advance.

♥ Gemäldegalerie
*Matthäikirchplatz (266 424242, www.smb.museum/gg). U2, S1, S2, S25 Potsdamer Platz. **Open** 10am-6pm Tue, Wed, Fri; 10am-8pm Thur; 11am-6pm Sat, Sun. **Admission** €10; €5 reductions. **Map** p100 K8.*

The Picture Gallery is a first-rate early European collection with many fine Italian, Spanish and English works on display, but the real highlights are the superb Dutch and Flemish pieces. Fans of Rembrandt can indulge themselves with around 20 paintings, the best of which include a portrait of preacher and merchant Cornelis Claesz Anslo and his wife, and an electric Samson confronting his father-in-law. Two of Franz Hals' finest works are here – the wild, fluid, almost impressionistic *Malle Babbe* (Mad Babette) and the detailed portrait of the one-year-old Catharina Hooft and her nurse. Other highlights include a couple of unflinching portraits by Robert Campin (early 15th century), a version of Botticelli's *Venus Rising*, and Corregio's brilliant *Leda with the Swan*. Look out too for a pair of Lucas Cranach Venus and Cupid paintings and his *Fountain of Youth*. Pick up the excellent (free) English-language audio guide.

Kunstgewerbemuseum

Matthäikirchplatz (266 424242, www.smb.
museum/kgm). U2, S1, S2, S25 Potsdamer
Platz. **Open** *10am-6pm Tue-Fri; 11am-6pm*
Sat, Sun. **Admission** *€8; €4 reductions.*
Map *p100 L8.*

The Museum of Decorative Arts reopened in
late 2014 after an extensive two-year revamp.
There are some lovely items in its collection
of European arts and crafts, stretching from
the Middle Ages through Renaissance,
Baroque and rococo to Jugendstil and
art deco. Additional features include an
impressive fashion gallery, covering 150 years
of fashion history, and the design collection
in the basement. **Other location** Schloss
Köpenick, Schlossinsel, Köpenick (266 3666).

Legoland Discovery Centre

Sony Center, Potsdamer Strasse 4 (301 0400,
www.legolanddiscoverycentre.de/berlin-en).
U2, S1, S2, S25 Potsdamer Platz. **Open**
10am-7pm daily; last entry 5pm. **Admission**
€18.50 (discounts available); free under-3s.
Map *p100 L8.*

Featuring rides, a 4D cinema, factory tour,
café and plenty of hands-on attractions for
Lego fans of all ages, the centre has plenty to
keep children entertained and is popular with
adults too. The walk-up price isn't cheap, but
discounts are available for families and when
booked online in advance. On rainy days, the
build and play zones will keep small hands
occupied for hours.

Museum für Film und Fernsehen

Sony Center, Potsdamer Strasse 2 (300 9030,
www.deutsche-kinemathek.de). U2, S1, S2,
S25 Potsdamer Platz. **Open** *10am-6pm Tue,*
Wed, Fri-Sun; 10am-8pm Thur. **Admission**
€7; €4.50 reductions; free to all 4-8pm Thur.
No cards. **Map** *p100 L8.*

Since 1963, the Deutsche Kinemathek
has been amassing films, memorabilia,
documentation and antique film apparatus.
In 2000, all this stuff found a home in this
roomy, well-designed exhibition space set
over two floors in the Sony Center. Striking
exhibits include the two-storey-high video
wall of disasters from Fritz Lang's adventure
films and a morgue-like space devoted to
films from the Third Reich. On a lighter note,
there's a collection of 'claymation' figures
from Ray Harryhausen films, such as *Jason
and the Argonauts*. But the main attraction is
the Marlene Dietrich collection of personal
effects, home movies and designer clothes.
Exhibitions are often linked with film
programming at the **Arsenal** cinema (*see
p220*) downstairs.

Musikinstrumentenmuseum

Tiergartenstrasse 1 (254 810, www.simpk.
de/mim_3.html). U2, S1, S2, S25 Potsdamer
Platz. **Open** *9am-5pm Tue, Wed, Fri;*
9am-8pm Thur; 10am-5pm Sat, Sun.
Admission *€6; €3 reductions; free under-18s.*
No cards. **Map** *p100 L8.*

More than 3,200 string, keyboard, wind and
percussion instruments (dating from the
16th century) are crammed into the small
Musical Instrument Museum, located next to
the Philharmonie. Among them are rococo
musical clocks, for which 18th-century princes
commissioned jingles from Mozart, Haydn
and Beethoven. Museum guides play obsolete
instruments such as the Kammerflugel; on
Saturdays at noon, the largest Wurlitzer organ
in Europe – salvaged from an American silent
movie house – is cranked into action.

Neue Nationalgalerie

Potsdamer Strasse 50 (266 424242, www.
smb.museum/nng). U2, S1, S2, S25 Potsdamer
Platz. **Closed** *until 2020.* **Map** *p100 L8.*

The Neue Nationalgalerie, a stark glass-and-
steel pavilion designed in the 1960s by Mies
van der Rohe, was built to house German
and international artworks from the 20th
century. The collection features key pieces by
Kirchner, Picasso, Gris and Léger. The Neue
Sachlichkeit is well represented by paintings
from George Grosz and Otto Dix, while the
Bauhaus contribution includes work from
Paul Klee and Wassily Kandinsky. The gallery
is currently closed for a major renovation (the
first in its history), masterminded by David
Chipperfield under the guiding principle 'as
much Mies as possible'. It should reopen in
summer 2020.

In the know
Street art

The Daimler Contemporary has positioned
various sculptures from its collection around
Potsdamer Platz. *The Boxers* by Keith
Haring (corner of Potsdamer Strasse and
Eichhornstrasse) comprises two figures
in primary blue and red, conjoined yet in
conflict, befitting both Berlin and this spot.
South of here, a spaceship-like contraption
perches on the shoulder of a building,
apparently scanning the streets below; this
is Auk de Vries's *Gelandet* ('Landed'). At the
point where this street opens into Marlene-
Dietrich-Platz, in front of the Spielbank
(casino), is Jeff Koons' *Balloon Flower*.
Between Haus Huth and the Arkaden shopping
mall is Robert Rauschenberg's *Riding Bikes*,
two neon-lit bicycles above a small pool.

Panoramapunkt

Kollhoff Tower, Potsdamer Platz 1, entrance on Alte Potsdamer Strasse (2593 7080, www.panoramapunkt.de). U2, S1, S2, S25 Potsdamer Platz. **Open** *Summer 10am-8pm daily. Winter 10am-6pm daily.* **Admission** *€7.50; €6 reductions. No cards.* **Map** *p100 L8.*

What's billed as 'the fastest elevator in Europe' shoots up to the 100-m-high (328-ft) viewing platform in the Kollhoff Tower. The building's north-east corner is precisely at the point where the borders of Tiergarten, Mitte and Kreuzberg all meet – and also on what was the line of the Wall. From this vantage point, you can peer through railings at the neighbouring postmodern high-rises at the landmarks of new Berlin. There are good views to the south and west; looking north, the DB Tower gets in the way.

Schwules Museum

Lützowstrasse 73 (6959 9050, www. schwulesmuseum.de). U1, U2, U3, U4 Nollendorfplatz. **Open** *2-6pm Mon, Wed, Fri, Sun; 2-8pm Thur; 2-7pm Sat.* **Admission** *€7.50; €4 reductions. No cards.* **Map** *p178 K9.*

The Gay Museum opened in 1985 in Kreuzberg but has since moved to this location. It is still one of very few in the world dedicated to homosexual life. The museum, library and archives are staffed by volunteers and survive mostly thanks to private donations and bequests (such as the archive of GDR sex scientist Rudolf Klimmer). The museum puts on regular exhibitions and shows an impressive collection of visual art, while the library and archives contain 8,000 books (500 in English), 3,000 international periodicals, photos and posters, plus TV, film and audio footage, all available to borrow.

Zoologischer Garten & Aquarium

Hardenbergplatz 8 (254 010, www.zoo-berlin. de). U2, U9, S5, S7, S75 Zoologischer Garten. **Open** *Zoo from 9am daily; closing times vary throughout the year. Aquarium 9am-6pm daily.* **Admission** *Single attraction €15.50; €8-€10.50 reductions. Combined admission €21; €10.50-€15.50 reductions.* **Map** *p100 H8.*

Germany's oldest zoo was opened in 1841 to designs by Martin Lichtenstein and Peter Joseph Lenné. With almost 14,000 creatures, it's one of the world's largest and most important zoos, with more endangered species in its collection than any zoo in Europe except Antwerp. It's beautifully landscaped, with lots of architectural oddities, and there are plenty of places for a coffee, beer or snack.

You can access the aquarium from within the zoo or through its own entrance on Olof-Palme-Platz by the Elephant Gate. More than 500 species are arranged over three floors,

and it's a good option for a rainy day. On the ground floor are the fish (including some impressive sharks); on the first you'll find reptiles (the crocodile hall is the highlight); while insects and amphibians occupy the second. The dark corridors and liquid ambience, with tanks lit from within and curious aquatic creatures drifting by, can be as absorbing as an art installation.

Restaurants & cafés

♥ Café Einstein €€

Kurfürstenstrasse 58 (2639 1919, www. cafeeinstein.com). U1, U2, U3, U4 Nollendorfplatz. **Open** *8am-midnight daily.* **Map** *p100 J9* ❸ *Austrian*

For a taste of Old World decadence, visit this Nollendorfplatz institution. It's set in a neo-Renaissance villa built in the 1870s by a wealthy industrialist; red leather banquettes, parquet flooring and the crack of wooden chairs all contribute to the historic Viennese café experience. You could come for a bracing breakfast of herb omelette with feta cheese and spinach, or, in the afternoon, enjoy a classic apple strudel and a *Wiener Melange* (a creamy Austrian coffee), all served with a flourish by the charming uniformed waiters.

♥ Cinco €€€€

Das Stue Hotel, Drakestrasse 1 (311 7220, www.5-cinco.com). S5, S7, S75 Tiergarten. **Open** *6.30-10pm Tue-Sat.* **Map** *p100 H8* ❹ *Spanish*

Chef Paco Pérez gained another Michelin star (his fifth) within Cinco's first year of opening. He supposedly keeps a camera trained on the kitchen 24/7, so he can quality-control all the way from Spain. The menu combines Catalan traditional cooking and the inventive plating of Spain's *nueva cocina*. Try the button mushroom royale with squid tartare and truffle or the pigeon, corn, mole and huitlacoche. Booking advised.

♥ Hugos €€€€

Hotel InterContinental Berlin, Budapester Strasse 2 (2602 1263, www.hugos-restaurant. de). U2, U9, S5, S7, S75 Zoologischer Garten. **Open** *6.30-10.30pm Tue-Sat.* **Map** *p100 H8* ❼ *Haute cuisine*

One of Berlin's best restaurants right now, and with the awards to prove it. Chef Thomas Kammeier juxtaposes classic French technique – the silver Christofle cheese trolley is a sight to behold – with New German flair. With tasting menus and wine pairings, expect dishes such as imperial caviar with pickled gherkin, shallot crumble and bonito jelly, or Australian roast beef with turnips, watercress and pear cabbage. Vegetarian menu available.

Zoologischer Garten

❤ Joseph-Roth-Diele €

*Potsdamer Strasse 75 (2636 9884, www. joseph-roth-diele.de). U1 Kurfürstenstrasse. **Open** 10am-midnight Mon-Fri. **No cards**. **Map** p100 K9* 8 *German*

A traditional Berlin book café, just a short stroll south of Potsdamer Platz, which pays homage to the life and work of interwar Jewish writer Joseph Roth. It's an amiable place, decorated in ochre tones and with comfortable seating, offering tea, coffee, wine, beer, snacks and great-value lunch specials such as meatloaf with mash.

Kin Dee €€€

*Lützowstrasse 81 (215 5294, www. kindeeberlin.com). U1 Kurfürstenstrasse. **Open** from 6pm Tue-Sat **Map** p100 K9* 9 *Thai*

In 2017, Kin Dee took over from Berlin-Thai institution Edd's. Part of the gastronomic network around Grill Royal, Kin Dee is proving a deserving successor. Head chef and owner Dalad crosses culinary boundaries, serving creative Thai cuisine with a focus on fresh, high-quality ingredients. Offering set menus of small plates, excellent vegetarian options and a well-chosen wine list, Kin Dee has gone down a storm.

Nordic Embassies Canteen €

*Rauchstrasse 1 (305 0500, www. nordicembassies.org). U2, U9, S5, S7, S75 Zoologischer Garten. **Open** 1-3pm Mon-Fri. **No cards**. **Map** p100 J8* 11 *Scandinavian*

The striking Nordic embassy complex, clad in maplewood and glass, houses an excellent lunch secret. The canteens of Berlin's civic buildings are all open to the public, so after 1pm you can tuck into the excellent subsidised food provided for the Scandinavian diplomats. The choice of a meat, fish and vegetarian dish changes daily.

Bars & pubs

Curtain Club

*Ritz-Carlton Hotel, Potsdamer Platz 3 (337 777, www.ritzcarlton.com). U2, S1, S2, S25 Potsdamer Platz. **Open** 11.30am-1am Mon-Thur; 11.30am-2am Fri-Sun. **Map** p100 L8* 1

Reeking of luxury, this wood-panelled and richly carpeted bar is slightly let down by its location in the ground-floor hotel foyer. Head barman Arnd Heissen specialises in essences; the Hypnose is a potent blend of rose petal-infused vodka and various aromatics. The rum tiki drinks come in comical skull-shaped ceramic mugs. There's a creative menu, beautifully presented, but the barmen will make you anything you ask for. Stay past 9pm Wednesday to Saturday for the live piano music.

Lebensstern

*Kurfürstenstrasse 58 (2639 1922, www.lebens-stern.de). U1, U2, U3, U4 Nollendorfplatz. **Open** 7pm-2am daily. **Map** p100 J9* 3

This smart bar above Café Einstein (*see p110*) became a second home for Quentin Tarantino when he was in Berlin to film *Inglourious Basterds*. He liked it so much, some scenes were even filmed here. If you can't find something among the list of 800 or so rums, there are over 200 gins to try. The cocktails are excellent too.

Victoria Bar

*Potsdamer Strasse 102 (2575 9977, www. victoriabar.de). U1 Kurfürstenstrasse. **Open** 6.30pm-3am Mon-Thur, Sun; 6.30pm-4am Fri, Sat. **No cards**. **Map** p100 K9* 4

Owner Stefan Weber has a humorous art collection, so works by Sarah Lucas and Martin Kippenberger adorn the walls of this sleek bar, which strikes a perfect balance between modernist layout and antique

As well as **Andreas Murkudis** (*see below*), the former *Tagesspiegel* newspaper complex on Potsdamer Strasse houses two excellent commercial galleries. **BlainSouthern** (644 931 510, www.blainsouthern.com) uses the vast space of the printing hall to powerful effect for big-name artists, including Damian Hirst and Douglas Gordon, while **Galerie Guido W Baudach** (3199 8101, www.guidowbaudach.com) curates shows by contemporary German artists, such as Thomas Zipp, Andreas Hofer and Thilo Heinzmann.

details. The drinks are superb. The menu is divided by liquor type: go fully decadent with an Alfonso, a mix of Dubonnet, sugar, bitters and champagne, or if you're feeling adventurous, try a Rosemary's Baby, an aged tequila sour with rosemary and sage.

Shops & services

♥ Andreas Murkudis

*Potsdamer Strasse 77 & 81E (680 798 306, www.andreasmurkudis.com). U2, S1, S2, S25 Potsdamer Platz. **Open** 10am-8pm Mon-Sat. **Map** p100 L9* ❶ *Fashion/Homewares*

The Murkudis brothers are a design duo with the Midas touch. This concept store (designed by one brother and housed in the former *Tagesspiegel* complex, whose move caused a mini-renaissance for Potsdamer Strasse several years ago) is white, stark and immense, with neon strip lighting. Clothes (by the other brother, as well as the likes of Dries van Noten and Maison Martin Margiela) are immaculately displayed among items of contemporary furniture, porcelain and homewares.

Kunst und Trödelmarkt

*Strasse des 17 Juni 110-114 (2655 0096, www.berliner-troedelmarkt.de). U2 Ernst-Reuter-Platz, or S5, S7, S75 Tiergarten. **Open** 10am-5pm Sat, Sun. **Map** p100 G7* ❸ *Market*

This second-hand market lies on the stretch of road west of Tiergarten S-Bahn station. You'll find good-quality, early 20th-century objects (with prices to match) alongside a jumble of vintage clothing, old furniture, records and books. Full of interesting stuff, and with a cast of eccentric locals to practise your haggling on, the market isn't a bad place to bring children, who enjoy hunting among the *Trödel* for treasures.

MOABIT

Situated north of the Tiergarten, bordered by canals and the River Spree, Moabit is a little pocket of central Berlin with an identity problem. Once a working-class residential district best known for its prison, Moabit has found itself unnervingly close to the action in recent years. In the streets around the **Arminiusmarkethalle**, an influx of students and artists chasing cheaper rents means new cafés and bars have sprung up alongside long-established favourites, while developers are building on both sides of the river, most noticeably around the hulking **Berlin Hauptbahnhof**. Close to the station and the impressive contemporary art collections of **Hamburger Bahnhof**, you'll find one of Berlin's favourite playgrounds, the spankingly luxurious **Vabali Spa**.

Sights & museums

Hamburger Bahnhof – Museum für Gegenwart

*Invalidenstrasse 50-51 (3978 3439, www.smb.museum/en/museums-institutions/hamburger-bahnhof/home.html). U55, S5, S7, S75 Hauptbahnhof. **Open** 10am-6pm Tue, Wed, Fri-Sun; 10am-8pm Thur. **Admission** (incl temporary exhibitions) €10; €5 reductions. **Map** p100 L5.*

This contemporary art museum opened in 1997 within a vast, grand neoclassical former train station. Outside is a stunning fluorescent light installation by Dan Flavin. Inside, the biggest draw is the controversial Friedrich Christian Flick Collection: some 2,000 works from around 150 artists (mainly from the late 20th century), with key pieces by Bruce Nauman and Martin Kipperberger. Flick, from a steel family whose fortune was earned partly from Nazi-era slave labour, paid for the refurbishment of the adjacent Rieckhalle to warehouse the (many large-scale) works, which are doled out in temporary, themed exhibitions. There are other shows too – an exciting Otto Mueller retrospective wowed the crowds – plus one of Berlin's best art bookshops.

Zentrum für Kunst und Urbanistik

*Siemensstrasse 27 (3988 5840, www.zku-berlin.org). U9, S45, S53 Westhafen. **Open** varies. **Admission** free. **Map** p100 G4.*

Describing itself as a laboratory for inter- and trans-disciplinary activities centered on the phenomenon of the city, the Zentrum for Kunst and Urbanistik hosts regular exhibitions, happenings and workshops. A lively arts centre run by a non-profit artists' collective, the ZKU is set in a former railway depot and surrounded by a freshly landscaped park. Check out their Facebook page for the latest events.

Restaurants & cafés

Freddy Leck sein Waschsalon €
Gotzkowskystrasse 11 (www.freddy-leck-sein -waschsalon.de). U9 Turmstrasse. **Open** *7am-11pm daily.* **No cards.** **Map** *p100 G5* ❺ *Café*

Need to check your email while drinking coffee and doing your laundry? Look no further than Freddy Leck's. A laundromat with an in-house café, free WiFi and glitzy chandeliers, this kitschy spot is one of Berlin's characterful, quirky corners.

♥ Garcia Kaffeebar €
Waldstrasse 59 (www.facebook.com/garcia. kaffeebar). U9 Turmstrasse. **Open** *8am-7pm daily.* **No cards.** **Map** *p100 G5* ❻ *Café*

A cosy, charming café serving breakfast, coffee, tea, a range of delicious sandwiches and cakes, plus a glass of wine and a cocktail or two, Garcia Kaffeebar is much beloved by its patrons. Offering a warm welcome hipster-Berlin style, Garcia makes coffee that's worth the schlep.

Restaurant Neumann's €€
Alt Moabit 126 (3929933, www. restaurantneumanns.de). U55, S5, S7, S75 Hauptbahnhof. **Open** *10am-midnight (or later) daily.* **Map** *p100 K6* ⓬ *German*

You'll find no avocado on sourdough here. This sizeable, über-traditional German eatery serves up massive portions of stick-to-your ribs grub, with the odd Austrian or Italian dish thrown in. Not far from the Hauptbahnhof and Reichstag, and with a pleasant summer terrace, Neumann's doesn't care that it's not fashionable and neither will you. Limited vegetarian options. Sunday brunch buffet.

Bars & pubs

Kallasch & Moab Barprojekt
Unionstrasse 2 (www.facebook.com/ moabiterbarprojekt). U9, S45, S53 Westhafen. **Open** *7pm-1.30am Wed; 7pm-3am Thur-Sat.* **Map** *p100 G4* ❷

With an unpretentious *Wohnzimmer* ('living room') atmosphere, fair prices and friendly staff, Kallasch & Moab is regularly hailed as Moabit's best bar. Regular live music and events, such as poetry slams and exhibitions, make it a great place to spend the evening. Non-smokers may find their eyes watering.

Shops & services

♥ Arminiusmarkthalle
Arminiusstrasse 2-4 (www. arminiusmarkthalle.com). U9 Turmstrasse. **Open** *10am-10pm Mon-Fri; 10am-6pm Sat.* **Map** *p100 H5* ❷ *Market*

Opened in 1898, the Arminiusmarkthalle has been selling Berliners their groceries for well over 100 years. Inside this traditionally built market hall, you'll find stands selling everything from cheese and wine to fresh fish and flowers. There are also are some fine *Imbisse*, where you can grab lunch or dinner, including a Peruvian *picanteria* and pisco bar. Overall, a highly recommended spot to wander, pick up some *Feinkosten* and people-watch.

♥ retro-nova
Wilsnacker Strasse 32 (www.retro-nova. de). U9 Birkenstrasse. **Open** *3-7pm Wed-Fri; noon-4pm Sat.* **Maps** *p100 J4* ❹ *Vintage furniture*

Carefully selected pre-loved furniture in a shop that favours 20th-century modernist designs. Run by two passionate enthusiasts; if you want it, they'll ship it. There are some real beauties here, but don't expect to pick up a masterpiece for peanuts.

♥ Vabali Spa
Seydlitzstrasse 6 (911 4860, www.vabali. de). U55, S5, S7, S75, Hauptbahnhof. **Open** *9am-midnight daily.* **Admission** *from €21.50.* **Map** *p100 K5* ❺

The perfect place to relax or detox from a night on the tiles, Vabali has proved a huge hit with Berliners. Set over a spectacular 20,000 square metres, with indoor and outdoor pools, 11 saunas and steam rooms, a jacuzzi, treatment rooms, a restaurant and gardens, Vabali's worth the ticket price. And with robes and towels for hire and swimming costumes surplus to requirements, you can just rock up on a whim.

Vabali Spa

Prenzlauer Berg & Mitte North

Prenzlauer Berg has been visibly transformed by Berlin's history. From 19th-century roots as a working-class district, it's become the most desirable neighbourhood for hip young families; the bijou children's clothing shops speak nothing of its previous life as a centre of GDR dissidence or post-Wall bohemia. Even if there aren't many major museums or sights to visit, the area still has fine examples of late 19th-century civic architecture, Berlin's biggest flea market at the Mauerpark and lots of great shopping. A blend of old and new, sleekly modern and charmingly quaint, Prenzlauer Berg is ideal for a weekend's exploring.

Following the S-Bahn ring westwards takes you across commercial Gesundbrunnen to reach working-class Wedding, the neighbourhood perennially touted as the next big thing. Wedding has never quite lived up to the hype, and nor does it seem to want to. Once you move away from the built-up concrete centre around the S-Bahn, the neighbourhood becomes friendlier and greener, sparsely dotted with cafés and bars. The waters of the Plötzensee attract Berliners on the hunt for some respite from the heat in summer, and there's a hidden rose garden in Humbolthain Park.

❤ **Don't miss**

1 Prater Biergarten *p123*
Berlin's oldest and loveliest beer garden.

2 Gedenkstätte Berliner Mauer *p125*
A grim insight into a city torn in two.

3 Mauerpark Flohmarkt *p124*
Sunday bargain-hunting has become an institution at Berlin's liveliest flea market.

4 Museum in der Kulturbrauerei *p119*
For a taste of what GDR life was really like.

5 Plötzensee *p199*
Berlin's one and only inner-city lake.

PRENZLAUER BERG & MITTE NORTH

Restaurants & cafés

1 A Magica *p119*
2 Anna Blume *p119*
3 Babel *p119*
4 The Barn *p120*
5 Bonanza *p120*
6 Café Pförtner *p127*
7 L'Escargot *p128*
8 Fischfabrik *p120*
9 Gugelhof *p120*
10 Konnopke's Imbiss *p120*
11 Lucky Leek *p121*
12 MontRaw *p121*
13 Mrs Robinson's *p121*
14 Oderquelle *p121*
15 Osmans Töchter *p121*
16 Pasternak *p121*
17 Sasaya *p122*
18 Shikgoo *p128*
19 Si An *p122*
20 Les Valseuses *p122*

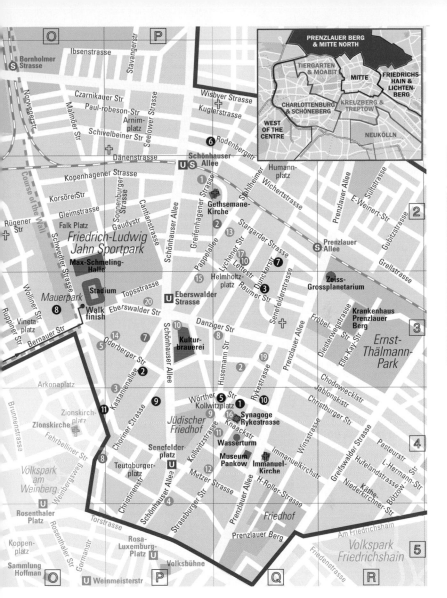

Bars & pubs

① Basalt Bar *p129*
② Becketts Kopf *p122*
③ Eschenbräu *p129*
④ F Bar *p129*
⑤ The Forsberg *p129*
⑥ Moritz Bar *p129*
⑦ Prater Biergarten *p123* ❤
⑧ Schwarze Pumpe *p122*
⑨ Vagabund Brauerei *p129*
⑩ Wohnzimmer *p122*

Shops & services

① D.nik *p122*
② Fein & Ripp *p123*
③ Goldhahn & Sampson *p123*
④ Hopfen & Malz *p129*
⑤ Kollwitzplatz Farmers'
Market *p123*
⑥ Leopoldplatz Flohmarkt *p129*
⑦ Lunettes Brillenagentur *p124*
⑧ Mauerpark Flohmarkt *p124*
⑨ Onkel Philipp's
Spielzeugwerkstatt *p124*
⑩ Saint George's *p124*
⑪ Temporary Showroom *p125*

PRENZLAUER BERG

Once a grey, depressing, working-class district, Prenzlauer Berg has undergone a facelift in the last two decades: its façades have been renovated, its streets cleaned, and its buildings newly inhabited by everyone from Russian artists to office workers. Worlds away from its grim wartime depiction in Hans Fallada's chilling novel *Alone in Berlin*, the district has seen galleries and cafés sprouting up, and century-old buildings have had coal heating replaced and private bathrooms installed. It's gone too far for some alternative types, but for many lifestyle émigrés from wealthier parts of Germany, there's no cooler part of town.

Laid out during the second half of the 19th century, Prenzlauer Berg was part of the city's Hobrecht-Plan expansion that coincided with the *Gründerzeit* – the building boom that followed German unification (*see p266*). It left behind wider streets and pavements, giving the area a distinctive open look. Although a few buildings still await restoration, the scrubbed and painted streets revive the impression of 19th-century boulevards.

The district's focal point is leafy **Kollwitzplatz**. The square is lined with bars, cafés and restaurants, and hosts an organic market on Thursdays. Knaackstrasse, heading south-east from Kollwitzplatz, brings you to one of the district's main landmarks, the **Wasserturm**. This water tower, constructed by English architect Henry Gill in 1852-75, provided running water for the first time in Germany. During the war, the Nazis used its basement as a prison and torture chamber; a plaque commemorates their victims. The tower has since been converted into swanky apartments.

Opposite the Wasserturm on Rykestrasse is the **Synagoge Rykestrasse**, a neo-romanesque turn-of-the-century structure that was badly damaged during Kristallnacht in 1938. After undergoing renovation in 1953, it was the only working synagogue in East Berlin. Now it stands peacefully in gentrified surrounds. Nearby, to the south-west of Kollwitzplatz, is the **Jüdischer Friedhof**, Berlin's oldest Jewish cemetery; it's fairly gloomy due to its closely packed stones and canopy of trees. The Impressionist painter Max Liebermann is buried here, and the tomb of famed soprano Sophie Löwe is, unusually, decorated with a carving of her face – usually prohibited by Judaism. To learn more about the district's history, look in at the **Museum Pankow** (Prenzlauer Allee 227, 902 953 917).

Moving on clockwise to the other side of Kollwitzplatz, Knaackstrasse extends north-west to the vast complex of the **Kulturbrauerei**, an old brewery that now houses a concert space, galleries, artists' studios, a market, a cinema and a museum. West from here, the area around Kastanienallee has plenty of good bars,

❤ Time to eat & drink

Caffeine snobbery
Bonanza *p120*, The Barn *p120*

Italian in a BVG bus
Café Pförtner *p127*

Brewery taps
Vagabund Brauerei *p129*, Eschenbräu *p129*

Kimchi as it should be
Shikgoo *p128*

❤ Time to shop

Heaven for bibliophiles
Saint George's *p124*

Farmers' goodies
Kollwitzplatz Farmers' Market *p123*

Beer connoisseurs
Hopfen & Malz *p129*

Wasserturm

In the know
Getting around

From the U2, which crosses Alexanderplatz, you can exit onto Eberswalder Strasse, which is about midway between Mauerpark and Kollwitzplatz. From there it's easy to walk to most places in Prenzlauer Berg in about ten or 15 minutes. The area is also well served by the M1 tramline. Bernauer Strasse U-Bahn (U8) and Berlin Nordbahnhof (S-Bahn) are best for reaching Gedenkstätte Berliner Mauer, but the area is also served by the M5, M8, M10 and M12 trams. Wedding and Gesundbrunnen are both accessible on the Ringbahn. Cycling isn't advised in this area due to the heavy traffic on the main streets.

shops and restaurants, including the **Prater** pub and beer garden (*see p123*). To the north-west, Eberswalder Strasse skirts the base of the **Mauerpark** (www. mauerpark.info). The site of an old train station, this area became a 'death strip' when the Wall went up, with a viewing platform for West Berliners to look into the East. It was turned into a community space in the 1990s, with two large sports halls, a graffiti-daubed section of the Wall and a home for the popular Sunday flea market (*see p124*). It's a lovely place to while away a summer afternoon among the drum circles, circus performers and assorted hippy types. To the north-east is the 'LSD' area – around Lychener Strasse, Stargarder Strasse and Dunckerstrasse – which is what passed for the GDR's druggy zone, and **Helmholtzplatz**, popular with young families. Situated just south of Schönhauser Allee S-Bahn on Stargarder Strasse is the striking neo-Gothic **Gethsemanekirche** (445 7745, www.ekpn.de), built in August Orth's typical red-brick style – he also built the Zionskirche. It served as an important meeting place for GDR dissidents in the late 1980s. A statue outside commemorates their sacrifice.

East of here, on the other side of Prenzlauer Allee, is **Ernst-Thälmann-Park**, named after the leader of the pre-1933 German Communist Party. (After the Wall fell, only pre-GDR figures remained memorialised in street names and monuments.) In its north-west corner stands the renovated **Zeiss-Grossplanetarium**, a fantastic GDR space that once celebrated Soviet cosmonauts. On the Greifswalder Strasse side of the park, just north of the Danziger Strasse corner, is a bombastic 1980s statue of Ernst Thälmann himself, raising a Communist fist. The statue was built with an amusing contemporary feature: a heated nose to melt any accumulating snow.

Sights & museums

❤ Museum in der Kulturbrauerei
Kulturbrauerei, Knaackstrasse 97 (4677 77911, www.hdg.de/berlin). U2 Eberswalderstrasse. **Open** *10am-6pm Tue, Wed, Fri-Sun; 10am-8pm Thur.* **Admission** *free.* **Map** *p116 P3.*

'Everyday Life in the GDR' is a fascinating permanent exhibition here, featuring hundreds of objects that show the contradictory nature of Communist life. Examples of leisure time include a Trabi roof-mounted tent, a mocked-up GDR living room and clothing customised to break the drab uniformity.

▶ *The Kulturbrauerei also hosts a Sunday food market, Street Food auf Achse (www. streetfoodaufachse.de), where you can try the latest taste trends.*

Zeiss-Grossplanetarium
Prenzlauer Allee 80 (4218 4510, www. planetarium.berlin). S8, S9, S41, S42, S85 Prenzlauer Allee. **Open** *9am-3pm Mon-Fri; 10am-4pm Sat.* **Admission** *€8; €6 reductions.* **Map** *p116 R3.*

This vast planetarium was constructed in 1987 as part of the city's 750th anniversary; at the time, its Cosmorama projector was one of the most advanced in Europe. Now, following renovation, it's described as one of the world's best star theatres, with illumination systems projecting onto a black velvet dome. There are a number of different shows that explore space and our planet, so check the listings.

Restaurants & cafés

A Magica €
Greifenhagener Strasse 54 (2280 8290, www.amagica.de). U2, S8, S9, S41, S42, S85 Schönhauser Allee. **Open** *noon-midnight Mon-Fri; 4pm-midnight Sat, Sun.* **Map** *p116 P2* ❶ *Pizza*

A real oasis of democratic Italian nosh, this pizzeria has been packing them in since 2007. It's a particular favourite with local young families, and for good reason: the Roman-style base is thin and flavoursome, and pizzas start at a mere €5. Or try the DIY option, building from a base of either tomato sauce, mint pesto or chickpea purée, then loading it with a long list of delicious toppings.

Anna Blume €
Kollwitzstrasse 83 (4404 8749, www.cafe-anna-blume.de). U2 Eberswalder Strasse. **Open** *8am-midnight daily; kitchen until 10pm.* **Map** *p116 Q3* ❷ *Café*

This café-cum-florist is named after a poem by Kurt Schwitters. There are expensive but high-quality pastries, plus sweet and savoury crêpes, soups and hot dishes. The terrace is lovely in summer, and the interior, not surprisingly, smells of flowers.

Babel €
Kastanienallee 33 (4403 1318). U2 Eberswalder Strasse. **Open** *11am-midnight daily.* **No cards.** **Map** *p116 P4* ❸ *Lebanese*

The crew at Babel have been throwing out Lebanese shawarma wraps for over a decade now, filled with the likes of grilled chicken, halloumi or crispy falafel. Although being on Prenzlauer Berg's most popular shopping street has meant prices have risen while

Ernst Thälmann statue

portions have shrunk, their *Teller* (plates) are still big enough to share, coming with a selection of fresh houmous, tabbouleh, pickled radish and famous green chilli sauce.

❤ The Barn €

Schönhauser Allee 8 (no phone, www. thebarn.de). U2 Senefelderplatz; U8 Rosenthaler Platz. **Open** *8.30am-6pm Mon-Fri; 10am-6pm Sat, Sun.* **No cards. Map** *p116 P4* ❹ *Café*

The Barn speciality coffee roastery is a shrine to the coffee bean. Owner Ralf Rüller has even made headlines for his serious approach: when he opened this second, more spacious branch (the original is in Mitte), customers were bemused by the industrial bollard set in the doorway. Ralf was taking a rather humourous stand against the area's 'yummy mummy' invasion by banning prams (and laptops and dogs), so there are no distractions from appreciation of the finished product. Try the pour-over Hario V60 for an alternative cupping method. **Other locations** Auguststrasse 58, Mitte ; Café Kranzler, Kurfürstendamm 18.

❤ Bonanza €

Oderberger Strasse 35 (0171 563 0795 mobile, www.bonanzacoffee.de). U2 Eberswalder Strasse. **Open** *8.30am-6pm Mon-Fri; 10am-6pm Sat, Sun.* **No cards. Map** *p116 O3* ❺ *Café*

Bonanza serves some of the best coffee in Berlin. The proprietors are concerned with every detail, from relationships with suppliers to roasting the beans in-house and getting the right steam temperature. The bar is dominated by a highly sensitive handmade Synesso Cyncra machine, and seating is minimal. The flat white is smooth and divine.

The cake selection is small – pretty much just carrot cake and brownies – but high grade.

Fischfabrik €

Danziger Strasse 24 (6431 4581, www. fischfabrik.eatbu.com). U2 Eberswalder Strasse. **Open** *10am-10pm Mon-Sat; 2-10pm Sun.* **No cards. Map** *p116 Q3* ❽ *Fish & chips*

For those craving some battered cod, this fish shop does a pretty decent chip supper, with Sarson's malt vinegar handily placed on every table. The fish is as fresh as it gets in Berlin, nicely steamed within a crispy shell, and the chips hit the spot even if they aren't really cut thickly enough. Perfect with a glass of the crisp house Riesling.

Gugelhof €€

Knaackstrasse 37 (442 9229, www.gugelhof. de). U2 Senefelderplatz. **Open** *5-11pm Mon-Fri; 10am-11pm Sat, Sun.* **Map** *p116 Q4* ❾ *Alsatian*

This restaurant pioneered the Kollwitzplatz scene in the 1990s. Food is refined but filling, service formal but friendly, and the furnishings comfortably worn. The *Bäckeoffe* – lamb, pork and beef marinated in Riesling, stewed and served in an earthenware pot with root veg and a bread-crust lid – displays the peasant flourishes of Alsace's regional cooking. There's also a fine selection of Alsatian *tartes flambées*. Breakfast is served until a leisurely 4pm at weekends. Reservations advised.

Konnopke's Imbiss €

Schönhauser Allee 44B, under U-Bahn tracks (442 7765, www.konnopke-imbiss.de). U2 Eberswalder Strasse. **Open** *10am-8pm Mon-Fri; 11.30am-8pm Sat.* **No cards. Map** *p116 P3* ❿ *Imbiss*

This venerable sausage stand (refurbished a few years ago) has been under the same family management since 1930. After coming up with a secret recipe for ketchup (not available after the Wall was erected), it was the first place to offer *Currywurst* in East Berlin and still serves probably the most famous – if not the best – *Currywurst* in the city. Expect a queue.

Lucky Leek €€-€€€
Kollwitzstrasse 54 (6640 8710, www.lucky-leek.com). U2 Senefelderplatz. **Open** *6-10pm Wed-Sun.* **No cards.** **Map** *p116 Q4* **11** *Vegan*

Chef Josita Hartanto started out at Charlottenburg's haute-cuisine La Mano Verde and has since carved out quite a following for her inventive vegan food. She's pushed the boundaries through clever plating and textural contrast, with dishes such as filo-spinach pockets of seitan with macadamia dumpling and brussel-sprout praline. For the full effect, opt for the five-course menu with a wine pairing.

MontRaw €€
Strassburger Strasse 33, (2578 2707, www.montraw.com) U2 Senefelderplatz or U8 Rosenthaler Platz. **Open** *8.30am-6pm Mon-Fri; 10am-6pm Sat, Sun.* **Map** *p116 P4* **12** *Middle Eastern*

Promising Middle Eastern recipes with a Mediterranean interpretation, MontRaw is about as far as you can get from houmous and kebabs. Fresh, clean fusion flavours are served

Bonanza

by a friendly, knowledgeable team in exquisite surroundings. Chef Ben Barabi serves us 'new Israeli food with a twist' inspired by the recipes of his childhood. Try the charred octopus served on a lentil puree with salsa verde and Jerusalem artichoke. The menu is small but carefully chosen, the wine-list reasonably priced. A smash hit since it opened in 2018; you're advised to book ahead.

Mrs Robinson's €€
Pappelallee 29 (5462 2839, www.mrsrobinsons.de). U2 Eberswalder Strasse. **Open** *6-11pm Mon, Thur-Sun.* **Map** *p116 Q2* **13** *Fusion*

This Asian-themed restaurant is run with creative enthusiasm by Israeli chef Ben Zviel and London-born partner Samina Raza. They serve finessed dishes resembling Japanese artwork, such as poached red prawn with lavender and hibiscus, alongside more traditionally comforting plates like the Infamous Fried Chicken and Caviar Bao.

Oderquelle €€
Oderbergerstrasse 27 (4400 8080, www.oderquelle.de). U2 Eberswalder Strasse. **Open** *6pm-late Mon-Sat; noon-late Sun.* **Map** *p116 P3* **14** *Austrian/German*

This simple yet cosy Prenzlauer Berg classic might be a tad more expensive than its rivals, but that's because it's better than them. The menu is short but changes regularly. Typical dishes are goose leg stuffed with vegetables on red-wine risotto or vegetable strudel in tomato sauce. It's particularly nice in summer, when you can sit outside and watch the world go by.

Osmans Töchter €€
Papelallee 15 (3266 3388, www.osmanstoechter.de). U2 Eberswalder Strasse. **Open** *5.30pm-midnight Mon-Sat; 5pm-midnight Sun.* **No cards.** **Map** *p116 P3* **15** *Turkish*

Although exposed light bulbs and mismatched wooden chairs are a Berlin cliché these days, it's refreshing to find a modern Turkish restaurant that doesn't resort to the usual cartoon orientalism. The menu is notable primarily for its homeliness: a network of Turkish housewives produces the range of *meze* salads and dips, as well as the *manti* (Turkish meat dumplings smothered in a garlicky yoghurt sauce). The juicy swordfish kebab is a particular draw.

Pasternak €€
Knaackstrasse 22-24 (441 3399, www.restaurant-pasternak.de). U2 Senefelderplatz. **Open** *9am-1am daily.* **Map** *p116 Q4* **16** *Russian*

This small bar and restaurant became home to a wave of Russian immigrants, many of them Jewish, following the fall of the Soviet Union. Food focuses on Russian and Ashkenazi classics, such as sweet and sour brisket or beef stroganoff. The lively atmosphere can get a little much sometimes – ask for a table in the small side room.

Sasaya €€

Lychener Strasse 50 (4471 7721, www.sasaya-berlin.de). U2 Eberswalder Strasse. **Open** *noon-3pm, 6-11.30pm Mon, Thur-Sun.* **No cards.** *Map p116 Q2* ⑰ *Japanese*

The lack of fresh fish available in Berlin poses a challenge for Japanese restaurants; there are scores of pan-Asian places serving 'discount' sushi, but the real thing is hard to come by. An authentic menu and a bustling atmosphere have kept Sasaya a long-term favourite. The sashimi is eye-poppingly fresh, but there are also fine cooked dishes, such as grilled horse mackerel and *kakuni* (braised pork belly). For a real taste of the ocean, try one of the dressed seaweed salads. Booking is essential.

Si An €

Rykestrasse 36 (4050 5775, www.sian-berlin.de). U2 Senefelderplatz, or tram M2, M10. **Open** *noon-midnight daily.* **No cards.** *Map p116 Q3* ⑲ *Vietnamese*

Si An was one of the first Viet restaurants to really up the ante on decor while making an effort to cook everything fresh. There are various *phos* and usually some sort of combination of curry, rice and meats, heaped with fresh herbs and vegetables. The approach has clearly paid off, as it now has a mini-empire of restaurants including Saigon street-food specialist District Mot (*see p91*) and tea house Chen Che.

Les Valseuses €€

Eberswalder Strasse 28 (7552 2032, www.lesvalseuses.de). U2 Eberswalder Strasse. **Open** *6.30pm-late daily.* **No cards.** *Map p116 P3* ⑳ *French*

This modern French bistro (owned by some of the team behind Mitte's popular Themroc) is remarkably good value: the 200g steak frites with béarnaise is a very reasonable €13.50. The specials board of French classics changes weekly – expect the likes of steak tartare with smoked garlic, or chicken with lemon and green olives. Team your meal with a 'natural' wine from the Languedoc. Local baker Ma Patissière has her ovens in the back and provides the excellent desserts.

Bars & pubs

Becketts Kopf

Pappelallee 64 (4403 5880, www.becketts-kopf.de). U2 Eberswalder Strasse. **Open** *8pm-late daily.* **No cards.** *Map p116 Q2* ②

This long-running cocktail bar is an oasis of fine drink in rather sparsely served Prenzlauer Berg. It follows the classic 'speakeasy' model: enter via an unmarked door and find yourself in rooms draped in red velvet. Settle back on the chesterfield sofas and enjoy the fresh air of the no-smoking room – a relative rarity in Berlin's bar scene. Try the Aviation, a paean to the classier days of air travel: a florid mix of gin, violet, maraschino and lemon. A grizzled portrait of playwright Samuel Beckett (not averse to a drink himself) keeps watch over proceedings.

Schwarze Pumpe

Choriner Strasse 76 (449 6939, www.schwarzepumpe-berlin.de). U2 Senefelderplatz; U8 Rosenthaler Platz. **Open** *10am-1am daily.* **No cards.** *Map p116 O4* ⑧

One of the first places to open after the Wall fell, Schwarze Pumpe is still a popular low-key neighbourhood bar, which has seen the street go from reclaimed derelict housing to luxury apartment living. It serves reasonably priced magnums of wine, draught beer and a decent menu of bar snacks, plus breakfast in the mornings.

Wohnzimmer

Lettestrasse 6 (445 5458, www.wohnzimmer-bar.de). U2 Eberswalder Strasse. **Open** *2pm-late daily.* **No cards.** *Map p116 Q2* ⑩

Immediately behind the door of this shabbily elegant 'living room' is a bar-like structure assembled from kitchen cabinets and assorted GDR furniture. Even if it's not the bohemian destination it used to be, Wohnzimmer still provides a sanctuary for hip, young Helmholtzplatz mothers during the day and for local barflies at night, who come for the strong cocktails.

Shops & services

D.nik

Wörther Strasse 14 (3064 8628, www.dnik-berlin.de). U2 Senefelderplatz. **Open** *10am-7pm Mon-Fri; 10am-6pm Sat.* **Map** *p116 Q4* ❶ *Toys*

The name spells 'child' backwards in German. Stock is carefully selected to fit into a design aesthetic of using sustainable materials and allowing for ergonomic play. You'll find modular Tukluk, which can be folded into

💙 Prater Biergarten

Kastanienallee 7-9 (448 5688, www. pratergarten.de). U2 Eberswalder Strasse. **Open** *6pm-late Mon-Sat; noon-late Sun. No cards.* **Map** *p116 P3* ❼

In the mid 16th century, brewing beer during the summer was outlawed in Bavaria due to the drink's rapid deterioration in the heat and the risk of fire spreading from the brewery kettles. Instead, brewers were encouraged to build cellars next to the River Isar in which to store beer for summer drinking. They discovered that if they planted lines of chestnut trees over these cellars, it kept the beer cooler and fresher for longer. After that, it was only second nature for drinkers to want to linger with a cool beer under their shady boughs, and thus the Bavarian tradition of the *Biergarten* was born. Refrigeration has technically done away with the need for beer gardens, but their popularity throughout Germany shows no sign of diminishing: enjoying a foaming *Stein* and a plate of *Wurst* in the open air is the essence of Southern German conviviality and hospitality.

Beer gardens in Berlin are generally open from April to September and are popular meeting spots after work or on a sunny weekend. These are places to hang loose and drink copious amounts of beer in good company, Prater Garten has been doing Berliners a brisk service since 1852. The enthusiastic beer-swilling, big wooden tables and platefuls of *Bratwurst* and

Bretzeln (pretzels) might make you feel as though you've been teleported down south to Munich. There's an indoor bar with a traditional German restaurant, but in summer you'll want to grab a house-brewed Pils and join the all-day buzz outdoors under the chestnut trees. Brunch is served from 10am to 4pm at the weekend, but, as is the case with all true beer gardens, you're also permitted to bring food from home to enjoy with beer bought on the premises: check out the sumptuous picnics laid out by locals. Prater opens early on sunny days, so be prepared to jostle for elbow room by noon even on weekdays.

▶ *There's also an open-air theatre here where productions by the Volksbühne (People's Theatre; see p255) are performed.*

gigantic, colourful geometric structures, playful furniture from young Swedish designers Little Red Stuga and cardboard building blocks.

Fein & Ripp
Kastanienallee 91-92 (4403 3250, www. feinundripp.de). U2 Eberswalder Strasse. **Open** *noon-7pm Mon-Sat.* **Map** *p116 P3* ❷ *Fashion*

A curious shop, which started out selling old stock discovered in a Swabian clothes factory – primarily cotton underwear in all shapes and sizes, from the 1920s to the '70s. They've now expanded into brands that continue traditional production methods: Frye's heavy leather prison boots, which come 'distressed', and Pike Brothers' stiff blue denim jeans. Unfortunately, dressing like a Depression-era hobo doesn't come cheap these days.

Goldhahn & Sampson
Dunckerstrasse 9 (no phone, www. goldhahnundsampson.de). U2 Eberswalder Strasse. **Open** *8am-8pm Mon-Fri; 9am-8pm Sat.* **Map** *p116 Q3* ❸ *Food & drink*

A charming deli that sells all sorts, from locally roasted Andraschko coffee to imported Japanese mayonnaise. There's also an assortment of international cookbooks, and you can sign up to a wide range of specialist cookery classes, such as macaroon baking or festive Jewish cuisine.

💙 Kollwitzplatz Farmers' Market
Kollwitzplatz (organic market 4433 9148, farmers' market 0172 327 8238 mobile). U2 Senefelderplatz. **Open** *noon-7pm Thur; 9am-4pm Sat.* **Map** *p116 Q4* ❺ *Market*

The Saturday farmers' market is popular with gourmets stocking up on weekend food

supplies and with locals out for a stroll and a snack. You'll find chocolates by Martin Franz, locally made tofu and fresh pasta. A Turkish-run stand sells the best *Gözleme* in town; another offers delicious and inexpensive fish soup. The Thursday market is slightly smaller and exclusively organic.

Lunettes Brillenagentur

Dunckerstrasse 18 (4471 8050, www.lunettes-selection.de). S8, S9, S41, S42, S85 Prenzlauer Allee; tram M2. **Open** *noon-8pm Mon, Tue, Thur, Fri; 10am-8pm Wed; noon-6pm Sat.* **Map** *p116 Q2* ❼ *Accessories*

Owner Uta Geyer has a knack for getting her hands on hard-to-find vintage spectacles frames, ranging from sleek 1920s pieces to rockabilly cat-eyes, classic aviators to glitzy Jackie Os. There's also a range of handmade frames, called Kollektion. Prices are surprisingly affordable.

❤ Mauerpark Flohmarkt

Bernauer Strasse 63-64 (0176 2925 0021 mobile). U8 Bernauer Strasse. **Open** *10am-6pm Sun.* **Map** *p116 Q3* ❽ *Market*

One of the biggest and busiest flea markets in Berlin sells everything from local designer clothes to cardboard boxes of black-market CDs. Students and residents hawk their things here; even if the market's massive popularity has meant prices creeping higher, you can still stumble upon a trove of rare records or vintage clothing.

Onkel Philipp's Spielzeugwerkstatt

Choriner Strasse 35 (449 0491, www.onkel-philipp.de). U2 Senefelderplatz. **Open** *9.30am-6.30pm Tue, Wed, Fri; 11am-8pm Thur; 11am-4pm Sat.* **Map** *p116 P4* ❾ *Toys*

Here's one for kids, both big and small: a toy-repair shop that's an Aladdin's cave of aged playthings, wooden toys, puzzles, trains, puppets and more. If you ask nicely, owner Philipp Schünemann lets you view his private GDR toy collection, a remote control unveiling a special surprise.

❤ Saint George's

Wörther Strasse 27 (8179 8333, www.saintgeorgesbookshop.com). U2 Senefelderplatz; tram M2. **Open** *11am-8pm Mon-Fri; 11am-7pm Sat.* **Map** *p116 Q4* ❿ *Books & music*

Founded by Paul and Daniel Gurner, twin brothers from England, Saint George's harks back to the heyday of London's Charing Cross Road. It's a sweet spot, where leather sofas coax readers to peruse at leisure. Housing around 10,000 English-language books, including plenty of biographies and contemporary fiction, it's also reliable for second-hand books in good condition.

Mauerpark

Temporary Showroom

*Kastanienallee 36A (6220 4564, www.temporaryshowroom.com). U2 Senefelderplatz. **Open** 11am-7pm Mon-Sat. **Map** p116 P4* ⓫ *Fashion*

Both a boutique stocking cult labels and a creative agency for young European designers, the Temporary Showroom rotates its stock regularly. There's technical shoeware from Adidas's experimental SLVR line to go with your patterned tracksuit from Switzerland's Julian Zigerli.

WEDDING & GESUNDBRUNNEN

The working-class industrial districts of Gesundbrunnen and Wedding, formerly on the western side of the Wall, are now politically part of Mitte, though few visitors venture very far into their largely grim surroundings. The big draw to the area is one of the few remaining stretches of the Wall, at the **Gedenkstätte Berliner Mauer** (Berlin Wall Memorial). Beyond this, Gesundbrunnen is home to a large African community and also to Turkish, Chinese and Arabic residents, giving it a refreshingly multicultural feel. Continually being hailed as the next area for gentrification, Wedding doesn't yet have anything like the restaurant or bar scene of Neukölln, but its low rents have encouraged artists to move their studios here. In 2013, a private group transformed the historic Wedding crematorium into **silent green Kulturquartier** (Plantagenstrasse 31, 1208 2210, www.silent-green.net), an independent space for experimentation in the arts. The result is fantastic and, for a former crematorium, just spooky enough. The buildings house a number of arts collectives and play host to film screenings and concerts. Elsewhere, a leisurely afternoon in **Volkspark Humbolthain** or a dip at **Plötzensee**, Berlin's only inner-city lake (*see p198* Berlin's bathing lakes), provide a welcome relief from the graffitied concrete surroundings. Just west of the lake

in Charlottenburg-Nord is a reminder of the terror inflicted by the Nazi regime on dissidents, criminals and anybody else they deemed undesirable. The **Gedenkstätte Plötzensee** (Plötzensee Memorial; Hüttigpfad, Charlottenburg-Nord, www. gedenkstaette-ploetzensee.de) preserves the execution shed of the former Plötzensee prison, where more than 2,500 people were killed between 1933 and 1945. There is little to see today, apart from the execution area behind the wall, with its meat hooks from which victims were hanged, and a small room with an exhibition. Excellent booklets in English are available.

▶ *Catch the S1 from Nordbahnhof, Humboldthain or Gesundbrunnen for the 40-minute journey to Oranienburg to visit KZ Sachsenhausen (see p128).*

Sights & museums
Anti-Kriegs-Museum

*Brüsseler Strasse 21 (4549 0110, tours 402 8691, www.anti-kriegs-museum.de). U9 Amrumer Strasse. **Open** 4-8pm daily. **Admission** free. **Map** fold-out map J2.*

The original Anti-War Museum was founded in 1925 by Ernst Friedrich, author of *War Against War*. In 1933, it was destroyed by the Nazis, and Friedrich fled to Brussels. He had another museum there from 1936 to 1940, when the Nazis again destroyed his work. In 1982, a group of teachers including Tommy Spree, Friedrich's grandson, re-established his museum in West Berlin. It now hosts films, discussions, lectures and exhibitions, as well as a permanent display that takes in World War I photos and artefacts from the original museum, children's war toys, information on German colonialism in Africa and pieces of anti-Semitic material from the Nazi era. Admission to the museum is free, but donations are welcome.

💜 Gedenkstätte Berliner Mauer

*Bernauer Strasse 111 (467 986 666, www. berliner-mauer-gedenkstaette.de). U8 Bernauer Strasse; S1, S2 Nordbahnhof. **Open** Documentation centre 10am-6pm Tue-Sun. **Admission** free. **Map** p116 N4.*

Immediately upon reunification, the city bought this stretch of the Wall on Bernauer Strasse to keep as a memorial. For a sense of how brutally Berlin was severed in two, a visit to this impeccably restored area of the Wall is a must. It extends along 1.4km (0.8 miles) of Bernauer Strasse and includes the death strip, watch tower and border fortifications. On this particular street, neighbours woke up one morning to find themselves in a different country from those on the opposite side of the road, as soldiers brandishing bricks and

Walking the Wall

Follow the route of the iconic barrier to see what remains today

Most of the Berlin Wall was demolished between June and November 1990. What had become the symbol of the inhumanity of the East German regime was prosaically crushed and reused for roadfill.

This walk sets out to trace the course of a small stretch of the Wall on the northern border of Mitte. Along the way you can see some of the remnants and gain an impression of how dramatically the border carved its way through the city.

The starting point is Berlin's central station – **Hauptbahnhof**, in former West Berlin. Exit the station into Invalidenstrasse, turning right along the street. Continue eastwards, passing on your left a Wilhelmine building, now a regional court, and the railway station turned art gallery, **Hamburger Bahnhof – Museum für Gegenwart** (*see p77*).

A little further on is the **Sandkrugbrücke**, located on a former border crossing into East Berlin. A stone by the bridge commemorates Günter Litfin, the first person to be shot dead attempting to escape to West Berlin (in 1961). The **Invalidenhaus** on the eastern side long predates the Cold War. Built in 1747 to house disabled soldiers, it was used in East German times as a hospital, ministry of health and supreme court. Today, it houses the Bundesministerium für Wirtschaft und Arbeit (Federal Ministry of Economics and Labour). Keeping this complex on your right, turn down the canalside promenade, continuing along until you get to the **Invalidenfriedhof**.

The Wall once ran straight through this graveyard – and a section remains. Headstones of the graves in the 'death strip' were removed so as not to impair the sightlines of border guards. The graveyard is a fascinating microcosm of Berlin history. Metres from the splendid 19th-century tombs of Prussian generals, a plaque commemorates members of the anti-Hitler resistance. Victims of air raids and the Battle of Berlin are buried in an adjacent mass grave. And it was here, in 1962, that West Berlin police shot dead an East Berlin border guard to save a 15-year-old boy who was in the process of escaping.

Just outside the graveyard is a former watchtower improbably standing in front of a new apartment building at the corner of Kieler Strasse. The observation post is closed in winter, but sometimes in summer you can look inside.

Between here and the corner of Chausseestrasse, few traces are left of the Wall, which ran roughly parallel to the canal before veering off to the right, close to the present helipad. At the end of Boyenstrasse, pavement markings indicating the Wall's former course briefly appear before vanishing under the new corner building.

Look down Chausseestrasse to note the line of powerful street lights indicating the site of another checkpoint, then continue on to Liesenstrasse. The **Liesenstrasse Friedhof** is the graveyard where 19th-century writer Theodor Fontane is buried. It was also part of East Berlin's border strip. A short section of the Wall appears before the railway bridge at the junction with Gartenstrasse.

The last leg of the walk takes you up Bernauer Strasse. Desperate scenes took place here in August 1961 as people jumped – three of them to their deaths – from the windows of houses that then stood on the

Bernauer Strasse

street's eastern side. The buildings were in
East Berlin, but the pavement before their
doors was in the West. The iconic photo of a
border guard leaping over barbed wire into the
West was snapped days earlier at the street's
northern end. In the 1960s and '70s, several
tunnels were dug from cellars in this area and
dozens escaped this way.

At the **Gedenkstätte Berliner Mauer** (see
p125), you can gain an impression of what the
border installation looked like – from below or
above. Steel rods delineate the Wall's route, and
in a grassy former death strip, neat elements
indicate the remains of submerged buildings,
barriers, security features and other deterrents.

A little further on is the oval **Kapelle der
Versöhnung** (Chapel of Reconciliation), built
on the site of an older church that was left
stranded in the death strip and finally blown
up in 1985 by the East German authorities.

The old patrol road remains in places, as do
some of the border illuminations – note, for
instance, the lights on Swinemünder Strasse
20. The plasterwork on the building at the
corner of Wolliner Strasse clearly reveals
where the eastern side of the Wall abutted
existing apartment blocks.

Between Wolliner Strasse and Schwedter
Strasse, you can still see the turning circle
once used by West Berlin buses. On the
eastern side, the tram still comes to an abrupt
halt in Eberswalder Strasse. Even so, it's hard
to believe that this whole area was once part
of the world's most heavily fortified border.
In the **Mauerpark**, where there is a popular
Sunday flea market (see *p124*), you can have
one last stroll along the Wall before heading to
the Eberswalder Strasse U-Bahn station.

mortar started to build what the East German
government referred to as the 'Anti-Fascist
Protection Wall'.

Don't miss the excellent **Documentation
Centre** across the street from the Wall,
which includes a very good aerial video
following the route of the Wall in 1990: it's
the best chance you have of really getting
your head around it. From the centre's
tower, you can look down over the Wall and
the **Kapelle der Versöhnung** (Chapel of
Reconciliation). Further down the road in
the old **Nordbahnhof** station is an excellent
exhibition, 'Border Stations and Ghost
Stations in Divided Berlin', which tells the
story of how East Germany closed and then
fiercely guarded stations through which West
German trains travelled during the Cold War.

▶ *For more on the Wall in this part of Berlin,
see opposite* Walking the Wall.

Volkspark Humbolthain

*Main entrance Brunnenstrasse 101. S1, S2,
S25, S41, S42, U8 Gesundbrunnen; S1, S2, S25,
S8 Humboldthain.* **Open** *Park 24hrs daily.
Pool 10am-6pm daily in summer.* **Admission**
Pool €5.50; €3.50 reductions. **Map** *p116 N2.*

On a warm summer's day, bring picnic
blankets and swimsuits to enjoy the green
pastures and open-air swimming pools of
Humbolthain, a park built on the remains
of rubble from World War II. For those
interested in history, there are guided tours
available from April to October of the partially
demolished Flak Tower, and for those who
simply want to perambulate, the hidden
rose garden with its high hedges is ideal for a
romantic stroll.

Restaurants & cafés

❤ Café Pförtner €€

*Uferstrasse 8-11 (5036 9854, www.pfoertner.
co). U8 Pankstrasse.* **Open** *9am-11pm Mon-
Fri; 11am-11pm Sat.* **No cards. Map** *p116
L1* ⑥ *Modern Italian*

Make the trip across town for the photo
opportunity this former bus repair station

Kapelle der Versöhnung

KZ Sachsenhausen

A reminder of Nazi horror

*Strasse der Nationen 22, Oranienburg (03301 2000, www.stiftung-bg.de). S1 Oranienburg (40 mins from Mitte), then 20-min walk. **Open** Mid Mar-mid Oct 8.30am-6pm Tue-Sun. Mid Oct-mid Mar 8.30am-4.30pm Tue-Sun. Grounds also open Mon. **Admission** free.*

Many Nazi concentration camps are open to the public as memorials and museums, and KZ Sachsenhausen is the nearest to Berlin.

As soon as he came to power, Hitler set about rounding up and interning his opponents. From 1933 to 1935, an old brewery on this site was used to hold them. The present camp received its first prisoners in July 1936 and was designated a *Schutzhaftlager* ('protective custody camp'). The first inmates were political opponents of the government – communists, social democrats, trade unionists – but soon the range of prisoners widened to include homosexuals, Jews and anyone guilty of 'anti-social' behaviour.

Around 6,000 Jews were brought here after Kristallnacht alone, with many later sent on to Auschwitz. Sachsenhausen saw some of the first experiments in organised mass murder: thousands of Russian POWs from the Eastern Front were killed at the camp's 'Station Z'.

The SS evacuated the camp in 1945 and began marching 33,000 inmates to the Baltic, where they were to be packed into boats and sunk in the sea. Some 6,000 died during the march, before the survivors were rescued by the Allies. Another 3,000 prisoners were found in the camp's hospital when it was captured on 22 April 1945.

After the German capitulation, the Russian secret police, the MVD, reopened Sachsenhausen as 'Camp 7' for the detention of war criminals; in fact, it was filled with anyone suspected of opposition. On 23 April 1961, the partially restored camp was opened to the public as a national monument and memorial. Following the fall of the GDR, mass graves were discovered, containing the remains of an estimated 10,000 prisoners.

Behind the parade ground – where morning roll-call was taken, and from where inmates were required to witness executions on the gallows – stand the two remaining barracks blocks. One is now a museum and the other is a memorial hall and cinema, where a film about the history of the camp is shown. Next door stands the prison block. It's a good idea to hire an audio guide (€3; available in English) at the gate.

Perhaps the grimmest site at Sachsenhausen is the subsiding remains of Station Z, the small extermination block. A map traces the path the condemned would have followed, depending on whether they were to be shot (the bullets were retrieved and reused) or gassed. All ended up in the neighbouring ovens.

affords. Situated along the narrow canal Panke, it's a little out of the way, but you'll quickly be won over by the inventive modern Italian food featuring flavours such as beetroot, melon and pork belly. Portions are a bit small and service can be lax, but eating in the converted BVG bus is an experience not to be missed.

L'Escargot €€-€€€

*Brüsseler Strasse 39 (453 1563, www. l-escargot.net). U6 Seestrasse. **Open** 5pm-midnight Tue-Sat; 5-11pm Sun. **No cards. Map** fold-out map J2 ❼ French/ Italian*

L'Escargot is nothing much from the outside, but a warm welcome awaits within: chef-patron Martino frequently welcomes guests and will discuss requirements and tastes before bustling into the kitchen. The cooking is a vague mix of French and Sicilian – the house speciality is a vast plate of garlicky snails – but the menu gallops cheerily across western Europe. Allow up to an hour for mains, as he cooks from scratch.

❤ Shikgoo €€

*Tegeler Strasse 25 (8501 2045). U6, U9 Leopoldplatz. **Open** 6pm-midnight Thur-Tue. **No cards.** fold-out map J3 ⓭ Korean*

This tiny restaurant is run by a hospitable Korean couple, who request shoes off when entering. It's a traditional Korean-style eaterie with low tables and cushions on the floor. Try the hot stone soup, and be sure to order extra kimchi.

Bars & pubs

Basalt Bar
*Utrechter Strasse 38 (www.facebook.com/ busaltberlin). U6, U9 Leopoldplatz. **Open** 8pm-late Tue-Sat. **No cards**. Map p116 K1* ❶

Black walls with an emerald-green tiled bar and an array of leafy jungle plants make this botanical-themed cocktail bar one of Wedding's best-looking secrets. The house cocktail, the Mescalmule, arrives in a bronze mug and is a daring concoction of smoked tequila, chili, cucumber and passionfruit. It's delicious.

♥ Eschenbräu
*Triftstrasse 67 (0162 493 1915 mobile, eschenbraeu.de). U6, U9 Leopoldplatz. **Open** 3pm-late daily. **No cards**. Map p116 K2* ❸

This brewery has an excellent microbrew prepared for almost every occasion and an enormous courtyard in which to sample them. There's also tasty *Flammkuchen* (German pizza), a far better choice of snack to share with some friends than the *Brezeln* (pretzels).

F Bar
*Grüntaler Strasse 9 (no phone, www.f-bar-berlin.com). U8 Pankstrasse. **Open** 6pm-late daily. **No cards**. Map p116 M1* ❹

This living-room-style bar is a home away from home for many in the neighbourhood; the friendly staff, cosy atmosphere and good beers (including Guinness on tap) always manage to keep guests staying longer than they planned. It's a little divey but incredibly welcoming.

The Forsberg
*Gerichtsstrasse 26 (0162 951 3544 mobile). S1, S2, S25, S8 Humboldthain. **Open** 6pm-late Thur-Sat. **No cards**. Map p116 L2* ❺

A stylish haunt in Wedding, which doubles up as the atelier of artist and bartender Charles Forsberg. It has a spacious, abandoned vibe, with enough touches of elegance to make it feel intriguing. The usual assortment of cocktails, beers and wines are on offer.

Moritz Bar
*Adolfstrasse 17 (0173 680 7670 mobile, www. moritzbar.com). U6, S41, S42 Wedding. **Open** 7pm-late daily. **No cards**. Map p116 K2* ❻

Wedding's very own living-room bar, complete with upcycled wooden counter, Augustiner by the bottle and assorted vintage furniture. The south German brothers who run the place offer special events, such as a weekly vegan food night, gay student Mondays and communal viewings of cult German TV detective series *Tatort*.

♥ Vagabund Brauerei
*Antwerpener Strasse 3 (5266 7668, www. vagabundbrauerei.com). U6 Seestrasse. **Open** 5pm-late Mon-Fri; 1pm-late Sat, Sun. **No cards**. Map p116 fold-out map U2* ❾

Three old friends from Maryland have fulfilled their dream of starting a craft brewery thanks to a wildly successful crowdfunding initiative. They run a homely taproom at the microbrewery, with a rotating menu of beers that includes their own citrusy American Pale Ale and unctuous Coffee Stout, as well as local guests from the likes of Heidenpeters and Eschenbräu.

Shops & services

♥ Hopfen & Malz
*Triftstrasse 57 (no phone, www.hopfenmalz. de). **Open** 3-8pm Mon-Thur; 2-8pm Fri; 11am-5pm Sat. Map fold-out map J3* ❹ *Bottle shop*

It looks a little shifty from the outside – almost like a run-down *Spätkauf* (late night shop) – but, in fact, this is an excellent specialist beer store, stocking a wide range of beers from microbreweries all over Germany, with a focus on Bavaria. It also has IPAs, ales and stouts from Belgium and the USA, as well as the largest selection of ciders in Berlin.

Leopoldplatz Flohmarkt
*Leopoldplatz on Müllerstrasse (www.bbm-maerkte.de). U6, U9 Leopoldplatz. **Open** Farmer's market 10am-5pm Tue, Fri; flea market 10am-4pm Sat, winter 3pm. Map p116 P1* ❻ *Market*

On Saturdays, this square is transformed into one of Berlin's best but least known flea markets. Forget Mauerpark, if you wantreal rummage bargains, wake up early and get ready to haggle. For a cheap breakfast post bargain-hunting, head over to **Simit Evi** for a selection of Turkish sesame breads (*simit*), savoury yoghurt dipping sauce and an ample serving of freshly cooked eggs. Tuesday and Friday's market sells fresh produce.

Friedrichshain & Lichtenberg

As Prenzlauer Berg and Mitte saw rents soar in the 1990s, Berlin's alternative squat community migrated to Friedrichshain and politicised this formerly working-class district. Much of the area is pretty bleak: one of the hardest hit during World War II, it is dominated by big communist-era housing blocks and slashed through by railway tracks. The area bordering the Spree contains the remains of industrial buildings, but, with the arrival of luxury apartments and hotels, the banks of the river here may soon be unrecognisable. Friedrichshain is also home to East Berlin's first post-war civic building project – a broad boulevard named originally Stalinallee and then Karl-Marx-Allee.

There's more to Friedrichshain today than a photoshoot at the East Side Gallery – though this is well worth a visit; there's a thriving alternative culture here, supporting flea markets and vegetarian restaurants. The district is also a nightlife hotspot, with a concentration of bars and clubs by Ostkreuz and along the Spree. Here too is the globally renowned club Berghain, a giant on the city's techno scene.

Further east, Lichtenberg has a couple of key former Stasi strongholds and the East Berlin Zoo.

❤ Don't miss

1 Gedenkstätte Berlin-Hohenschönhausen *p140*
Ex-inmates lead tours of this Stasi prison.

2 East Side Gallery *p135*
Colourful murals adorn what's left of the Wall.

3 Berghain *p243*
Dance the weekend away in the infamous temple to techno.

4 Karl-Marx-Allee *p134*
Look east on this formidable Stalinist avenue.

5 Oberbaumbrücke *p132*
Berlin's most photogenic bridge.

Test The Best (Test The Rest) by Birgit Kinder, East Side Gallery

FRIEDRICHSHAIN

The most atmospheric way to enter Friedrichshain is to cross the River Spree from Kreuzberg over the **Oberbaumbrücke**. This double-decker brick bridge, described as the most beautiful in Berlin, connects the two formerly divided districts and has become a beautiful monument to reunification. Whether you walk, cycle, drive or take the U1 across, you'll be spoilt by the views: look west to see the iconic Fernsehturm and east to see *Molecule Man*, a 30-metre (98-foot) aluminum sculpture of three men rising out of the Spree. Designed by American sculptor Jonathan Borofsky, *Molecule Man* is representative of the coming together of the three neighbouring districts (Friedrichshain, Kreuzberg and Treptow), and, says the artist, of mankind itself. The bridge itself dates back to 1732, when it was a wooden drawbridge, but the distinctive Brick Gothic version was designed and built in 1896 by architect Otto Stahn, with a U-Bahn track installed on the top deck just a few years later in 1902. The bridge was damaged in the war and then used as a border gate for the GDR; it was not fully reconstructed until six years after the fall of the Wall. Today, the lower walkway doubles up as an unofficial bazaar, occupied by a miscellany of buskers and street vendors.

After crossing the Spree, you'll arrive at Warschauer Strasse U-bahn station, frequented by some surprisingly talented buskers but also by pickpockets who find cover in the jostling crowds just outside the station. Head west from here to visit the **East Side Gallery** (*see p135*) on Mühlenstrasse ('Mill Street'; the old mill is at no.8), along the north bank of the Spree. This 1.3-km (0.8-mile) stretch of former Wall was turned into a mural memorial in 1990 and remains one of the city's most photographed sights. At the eastern end (accessed via an incongruous pirate-themed bar-restaurant) is the **Wall Museum**, which documents the Wall's fascinating history. The industrial buildings hereabouts have been renovated and rechristened **Oberbaum City**, and are now home to loft spaces, offices and studios. Both Universal Music and MTV-Europe have their German HQs here, as part of the ongoing development of the vast **Mediaspree** complex, which has met much opposition.

FRIEDRICHSHAIN & LICHTENBERG

Restaurants & cafés

1. Butterhandlung *p136*
2. Café Schönbrunn *p136*
3. Goodies *p136*
4. Hako Ramen *p136*
5. Mutzenbacher *p136*
6. Nil *p137*
7. Santa Cantina *p137*
8. Schneeweiss *p137*
9. Silo Coffee *p137*
10. Spätzle & Knödel *p137*
11. Vöner *p137*

Bars & pubs

1. Briefmarken Weine *p137*
2. Chapel Bar *p137*
3. CSA *p138*
4. Hops & Barley *p138*

Shops & services

1. Big Brobot *p138*
2. Dollyrocker *p138*
3. Flohmarkt am Boxhagener *Platz p138*
4. Olivia *p138*
5. Shakespeare & Sons *p139*
6. Urban Spree Bookshop & *Gallery p139*

FRIEDRICHSHAIN & LICHTENBERG

132

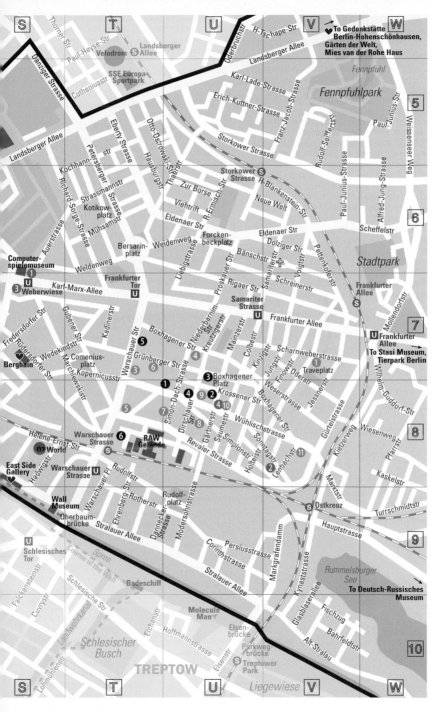

S · Thorner Str · Paul-Heyse-Str · T · U · Oberbaumstr · H-Tschape-Str · V · W

To Gedenkstätte
Berlin-Hohenschönhausen,
Gärten der Welt,
Mies van der Rohe Haus

Velodrom · S · Landsberger Allee · Landsberger Allee

Danziger Strasse · Cotheniusstr · SSE Europa-Sportpark

Karl-Lade-Strasse · Fennpfuhl

Fennpfuhlpark

Erich-Kuttner-Strasse · Franz-Jacob-Strasse · 5

Landsberger Allee · Eberty Strasse · Otto-Ostrowski-Strasse · Hausburgstr · Thaerstr · Storkower Strasse · Rudolf-Seiffert-Str · Paul-Junius-Str · Weissenseer Weg

Kochhannstr · Petersburger Strasse · str · Zur Borse · Paul-Junius-Strasse

Richard-Sorge-Strasse · Strassmannstr · Viehtrift · R-Ermisch-Str · Storkower Strasse · S · H-Blankenstein-Str · Neue Welt · Scheffelstr · Alfred-Jung-Strasse · 6

Kotikow-platz · Mühsamstr · Eldenaer Str · Forcken-beckplatz · Eldenaer Str · Stadtpark

Auerstrasse · Bersarin-platz · Weidenweg · Liebigstrasse · Bänschstr · Dolziger Str · Vogtstr · Pettenkoferstr

Computer-spielemuseum · 1 · Weldenweg · Proskauer Str · Rigaer Str · Samariterstr · Schreinerstr · Frankfurter Allee

3 · Weberwiese · Frankfurter Tor · U · Karl-Marx-Allee · Samariter Strasse · U · S

Fredersdorfer Str · Gubener Str · Kadinerstr · Boxhagener Str · Niedebarnim-Str · Mainzerstr · Colbestr · Frankfurter Allee · Mollendorfstr · 7

Rüdersdorfer Str · Wedekindstr · Warschauer Str · 5 · Grünberger Str · 4 · Kreutzigerstr · Scharnweberstrasse · U · Frankfurter Allee · To Stasi Museum, Tierpark Berlin

Berghain · Comenius-platz · 3 · 6 · 3 · Boxhagener Platz · Kinzigstr · Jungstr · 1 · Traveplatz · Wilhelm-Guddorf-Str

Marchlewskistr · Kopernicusstr · 1 · 4 · 9 · 2 · Krossener Str · Einowstr · Oderstr · Weserstrasse · Jessnerstr

Simon-Dach-Strasse · 5 · 7 · 4 · 10 · Gärtnerstr · Seumestr · Wühlischstrasse · Boxhager Str · Sonntagstr · Güntelstrasse · Kietzerweg · Wiesenweg · Pfarrstr

Helene-Ernst-Str · Warschauer Strasse · 6 · RAW Gelände · Dischauer Str · Simplonstr · Hostelstr · Lenbachstr · 11 · Kaskelstr · 8

O2 World · Hedwigstr · Warschauer Strasse · U · S · Revaler Strasse · 2

East Side Gallery · Warschauer Pl · Rudolfstr · Ehrenbergstr · Rotherstr · Danneckerstr

Wall Museum · Oberbaum-brücke · Stralauer Allee · Rudolf-platz · Modersohnstrasse · Ostkreuz · Turrschmidtstr · 9

U · Schlesisches Tor · Falckensteinstr · Cuvrystr · Course of the Wall · Spree · Schlesische Str · Schlesische Str · Persiusstrasse · Corinthstrasse · Stralauer Allee · Markgrafendamm · Kynaststrasse · Hauptstrasse · Rummelsburger See · To Deutsch-Russisches Museum

Lohmühlenstr · Landwehrkanal · Badeschiff · Eichenstr · Molecule Man · Hoffmannstrasse · Elsen-brücke · Eisenstr · Glasblaserallee · Fischzug · Alt-Stralau · Bahrfeldtstr · 10

Schlesischer Busch · TREPTOW · Parkweg-brücke · S · Treptower Park · Liegewiese

S · T · U · V · W

FRIEDRICHSHAIN & LICHTENBERG

133

▶ *For the best photograph of the Oberbaumbrücke, stand on the north bank of the Spree at Friedrichshain during golden hour, just before sunset.*

Back at Warschauer Strasse, head north on a bridge above the S-Bahn lines, and then take the stairs leading down to your right to enter **RAW Gelände**. This former train repair yard is now a culturally vital urban space home to a mishmash of street-food stands, the **Urban Spree** book shop and art gallery, a Sunday flea market, bars, bookshops, street art and a well-attended skate park. Heading north from here, you'll pass through the shops, bars and restaurants of **Simon-Dach-Kiez**, which, sadly, have turned the area's non-conformist values into something of a boozy tourist industry. Boxhagener Platz is a pleasant exception; aside from the excellent weekly flea market and farmers' market (try the mackerel bun), there are also plenty of decent places on the square to refuel.

East of here is the notorious techno club **Berghain** (*see p243*), located in a former power plant on Am Wriezener Bahnhof.

If you want to find out what all the fuss is about, be prepared to wait silently in line for at least an hour and to hear 'nicht Heute' ('not today') from the grim-faced bouncers. Not prepared to risk it? Some of Berlin's best nightlife can be found around Ostkreuz at places such as **Salon zur Wilden Renate** (*see p242*) and **Buttons** at **:// about blank** (*see p242*). Open-air, water-facing venues, such as **Kater Blau** (*see p242*) are a must for partygoers in the warmer months.

North-west of Simon-Dach-Kiez, the twin towers of **Frankfurter Tor**, built in the Stalinist style between 1953 and 1956, mark the eastern end of **Karl-Marx-Allee**, the GDR's grand construction project, created with lightning speed in the 1950s. The stretch east from Lichtenberger Strasse truly impresses in its communist monumentalism, with rows of grand apartment blocks draped in stone and Meissen tiles stretching to Frankfurter Tor and beyond. To take a break from the socialist bombast, visit the **Computerspiele Museum** (Computer Games Museum) or spend some time exploring the huge

Molecule Man

💜 Time to eat, drink & shop

Linger over brunch
Silo Coffee *p137*, Café Schönbrunn *p136*

Pretend you're in the Alps
Schneeweiss *p137*, Spätzle & Knödel *p137*

Food market finds
Dong Xuan Center *p141*, Flohmarkt am Boxhagener Platz *p138*

Indulge your oenophilia
Briefmarken Weine *p137*

Nightcap cocktail
Chapel Bar *p137*

Veggie fast food
Vöner *p137*, Nil *p137*

▶ *For Friedrichshain's extensive nightlife options, see p230 and p242.*

In the know
Getting around

The two main transport hubs for Friedrichshain are Warschauer Strasse, on the U1 line, and Frankfurter Tor, served by the U5, which runs directly through the middle of the district. The Ostbahnhof and Ostkreuz stations can be reached by both S-Bahn and regional lines. For the *fussfaul* (foot-lazy), tram lines run along Boxhagener Strasse, Wülischstrasse and Warschauer Strasse.

❤ East Side Gallery

Mühlenstrasse (www.eastsidegallery-berlin. de). U1, S5, S7, S75 Warschauer Strasse or S5, S7, S75 Ostbahnhof. **Open** *24hrs daily.* **Admission** *free.* **Map** *p132 S8.*

Running along the River Spree for 1.3km (0.8 mile) from Oberbaum Bridge to Ostbahnhof is one of Berlin's most photographed tourist sights. This is the largest remaining section of the Wall still standing, and it is decorated with 101 paintings by international artists from 1990. Dmitri Vrubel's striking portrait depicting Brezhnev and Hönecker's kiss – a Soviet sign of great respect – is easily its most iconic image. The murals were steadily defaced in the ensuing years, and controversy still rages over the gallery's 2009 restoration, with certain artists objecting to copies being painted over their originals. In 2017, in an attempt to prevent further vandalism, a metre-high (three-foot) metal fence was erected around the perimeter of the Wall, an irony not lost on visitors.

Although the Wall is undeniably shabby and there's better street art to be seen elsewhere in the city, the East Side Gallery remains a lasting physical testimony to the story of the city's division and reunification.

However, visiting the East Side Gallery will not give you a sense of the reality of living with the Wall: the reinforced concrete, barbed wire and patrolling Soviet guards who were ordered to shoot on sight. For that, you could check out the convenient but pricey **Wall Museum** (Mühlenstrasse 78-80, 9451 2900, www.thewallmuseum.com, €12.50, €6.50 reductions), or, better still, visit Gedenkstätte Berliner Mauer (*see p125*) and Haus am Checkpoint Charlie (*see p147*).

FRIEDRICHSHAIN & LICHTENBERG

RAW Gelände *p134*

Butterhandlung offers modern European dining, with a Brazilian twist. Try the truffle risotto or indulge yourself with a piece of their decadent banoffee pie. Once you've finished eating, head to the secret bar in the back for a cocktail and some live music. It's popular, so make a reservation.

♥ Café Schönbrunn €€
Volkspark Friedrichshain (4530 56525, www.schoenbrunn.net). Bus 200; Tram M4, M6, M8. **Open** *10am-late daily.* **Map** *p132 R5* ❷
Café

A favoured hangout for those who love to while away lazy Sundays in the park. A couple of years ago, this waterside place sold basic coffee and snacks to an elderly crowd, but now older parkgoers sip their first afternoon beer on the terrace while the in-crowd tucks into a post-clubbing breakfast. The unspectacular concrete front is unchanged, and the lounge furniture is pure 1970s.

Goodies €
Warschauer Strasse 69 (no phone, www.goodies-berlin.de). U1, S5, S7, S75 Warschauer Strasse. **Open** *7.30am-7pm Mon-Fri; 9am-7pm Sat, Sun.* **No cards.** **Map** *p132 T7* ❸ *Vegetarian*

If an excess of döner kebabs is getting you down, head to the original branch of the vegetarian Goodies chain, a great place to load up on superfood smoothies and tofu bagels. Friendly staff and comfy sofas facilitate lingering. Their outlets inside supermarket chain Veganz are, unsurprisingly, vegan. **Other locations** throughout the city.

Hako Ramen €
Boxhagener Strasse 26 (www.facebook.com/HakoRamenBerlin). U5 Frankfurter Tor. **Open** *5-10pm Mon-Thu; 5-11pm Fri; 2-11pm Sat, Sun.* **Map** *p132 U7* ❹ *Japanese*

A traditional Japanese ramen bar that also caters to vegetarians. You can take a place at the bar and watch your *tan tan* or *tonkotsu* being freshly prepared, or, if you prefer, sit at one of the more private tables at the back. This place has been fiercely embraced by Berliners, who appreciate the incredible broth.

Mutzenbacher €€
Libauerstrasse 11 (9561 6788, www.mutzenbacher-berlin.de). U1, S5, S7, S75 Warschauer Strasse. **Open** *4pm-midnight Mon-Fri; 10am-midnight Sat, Sun.* **No cards.** **Map** *p132 T8* ❺ *Austrian*

Named after fictional Viennese prostitute Josephine Mutzenbacher, star of a famous 1906 erotic novel, this place offers inventive

Volkspark Friedrichshain on the northern edge of the district, whose hilly topography was formed from the rubble of World War II bombing. The park has an open-air stage, an imposing fountain of fairy-tale characters (*Märchenbrünnen*) and the popular **Café Schönbrunn**. The graves of fighters who fell in March 1848 in the battle for German unity are here too.

Sights & museums
Computerspiele Museum
Karl-Marx-Allee 93A (6098 8577, www.computerspielemuseum.de). U5 Weberwiese. **Open** *10am-8pm daily.* **Admission** *€9; €6 reductions.* **Map** *p132 S6.*

This excellent museum traces the history of video games with interactive displays and well-curated installations from early arcade classics, such as Pong, to groundbreaking genre-definers, such as Sim City. It's a great way for families with older kids to while away a few hours. Adult gamers will love it too, if they don't mind waiting their turn behind the younger crowds.

Restaurants & cafés
Butterhandlung €€€
Scharnweberstrasse 54 (6891 5679, www.butterhandlung.de) U5, S8, S41, S42, S85 Frankfurter Allee. **Open** *5-11pm Mon-Sat; noon-11pm Sun. p132 V7* ❶ *Modern European*

Austrian cuisine in surroundings befitting Friedrichshain's punkier vibe. A mounted boar's head made from glass shards looks on as fetching waitstaff in Lederhosen bring out *Rindsvögerl* (braised beef rolls) with red cabbage or *Fleischkäse* (meatloaf).

♥ Nil €

Grünberger Strasse 52 (2904 7713, www. nil-imbiss.de). U5 Frankfurter Tor. **Open** *11am-11.30pm daily.* **No cards.** *Map p132 T7* 6 *Imbiss/Sudanese*

In a city full of vegetarians, Nil was an instant hit with its Sudanese spin on the falafel wrap: it's fried to order for extra crispness and served with plenty of fresh salad and the magic ingredient, a creamy peanut sauce. **Other locations** Oppelner Strasse 4, Kreuzberg (4881 6414).

Santa Cantina €-€€

Simon-Dach-Strasse 22 (2236 0175, www. santaberlin.com/santa-cantina). U1 Warschauer Strasse. **Open** *5pm-late Mon-Fri; noon-late Sat; 11am-late Sun.* **Map** *p132 U8* 7 *Tex Mex*

Like its older sister Santa Maria in Kreuzberg, Santa Cantina serves modern Mexican that's a cut above the usual German Tex-Mex offerings. Winning hearts and minds with its 'Taco Tuesdays' and affordable margaritas, Santa Cantina has a menu that's adventurous, fresh and delicious. At weekends, come for brunch, but be prepared to fight for a table. There's a good selection of craft beers and wines, too. **Other location** Santa Maria, Oranienstrasse 170, Kreuzberg (9221 0027).

♥ Schneeweiss €€-€€€

Simplonstrasse 16 (2904 9704, www. schneeweiss-berlin.de). U1, S5, S7, S75 Warschauer Strasse. **Open** *6pm-1am Mon-Fri; 10am-1am Sat, Sun.* **Map** *p132 U8* 8 *Southern German/Austrian*

With its statement 'snow-white' decor, Schneeweiss certainly lives up to its name. The menu offers 'Alpine' dishes – essentially a fusion of Italian, Austrian and south German cuisine. There are daily lunch and dinner menus, plus breakfast, snacks, shakes and schnitzels throughout the day. Although upmarket for the area, it's great quality for the price and deservedly popular, so do book.

♥ Silo Coffee €€

Gabriel-Max Strasse 4 (0151 6451 8685 mobile, www.silogoods.com). U5 Frankfurter Tor. **Open** *8.30am-5pm Mon-Fri; 9.30am-7pm Sat; 10am-7pm Sun.* **Map** *p132 U8* 9 *Café*

It's a well-known fact that Berliners are lazy and reluctant to leave their home districts, favouring local hotspots over schlepping across town. However, Silo's classic but expertly prepared breakfast menu – including oven-baked pancakes, avocado toast, baked eggs, and of course, the house-roasted Fjord Coffee – pulls Berliners in from all over the city. Homesick Australians will also find comfort here. You may have to wait for a table, particularly at weekends.

♥ Spätzle & Knödel €-€€

Wühlischstrasse 20 (2757 1151, www. spaetzleknoedel.de). U1, S5, S7, S75 Warschauer Strasse or tram M13. **Open** *5-11pm Mon-Sat; 3-11pm Sun.* **No cards.** *Map p132 U8* 10 *Bavarian*

A bare-bones eaterie – literally a brick-walled room with wooden tables – catering to southern German appetites with plates piled high with cheesy Spätzle or dumplings, topped with a choice of goulash, roast pork or mushroom sauce.

♥ Vöner €

Boxhagener Strasse 56 (0176 9651 3869 mobile, www.voener.de) S4, S41, S42, S5, S7, S75, S8, S86 Ostkreuz. **Open** *noon-10pm Mon-Thu; noon-11pm Fri-Sun.* **Map** *p132 V8* 11 *Vegan*

Vegans, vegetarians and all those exhausted by Germany's love for *Fleisch* will find respite at this hip café. Here you're free to indulge in classic hangover or munchie food normally off-limits to veggies, including *Currywurst*, döner kebabs and seitan nuggets – all without any risk of getting the dreaded meat sweats.

Bars & pubs

♥ Briefmarken Weine

Karl-Marx-Allee 99 (4202 5292, www. briefmarkenweine.de). U5 Weberwiese. **Open** *7pm-midnight Mon-Sat.* **Map** *p132 S7* 1

Situated on Karl-Marx-Allee, former East German stamp shop turned Italian antipasti and wine purveyor, Briefmarken retains much of its old charm. Briefmarken is a mini oasis of regional Italian wine, fresh mozzarella antipasti and quiet candlelit conversations, and easy to distinguish by its neon green sign.

♥ Chapel Bar

Sonntagsstrasse 30 (0157 3200 0032 mobile, www.chapel.berlin) S3, S41, S42, S5, S7, S75, S8, S85 Ostkreuz. **Open** *6pm-1am Tue, Wed; 6pm-2am Thu; 6pm-3.30am Fri, Sat.* **No cards.** *Map p132 V8* 2

With artfully distressed walls, amber glowing table lamps and an eclectic assortment of vintage furniture, Chapel is evocative of dark smoky jazz joints. What really sets this place apart from other Berlin bars is the high quality of the artisan cocktails. The bar staff are happy to design you a signature drink, to play around with something experimental (artichoke liquor anyone?), or to simply rustle up an old favourite. The gin basil smash is superb.

CSA

*Karl-Marx-Allee 96 (2904 4741, www.csa-bar.de). U5 Weberweise. **Open** 7pm-late Mon-Sat; by reservation only Sun. **No cards**. **Map** p132 S7* ❸

This ultra-modern bar, housed in the old Czech Airlines building, has the feel of a futuristic airport lounge as dreamed up in the 1970s. The angular furniture and white plastic fittings contrast magnificently with its shabby location and the vast concrete sweep of Karl-Marx-Allee. The atmosphere is relaxed; the design-conscious crowd come for the excellent drink selection.

Hops & Barley

*Wühlischstrasse 22-23 (2936 7534, www. hopsandbarley.eu). U1, S5, S7, S75 Warschauer Strasse. **Open** 5pm-2am Mon-Fri, Sun; 3pm-4am Sat. **No cards**. **Map** p132 U8* ❹

Big Brobot

Interesting hop varieties are used here to produce traditional German beers, such as the top-fermenting *Weiz* (wheat) and *Dunkles* (dark), as well as *Apfelwein* (apple wine, or cider to you and me), a drink rarely seen in Berlin pubs. The heavy wooden bar is complemented by green and white tiling, with the large brewing kettles in pride of place along one side.

Shops & services

Big Brobot

*Kopernikusstrasse 19 (7407 8388, www. bigbrobot.com). U5 Frankfurter Tor. **Open** 11am- 8pm Mon-Fri; 11am-6pm Sat. **Map** p132 T8* ❶ *Gifts & souvenirs*

A paradise for graphics nerds, with hundreds of collectible toys, comics and books on tattoo art or vintage typography. Big Brobot also stocks high-end skate labels such as Stüssy and Kid Robot. The refreshingly unpretentious staff are happy to help.

Dollyrocker

*Gärtnerstrasse 25 (5471 9606). U5 Samariterstrasse. **Open** 10am-7pm Mon-Fri; 11am-5pm Sat. **No cards**. **Map** p132 U8* ❷ *Kids' clothes*

Designers (and mothers) Gabi Hartkopp and Ina Langenbruch upcycle high-quality textiles to create colourful, adorable clothing and accessories for kids aged up to seven. Under their sewing machine needles, a man's shirt becomes a boy's T-shirt, women's designer jeans become a girl's dress – each piece is unique. Handmade leather shoes are also sold.

❤ Flohmarkt am Boxhagener Platz

*Boxhagener Platz (Flea market 0152 1134 2683 mobile, Farmers' market 0178 476 2242 mobile). U5 Samariterstrasse. **Open** 9am-3.30pm Sat; 10am-6pm Sun. **No cards**. **Map** p132 U7* ❸ *Market*

The Boxi market used to be more of a makeshift affair, full of bric-a-brac and punk clothing but, much like the surrounding area, it's now got with the times, offering a thriving farmers' market on Saturdays, and handicrafts, art and vintage clothing on Sundays. Stock up on local organic vegetables while chomping on a *lahmacun* (Turkish flatbread) roll.

Olivia

*Wühlischstrasse 30 (6050 0368, www.olivia-berlin.de). U1, S5, S7, S75 Warschauer Strasse. **Open** noon-7pm Mon-Sat; 1-6pm Sun. **No cards**. **Map** p132 U8* ❹ *Food & drink*

Urban Spree

The cutesy boutique of a chocolatier, with beautiful hand-painted biscuits, lots of cocoa varieties and signature cakes, which come baked in a jar. The Chilli Schokoladen Torte is recommended.

Shakespeare & Sons
Warschauer Strasse 74 (4000 3685, www. shakesbooks.de, www.finebagels.com) U5 Frankfurter Tor. **Open** *8am-8pm Mon-Sat; 10am-8pm Sun.* **Map** *p132 T7* ❺ *Books*

Those looking for a respite from the bustle of Simon-Dach-Kiez would do well to retreat to this English- and French-language bookshop. With coffee and bagels provided by in-house Jewish-American bakery Fine Bagels, Shakespeare & Sons has a well-curated selection of reading matter, knowledgeable staff and plenty of solitary spots for you to hunker down in peace.

Urban Spree Bookshop & Gallery
Revaler Strasse 99 (7407 8597, www. urbanspree.com). U1, S5, S7, S75 Warschauer Strasse. **Open** *General noon-midnight Mon-Thur, Sun; noon-3am Fri, Sat. Shop & gallery noon-6.30pm Tue-Sun.* **No cards.** **Map** *p132 T8* ❻ *Books & art*

Run by the team behind the now-closed HBC, Urban Spree's ground-floor space functions as a gallery devoted to street art, graffiti and photography. There's also an excellent bookshop specialising in these topics, with limited editions and books from small publishers such as Fabulatorio. Gigs and performances also take place here, and a visit to the on-site *Biergarten* is highly recommended.

LICHTENBERG

Most of the neighbourhoods in the old East have little to offer the visitor, lumbered with a legacy of unemployment, Plattenbau high-rise housing and lingering pockets of neo-Nazi support. East of Friedrichshain, Lichtenberg is famously unappealing, though it does contain the **Tierpark Berlin-Friedrichsfelde** (Berlin-Friedrichsfelde Zoo) and both the **Stasi Museum**, more properly known as the **Forschungs- und Gedenkstätte Normannenstrasse**, and the **Gedenkstätte Berlin-Hohenschönhausen** (*see p140*), a former Stasi prison turned chilling exhibit of state oppression. The **Deutsch-Russisches Museum** documents the somewhat troubled history of Russian-German relations during the last century.

Sights & museums
Deutsch-Russisches Museum
Zwieseler Strasse 4 (5015 0810, www. museum-karlshorst.de). S3 Karlshorst. **Open** *10am-6pm Tue-Sun.* **Admission** *free.*

After the Soviets took Berlin, they commandeered this former German officers' club as HQ for the military administration. It was here, on the night of 8-9 May 1945, that German commanders signed the unconditional surrender, ending the war in Europe. This stern museum surveys over 70 years of German-Soviet relations. Divided into 16 rooms, with the surrender room left in its original state, it takes us through the wars of the 20th century, plus assorted pacts, victories and capitulations. Buy an English guide, as the exhibits are labelled in German and Russian. English tours can be booked.

❤ Gedenkstätte Berlin-Hohenschönhausen

Genslerstrasse 66 (9860 8230, www.stiftung-hsh.de). Tram M5, M6. **Open** *Exhibition 9am-6pm daily. Guided tours (in German) 10am-4pm hourly; (in English) 10.30am, 12.30pm, 2.30pm daily.* **Admission** *€6; €1-3 reductions. No cards.*

It's claimed that at some point in their lives, one in three citizens worked as unofficial informers for East Germany's Ministerium für Staatssicherheit, better known as the Stasi. There were around 90,000 full-time agents and 175,000 *Inoffizielle Mitarbeiter* (unofficial employees, aka informers) – that's around 2.5 per cent of those aged between 18 and 60. One thing's for sure: the secret police apparatus was the most pervasive in the history of state-sponsored repression; compare, for example, the Gestapo, which in its 1940s heyday only had about 30,000 members.

The Stasi's grip on everyday life in the GDR was exhaustive, with hidden cameras and microphones, a network of informers and infamous secret prisons where political prisoners were held, brutalised, and psychologically broken before being sent to labour camps. A visit to this sprawling former remand prison is gut-wrenchingly bleak. First the site of a canteen for the Nazi social welfare organisation, the building was turned into 'Special Encampment No.3' by the Soviets before being expanded by the Stasi. Excellent and highly personal guided tours are led daily by ex-prisoners; their personal testimony adds chilling immediacy to the bureaucratically spare interrogation rooms, the concrete 'tiger cage' in which 30 minutes of walking per day was permitted and the cramped cells where prisoners were forced to sleep in a mandated position. The museum houses a permanent exhibition, which reveals the stories of former prisoners during their incarceration, and there are temporary exhibitions which change throughout the year, often curated from the memorial's own immense collection of 15,000 historical artefacts from the GDR.

▶ *For further insights into the structure and methods of the Stasi, visit Forschungs- und Gedenkstätte Normannenstrasse, better known as the Stasi Museum (see opposite).*

Gärten der Welt Marzahn

Eisenacher Strasse 99, Marzahn (700 906 778, www.gruen-berlin.de/gaerten-der-welt). S7 Marzahn then bus 195. **Open** *9am-sundown daily.* **Admission** *Summer €7; €3 reductions. Winter €4; €2 reductions.*

Originally built in 1986 as the GDR equivalent to the similar Britz gardens in Neukölln, this existed as an eastern peripheral oddity until the millennium, when it was turned into the sparkling collection of specialist gardens that exists today. The Chinese garden is the largest in Europe; and there are similarly authentic Korean, Balinese and Italian gardens. Kids will love the fiendish hedge maze.

Mies van der Rohe Haus

Oberseestrasse 60 (9700 0618, www.miesvanderrohehaus.de). Tram M5, 27. **Open** *11am-5pm Tue-Sun.* **Admission** *free.*

Ludwig Mies van der Rohe designed this L-shaped modernist gem in 1933 for Karl Lemke, the owner of a Berlin graphic-art and printing firm. Lemke and his wife lived here until 1945, when the Red Army stormed in and used it as a garage. From 1960 until the fall of the Wall, it was a laundry for the Stasi; these days, it hosts art exhibitions.

Stasimuseum (Forschungs- und Gedenkstätte Normannenstrasse)

Ruschestrasse 103 (553 6854, www.stasimuseum.de). U5, S8, S9, S41, S42, S85 Frankfurter Allee; U5 Magdalenenstrasse. **Open** *10am-6pm Mon-Fri; 11am-6pm Sat, Sun. Tours (in English) 3pm Mon, Sat, Sun.* **Admission** *€6; €4.50 reductions. No cards.*

In January 1990, a few weeks after the Wall was breached, crowds stormed the Stasi headquarters at Normannenstrasse to vent anger at their former tormentors and to prevent the destruction of secret documents, which Stasi agents had been working overtime with shredders to destroy. Thanks to their efforts, many of the six million or so files were saved; since reunification they have been administered by a special authority charged with reviewing them and making them available to prosecutors and everyday people curious to find out what the Stasi knew about them. Not surprisingly, the files contained embarrassing revelations, with many people being listed as unofficial informers, a status hard to dispute or verify.

Visitors can explore the former headquarters and see displays of bugging devices and spy cameras concealed in books, plant pots and car doors. You can even poke around the offices of secret police chief Erich Mielke – his old uniform still hangs in the wardrobe – and apply at the front desk to see your own Stasi records, should any exist.

Stasimuseum

Since early 2015, a permanent exhibition has explored the Stasi's structure, methods and activities, giving an insight into the most insidious police surveillance state in all of history. Tours are also offered of the Stasi Archives next door.

Tierpark Berlin-Friedrichsfelde

Am Tierpark 125 (515 310, www.tierpark-berlin.de). U5 Tierpark. **Open** *Late Mar-mid Sept 9am-6pm daily. Mid Sept-late Mar 9am-4.30pm daily.* **Admission** *€14; €6-€7 reductions.*

East Berlin's zoo is still one of Europe's largest, with an impressive amount of roaming space for the herd animals, although others are still kept in rather small cages. Residents include bears, big cats, elephants and penguins. One of the continent's biggest snake farms is also here. In the north-west corner is the Baroque Schloss Friedrichsfelde.

Shops & services

♥ Dong Xuan Center

Herzbergstrasse 128-139 (5544 0342, www.dongxuan-berlin.de). Tram M8, 21. **Open** *10am-8pm Mon, Wed-Sun. Food & drink*

Four cavernous warehouses stand on the former site of an enormous coal and graphite processing plant (it was demolished in the 1990s and the land underwent extensive 'detoxification'). Tradesmen hawk all sorts of wares for businesses affiliated with the Vietnamese community, from wholesale nail-salon supplies to glitzy chandeliers, but of most interest are the enormous food halls. The offal butchers and rare South-east Asian herbs will transport you straight to downtown Saigon.

Kreuzberg & Treptow

Kreuzberg is divided quite firmly into halves, according to its old postcodes – Kreuzberg 36, the eastern part, is scruffy and hip, great for a night out; Kreuzberg 61, in the west, is quieter, prettier, duller after dark but lovely during the day. Further east, Treptow is a quiet residential area concealing leafy Treptower Park, a huge war memorial and an abandoned amusement park. Following the Spree east leads to far-flung Köpenick, frequented by day trippers for its Baroque water palace and easy access to Grosser Müggelsee, one of Berlin's largest and most popular lakes.

❤ Don't miss

1 Sowjetisches Ehrenmal am Treptower Park *p162*
One of Berlin's most awesome public monuments, sequestered in a peaceful corner of Treptower Park.

2 Haus am Checkpoint Charlie *p147*
The longest running museum dedicated to the Wall charts the daring escapes from East to West.

3 Jüdisches Museum *p149*
Daniel Libeskind's masterful representation of the history of Judaism and Germany.

4 Markthalle Neun *p160*
This bustling covered market was created through community effort.

5 Badeschiff *p161*
Lounge by the pool in the day; party in the open air at night.

In the know
Getting around

The most enjoyable way to explore both Kreuzberg and Treptow is by bike, thanks to the numerous green parks and residential spaces – just watch out for the cobblestones on the side roads. Kreuzberg is well served by the U-Bahn, with the U1 running from east to west through the centre, and the U6, 7 and 8 covering the rest of the district. Note that, even if you use the U-Bahn, you're likely to do some walking, as distances between stations are significant. Treptow is served primarily by the S-Bahn to Treptower Park. Day trippers to Köpenick have two main options: to visit the Schloss, take the S47 to Spindlersfeld from where it's a 15-minute walk across the River Dahme; for the Müggelsee, take the S3 to Friedrichshagen. Alternatively, it's about an hour's cycle ride from Kreuzberg.

Sowjetisches Ehrenmal am Treptower Park

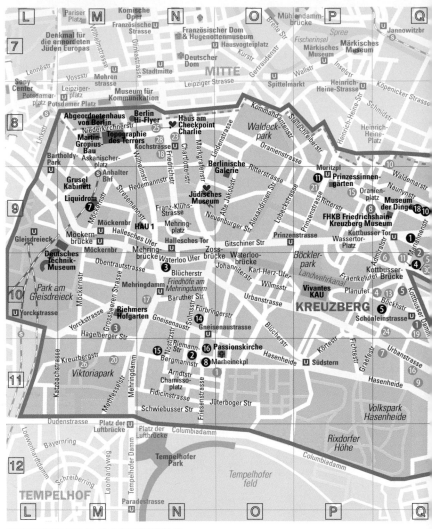

KREUZBERG & TREPTOW

Restaurants & cafés

1 Austria Das Original *p151*
2 Bar Raval *p154*
3 Burgermeister *p154*
4 Il Casolare *p154*
5 Cocolo *p154*
6 Doyum Grillhaus *p155*
7 Figl *p155*
8 Five Elephant *p156*
9 Hamy Café-Foodstore *p156*
10 Henne *p156*
11 Horvath *p156*

12 Jolesch *p156*
13 KaffeeBar Jenseits des Kanals *p157*
14 Lode & Stijn *p157*
15 Max Und Moritz *p157*
16 Mo's King of Falafel *p157*
17 Mustafa's Gemüse Kebap *p151*
18 Nobelhart & Schmutzig *p150*
19 Olivio Pasta Bar *p151*
20 Osteria No.1 *p151*
21 Parker Bowles *p157*

22 Richard *p157*
23 Sale e Tabacchi *p150*
24 St Bart's *p157*
25 Tim Raue *p150*
26 Tomasa Villa Kreuzberg *p151*
27 Weltrestaurant Markthalle *p158*
28 Westberlin *p150*
29 White Crow Café *p161*
30 Zola Pizza *p158*

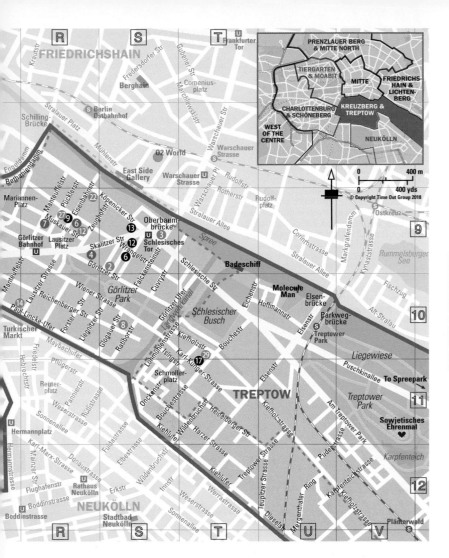

Bars & pubs

1 Bei Schlawinchen *p158*
2 DasHotel Bar *p158*
3 Galander Kreuzberg *p152*
4 John Muir *p158*
5 Marques Bar *p158*
6 Schwarze Traube *p158*
7 Tante Lisbeth *p159*
8 Würgeengel *p159*

Shops & services

1 Alimentari e Vini *p159*
2 Another Country *p152*
3 Hallesches Haus *p152*
4 Hard Wax *p159*
5 Kado *p159*
6 Kumru Kuruyemis *p160*
7 Liquidrom *p152*
8 Marheineke Markthalle *p153*
9 Markthalle Neun *p160*
10 Modern Graphics *p160*
11 Modulor *p160*

12 Motto *p160*
13 Overkill *p160*
14 Paul Knopf *p153*
15 Picknweight Concept Store *p153*
16 Space Hall *p153*
17 Vintage Berlin *p163*
18 Voo Store *p160*

NORTH-WEST KREUZBERG

The north-western portion of Kreuzberg, bordering Mitte, is not the prettiest, but it's where you'll find most of the area's museums and tourist sights. The most prominent is Daniel Libeskind's sensational **Jüdisches Museum** (*see p149*) on Lindenstrasse, an example of architecture at its most cerebral, and a powerful sensory experience. Behind it, on Alte Jakobstrasse, is the **Berlinische Galerie**, home to Berlin's permanent collection of art, photography and architecture. From there it's only a few minutes' walk to the **König Gallery** (Dessauerstrasse 6-7, 2610 3080, www. johannkoenig.de), which represents some of the hottest artists around, including Monica Bonvinci. It's run by one of Berlin's leading art aficionados, the bona fide iconoclast Johann König. West of here, close to the Landwehrkanal, is the enjoyable **Deutsches Technikmuseum Berlin** (German Museum of Technology) with a 1930s Junkers JU 52 plane mounted on the roof.

Over the canal to the north is the site of Anhalter Bahnhof, which was once the city's biggest and busiest railway station. Only a tiny section of façade remains, preserved in its bombed state near the S-Bahn station that bears its name. On Stresemannstrasse, the Bauhaus-designed **Europahaus** was heavily bombed during World War II, but the lower storeys remain. On the north side of the street, Berlin's *Landtag* (parliament), the **Abgeordnetenhaus von Berlin** (Berlin House of Representatives), meets in what was formerly the Prussian parliament. Its surprisingly good canteen is open to the public when parliament is not sitting. Dating from the 1890s, the building was renovated in the early 1990s. Opposite stands the **Martin-Gropius-Bau**, a venue for major art shows. The building was modelled on London's South Kensington museums – the figures of craftspeople on the external reliefs reveal its origins as an applied arts museum.

Next to it is a mostly deserted block that once held the Prinz Albrecht Palais, which the Gestapo took over as its headquarters. In the basement's 39 cells, political prisoners were held, interrogated and tortured. The land was flattened after the war. In 1985, during an acrimonious debate over the design of a memorial to be placed here, a group of citizens staged a symbolic 'excavation'. To their surprise, they hit the Gestapo's basement, and plans were then made to reclaim the site. Today, there's an open-air exhibition about the rise of National Socialism and a documentation centre, the **Topographie des Terrors**.

Along the site's northern boundary on Niederkirchnerstrasse is one of the last few remaining stretches of the **Berlin Wall**, pitted and threadbare after thousands of 1990 souvenir-hunters pecked away at it with hammers and chisels. The stark building opposite is Hermann Göring's fortress-like Luftfahrministerium (Air Ministry), a rare relic of the Nazi past, which survived the allies' bombs and is now the Federal Finance Ministry.

Walking east, Niederkirchnerstrasse turns into Zimmerstrasse, which intersects Friedrichstrasse, where Checkpoint Charlie once stood and where the **Haus am Checkpoint Charlie** (*see opposite*) documents the history of the Wall. Most of the space where the border post once stood has been claimed by new buildings, though

---

♥ Time to eat & drink

Coffee and a croissant
Five Elephant *p156*, White Crow Café *p161*

Cheap and cheerful lunch
Hamy Café-Foodstore *p156*, Markthalle Neun *p160*, Olivio Pasta Bar *p157*

Daytime drinking
Biergarten Freiheit Fünfzehn *p163*, Bei Schlawinchen *p158*

Contemporary bistros
Lode & Stijn *p157*, Nobelhart & Schmutzig *p150*

Artisanal cocktails
Marques Bar *p158*, Schwarze Traube *p158*

♥ Time to shop

Stock up on vinyl
Hard Wax *p159*, Space Hall *p153*

The latest designer togs
Voo Store *p160*, Overkill *p160*

Tempting homewares
Hallesches Haus *p152*

Get crafty
Modulor *p160*

Read all about it
Another Country *p152*, Modern Graphics *p160*, Motto *p160*

❤ Haus am Checkpoint Charlie

*Friedrichstrasse 43-45 (253 7250, www.
mauermuseum.de). U6 Kochstrasse.* **Open**
9am-10pm daily. **Admission** *€14.50; €6.50-
€9.50 reductions.* **Map** *p144 N8.*

A little tacky, but essential for anyone
interested in the Cold War, this private
museum opened not long after the GDR
erected the Berlin Wall in 1961, making it
the oldest documentation of the Wall in
existence. The founder of the museum, Dr
Rainer Hildebrandt, opened it as a non-
violent protest against the Wall, with the
purpose of recording the events that were
taking place at this, the best-known crossing
point. He believed that it was essential to
be 'as close as possible to the injustice itself,
where human greatness fully unfolds'. Haus
am Checkpoint Charlie is not just a testament
to the unfolding of history but played an
active role in planning and assisting escapes.

The exhibition charts the history of the
Wall and details the ingenious and
hair-raising ways people escaped from the
GDR – as well as exhibiting some of the
actual contraptions that were used, such
as a home-made hot-air balloon, a mini-
submarine and getaway cars. Today, the
museum also features permanent displays
that look beyond Berlin and Germany
towards other forms of non-violent protest.

For some *Ostalgie* (nostalgia for the GDR),
head a few steps down from the Haus am
Checkpoint Charlie to the **Trabi Museum**
(Zimmerstrasse 14-15, 3020 1030, www.
trabi-museum.com) dedicated to the cult
Eastern bloc vehicle. And, to really max out
on German kitsch, especially if you have
bored and hungry kids in tow, finish off your
visit with a trip to the nearby **Deutsches
Currywurst Museum** (Schützenstrasse 70,
8871 8647, currywurstmuseum.com).

KREUZBERG & TREPTOW

there is an open-air exhibition in the dead space north of the old checkpoint. The actual site of the borderline is memorialised by Frank Thiel's photographic portraits of an American and a Soviet soldier. The small white building that served as a gateway between East and West is now in the **Alliierten Museum** (*see p203*) – the one in the middle of the street is a replica.

Just to the south is Kochstrasse. In 2008, the eastern stretch, containing the towering headquarters of right-wing media magnate Axel Springer, was renamed Rudi-Dutschke-Strasse in honour of one of Germany's most famous student revolutionaries. In April 1968, Dutschke was the victim of an attempted assassination, shot in the head and chest after various Springer publications had called on their readers to 'eliminate the troublemakers' and 'stop the terror of the young reds.' His supporters demonstrated outside the Springer building, claiming the publisher was partially responsible for the shooting. Dutschke died some years later of complications arising from his injuries. The street is home to art dealer **Alexander Levy**'s boxy exhibition space at no.26 (2529 2221, www. alexanderlevy.net), which showcases quality art with an experimental edge.

Sights & museums

Berlin Hi-Flyer
Corner of Wilhelmstrasse & Zimmerstrasse (226 678 811, www.air-service-berlin.de). U6 Kochstrasse. **Open** *10am-7pm daily.* **Admission** *€23; €10-€18 reductions.* **Map** *p144 M8.*

This helium balloon has hovered 150m (490ft) above Berlin in various different guises since 1999 and, somewhat bewilderingly, is now one of the city's leading tourist attractions – as well as one of its most expensive. You do get a lovely view but, given that the panorama from the dome of the (free) Reichstag is almost as good, you might wish to give this one a miss.

Berlinische Galerie
Alte Jakobstrasse 124-128 (7890 2600, www. berlinischegalerie.de). U6 Kochstrasse. **Open** *10am-6pm Mon, Wed-Sun.* **Admission** *€8; €5 reductions; free under-18s.* **Map** *p144 O9.*

Founded in 1975, the Berlinische Galerie moved into this spacious renovated industrial building near the Jewish Museum in 2004. It specialises in art created in Berlin, dating from 1870 to the present, including painting, sculpture, photography and architecture. Its collections cover Dada Berlin, the Neue Sachlichkeit and the Eastern European avant-

garde. Enjoy half-price admission every first Monday of the month.

▶ *Visitors pay the reduced price if they have bought a ticket to the Jüdisches Museum (see p149) within the previous 48 hours.*

Deutsches Technikmuseum Berlin
Trebbiner Strasse 9 (902 540, www.sdtb.de). U1, U7 Möckernbrücke. **Open** *9am-5.30pm Tue-Fri; 10am-6pm Sat, Sun.* **Admission** *€8; €4 reductions.* **Map** *p144 M9.*

Opened in 1982 in the former goods depot of the Anhalter Bahnhof, the German Museum of Technology is an eclectic, eccentric collection of new and antique industrial artefacts. The rail exhibits have pride of place, with the station sheds providing an ideal setting for locomotives and rolling stock from 1835 to the present. Other displays focus on the industrial revolution; street, rail, water and air traffic; computer technology; and printing technology. Behind the main complex is an open-air section with two functioning windmills and a smithy. Oddities, such as 1920s vacuum cleaners, make this a fun place for implement enthusiasts. The nautical wing has vessels and displays on inland waterways and international shipping, while another wing covers aviation and space travel. Electronic information points offer commentaries in English on subjects from the international slave trade to the mechanics of a space station. The Spectrum annex, at Möckernstrasse 26, houses over 200 interactive devices and experiments.

Martin-Gropius-Bau
Niederkirchnerstrasse 7 (254 860, www. gropiusbau.de). S1, S2, S25 Anhalter Bahnhof; U6 Kochstrasse **Open** *10am-7pm Mon, Wed-Sun.* **Admission** *varies.* **Map** *p144 M8.*

Cosying up to where the Wall once stood (a short, pitted stretch still runs nearby along the south side of Niederkirchnerstrasse), the Martin-Gropius-Bau is named after its architect, uncle of the more famous Walter. Built in 1881, it has been renovated and is now used for large-scale art exhibitions.

Topographie des Terrors
Niederkirchnerstrasse 8 (2545 0950, www. topographie.de). S1, S2, S25 Anhalter Bahnhof; U6 Kochstrasse. **Open** *Outdoor exhibition 10am-dusk daily. Indoor exhibition 10am-8pm daily.* **Admission** *free.* **Map** *p144 M8.*

Essentially a piece of waste ground, this was once the site of the Prinz Albrecht Palais, headquarters of the Gestapo, and the Hotel Prinz Albrecht, which housed offices of the Reich SS leadership. These buildings formed

❤ Jüdisches Museum

*Lindenstrasse 9-14 (2599 3300, guided tours 2599 3305, www.jmberlin.de). U1, U6 Hallesches Tor. **Open** (last entry 1hr before closing) 10am-8pm daily. **Admission** €8; €3 reductions. **Map** p144 N9.*

The idea of a Jewish museum in Berlin was first mooted in 1971, the 300th birthday of the city's Jewish community. In 1975, an association was formed to acquire materials for display; in 1989, a competition was held to design an extension to the Baroque Kollegienhaus to house them. Daniel Libeskind emerged as the winner, the foundation stone was laid in 1992 and the permanent exhibition finally opened in 2001.

The ground plan of Libeskind's remarkable building is in part based on an exploded Star of David, in part on lines drawn between the site and former addresses of figures in Berlin's Jewish history, such as Mies van der Rohe, Arnold Schönberg and Walter Benjamin. The entrance is via a tunnel from the Kollegienhaus. The underground geometry is startlingly independent of the above-ground building. One passage leads to the exhibition halls, two others intersect en route to the Holocaust Tower and the ETA Hoffmann Garden, a grid of 49 columns, tilted to disorientate. Throughout, diagonals and parallels carve out surprising spaces, while windows slash through the structure and its zinc cladding like the knife-wounds of history. And then there are the 'voids' cutting through the layout, negative spaces that stand for the emptiness left by the destruction of German Jewish culture.

The permanent exhibition struggles in places with such powerful surroundings.

What makes it engaging is its focus on the personal: it tells the stories of prominent Jews and what they contributed to their community, and to the cultural and economic life of Berlin and Germany. After centuries of prejudice and pogroms, the outlook for German Jews seemed to be brightening. Then came the Holocaust. The emotional impact of countless stories of the eminent and the ordinary, and the fate that almost all shared, is hard to convey adequately in print. The museum is undoubtedly a must-see, but expect long queues and big crowds.

▶ *Visitors pay the reduced price if they have bought a ticket to the Berlinische Galerie (see p148) within the previous 48 hours.*

Memory Void

Libeskind building

Topographie des Terrors p148

the centre of the Nazi police-state apparatus: it was from here that the Holocaust was managed and the Germanisation of the east was dreamed up. There's an outdoor exhibition that gives a fairly comprehensive chronology of Hitler's rise to power, as well as an indoor documentation centre. A segment of the Berlin Wall runs along the site's northern boundary.

Restaurants & cafés

♥ Nobelhart & Schmutzig €€€
Friedrichstrasse 218 (2594 0610, www. nobelhartundschmutzig.com). U6 Kochstrasse. **Open** *from 6.30pm Tue-Sat.* **Map** *p144 N8* ⑱ *Contemporary*

This restaurant's tagline is 'vocally local' – meaning they refuse to import food from beyond the capital and its immediate surroundings. Sadly, this means no chocolate. However, chef and sommelier Billy Wagner has ways of helping you temporarily forget: he uses neglected traditional methods to create a seasonally shifting menu of bold, contemporary flavours that evoke, impossibly, the authentic taste of Berlin. The outside is nondescript, visible only to those in the know, and you must ring a bell before you are ushered into the eatery – a long wooden table with just 28 seats. Booking essential.

Sale e Tabacchi €€
Rudi-Dutschke-Strasse 25 (252 1155, www. sale-e-tabacchi.de). U6 Kochstrasse. **Open** *from 11am daily.* **Map** *p144 N8* ㉓ *Italian*

An old-school Italian restaurant, ideal for larger groups looking for some southern decadence and creaky, middle-aged Italian

waiters. Food is simple and delicious rather than spectacular, but it's the ambience – a comfortable fug of cosiness and quiet affluence (the restaurant is owned by the left-leaning *Tageszeitung* newspaper) – that's the big draw.

Tim Raue €€€€
Rudi-Dutschke-Strasse 26 (2593 7930, www. tim-raue.de). U6 Kochstrasse. **Open** *noon-1pm, 7-9pm Wed-Sat.* **Map** *p144 N8* ㉕ *Fine dining*

In contrast to many of Berlin's fine-dining establishments, this small restaurant, decorated with Chinese ceramics and dark wood furniture, prides itself on its informality. Not that this detracts from the exacting dishes. The tasting menu might include *amuse-bouches* of spicy cashews, prawn sashimi and marinated pork belly, moving on to main courses of wagyu beef, lobster, Australian winter truffle and tofu, all flaunting Japanese techniques and served with blobs, smears or foams of contrasting flavours and colours. Book ahead.

Westberlin €
Friedrichstrasse 215 (2592 2745, www. westberlin-bar-shop.de). U6 Kochstrasse. **Open** *8.30am-7pm Mon-Fri, 10am-7pm Sat, Sun.* **Map** *p144 N8* ㉓ *Café*

A minimal café in a built-up part of Berlin, it's a small oasis of third-wave coffee and Scandinavian cool in a rather barren part of the tourist centre. Don't be deceived by its almost lifeless stylings, the place is always buzzing. Grab a magazine and quickly claim a spot before settling down with a flat white and a *Franzbrötchen*.

SOUTH-WEST KREUZBERG

The more sedate western part of Kreuzberg incorporates some of the most picturesque corners of West Berlin. **Viktoriapark** contains the actual Kreuzberg ('Cross Hill') after which the borough is named. A landscaped waterfall cascades down the hill in summer, and paths wind their way to the summit, where Schinkel's 1821 monument commemorates victories in the Napoleonic Wars – many of the streets nearby are named after battles and generals of that era. From this commanding view over a mainly flat city, the landmarks of both East and West spread out before you: Friedrichstrasse is dead ahead; the Europa-Center off to the left; the Potsdamer Platz high-rises in between; the Fernsehturm over to the right. The park also has a legendary *Biergarten*, **Golgatha** (www.golgatha-berlin.de), where you can drink and dance in the open air until the small hours.

Back on ground level, the streets north of the park lead to one of Berlin's most attractive courtyard complexes. **Riehmers Hofgarten** is cobbled, closed to traffic and often used as a film location due to its 19th-century feel.

Bergmannstrasse, which runs east from here, is the main hub of local activity. This street of cafés, junk shops, bookstores and record shops is livelier than ever by day, although uneventful by night. It leads to **Marheinekeplatz**, where the old Markthalle is now a sort of luxury mall full of speciality food stalls. **Zossener Strasse**, north from here, also bustles.

Bergmannstrasse continues east past a large cemetery to Südstern. Here is the entrance to the **Volkspark Hasenheide**, the other of the neighbourhood's large parks, with a good view from atop the Rixdorfer Höhe. The streets just south of Bergmannstrasse also resemble a movie set. Many buildings survived wartime bombing, and the area around **Chamissoplatz** has been immaculately restored – the cobbled streets are lined with houses still sporting their Prussian façades and illuminated by gaslight at night.

Restaurants & cafés

▶ *Don't miss the excellent café at Hallesches Haus (see p152).*

Austria Das Original €€
*Bergmannstrasse 30 (694 4440, www. austria-berlin.de). U7 Gneisenaustrasse. **Open** 6pm-midnight Mon; noon-midnight Tue-Sun. Map p144 O11* ❶ *Austrian*

With a collection of antlers, this place does its best to look like a hunting lodge. The *Schnitzel* famously spills over the edge of the plate. Literary types may recall it has a cameo in the Pulitzer prize-winning novel *Middlesex*, written by a regular diner, Jeffrey Eugenides, when the narrator declares, 'I don't like anyone who doesn't like Austria.' Book at weekends and in summer – when the outdoor seating on a tree-lined square comes into its own.

Mustafa's Gemüse Kebap €
*Mehringdamm 32 (no phone, www. mustafas.de). U6, U7 Mehringdamm. **Open** 10.30am-2am daily. **No cards. Map** p144 M11* ❶ *Imbiss*

Easily the most popular kebab stall in town – don't be surprised by half-hour waits, especially for the chicken kebabs. But it's the vegetarian option that's really worth the wait: grilled peppers, aubergines and fried potatoes, finished with crumbled feta and a squirt of lemon juice to really make it sing.

Osteria No.1 €€
*Kreuzbergstrasse 71 (5779 2999, www. osteria1-berlin.com). U6, U7 Mehringdamm. **Open** noon-midnight daily. **Map** p144 M11* ❷ *Italian*

Most of Berlin's best Italian chefs paid their dues at this 1977-founded establishment, learning their lessons from a family of restaurateurs from Lecce. There's an excellent lunch menu and, in summer, one of Berlin's loveliest garden courtyards. Kids eat free on Sundays. Booking recommended.

Tomasa Villa Kreuzberg €€
*Kreuzbergstrasse 62 (8100 9885, www. tomasa.de). U6, U7 Mehringdamm. **Open** 9am-midnight daily. **Map** p144 M11* ❷

Positioned favourably close to Viktoriapark and the Kreuzberg waterfall, this café serves brunch – from full English to a more traditional German spread of breads, boiled eggs and fruit – on a grand scale. It's family-friendly, so expect some noise.

In the know
Curry 36

Don't be put off by the endless queues outside **Curry 36** (Mehringdamm 36, 25800 88336, www.curry36.de): service is swift, and, if you're in the area, it's a cheap and cheerful way to participate in a Berlin tradition. Is it the best *Currywurst* in the world? Probably not, but then again, this is one seriously hyped hot dog.

Bars & pubs

Galander Kreuzberg
Grossbeerenstrasse 54 (3850 9030, www.
galander.berlin/galander-kreuzberg). U7
Gneisenaustrasse. **Open** *6pm-late daily.*
Map *p144 M10* ❸

This low-lit haven, complete with squishy
leather armchairs and a piano at the back,
offers a decadent array of spirits and
home-made cordials to please the most
demanding cocktail connoisseur. The
friendly and attentive staff are brimming with
encyclopaedic knowledge on mixology and
won't hesitate to create something special or
even regale you with a tune. The basil smash
is divine.

Shops & services

♥ Another Country
Riemannstrasse 7 (6940 1160, www.
anothercountry.de). U7 Gneisenaustrasse.
Open *2-8pm Mon; 11am-8pm Tue-Fri; noon-*
6pm Sat. **Map** *p144 N11* ❷ *Books & music*

This second-hand bookshop was established
by Sophia Raphaeline long before the area
was laden with cafés, restaurants and shops,
and offers a window into Kreuzberg of the
past. It now has legendary status but retains a
whiff of bohemia. The rooms have the feel of
a private study, with piles of books laid out on
tables and a fridge for beers; a projector is set
up for film nights, and quizzes and dinners
are also held.

♥ Hallesches Haus
Tempelhofer Ufer 1 (no phone, hallescheshaus.
com). U1, U6 Hallesches Tor. **Open** *10am-7pm*
Mon-Fri; 10am-6pm Sat, Sun. **Map** *p144*
N10 ❸ *Homewares*

Succulents, copper kettles, angora wool
throws, over-sized lightbulbs, seaweed and
samphire unguents – there is a dizzying array
of artfully curated knick-knacks and treasures
to buy here, all tastefully arranged on wooden
crates and industrial shelving. There's also
a very good café, with a locally sourced,
seasonal menu and plenty of places to sit and
mull over those pretty things you never knew
you needed.

Liquidrom
Möckernstrasse 10 (2580 07820, www.
liquidrom-berlin.de/en). S1, S2, S25 Anhalter
Bahnhof; U1 U7 Möckernbrücke. **Open**
9am-midnight Mon-Thur, Sun; 9am-1am
Fri, Sat. **Admission** *from €19.50.* **Map** *p144*
M9 ❼ *Spa*

The highlight of this spa is the enormous
heated salt pool where you can float and zen
out to the ambient underwater music. It's
especially good in the evenings, as there's a
psychedelic light show playing between water
and ceiling, which is spoiled by the natural
light of the day. Nudity is mandatory in the
saunas, so try to think like a German. Be
mindful of the time slot you pay for, as they
charge extra if you overstay. Look out for DJ
nights at the weekends.

Hallesches Haus

Another Country

Marheineke Markthalle

*Marheinekestrasse 15 (5056 6536, meine-markthalle.de). U7 Gneisenaustrasse. **Open** 8am-8pm Mon-Fri; 8am-6pm Sat. **Map** p144 N11* **8** *Market*

A lovely covered market with French butchers, Italian charcuterie, flowers and organic produce, as well as plenty of prepared foods to take away. You'll find a Veganz supermarket upstairs, and a variety of snack bars with seating along the front wall.

Paul Knopf

*Zossener Strasse 10 (692 1212, www. paulknopf.de). U7 Gneisenaustrasse. **Open** 9am-6pm Tue, Fri; 2-6pm Wed, Thur. **No cards**. **Map** p144 N10* **14** *Accessories*

A Kreuzberg institution stocking buttons in every shape, colour and style you can think of. Whatever you're seeking, Paul Knopf ('Button') will help you find it. His patient and untiring service is remarkable considering most transactions are for tiny sums.

Picknweight Concept Store

*Bergmannstrasse 102 (694 3348, www. picknweight.de). U7 Gneisenaustrasse. **Open** 11am-8pm Mon-Sat. **Map** p144 N11* **15** *Fashion*

Part of the Made in Berlin chain, this shop is mostly known for its gimmick of selling clothes by the 'kilo'. Up for grabs are jeans, leather jackets and dresses, including party stunners and fetching Bavarian dirndls, plus the odd gem from the 1950s.

♥ Space Hall

*Zossener Strasse 33 & 35 (694 7664, www. space-hall.de). U7 Gneisenaustrasse. **Open** 11am-8pm Mon-Wed, Sat; 11am-10pm Thur, Fri. **Map** p144 N11* **16** *Music*

A favourite of Berlin's resident DJs and producers, Space Hall has a huge selection of new and second-hand CDs and vinyl. Techno, house and electronica are the mainstay, but there's also hip hop, indie and rock.

EAST KREUZBERG

In the 1970s and '80s, the eastern half of Kreuzberg, north of the Landwehrkanal, was right at the eastern edge of inner West Berlin. Enclosed by the Wall and the canal, and mostly ignored by the rest of the city, its decaying tenements came to house Berlin's biggest and most militant squat community. The area was full of punky left-wing youths on a draft-dodging mission – a loophole meant residents were exempt from military service – and guest-worker Turks who came to the area because rents were cheap and people mostly left them alone.

No area of West Berlin has changed so much since the fall of the Wall. This once-isolated pocket found itself recast as desirable real estate. Much of the alternative art scene shifted north to Mitte, but gentrification was slow to take off and, slowly, Kreuzberg regained its appeal for young bohemia.

Enough of the anarchistic old guard stayed behind to ensure that the area retains a distinctive atmosphere. It's an earthy kind of place, full of cafés, bars and clubs, and dotted with independent cinemas; it's also an important nexus for the city's gay community.

Oranienstrasse is the area's main drag, with plenty of bars and clubs, as well as the quirky **Museum der Dinge**. The hideous pre-fab development immediately to the north of Kotbusser Tor U-Bahn station – Kotti for short – was once a no-go area after dark, but now it's a popular nightspot, with bars such as **Monarch** and the **Paloma Bar**. The area is also the centre of Turkish Berlin (*see p155 The Turkish Capital*) and bustles with kebab shops and Anatolian travel agents.

Rather gentler these days is **Wiener Strasse**, running alongside the old Görlitzer Bahnhof, where more bars and cafés await. A couple of blocks further south lies chi-chi **Paul-Lincke-Ufer**, a canalside street lined with smart cafés and restaurants and the district's most desirable houses. South-west is **Graefekiez**, a green and gentrified neighbourhood full of cafés and boutique shops catering to hip young families.

Further north of Kotti is the innocuous Moritzplatz roundabout, previously a no-man's-land, which now has several notable businesses centred around the Aufbau publishing building: the fantastic **Modulor** craft shop, a Vietnamese *bahn mi* café and the **Prince Charles** night-club (*see p245*). It's also the site of the **Prinzessinnengarten** (http:// prinzessinnengarten.net), a massive community effort that transformed a wasteland into an oasis of organic vegetables and beehives, with regular workshops for children. Heading towards Oranienplatz, there are several art galleries of note: local institution **DAAD Galerie** (Oranienstrasse 161, 6980 7607, www.daadgalerie.de), the offbeat and idiosyncratic **Klemms** (Prinzessinnenstrasse 29, 4050 4953, www.klemms-berlin.com), and the small but perfectly formed **Chert Lüdde** gallery (Ritterstrasse 2A, 3551 2054, http://chertluedde.com).

The U1 line runs overhead through the neighbourhood along the middle of **Skalitzer Strasse**. The onion-domed Schlesisches Tor station was once the end of the line, but these days the train continues one more stop across the Spree to Warschauer Strasse. You can also walk across the **Oberbaumbrücke** (*see p132*) into Friedrichshain and the post-industrial nightlife district around Mühlenstrasse. The area around Schlesisches Tor station, along **Schlesische Strasse** and over the canal towards the next borough of Treptow is another hotspot. Sometimes called the Wrangelkiez, this buzzing area has become such a tourist draw that local residents held a crisis meeting a few years ago to complain about the noise levels.

Sights & museums

FHXB Friedrichshain-Kreuzberg Museum

Adalbertstrasse 95A (5058 5233, www.fhxb-museum.de). U1, U8 Kottbusser Tor. **Open** *noon-6pm Tue-Fri; 10am-6pm Sat, Sun.* **Admission** *free.* **Map** *p144 Q9.*

A council-run museum about Kreuzberg's turbulent history. The permanent exhibition catalogues both the area's Turkish immigrant heritage and its radical political legacy.

Museum der Dinge

Oranienstrasse 25 (9210 6311, www.museumderdinge.de). U1, U8 Kottbusser Tor. **Open** *noon-7pm Mon, Thur-Sun.* **Admission** *€6; €4 reductions. No cards.* **Map** *p144 Q9.*

On the top floor of a typical Kreuzberg apartment block, the 'Museum of Things' contains every kind of small object you could imagine in modern design from the 19th century onwards – from hairbrushes and fondue sets to beach souvenirs and Nazi memorabilia. It's not a musty collection but a sleek and minimalist space organised by themes such as 'yellow and black' or 'functional vs kitsch', rather than by era or type, so that the 'things' appear in new contexts. It can get a little confused at times – hardly surprising, given the 20,000 objects – but it's a fascinating place. There's a great shop too.

Restaurants & cafés

Bar Raval €€

Lübbener Strasse 1 (5316 7954, www.barraval.de). U1 Görlitzer Bahnhof. **Open** *6-11pm Mon-Thur, Sun; 6pm-midnight Fri, Sat.* **Map** *p144 S9* ❷ *Spanish*

Bar Raval, owned by actor Daniel Brühl and restaurateur Atilano González, features traditional Spanish tapas dining in a contemporary setting. The open-plan kitchen serves classics, including salt-cod fritters, tortilla and succulent bellota ham. The regional monthly specials feature the likes of Valencian monkfish in paprika sauce or Basque veal cheeks in red wine.

Burgermeister €

Oberbaumstrasse 8 (2388 3840, www.burgermeister.de). U1 Schlesisches Tor. **Open** *11am-3am Mon-Thur; 11am-4am Fri; noon-4am Sat noon-3am Sun.* **No cards.** **Map** *p144 S9* ❸ *Burgers*

The hollowed-out remains of an old public toilet under the tracks of the U1 serve as the kitchen for this popular burger joint. A small glasshouse is erected in winter for people to fuel up on a cheeseburger and the famous chilli fries before (or after) clubbing. You might have to queue to get in. **Other location** Skalitzer Strasse 136, Kreuzberg.

Il Casolare €

Grimmstrasse 30 (6950 6610). U1, U8 Kottbusser Tor. **Open** *noon-midnight daily.* **No cards.** **Map** *p144 Q10* ❹ *Pizza*

Italian punks opened this pizzeria, which explains all the old NoFX tour posters adorning the walls. It's now a small chain, but the Kreuzberg branch is still the best, with outdoor terrace seating on Planüfer overlooking the canal. Service can be brusque, but the thin, crispy pizza bases are great. **Other locations** Il Ritrovo, Gabriel-Max-Strasse 2, Friedrichshain (2936 4130); I Due Forni, Schönhauser Allee 12, Prenzlauer Berg (4401 7333).

Cocolo €

Paul-Lincke Ufer 39-40 (9833 9073, www.kuchi.de). U1, U8 Kottbusser Tor. **Open** *noon-11pm Mon-Sat; 6-11pm Sun.* **No cards.** **Map** *p144 Q10* ❺ *Japanese*

This ramen bar sparked Berlin's on-going obsession with bone broth and expanded from a tiny bar in Mitte to this spacious branch by the canal in Kreuzberg. All the classic ramen styles are served, but the cognoscenti always pick *tonkotsu*: the pork stock is kicked up to a piggy 11/10 by the addition of liquor derived from boiling bones, collagen and fat for hours. It's then topped

The Turkish Capital

From Gastarbeiter *to German citizens*

Turkish food is a Berlin staple; in fact, Berliners maintain that the döner kebab, served in a Turkish flatbread to increase portability, was 'invented' in the city. A number of people lay claim to this stroke of culinary genius, but it is most often attributed to the late Mehmet Aygun, founder of Kreuzberg's Hasir restaurant chain, who definitely profited most from the innovation. But Turkish culture stretches well beyond street food. Berlin is home to the world's largest Turkish community outside Turkey, concentrated in the neighbourhoods of Kreuzberg and Neukölln. The combination of Turkish families living side by side with punks and squatters has created unique communities and culture in these areas. The sound of *Turkendeutsche*, the hybrid language of the immigrant population, fills the air around Oranienstrasse, while Turkish–German rappers such as Cartel and Azziza-A spit lyrics on bar stereos. The weekly Turkischer Markt (*see p171*) on the Maybachufer in Neukölln showcases the Turks' more traditional side, while Turkish gay nights at nightclub SO36 (*see p246*) reveal a corresponding cosmopolitanism. Berlin's homegrown Turkish football club, Türkiyemspor, is also fêted as a model of integration.

However, this meeting of cultures has had a difficult history and faces increased challenges in the present. The fast flow of immigration began in 1961 as a direct consequence of the building of the Berlin Wall. East German workers were cut off from jobs in the West, so thousands of *Gastarbeiter* ('guest workers') were recruited from Turkey to provide cheap labour. The West German authorities proved to be ungracious hosts. The 'guest workers' were considered no more than a temporary necessity, and the Nationality Act (or 'Blood Law') of 1913, which based German citizenship on heredity, meant that no person born of Turkish parents could be granted a German passport. The Turkish community thus remained apart from mainstream society for many decades. As recently as 2004, a report found that up to 60 per cent of children in Kreuzberg nursery schools couldn't speak a single word of German.

Popular antagonism peaked in 1990, amid fears that large numbers of foreign settlers would destabilise Germany's national identity and hinder a successful reunification. The then-Chancellor, Helmut Kohl, declared that Germany was 'not a land of immigration', and some scandalous acts of anti-immigrant violence happened around this time. Attitudes softened in the years following reunification, and, in 2001, a new law granted citizenship to any child born on German soil, provided their parents had been legally resident for at least eight years. However, tensions flared again in 2010, when a book criticising multiculturalism, by ex-senator Thilo Sarrazin, became a national bestseller, with Sarrazin accused of Islamophobia and racism.

More recently, the influx of refugees from Syria and other war-torn parts of the Middle East that resulted from Chancellor Angela Merkel's well-intentioned open-door policy has further fuelled Islamophobia. The rise of the far-right populist AfD (Alternative for Deutschland) in the 2017 general election and comments in 2018 by the interior minister, Horst Seehofer, that 'Islam does not belong in Germany' have destabilised the situation not only for newcomers but also for long-term Muslim residents. What's more, Turkey's involvement in the Syria conflict has inflamed tensions between Turkish and Kurdish groups in Germany.

While Berlin is not free from far-right rallies and marches, these are always dwarfed by opposing counter-demonstrations. In May 2018, a 5,000-strong AfD rally was met by over 20,000 protestors, including 100 clubs who participated in a 'Bass away the AfD' demonstration: DJs played from boats and floats along the Spree, drowning out the AfD's speeches beneath techno and revelry. This characteristic Berlin response to racism and division rings a hopeful note as the city adapts to the new wave of migrants seeking safety and stability here.

KREUZBERG & TREPTOW

with a soft-boiled egg, pickled ginger, crispy seaweed, slices of roast pork and braised sweet pork belly. **Other location** Gipsstrasse 3, Mitte (2838 6622).

Doyum Grillhaus €-€€

*Admiralstrasse 36 (6165 6127). U1, U8 Kottbusser Tor. **Open** 7am-midnight daily. **No cards**. Map p144 Q10* ⑥ *Turkish*

One of the best *ocakbasi* (Turkish grillhouses) in Kotti is somehow hidden in plain sight.

Tourists flock to the overrated Hasir, but the Turkish locals come to this beautifully tiled dining room for a plate of *iskender* kebab smothered in yoghurt sauce, or succulent minced lamb *adana*. No alcohol allowed.

Figl €€

*Urbanstrasse 47 (7229 0850, www.gasthaus-figl.de). U7, U8 Hermannplatz. **Open** 6pm-midnight daily. **No cards**. Map p144 Q11* ⑦ *Pizza*

Figl occupies a former *Kneipe* (pub) and has kept the beautiful original fittings: the dark wood bar, a giant ceramic coal heater and, best of all, a two-lane skittle alley in the basement. The menu is based around beefed-up *Flammkuchen*: Alsatian flatbread usually topped with crème fraiche, smoked bacon and red onion. Here, they use the stone oven to full effect, putting Tyrolean flavours (blood sausage, ham, apple and *Bergkäse*) on what is more like a pizza base, as well as offering Italian toppings of artichoke, anchovies, taleggio or plain marinara.

❤ Five Elephant €€
Reichenberger Strasse 101 (9608 1527, www. fiveelephant.com). U1 Görlitzer Bahnhof. Open 8.30am-7pm Mon-Fri; 10am-7pm Sat, Sun. No cards. Map p144 S10 ⑧ *Café*

You can feel the love at this café and roastery run by a charming Austro-American couple: she bakes the cakes; he roasts the beans. There's a selection of traditional cakes and tarts, but the Philadelphia cheesecake is transcendental: a wafer-thin layer of spice is all that separates the custardy interior from the velvety top. No WiFi, so bring a book if you plan to stay a while.

❤ Hamy Café-Foodstore €
Hasenheide 10 (6162 5959, www.hamycafe. com). U7, U8 Hermannplatz. Open noon-midnight daily. No cards. Map p144 Q11 ⑨ *Vietnamese*

Don't panic if there's no room here: get others to budge up and share their table, or wait – service is so speedy it won't take long. There are three specials a day, all priced at €4.90: glass noodle salad with octopus, perhaps, or a golden chicken curry. Tofu can be substituted

for meat or fish. Alcohol is served, but you may prefer to skip the beer in favour of fresh lime juice or lassi.

Henne €
Leuschnerdamm 25 (614 7730, www.henne-berlin.de). U1, U8 Kottbusser Tor. Open 5pm-midnight Tue-Sun. No cards. Map p144 Q8 ⑩ *German*

There's just one thing to order at Henne: half a crispy fried chicken. The only decisions you need to make after that are whether you want cabbage or potato salad, and which beer to go for (try the Franconian Landbier). Check out the letter over the bar from JFK, regretting missing dinner here. The leafy beer garden is pleasant in summer.

Horvath €€€
Paul-Lincke-Ufer 44A (6128 9992, www. restaurant-horvath.de). U1, U8 Kottbusser Tor. Open 6.30-10pm Wed-Sun. Map p144 Q10 ⑪ *Contemporary German*

Operating outside the usual Berlin luxury hotel system, Austrian chef Sebastian Frank gained a Michelin star in 2011 at this canalside restaurant. Enjoy a tasting menu of typical rustic German ingredients transformed through novel techniques: onion, pigeon and kohlrabi, or sturgeon, rib and celery, are charred, abstracted and perfectly plated. The Austrian wine list is excellent. Booking advised.

Jolesch €€
Muskauer Strasse 1 (612 3581, www. jolesch.de). U1 Görlitzer Bahnhof. Open 11.30am-midnight Mon-Fri, Sun; 5pm-midnight Sat. Map p144 R9 ⑫ *Austrian*

All a proper *Wiener Schnitzel* (made with veal) requires is a slice of lemon and a side of potato and cucumber salad to cut through the fat. The classics here are undisputedly good but are complemented by a chef's menu of seasonal and often adventurous dishes, such as venison with quince, or hay-smoked lamb's tongue. For dessert, share a plate of *Kaiserschmarrn*; the fluffy, eggy pancake with plum sauce was an imperial favourite.

KaffeeBar Jenseits des Kanals €

Graefestrasse 8 (no phone, www.kaffeebar-berlin.com). U8 Schönleinstrasse. **Open** *7.30am-7pm Mon-Fri; 9.30am-7pm Sat, Sun.* **No cards. Map** *p144 Q10* ⑬ *Café*

Finally, Graefekiez gets a well-pulled espresso. Freshly baked cakes, panini and croissants make loitering at this comfy café most enjoyable, as does the almost over-the-top avocado eggs benedict.

❤ Lode & Stijn €€€

Lausitzer Strasse 25 (6521 4507, www.lode-stijn.de). U1 Görlitzer Bahnhof. **Open** *6-10pm Tue-Sat.* **Map** *p144 R10* ⑭ *Contemporary*

A contemporary dining experience and part of a wave of chic bistro restaurants sweeping Berlin. Lode & Stijn offers a tri-weekly rotating seasonal set menu with a no-nonsense approach to cooking (the beef *Bitterballen* are to die for). A shorter version of the set menu is served at the bar. Booking is recommended.

Max Und Moritz €€

Oranienstrasse 162 (6951 5911, www.maxundmoritzberlin.de). U8 Moritzplatz **Open** *from 5pm daily.* **No cards. Map** *p144 P9* ⑮ *German*

Those craving meat-heavy comfort food will be left groaning after a visit to this traditional beerhouse, which has been serving hearty German dishes, just like *Oma* used to make, since 1902. Service can take a while, so order a bottle of *Rotwein* and take in the candlelit atmosphere, safe in the knowledge that when your food does arrive, it will be delicious and plentiful.

Mo's King of Falafel €

Urbanstrasse 68 (7407 3666). U7, U8 Hermannplatz. **Open** *1-11pm daily.* **No cards. Map** *p144 Q11* ⑯ *Imbiss*

It's actually Mo's wife who forms the little chickpea balls at this hole-in-the-wall joint. Enormous wraps stuffed with freshly fried falafel and salad cost just a few euros. Expect to queue in summer months.

❤ Olivio Pasta Bar €

Schönleinstrasse 29 (6110 1695). U8 Schönleinstrasse. **Open** *noon-11pm daily.* **Map** *p144 Q10* ⑲ *Italian*

This hole-in-the-wall Italian is easy to overlook from the outside, but it's worth seeking out for its authentic pasta dishes and for pizza that's handmade to order and generously laden with fresh ingredients: for €6, it simply cannot be beaten. Skip the wholewheat option (which is dry) and stick to the superb original. Grab a table outside if the weather allows, as the indoor seating area is cramped.

Parker Bowles €€€

Prinzenstrasse 85D (5527 9099, www.parker-bowles.com). U8 Moritzplatz. **Open** *Delicatessen 9am-6pm Mon-Sat. Restaurant 9am-6pm Mon-Wed; 9am-late Thur-Sat.* **Map** *p144 P9* ㉑ *Modern European*

Cheekily named by the team behind the Prince Charles club next door (geddit?; *see p245*), this low-key yet elegant supper club serves an eclectic menu of vegetarian, paleo, meat and fish specialities, many sourced from local producers. Chef Sebastian Pfister tends towards the surreal in his juxtapositions and flavours – horseradish ice-cream, anyone? – but Parker Bowles is a welcome and delightful addition to the Aufbauhaus complex at Moritzplatz.

Richard €€€

Köpenicker Strasse 174 (4920 7242, www.restaurant-richard.de). U1 Görlitzer Bahnhof. **Open** *7pm-midnight Tue-Sat.* **No cards. Map** *p144 R9* ㉒ *Fine dining*

Headed up by Swiss-born painter turned chef Hans Richard, this beautifully decorated dining room claims to 'look to Paris' for inspiration for its tasting menus. One menu is, refreshingly, vegetarian, even if distinctly un-Parisian.

St Bart's €€€

Graefestrasse 71 (4075 1175, www.stbartpub.com). U8 Schönleinstrasse. **Open** *Bar 4pm-midnight Mon-Thur, Sun; noon-midnight Fri, Sat. Kitchen 6-10pm Mon-Thur, Sun; noon-3pm, 6-10pm Fri, Sat.* **Map** *p144 Q10* ㉔ *Gastropub*

This surprising little gastropub serves up a sumptuous feast of simple yet powerful flavours. The menu features the likes of burnt Jerusalem artichokes, green asparagus, lentils and goats cheese and heavenly buttermilk fried chicken. Everything comes paired with home-made sauces, and the booze menu is unpretentiously priced.

Weltrestaurant Markthalle €€

*Pücklerstrasse 34 (617 5502, www.
weltrestaurant-markthalle.de). U1 Görlitzer
Bahnhof. **Open** noon-late daily. **Map** p144
R9* 27 *German*

This unpretentious *Schnitzel* restaurant and
bar, with chunky tables and wood-panelled
walls, is popular with locals and big groups.
Breakfast is served until 4pm, lunch specials
from noon, while dinner brings such hearty
dishes as wild boar and red snapper. It's also
fun just to sit at the long bar and sample the
selection of grappas. After dinner, see what's
on downstairs at the Auster Club.

Zola Pizza €

*Paul-Lincke-Ufer 39-40 (01514 3596561
mobile). U8 Kottbusser Tor. **Open** noon-10pm
daily. **No cards**. **Map** p144 Q10* 30 *Pizza*

A drop-in Neapolitan-style pizza joint hidden
away behind Concierge Coffee (also a must
try) by the Landwehrkanal. The enormous
wood-burning oven is an arresting centrepiece, and 90 seconds is all the sourdough
crust needs to be perfectly charred and
bubbling.

Bars & pubs

▶ *There are some great LGBT bars in
Kreuzberg; whatever your persuasion, don't
miss Barbie Deinhoff's (see p231).*

❤ Bei Schlawinchen

*Schönleinstrasse 34 (no phone). U8
Schönleinstrasse. **Open** 24hrs daily.
No cards. **Map** p144 Q10* 1

This dive bar situated just off Kottbusser
Damm is a unique example of a Berlin
Kneipe (pub), with its bizarre decorations
of dolls, old bicycles and instruments. High
unemployment in the neighbourhood means
that it's usually rammed all day, with rowdy
characters propping up the bar or hammering
away at the table football. Naturally, the beer
is both cheap and plentiful. Rumour has it,
they haven't closed since 1978...

DasHotel Bar

*Mariannenstrasse 26a (8411 8433, www.
dashotel.org). U8 Kottbusser Tor. **Open**
4pm-late daily. **No cards**. **Map** p144 Q9* 2

Das Hotel occupies some attractive old
altbau buildings, with an ice-cream parlour,
brasserie, bar and dive club – pretty much
everything except for actual hotel rooms.
The bar is all candles and old pianos, and a
Spanish DJ gets the downstairs dancefloor
going on weekends. There are some 'secret'
rooms to rent – phone or email for details.

Markthalle Neun *p160*

John Muir

*Skalitzerstrasse 51 (0174 746 2881 mobile,
www.johnmuirberlin.com). U1 Görlitzer
Bahnhof. **Open** 6pm-late Mon-Sat. **No
cards**. **Map** p144 R9* 4

This bar aims to bring a Brooklyn flavour to
Kreuzberg 36, with its mounted trophy heads
and red-brick walls. It's craft beer night on
Mondays, and the experimental cocktail
menu changes monthly, featuring whimsical
names such as Black Beer'd (cognac, black
beer, lime, orange and bitters).

❤ Marques Bar

*Graefestrasse 92 (6162 5906). U8
Schönleinstrasse. **Open** 7pm-late daily.
No cards. **Map** p144 Q10* 5

Below a rather average Spanish restaurant
is this 1920s time-capsule of a cocktail
bar, where the decor is suitably solid and
mahogany. A host takes you to an available
table and asks for your preferred 'flavour
profile' (ie what kind of drink you usually
like). Then the bar staff do their magic,
working with hundreds of booze varieties
(plus over 30 tonics), vintage glassware and
fist-sized rocks of ice.

❤ Schwarze Traube

*Wrangelstrasse 24 (2313 5569). U1 Görlitzer
Bahnhof. **Open** 7pm-late daily. **No cards**.
Map p144 R9* 6

In the know
Schwarzlicht Minigolf

Situated beneath the Görlitzer Park café are five rooms of neon mini-golf (www.indoor-minigolf-berlin.de). The UV psychedelic extravaganza element is a little cheesy, but it's good fun for groups. Bear in mind that Görlitzer Park is frequented by overzealous drug dealers after dark; avoid passing through alone.

masterpiece *The Exterminating Angel*, in which a group of bourgeois worthies find themselves inexplicably unable to leave a lavish dinner party. The smartly dressed waiting staff, glass-latticed ceiling and leather booths certainly evoke an old-world sensibility, but it's still accessibly priced.

Shops & services

Alimentari e Vini
Skalitzer Strasse 23 (611 4981, www.alimentari.de). U1, U8 Kottbusser Tor. **Open** *9am-8pm Mon-Fri; 9am-4pm Sat.* **Map** *p144 Q9* **❶** *Food & drink*

This well-established Italian delicatessen was one of the first places in Berlin to import goods direct from artisan producers. San Daniele hams, creamy burrata and fresh pastas are all stocked. **Other locations** Marheinekeplatz 15, Kreuzberg (6953 9793); Arminiusstrasse 2-4, Moabit (3983 5088).

❤ Hard Wax
Paul-Lincke-Ufer 44A (6113 0111, www.hardwax.de). U1, U8 Kottbusser Tor. **Open** *noon-8pm Mon-Sat.* **Map** *p144 Q10* **❹** *Books & music*

Up a staircase at the back of a Kreuzberg courtyard lies this vinyl mecca, famous for its flawless selection of dub, techno and reggae. It was opened by dub techno pioneers Basic Channel, and many of the city's biggest DJs (Marcel Dettmann, DJ Hell) started out by working here. Beware – it's infamous for its haughty service.

Kado
Graefestrasse 20 (6904 1638, www.kado.de). U8 Schönleinstrasse. **Open** *9.30am-6.30pm Tue-Fri; 9.30am-3.30pm Sat.* **No cards.** **Map** *p144 Q10* **❺** *Food & drink*

A mind-boggling selection of liquorice from all over the world is beautifully presented in row upon row of glass jars at Kado. All shapes, sizes and varieties are available.

This bar on a quiet backstreet shot to fame when the slight but magnificently bearded owner, Atalay Aktas represented Germany at the 2013 World Class Bartender of the Year final. Aktas describes his ideal ambience as 'noble trash'. It's all about the detail here – ask bar staff for a custom-made cocktail to suit your taste, or request a classic.

Tante Lisbeth
Muskauer Strasse 49 (6290 8742, www.pyonen.de/tantelisbeth). U1 Görlitzer Bahnhof. **Open** *4pm-late Mon-Fri; 2pm-late Sat, Sun.* **No cards.** **Map** *p144 R9* **❼**

For those wishing to give their lungs a break, this spacious bar has a separate smoking room, as well as a folksy granny-flat aesthetic; but hidden downstairs is the real reason to come: a 1970s bowling alley. Book it online and bring a group down to enjoy the wood-panelled clubhouse with original fittings. Make sure to order a *Herrengedeck* too – a 'gentlemen's menu' consisting of a beer and schnapps.

Würgeengel
Dresdener Strasse 122 (615 5560, www.wuergeengel.de). U1, U8 Kottbusser Tor. **Open** *7pm-late daily.* **No cards.** **Map** *p144 Q9* **❽**

It's a bit of a mouthful, but this sultry boozer is named after Luis Buñuel's absurdist movie

Modern Graphics

Kumru Kuruyemis
Wrangelstrasse 46 (3013 0216). U1 Schlesisches Tor. **Open** *10am-8.30pm Mon-Sat.* **No cards.** *Map p144 S9* **6** *Food & drink*

There are plenty of nut shops to feed the Turkish community's deep love of roasted sunflower seeds, pistachios and fried corn. But Kumru Kuruyemis is a step up, stocking unshelled salty almonds and *churchkhela*, a string of nuts dipped in grape must then dried like a sausage.

♥ Markthalle Neun
Eisenbahnstrasse 42-43 (610 734 73, www. markthalleneun.de). U1 Görlitzer Bahnhof. **Open** *General 8am-8pm daily. Market noon-6pm Fri; 10am-6pm Sat. Street food 5-10pm Thur.* **No cards.** *Map p144 R9* **9** *Market*

During the late 19th century, 14 municipal covered markets were opened to replace traditional outdoor markets and improve hygiene standards. Local residents saved this one from closure in 2009, filling it with stalls serving heritage veg and locally sourced meats. It's also home to the excellent Heidenpeters microbrewery and the Sironi bakery from Milan. Aligned with the Slow Food movement, the market hosts regular themed events, including the hugely popular and influential **Street Food** showcase on Thursday evenings (www.facebook.com/StreetFoodThursday) and **Cheese Berlin**, where'll you find a multitude of artisanal European cheeses.

♥ Modern Graphics
Oranienstrasse 22 (615 8810, www.modern-graphics.de). U1, U8 Kottbusser Tor. **Open** *11am-8pm Mon-Sat.* **Map** *p144 Q9* **10** *Books & magazines*

Shelves of European and alternative comics, plus graphic novels, anime, T-shirts and calendars. **Other location** Europa-Center, Tauentzienstrasse 9-12, Charlottenburg (8599 9054).

♥ Modulor
Prinzenstrasse 85 (690 360, www.modulor. de). U8 Moritzplatz. **Open** *9am-8pm Mon-Fri; 10am-6pm Sat.* **Map** *p144 P9* **11** *Art & craft supplies*

A paradise for the crafty, with everything laid out over several floors. There are rolls of synthetic materials for product designers or fashion students, but also more traditional art supplies – pencils, chalks, charcoals, oils and acrylics. Services include cutting, laser etching and tool rental.

♥ Motto
Skalitzer Strasse 68 (4881 6407, www. mottodistribution.com). U1 Schlesisches Tor. **Open** *noon-8pm Mon-Sat.* **Map** *p144 S9* **12** *Books & magazines*

Tucked away in a disused frame factory in a courtyard off Schlesisches Tor, Motto is Swiss by origin and Swiss in its super design-consciousness. Fanzines, back issues, artists' books, posters, rare print-runs and cult classics are spread in a come-hither way across a long central table.

♥ Overkill
Köpenicker Strasse 195A (6107 6633, www. overkillshop.com). U1 Schlesisches Tor. **Open** *11am-8pm Mon-Sat.* **Map** *p144 S9* **13** *Accessories*

At this urban culture hotspot, you'll find limited runs of Adidas, Asics and Nike shoes in unusual colours, as well as sprays, markers and caps for the budding street artist.

♥ Voo Store
Oranienstrasse 24 (6110 1750, www.vooberlin. com). U1, U8 Kottbusser Tor. **Open** *10am-8pm Mon-Sat.* **Map** *p144 Q9* **18** *Fashion*

The Voo concept store brings sleek fashions to an area usually associated with punkier looks. Expect well-crafted outerwear from minimal Swedish favourite Acne, classic New Balance sneakers, and a selection of accessories. At the in-store coffee bar, **Companion Coffee**, you can get a fine macchiato while perusing upmarket magazines such as *The Travel Almanac*.

TREPTOW

The canal and lack of U-Bahn keeps this large district just east of Kreuzberg relatively isolated. From Schlesisches Tor U-Bahn station, walk down Schlesische Strasse, where you'll see the vast murals by Italian street artist Blu: on the left, two figures representing West and East Berlin de-masking each other; on the right, a besuited man shackled in gold chains. Over the bridge is the canalside DJ bar **Club Der Visionaere** (*see p244*), open pretty much all hours in summer, while to the left is the **Arena Berlin** complex, which houses the

In the know
♥ **Badeschiff**

The **Badeschiff** (Eichenstrasse 4, 0162 545 1374, www.arena-berlin.de/badeschiff) is a former barge docked on the banks of the Spree that has been converted into a heated open-air swimming pool. The pool is open from May to September and a day ticket costs €5.50 (€2-€3 reductions). In winter, it becomes a covered sauna.

Badeschiff, a swimming pool suspended in the Spree (*see below* In the know). On the right is one of only three remaining GDR watchtowers, overlooking a former 'death strip' of the Wall that ran down the canal.

The grand tree-lined Puschkinallee with its 19th-century mansions neatly segues into the leafy **Treptower Park**, location of the **Sowjetisches Ehrenmal** (Soviet War Memorial; *see p162*). Slightly off the beaten track, the memorial gets fewer visitors than it deserves – it's easily the most impressive Communist monument in Berlin. Treptower Park covers a huge area and is worth exploring; combine your visit to the memorial with a stroll to the nearby *Karpfenteich* (carp pond) and a bike ride along the Spree to the charming **Insel der Jugend** (8096 1850, www.inselberlin.de), a tiny landscaped islet, connected to the mainland by Germany's first composite steel bridge, built in 1915. The wooded island has served various functions over the years, most recently as a GDR youth centre. It's now a lovely small park, with a bar/café that hosts puppet-theatre workshops and other family-friendly events, plus open-air raves in summer. The old Neukölln coat of arms is displayed on the bridge's tower. On a pleasant day it makes an agreeable detour.

Alternatively, continue along the dirt tracks, popular with joggers and mountain bikers, to one of Berlin's best-known secrets, the abandoned **Spreepark** (www.berliner-spreepark.de). A massively popular amusement park in GDR days, it sank into debt after the Wall fell. Now the rides are all overgrown and the ferris wheel creaks eerily in the wind – it's wonderfully atmospheric. Security is tight, but guided tours are available from the main gate (often booked up well in advance; check the websites). In early 2014 the site was purchased by the city who gave responsibility for developing the park to Grün Berlin. Their plans include restoring the 40-metre Ferris wheel and opening up a café by the Spree for tourists; however, this still seems a long way off.

Restaurants & cafés

♥ White Crow Café €

Bouchéstrasse 15 (no phone, www.facebook.com/blacksheepcafeberlin). S8, S9, S41, S42 Treptower Park. **Open** *8am-6pm Mon-Fri; 9am-6pm Sat; 9am-3pm Sun.* **Map** *p144 T10* ㉙ *Vegan*

Formerly known as the Black Sheep, this modern vegan café serves a selection of freshly made croissants, wraps and raw treats alongside speciality coffee from local Berlin establishments, The Barn and Passenger. It also serves the best *kombucha* in Berlin.

❤ Soviet Memorial (Sowjetisches Ehrenmal am Treptower Park)

Treptower Park (www.treptowerpark.de). S8, S9, S41, S42 Treptower Park. **Map** *p144 V11.*

This Soviet war memorial (one of three in Berlin) and military cemetery is tucked away in beautiful Treptower Park. Architect Yakov Belopolsky's design to commemorate the loss of 80,000 Soviet soldiers was unveiled just four years after World War II ended, on 8 May 1949, and its epic scale and brawny symbolism made it a war memorial for all East Germany. During the GDR era, the monument was part of the obligatory itinerary for Westerners during trips to the East, and it also played its part in installing reverence for the Soviet Union among East Germans. Parts of the monument are created from the marble of Hitler's demolished New Chancellery.

On entering, you're greeted by statues of two kneeling soldiers, and the view unfolds across a geometrical expanse flanked by 16 stone sarcophagi, one for each of the 16 Soviet republics, which mark the burial site of the 5,000 Soviet soldiers who died in the final Battle of Berlin in spring 1945. At the end is a 12-m (40-ft) statue of a Soviet soldier holding a rescued German child and a massive lowered sabre, a broken swastika crushed beneath his boot. It is claimed that this depicts the deeds of Sergeant of Guards Nikolai Masalov, who risked a hail of German gunfire to save the life of a three-year-old German girl. While the origins of the story are disputed, the symbolism cannot be lost on anyone: it's an arresting image, whether surrounded by foliage in summer, or bleak snow in winter. When you visit, don't be surprised to see flowers and miniature bottles of vodka inside the small memorial hall – even today visitors come to pay their respect to the fallen Soviets.

Shops & services

Vintage Berlin

*Karl-Kunger-Strasse 54 (5321 2305, www. vintageberlin.de). S8, S9, S41, S42 Treptower Park. **Open** noon-7pm Mon-Fri; 11am-4pm Sat. **Map** p144 T11* **🆗** *Vintage fashion*

These guys really know how to dress a window: colliding prints, wide collars and billowing '80s sleeves have never looked so chic. Like most vintage clothes shops, the selection favours women, but there are enough zig-zagging shirts and scratchy woollen jumpers to merit a rummage for men too.

KÖPENICK & AROUND

The name Köpenick is derived from the Slavonic *copanic*, meaning 'place on a river'. The old town, around 15 kilometres (nine miles) south-east of Mitte, stands at the confluence of the Spree and Dahme and, having escaped bombing, decay and development by the GDR, still maintains much of its 18th-century character. This is one of the most sought-after areas of East Berlin, with handsome shops, cafés and restaurants clustered around the old centre. With its historic buildings and extensive riverfront, it's a fine place for a Sunday afternoon wander.

The imposing **Rathaus** (town hall) is a good example of Wilhelmine civic architecture. It was here in 1906, two years after the building's completion, that Wilhelm Voigt, an unemployed cobbler who'd spent half his life in jail, dressed up as an army captain and ordered a detachment of soldiers to accompany him into the Treasury, where they emptied the town coffers. He instantly entered popular folklore. Carl Zuckmeyer immortalised him in a play as *Der Hauptmann von Köpenick* (Captain of Köpenick), and the Kaiser eventually pardoned him because he'd proven the absolute obedience of the Prussian soldiery. His theft is re-enacted every June during the Köpenicker summer festival.

Close by, on a man-made island, is the grand white complex of **Schloss Köpenick** (1677-90), with a medieval drawbridge, Renaissance gateway and Baroque chapel.

A couple of kilometres east of Köpenick, the village of **Friedrichshagen** has retained its independent character. The main street, Bölschestrasse, is lined with steep-roofed Brandenburg houses and ends at the shores of a large lake, the **Grosser Müggelsee**; boat tours are available. Friedrichshagen is particularly enjoyable when the **Berliner Burgerbräu**, a family-owned brewery

since 1869, throws open its gates for its annual summer celebration. Stalls line Bölschestrasse; the brewery lays on music, and people lounge about on the lakeshore with cold beers. The Bräustübl restaurant, next to the brewery, serves hearty Berlin cuisine.

Sights & museums

Schloss Köpenick

*Schlossinsel 1 (2664 24242, www.smb. museum/museen-und-einrichtungen/schloss-koepenick). S47 Spindlersfeld. **Open** Apr-Sept 11am-6pm Tue-Sun. Oct-Mar 11am-5pm Thur-Sun. **Admission** €6; €3 reductions.*

Furniture and decorative art pieces from the Kunstgewerbemuseum (Museum of Decorative Arts; *see p109*) are presented in a series of rooms arranged according to period (Renaissance, Baroque and rococo) beneath carefully restored ceiling paintings. There's also an exhibition on the history of the island, plus a riverside café.

Restaurants & cafés

Kid Creole €€

*Bölschestrasse 10, Friedrichshagen (6507 6680, www.kidcreole.de). S3 Friedrichshagen. **Open** 4pm-midnight daily. Cajun*

A leafy courtyard in forgotten Friedrichshagen is possibly the least likely setting for Kid Creole. This restaurant packs the flavours of Louisiana into traditional creole dishes and southern American comfort food. Come hungry and ready to choose between the likes of jambalaya, gumbo and cajun alligator served with a side of creamy sweet potato. Book ahead to avoid disappointment; it's a little on the small side.

Bars & pubs

❤ Biergarten Freiheit Fünfzehn

*Freiheit 15, Köpenick (6588 7825, www. freiheit15.com). S47 Spindlersfeld. **Open** Summer 2pm-late Mon-Fri; 11am-late Sat, Sun.*

When it's one of those glorious Berlin sunny days, and you've worked up a tan and a thirst lounging by the Müggelsee, don't trek straight back into town: head instead for Freiheit Fünfzehn. It offers the usual German pick-me-ups – beer and *Currywurst* – but its biggest draw is the large, open beer garden, dotted with deckchairs and tables overlooking the river Dahme. There are often music events and parties on weekend evenings, so head home early to avoid the more boisterous crowds.

Neukölln

Neukölln is, arguably, Berlin's hippest district. With a vibrant ethnic mix dominated by the Turkish community, it's also home to plenty of bohemians and artists. While gritty bars and pubs are giving way to boutiques and high-end eateries, gentrification is patchy and has yet to creep far beyond the Ringbahn, the S-Bahn line that encircles Berlin's inner districts. At its northernmost tip, the area hugging the canal is known as Kreuzkölln and is fertile ground for charming cafés and restaurants. Following Weserstrasse south-east takes you past living-room bars and cocktail joints towards the picturesque 18th-century 'village' of Rixdorf. Cross Karl-Marx-Strasse westwards and you'll be in Schillerkiez, another café and dining hotspot that is gateway to the vast expanse of Tempelhofer Feld.

❤ Don't miss

1 Tempelhofer Feld *p173*
Rent bikes to explore this decommissioned airport, now one of the largest urban parks in Europe.

2 Türkischer Markt *p171*
Street food meets handicrafts meet fruit and veg at this bustling market.

3 Rixdorf *p172*
This 18th-century bohemian village is an oasis of calm in the middle of the city.

4 Stadtbad Neukölln *p175*
Swim, sauna and steam in one of Europe's most beautiful and historic public baths.

5 Britzer Garten *p175*
Plenty of attractions here for the young and young at heart, including a windmill and a narrow-gauge railway.

Schmettau Statue in Hermannplatz

KREUZKÖLLN

The small strip bordering the canal just across from Kreuzberg was, until about 15 years ago, a quiet, predominantly working-class area with a large Turkish population. But these days you are as likely to hear English, French, Spanish, Swedish, Italian and Japanese as Turkish on the streets. The past decade has seen a restaurant and café boom, with many ventures led by the city's international new arrivals. Pull up a chair, sip a flat white and watch the young and hopeful living their Berlin dream.

Home to the lively **Türkischer Markt** and **Nowkoelln Flowmarkt**, the canalside Maybachufer is just across the Kottbusser Brücke and makes for a jolly stroll. From here, head south for espresso bars and vintage fashion, making sure to stop for some of the city's best pistachio ice-cream at **Fräulein Frost** – after school, it's overrun by sugar-high toddlers. Quiet by day, Weserstrasse comes alive at night and is conveniently adjacent to the Levantine food paradise that is **Sonnenallee**. These days, Sonnenallee is awash with shisha smoke and baklava, but 30 years ago it was home to a little-known East–West border crossing. Check out Leander Haussmann's controversial 1999 film comedy *Sonnenallee*, about youth culture in the East, which kicked off the whole *Ostalgie* trend – a rose-tinted view of more 'innocent' times in the GDR.

Restaurants & cafés

❤ Ankerklause €

Kottbusser Damm 104 (693 5649, www.anklerklause.de). U8 Schönleinstrasse. **Open** *4pm-late Mon; 10am-late Tue-Sun.* **No cards. Map** *p166 Q10* ❶ *International*

Café by day and bar by night, the nautically themed Ankerklause has firmly resisted the temptation to gentrify itself, despite its enviable location, with balcony seating hanging over the canal. The coffee is average, and you might want to avoid drinking too much of the house wine, Chateau Migraine, but the breakfasts and cakes are hearty and delicious. Give market days a skip (Tuesdays and Fridays), when it's inevitably rammed.

❤ Azzam €

Sonnenallee 54 (3013 1541). U7, U8 Hermannplatz. **Open** *8am-midnight daily.* **No cards. Map** *p166 R11* ❷ *Lebanese*

People flock from all over the city to sample Azzam's houmous, made fresh throughout the day. The grilled minced lamb is perfectly

NEUKÖLLN

Restaurants & cafés

❶ Ankerklause *p166*
❷ Azzam *p166*
❸ Berlin Burger International *p168*
❹ Café Brick *p168*
❺ Café Rix *p172*
❻ Café Vux *p172*
❼ Coda *p168*
❽ Chez Dang *p169*

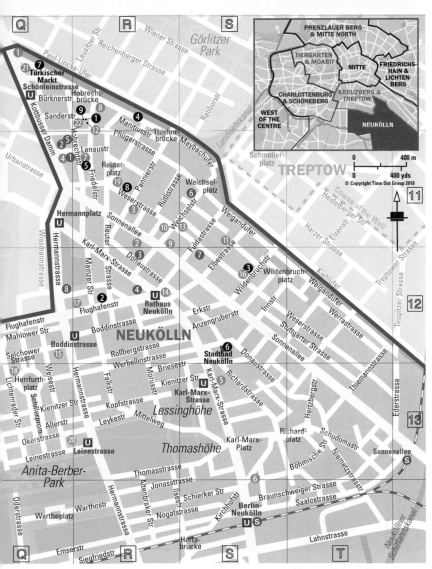

NEUKÖLLN

9 City Chicken *p169*
10 Dr To's *p169*
11 Eins 44 *p169*
12 Fräulein Frost *p169*
13 Gastón Tapas Bar *p169*
14 Imren Grill *p169*
15 Isla *p174*
16 K-Fetish *p169*
17 Lavanderia Vecchia *p174*
18 La Pecora Nera *p174*
19 Pizza a Pezzi *p169*
20 Rundstück Warm *p174*

21 Le Sainte Amour *p170*
22 Sing Blackbird *p170*

Bars & pubs

1 Galatea *p170*
2 Geist im Glas *p170*
3 Das Gift *p170*
4 Klunkerkranich *p174*
5 Mama *p170*
6 Nathanja & Heinrich *p171*
7 Tier *p171*
8 Villa Neukölln *p174*

Shops & services

1 Aura *p171*
2 Fantasiakulisse *p175*
3 Let Them Eat Cake *p171*
4 Nowkoelln Flowmarkt *p171*
5 Oye Kreuzkölln *p171*
6 Stadtbad Neukölln *p175*
7 Türkischer Markt *p171*
8 Vin Aqua Vin *p171*
9 Vintage Galore *p171*

seasoned, and the falafel a crunchy, sesame-speckled delight. You get a lot for your money too: each dish comes with raw veg, bitter olives, garlicky mayo or tahini sauce, and a basket of stacked pitta bread, which doubles as cutlery.

Berlin Burger International €
*Pannierstrasse 5 (0160 482 6505 mobile, www.berlinburgerinternational.com). U7, U8 Hermannplatz. **Open** noon-11pm Mon-Thur; noon-midnight Fri, Sat; noon-10pm Sun. **No cards**. **Map** p166 R11* ❸ *Imbiss*

A proper hole-in-the-wall. The pavement tables are constantly packed, whatever the season: BBI has punters hooked on stacked hamburgers, served with three types of salad, and with a small amount of lamb mince in the patty for extra succulence.

Café Brick €
*Lenaustrasse 1 (223 52595, www.brick-coffee.com). U7, U8 Hermannplatz; U8 Schönleinstrasse. **Open** 9am-10pm Mon-Thur; 9 am-midnight Fri; 10am-midnight Sat; 10am-10pm Sun. **Map** p166 Q11* ❹ *Café*

A welcome addition to this end of Kottbusser Damm, Café Brick makes the best coffee around. Small but beautiful, this cosy neighbourhood spot offers delicious and fairly priced cakes, bagels and sandwiches. With free WiFi, a laid-back vibe and a cheeky little cocktail list, you may find yourself spending a lot longer here than intended.

♥ Coda €€
*Friedelstrasse 47 (9149 6396, www.coda-berlin.com). U7, U8 Hermannplatz; U8 Schönleinstrasse. **Open** 7pm-late Tue, Thur-Sat. **Map** p166 R11* ❼ *Fine dining*

Offering a menu composed entirely of desserts and drinks, concept restaurant Coda is due a Michelin star any day now. Masterminded by chef René Frank, with an emphasis on the surprising and experimental, plates are artfully composed using the freshest ingredients. You'll find no unctuous, stodgy puddings here. Come by for the full blow-out six-course tasting menu, which pairs desserts with drinks (from €98). Or head to the bar for a single exquisite pud and a superlative cocktail.

Ankerklause *p166*

♥ Time to eat, drink & shop

Canal-side chilling
Ankerklause *p166*

Lebanese fast food
Azzam *p166*

Vintage finds
Aura *p171*, Sing Blackbird *p170*, Vintage Galore *p171*

Essential Kreuzkölln
Türkischer Markt *p171*

On-trend dining
Eins44 *p169*, Coda *p168*

Late-night drinking
Villa Neukölln *p174*, Geist im Glas *p170*

In the know
Getting around

Neukölln is well served by public transport, including the U7, U8 and various S-Bahn lines. Bus services include the notorious M41, a ride on which will immerse you in a perfect microcosm of the district's diverse communities.

Chez Dang €

Friedelstrasse 31 (5305 1205, www.chez-dang.com). U8 Schönleinstrasse. **Open** *11.30am-11.30pm Mon-Fri.* **No cards.** **Map** *p166 R10* ❽ *Vietnamese*

Steer clear of nearby Jimmy Woo and head to Chez Dang for a fresh and healthy Vietnamese fix. This family-run restaurant has pictures of the owner's grandparents on the walls, and the menu is far more inventive than the usual fast-food noodle joints.

City Chicken €

Sonnenallee 59 (624 8600). U7 Rathaus Neukölln. **Open** *8.30am-2am daily.* **No cards.** **Map** *p166 R11* ❾ *Rotisserie*

Kreuzberg's Hühnerhaus gets a run for its money at City Chicken, the scene of frenzied rotisserie action. There's only really one option: a silver platter with half a roast chicken, a pile of fries, garlicky mayonnaise, assorted pickles and some pitta to mop up the juices.

Dr To's €€

Weichselstrasse 54 (0152 16667022, www.dr-tos.de). U7 Rathaus Neukölln. **Open** *6pm-midnight Mon-Sat.* **No cards.** **Map** *p166 R11* ❿ *Asian*

Menus that describe their food as 'Asian' are often a bad sign in Berlin, but at Dr To's you'll find thoughtful and creative tasting plates, such as Japanese roast beef with fresh mint and pomegranate, and calamari salad with green beans, seaweed and miso. Portions are small so don't under order.

❤ Eins44 €€€

Elbestrasse 28/29 (6298 1212, www.eins44. com). U7 Rathaus Neukölln. **Open** *12.30-2.30pm, 7pm-midnight (last orders 10.30pm) Tue-Fri; 7pm-midnight (last orders 10.30pm) Sat.* **Map** *p166 S11* ⓫ *Fine dining*

Situated in a former schnapps factory, Eins44 pairs industrial design with fine dining. Proving there's a place for high-end eating in down-and-dirty Neukölln, the restaurant serves both lunch and dinner. Lunches tend towards the classic, while in the evenings you can select three (€46) or up to six courses (€73) from flexible menus featuring highly seasonal dishes, such as venison with shiitake mushrooms, radish and ginger, and prawns served with yellow beetroot and vermouth. Wine pairings are recommended.

Fräulein Frost €

Friedelstrasse 39 (9559 5521). U8 Schönleinstrasse. **Open** *2-8pm daily.* **No cards.** **Map** *p166 R11* ⓬ *Ice-cream*

The opening of the city's numerous ice-cream parlours is Berliners' favourite herald of

spring, and Fräulein Frost is one of the best. Sledges provide outside seating (and fun) for kids. Refresh yourself with their signature GuZiMi (cucumber, lemon, mint) or go all out with a velvety pistachio, a buttermilk orange, or Elvis's favourite, the divine Graceland.

Gastón Tapas Bar €-€€

Weichselstrasse 18 (01521 587 8084, www. facebook.com/gastontapasbar). U7 Rathaus Neukölln. **Open** *5.30pm-1am daily.* **No cards.** **Map** *p166 S11* ⓭ *Tapas*

A lively bar-restaurant on the corner of Weserstrasse. In summer, diners spill out onto tables on the street. Serving up tasty traditional Spanish tapas, and with a thoughtfully selected but fairly limited wine list, Gaston is popular with a young, international crowd. Worth booking ahead.

Imren Grill €

Karl-Marx-Strasse 75 (no phone, www. imren-grill.de). U7 Rathaus Neukölln. **Open** *9am-3am daily.* **No cards.** **Map** *p166 R12* ⓮ *Imbiss*

Part of a small chain, Imren Grill provides some of the best Turkish snacks in town. Lunch specials include baked fish with stew and rice – but first things first: order the classic *Döner im Brot* (kebab in toasted bread), with its stuffing of lamb grilled in neck fat, fresh salad, sesame sauce and chilli flakes. **Other locations** Boppstrasse 4, Kreuzberg; Boppstrasse 10, Kreuzberg; Badstrasse 46, Wedding; Müllerstrasse 134, Wedding.

K-Fetisch €

Wildenbruchstrasse 86 (6808 0362, www. kfetisch.blogsport.de). U7 Rathaus Neukölln. **Open** *10am-midnight Tue-Sat; 11am-10pm Sun.* **No cards.** **Map** *p166 S12* ⓰ *Café*

The fetish in question in coffee, and it is as good as you would expect at this lively leftist collective café. K-Fetisch provides atmosphere, board games, a great selection of pastries and snacks, including vegan options, and there's a laptop ban in about 80% of the premises. There's plenty of political reading material, if you feel so inclined, but sitting back and enjoying the coffee is a perfectly acceptable alternative to getting involved. Deservedly popular; you may have to wait for a table.

Pizza a Pezzi €

Weserstrasse 208 (6178 9619, www.pizza-a-pezzi.de). U7, U8 Hermannplatz. **Open** *10am-midnight daily.* **No cards.** **Map** *p166 R11* ⓳ *Pizza*

This blue-tiled pizzeria has plenty of seating in its large corner location. It offers excellent *al taglio* style pizzas – pre-made small squares finished to order in the oven – as well as standard whole pizzas, missable baked pastas and a fabulous tiramisu.

Le Saint Amour €
*Maybachufer 2 (6956 4600, lesaintamour. de). U8 Schönleinstrasse. **Open** 6.30pm-midnight Tue-Sat. **Map** p164 Q10* **㉑** *French*

Charming, unpretentious and ever so slightly kitsch, Le Saint Amour features a small menu of authentic Lyonnaise cuisine. Beloved by French locals who hail it the best of its kind in Berlin, Le Saint Amour manages to deliver reasonable prices, excellent service and delectable food in a cosy canal-side location. Try the frogs legs, lamb chops and the divine chocolate fondant. But, bear in mind that options for vegetarians are limited.

❤ Sing Blackbird €
*Sanderstrasse 11 (5484 5051, www.facebook. com/singblackbird). U8 Schönleinstrasse. **Open** 1-7pm daily. **No cards**. **Map** p166 R10* **㉒** *Café*

An instant hit on opening, this charming vegetarian café doubles up as an excellent vintage clothes shop, where you can bring in your clothes for trade or credit. The café does cakes and is also home to the cold-pressed Daily Dose juice company.

Türkischer Markt

Bars & pubs

Galatea
*Lenaustrasse 5 (6583 4970, www. facebook.com/GalateaWineBerlin). U7, U8 Hermannplatz. **Open** 7.30pm-1am Wed, Thur; 7.30pm-2am Fri, Sat. **Map** p166 Q11* **❶**

A Spanish wine bar, Galatea offers *pinchos* alongside a wine list featuring a rounded selection of Iberian wines. Friendly and popular with local music lovers, Galatea hosts live concerts a few nights a week. Expect an enthusiastic crowd and anything from swing to folk and jazz.

❤ Geist im Glas
*Lenaustrasse 27 (0176 5533 0450 mobile, www.facebook.com/geistimglas). U7, U8 Hermannplatz. **Open** 7pm-late Mon-Fri; 10am-late Sat, Sun. **No cards**. **Map** p166 Q11* **❷**

The space here is built up with wooden platforms, and there's great attention to detail in the decor, including Victorian curios laid into the bar and an esoteric toilet. The speciality is infused alcohols, shots of which are poured out of a giant bottle at the bar or mixed into house cocktails, such as the Geist Russian, a rich blend of vodka infused with

vanilla, cinnamon, Kahlúa and cream. The weekend brunch features *huevos rancheros*, chicken with waffles and fabulous bloody marys, but you'll need to get there early.

Das Gift
*Donaustrasse 119 (no phone, www.dasgift. de). U7, U8 Hermannplatz. **Open** 5pm-late Mon-Fri; noon-late Sat-Sun. **No cards**. **Map** p166 R12* **❸**

Owned by Barry Burns, a member of Scottish post-rock band Mogwai, Das Gift is his attempt at mashing a Glaswegian pub into a Berlin *Kneipe*. Lots of ales and single malts behind the bar, regular pie nights and a rowdy pub quiz go some way towards comforting the homesick Brit expats that frequent the place.

Mama
*Hobrechtstrasse 61 (0157 7386 4042 mobile, www.facebook.com/mamabarberlin). U7, U8 Hermannplatz. **Open** 7pm-late daily. **No cards**. **Map** p166 Q11* **❺**

Nearer to a grandmother in Neukölln years, Mama was one of the area's first bars to nail down the look with its GDR living-room furniture, intricate murals and sound system veering towards Balkan beats. The unpasteurised Svijany beer on tap is excellent.

Nathanja & Heinrich
Weichselstrasse 44 (no phone, www. nathanja-heinrich.de). U7 Rathaus Neukölln. Open 3pm-late Mon-Fri; 1pm-late Sat-Sun. No cards. Map p166 S11 **6**

Serving up a devastatingly good gin basil smash, Nathanja & Heinrich put equal effort into their beer selection. This beautiful bar – full of wood, mirrors and fresh flowers – hosts plenty of freelancers tapping at their MacBooks over coffee during the day. In the evenings, it's crowded with hipsters sipping mixed drinks late into the night.

Tier
Weserstrasse 42 (no phone, www.tier.bar). U7 Rathaus Neukölln. Open 7pm-late daily. No cards. Map p166 S12 **7**

Seen through the frosted windows, Tier's long bar could be a facsimile of Hopper's iconic *Nighthawks*. The vinyl collection sticks to the trusted classics, as does the cocktail menu, though there's a rotating experimental special. Large groups not permitted.

Shops & services

❤ Aura
Sanderstrasse 13 (178 148 4444 mobile, www. auraberin.com). Transport. Open 1-8pm Mon-Fri; noon-7pm Sat. Map p166 R10 **1** *Vintage fashion*

Set next to two other vintage shops (Vintage Galore and Sing Blackbird; *see opposite*), Aura has a back room bursting at the seams with a vast collection of vintage Japanese kimonos in jewel-like colours. The front room is devoted to vintage ladies' wear and accessories, including sunglasses. A good place for unusual finds and not over-priced.

Let Them Eat Cake
Weserstrasse 164 (6096 5095). U7 Rathaus Neukölln. Open 1-7pm Mon-Sat. Map p166 S12 **3** *Fashion/Gallery*

This Swedish vintage shop with an adjoining gallery space specialises in chunky 1990s clothing and designer jewellery.

Nowkoelln Flowmarkt
Maybachufer between Friedelstrasse and Pannierstrasse (no phone, www.nowkoelln. de). U8 Schönleinstrasse. Open Apr-Nov 10am-6pm every 2nd Sun. Closed Dec-Mar. No cards. Map p166 R10 **4** *Flea market*

This massively popular canalside flea market has grown considerably in recent years.

Plenty of local trendsters hawk vintage apparel, and there's a strong food section with smoked fish sandwiches, *Käsespätzle* and hot apple pie on offer. Note that the market doesn't operate over winter. **Other location** Prinzessinnengärten, Kreuzberg (no phone, www.kreuzboerg.de).

▶ *For details of the weekly Türkischer Markt at this location, see below.*

Oye Kreuzkölln
Friedelstrasse 49 (8937 2815, www.oye-records.com). U7, U8 Hermannplatz. Open 1-8pm Mon-Fri; 2-8pm Sat. Map p166 R11 **5** *Books & music*

The southern branch of Oye Records, this small shop packs in a quality pick of house, techno and bass vinyl. Big-name DJs often do in-store events. **Other location** Oderberger Strasse 4, Prenzlauer Berg (6664 7821).

❤ Türkischer Markt
Maybachufer between Kottbusser Damm and Hobrechtstrasse (no phone, www. tuerkenmarkt.de). U8 Schönleinstrasse. Open 11am-6.30pm Tue, Fri, Sat. No cards. Map p166 Q10 **7** *Market*

On Tuesdays and Fridays, the Maybachufer buzzes with traders selling fruit, veg, organic and artisanal produce and street food. On Saturdays, the groceries give way to crafts, jewellery, a German-only wine stand, plants and haberdashery. The market continues to be very much a local affair, and it's a great, if somewhat hectic, introduction to the neighbourhood. Once you've run the gamut of the market, you can relax with a beverage of choice and check out the buskers performing at the far end.

Vin Aqua Vin
Weserstrasse 204 (9405 2886, www. vinaquavin.de). U7, U8 Hermannplatz. Open 4pm-midnight Mon-Wed; 3pm-midnight Thur, Fri; 2pm-midnight Sat. No cards. Map p166 R11 **8** *Food & drink*

This wine bar and shop stocks an impeccable selection from all the trendiest regions (Ribera del Duero, Languedoc, Douro) and from plenty of small German vintners. Regular tasting events.

❤ Vintage Galore
Sanderstrasse 12 (6396 3338, www. vintagegalore.de). U8 Schönleinstrasse. Open 2-8pm Wed-Fri; noon-6pm Sat. Map p166 R10 **9** *Homewares*

Vintage Galore is one of the best places for authentic mid-century Danish furniture: it stocks everything from floor lamps to snack plates in the distinctive rounded teak style.

SCHILLERKIEZ & RIXDORF

As rents shot up in Kreuzkölln, and following the closure of Tempelhof Airport in 2008, the now-peaceful **Schillerkiez** quickly became recognised as one of Berlin's most desirable neighbourhoods. With leafy Herrfurthplatz at its heart, Schillerkiez stretches from Hermannstrasse in the east to the awesome **Tempelhofer Feld** (*see p173*) in the west. Much quieter than raucous Weserstrasse, it's an area where Spanish restaurateurs, Swedish fashion designers and English bar-owners throw in their lot with the Turkish kebab shops and betting parlours.

East of the busy shopping street of Karl-Marx-Strasse is the historic and charming village of **Rixdorf**, centred around Richardplatz. Buildings dating from the original early 18th-century Bohemian settlement include a blacksmith and farmhouse, as well as the older 15th-century Bethlehemskirche. There's even a horse-and-carriage business still in operation, and the square regularly holds traditional events including a Christmas craft market.

For a break from sightseeing and window-shopping, take a dip at the marvellous **Stadtbad Neukölln**.

Restaurants & cafés

Café Rix €-€€
Karl-Marx-Strasse 141 (686 9020, www.caferix.de). U7 Karl-Marx-Strasse. **Open** *9am-midnight Mon-Thur; 9am-1am Fri, Sat; 10am-midnight Sun.* **No cards.** **Map** *p166 S13* **5** *Café*

Hidden behind the noisy shopping street of Karl-Marx-Strasse is this oasis – a grand café housed in a former 19th-century ballroom. There's a lovely courtyard where you can enjoy a coffee and cake or the breakfast menu, which is served until 5pm.

Café Vux €
Wipperstrasse 14 (no phone, www.vux-berlin.com). U7, S41, S42, S45, S46, S47 Neukölln. **Open** *noon-7pm Wed-Sat; noon-6pm Sun.* **No cards.** **Map** *p166 S13* **6** *Café*

In the know
Picnic in the park

Just past the Leinestrasse U-Bahn stop and hidden down Jonasstrasse is the secluded baroque-style **Körnerpark**. Built on reclaimed land, it creates the wonderful illusion of being completely hidden from the rest of the city and makes for a perfect picnic spot.

Tempelhofer Feld

Main entrance at Herfurthstrasse and Oderstrasse (www.gruen-berlin.de/ tempelhofer-feld). U8 Boddinstrasse. **Open** *dawn-dusk daily.* **Admission** *free. Tours €12; reductions from €6.* **Map** *p166 O12.*

Famous for its Nazi and Cold War history, Tempelhof Airport ceased operation in 2008. Now you can stroll down the runways where World War II Stuka dive-bombers took off and where, during the Berlin Airlift of 1948 when the Soviets blockaded West Berlin, the Western Powers landed supplies for the city's 2.5 million residents in one of the greatest feats in aviation history. Today, the 368-hectare open space of runways and grasslands is much enjoyed by – among others – walkers, kite-surfers, cyclists, runners, skaters and goshawks. There are designated sections for dogs to run free, basketball courts, a baseball field, beer gardens and even small allotments where Berliners can grow their own veg. Few experiences can compare with zooming down the central runway on two wheels, filling your lungs with the famously inspiring 'Berliner Luft'. However, the future of the *Feld* is far from secure. Berlin needs money, and developing at least part of the land would bring much-needed funds to the city's coffers. Controversially, Berliners voted against building on this vast space in a 2014 city-wide referendum, despite promises of affordable housing and a new library. In 2015, the airport buildings became temporary shelter for up to 3,000 refugees seeking sanctuary in Germany; the numbers have since dwindled to a few hundred. By 2018 it was unclear whether the huge hangars would return to hosting concerts and trade fairs, such as fashion extravaganza Bread & Butter, or be re-purposed to house a proposed creative district, visitor centre, rooftop gallery and a museum about the Berlin Airlift. One thing is certain, however: Berliners won't be giving up this grand open-air playground without a fight.

▶ *The park has more than 10 entrances spread across the districts of Neukölln, Kreuzberg and Tempelhof. These can be found on the park's website, under 'visitor information' alongside detailed opening hours. A comprehensive tour of the airfield can be booked at touren@berlinkompakt.net.*

NEUKÖLLN

This Brazilian-run café brings to mind a twee tea parlour. Enjoy incredible vegan versions of classics such as black forest gateau and coconut cheesecake.

Isla €
*Hermannstrasse 37 (no phone, www. facebook.com/Islacoffeeberlin). U8 Boddinstrasse. **Open** 7.30am-6pm Mon-Fri; 9am-6pm Sat, Sun. **Map** p166 Q12* ⑮ *Café*

A delicious brunch, lunch and coffee outfit, Isla has a zero-waste policy, a cool, minimalist interior and friendly waiting staff. Try the pea, houmous, spinach and cheese sandwiches. Weekdays are popular with the freelancer crowd, but the weekend laptop ban leaves space for brunching. In 2018, the staff were also hosting pop-up dining events.

Lavanderia Vecchia €€
*Flughafenstrasse 46 (6272 2152, www. lavanderiavecchia.de). U8 Boddinstrasse. **Open** noon-3pm, 7.30pm-midnight Tue-Fri; 7.30pm-midnight Sat. **Map** p166 R12* ⑰ *Italian*

This cute Italian joint has white linen strung along the ceiling, as a nod to the building's original role as a laundry house. Tricky to locate, it's in a courtyard set back from the street. There's just one set menu for dinner (booking essential), costing €65 a head including wine. Changing weekly, it features lots of classic antipasti (*vitello tonnato*, squid salad, sardines), followed by a pasta starter and homely mains, accompanied by a choice of wines from the Sabina region of Italy. Lunch is a more affordable affair.

La Pecora Nera €€
*Herrfurthplatz 6 (6883 2676, www. pecoraberlin.de). U8 Boddinstrasse. **Open** 6pm-late Tue-Sun. **No cards. Map** p166 Q13* ⑱ *Italian*

Schillerkiez really upped its restaurant game with the arrival of La Pecora Nera, a charming Venetian place with an authentic menu and excellent choice of wines. The speciality is *bigoli*, a buckwheat pasta peculiar to the Veneto region. There are fish specials on Fridays.

Rundstück Warm €
*Okerstrasse 40 (5485 6849). U8 Leinestrasse. **Open** 6-11pm Mon-Fri; 4-11pm Sat, Sun. **No cards. Map** p166 Q13* ⑳ *Burgers*

Headed by an excellent Guatemalan chef, this little burger place adjoins a larger bar next door. Spanish tiles line the wall, and charred *padrón* peppers are available as a side to the juicy burgers, as are home-made chilli sauces of varying intensity.

Bars & pubs

Klunkerkranich
*Karl-Marx-Strasse 66 (no phone, www. klunkerkranich.de). U7 Rathaus Neukölln. **Open** 4pm-2am; Wed-Fri; noon-2am Sat, Sun. **No cards. Map** p166 R12* ④

This rooftop bar with a view over the city is tricky to find but worth the effort. It's set on top of the Neukölln Arcaden shopping centre; to get there take a lift to the fifth-floor parking lot and walk up. Extremely popular in summer, Klunkerkranich hosts regular events; check out the website to see what's on. When DJs are playing, expect a cover charge of €5.

♥ Villa Neukölln
*Hermannstrasse 233 (6272 8948, www. villaneukoelln.de). U8 Boddinstrasse. **Open** 4.30pm-2.30am Mon, Tue; 4.30pm-4am Wed, Thur; 2.30pm-4am Fri-Sun. **No cards. Map** p166 Q12* ⑧

A much-loved institution, Villa Neukölln is the definition of shabby-chic. With two front rooms, one a haven for smokers, and plenty of street-side seating in good weather, the real draw is the old ballroom out back. Part the velvet curtains to find yourself in a different era. Hosting swing nights, concerts and dancing lessons, the Villa scores high on character and low on attitude. Pop in for a drink or check the website to see what's on.

Britzer Garten

Shops & services

Fantasiakulisse

Flughafenstrasse 32 (0178 335 7354 mobile, www.fantasiakulisse.de). U8 Boddinstrasse. **Open** *10am-6pm Mon-Fri; or by appointment.* **No cards.** **Map** *p166 R12* ❷
Gifts & souvenirs

Flughafenstrasse is junk-shop central, and Fantasiakulisse is a particular treasure chest, rammed full of the eccentric owner's film memorabilia, theatre props and mannequin collection.

❤ Stadtbad Neukölln

Ganghoferstrasse 3 (682 4980, www. berlinerbaeder.de/baeder/stadtbad-neukoelln). U7 Rathaus Neukölln. **Open** *sauna 10am-10.30pm Mon-Sun; pool varied Mon-Sun.* **Admission** *sauna from €16, reductions €13. Pool from €3.50, reductions €2.* **No cards.** **Map** *p166 S12* ❻

Built for Berlin's workers and first opened in 1914, Stadtbad Neukölln is a jewel. Architect Reinhold Kiehl drew inspiration from the ancient thermal baths of classical Rome, and the two large pools and assortment of saunas, steam rooms and plunge pools feature statues of Greek gods, pillars, mosaics, fountains, cupolas and a café-bar. Splashing about in such palatial surroundings is an unforgettable experience. While the changing rooms are basic, the sauna complex, is excellent, and though they're not quite fit for serious lane swimming, Stadtbad Neukölln's two pools are perfect for families and recreational swimmers. Check the hours on the website before showing up, though, since Berlin's pools are infamous for last-minute schedule changes.

DEEP NEUKÖLLN

In years to come this area may become a part of the city to watch, but, at present, there's not a lot to draw you past Berlin's Ringbahn into what you may hear referred to as 'Deep Neukölln', an area made up of districts Britz, Buckow and Rudow. Still, for fans of architecture or families looking for some respite from the city, there are a couple of worthwhile attractions. Heading far south into Britz, you'll find **Hufeisensiedlung** (Lowise-Reuter-Ring, U7 Parchimer Allee), a vast housing estate that is one of Berlin's six modernist estates to be listed as a UNESCO World Heritage Site. Built in the late 1920s by Bruno Taut and Martin Wagner with some of the Garden City movement's ideals, the large horseshoe-shaped complex contains 1,200 flats overlooking a large green space. Many of the flats retain their original Bauhaus fittings and distinctive brightly coloured doors. Also in Britz, the **Britzer Garten** (www.gruen-berlin.de) is perfect for small children. The immaculately manicured gardens with their once-futuristic architecture look like something out of the *Teletubbies*, and there are farm animals, playgrounds, a narrow-gauge railway, a working 19th-century windmill and plenty of food and drink options.

Charlottenburg & Schöneberg

The old heart of West Berlin runs all the way from the Tiergarten to Spandau, from Tegel Airport in the north to wealthy, residential Wilmersdorf in the south. Often derided as staid and stagnant in comparison to its edgier eastern neighbours, Charlottenburg is undeniably bourgeois – the fur coat/small dog quotient is high – but it's far from boring. As well as charming hotels and lovely squares, it boasts the magnificent Schloss Charlottenburg and the Kurfürstendamm shopping street as well as some odd seedy little corners. It's also where you'll find department store KaDeWe, Berlin's answer to Harrods. East of Wilmersdorf is Schöneberg, also well-heeled and residential. Berlin's long-established gay scene is focused on its northern reaches.

❤ **Don't miss**

1 KaDeWe *p54*
Forget the other mall upstarts, there's only one KaDeWe.

2 Berlin by boat *p186*
Float along the Spree from the Schlossbrücke.

3 Schloss Charlottenburg *p187*
The palace gardens have been restored to their Baroque glory.

4 Thai Park *p189*
Bangkok meets Berlin in the Preussenpark.

5 Kaiser-Wilhelm-Gedächtnis-Kirche *p181*
Nicknamed the 'Hollow Tooth', this bombed-out church is a reminder of the devastation of war.

6 Story of Berlin *p182*
A child-friendly museum telling the city's turbulent tale.

7 Museum Berggruen *p187*
An outstanding collection of 20th-century art.

Kaiser-Wilhelm-Gedächtnis-Kirche

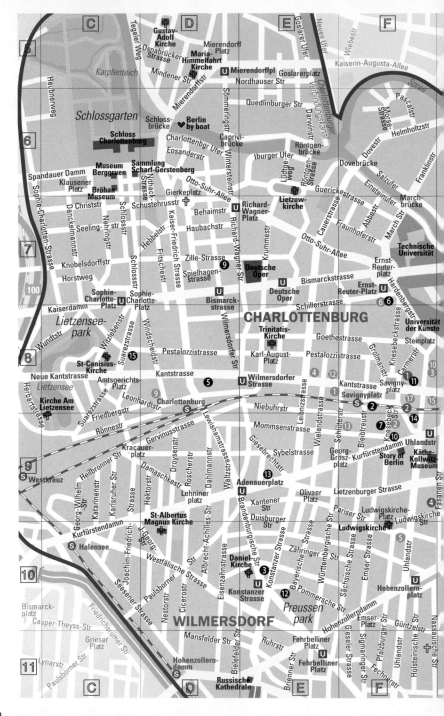

CHARLOTTENBURG & SCHÖNEBERG

Restaurants & cafés

1. 893 Ryotei *p182*
2. 1900 Café Bistro *p182*
3. Arirang *p183*
4. Aroma *p183*
5. Benedict *p189*
6. Brot & Butter *p183*
7. Café Aroma *p191*
8. Double Eye *p191*
9. Gasthaus Lentz *p188*
10. Glass *p183*
11. Ixthys *p191*
12. Lon Men's Noodle House *p183*
13. Marjellchen *p183*
14. Neni *p183*
15. Paris Bar *p183*
16. Renger-Patzsch *p193*
17. Schwarzes Café *p183*
18. Sissi *p193*
19. Tian Fu II *p189*
20. Witty's *p184*
4. Rum Trader *p189*
5. Stagger Lee *p193*

Bars & pubs

1. Dicke Wirtin *p184*
2. Diener Tattersall *p184*
3. Green Door *p193*

Shops & services

1. Antiquariat Thomas Mertens *p193*
2. Bücherbogen *p184*
3. Erich Hamann Bittere Schokoladen *p189*
4. Garage *p193*
5. Harry Lehmann *p188*
6. Manufactum *p184*
7. Marga Schoeller Bücherstube *p185*
8. Michas Bahnhof *p193*
9. Rogacki *p188*
10. Steiff Galerie *p185*
11. Stilwerk *p185*
12. Thai Park *p189*
13. Veronica Pohle *p185*
14. Viniculture *p185*
15. Wald Königsberger Marzipanp188
16. Winterfeldtplatz Market *p193*

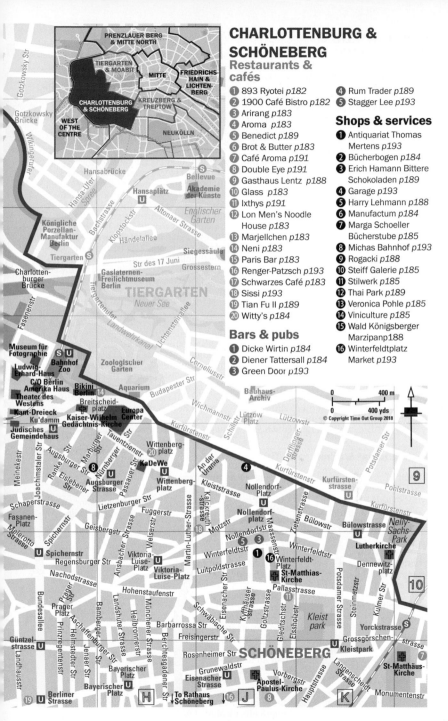

BAHNHOF ZOO & THE KU'DAMM

During the Cold War, **Bahnhof Zoo** (Zoo Station or Bahnhof Zoologischer Garten, to give it its full name) was the main entry point to the West. It was a spooky anomaly: slap in the middle of West Berlin but policed by the East Berlin authorities, who controlled the intercity rail system. It became a seedy hangout for junkies and sex workers, and served as the central backdrop to the infamous cult film *Christiane F*. In the 1990s, attempts were made to spruce it up with chain stores and fast-food outlets, but with the opening of Berlin Hauptbahnhof, it was relegated to just another regional train stop.

The original building on Hardenbergplatz was designed in 1882 by Ernst Dircksen, with modern glass sheds added in 1934. The surrounding area, with its sleaze and shopping, cinemas and crowds, is the gateway to the **Kurfürstendamm**, the main shopping street of western Berlin. On the other side of the square is the entrance to the **Zoologischer Garten** itself, in Tiergarten (*see p110*). Fans of photography, and of Helmut Newton in particular, shouldn't miss the **Museum für Fotografie** (Museum of Photography), behind the station.

The most notable landmark nearby is the fractured spire of the **Kaiser-Wilhelm-Gedächtnis-Kirche** (Kaiser Wilhelm Memorial Church) in Breitscheidplatz. Close by is the 22-storey **Europa-Center**, whose Mercedes star can be seen from much of the rest of the city. It was built in 1965 – and it shows. Intended as the anchor for the development of a new western downtown, it was the first of Berlin's genuinely tall buildings; now, it's the grande dame of the city's shopping malls. The exterior looks best when neon-lit at night. The strange sculpture in front (erected in 1983) is officially called *Weltenbrunnen* (Fountain of the Worlds), but is nicknamed '*Der Wasserklops*' ('Water Meatball').

Running along the south of the Europa-Center, **Tauentzienstrasse** is the westernmost piece of the Generalzug, a sequence of streets laid out by Peter Joseph Lenné to link the new west end of the city with Kreuzberg and points east. Constructed around 1860, they're all named after Prussian generals from the Napoleonic wars: Tauentzien, Kleist, Bülow and so on. The tubular steel sculpture in the central reservation was commissioned for the city's 750th anniversary in 1987 and represents the then-divided city.

North of Breitscheidplatz, the 1950s 'Zentrum am Zoo' complex overlooking the Zoo, which includes the Bikini Haus and the Zoo Palast cinema (*see p222*), has been reimagined as **Bikini Berlin**: a group of listed buildings that have become a sort of mega-hub combining shopping, work spaces, a spa and the stylish **25hours Hotel** (*see p299*). West of it rises the 32-storey Zoofenster, which contains the luxury hotel **Waldorf Astoria Berlin** on its upper floors.

Tauentzienstrasse continues east past **KaDeWe** (*see p54*), still the largest

---

❤ Time to eat & drink

Brunch
1900 Café Bistro *p182*, Benedict *p189*

People-watching
KaDeWe food hall *p54*, Rogacki *p188*

A taste of the Orient
Aroma *p183*, Arirang *p183*, Thai Park *p189*

Guilt-free fast food
Witty's *p184*

West Berlin revisited
Schwarzes Café *p183*, Diener Tattersall *p184*

Fine cocktails
Rum Trader *p189*, Green Door *p193*, Stagger Lee *p193*

❤ Time to shop

Sustainable homewares
Manufactum *p184*, Stilwerk *p185*

Classic toys
Steiff Galerie *p185*, Michas Bahnhof *p193*

Satisfying a sweet tooth
Wald Königsberger Marzipan *p188*, Erich Hamann Bittere Schokladen *p189*

Dietrich's perfumery
Harry Lehmann *p188*

Read all about it
Bücherbogen *p184*, Marga Schoeller Bücherstube *p185*

A taste of the country
Winterfeldplatz Market *p193*

In the know
Getting around

Charlottenburg is well-served by U-Bahn, S-Bahn and bus lines. The 15-minute journey by S-Bahn from Mitte to Charlottenburg is a treat, offering views over Museum Island, the River Spree, Tiergarten and the zoo; join the S5, S7 or S75 and jump off at Zoologischer Garten or Savignyplatz. Nollendorfplatz is the main U-Bahn station serving north Schöneberg; for Kleistpark and around, use the U7.

department store in continental Europe, and ends at a large pedestrianised square, **Wittenbergplatz**. The 1911 neoclassical U-Bahn station here (by Alfred Grenander) is a listed building and has been wonderfully restored with wooden kiosks and old ads on the walls. A block further east is the huge steel sculpture at **An der Urania**, with its grim monument to children killed in Berlin traffic. This marks the end, or the beginning, of the western 'downtown'.

Leading south-west from the Kaiser Wilhelm Memorial Church, the **Kurfürstendamm** (or Ku'damm, as it's universally known) is named after the Prussian Kurfürst ('Elector'); for centuries it was nothing but a track leading from the Elector's residence to the royal hunting palace in the Grunewald. In 1881, Bismarck insisted it be widened to 53 metres (174 feet) as Berlin's answer to the Champs-Elysées. Heaving with cafés, fashionable boutiques, bars and clubs, it was the focal point for decadent Berliners in the city's 1920s 'Babylon on the Spree' days.

Today, the Ku'damm remains an elegant tree-lined shopping boulevard, dedicated to separating you from your cash. If you tire of shopping, there are cinemas (mostly showing dubbed Hollywood fare) and a full range of restaurants (from classy to burger joints). There's also an entertaining museum-cum-attraction called the **Story of Berlin**. Bleibtreustrasse to the north has more shops and several outrageous examples of 19th-century Gründerzeit architecture.

The side streets to the south are quieter but even more upmarket. Of the many villas erected here in the 19th century few survive today; one sizeable exception on Fasanenstrasse contains the **Käthe-Kollwitz-Museum**, the Villa Griesbach auction house and the Literaturhaus Berlin, with its **Café im Literaturhaus**. The villas soon made way for upmarket tenement buildings with huge apartments. About half of these were destroyed in the war and replaced by functional offices, but many bombastic old structures remain.

At the north-west corner of the intersection of the Ku'damm and Joachimstaler Strasse is the **Neues Kranzler-Eck**, a Helmut Jahn-designed ensemble built around the famous old Café Kranzler, with a 16-storey tower and pedestrian courtyards including a habitat for parrots. Other notable buildings include Josef Paul Kleihues's **Kant-Dreieck** (Fasanenstrasse/Kantstrasse), with its large metal 'sail', and Nicholas Grimshaw's **Ludwig-Erhard-Haus** for the Stock Exchange at Fasanenstrasse 83-84. Back towards the Kurfürstendamm

end of Fasanenstrasse is the **Jüdisches Gemeindehaus** (Jewish Community House) and, opposite, the **Zille-Hof** flea market.

Kantstrasse runs more or less parallel to the Ku'damm at the Zoo end; it contains the grandiloquent **Theater des Westens**, Berlin's central venue for musicals, and many of Berlin's best Asian restaurants. Since the opening of the **Stilwerk** design centre, the stretch between Fasanenstrasse and Savignyplatz has become a centre for designer homeware shops. The environs of leafy **Savignyplatz**, meanwhile, are dotted with chic restaurants, cafés and shops, particularly on Grolmanstrasse and in the Savignypassage. Knesebeckstrasse includes the legendary **Marga Schoeller Bücherstube**, which secretly sold forbidden literature during the Nazi years.

Sights & museums

C/O Berlin Amerika Haus
Hardenbergstrasse 22-24 (284 441 662, www.co-berlin.org). U2, U9, S5, S7, S75 Zoologischer Garten. **Open** *Exhibition and bookshop 11am-8pm daily. Café 10am-8pm daily.* **Admission** *€10; €6 reductions.* **Map** *p178 G8.*

Built by the US in the 1950s to promote transatlantic cultural exchange, Amerika Haus housed embassy offices until the new Pariser Platz site was completed in 2006. Since 2014, following extensive renovations, it has been an exhibition space for the much-loved photography gallery C/O Berlin, which exhibits museum-quality photography and visual media from around the world.

❤ Kaiser-Wilhelm-Gedächtnis-Kirche
Breitscheidplatz (218 5023, www. gedaechtniskirche.com). U2, U9, S5, S7, S75 Zoologischer Garten. **Open** *9am-7pm daily. Guided tours 10.15am-3.15pm hourly Mon, Fri, Sat; 12.15-3.15pm hourly Tue-Thur, Sun.* **Admission** *free.* **Map** *p178 G8.*

The Kaiser Wilhelm Memorial Church is one of Berlin's best-known sights and one of its most dramatic at night. The neo-romanesque structure was built in 1891-95 by Franz Schwechten in honour of – you guessed it – Kaiser Wilhelm I. Much of the building was destroyed during an Allied air raid in 1943. These days, the church serves as a stark reminder of the damage done by the war, although some might argue it improved what was originally a profoundly ugly building. Inside the rump of the church is a glittering art nouveau-style ceiling mosaic depicting members of the House of Hohenzollern on pilgrimage towards the cross. There's also a cross made from nails from Coventry's war-destroyed cathedral, and photos of the church before and after the war. The wrap-around blue stained glass in the chapel is simply stunning. Guided tours in English can be booked.

Käthe-Kollwitz-Museum

Fasanenstrasse 24 (882 5210, www.kaethe-kollwitz.de). U1, U9 Kurfürstendamm. **Open** *11am-6pm daily.* **Admission** *€7; €4 reductions; free under-18s. No cards.* **Map** *p178 F9.*

Käthe Kollwitz's powerful, deeply empathetic work embraces the full spectrum of life, from the joy of motherhood to the pain of death (with a particular fascination for the latter). A committed socialist and pacifist, she is held in great esteem by Berliners. The collection includes her famous lithograph *Brot!*, as well as charcoal sketches, woodcuts and sculptures, all displayed to impressive effect in this grand villa off the Ku'damm. For refreshments, the Café im Literaturhaus next door is a lovely spot.

Museum für Fotografie

Jebensstrasse 2 (266 424242, www.smb. museum/mf). U2, U9, S5, S7, S75 Zoologischer Garten. **Open** *11am-7pm Tue, Wed, Fri-Sun; 11am-8pm Thur.* **Admission** *€10; €5 reductions.* **Map** *p178 G8.*

Shortly before his death in 2004, Berlin-born Helmut Newton – who served his apprenticeship elsewhere in Charlottenburg at the studio of Yva – donated over 1,000 of his nude and fashion photographs to the city and provided funds towards the creation of a new gallery. This museum, doubling as a home for the Helmut Newton Foundation (www.helmutnewton.com), was the result. Housed in a former casino behind Bahnhof Zoo, it's now the largest photographic gallery in the city. The ground and first floors are dedicated to Newton's work. Six colossal nudes, modelled on 1930s Nazi propaganda photos, glare down at you on entering the building and set the tone for the big, garish, confrontational pieces that dominate the exhibits. The top floor has changing shows on the history of photography, drawn from the collection of the Berlin State Museums.

❤ Story of Berlin

Kurfürstendamm 207-208 (8872 0100, www. story-of-berlin.de). U1 Uhlandstrasse. **Open** *10am-8pm daily; last entry 6pm.* **Admission** *€12; €5-€9 reductions.* **Map** *p178 F9.*

If you're interested in the city's turbulent history, the Story of Berlin is a novel way of approaching it. The huge space is filled with well-designed rooms and multimedia exhibits

Story of Berlin

created by a wide range of authors, designers and film and stage specialists, telling Berlin's story from its founding in 1237 to the present day. The 20 themed displays are labelled in both German and English and are fairly child-friendly. Underneath all this is a massive nuclear shelter. Built by the Allies during the 1970s, the low-ceilinged, oppressive bunker is still fully functional and can hold up to 3,500 people. Guided tours of the bunker are included in the price of the ticket.

Restaurants & cafés

893 Ryotei €€€

Kantstrasse 135 (9170 3121, www.893ryotei. de). S5, S7, S75 Savignyplatz. **Open** *Restaurant 6.30-11pm Tue-Sat.* **No cards.** **Map** *p178 E8* ❶ *Japanese*

From the outside, 893 Ryotei looks like a low-end supermarket covered in graffiti, but step inside and you'll find yourself in a beautifully lit, plush interior with an open kitchen, central marble-topped bar and plenty of – usually full-tables. Serving modern Japanese cuisine with a Nikkei twist (sashimi taquitos anyone?), the seafood is to die for, which isn't something you often say in Berlin. Brought to the city by Duc Ngo, the brains behind Cocolo and Kuchi, with 893 Ryotei he's done it again. Book ahead.

❤ 1900 Café Bistro €

Knesebeckstrasse 76 (8871 5871). S5, S7, S75 Savignyplatz. **Open** *8am-7pm Mon-Fri; 9am-7pm Sun.* **No cards.** **Map** *p178 F9* ❷ *Café*

Booking is recommended for weekend brunch at this kitschy café, where plates overflow with cold cuts, cheese and fruit. Traditional tray-baked crumble cakes and a salad menu are also available.

❤ Arirang €
*Uhlandstrasse 194 (4502 1248). U2, U9, S5, S7, S75 Zoologischer Garten. **Open** noon-11pm daily. **No cards**. **Map** p178 F8* ❸ *Korean*

This fabulous restaurant used to be a closely guarded secret in a shabby Wedding location, but in 2014 it moved to Charlottenburg. There's nothing special about the surroundings or the service, but the food is authentic. As is the norm in Korea, dishes are served with a selection of kimchi, pickled salads and rice, so take care not to over-order. The fiery kimchi and noodle stew, and the spring onion and seafood pancakes are perfect for sharing.

❤ Aroma €-€€
*Kantstrasse 35 (3759 1628). S5, S7, S75 Savignyplatz. **Open** noon-2.30am daily. **No cards**. **Map** p178 E8* ❹ *Chinese*

If you're hankering for a dim sum fix, head to Aroma in Berlin's mini Chinatown on Kantstrasse. You can enjoy assorted dumplings in the traditional, genteel tea-time style of *yum cha* or as part of a full dinner with more substantial plates. Go with classics such as *har gao* (steamed shrimp dumplings), fried turnip cakes or *cheong fun*, pillowy steamed rice noodle rolls stuffed with prawn or beef.

Brot & Butter €
*Hardenbergstrasse 4-5 (2630 0346). U1, U2 Ernst-Reuter-Platz. **Open** 8am-8pm Mon-Fri; 8am-6pm Sat. **No cards**. **Map** p178 F7* ❻ *Café*

The on-site bakery of the magnificent Manufactum craft-oriented department store (*see p184*) does vast sourdough loafs and traditional crusty baguettes. The café serves almond croissants, small lunch specials and mixed plates of charcuterie. Don't miss the indulgent raw-milk butter.

Glass €€€-€€€€
*Uhlandstrasse 195 (5471 0861, www. glassberlin.de). U2, U9, S5, S7, S75 Zoologischer Garten. **Open** 6-11pm Tue-Sat. **Map** p178 F8* ❿ *Fine dining*

Inside a brutalist apartment building, chef Gal Ben-Moshe spins straw into culinary gold. The Arab-influenced set menu of six to eight courses features starters impaled on smoking cinnamon sticks; soups adorned with savoury sorbets; and finely tuned, playful desserts. Wine pairings are available.

Lon Men's Noodle House €
*Kantstrasse 33 (3151 9678). S5, S7, S75 Savignyplatz. **Open** noon-11pm daily. **No cards**. **Map** p178 E8* ⓬ *Taiwanese*

This tiny hole-in-the-wall spot knocks out Taiwanese classics such as noodle soups and *gua bao* (rice buns filled with duck) as well as more esoteric plates of dressed beef tongue or pigs' ears sliced finely over rice noodles.

Marjellchen €€
*Mommsenstrasse 9 (883 2676, www. marjellchen-berlin.de). S5, S7, S75 Savignyplatz. **Open** 5pm-midnight daily. **No cards**. **Map** p178 F9* ⓭ *German*

Not many places like Marjellchen exist any more. It serves specialities from East Prussia, such as Masurian jugged game or beef with prunes, in an atmosphere of old-fashioned *gemütlichkeit* (homely cosiness). The beautiful bar and great service are further draws, and the larger-than-life owner recites poetry and sometimes sings.

Neni €€-€€€
*25hours Hotel, Bikini Berlin, Budapester Strasse 40 (1202 21200, www.neniberlin.de). U2, U9, S5, S7, S75 Zoologischer Garten. **Open** noon-11pm Mon-Fri; 12.30-11pm Sat, Sun. **No cards**. **Map** p178 G8* ⓮ *Middle Eastern*

A top-floor restaurant in Charlottenburg's fanciest boutique hotel (*see p299*), Neni offers views to die for. The menu encourages diners to share plates of Middle Eastern-style food, such as *sabich* (fried aubergine, houmous and salad), *chraime* (cod in tomato stew) and slow-roasted lamb shoulder.

Paris Bar €€€
*Kantstrasse 152 (313 8052, www.parisbar. net). S5, S7, S75 Savignyplatz. **Open** noon-late daily. **Map** p178 F8* ⓯ *Brasserie*

Owner Michel Wurthle's friendship with Martin Kippenberger and other artists of his generation is clear from all the art hanging here. Paris Bar, with its salon-like appeal, is one of Berlin's most established arty hangouts. It attracts a crowd of rowdy regulars, and newcomers can feel left out if seated in the rear. The pricey food, it has to be said, isn't nearly as good as the staff pretend. Book ahead.

❤ Schwarzes Cafe €-€€
*Kantstrasse 148 (313 8038, www. schwarzescafe-berlin.de). S5, S7, S75 Savignyplatz. **Open** 24 hours Wed-Mon; from 10am Tue. **No cards**. **Map** p178 F8* ⓱ *Cafe*

A Charlottenburg institution, Schwarzes Café is open round the clock, closing only between 3am and 10am on Tuesday mornings. The

Bikini Berlin

menu features hearty middle-European fare, including *Schnitzel* and *Knödel*. If you come to eat, you won't leave hungry. Noisy and sociable, this is an unpretentious spot with a big student following.

❤ Witty's €
Wittenbergplatz 5 (6391 1666, www.wittys-berlin.de). U1, U2, U3 Wittenbergplatz. **Open** *10am-midnight Mon-Sat; 11am-midnight Sun.* **No cards.** **Map** *p178 H9* ⑳ *Imbiss*

Yearning for an authentic sausage fix but concerned about the industrially processed content of your average Imbiss offering? Look no further. Witty's features a fully organic menu of Berlin staples, including *Currywurst* and fries. Gluten-free options available.

Bars & pubs
Dicke Wirtin
Carmerstrasse 9 (312 4952, www.dicke-wirtin.de). S5, S7, S75 Savignyplatz. **Open** *11am-late daily.* **No cards.** **Map** *p178 F8* ❶

The 'Fat Landlady' is a proper German pub: nine beers on tap, bizarre house schnapps (tiramisu liqueur, anyone?) and dirt-cheap prices for the area. If you get tipsy, there are plenty of *Schmalz-* (lard-) heavy treats to bring you back to earth.

❤ Diener Tattersall
Grolmanstrasse 47 (881 5329, www.diener-berlin.de). S5, S7, S75 Savignyplatz. **Open** *6pm-late daily.* **No cards.** **Map** *p178 F8* ❷

Ex-boxer Franz Diener took this place over in 1954 and, with his artist friends, turned it into one of the central hubs of West Berlin cultural life. The chattering classes flocked here from concert halls and theatres to gossip and to

spot off-duty actors drinking the night away. In a city fascinated with *Ostalgie* and the rapid rhythms of gentrification, raise a toast (or four) to this previous age of West Berlin bohemians.

Shops & services

▶ *KaDeWe is still the queen of consumerism in these parts; see p54. For fashion and designer homewares, check out the permanent retailers and pop-ups in Bikini Berlin. Highlights include the Artek Concept Store and Samsø & Samsø.*

❤ Bücherbogen
Stadtbahnbogen 593, Savignyplatz (3186 9511). S5, S7, S75 Savignyplatz. **Open** *10am-8pm Mon-Fri; 10am-6pm Sat.* **No cards.** **Map** *p178 F8* ❷ *Books & music*

An art-lover's dream, this massive bookshop takes up three whole railway arches, with rows of books on art, design and architecture, plus exhibition catalogues and lots of rare or out-of-print volumes.

❤ Manufactum
Hardenbergstrasse 4-5 (2403 3844, www.manufactum.de). U1, U2 Ernst-Reuter-Platz. **Open** *10am-8pm Mon-Fri; 10am-6pm Sat.* **Map** *p178 F7* ❻ *Department store*

Founded in 1988 by a high-profile Green Party politician as a counterpoint to cheap mass production, Manufactum quickly developed a cult following for its ironic catalogue blurbs and impeccable selection of products. It continues in the same vein today, with an emphasis on German-made goods that demonstrate high production values, classic design and sustainability. Prices reflect the quality.

❤ Marga Schoeller Bücherstube
Knesebeckstrasse 33 (881 1112, www.
margaschoeller.de). S5, S7, S75 Savignyplatz.
Open *9.30am-7pm Mon-Wed; 9.30am-8pm*
Thur, Fri; 9.30am-6pm Sat. **Map** *p178 F9* ❼
Books

This bookshop (established 1930) won
renown when owner Marga shook a fist
at the Nazi regime by removing all Nazi-
related texts from her shelves. In the '70s,
it relocated down the road from its original
Ku'damm spot. English books are displayed
in an inviting alcove. It goes further than
most to provide new non-fiction titles,
from philosophical and political texts to
theatre studies.

❤ Steiff Galerie
Kurfürstendamm 38 (8862 5006, www.steiff.
de). U1 Uhlandstrasse. **Open** *10am-8pm Mon-*
Sat. **Map** *p178 F9* ❿ *Gifts & souvenirs*

Inventor of the teddy bear (so named in the
US after a hunting story involving 'Teddy'
Roosevelt), Steiff has been in business since
the late 19th century. The company's whole
range of artisan animals (not just bears) are
here. Prices are aimed at adult hobbyists
rather than kids.

❤ Stilwerk
Kantstrasse 17 (315 150, www.stilwerk.de). S5,
S7, S75 Savignyplatz. **Open** *10am-7pm Tue-*
Sat. **Map** *p178 F8* ⓫ *Homewares*

This huge design marketplace offers high-end
products from an array of retailers, including
modern furnishings and kitchens, lighting
and bathroom fittings, plus interior items.
There's also a fourth-floor showcase for work
from local design studios.

Veronica Pohle
Kurfürstendamm 64 (883 3731, www.
veronicapohle.de). U7 Adenauerplatz. **Open**
10.30am-7.30pm Mon-Fri; 11am-6.30pm Sat.
Map *p178 E9* ⓭ *Fashion*

Womenswear from top international labels
such as Missoni, Roberto Cavalli, Vivienne
Westwood, Diane von Fürstenberg and
Alexander McQueen.

Viniculture
Grolmanstrasse 44-45 (883 8174, www.
viniculture.de). S5, S7, 75 Savignyplatz. **Open**
11am-8pm Mon-Fri; 10am-6pm Sat. **Map** *p178*
F9 ⓮ *Wine*

Viniculture was pushing biodynamic and
'natural' wines years before they became
fashionable. Stock comes from France,
Germany, Austria and Italy, and there's
a programme of tasting seminars, often
in English.

SCHLOSS CHARLOTTENBURG & AROUND

The palace that gives Charlottenburg its
name lies about three kilometres (two miles)
north-west of Bahnhof Zoo. In contrast to
the commercialism and crush of the latter,
this part of the city is quiet, wealthy and
serene. **Schloss Charlottenburg** was built
in the 17th century as a summer palace for
Queen Sophie-Charlotte, wife of Friedrich
III (later King Friedrich I), and was intended
as Berlin's answer to Versailles. It's not a
very convincing answer, but there's plenty
of interest in the buildings and outside;
the apartments of the New Wing and the
gardens are the main attractions.

In front of the entrance is the **Museum
Berggruen**, with work by Picasso and other
modernists, and the **Bröhan-Museum**,
which showcases art nouveau and art deco
pieces. The arrival across the street in 2008
of the **Sammlung Scharf-Gerstenberg**,
which traces the lines between fantastic
and surrealist work, firmly established this
corner of town as a stronghold for early
20th-century art.

There are few eating, drinking or
shopping opportunities in the immediate
vicinity of the palace, but if you head down
Schlossstrasse and over Bismarckstrasse,
the streets south of here – particularly those
named after philosophers (Leibniz, Goethe)
– have many interesting small shops selling
antiques, books and the fashions favoured
by well-to-do locals.

▶ *For details of the Gedenkstätte Plötzensee,*
a former Nazi prison and execution centre in
Charlottenburg-Nord, see p125.

Sights & museums
Bröhan-Museum
Schlossstrasse 1A (3269 0600, www.broehan-
museum.de). U2 Sophie-Charlotte-Platz; U7
Richard-Wagner-Platz. **Open** *10am-6pm*
Tue-Sun. **Admission** *€8; €5 reductions;*
free under-18s. Special exhibitions varies.
Map *p178 C6.*

This quiet museum contains three floors
of international art nouveau and art deco
pieces that businessman Karl Bröhan began
collecting in the 1960s and donated to the
city of Berlin on his 60th birthday. The
paintings, sculptures, furniture, porcelain,
glass and silver date from 1890 to 1939 and are
thoughtfully laid out, although the labelling
is in German only. Among the pieces of fine
art, Hans Baluschek's paintings of social life
in the 1920s and '30s, and Willy Jaeckel's
portraits of women are the highlights. The
furniture is superb too.

❤ Berlin by boat

While Berlin's claims to be the 'Prussian Venice' may meet with deserved scepticism, the German capital is still an engagingly watery place. The River Spree meanders through Berlin on its journey from the Czech Republic to the Elbe, creating a maze of interlocking rivers, lakes and canals that are an integral part of the German capital. In fact, all the materials used to build the city arrived via barges, so it simply wouldn't exist without its waterways. Today, they're more for pleasure than industry – nothing beats a sundowner on the banks of the Spree – although in and around Tegeler See, there are isolated houses on islands that can still only be reached by boat.

A range of city-centre tours is offered by **Stern und Kreis** (www.sternundkreis.de), **Reederei Winkler** (www.reederei winkler.de) and **Reederei Riedel** (www.reederei-riedel.de). Circular tours of the Spree and the Landwehrkanal usually last three to four hours and take in the city's top sights, including the Reichstag and Museum Island; they also pass under Berlin's numerous bridges, including the picturesque Oberbaumbrücke. Passengers can hop on and off at landing stages en route, and basic food and drink is served on board. For a complete tour, expect to pay around €19 per adult. Shorter trips and evening sailings are also available. There are convenient landing stages at the Schlossbrücke in Charlottenburg, at the Haus der Kulturen der Welt in Tiergarten, at Märkisches Ufer, at Jannowitzbrücke and in the Nikolaiviertel. Note that many services operate only from mid-March to late November.

A short train journey (20-30 minutes) to Wannsee (*see p201*) offers more boating opportunities. Stern & Kreis's Seven Lakes Trip (7-Seen-Rundfahrt) gives a chance to ogle some of Berlin's poshest backyards as the boat slides gently past the handsome mansions surrounding the Kleiner Wannsee. Or you can take a round trip to Potsdam and Sanssouci. For further details of these and other options, consult the operator's website. However, savvy visitors on a budget may prefer to take advantage of the hourly year-round **BVG ferry** from Wannsee to Kladow, which is part of the local transport network; a standard A-B zone ticket (€2.80) is valid for both the S-Bahn journey to Wannsee and the ferry. It's a beautiful ride, and there's even a decent pub by the pier in a quasi-rural setting on the other side. Other BVG passenger ferries, including a rowing boat service, operate on and around the Müggelsee (*see p199*).

♥ Museum Berggruen

*Westlicher Stülerbau, Schlossstrasse 1
(266 424 242, www.smb.museum/mb). U2
Sophie-Charlotte-Platz; U7 Richard-Wagner-
Platz.* **Open** *10am-6pm Tue-Fri; 11am-6pm
Sat, Sun.* **Admission** *€10; €5 reductions.*
Map *p178 C6.*

Heinz Berggruen was one of Picasso's dealers
in Paris and went on to become a major
modernist collector. In 2000, he sold his
entire collection to Berlin for a knockdown
$100 million; it is now displayed across three
easily manageable circular floors. Inevitably,
the astonishingly prolific and diverse output
of Pablo Picasso dominates. Some of the
many highlights include the 1942 *Reclining
Nude* and his late-period *The Woman of
Algiers* (1955). Works by Braque, Giacometti,
Cézanne and Matisse also feature, while
most of the second floor is given over to the
wonderful paintings of Paul Klee.

Sammlung Scharf-Gerstenberg

*Schlossstrasse 70 (266 424242, www.
smb.museum/en/museums-institutions/
sammlung-scharf-gerstenberg). U2 Sophie-
Charlotte-Platz.* **Open** *10am-6pm Tue-Fri;
11am-6pm Sat, Sun.* **Admission** *€10; €5
reductions.* **Map** *p178 C6.*

Housed in the eastern Stüler building and in
the Marstall (stables wing) opposite Schloss
Charlottenburg, this gallery exhibits works
by the Surrealists and their forerunners.
Featured artists range from Piranesi, Goya
and Redon to Dalí, Magritte and Ernst. The
original collection was amassed by Otto
Gerstenberg around 1910 and added to by his
grandsons, Walter and Dieter Scharf.

♥ Schloss Charlottenburg

*Spandauer Damm 10-22 (0331 969 4200,
www.spsg.de). U2 Sophie-Charlotte-Platz;
U7 Richard-Wagner-Platz.* **Open** *Apr-
Oct 10am-5.30pm Tue-Sun. Nov-Mar
10am-4.30pm Tue-Sun. Belvedere &
Mausoleum closed Nov-Mar.* **Admission**
*Combined ticket €17; €13 reductions; for
individual ticket prices, see text below.
Guided tour of the state apartments €8, €5
reductions (German only). Gardens free.*
Map *p178 C6.*

Elector Friedrich III (later King Friedrich I)
built this sprawling palace and gardens in
1695-99 as a summer home for his queen,
Sophie-Charlotte, who gave her name to
both the palace and the wider district. Later
kings also summered here, tinkering with
and adding to the buildings. The palace was
severely damaged during World War II but
has since been restored and now stands as the
largest surviving Hohenzollern palace.

Each of the outbuildings has a separate
admission charge, so the easiest option is
to buy the combined ticket, which allows
entrance to all parts of the palace, except
the state and private apartments of King
Friedrich I and Queen Sophie-Charlotte
in the Altes Schloss (Old Palace), which
are only accessible on a guided tour. This
tour takes in more than 20 rooms, some
of staggering Baroque opulence, and
certainly has its highlights (particularly the
Porcelain Cabinet), but it can be skipped,
as there's plenty of interest elsewhere.
The upper apartments in the **Old Palace**
(€10; €7 reductions) can be visited without
a guided tour but are a bit of a silver and
porcelain overload.

The one must-see is the **Neue Flügel**
or New Wing (€10; €7 reductions), also
known as the Knobeldorff Wing (after its
architect). The upper floor contains the
state apartments of Frederick the Great
and the winter chambers of his successor,
King Friedrich Wilhelm II. The contrast
between the two sections is fascinating:
Frederick's rooms are all excessive rococo
exuberance (the wildly over-the-top Golden
Gallery practically drips gilt), while Friedrich
Wilhelm's far more modestly proportioned
rooms reflect the more restrained classicism
of his time. Frederick the Great was a big
collector of 18th-century French painting,
and some choice canvases hang from the
walls, including Watteau's masterpiece *The
Embarkation for Cythera*. Also worth a look
are the apartments of Friedrich Wilhelm III
in the New Wing.

By the east end of the New Wing stands
the **Neue Pavillon** (New Pavilion), also
known as the Schinkel Pavilion. It was
built by Karl Friedrich Schinkel in 1824 for
Friedrich Wilhelm III – the king liked it so
much that he chose to live here in preference
to the grandeur of the main palace. Inside
is an excellent permanent exhibition on the
architect's legacy.

The huge, impeccably kept gardens are
one of the palace's main draws. Laid out
in 1697 in formal French style, they were
reshaped in a more relaxed English style
in the 19th century. Within them, you'll
find the **Belvedere** (Apr-Oct only; €4, €3
reductions), a three-storey structure built
in 1788 as a tea house, now containing a
collection of Berlin porcelain. Also in the
gardens is the sombre **Mausoleum** (Apr-
Oct only; €3), containing the tombs of
Friedrich Wilhelm III, his wife Queen Luise,
Kaiser Wilhelm I and his wife. Look out for
temporary exhibitions in the Orangerie.
There's a café and restaurant at the front of
the palace. Note: the entire palace is closed
on Mondays.

Schloss Charlottenburg p187

Restaurants & cafés

Gasthaus Lentz €
*Stuttgarter Platz 20 (324 1619, www.
gasthaus-lentz-berlin.de). S5, S7, S75
Charlottenburg; U7 Wilmersdorfer Strasse.*
Open *9am-1am daily.* **No cards.** **Map** *p178
D8* 9 *Café*

Bespectacled Charlottenburgers take their
time with a newspaper and coffee here. Daily
specials of German classics usually involve
something porky with potatoes and salad. A
local institution and good value.

Shops & services

♥ Harry Lehmann
*Kantstrasse 106 (324 3582, www.parfum-
individual.de). S5, S7, S75 Charlottenburg; U7
Wilmersdorfer Strasse.* **Open** *9am-6.30pm
Mon-Fri; 9am-2pm Sat.* **No cards.** **Map** *p178
D8* 5 *Perfume*

In business since 1926, Harry Lehmann's is
a jewel of a store where perfumes are sold by
weight. Famously, Marlene Dietrich was a fan
of the lavender scent. You can choose your
own favourite from the rows of glass flacons,
or the staff will concoct you a mix to take
away in a beautiful retro bottle.

♥ Rogacki
*Wilmersdorfer Strasse 145-146 (343 8250,
www.rogacki.de). U7 Bismarckstrasse.*
Open *9am-6pm Mon-Wed; 9am-7pm Thur;
8am-7pm Fri; 8am-4pm Sat.* **Map** *p178 D7* 9
Food & drink

A trip to Rogacki, a German-Polish
delicatessen-cum-food market, is like stepping
back in time. The draw here is the fish:
specialities include *Bratherings* (fried and
brined herring), *Rollmops* (pickled herrings
rolled around gherkin) and *Senfgurken* (white
gherkins from Spreewald). Alongside the
excellent quality produce, you'll find gourmet
islands inside where you can pull up a stool
and order a *Fischbrötchen* or oysters and wine
for much less than you'll pay at the KaDeWe.
Excellent for people-watching!

♥ Wald Königsberger Marzipan
*Pestalozzistrasse 54A (323 8254). S5, S7, S75
Charlottenburg; U7 Wilmersdorfer Strasse.*
Open *10am-6.30pm Mon-Fri; 10am-3.30pm
Sat.* **No cards.** **Map** *p178 C8* 15 *Food & drink*

Irmgard Wald and her late husband arrived
in Berlin after the war, when the Soviets
changed Prussian Königsberg to Kaliningrad,
to begin their confectionery business anew.
In 2005, Frau Wald handed over control to
her charming American-born granddaughter.
The company still produces fresh, soft, melt-
in-your-mouth marzipan.

WILMERSDORF

Following Uhlandstrasse south of Kurfürstendamm, things get steadily quieter and leafier as you enter the traditionally middle-class residential area of **Wilmersdorf**. There are few sights of note – except for curiosities such as the ex-Nazi town hall at **Fehrbelliner Platz** and the **Künstlerkolonie Berlin**, a 1920s artists' commune on the border of Steglitz – but it's a great place to get a feel for how the other half of Berlin lives, away from the street art and piercings of the East. The area was farmland until the mid 19th century, when a property boom led to the phenomenon of the *Millionenbauern* (peasant millionaires), farmers handsomely paid off by developers. It rapidly developed into an affluent neighbourhood and was home to a large Jewish population during the Weimar years. Visit at the weekend to explore the flea market on Fehrbelliner Platz and pick up a uniquely Berlin souvenir. Then, saunter north into Preussen Park to have your tastebuds tickled by the Thai flavours on offerings at Europe's largest and most informal Asian streetfood market.

▶ *From Fehrbelliner Platz, it's a five-minute bus journey (bus 115) to the Brücke-Museum (see p203), a villa devoted to German Expressionism.*

Restaurants & cafés
♥ Benedict €€
*Uhlandstrasse 49 (9940 40997, www.benedict-breakfast.de). U3, U9 Spichernstrasse. **Open** Restaurant 24hrs daily. Bakery 7.30am-6.30pm daily. **Map** p178 F10* ⑤ *Breakfast*

Brunch is the quintessential Berlin meal, but in recent years locals have been hankering after something more than the eggs, cold cuts and cheese that make up the typical offering. Since it opened in 2017, Benedict has been overwhelming Berliners with its menu, which fuses the flavours of Tel Aviv and New York, and serves them with European flair. Eggs Benedict may be the titular dish, but the menu runs from *shakshuka* (baked eggs in tomato sauce), to a Russian breakfast, to the most mouth-watering pancakes in town.

Tian Fu II €€
*Berliner Strasse 15 (8639 7780, www.tianfu.de). U7, U9 Berliner Strasse. **Open** noon-11pm daily. **No cards. Map** p178 G11* ⑲ *Chinese*

Chilli-lovers can find it hard to get their fix in a spice-shy country, but Tian Fu II provides some real Sichuan fire, of both the

hot and numbing type. Kick things off with traditional cold starters such as tripe salad with Sichuan peppercorn or seaweed salad in black vinegar dressing, then dive into a fiery fish stew swimming in red chillies. **Other location** Uhlandstrasse 142, Charlottenburg (861 3015).

Bars & pubs
♥ Rum Trader
*Fasanenstrasse 40 (881 1428). U3, U9 Spichernstrasse. **Open** varies. **No cards.** **Map** p178 F9* ④

Subtitled the 'Institute for Advanced Drinking', this tiny bar is a Berlin classic, thanks to its eccentric owner, Gregor Scholl, who is ever present, smartly dressed in bow tie and waistcoat. There is no menu: Scholl will ask which spirit you like and whether you want something '*süss oder sauer*' (sweet or sour). Don't waste his time (or talent) by asking for a mojito. Hugely atmospheric and with room for only 15 guests, Rum Trader is best avoided if you're on a budget.

Shops & services
♥ Erich Hamann Bittere Schokoladen
*Brandenburgische Strasse 17 (873 2085, www.hamann-schokolade.de). U7 Konstanzer Strasse. **Open** 9am-6pm Mon-Fri; 9am-1pm Sat. **Map** p178 E10* ③ *Food & drink*

This beautiful Bauhaus building houses Berlin's oldest functioning chocolate factory. Everything is still done with an eye to period detail: chocolate thins are boxed by hand in beautifully old-fashioned packaging, while the signature chocolate 'bark' is still made in the original purpose-built machine.

♥ Thai Park
*Preussenpark. U7 Konstanzer Strasse. **Open** varies. **Admission** free. **Map** p178 E10* ⑫ *Food market*

Thai Park began when Thai Berliners started an impromptu foodie get-together in this sedate little park. When other visitors to the park started asking if the food was for sale, the Thai locals saw a business opportunity and set up shop from their picnic blankets, knocking up authentic pad thai or green papaya salad with nothing more than portable gas burners and Tupperwares full of ingredients. The city authorities turned a blind eye, and, soon, what had been a few noodle and saté stands had burgeoned into the largest Thai street-food market outside Asia. Still an informal set-up with no official hours, Thai Park is busiest on Sundays,

Thai Park p189

though stalls sometimes open on weekdays as well in good weather. With a carnival atmosphere – helped by the caipirinhas and massages on offer alongside all the food – this is a great place to bring a blanket and savour delicious soups, dumplings and deep-fried treats alfresco. Children romp, clubgoers wearing shades feed their hangovers, while the Thais catch up on the week's gossip. In 2018, there was talk of the city authorities shutting down the whole operation but, to date, the entrepreneurs of Thai Park continue to cook, indifferent to the controversy, in true Berlin style.

In the know
Marlene Dietrich

Berlin is rightfully proud of Marlene Dietrich, the city's most iconic actress. Born in 1901 on Schöneberg's Rote Insel, she first found fame in silent films and on stage. Her breakthrough film was *Der Blaue Engel* (*The Blue Angel*, 1930), filmed at the Babelsberg studios (see p178), whose success enabled her to move to Hollywood. In the 1930s, Dietrich spurned Nazi offers to return to Germany and instead became a key figure in the effort to raise Allied war bonds. Her film career subsided, but she continued to perform on stage as a cabaret artist for several decades, until ill health forced her to retire. She died in Paris in 1992. Her will stated that she was to be buried in Schöneberg, but only after the Wall fell. Her grave can be found in the Städtischer Friedhof III cemetery on Stubenrauchstrasse.

SCHÖNEBERG

Geographically and atmospherically, Schöneberg lies between Charlottenburg and Kreuzberg but has a charm all of its own. It's an interesting part of town, mostly built in the late 19th century. Though largely devoid of conventional sights, Schöneberg is rich in reminders of Berlin's recent history. With beautiful squares, such as Viktoria-Luisa Platz, grand buildings and one of Europe's oldest, wildest and wealthiest gay communities, it's a beautiful neighbourhood to wander through before browsing the antique shops or grabbing a cocktail.

Schöneberg means 'beautiful hill' – which is odd, because the borough is flat. It does, however, have an 'island' of sorts: the triangular **Schöneberger Insel** is carved out by the two broad railway cuttings that carry the S1, S2 and S25 lines; an elevated stretch of lines S41, S42 and S45 provides the southern boundary. In the 1930s, this area became known as the Rote Insel ('Red Island'), because it was one of the last bits of Berlin to resist Nazification, thanks to its socialist-leaning population and its limited access over a handful of bridges. There's a fine view from Monumentenbrücke, on the east side, towards Kreuzberg's Viktoriapark. On the north-west edge is **St Matthäus-Kirchhof**, a graveyard that is the last resting place of the Brothers Grimm.

West along Langenscheidtstrasse leads you towards Kleistpark U-Bahn Station, from where Schöneberg's main street stretches north as Potsdamer Strasse and south-west as Hauptstrasse. David Bowie and Iggy Pop once resided at Hauptstrasse 155. To the west is **Rathaus Schöneberg**, which served as West Berlin's town hall during the Cold War. John F Kennedy made his famous 'Ich bin ein Berliner' speech (*see p191* In the know) in the square outside, which now bears his name, and Mayor Walter Momper welcomed East Berliners to the West here in 1989.

From here, Belziger Strasse leads back in the direction of **Kleistpark**. The entrance to Kleistpark from Potsdamer Strasse is an 18th-century double colonnade, moved here from near Alexanderplatz in 1910. The mansion in the park was originally a law court but, during the Cold War, became headquarters for the Allied Control Council. After the 1972 treaty that formalised the separate status of East and West Germany, the building stood virtually unused apart from occasional Allied Council meetings. The American, British and French representatives would observe a ritual pause before each of these meetings, as if expecting the Soviet delegate, who had last attended in 1948, to turn up. In 1990, a Soviet finally did rejoin the council, and the Allies were able to hold a last meeting to formalise their withdrawal from the city in 1994. This may be the place where the Cold War officially ended.

On the north-west corner of Potsdamer Strasse's intersection with Pallasstrasse stood the Sportpalast, site of many Nazi rallies and the scene of Goebbels' famous 'Total War' speech of 18 February 1943. In its place stands a shabby block of flats. One part of the complex straddles Pallasstrasse and rests on the huge concrete hulk of a Nazi air-raid shelter, which planners were unable to destroy (*see p280*).

At the west end of Pallasstrasse stands **St-Matthias-Kirche**. South from here, Goltzstrasse is lined with cafés, bars and interesting shops. To the north of the church is **Winterfeldtplatz**, site of bustling Wednesday- and Saturday-morning markets that help support the surrounding cafés and restaurants.

Nollendorfplatz to the north is the hub of Schöneberg's nightlife. The theatre on the square has had many incarnations. In the Weimar era, it was home to experimental director Erwin Piscator; under the Third Reich, Hitler came here to watch Zara Leander shows; in the 1980s, it was the infamous Metropol disco.

Outside Nollendorfplatz U-Bahn, the small 'pink triangle' memorial to homosexual men killed in concentration camps is a reminder of the area's history. Though many flock to the younger and more contemporary scenes in Kreuzberg and Neukölln, north Schöneberg is, historically, Berlin's gay district. Motzstrasse has been a major artery of Berlin's gay life since the 1920s, and Christopher Isherwood, just one of Schöneberg's many literary greats,

chronicled Berlin from his rooming house at Nollendorfstrasse 17. Gay Schöneberg continues round the corner, across Martin-Luther-Strasse and along Fuggerstrasse. The **Schwules Museum** is just to the north (*see p110*).

Restaurants & cafés

Café Aroma €€
Hochkirchstrasse 8 (782 5821, www.cafc aroma.de). U7, S1, S2 Yorckstrasse. **Open** *5pm-midnight Mon-Sat; 11am-midnight Sun.* **Map** *p178 L11* **7** *Italian*

In a brunch-mad city, this lovely Italian trattoria is a Berlin foodie favourite for its multi-course marathon of cold cuts, poached salmon, fried risotto balls and roast vegetables. One of the first restaurants to sign up to Germany's Slow Food association in the early 1990s, it takes pains to source sustainable and authentic produce.

Double Eye €
Akazienstrasse 22 (0179 456 6960 mobile, www.doubleeye.de). U7 Eisenacher Strasse. **Open** *9.30am-6.30pm Mon-Fri; 10am-3.30pm Sat.* **No cards.** **Map** *p178 J11* **8** *Café*

Double Eye was one of the first of Berlin's third-wave coffee shops, and it's still one of the best, drawing queues for its cheap but potent espressos and creamy custard tarts.

Ixthys €
Pallasstrasse 21, on Winterfeldtplatz (8147 4769). U1, U2, U3, U4 Nollendorfplatz. **Open** *noon-10pm Mon-Sat.* **Map** *p178 J10* **11** *Korean*

Reams of handwritten scripture adorn the wall at this Christian Korean café, and the menu has bizarre flow diagrams explaining man's relationship with original sin. Brisk service brings *bulgogi*-marinated meats, or spicy broths, but the star of the show is the *bibimbap*, a classic dish of rice, layered with sautéed vegetables, chilli paste and sliced beef, crowned with a glistening fried egg and served in a scalding stone bowl so it will continue sizzling on the table.

In the know
Ich bin ein Berliner

Contrary to widely held belief, President Kennedy did not call himself a doughnut in front of half a million Berliners in 1963. A *Berliner* is only a doughnut in the north and west of Germany; in Berlin, doughnuts are known as *Pfannkuchen*. What's more, his addition of the indefinite *ein* was grammatically correct, implying solidarity with the city's embattled citizens.

❤ Berlin brunch

Breakfast in Berlin is a big deal. Whether you're up bright and early and fancy a leisurely morning meal, or you've been partying all night and need a calorie hit before crashing out, Berlin's brunch culture will see you right. The offer ranges from a simple duo of (excellent) coffee and a pastry, through a traditional German *Frühstuck* of bread rolls (called *Schrippen* in Berlin), cheese and salami, to increasingly elaborate spreads complete with muesli, fruit, yoghurt, cured meats, eggs and authentic dishes from around the globe. Highlights include Aussie comfort food – think lashings of avocado, eggs and unbeatable coffee – at **Silo Coffee** (*see p137*); pastries and crêpes surrounded by freshly cut flowers at **Anna Blume** (*see p119*); a post-clubbing refuel in the fresh air at **Café Schönbrunn** (*see p136*) and hearty portions in a cutesy setting at **1900 Café Bistro** (*see p182*). Other reliable brunch spots include **Barcomi's** and **Café Fleury** in Mitte (*see p90*), **Isla** (*see p174*) in Neukölln and **Café Aroma** in Schöneberg. For something different, try **La Femme** (Kottbusser Damm 77, 5360 4057, www.lafemme-breakfast.

de) in Kreuzberg, which serves traditional Turkish treats such as white cheese, *sucuk* (sausage), olives, eggs and fresh *simit* (a pretzel-shaped sesame-seeded breadstick). But perhaps the go-to spot right now is **Benedict** in Wilmersdorf (*see p189*), which has taken the city's infatuation with the meal to new heights by serving nothing but breakfast 24 hours a day. Luxury egg dishes and pancakes are the stars of its extensive international menu.

For many Berliners, lingering over brunch is an essential part of their week. Berliners rise indecently late at the weekend, but by 11am on a Saturday morning, the whole city seems to be out scouting for brunch; popular spots become jammed, and there's often a wait for tables, followed by incredibly slow service. By the time your food comes, you'll be close to tears. To avoid such an unpleasant start to your weekend, get to your venue of choice no later than 10.35am, so you can pick your table, place your order and sit back smugly sipping on that first latte-macchiato of the day, watching the frustration of those a bit slower off the mark.

Benedict *p189*

Renger-Patzsch €€

Wartburgstrasse 54 (784 2059, www.renger-patzsch.com). U7 Eisenacher Strasse. **Open** *6pm-late Mon-Sat; kitchen until 10.30pm.* **Map** *fold-out map J11* **16** *German*

The pan-German food – soup and salad starters, a sausage and sauerkraut platter, plus meat and fish dishes that vary daily – is finely prepared by versatile chef Hannes Behrmann, formerly of Le Cochon Bourgeois. House speciality is Alsatian tarte flambée: a crisp pastry base with toppings in seven variations. Expect substantial portions and a *Gasthaus* vibe. Communal seating is at long wooden tables and, in summer, there's a nice garden on this beautiful corner.

Sissi €€-€€€

Motzstrasse 34 (2101 8101, www.sissi-berlin. de). U1, U2, U3, U4 Nollendorfplatz. **Open** *from 5pm daily.* **Map** *p178 J10* **18** *Austrian*

Sissi is just darling! Some of the best *Schnitzel* in town and other hearty Austro-German dishes are complemented by excellent wines and attentive service. It's much bigger than it looks, thanks to a sizeable upstairs dining area, and the bright pink walls and an abundance of candlelight ensure the atmosphere is warm and inviting.

Bars & pubs

❤ Green Door

Winterfeldtstrasse 50 (215 2515, www. greendoor.de). U1, U2, U3, U4 Nollendorfplatz. **Open** *6pm-3am Mon-Thur, Sun; 6pm-4am Fri, Sat.* **No cards.** **Map** *p178 J10* **3**

Behind an actual green door (ring the bell for entry) lies this popular cocktail bar, which attracts a solid crowd of upmarket regulars as well as booze tourists on the Berlin quality cocktail trail. Inside it's quietly classy with a touch of kitsch. The impressive drinks menu runs the gamut of spirit-based mixology and includes the house Green Door cocktail, a refreshing mix of champagne, lemon, sugar and mint.

❤ Stagger Lee

Nollendorfstrasse 27 (2903 6158, www. staggerlee.de). U1, U2, U3, U4 Nollendorfplatz. **Open** *7pm-late daily.* **Map** *p178 J10* **5**

This vaudeville bar takes its name from a 1920s folk song about the true-life exploits of a violent pimp from St Louis, Missouri. Low-hanging saloon lamps, Victorian wallpaper and an enormous mechanical till add to its faux-Americana charm. The cocktails are outstanding. If you're choosing between here and the Green Door, pick Stagger Lee if you're all about the rye – but they're both excellent.

Shops & services

Antiquariat Thomas Mertens

Winterfeldtstrasse 51 (251 9203, http:// antiquariat-thomas-mertens.business. site). U1, U2, U3, U4 Nollendorfplatz. **Open** *11am-6pm Mon-Fri; 10.30am-3pm Sat.* **Map** *p178 J10* **1** *Antiques & books*

Schöneberg's a good district for antique and vintage shopping of all kinds, with a number of rare and second-hand bookshops to cater for bibliophiles. It's easy to lose track of time at Thomas Mertens as you browse the antique maps and first editions. Like most places, it's diversified, so you'll also find art and fascinating curios.

Garage

Ahornstrasse 2 (211 2760, www.kleidermarkt. de). U1, U2, U3, U4 Nollendorfplatz. **Open** *11am-7pm Mon-Fri; 11am-6pm Sat.* **Map** *p178 J9* **4** *Fashion*

Barn-like Garage sells cheap second-hand clothing priced by the kilo. The large selection is well organised, making it easy to root out last-minute party gear. A great place for '60s gear or to pick up fancy dress. On Wednesdays, there's a 30% discount 'happy hour' from 11am-1pm.

❤ Michas Bahnhof

Nürnberger Strasse 24A (218 6611, www. michas-bahnhof.de). U3 Augsburger Strasse. **Open** *10am-6.30pm Mon-Fri; 10am-3.30pm Sat.* **Map** *p178 G9* **8** *Gifts & souvenirs*

Unsurprisingly in such an engineering-mad country, Berlin has some fantastic model-train shops, and Michas Bahnhof is one of the best. The small space is rammed with engines, old and new, from around the world – and everything that goes with them.

❤ Winterfeldtplatz Market

Winterfeldtplatz (0175 437 4303 mobile). U1, U2, U3, U4 Nollendorfplatz. **Open** *8am-1pm Wed; 8am-4pm Sat.* **Map** *p178 J10* **16** *Food & drink*

In the leafy square surrounding St-Matthias-Kirche, this thriving farmers' market buzzes with life twice a week. There are more than 250 stalls; some stock traditional market tat, but most offer high-end gastronomic produce. The emphasis is on the local and seasonal, such as wild herbs and edible flowers, foraged mushrooms and local salami. Plenty of vendors serve cooked food; look out for Bauer Lindner, which sells *Bratwurst* made from their own pigs raised organically in Brandenburg.

West of the Centre

As it consists of two cities – once divided and now fused back together – it's not surprising that Berlin sprawls for miles in every direction. Although most of the fun stuff is in the gentrified East, and the key sites are in the centre, the outlying western boroughs are well worth exploring. Sleepy, a touch staid but with plenty of culture and history, the western districts feel a world away from the *Plattenbauten* (high-rises) and industrial sites in the East. Visiting the leafy streets and villas of Grunewald and Wannsee is like stepping back in time. The most popular excursion is to Potsdam, located just beyond the confines of the city in the state of Brandenburg. Potsdam is to Berlin what Versailles is to Paris.

❤ Don't miss

1 Bathing lakes *p198*
Skinny dip like a local all year round in one of Berlin's many lakes.

2 Brücke-Museum *p203*
Discover the best of German Expressionist painting in this beautiful villa.

3 Berliner Teufelsberg *p203*
Abandoned ex-spy station with a stunning city view.

4 Olympiastadion *p197*
The Olympic rings hover in the sky at this Nazi-era stadium.

5 Grunewald *p201*
Outdoor fun with forest, lakes and Cold War sites.

6 Park Sanssouci *p206*
Stroll through the park like Frederick the Great.

In the know
Getting around

Berlin's late 19th-century expansion into a hinterland of lakes and forests coincided with the age of railways, meaning public transport will whisk you to most of the far-flung districts. The S1 and S7 are the most useful lines for the sights mentioned in this chapter. The S1 runs all the way to Potsdam in 50 minutes, or you could take a faster regional train from Alexanderplatz, Hauptbahnhof or Zoo (25 minutes). Cycling is a great way to explore. Either pick up your wheels in the city and put your bike on the S-Bahn (remembering to buy a *Fahrrad* ticket), or pop into Pedales Bike Rental (potsdam-per-pedales.com) at Griebnitzsee S-Bahn station to rent a bike – or kayak, or SUP – by the day, hour, or week.

Grunewald

Funkturm

WESTEND

A couple of kilometres south-west of Schloss Charlottenburg, at the western end of Neue Kantstrasse, stands the futuristic **International Conference Centre** (ICC). Built in the 1970s, it's used for pop concerts, political rallies and the like. Next door, the even larger **Messe- und Ausstellungsgelände** (Trade Fair & Exhibition Area) plays host to trade fairs ranging from electronics to food to aerospace. Within the complex, the **Funkturm** (Radio Tower) offers panoramic views. Nearby, Hans Poelzig's **Haus des Rundfunks** (Masurenallee 9-14) is an expressive example of brick modernism.

Another couple of kilometres to the north-west, the imposing columns and conjoined rings of the **Olympiastadion** loom large. One of the few pieces of Fascist-era architecture still standing in Berlin, it was extensively renovated for the 2006 World Cup Final. Immediately south of Olympiastadion S-Bahn station is the **Corbusierhaus**, a huge multicoloured apartment block. Designed by Le Corbusier, it was constructed for the International Building exhibition of 1957. From here, a ten-minute walk along Sensburger Allee brings you to the sculptures of the **Georg-Kolbe-Museum** and its charming garden café.

Sights & museums

Funkturm

Messedamm (3038 1905, www.funkturm-messeberlin.de). U2 Theodor-Heuss-Platz or Kaiserdamm. **Open** *Platform 2-10pm Tue-Fri; 11am-10pm Sat, Sun. Restaurant 6-11pm Tue-Fri; 11.30am-11pm Sat, Sun.* **Admission** *€5; €3 reductions. No cards.* **Map** *p197.*

The 147-m (482-ft) Radio Tower was built in 1926 and looks a bit like a smaller version of the Eiffel Tower. There's a zippy lift up to the observation deck, but challenge-seekers can attempt the 610 steps; vertigo sufferers can seek solace in the restaurant, only 55m (180ft) from the ground. The tower closes in summer for repairs, so ring ahead.

Georg-Kolbe-Museum

Sensburger Allee 25 (304 2144, www.georg-kolbe-museum.de). S3, S9 Heerstrasse or bus X34, M49, X49. **Open** *10am-6pm daily.* **Admission** *€7; €5 reductions; free under-18s. No cards.* **Map** *p197.*

Georg Kolbe's former studio has been transformed into a showcase for his work. The Berlin sculptor, regarded as Germany's best in the 1920s, focused on naturalistic

Olympiastadion

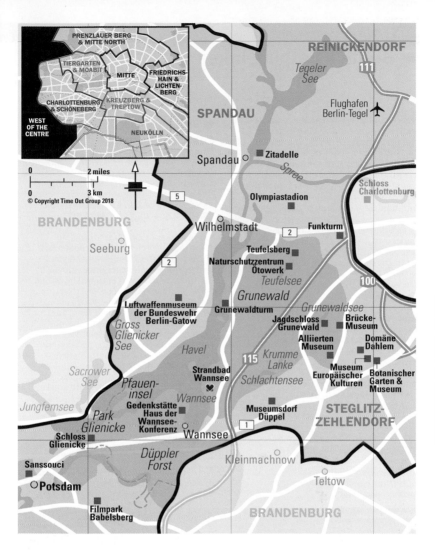

human figures. There are examples of his earlier graceful pieces, as well as his later more sombre and bombastic works, created in accordance with Nazi aesthetic ideals. His famous *Figure for Fountain* is in the sculpture garden, where there's also a great café for coffee and cake.

❤ Olympiastadion

*Olympischer Platz 3 (2500 2322, www. olympiastadion-berlin.de). U2 Olympia-Stadion or S3, S9 Olympiastadion. **Open** varies. **Admission** €8; €5.50 reductions. Guided tours €11; €9.50 reductions. No cards. **Map** p197.*

Built on the site of Berlin's original 1916 Olympic stadium, the current structure was designed by Werner March and opened in 1936 for the infamous 'Nazi Olympics' (you can see where the swastikas were removed from the old bell). The 74,000-seat stadium underwent a major and long-overdue refitting for the 2006 World Cup, including better seats and a roof over the whole lot. Home of Hertha BSC, it also hosts the German Cup Final, plus other sporting events and concerts. You can book a guided tour at the visitor centre by the Osttor (eastern gate). After the war, the former *Reichssportfeld* became the headquarters of the British military occupation forces.

❤ Berlin's bathing lakes

Brandenburg, the state that encircles Berlin, is known as the land of 3,000 lakes, and a visit to one is the perfect antidote to any of the Berlin vices – beer, cigarettes, sausage – to which you may have succumbed. Starkly beautiful in winter and inviting in summer, a good number of the lakes are reachable by public transport, and, if you bring a bike, you stand a good chance of finding your own private lakeside sunbathing patch. Whether for sailing, swimming or strolling, each lake has its own distinct character, and every Berliner has his or her favourite. Striking out in any direction from Berlin, you'll be spoilt for choice.

If you've got the time and are feeling adventurous, you'll find quieter, more idyllic lakes by going that bit further. The **Tonsee** south of Berlin, **Liepnitzsee** in the north and **Straussee** in the east, all make lovely day trips.

The municipal bathing beaches – *Strandbäder* – are run by the city. You pay an entrance fee for access to showers, toilets, changing rooms and the services of a lifeguard. Usually, one end of the beach is favoured by nudists. Freikörperkultur (FKK), German for nudism, has a long history in these parts. Berliners are untroubled by the sight of a naked body, and at most lakes no one will care if you suit up or not.

▶ *For details of all the city's* Strandbäder *and other swimming pools, see www. berlinerbaeder.de.*

❤ Best for families
Strandbad Wannsee
Wannseebadweg 25, Nikolassee (2219 0011, www.berlinerbaeder.de/baeder/strandbad-wannsee). S1, S7 Nikolassee then 10-min walk, or Berlin Wannsee then shuttle bus. **Open** *Apr-mid Sept; see the website for daily opening times. No swimming in Apr.* **Admission** *€5.50, €3.50 reductions.* **Map** *p197.*

Lie on the sandy beach at Strandbad Wannsee to watch the sailing boats dart up and down the River Havel and you'll be partaking in an experience enjoyed by Berliners for nearly a century. The waters of the Wannsee (an inlet of the river) are extensive and, in summer, warm enough for comfortable swimming; there's a strong current, though, so don't stray beyond the floating markers. Between May and September, there are boats, pedalos and two-person wicker sunchairs, called *Strandkörbe*, for hire, plus a playground and slides. Service buildings house showers, toilets, shops, cafés and kiosks. Children love it here.

❤ Best for rowing
Schlachtensee
S1 Schlachtensee. **Map** *p197.*

A circuit of the Schlachtensee is 5.5km (3.5 miles), which is the perfect distance to work up an appetite that you can happily sate

Schlachtensee

WEST OF THE CENTRE

at the **Fischerhütte** (*p204*). In summer, there are rowing boats and paddle boards for hire (www.stch-paddler.com), and the particularly clean waters are ideal for a dip. The lake is just across the road from the station, but you may have to walk a few minutes along its perimeter to find a secluded spot.

♥ Best for skinny-dipping

Teufelsee
S7 Grunewald, then 15-min walk. **Map** *p197.*

This small lake in the Grunewald is surround by a pleasant green meadow, ideal for stretching out on. On the lake itself, floating rafts draw swimmers who compete for space with the ducks. Prudes beware: naked swimming and sunbathing are common here.

♥ Best for sunset swimming

Strandbad Plötzensee
Nordufer 26, Wedding (8964 4787, www. strandbad-ploetzensee.de). S41, S42 Beusselstrasse, or U9, S41, S42 Westhafen then 20-min walk. **Open** *May-Sept 9am-7pm daily (longer hours in good weather).* **Admission** *€5 (€3 reductions).*

Only 30 minutes from Alexanderplatz, Plötzensee is the perfect spot to relax with a swim after a strenuous day's exploring. The Strandbad has 740m of sand, and there are plenty of refreshments on offer, so you can have a dip, crack open a beer – and still be back in the centre in time for dinner.

♥ Best for hiking

Müggelsee
S3 Friedrichshagen.

Officially Berlin's largest lake, Müggelsee in the east is over 4km (2.5 miles) long and 2.5km (1.5 miles) wide, so hiking round the lake is a great way to stretch your legs. If you're planning to do the whole circuit, you'll have to take the tiny ferry between Müggelwerder and Müggelhort, which runs once an hour in summer; the crossing takes 10 minutes. Once over, follow the lake round and after 30 minutes you'll come to a lovely

beer garden. There are plenty of sandy little spots to take a dip, but if you're looking for facilities, then head for Strandbad Müggelsee (www.strandbad-mueggelsee. de) – although the large colony of ducks here can make swimming a challenge!

Müggelsee

Strandbad Wannsee

SPANDAU

Berlin's western neighbour and eternal rival, Spandau is a little Baroque town that seems to contradict everything about the city of which it is now, reluctantly, a part. Spandauers still talk about 'going into Berlin' when they head off to the rest of the city. Berliners, meanwhile, basically still consider Spandau to be part of old West Germany, though travelling there is easy on the U7, alighting at either Zitadelle or Altstadt Spandau, depending on which sights you want to visit. There's nothing thrilling to see, but it makes for a low-key escape from the city.

The **Zitadelle** (Citadel) contains in one of its museums Spandau's original town charter, dating from 1232, a fact Spandauers have used ever since to argue their historical primacy over Berlin. The old town centre is mostly pedestrianised, with 18th-century townhouses interspersed with chain burger joints and department stores. One of the prettiest buildings is the former Gasthof zum Stern in Carl-Schurz-Strasse; older still are houses in Kinkelstrasse and Ritterstrasse – but the best-preserved district is north of Am Juliusturm in the area bounded by Hoher Steinweg, Kolk and Behnitz. Steinweg contains a fragment of the old town wall from the first half of the 14th century; Kolk has the **Alte Marienkirche** (1848); and in Behnitz, at no.5, stands the elegant Baroque **Heinemannsche Haus**. In Reformationsplatz, the **Nikolaikirche** has a brick nave dating from 1410-50; the west tower was added in 1468, and there are later enhancements by Schinkel.

Many will know the name Spandau from its association with Rudolf Hess. Hitler's deputy, who flew to Britain in 1940 for reasons that are still disputed, was held in the Allied prison here after the Nuremberg trials, and remained here (alone after 1966) until his suicide in 1987 at the age of 93. The prison, a 19th-century brick building at Wilhelmstrasse 21-24, was then demolished to make way for a supermarket for the British forces. Some distance south of Spandau is the **Luftwaffenmuseum der Bundeswehr Berlin-Gatow**.

Sights & museums

Luftwaffenmuseum der Bundeswehr Berlin-Gatow

Kladower Damm 182, Gatow (3687 2601, www.luftwaffenmuseum.de). U7 Rathaus Spandau, then bus 135, then 15-min walk. **Open** *10am-6pm Tue-Sun.* **Admission** *free.* **Map** *p197.*

For propeller heads only, this museum is on the far western fringes of the city at what was formerly the RAF base in divided Berlin; it's a long journey by public transport followed by a 15-minute walk from the bus stop (or you can get a cab from the U-Bahn station). Then there's a lot more walking to take in more than 100 aircraft scattered around the airfield, plus exhibits in two hangars and the former control tower. The emphasis is on the history of military aviation in Germany since 1945, although there's also a World War I triplane, a restored Handley Page Hastings (as used during the Berlin Airlift) and a whole lot of missiles.

Zitadelle

Am Juliusturm 64 (354 9440, tours 334 6270, www.zitadelle-spandau.net). U7 Zitadelle. **Open** *10am-5pm daily.* **Admission** *€4.50; €2.50 reductions. No cards.* **Map** *p197.*

The bulk of the Zitadelle was constructed between 1560 and 1594 in the style of an Italian fort to dominate the confluence of the Spree and Havel rivers. Since then it has been used as everything from a garrison to a prison to a poison-gas laboratory. The oldest structure here (and the oldest secular building in Berlin) is the Juliusturm, probably dating back to an Ascanian fortress from about 1160. The present tower was home until 1919 to 120-million gold Marks, a small part of the five billion paid as French reparations to Germany in 1874 after the Franco-Prussian War. There are two museums within the Zitadelle: one tells the story of the building with models and maps; the other covers local history.

Restaurants & cafés

Brauhaus Spandau €-€€

Neuendorferstrasse 1 (353 9070, www. brauhaus-spandau.de). U7 Altstadt Spandau. **Open** *10am-late daily. German*

This large beer hall is about as German as they come: a large dining room with gallery, big hunks of pork and potato on the plate and mugfuls of frothy home-brewed beer. The food is stodgy but hits the spot, and they have dark, light and seasonal beers, which you can order in a gut-busting litre glass.

SOUTH-WEST BERLIN

South-west Berlin contains some of the city's wealthiest suburbs and, in the days of division, was the American sector; various landmarks survive from this time.

Dahlem and around

The museum complex at Dahlem was built to house the world-class **Ethnologisches Museum** (Ethnological Museum), the **Museum für Asiatische Kunst** (Museum of Asian Art) and the **Museum Europäischer Kulturen** (Museum of European Cultures). However, it is unclear what will become of the current museum buildings once the ethnographic and Asian art collections move permanently to the Humboldt Forum in 2019 (*see p79*) and the Museum of European Cultures possibly relocates to the Kulturforum near Potsdamer Platz.

Surrounding the museums is the campus of the **Freie Universität**, some of whose departments occupy former villas seized by the Nazis from their Jewish owners. Nearby, opposite the Dahlem-Dorf cemetery, is the **Domäne Dahlem** working farm – a great place to take kids. Two other worthwhile museums can be found on the edge of the **Grunewald** (*see below*): the **Brücke-Museum** displays a collection of expressionist paintings and prints, while the **Alliierten Museum** (Allied Museum) has exhibits from the early years of the Cold War.

Ten minutes' walk east from Dahlem along Königin-Luise-Strasse is the **Botanischer Garten & Botanisches Museum** (Botanical Garden & Museum), while, west of Dahlem, in Zehlendorf, is the reconstructed 14th-century village at **Museumsdorf Düppel**.

♥ Grunewald

The western edge of Zehlendorf is formed by the Havel River and the extensive Grunewald, the largest of Berlin's many forests. Due to its easy accessibility by S-Bahn, its lanes and pathways fill with walkers, runners, cyclists and horse riders at weekends. At the station itself, take a moment to visit **Gleis 17**, the platform from where as many as 50,000 Berlin Jews were deported to the death camps. Metal plaques give the dates and destinations of the transports.

Heading west into the forest, one popular destination is the **Teufelsee**, a tiny lake packed with nudist bathers (and mosquitos) in summer, reached by heading west from the station along Schildhornweg for 15 minutes (*see p198* Berlin's bathing lakes). Close by is a wonderful eco park, **Naturschutzzentrum Ökowerk** (www.oekowerk.de) and the legendary **Teufelsberg**, a by-product of wartime devastation that became Berlin's highest point; a railway was laid from Wittenbergplatz to carry the 25 million cubic metres of rubble to this spot. There are great views from the summit and an eerie abandoned spy structure on the top. For years, there has been talk of replacing the Cold War-era, US electronic listening post with a hotel and conference centre, but, for now, you can pay an entrance fee and wander freely or take a tour of the spooky site.

On the west side of the Grunewald, halfway up Havelchaussee, is the **Grunewaldturm**, a tower built in 1897 in memory of Wilhelm I. It has an observation platform 105 metres (344 feet) above the Havel River, with expansive views west as far as Spandau and Potsdam. There's a restaurant at the base and another over the road, both with garden terraces. A short walk south along Havelufer leads to the ferry to **Lindwerder Insel**, which also has a restaurant. To the north, a little way into the forest, ex-Velvet Underground singer Nico, who grew up in Schöneberg, is buried among the trees in the **Friedhof Grunewald-Forst**.

South of Grunewald station, meanwhile (and to the east of the A115, which bisects the forest), is a string of lakes. The **Grunewaldsee** has the 16th-century **Jagdschloss Grunewald** (Grunewald Hunting Lodge) at its far end. This is the kind of building that once maintained the country life of the Prussian Junkers (landed gentry). To the south-west, **Krumme Lanke** and **Schlachtensee** (*see p198* Berlin's bathing lakes) are pleasantly clear urban lakes, perfect for picnicking, swimming or rowing – and each with its own train station. There's a particularly lovely beer garden and restaurant at Schlachtensee called the **Fischerhütte**.

Wannsee and Pfaueninsel

At the south-west edge of the Grunewald, you'll find boats and beaches in summer, and castles and forests all through the year. The **Grosser Wannsee** is a wide inlet of the Havel, with the **Strandbad Wannsee**, the largest inland beach in Europe, on its eastern shore (*see p198* Berlin's bathing lakes). A small bridge north of the beach leads to **Schwanenwerder**, once the exclusive private island retreat of Goebbels and now home to the Aspen Institute, an international think-tank.

The town of Wannsee is clustered around the south-west of the bay and is dominated by a long promenade, Am Grossen Wannsee, scattered with hotels and fish restaurants. A short distance from Wannsee S-Bahn station along Bismarckstrasse is a little garden where German dramatist Heinrich von Kleist shot himself in 1811; the beautiful view of the **Kleiner Wannsee** was the last thing he wanted to see. To the north, the **Gedenkstätte Haus der Wannsee-Konferenz** is an elegant Gründerzeit mansion – now a museum – where a group of prominent Nazis met in January 1942 to plan their monstrous 'Final Solution' for the extermination of the Jewish race.

From Wannsee, bus 218 scoots through **Düppeler Forst** to a pier on the Havel, from where it's a brief ferry ride to **Pfaueninsel** (Peacock Island; €8 return). Friedrich Wilhelm II purchased the island in 1793, and built a castle for his mistress, but he died in 1797 before they had a chance to move in. Its first residents were Friedrich Wilhelm III and Queen Luise, who spent much of their time together on the island, even setting up a farm there. A royal menagerie was later developed. Most of the animals were moved to the new Tiergarten Zoo in 1842; now peacocks, pheasants, parrots, goats and sheep remain. Surviving structures include the **castle** (Mar-Nov Tue-Sun 10am-5.30pm; €6, €5 reductions); Jakobsbrunnen (Jacob's Fountain); a copy of a Roman temple; the Kavalierhaus (Cavalier's House), built in 1803 from an original design by Schinkel; and the Swiss cottage, also based on a Schinkel plan. All are linked by winding paths laid out in the English manner by Peter Joseph Lenné. A walk around the island – with its monumental trees, rough meadows and views over the Havel – provides one of the most complete sensations of escape to be had within the borders of Berlin.

Back on the mainland, a short walk south along Nikolskoer Weg is the **Blockhaus Nikolskoe** (805 2914, www.blockhaus-nikolskoe.de), a huge wooden chalet built in 1819 by Friedrich Wilhelm II for his daughter Charlotte, and named after her husband, the future Tsar Nicholas of Russia. There's a magnificent view from the terrace, where you can sit back and enjoy some typical Berlin dishes or coffee and cakes.

Glienicke

West of Wannsee, and only a couple of kilometres from Potsdam, Glienicke was once the south-westernmost tip of West Berlin. The suspension bridge over the Havel here was named **Brücke der Einheit** (Bridge of Unity) because it joined Potsdam

Pfaueninsel

with Berlin. After the building of the Wall, it was painted different shades of olive green on the East and West sides; it was used only by Allied soldiers and for top-level prisoner and spy exchanges – Anatoly Shcharansky was one of the last, in 1986. The Tom Hank's film *The Bridge* dramatises this corner of Cold War history.

The main reason to come here is **Park Glienicke**. Its centrepiece is **Schloss Glienicke** (0331 969 4200, www.spsg. de, closed Mon), originally a hunting lodge designed by Schinkel for Prinz Carl von Preussen, who adorned the garden walls with ancient relics collected on his Mediterranean holidays and decided to simulate a walk from the Alps to Rome in the densely wooded park. The summer houses, fountains and follies are all based on original Italian models, and the woods and fields around them make an ideal place for a Sunday picnic, since this park is little visited. The Schloss hosts regular classical music concerts. At the nearby inlet of Moorlake, there's a restaurant in an 1842 hunting lodge.

Sights & museums

Alliierten Museum

Clayallee 135, at Huttenweg (818 1990, www. alliiertenmuseum.de). U3 Oskar-Helene-Heim then 10 mins walk, or bus 115. **Open** *10am-6pm Tue-Sun.* **Admission** *free.*

The Allies arrived as conquerors, kept West Berlin alive during the 1948 Airlift and finally went home in 1994. In what used to be a US Forces cinema, the Allied Museum is mostly about the period of the Blockade and Airlift, documented with photos, tanks, jeeps, planes, weapons and uniforms. Outside is the former guardhouse from Checkpoint Charlie and an RAF Hastings TG 503 plane. Guided tours in English can be booked in advance.

♥ Berliner Teufelsberg

Teufelsseechaussee 10 (www.teufelsberg-berlin.de). **Open** *Tours noon-8pm Wed-Sun. Tickets €5-€15. No cards.* **Map** *p197.*

During the Cold War, the Allies built this listening station on the top of one of Berlin's highest hills to eavesdrop on what the East Germans were up to on the other side of the Wall. The site was abandoned when the Iron Curtain fell, and soon became a favourite spot for urban explorers and ravers looking for a trippy place to throw an open-air party. The days of illegally exploring the site are now over, but the situation is still a bit disorganised. You can buy a ticket to explore the Teufelsberg online or at the site, but if you choose the latter, bring cash or you'll be turned away. Guided tours taking you through the decrepit structure are offered in German and English and cost extra, as does bringing in a camera (but not a smartphone). Beyond Teufelsberg's varied history, it's the stunning view over the city, the wild graffiti and the unnerving acoustics of the giant radar dome that are the real draws. Keep an eye on children; there's no health and safety here.

Botanischer Garten & Botanisches Museum

Königin-Luise-Strasse 6-8 (8385 0100, www.botanischergartenberlin.de). S1 Botanischer Garten then 15 mins walk. **Open** *Garden May-July 9am-8pm daily. Museum 10am-7pm daily.* **Admission** *Garden & Museum €6; €3 reductions. Museum only €2.50; €1.50 reductions. No cards.* **Map** *p197.*

The Botanical Garden was landscaped at the beginning of the 20th century. Today, it's home to 18,000 plant species, 16 greenhouses and a museum. The gardens make for a pleasant stroll, but the museum is a bit dilapidated and there's no information in English. Every Monday, the staff run a wild

mushroom advice workshop, so feel free to forage away in the nearby forests.

♥ Brücke-Museum

Bussardsteig 9 (831 2029, www.bruecke-museum.de). U3 Oskar-Helene-Heim then bus 115. **Open** *11am-5pm Mon, Wed-Sun.* **Admission** *€6; €4 reductions. No cards.* **Map** *p197.*

This small but satisfying museum – reputedly a favourite of David Bowie – is dedicated to the work of *Die Brücke* (The Bridge), a group of expressionist painters that was founded in Dresden in 1905 before moving to Berlin. A large collection of oils, watercolours, drawings and sculptures by the main members of the group – Schmidt-Rottluff, Heckel, Kirchner, Mueller and Pechstein – is rotated in temporary exhibitions.

Domäne Dahlem

Königin-Luise-Strasse 49 (666 3000, www. domaene-dahlem.de). U3 Dahlem-Dorf. **Open** *Museum 10am-5pm Wed-Sun.* **Admission** *Museum €5; €3 reductions. No cards.* **Map** *p197.*

On this organic working farm, children can see how life was lived in the 17th century. Craftspeople preserve and teach their skills. It's best to visit during one of the several annual festivals, when kids can ride ponies, tractors and hay wagons. There's also a farm shop and, in good weather, a garden café.

Gedenkstätte Haus der Wannsee-Konferenz

Am Grossen Wannsee 56-58 (805 0010, www. ghwk.de). S1, S7 Wannsee then bus 114. **Open** *10am-6pm daily.* **Admission** *free.*

On 20 January 1942, a group of leading Nazis, chaired by Heydrich, gathered here to draw up plans for the Final Solution. Today, this infamous villa has been converted into the Wannsee Conference Memorial House, a place of remembrance, with a photo exhibit on the conference and its genocidal consequences. Call in advance if you want to join an English-language tour, though the information is in both English and German.

Museum Europäischer Kulturen

Arnimallee 25 (266 426802, www.smb. museum/en/museums-institutions/museum-europaeischer-kulturen/home.html). U3 Dahlem-Dorf. **Open** *10am-5pm Tue-Fri; 11am-6pm Sat, Sun.* **Admission** *€8; €4 reductions.* **Map** *p197.*

The museum covers everyday European culture from the 18th century to the present. One highlight is a mechanical model of the Nativity, displayed during Advent. Exhibitions will continue here until at least July 2019; thereafter the museum may relocate to the Kulturforum; check the website for updates.

Museumsdorf Düppel

*Clauertstrasse 11 (802 6671, www.dueppel.de). S1 Mexikoplatz then bus 118, 622. **Open** Apr-Oct 10am-6pm Sat, Sun. **Admission** €3.50; free-€2.50 reductions. No cards.*

At this reconstructed 14th-century village, built around archaeological excavations, workers demonstrate medieval handicrafts, technology and farming techniques. Kids can enjoy ox-cart rides.

Restaurants & cafés

There are several restaurants next to Grunewald station, and on the other side of the motorway at Schmetterlingsplatz; these are open from April to October.

Fischerhütte am Schlachtensee €€

*Fischerhüttenstrasse 136 (8049 8310, www. fischerhuette-berlin.de). U1 Krumme Lanke or S1 Mexikoplatz. **Open** 10am-midnight daily. German*

Overlooking the lake is the Fischerhütte, encompassing both a large beer garden and a more formal restaurant inside. It was built in the mid-18th century as a rest house on the road between Berlin and Potsdam. The restaurant has plenty of old photos from its heyday in the 1920s, when the lakes were Berlin's answer to the French Riviera. Grab a *Bratwurst* and beer at the lakeside if you don't fancy a sit-down dinner.

Krasselts €

*Steglitzer Damm 22, Steglitz (796 9147, www. krasselts-berlin.de). U9, S1 Rathaus Steglitz. **Open** 10am-11pm Mon; 10am-midnight Tue-Sat; 11am-11pm Sun. Imbiss*

Still family-run, Krasselts has been knocking out the Berlin street-food classic of *Currywurst* for over half a century. They closely guard their secret sauce recipe and make all their own sausages. East Germans traditionally ate their sausage with skin, but these days the distinction has mostly disappeared. Enjoy at a standing table with a side of fries or a crusty white roll.

Luise €-€€

*Königin-Luise-Strasse 40-42, Dahlem (841 8880, www.luise-dahlem.de). U3 Dahlem-Dorf. **Open** 10am-late daily. Brasserie*

This traditional Berlin brasserie does all sorts, with a pizza menu (the buffalo mozzarella is made locally in Brandenburg), German snacks such as *Currywurst*, and breakfast too. It's near the Freie Universität, so the large,

lovely beer garden gets packed with students. Convenient for those visiting the museums, Luise also offers a very decent all-you-can-eat brunch buffet on Sundays.

Waldhaus an der Havelchaussee €€

*Grunewaldturm, Havelchaussee 66 (304 0595). S7 Grunewald then bus 218. **Open** 10.30am-6pm Tue-Sun. **No cards**. German*

Enjoy old school Berliner hospitality at this lovely forest house situated in the beautiful Grunewald. Eat inside in the historic restaurant, or among the lushly terraced gardens when the weather's fine. Serving seasonal specialities, such as white asparagus with hollandaise, traditional German cuisine and delicious cakes, the Waldhaus is the perfect spot to satisfy an appetite worked up by a stroll, jog or swim.

POTSDAM & BABELSBERG

Potsdam is the capital of the state of Brandenburg. Located just outside Berlin's city limits to the south-west, it's the capital's most beautiful neighbour. Known for its 18th-century Baroque architecture, it's a magnet for tourists.

For centuries, Potsdam was the summer residence of the Hohenzollerns, who were attracted by the area's gently rolling landscape, rivers and lakes. Despite the damage wrought during World War II and by East Germany's socialist planners, much remains of the legacy of these Prussian kings. The best-known landmark is Sanssouci, the huge landscaped park created by Frederick the Great – one of three royal parks flanking the town.

Potsdam has changed considerably since reunification. In East German times, a lack of political will and economic means led to much of the town's historic fabric falling into disrepair or being destroyed. In 1990, though, Potsdam was assigned UNESCO World Heritage status and some 80 per cent of the town's historic buildings have since been restored.

The end of East Germany also marked the end of Potsdam's historic role as a garrison town. Until the Soviet withdrawal, some 10,000 troops were stationed here. With their departure, vast barracks and tracts of land to the north of the town were abandoned. The area is currently being redeveloped for civilian use, including the BUGA or Volkspark, with its **Biosphäre** (Georg-Hermann-Allee 99, 0331 550 740, www.biosphaere-potsdam.de). The indoor tropical park is spread over 7,000 square metres (75,340 square feet) and houses over 20,000 plants, plus iguanas, snakes, frogs and geckos. It's an ideal place to take kids on a rainy day.

The Old Town

One of the most dominant historical buildings in the Old Town is the 19th-century **Nikolaikirche** (Am Alten Markt, 0331 270 8602, www.nikolaipotsdam. de), whose huge dome is a landmark of the Alter Markt (old market). The **Alter Markt** was left in ruins by World War II bombing and Soviet artillery fire; during the GDR years, there was no cohesive plan for reconstruction, although both the Nikolaikirche and the rather more graceful 18th-century **Altes Rathaus** (old town hall) were rebuilt in the 1960s. The Altes Rathaus is now used for exhibitions and lectures, and houses the **Potsdam Museum** (Am Alten Markt 9, 0331 289 6868, www.potsdam. de/potsdam-museum, closed Mon), with a permanent display on the history of the city.

The **Stadtschloss** (city palace), to the south, was also substantially damaged during World War II, and the East German authorities demolished the rest of it in 1960. In 2007 a decision was made to reconstruct the Stadtschloss and restore the Alter Markt to its former glory. A historically accurate reconstruction of the palace was completed in 2014, which now houses the Brandenburg state parliament.

At the southern end of the square is the state-of-the-art **Museum Barberini**, (Humboldtstrasse 5-6, 0331 2360 14499, www.museum-barberini.com, closed Tue, €10-€14), rebuilt on the site of the 18th-century Barberini Palace. It opened in 2017 to house a permanent collection of art produced in the GDR and to host temporary exhibitions from around the world. There's a café with a lovely view of the Alter Markt. Opposite the palace, the park behind the vast Hotel Mercure was once part of the palace gardens. Later, Friedrich Wilhelm I, the Soldier King, turned it into a parade ground.

The low red building to the west of the Stadtschloss is the former Marstall, or royal riding stables. Dating from 1685 and originally an orangery, it's one of the oldest buildings in town. Today it houses the **Filmmuseum Potsdam** (Breite Strasse 1A, 0331 271 8112, www.filmmuseum-potsdam. de, closed Mon), which explores nearly a century of film-making at the Babelsberg studios (*see p207*). The on-site cinema regularly shows films, and guided tours are available in English.

Nearby, Neuer Markt survived the war intact. At no.1 is the house where Friedrich Wilhelm II was born. The Kutschstall, originally the royal coaching stables, now houses the **Haus der Brandenburgisch-Preussischen Geschichte**(0331 620 8550, www.hbpg.de, closed Mon, €3.50-€4.50s), charting 900 years of Brandenburg history through artwork and everyday artefacts.

Baroque and Dutch quarters

Potsdam's impressive Baroque Quarter is bounded by Schopenhauerstrasse, Hegelallee, Hebbelstrasse and Charlottenstrasse. Some of the most appealing houses can be found in Gutenbergstrasse and Brandenburger Strasse, the city's pedestrianised shopping drag. Note the pitched roofs with space to accommodate troops – the Soldier King built the quarter in the 1730s. Just around the corner is **Gedenkstätte Lindenstrasse**, (Lindenstrasse 54, 0331 289 6136, www. gedenkstaette-lindenstrasse.de, closed Mon, €1-€2), a detention centre that was used by both the Nazis and the Stasi to house thousands of political prisoners. It is now a memorial and museum to victims of political persecution and violence.

Three Baroque town gates – **Nauener Tor**, **Jäger Tor** and **Brandenburger Tor** – stand on the northern and western edges of the quarter. East from here, two churches bear witness to Potsdam's cosmopolitan past. The Great Elector's 1685 Edict of Potsdam promised refuge to Protestants suffering from religious persecution in their homelands, sparking waves of immigration. The **Französische Kirche** on Hebbelstrasse was built for the town's Huguenot community, while **St Peter & Paul's** in Bassinplatz was built for Catholic immigrants.

The **Holländisches Viertel**, or Dutch Quarter, is the most attractive part of Friedrich Wilhelm I's new-town extension. As part of a failed strategy to lure skilled Dutch immigrants to the town, the king had Dutch builders construct 134 gable-fronted houses. In **Jan Bouman Haus** (Mittelstrasse 8, 0331 280 3773, www.jan-bouman-haus.de), you can see an original interior. Today, this area is filled with upmarket boutiques and restaurants.

Alexandrowka

Another Potsdam curiosity is the Russian colony of Alexandrowka, 15 minutes' walk north from the town centre. The settlement consists of 13 wooden-clad, two-storey dwellings with steeply pitched roofs laid out in the form of a St Andrew's Cross. There's even a Russian Orthodox church with an onion dome. Services are still held in the **Alexander-Newski-Kapelle**.

Alexandrowka was built in 1826 by Friedrich Wilhelm III to commemorate the death of Tsar Alexander I, a friend from the Wars of Liberation against Napoleon. The settlement became home to surviving members of a troupe of Russian musicians given into Prussian service by the Tsar in 1812. Russian specialities are served by waitresses in folkloric costume at the **Teehaus Russische Kolonie** (Alexandrowka 1, 0331 200 6478, closed Mon). Nearby is the tiny **Alexandrowka Museum** (Russische Kolonie 2, 0331 817 0203, www.alexandrowka.de, closed Wed).

The area around and to the north of Alexandrowka became the focus of a different Russian presence during the Cold War, when Soviet forces took over buildings that had been used by the Prussian army in the 19th century and later by the Nazis. One such building is the castle-like **Garde-Ulanen-Kaserne** in Jägerallee, near the junction with Reiterweg.

The recently restored Belvedere, at the top of the hill to the north of Alexandrowka, is the town's highest observation point.

Potsdam's royal parks and palaces

Back towards the town centre is Potsdam's biggest tourist magnet, the sprawling **Park Sanssouci**. A legacy of King Friedrich II (Frederick the Great), 'Sans souci' means 'without worry' and reflects the king's desire for a sanctuary where he could pursue his philosophical, musical and literary interests. He initially had the famous vineyard terraces and formal garden built, before adding the rococo palace, **Schloss Sanssouci** (Maulbeerallee, 0331 969 4200, www.spsg.de, closed Mon, €8-€12), where Voltaire was one of many guests. The palace is flanked to the west by the ornate **Neue Kammern** (New Chambers, closed Nov-Mar and closed Mon, €5-€6) and to the east by the **Bildergalerie** (Picture Gallery, closed

Nov-Apr and closed Mon, €5-€6), built to house Friedrich II's extensive art collection, including some Flemish and Dutch masters. Spreading out from these buildings are acres of grandly elegant gardens, which conceal several other features, including the Orangery; the Spielfestung, or toy fortress, built for Wilhelm II's sons, with a toy cannon that can be fired; the Chinesisches Teehaus (Chinese Tea House), with its collection of Chinese and Meissen porcelain; and the Drachenhaus (Dragonhouse), a pagoda-style café. It's free to wander through the park, and its size means you can always find your own grassy corner for a picnic.

After victory in the Seven Years' War, Friedrich II built the huge **Neues Palais** (0331 969 4200, www.spsg.de, closed Tue, €6-€8) to the west of Sanssouci. The parkland between the two palaces was expanded and landscaped by Friedrich Wilhelm IV, and the monumental building was used by Kaiser Wilhelm II as his favoured residence. Long-term, extensive renovations are ongoing. In the park's south-west corner lies **Schloss Charlottenhof**, with its copper-plate engraving room, built in the 1830s on the orders of crown prince Friedrich Wilhelm IV. Outside Sanssouci, on Breite Strasse, is the **Dampfmaschinenhaus**. It pumped water for Sanssouci's fountains but was built to look like a mosque.

North-east of the town centre is another large park complex, the **Neuer Garten**, designed on the orders of Friedrich Wilhelm II. The king died a premature death in the neoclassical **Marmorpalais** (0331 969 4200, www.spsg.de, closed Mon-Fri in winter), allegedly as a result of his dissolute lifestyle. At the park's most northern corner is **Schloss Cecilienhof** (0331 969 4200, www.spsg.de, closed Mon), the last royal palace to be built in Potsdam. This incongruous, mock-Tudor mansion was built for the Kaiser's son and his wife. Spared wartime damage, it hosted the Potsdam Conference in summer 1945, where Stalin, Truman and Churchill (later replaced by Clement Attlee) met to discuss Germany's future. Inside, you can see the round table where the settlement was negotiated.

During the conference, the Allied leaders lived across the Havel river in one of Babelsberg's secluded 19th-century villa districts. Stalin stayed in Karl-Marx-Strasse 27; Churchill stayed in Villa Urbig at Virchowstrasse 23, one of Mies van der Rohe's early buildings; and Truman stayed in Truman-Villa at Karl-Marx-Strasse 2. These buildings can be viewed from the outside only.

Potsdam's third and most recent royal park, **Park Babelsberg**, fell into neglect

Schloss Sanssouci

during the GDR because it lay so near to the border. **Schloss Babelsberg**, a neo-Gothic extravaganza inspired by Windsor Castle, nestles among its wooded slopes. Another architectural curiosity is the **Flatowturm**, an observation tower in mock medieval style close to the Glienicker See.

Also on the east side of the Havel river, not too far south of Potsdam's main station, is Erich Mendelsohn's expressionist **Einsteinturm**, built to house an observatory that could confirm the General Theory of Relativity. Built in 1921, it was one of the first products of the inter-war avant-garde.

On nearby Brauhausberg, there's one last reminder of Potsdam's complex, multi-layered past. The square tower rising up from the trees is the present seat of Brandenburg's state parliament. In East German days, the building was known as the 'Kremlin' because it served as local Communist Party headquarters.

Babelsberg

The main attraction in Potsdam's eastern neighbour, Babelsberg, is the film-studio complex, sections of which are open to the public in theme-park form. In the 1920s, this was the world's largest studio outside Hollywood, and it was here that Fritz Lang's *Metropolis*, Josef von Sternberg's *The Blue Angel* and other masterpieces were produced. During the Nazi period, it churned out thrillers, light entertainment and propaganda pieces such as Leni Riefenstahl's *Triumph of the Will*. More than 700 feature films were made here during the Communist era.

The studios were privatised after reunification and now there are modern facilities for all phases of film and TV production. **Filmpark Babelsberg** (Grossbeerenstrasse 200, 0331 721 2750, www.filmpark.de, closed Nov-Mar, €15-€22) has an assortment of attractions, ranging from themed restaurants and rides to set tours and stunt displays, but it's pretty tacky.

Restaurants & cafés

Café Heider (Friedrich-Ebert-Strasse 31, 0331 270 5596, €-€€) offers excellent coffee and cake, plus a wide range of main dishes. **Backstoltz** (Dortustrasse 59, 0331 2012 929, €) is a cosy *croissanterie*, good for a light breakfast or lunch. There's also a range of cafés, pubs and restaurants along pedestrianised Brandenburger Strasse, most with tables outside in summer, and on nearby Lindenstrasse and Dortustrasse.

Experience

Events	210
Film	216
LGBT	224
Nightlife	236
Performing Arts	248

Bar jeder Vernunft *p257*

Events

The calendar is packed throughout the year, but the city is at its most celebratory and hedonistic in late spring and early summer

The German capital has long eschewed high-profile, glitzy events in favour of homegrown, local efforts. In fact, part of the city's dishevelled charm is the resourcefulness of its inhabitants, their willingness to take to the streets and create their own low-budget fun. May Day is a typical Berlin combination of street parties and demonstrations, heralding a summer season spent happily bouncing from one celebration of cultural diversity to another. The end of the year is also marked in customary Berlin style – with fireworks recklessly launched from hilltops and cars.

However, despite its counter-culture reputation, Berlin has been steadily gaining international recognition in certain spheres. Music festivals are particularly numerous, covering every genre from early music to the latest avant-garde creations. Berlin's Art Week and Gallery Weekend have put the city on the map for contemporary art, and the twice-yearly Fashion Week is gaining ground on the international catwalk. With the prestigious Berlin International Film Festival sprinkling a little stardust over the wintry city each February, it may finally be time for Berlin to dust off its black tie and heels.

Karneval der Kulturen *p213*

Spring

MaerzMusik – Festival für Zeitfragen
Various venues (254 890, www. berlinerfestspiele.de). Date late Mar.

A holdover from the more culture-conscious days of the old East Germany, this ten-day contemporary music festival invites international avant-garde composers and musicians to present new works.

Gallery Weekend
Various venues (2844 4387, www.gallery-weekend-berlin.de). Date late Apr.

Around 50 galleries time their openings for the last weekend in April, making for an arty extravaganza attended by leading dealers and ordinary art-lovers.

Kirschblütenfest
Berliner Mauerweg, Teltow (www. hanamifest.org). S25, S26 Lichterfelde Süd. Date late Apr.

Taking place just on Berlin's border with Brandenburg, this one-day Hanami Cherry Blossom Festival celebrates Japan's generous gift to Berlin upon the city's reunification. Over 70 stands offer Japanese goodies, from calligraphy to regional specialities, as well as the chance for a leisurely walk around the Teltow canal, which once divided East and West Germany..

ILA Berlin Air Show
Berlin ExpoCenter Airport, Messestrasse 1, Schönefeld (3038 2153, www.ila-berlin.de). S9, S45 Flughafen Berlin-Schönefeld. Date late April/May.

This popular biennial event – the next is in 2020 – is held at Schönefeld airport over six days. It features around 1,000 exhibitors from

Deutsch-Amerikanisches Volksfest *p214*

40 countries, with aircraft of all kinds and a serious focus on space travel.

May Day
Around Kottbusser Tor, Kreuzberg. U1, U8 Kottbusser Tor. Date 1 May.

An annual event since 1987, when Autonomen engaged in violent clashes with police. The riots have quietened in recent years,

---

♥ Best events

Berlinale *p218*
International film talent descends upon Berlin each winter.

Christopher Street Day Parade *p213*
Berlin's pride parade is as fabulous as you'd expect.

JazzFest Berlin *p215*
One of the most renowned jazz festivals on the continent.

Karneval der Kulturen *p213*
Kitsch, cocktails and colourful food stalls from around the world.

Lange Nacht der Museen *p214*
Museum-hopping all night long.

Transmediale *p215*
A high-brow celebration of digital arts culture.

In the know
ITB Berlin

The world's biggest tourism trade fair draws in a staggering 180,000 visitors, journalists and tourism insiders to the city each March. Even if you're not interested in the show itself, bear in mind that the flocks of international attendees travelling on company expenses mean that hotel rooms are booked up weeks in advance at this time, and prices are inflated accordingly.

but Kreuzberg is still very lively on 1 May, especially at Spreewaldplatz near Kotti. During the day, there are lots of street parties and music, as well as protests. However, as night draws in, alcohol-fuelled misadventures spoil the atmosphere. Be sure to withdraw cash the night before (ATMs shut down on the day) and to make solid plans with friends, as mobile service is erratic, too.

Theatertreffen Berlin
Various venues (254 890, www. berlinerfestspiele.de). Date May.

A jury picks out ten of the most innovative and controversial new theatre productions from companies across Germany, Austria and Switzerland, and the winners come to Berlin to perform their pieces over two weeks in May.

Deutschland Pokal-Endspiel
Olympiastadion, Olympischer Platz 3, Charlottenburg (300 633, https:// ticketportal.dfb.de). U2 Olympia-Stadion; S3, S9 Olympiastadion. Date late May.

The domestic football cup final has been taking place at the Olympiastadion every year since 1985. It regularly attracts some 65,000 fans, and tickets are very hard to come by.

❤ Karneval der Kulturen
Kreuzberg (3465 55960, www.karneval-berlin.de). Date May/June.

Inspired by London's Notting Hill Carnival and intended as a celebration of Berlin's ethnic and cultural diversity, this long holiday weekend (always Pentecost) centres on a 'multi-kulti' parade (on the Sunday) involving dozens of floats, hundreds of musicians and thousands of spectators. The parade and festival snake from the Hallesches Tor area to Hermannplatz.

Summer
Fête de la Musique
Various venues (4171 5289, www. fetedelamusique.de). Date 21 June.

A regular summer solstice happening since 1995, this music extravaganza of bands and DJs takes place across the city. The selection is mixed, with everything from heavy metal to *Schlager*.

48 Stunden Neukölln
Various venues (6824 7821, http://48-stunden-neukoelln.de). Date late June.

For one weekend, under-the-radar artists transform studios, cafés and even apartment buildings into temporary exhibition spaces in Berlin's most hyped neighbourhood. The casual entry requirements mean the art on display ranges from the weird and wonderful to the utterly dire. Best encountered with beers and an open mind.

Berlin Philharmonie at the Waldbühne
Waldbühne, Am Glockenturm, Charlottenburg (administration 7473 7500, box office 01806 570070, www.waldbuehne-berlin.de). S3, S9 Pichelsberg then shuttle bus. Tickets €23-€75. Date June/July.

The Philharmonie ends its season with an open-air concert that sells out months in advance. Over 20,000 Berliners light the atmospheric 'forest theatre' with candles once darkness falls.

Berlin Fashion Week
Various venues (www.fashion-week-berlin. com). Date early July & late Jan.

OK, so it's not quite Paris, but Berlin's twice-yearly style shindig is gradually becoming a serious event on the fashion calendar. In recent years, there's been a focus on young talent and 'green fashion', which can be seen at the Ethical Fashion Show and at the Greenshowroom.

Classic Open Air
Gendarmenmarkt, Mitte (3157 540, www. classicopenair.de). U6 Französische Strasse. Tickets €43-€105. Date early July.

Big names usually open this concert series held over five days in one of Berlin's most beautiful squares.

Lesbisch-Schwules Stadtfest
Nollendorfplatz & Motzstrasse, Schöneberg (2147 3586, www.regenbogenfonds.de). U1, U2, U3, U4, Nollendorfplatz. Date late July.

The Lesbian & Gay Street Fair takes over Schöneberg every year, filling several blocks in West Berlin's gay quarter. Participating bars, clubs, food stands and musical acts make this a dizzying, non-stop event that also serves as a kick-off for the Christopher Street Day Parade (*see below*).

❤ Christopher Street Day Parade
2362 8632, www.csd-berlin.de. Date Sat in late July.

Originally organised to commemorate the 1969 riots outside the Stonewall Bar on Christopher Street in New York, this fun and flamboyant parade has become one of the summer's most enjoyable and inclusive street parties. Hundreds of thousands of people march for and celebrate the rights of LGBT people each year. Check the website for details of the route.

Deutsch-Amerikanisches Volksfest
Marienpark, Alt-Mariendorf (03322 4288 245, www.deutsch-amerikanisches-volksfest.de). U6 Alt-Mariendorf, then 20-min walk. **Tickets** *€2; free under-14s.* **Date** *July/Aug.*

Established by the US forces stationed in West Berlin, the German-American Festival lasts about three weeks and offers a tacky but popular mix of carnival rides, cowboys doing lasso tricks, candy floss, hot dogs and Yankee beer.

Tanz im August
Various venues (2590 0427, www.tanzimaugust.de). **Tickets** *€15-€35.* **Date** *Aug.*

This three-week event is Germany's leading modern dance festival, with big-name participants.

Internationales Berliner Bierfestival
Karl-Marx-Allee, from Strausberger Platz to Frankfurter Tor, Friedrichshain (6576 3560, www.bierfestival-berlin.de). U5 Frankfurter Tor. **Admission** *free.* **Date** *Aug.*

Describing itself as 'the world's longest beer garden', with a 2011 Guinness World Record to prove it, this two-day festival has been running for nearly 20 years, showcasing hundreds of beers from over 80 countries and bringing conviviality to the city's premier Stalinist boulevard.

Young.euro.classic
Konzerthaus, Gendarmenmarkt 2, Mitte (8847 13911, www.young-euro-classic.de). U6 Französische Strasse. **Tickets** *€17-€29.* **Date** *Aug.*

This summer concert programme brings together youth orchestras from around Europe for two weeks.

♥ Lange Nacht der Museen
Various venues (2474 9888, www.lange-nacht-der-museen.de). **Tickets** *€18; €12 reductions; free under-12s.* **Date** *last Sat in Aug.*

Around 100 museums, collections, archives and exhibition halls stay open into the early hours of the morning, with special events, concerts, readings, lectures and performances. A ticket gets you free travel on special shuttle buses and regular public transport. Lange Nacht der Museen is the final night of Berlin's MuseumsSommer, in which museums around the city host special open-air events throughout July and August.

Autumn
Musikfest Berlin
Various venues (2548 9244, www.berlinerfestspiele.de). **Date** *Sept.*

This major classical music festival, held over the space of three weeks, presents more than 70 works by 25 composers. Orchestras, instrumental and vocal ensembles, and numerous soloists take part, with many from abroad (Sweden, Denmark, Israel, the UK and the United States in recent years).

Internationales Literaturfestival Berlin
Various venues (2787 8665, www.literaturfestival.com). **Date** *Sept.*

A major literary event, with readings, symposiums and discussions over ten days, drawing well-known authors and rising stars from around the world.

Berlin Marathon
Finish line at Brandenburger Tor (www.bmw-berlin-marathon.com). **Date** *last Sun in Sept.*

Fewer than 300 people took part in the inaugural Berlin Marathon in 1974; now, it's one of the biggest and most popular road races in the world with more than 40,000 runners, plus a million spectators lining the route to cheer them on.

Berlin Art Week
Various venues (www.berlinartweek.de). **Date** *late Sept.*

Berlin Art Week has become the highlight of the contemporary art calendar in the city

Berlin Marathon

Gendarmenmarkt

Winter

Christmas markets

Kaiser-Wilhelm-Gedächtniskirche, Breitscheidplatz, Charlottenburg (213 3290, www.weihnachtsmarkt-deutschland.de). U2, U9, S3, S5, S7, S9 Zoologischer Garten. **Open** *11am-10pm daily.* **Date** *Dec.*

Traditional markets spring up across Berlin during the Christmas season, offering toys, mulled wine and gingerbread. This is one of the biggest. There's another good one in Spandau (*see p200*).

Silvester

Date *31 Dec.*

Given Berliners' enthusiasm for tossing firecrackers out of windows, New Year's Eve is always going to be vivid, noisy and hazardous. Thousands celebrate at the Brandenburger Tor. Thousands more trek up the Teufelsberg in the Grunewald or head to Viktoriapark in Kreuzberg to watch the fireworks across the city. Be careful out there!

Grüne Woche

Messegelände am Funkturm, Messedamm 22, Charlottenburg (30380, www. gruenewoche.de). U2 Kaiserdamm; S3, S9 Messe Süd; S41, S42, S46 Messe Nord. **Tickets** *€5-€15.* **Date** *Jan.*

The best thing about this ten-day show dedicated to food, agriculture and horticulture is the opportunity to sample food and drink from the far corners of Germany and across the planet.

Ultraschall Berlin – Festival für Neue Musik

Various venues (ultraschallberlin.de). **Tickets** *€15-€18; €70 festival pass.* **Date** *mid Jan.*

Ultrasound Berlin focuses on new music played in high-profile venues by some of the world's leading specialist ensembles. Concerts are broadcast live, and there are talks by composers and other events.

💜 Transmediale

Haus der Kulturen der Welt, John-Foster-Dulles-Allee 10, Tiergarten (www. transmediale.de). U55, S3, S5, S7, S9 Hauptbahnhof. **Date** *late Jan/early Feb.*

One of the world's largest international festivals for media art and digital culture, with exhibitions and screenings from artists working in video, TV, computer animation, internet and other visual media.

💜 Berlinale

See p218 Berlinale

---

since the inaugural event in 2012. Around 50 participating institutions put on events, art fairs (notably ABC Contemporary and Positions Berlin) and wildly popular opening nights. Even the bigger venues, such as Tempelhof Airport and the Hamburger Bahnhof, struggle to handle the swarms of art scenesters at peak times.

Tag der Deutschen Einheit

Date *3 Oct.*

The Day of German Unity is a public holiday commemorating the day, back in 1990, when two Germanies became one. Head to the Brandenburg Gate to party with up to one million other revellers.

Festival of Lights

Various venues (www.festival-of-lights.de). **Date** *mid Oct.*

For ten days every year, Berlin's world-famous sights and monuments become the canvas for spectacular light and video projections. The illuminations are switched on at 7pm nightly.

💜 JazzFest Berlin

Various venues (254 890, www. berlinerfestspiele.de). **Date** *1st wknd in Nov.*

A fixture since 1964, JazzFest Berlin is one of the oldest and most prestigious in Europe, showcasing a wide range of jazz from an array of internationally renowned artists; past guests have included Miles Davis and Duke Ellington. Curator and jazz player Nadin Deventer took over as artistic director in 2018.

Berliner Märchentage

Various venues (3470 9479 www.berliner-maerchentage.de). **Date** *Nov.*

The fortnight-long Berlin Fairytale Festival celebrates tales from around the world, with some 400 storytelling and music events taking place in a carnival atmosphere, for children and adults. The central theme varies each year.

Film

*In the hope of living up to the city's cinematic heyday, Berlin's movie
theatres are getting creative*

The first moving picture show to be presented to a paying
audience took place in Berlin's Wintergarten on 1 November
1895, when the Skladanowsky brothers premiered their Bioscop,
an early film projector. Within two decades Berlin had become
a centre for groundbreaking cinema. During the 1920s and
'30s, pioneering directors Friedrich Wilhelm Murnau and Fritz
Lang revolutionised film-making, while the Kurfürstendamm's
famously grand film halls, such as the Ufa Palast Am Zoo
and the Marmorhaus, offered a swinging good time for
fashion-conscious patrons.

A few wars and political shifts later, cinema remains an
important piece of the city's cultural jigsaw. Though the scene
here may not quite compare to that of London or New York –
or even to the Berlin of the 1920s – the near 300 screens and
remaining bastions of independent film suggest that cinema,
in all its forms, is thriving in the city. In fact, thanks to a cast
of old-school arthouse joints and blockbuster multiplexes,
the world-class Berlinale and a handful of DIY genre festivals,
it's hard to say if Berlin's glory days of cinema are long
gone or just beginning.

Berlin's screen scene

Indie mainstays such as **Arsenal**, **FSK**, and **Kino Central** have managed to tough it out in the face of gentrification, and Moviemento and Xenon still thrive, buoyed by their long-appreciated individuality. **Babylon** (Mitte) has spiced up its once-stodgy schedule, and the old **Zeughaus Kino** still sells tickets, remarkably, for the price of some döner kebabs. Nowadays, all seem to have more English-language programming in evidence. For monophones, all-English venues run by Yorck cinemas include the **Odeon**, **Babylon Kreuzberg** and **Rollberg**, plus all eight screens at the **Cinestar IMAX Sony Center**.

There are two film museums: the **Museum für Film und Fernsehen** (*see p109*) on Potsdamer Platz, which includes a special exhibition about Berlin's favourite daughter, Marlene Dietrich; and the **Filmpark Babelsberg**, near Potsdam (*see p207*). Berlin even has its own answer to the Hollywood Walk of Fame: the rather underwhelming **Boulevard der Stars** on Potsdamer Strasse.

Film festivals

The **Berlin International Film Festival**, or **Berlinale** (*see right*), in February, is the biggest and most prominent of the international film festivals, but it's far from the only game in town.

The ten-day **Fantasy Film Festival** (www.fantasyfilmfest.com) shows the latest in fantasy, splatter, horror and sci-fi from the US, Hong Kong, Japan and Europe. Films – most in English or with English subtitles – are often premières, with occasional previews, retrospectives and rarities. It takes place around late August/early September.

With plenty of cultural subsidies to go round and a relatively international audience, Berlin is awash with film festivals focusing on specific countries. **Alfilm** (www.alfilm.de), in April, represents Arabic cinema, with films from Egypt, Syria, Palestine and Iran. Australia has **Down Under Berlin** (www.downunderberlin.de)

❤ Berlinale

Various venues (259 200, www.berlinale.de).
Tickets €7-€16; €100 festival pass. **Date** *mid Feb.*

For more than 60 years, the Berlinale (or Internationale Filmfestspiele Berlin, to use its official title) has been the city's biggest cultural event, as well as one of the world's three most prominent film festivals.

Born out of the Cold War, the Berlinale developed from a propaganda showcase, supported by the Allies, into a genuine meeting place – and frequent collision point – for East and West. Whether it was the 1959 French boycott over Stanley Kubrick's indictment of war, *Paths of Glory*, the jury revolt over the pro-Vietnamese film *OK* in 1970, or the 1979 Eastern Bloc walk-out over the depiction of Vietnamese people in *The Deer Hunter*, the festival's drama was never confined to the screens. The years following the fall of the Berlin Wall were particularly exciting: the mood and energy of the festival reflected the joy and chaos of the changing city. The future direction of the Berlinale will again be up for grabs once long-term festival director Dieter Kosslick steps down in 2019.

Although Potsdamer Platz is the focus of the festival, screenings take place around the city, including at Alexanderplatz, in the Zoo Palast cinema in Tiergarten and in a renovated crematorium (silent green Kulturquartier) in Wedding. In this way, the Berlinale offers the chance not

Marlene Dietrich

FILM

only to watch undiscovered movies and rub shoulders with fellow film buffs and industry leaders, but to experience Berlin's unique architectural and cultural heritage. In recent years, the festival has taken on more of the glamour and celebrity of its two major rivals, Cannes and Venice. What remains the same, however, is the chance to see arguably the widest and most eclectic movie mix of any film festival anywhere. The films are presented in nine sections, of which the following are the most significant.

International Competition

Films compete for the festival's most prestigious awards – the Golden and Silver Bears – and the winners are announced at the closing night gala. A rise in celebrity attendance at the festival saw a much-criticised shift towards conservative, US-centric films in recent years, with the festival performing a balancing act between maintaining its authentic, experimental feel while accepting a degree of commercial success. However, critics were left politely bewildered and, in some cases, openly hostile, when the judges announced the 2018 winner of the Golden Bear to be the intimate, unsettling *Touch Me Not* by avant-garde Romanian director Adina Pintilie, while the crowd-pleasing *Isle of Dogs* (Wes Anderson) took silver – a timely reminder, perhaps, of the festival's enduring maverick values.

International Forum of Young Cinema

Some devotees claim this is the real Berlin festival, and the place where discoveries are made. Born out of the revolt that dissolved the Competition in 1970, the Forum has no format or genre restrictions, and provides a platform for challenging, eclectic fare that you won't see elsewhere.

Panorama

Originally intended to showcase films that fell outside the guidelines of the Competition, Panorama shines a spotlight on world independent arthouse movies, gay and lesbian works and political films.

Perspektive Deutsches Kino

Perspektive reflects the festival's focus on the next generation of German cinema. It is a big audience favourite, helped by the fact that all films are shown with English subtitles. If you think German cinema has a bad rep, this is where to break down the stereotypes.

Retrospective

Perhaps the festival's best bet for sheer movie-going pleasure, the Retrospective often concentrates on the mainstream, but it's an opportunity to experience classics and rarities on the big screen. Themes have ranged from great directors, such as Louis Buñuel, Fritz Lang and Ingmar Bergman, to subjects including 1950s glamour girls, Weimar cinema, science fiction and even Nazi entertainment films.

Buying tickets

Films are usually shown three times. Tickets range in price from €8 to €20 and can be bought up to three days in advance (four days for Competition repeats) at the main ticket office in the Potsdamer Platz Arkaden (Alte Potsdamer Strasse, Tiergarten, 259 2000) as well as at cinemas Kino International (Karl-Marx-Allee 33) and Haus der Berliner Festspiele (Schaperstrasse 24). Other official partners are announced before the festival. Tickets are also available online, but on the day of screening they can only be bought at the theatre box office; last-minute tickets are often available. Queues for advance tickets can be long and online tickets go fast, so plan well ahead. From January onwards, check for updates and programme information at www.berlinale.de.

Berlinale bear

in September, and Latin America has the excellent **Lakino** (www.lakino.com) in October. The **Asian Film Festival Berlin** (www.asianfilmfestivalberlin.de) is also held in autumn.

The **InterFilm Short Film Festival** (www.interfilm.de), in November, has been going since 1984, growing from a DIY affair into an international event with big buck prizes. It shows more than 500 short films from 88 countries. Unsurprisingly, the **Porn Film Festival Berlin** (www.pornfilmfestivalberlin.de) is also extremely popular. It presents films, art videos and shorts that transgress the fine line between art and pornography. It's usually held in October and there are lots of related parties and talks.

Queer films of all kind are put under the spotlight at the **Xposed International Queer Film Festival** (www.xposedfilmfestival.com) in May and June, but the LGBT film event with the highest profile is the Teddy Award (www.teddyaward.tv), which is presented as an official award during the Berlinale by an independent jury.

New film-related festivals and events regularly crop up in Berlin, and some prove to have staying power. A welcome addition to Berlin's genre festival scene is the **Final Girls Film Festival** (www.finalgirlsberlin.com) dedicated to horror films written, directed or produced by women. At the more experimental end, **Transmediale** (www.transmediale.de, *see p215*) is a five-day international programme of digital presentations, installations and performances, which leaves a month-long exhibition in its wake.

Information

Check listings in *Tip* (www.tip-berlin.de) and *Zitty* (www.zitty.de). *Exberliner* lists current film details in print, as does *[030]*, which is available free in many bars. A handy alphabetical film list that's searchable by language can be found online at www.berlinien.de/kino/kinoprogramm.html.

Watch for the notation OV or OF ('original version' or 'Originalfassung'), OmU ('original with subtitles') or OmE ('original with English subtitles'). But watch out – OmU might well be a French or Chinese movie with German subtitles. The cinemas listed below are those most likely to be showing films in English.

Many cinemas have a 'Kinotag' on either Monday, Tuesday or Wednesday, when they offer reduced admission and deals on pre-paid tickets. Even full-price tickets are generally cheaper than in many other capital cities.

Cinemas

Arsenal

Sony Center, Potsdamer Strasse 2, Tiergarten (2695 5100, www.arsenal-berlin. de). U2, S1, S2, S25 Potsdamer Platz. **Tickets** *€8; €3 reductions. No cards.* **Map** *p100 L8.*

With two state-of-the-art screening rooms in the Sony Center, Berlin's own cinematheque is a welcome corrective to its multiplex neighbours, offering a brazenly eclectic programme that ranges from classic Hollywood to contemporary Middle Eastern cinema, Russian art films to Italian horror movies, niche documentaries to retrospectives of cinema's leading lights. Also check out its ongoing series of iconic films, Magical History Tour. The Arsenal shows plenty of English-language films and some foreign-language films with English subtitles.

▶ *The Arsenal is one of the core venues for the Berlin International Film Festival (see p218 Berlinale).*

❤ Astor Film Lounge

Kurfürstendamm 255, Charlottenburg (883 8551, www.astor-filmlounge.de). U1, U9 Kurfürstendamm. **Tickets** *€12-€18.* **Map** *p178 G8.*

The first 'premium cinema' in Germany offers a luxury cinematographic experience, complete with a welcome cocktail, doorman and valet parking. The building dates from 1948, when a café was converted into a small cinema called the KiKi (Kino im Kindl). It was later redesigned and renamed the Filmpalast and become one of West Berlin's classiest *Kinos*. After thorough renovations and another name change, it's still a grand example of 1950s movie-going luxury, with an illuminated glass ceiling, comfortable seats and a gong to announce the show.

Babylon

Rosa-Luxemburg-Strasse 30, Mitte (242 5969, www.babylonberlin.de). U2, U5, U8, S5, S7, S75 Alexanderplatz, or U2 Rosa-Luxemburg-Platz. **Tickets** *€7-€9; €4 reductions. No cards.* **Map** *p68 P5.*

Housed in a restored landmark building by Hans Poelzig, the former Filmkunsthaus Babylon has reinvented itself with a much more active programming policy. While it nominally focuses on new German independent cinema, English-language fare is on the up, particularly in its monthly Schräge Filme (Weird Films) programme; and its foreign-language film screenings tend to have English subtitles. It also hosts regular international film fests, such as Chilean Cinema Week and even a North Korean film festival.

Babylon Kreuzberg

Dresdener Strasse 126, Kreuzberg (6160 9693, www.yorck.de). U1, U8 Kottbusser Tor. **Tickets** *€7-€9. No cards.* **Map** *p144 Q9.*

Another Berlin perennial, this twin-screen theatre runs a varied programme featuring indie crossover and UK films. Once a local Turkish cinema, its films are almost all English-language and it offers a homely respite from the multiplex experience.

CineStar IMAX Sony Center

Potsdamer Strasse 4, Tiergarten (0451 7030 200, www.cinestar.de). U2, S1, S2, S25 Potsdamer Platz. **Tickets** *€7-€11.50; 3D films €10-€14.50.* **Map** *p100 L8.*

CineStar has eight screens showing films exclusively in their original language, mostly English. Despite a few random sparks of creativity, what's shown is largely mainstream fare and all major releases tend to appear here, shown in both 3D and 2D versions on its massive IMAX screen. Counteract the high prices by buying the Five-Star ticket – five (2D) films for €32.50.

Colosseum

Schönhauser Allee 123, Prenzlauer Berg (4401 9200, www.uci-kinowelt.de). U2, S8, S9, S41, S42 Schönhauser Allee. **Tickets** *€5.90-€11.20; reductions from €3.80.* **Map** *p116 P2.*

Built in 1924 from a stable for the horses that pulled the first trams, the Colosseum was restored by the Soviets to become the finest cinema in East Berlin. Although it was turned into a multiplex in the late 1990s, the original auditorium is still in use, restored to its 1950s splendour. In the lobby you can still see the brick walls of the stables, complete with the rings used to tie up the horses.

Delphi Filmpalast am Zoo

Kantstrasse 12A, Charlottenburg (312 1026, www.delphi-filmpalast.de). U2, U9, S5, S7, S75 Zoologischer Garten. **Tickets** *€7-€10.* **Map** *p178 G8.*

The Delphi was originally a 1920s dance palace. Bombed out during the war, it was rebuilt as the Delphi Filmpalast and became a major Cinemascope and 70mm venue, where films such as *Ben Hur* and *My Fair Lady* would run for up to a year. It's the last cinema in the city still to have balcony seating. Now part of the excellent Yorck cinema group, it shows mainly new German arthouse films. Just next door, at Kantstrasse 10, is another fabulous Yorck cinema, Delphi LUX (322 931040), which serves as a designated audience cinema for the European Film Awards.

Filmtheater Am Friedrichshain

Bötzowstrasse 1-5, Friedrichshain (4284 5188, www.yorck.de). Bus 200. **Tickets** *€7-€9; €5.50 under-12s. 3D films €9.50-€11.50.* **Map** *p132 R5.*

This charming five-screen cinema is right on the park in Friedrichshain and has a lovely beer garden that's open during the summer.

FSK

Segitzdamm 2, Kreuzberg (614 2464, www.fsk-kino.de). U1, U8 Kottbusser Tor, or U8 Moritzplatz. **Tickets** *€7-€8. No cards.* **Map** *p144 P9.*

Named after the state film rating board, this two-screen cinema is deep in the heart of Turkish Kreuzberg. It shows a lot of foreign-language films, mostly with German subtitles, but occasionally has American or British indie films and documentaries.

Hackesche Höfe Kino

Rosenthaler Strasse 40-41, Mitte (283 4603, www.hoefekino.de). U8 Weinmeisterstrasse, or S3, S5, S7, S9 Hackescher Markt. **Tickets** *€7.50-€9. No cards.* **Map** *p68 O5.*

The four-storey walk up hasn't stopped this place from becoming one of the area's best-attended cinemas. It shows mostly foreign-language films, with documentaries and occasional indie features in English.

Kino Central

Rosenthaler Strasse 39, Mitte (2859 9973, www.kino-central.de). U8 Weinmeisterstrasse, or S3, S5, S7, S9 Hackescher Markt. **Tickets** *€7-€8.50. No cards.* **Map** *p68 O5.*

Still hanging in there with a programming attitude that's uniquely its own, this cinema is worth a look for its various culture series and discussions, though in recent times it

---

In the know
Outdoor cinemas

In the warmer months, Berlin's *Freiluftkino*s open for business in some of Berlin's largest parks: Volkspark Friedrichshain, Rehberge (Wedding), and Hasenheide (Neukölln). There are a handful of smaller venues scattered throughout the city, too, as far out as Spandau. The films shown are often a season behind, so this may not be the thing for hardcore cinephiles, but it's an undeniably enjoyable way to spend a summer evening – just don't forget the cold *Späti* beer as well as bug spray to fend off the mosquitos.

has become something of a tourist hotspot, tucked into a grungy courtyard and next to a smoky bar. In summer, there's an outdoor cinema in the back courtyard.

Kino International
Karl-Marx-Allee 33, Mitte (2475 6011, www. yorck.de). U5 Schillingstrasse. **Tickets** *€7-€9.50. No cards.* **Map** *p68 Q6.*

The monumental post-Stalinist architecture of Kino International belies a modest 551-seat auditorium, but the real reason to come here is for the lobby, with its crystal chandeliers and upholstered seating. A first-class example of 1960s GDR chic, it overtook the Colosseum as East Berlin's premier cinema, and became a common venue for Communist Party functions and socialist shindigs.

▶ *Kino International is also the home of the gay and lesbian Club International, which shows LGBT films every Monday ('Mongay') at 10pm.*

Moviemento
Kottbusser Damm 22, Kreuzberg (692 4785, www.moviemento.de). U7, U8 Hermannplatz, or U8 Schönleinstrasse. **Tickets** *€7.50-€8.50; €5 reductions. No cards.* **Map** *p144 Q11.*

This cosy upstairs cinema in Kreuzberg is one of the last bastions of Berlin's original alternative cinema scene. There's very imaginative programming, with the occasional English film, but emphasis is placed on foreign-language film weeks and themed festivals.

Neues Off
Hermannstrasse 20, Neukölln (6270 9550, www.yorck.de). U7, U8 Hermannplatz. **Tickets** *€7-€9.* **Map** *p166 Q12.*

This beautifully decorated single-screen cinema is hidden in plain sight by a row of concrete apartment buildings just up the hill from Hermannplatz. It opened in the 1920s under the name Rixdorfer Lichtspiele and charms down to the smallest details. The original Sarotti kiosk is a highlight, and the typically simple programme feels refreshing rather than limited.

Odeon
Hauptstrasse 116, Schöneberg (7870 4019, www.yorck.de). U4, S42, S46 Innsbrucker Platz, or S1, S41, S42, S46 Schöneberg. **Tickets** *€7-€9. No cards.* **Map** *fold-out map J2.*

The Odeon is one of the final hold-outs from the age of single-screen neighbourhood

cinemas and should be appreciated just for that fact. Set deep in Schöneberg, it's exclusively English-language, providing a reasonably intelligent, though increasingly mainstream, selection of Hollywood and UK fare.

Rollberg
Rollbergstrasse 70, Neukölln (6270 4645, www.yorck.de). U8 Boddinstrasse. **Tickets** *€6-€8.50. No cards.* **Map** *p166 R12.*

One of the three excellent cinemas in Neukölln run by the Yorck group, Rollberg is hidden inside a nondescript shopping centre beside a Rewe supermarket. It shows a healthy mix of Hollywood action flicks and arthouse cinema, all in their original language.

Xenon
Kolonnenstrasse 5-6, Schöneberg (7800 1530, www.xenon-kino.de). U7 Kleistpark. **Tickets** *€5.50-€7.50; children's films €4-€5. No cards.* **Map** *p178 K11.*

Only in Berlin would a dedicated queer cinema also be a multiple award-winner for children's programming. Those who have come of age can find specific gay and lesbian programming, as well as more mainstream independent films.

Zeughaus Kino
Deutsches Historisches Museum, Unter den Linden 2, Mitte (2030 4770, www.zeughauskino.de). U6 Französische Strasse. **Tickets** *€5. No cards.* **Map** *p68 O6.*

The Zeughaus Kino has a variety of interesting film series and often hosts touring retrospective shows. It makes a concerted effort to get the original versions of movies, and foreign-language films sometimes appear with English subtitles. The entrance is by the River Spree.

Zoo Palast
Hardenbergstrasse 29A, Charlottenburg (01805 222 966 premium phone, www.zoopalast-berlin.de). U2, U9, S5, S7, S75 Zoologischer Garten. **Tickets** *€11-€12.50; 3D films €13-€17.50.* **Map** *p178 G8.*

In the Cold War, West Berlin premières were always held in this striking 1950s building, which in a different reincarnation during the Nazi era was the venue for Albert Speer's most spectacular light shows. Much like the surrounding Zoo area, it fell into disrepair after 1990 but reopened in late 2013 with seven new screens showing traditional multiplex blockbuster fare.

Berlin on Screen

The city has played a starring role since the birth of film

Berlin's beauty may be rough and ready, but the city loves being on camera, either as itself or standing in for other locales. Every year, more than 100 films are shot on location in the German capital. Here are some of the best.

Der Blaue Engel (Josef von Sternberg, 1929)
Coinciding with the Wall Street Crash and the rise of Hitler, *The Blue Angel* was a turning point for German cinema, as the first sound picture produced at Berlin's Babelsberg Studios. A torrid story about a college professor obsessed with a nightclub singer (a then-unknown Marlene Dietrich), it still flickers alluringly.

Cabaret (Bob Fosse, 1971)
The evergreen musical based on British expat Christopher Isherwood's sleazy account of life in 1930s Weimar Berlin, *Cabaret*'s blend of camp, theatricality and decadence is as vibrant as ever. Liza Minnelli is mesmerising as showgirl Sally Bowles, negotiating love amid the city's dives and music halls, against a creeping backdrop of Nazism.

Christiane F (Uli Edel, 1981)
Set in and around the bleak Gropiusstadt housing projects in Neukölln and the Zoo station, this hard-hitting movie recounts the descent of Christiane F, a teenage drug addict and prostitute, into the dark side of 1980s West Berlin. The David Bowie soundtrack fits the mix of neon and squalor.

Deutschland 83 (Anna & Joerg Winger, 2015)
This sleeper hit TV series made history by being the first German-language drama to broadcast on a US network, Sundance TV. Tense Cold War espionage, a delightful 1980s soundtrack and authentic props from East Germany make it well worth a watch. The second season, *Deutschland 86*, screened in 2018, with *Deutschland 89* to follow in due course.

The Edukators (Hans Weingartner, 2004)
Sinister crime comedy caper with three would-be radicals in the heart of Berlin getting more than they bargained for when they take a wealthy hostage.

Goodbye Lenin! (Wolfgang Becker, 2003)
A devoted Socialist woman wakes up from a coma post-reunification. Her son, fearful of what the shock of discovering the demise of the GDR would do to her, goes to extraordinary lengths to pretend the world is the same as before 1989. A charming and affecting comedy, set almost entirely within former East Berlin.

Der Himmel über Berlin (Wim Wenders, 1987)
One of the best-known films about the divided city, *Wings of Desire* sees angels descend from the skies to peer into the hearts and minds of everyday Berliners, soothing those in distress. One angel (Bruno Ganz) falls in love with a trapeze artist – becoming human in the process. Against a backdrop of a grimy Wall and austere monochrome views of Berlin, Wenders' masterpiece is a loving ode to the city.

Das Leben der Anderen (Florian Henckel von Donnersmarck, 2006)
The Lives of Others is a gripping, heart-rending drama about an emotionally crippled Stasi officer detailed to spy on a renegade playwright and his girlfriend during the 1980s. Filmed on location around East Berlin, including at the old Stasi HQ in Lichtenberg, it captures the grim austerity and repression of the Communist state in its final years.

Oh Boy (Jan-Ole Gerster, 2012)
This black-and-white tragicomedy is a deadpan take on a globalised Berlin from the eyes of Niko Fischer (Tom Schilling), a law school dropout searching for an elusive cup of 'normal' coffee. *Oh Boy* is full of atmosphere, and worth watching for the gorgeous jazz soundtrack alone, featuring Berlin's Cherilyn MacNeil and The Major Minors.

One, Two, Three (Billy Wilder, 1961)
James Cagney is brilliant as the Pepsi exec whose daughter falls for East Berlin communist Horst Buchholz.

Possession (Andrzej Zulawski, 1981)
Sam Neill and Isabel Adjani star in cult psychosexual horror flick, which uses its West Berlin backdrop to compellingly weird effect.

Victoria (Sebastian Schipper, 2015)
Despite being shot in one single take between 4.30 and 7am, *Victoria* is no gimmick. With a mere 12 pages of script, the 138-minute film requires some athletic improvisation from its cast as it follows them through Kreuzberg and Mitte in the pre-dawn hours. The result offers a glimpse into the underbelly of Berlin's nightlife, with a hilariously accurate blend of accented English and broken German dialogue.

LGBT

Berlin's queer scene is diverse, innovative and extensive

Tourists and Bavarians alike may moan about the *Berliner Schnauze*, but it's exactly this gruff nonchalance that characterises the average Berliner's staunch tolerance for alternative lifestyles. Grouchy Berliners may accost you for failing to separate your recycling properly, but they don't give a damn about how, or with whom, you spend your nights. Berlin has one of the world's most active queer scenes, but this hasn't appeared out of nowhere; in years past, the city has borne witness to dramatic swings in acceptance and persecution. Today, the city practises a never-again stance towards gay intolerance. Alternative lifestyles of all stripes are considered normal and are even celebrated on giant billboards in U-Bahn stations.

You won't need to search hard to uncover Berlin's gay scene: it'll find you in about ten minutes. Venues and events are spread throughout the city, but some areas are still gayer than others, especially Schöneberg, as well as parts of Prenzlauer Berg, Mitte and Kreuzberg.

Berlin's gay history

Historically, Berlin has acted as a tolerant, catch-all city for people of different religions, races and sexual orientations – even when the rest of Germany wasn't quite on board. Berlin was the capital of a kingdom whose 18th-century king, Frederick the Great, was rumoured to discuss and delve into homoerotic activities (just check out some of the art at his men-only summer retreat, **Sanssouci** – *see p206*). Later, in 1897, the first institution in the world with an emancipatory homosexual agenda was founded in Berlin – the Wissenschaftlich-Humanitäres Komitee (Scientific-Humanitarian Committee).

The 1920s accelerated and cemented Berlin's role as Europe's gay capital. The Weimar era (1918-33) brought an anything-goes spirit to the city: gay and lesbian bars flourished, drag performances were popular, and an open sexual culture, not to mention a depressed national currency, attracted homosexual tourists from across the globe. The scene gave the world a first glimpse at what we might recognise as a modern gay community and was frequented by Marlene Dietrich, Anita Berber and Christopher Isherwood. This freewheeling period ended with the election of the Nazis in 1933, after which homosexuals, especially in 'depraved' Berlin, were persecuted by the state. Thousands of gay men were forced to wear a pink triangle in concentration camps, many perishing in the bloody years of World War II. Lesbians, along with the homeless, disabled, and other 'asocials' were lumped together with a black triangle. Today, the gay victims of National Socialism are commemorated in a striking memorial in the Tiergarten that was unveiled in 2008 (*see p82*).

During the occupation and the Cold War (1945-89), gay culture existed on both sides of a divided Berlin, though mostly underground. West Berlin, in particular, saw a surge in its gay ranks, as many young men were attracted to the only city in West Germany where citizens were exempt from military service. In 1994, the notorious Paragraph 175, which had criminalised homosexual contact in Germany since 1871, was repealed by the newly unified nation, and, in 2017, gay marriage was legalised to little controversy.

The scene today

In West Berlin's Schöneberg district, gays and lesbians trod separate paths for decades. Across the wall in East Berlin, however, homosexuals of both sexes shared bars and clubs, making common cause under the Communists. These traditions can still be felt today. The expansion of the gay scene into other parts of the city means that mixed venues predominate, though most places tend to lean one way or the other. **Schöneberg** still has the highest concentration of gay shops, bars, restaurants and organisations – especially the tourist-friendly venues around Motzstrasse and Fuggerstrasse – though these skew heavily towards the masculine. Roving monthly parties, as well as the overlap with other political movements, have resulted in a diffusion – or a fracturing, in some cases – of the scene into **Kreuzberg**, **Prenzlauer Berg**, **Mitte** and **Friedrichshain**. Traditionally Turkish **Neukölln** also has its share of queer go-to spots; the contrasting cultures coexist, for the most part, seamlessly. While the gay

❤ Best queer venues

Alaska Bar *p233*
Vegan tapas in the heart of Neukölln.

Gayhane at SO36 *p231*
Arabic pop hits at the iconic Xberg institution.

Horse Meat Disco *p229*
This hard-hitting party aims to please.

Neues Ufer *p234*
Bowie's old haunt – he lived two doors down.

Schwules Museum *p110*
Europe's foremost queer museum.

Travesty at SO36

scene in Schöneberg is, on the surface, apolitical; the mixed queer scene elsewhere rubs elbows with general leftist and feminist movements.

Few cities can compete with Berlin's network of lesbian institutions, but there aren't many lesbian-only bars. For mixed bars and club nights, check *Siegessäule* (*see below*) or *L-mag* (www.l-mag.de), a quarterly free lesbian magazine. Younger queer women tend to favour mixed venues such as **SchwuZ** (*see p233*), **SO36** (*see p246*), **Möbel-Olfe** (*see p231*) and **Silver Future** (*see p233*), but nights such as **L-Tunes** (*see p232*) are also popular. Many parties that were once referred to as 'women only' now use the more inclusive label FLTI, which stands for women (*Frauen*), lesbian, trans and intersex.

The LGBT scene as a whole includes much more than the venues listed here: there are sex parties for every taste and perversion, as well as gay saunas (*see p235* In the know), cruising parks and stigma-free darkrooms in many bars. If that's not your thing, queer art and history are documented at the Schwules Museum (*see p110*), which also has an archive, and the queer community organises plenty of cultural and recreational events throughout the year (*see p232* Queer Life). Summer is the most exciting time of year, when all contingents come together to play, party and protest. The **Lesbisch-Schwules Stadtfest** (*see p213*) on Nollendorfplatz in mid June is followed by the **Christopher Street Day** (*see p213*), Germany's version of Pride, which includes a flamboyant annual parade through Tiergarten. Alternative parades in other parts of town celebrate every shade of the queer rainbow.

Displays of affection between gays in public are rarely of interest to passers-by, but bigots do exist and so does anti-gay violence, usually perpetrated by groups of macho teenagers or right-wing skinheads. But violence is rare and, compared to other cities, Berlin is an easy-going place.

Leather, sex & fetish

The hardcore and fetish scene in Berlin is huge. These days, leather gays are outnumbered by a younger hardcore crowd and skinhead types who prefer rubber and uniforms. Places to obtain your preferred garb are plentiful, as are opportunities to show it off, including the eternally crowded **Easter Berlin** leather and fetish event in spring (www.easterberlin.de) and the associated **Skin Berlin** in the autumn, plus various fetish parties and events.

Though the most visible elements of the fetish scene cater to gay men, there are plenty of venues for women, trans and intersex folks, the pinnacle of which is the

Easter weekend WLTI **Osterkonferenz** (www.osterkonferenz.com), which offers BDSM workshops and play parties for keen partakers from all over Europe. **KitKatClub** (*see p240*) hosts parties for all, and many other Kreuzberg venues offer mixed gender and women-only nights. Some are exclusively queer, while others welcome straight couples too. In September, the **Folsom Europe** (http://folsomeurope. info) leather and BDSM street fair attracts an eager crowd, with one or two parties exclusively for non-men.

In general, expect to pay between €5 and €20 for admission to most parties. Most clubs have something on offer multiple nights a week, always in accordance with a specific theme or crowd. Many have strict dress codes, some none at all; check the websites for specifics.

Cruising

Cruising is a popular and legal pursuit in Berlin. Most action takes place in parks, in the daytime, often just metres away from the general public, who don't seem to care. There is no taboo about nudity in parks. And don't panic or jump into a bush when encountering the police – they are actually there to protect you from gay-bashers, and they never hassle cruisers.

In the **Tiergarten** (*see p103*), the Löwenbrücke is the cruising focal point – but the whole corner south-west of the Siegessäule becomes a bit of a gay theme park in summer, when daytime finds hundreds of gays sunning themselves on the Tuntenwiese ('faggot meadow'). **Volkspark Friedrichshain** (*see p136*) and **Hasenheide** (*see p151*) both offer friendly and relaxed cruising spots with a slightly younger crowd. In Friedrichshain, check the slopes right off Friedenstrasse, and in Hasenheide, head for the south-west corner of the park, near Columbiadamm. In **Grunewald** (*see p201*), head for the woods behind the car park at Pappelplatz; it's a popular daytime spot, but also frequented at night by bikers. **Wannsee** (*see p201*) is home to Europe's largest inland beach as well as a patch of sand traditionally occupied by gay men – just walk all the way to the end of the beach to the far reaches of the FKK (nudist) zone.

Information

For helplines, information and counselling services, *see p307*. The best way to find one-off events, parties and festivals is by checking *Blu* (www.blu.fm) and *Siegessäule* (www.siegessaeule.de), free monthly magazines available online or at most LGBT venues. *Siegessäule* lists all gay and

Christopher Street Day Parade *p213*

lesbian venues and pinpoints them on a map. It also publishes *Kompass* (www.siegessaeule-kompass.de), a classified directory in German of everything gay or lesbian. You can find English information in pocket-sized Gay City Guides for individual districts.

MITTE

Not just a place for museums and monuments, Mitte offers a *klein aber fein* (small but perfectly formed) smattering of queer culture, right in the middle of it all. **KitKatClub** (*see p240*) blurs lines as a sex, fetish and party venue for all.

Cafés & bars

Besenkammer

Rathausstrasse 1 (242 4083). U2, U5, U8, S5, S7, S75 Alexanderplatz. **Open** *24hrs daily.* **No cards.** **Map** *p68 P6. Gay*

The oldest gay pub in the city, Besenkammer ('broom closet') is a tiny place under the S-Bahn tracks at Alexanderplatz, and it virtually never closes. It's probably not a bar you'd spend a whole night in, but well-worth the trip for the queer history: it was a refuge for gay men in the GDR, and, in 1973, gay activist Michael Eggert met here with sympathisers from the West. Their discussion inspired movements that would radically change views on sexuality in East Germany.

Betty F***

Mulackstrasse 13 (no phone, www.bettyf.de). U8 Weinmeisterstrasse. **Open** *8pm-late daily.* **No cards.** **Map** *p68 O5. Gay*

A quirky basement space near Hackescher Markt that offers everything from theatre performers to live classical music. Mostly, though, men of all ages gather here in the evening for an anything-goes atmosphere that strikes a good balance between edgy and casual.

Café Seidenfaden

Dircksenstrasse 47 (283 2783, www.frausuchtzukunft.de). U8 Weinmeister Strasse, or S5, S7, S75 Hackescher Markt. **Open** *8am-4pm Mon-Fri.* **No cards.** **Map** *p68 O6. Lesbian*

This place is run by women from a therapy group of former addicts. There are readings and exhibitions, but absolutely no drugs or alcohol. It's packed at lunchtime, and there's even a yoga class from 4pm on Fridays.

TheLiberate

Kleine Präsidentenstrasse 4 (8867 7778, www.theliberate.com). S5, S7, S75 Hackescher Markt. **Open** *7pm-late Wed-Sun.* **Map** *p68 O6. Mixed*

It's not a card-carrying gay bar, but TheLiberate is popular with well-to-do guys from the fashion world. Slathered in gold-shimmering velvet and leather, it's a swanky and, for Berlin, expensive affair. Come at the weekend, and all three rooms are chock-a-block with scenesters and champagne cocktails.

Clubs & one-nighters

GMF

Club Weekend, Alexanderstrasse 7 (2809 5396, www.gmf-berlin.de). U2, U5, U8, S5, S7, S75 Alexanderplatz. **Open** *11pm-late Sun.* **Admission** *€10. No cards.* **Map** *p68 Q6. Mixed*

Berlin's ultimate and longstanding Sunday disco is housed in Club Weekend, which towers over Alexanderplatz. There's an open-air terrace, a smoking section and two floors, split into two musical realms: pop and techno. It welcomes everyone but draws a very heavy gay presence.

❤ Horse Meat Disco

Bauakademie, Schinkelplatz (no phone, www.horsemeatdiscoberlin.com). U2 Hausvogteiplatz. **Open** *varies.* **Admission** *€10. No cards.* **Map** *p68 O6. Mixed*

It may have been born in London's Vauxhall, but Horse Meat Disco has matured in Berlin. Resident DJs call it 'the queer party for everyone', though, as with many sex-themed clubs, it attracts a lot of gay men. Whoever is there, it's a fantastic party, inspired by the heydey of New York City nightlife.

Revolver

KitKatClub, Köpenicker Strasse 76 (no phone, www.revolverparty.com). U8 Heinrich-Heine-Strasse. **Open** *2nd Fri every mth.* **Admission** *€10. No cards.* **Map** *p68 Q7. Gay*

Relocated from London to Berlin in 2013, Revolver hosts international and local DJs from the underground scene. Neither too sleek or too kitsch, it's simply a good mix of gay subculture and high-quality electronic music.

PRENZLAUER BERG

Less centralised than in the West, Prenzlauer Berg's queer scene is scattered but homey. The bars provide a blurred glimpse into gay life in the GDR, so expect to hear more German than English.

Cafés & bars

Flax

Chodowieckistrasse 41 (2578 2573, www.flax-berlin.de). S8, S9, S41, S42, S85 Greifswalder Strasse; tram M4, M10. **Open** *6pm-late Tue-Sun.* **No cards.** **Map** *p116 R4. Mixed*

It may be on the edge of the Prenzlauer Berg gay scene, but Flax has developed into one of the most popular café/bars in the district, mainly pulling in a young mixed crowd. There's a very German buffet and table tennis

on Wednesdays, and karaoke on the first Friday of the month.

Marietta

Stargarder Strasse 13 (4372 0646). U2, S8, S9, S41, S42, S85 Schönhauser Allee. **Open** *6pm-late Mon-Sat.* **No cards.** **Map** *p116 Q2. Mixed*

Hot bartenders and a large room done up like a GDR office waiting room circa 1979 draw locals to Marietta every night. On Wednesdays, the place is crammed with young men gossiping, laughing and boozing, though it's not exclusively gay.

Perle

Sredzkistrasse 64 (4985 3450, www.barperle.de) U2 Eberswalder Strasse. **Open** *7pm-late Tue-Sat.* **Map** *p116 Q3. Gay*

Delicious beverages abound at this small, austerely designed cocktail bar on Prenzlauer Berg's eastern fringe. Most nights, gay men line the bar sipping martinis, or gather round the large table in the elevated back room. A street-side patio doubles the capacity in summer.

Shops & services

Black Style

Seelower Strasse 5 (4468 8595, www.blackstyle.de). U2, S8, S9, S41, S42, S85 Schönhauser Allee. **Open** *1-6.30pm Mon-Wed; 1-8pm Thur, Fri; 11am-6pm Sat.* **Map** *p116 P1. Fetish gear*

From fashion to butt plugs, if it's made out of rubber or latex, Black Style has got it. High quality, reasonable prices and a big variety. Mail order too.

Leather, sex & fetish venues

Stahlrohr 2.0 (Paul-Robeson Strasse 50, www.stahlrohr.info) is a cruisy gay pub with a large darkroom that hosts sex parties for every taste; the Underwear Party and Karaoke Sex are highlights, as is the Youngster Party (for those aged 18-28) on Tuesdays.

WEDDING

Although it's rife with opportunities for making 'gay Wedding' jokes, there's not such a strong LGBT scene established in the district. Of course, most of Berlin's nightlife is at least a little bit gay, and Wedding's perennial 'up-and-coming' status offers the reassurance that new places will pop up any minute now, or so we're told.

Nollendorfplatz

Cafés & bars

Café Cralle
*Hochstädter Strasse 10A (455 3001, www.
cafecralle.wordpress.com). U9 Nauener
Platz.* **Open** *7pm-late daily.* **No cards.**
Map *p116 K1. Mixed*

This popular FLTI collective is rather
politically oriented, but there's nothing
aggressive about it. It's a cosy respite from
the busy streets of Wedding, with readings,
a well-stocked bar and snacks. The strength
of the place comes from the limited options
in the neighbourhood; whereas the scene
elsewhere can feel fractured, Wedding queers
are joyfully lumped together here.

Clubs & one-nighters

Gay Wedding
*Moritz Bar, Adolfstrasse 17 (0173 680 7670
mobile, www.moritzbar.com). U6, S41, S42
Wedding.* **Open** *7pm-late Mon.* **No cards.**
Map *p116 L2. Mixed*

Deep in the heart of Wedding, Moritz Bar
makes for a cheerful evening any day of the
week, but on Monday, 'Gay Wedding' visitors
will be greeted with pop music and a 2-for-1
deal on gin and tonics. Something between
a bar and a club night, it's ideal for making
friends. The crowd is relaxed and skews
student-heavy.

FRIEDRICHSHAIN

Cafés & bars

Grosse Freiheit 114
*Boxhagener Strasse 114 (7072 8306, www.
grosse-freiheit-114.de). U5 Frankfurter Tor.*
Open *8pm-late Wed-Sun.* **No cards.**
Map *p132 U7. Gay*

The name promises 'big freedom', and
the bar delivers, with a distinctly open
policy to all kinds of gay fellows looking
for a good time, either at the bar or in the
darkrooms. It's particularly popular with
older locals, although the changing nature
of the neighbourhood is slowly bringing
in the under-40 crowd too. Note that the
big freedom here only applies to men: no
women allowed.

Himmelreich
*Simon-Dach-Strasse 36 (2936 9292, www.
himmelreich-berlin.de). U5 Frankfurter Tor;
U1, S5, S7, S75 Warschauer Strasse.* **Open**
6pm-late Mon-Sat; 4pm-late Sun. **No cards.**
Map *p132 U8. Mixed*

A colourful and comfortable lounge serving
snacks and coffee in the earlier hours and
drinks well into the night. Tuesday evenings
were once called 'Women's Lounge', but in
recent years the bar has opted for a more
inclusive 'Queer Night,' which still serves a
lesbian-heavy crowd. On Wednesdays, there's
a 2-for-1 happy hour.

Zum Schmutzigen Hobby
*Revaler Strasse 99 (3646 8446). U1, S5, S7,
S75 Warschauer Strasse.* **Open** *from 6pm
daily.* **No cards.** **Map** *p132 T8. Mixed*

In 2010, famed drag queen Nina Queer moved
her popular watering hole from Prenzlauer
Berg to this graffiti- and bottle-strewn
party zone of reclaimed buildings next to
the Spree. Nina has since left the bar, but it
remains as good as ever. It's intensely fun,
especially later in the night when loud US
pop hits fill the air. The large outdoor patio
hosts viewing parties for *Germany's Next Top
Model*, Eurovision and other TV events of
gay interest.

Clubs & one-nighters

Just a short walk from the punk *Kneipen*
and happy-hour chain restaurants, in the
areas surrounding Warschauer Strasse, are
some of Berlin's most visited gay clubs –
and clubs, period. **Berghain**'s (*see p243*)
legendary popularity extends to a large
queer clientele. In the same building, **Lab.
oratory**'s sprawling hardcore sex den is the

LGBT

place for fetish-friendly gays, complete with all the props and weekend specials (www.lab-oratory.de). Nearby, **Monster Ronson's Ichiban Karaoke** (*see p242*) hosts Berlin's most celebrated drag night, 'The House of Presents' (Tuesdays from 9pm), with a newcomer's show that welcomes folk of all genders to give it their best.

KREUZBERG

A hub for leftist culture of all kinds, Kreuzberg's answer to the gay bar is noticeably more political than Schöneberg's, but there are still plenty of places to drink up and dance, no matter what's on the news. **SO36** (*see p246*) is long-time Kreuzberg favourite whose Gay Oriental Night (Gayhane – House of Halay) on the last Saturday of the month is not to be missed.

Cafés & bars
Barbie Deinhoff's
Schlesische Strasse 16. U1 Schlesisches Tor. **Open** *from 7pm-late daily.* **No cards.** **Map** *p144 S9. Mixed*

Sure, this is a queer performance space, but most people come to its bright, casual rooms for the young, mixed crowd, the top-notch local DJs and the hilarious art adorning the walls. Two-for-one Tuesdays are popular, attracting a particularly skint Kreuzberg crowd.

Café Melltta Sundström
Mehringdamm 61 (no phone, www.melitta-sundstroem.de). U6, U7 Mehringdamm. **Open** *2pm-3am daily.* **No cards.** **Map** *p144 N11. Mixed*

By day, this place serves as a cosy café for students; in the evening, it's brimming with a cheerful and rather well-behaved crowd — this is Bergmannkiez, after all. It once served as the entrance to SchwuZ (*see p233*), now in Neukölln. Without the legendary club pumping music all night long, owner Bernhard Sachse is thrilled he can now get to bed a few hours earlier.

Möbel-Olfe
Reichenberger Strasse 177, corner of Dresdener Strasse (2327 4690, www.moebel-olfe.de). U1, U8 Kottbusser Tor. **Open** *6pm-late Tue-Sun.* **No cards.** **Map** *p144 Q9. Mixed*

The vast 1960s estate that houses a large number of Turkish families is also home to Möbel-Olfe, a popular alternative gay bar. Old chairs are glued to the ceiling as a cheeky nod

to the space's original function as a furniture shop. Tuesday's *Mädchendisko* (girl's disco) is popular with women, lesbian and trans folk of all backgrounds; Thursdays are a sweaty affair more geared towards the men.

♥ Roses
Oranienstrasse 187 (615 6570). U1, U8 Kottbusser Tor. **Open** *10pm-6am daily.* **No cards.** **Map** *p144 Q9. Mixed*

Whatever state you're in (the more of a state, the better), you'll fit in just fine at this boisterous den of glitter. It draws customers of all sexual preferences, who mix and mingle and indulge in excessive drinking amid the plush, kitsch decor. No place for uptights, always full, very Kreuzbergish.

Südblock
Admiralstrasse 1-2 (6094 1853, www.suedblock.org). U1, U8 Kottbusser Tor. **Open** *11 am-late Mon-Sat; 10am-late Sun.* **No cards.** **Map** *p144 Q9. Mixed*

A former beer-slinger from Möbel-Olfe (*see above*) opened this bar for Kreuzberg's increasingly large gay population in 2010. Located under one of the wrap-around housing developments at Kottbusser Tor, the mixed (but girl-heavy) crowd enjoy nightly drinks and dancing, as well as many one-off rock parties. Südblock also serves food, ranging from breakfast to midnight snacks, and in the warmer months, resembles a chilled-out *Biergarten* more than a club.

Shops & services
Other Nature
Mehringdamm 79 (2062 0538, www.other-nature.de). U7 Mehringdamm. **Open** *11am-8pm Mon, Wed-Fri; 11am-6pm Tue; 11am-7pm Sat.* **Map** *p144 N11.*

This alternative and vegan sex shop focuses heavily on sex-positive education across the gender spectrum. You'll find vibrators, dildos and vegan lube along with a small selection of gorgeous harnesses and other kink supplies. There's also a selection of books and postcards in the back room. The products are well worth the prices, and the owner, Sara Rodenhizer, is extremely helpful.

Playstixx
Heimstrasse 6 (6165 9500, www.playstixx.de). U7 Gneisenaustrasse. **Open** *1-7pm Tue-Fri; noon-5pm Sat.* **No cards.** **Map** *p144 O11.*

The dildos on offer at this workshop, run by sculptress Stefanie Dörr, are more likely to come in the form of bananas, whales, fists and dolphins than phalluses. Most are made of non-allergenic, highly durable silicon.

Queer Life

There's more to Berlin's LGBT scene than sex clubs and fetish shops

Once you move past (or through) the smut of Berlin's gay scene, you'll find a whole range of wholesome activities for both locals and tourists. For the athletically inclined, rugby team **Berlin Bruisers** (www.berlinbruisers.com) holds an open practice every Sunday, and **Bear City Roller Derby** (www.bearcityrollerderby.com) puts on newbie roller-skating courses as well as matches, which draw a big queer crowd. Founded in 2016 by trans and genderqueer activists, **Queerclimb** (www.queerclimb.com) is great for meeting new people while learning the literal ropes of climbing and bouldering.

For the less sporty, **Queer Stories** (www.facebook.com/qtinac) is a long-running English-language reading and concert series featuring writers, musicians and filmmakers, as well as an open-mic session for all-comers and a pre-performance buffet. **Transnational Queer Underground** (www.tqu-berlin.net) puts on a smorgasbord of events, ranging from DIY screen-printing workshops to art exhibitions, and sells a fun range of handmade stickers, bags and shirts, all of which make fantastic souvenirs. There are tons of recurring events throughout the year, too, such as the **Queer Zinefest** (www.queerzinefestberlin.net) and **Queer Summer Splash** (www.berlinerbaeder.de), held at the outdoor swimming centre on Prinzenstrasse.

Berlin Bruisers

Clubs & one-nighters

GentleWomansClub
Freudenzimmer, Mehringdamm 61 (0174 8496696 mobile, www.girlstownberlin.tumblr.com). U6, U7 Mehringdamm. **Open** *varies.* **No cards.** **Map** *p144 N11. Lesbian*

GentleWomansClub is relatively new on the scene but has made a big splash. It's technically open to all genders, though girls tip the scale. Sometimes there's a round of speed-dating in the early hours, all in good fun.

Girlstown
Gretchen, Obentrautstrasse 1 (www.girlstownberlin.tumblr.com). U6, U7 Mehringdamm. **Open** *varies.* **No cards.** **Map** *p144 N10. Lesbian*

Once every two months or so, queer women of all ages take over Gretchen. Earlier in the night there's an unfortunate amount of chart music on, but the party really gets going in the pre-dawn hours. It's not particularly raunchy, but great for a good, old-fashioned dance.

Irrenhouse by Nina Queer
Musik & Frieden, Falckensteinstrasse 47-48 (2391 9994). U1 Schlesisches Tor. **Open** *11pm-late 3rd Sat of mth.* **Admission** *€8-€10. No cards.* **Map** *p144 S9. Gay*

This popular one-nighter is true to its name: 'Madhouse'. Famed hostess Nina Queer attracts a bizarre mixture of party kids, trashy drag queens and other flotsam of the night to dance to house and chart music under even more bizarre video installations. Popular and shrill, with candy distributed for free all night and a darkroom out back.

L-Tunes
Spindler & Klatt, Köpenicker Strasse 16-17 (https://l-tunes.com). **Open** *from 10pm last Sat every mth.* **Admission** *€5-€10. No cards.* **Map** *p144 R8. Lesbian*

For lesbians and all their friends, L-tunes takes place on the last Saturday of the month, with music ranging from classic pop to electronica. Spindler & Klatt is the usual venue these days, with a gorgeous terrace overlooking the Spree, but check the website for changes.

Leather, sex & fetish venues

In Kreuzberg, the fetish scene is more mixed. **Club Culture Houze** (Görlitzerstrasse 71, www.club-culture-houze.de) offers gay nights, 'bi' nights, kinky SM and vanilla parties and everything in-between, which makes it a go-to for newbies. The small and plucky **Ficken 3000** (Urbanstrasse 70, www.ficken3000.com) has an extensive basement cruising dungeon, plus an all-welcome bar upstairs. Just down the street from Ficken, **Triebwerk** (Urbanstrasse 64, http://club-triebwerk.business.site) attracts Kreuzberg gays of every denomination for a varied set of weekly parties. **Quälgeist** (Lankwitzer Strasse 42, www.quaelgeist-berlin.de) is a beloved SM institution and the first to organise SM parties for beginners as well as bondage and 'slave' nights. There's usually a dress code.

NEUKÖLLN

There are fewer outright LGBT establishments than in Kreuzberg, but queer politics permeate much of the nightlife anyway, which some prefer to the homogeneity of Motzstrasse.

Cafés & bars
♥ Alaska Bar
*Reuterstrasse 85 (2391 4138). U8 Boddinstrasse. **Open** 6pm-late Tue-Sun. **Map** p166 R12. Mixed*

This vegan café and bar is a mainstay in Reuterkiez. It attracts a truly varied crowd, and, though it may not seem so from the outside, it's very unpretentious. The vegan tapas make great bar snacks, and the wine is surprisingly good. Alaska hosts the occasional churro or taco night, too, which you can expect to be packed.

Silver Future
*Weserstrasse 206 (7563 4987, www.silverfuture.net). U7, U8 Hermannplatz. **Open** 5pm-2am Mon-Thur, Sun; 5pm-3am Fri, Sat. **Map** p166 R11. Mixed*

Neukölln is the new frontier of cool in Berlin, and this is its longstanding queer destination. 'You are now leaving the heteronormative zone' announces a playful sign above the bar – and it's not kidding. Fun for groups of any sexual or gender definition, this neighbourhood bar is welcoming, witty and charmingly rough around the edges.

Clubs & one-nighters
CockTail D'Amore
*Griessmuehle, Sonnenallee 221 (www.cocktaildamore.tumblr.com). S41, S42 Sonnenallee. **Open** midnight-next day 1st Sat of mth. **Admission** varies. No cards. **Map** p166 U13. Mixed*

This alternative party series keeps things fresh with frequent new locations and everlasting DJ sets from its organisers Discodromo and Boris (of Berghain fame). Men, as well as an increasing crowd of other types, come from across the city, eager to dance well into the next day. The vibe can be a bit snobby at first, but as the night wears on, it gets easier to befriend patrons on the dance floor and in the outdoor chill-out space.

The Real Housewives of Neukölln
*www.facebook.com/therealhousewivesofneukolln. **Admission** varies. No cards. Mixed*

The queens of the absurdist drag performances are real royalty. Events are held at various venues throughout the city, with house music, techno, disco, and more. Wherever the party takes place, finding it is never a bad idea.

SchwuZ
*Rollbergstrasse 26 (5770 2270, www.schwuz. de). U7 Rathaus Neukölln; U8 Boddinstrasse. **Open** & admission varies. **No cards**. **Map** p166 R12. Mixed*

One of Berlin's longest-running dance institutions, SchwuZ moved into the old Kindl brewery in 2013. A variety of mainstream and more underground events takes place throughout the week attracting a mixed and ready-to-mingle crowd who take full advantage of the warehouse-like space and multiple dancefloors.

SCHÖNEBERG

The undeniable hub for Berlin's historic gay culture is right here, smack-dab in the middle of Schöneberg's *Altbau* apartments, cute cafés and organic markets. There may be a lot happening elsewhere in the city, but if you're looking for a gay-centric one-stop-shop, this is it.

Cafés & bars

Barbiche

Potsdamer Strasse 151 (www.berlin-ist-eine-frau.com/barbiche). U2 Bülowstrasse. **Open** *5pm-midnight Tue-Sat.* **No cards.** **Map** *p178 K10. Mixed*

Lena Braun, the mastermind behind Kreuzberg's infamous Barbie Deinhoff's (*see p231*), has opened a new café, gallery and co-working space among the sex clubs of Schöneberg. Fantastic exhibitions, including a homage to the fashion label Palomo Spain, are on display, and queers from all over town come over for performance nights such as 'Electric Cabaret'.

Begine

Potsdamer Strasse 139 (215 1414, www.begine.de). U2 Bülowstrasse. **Open** *5pm-late Mon-Fri; 7pm-late Sat.* **No cards.** **Map** *p178 K10. Lesbian*

This venerable women's café frequented by a slightly older crowd of lesbians is part of the 'Meeting Point and Culture for Women' centre. From concerts and cabaret to readings and quiz nights, it has a jam-packed programme.

Café Berio

Maassenstrasse 7 (216 1946, www.cafeberio.de). U1, U2, U3, U4 Nollendorfplatz. **Open** *6am-3am daily.* **No cards.** **Map** *p178 J10. Gay*

One of the best daytime cafés in Berlin, this Parisian-style café is full of attractive, trendy young men (including the waiters), with a good people-watching terrace in summer. Decent food is served all day, should you get hunger pangs at an ungodly hour. It's a gay café historically, but no one will be turned away.

Hafen

Motzstrasse 19 (211 4118, www.hafen-berlin.de). U1, U2, U3, U4 Nollendorfplatz. **Open** *8pm-late daily (from 7pm in summer).* **No cards.** **Map** *p178 J9. Gay*

A red, plush and vaguely psychedelic bar in the centre of Schöneberg's gay triangle. It's popular with the fashion-conscious, especially at weekends, when it provides a safe haven from nearby heavy cruising dens. It's usually very crowded, especially for Quizz-o-Rama, a pub quiz (in English) intermittently scheduled.

Heile Welt

Motzstrasse 5 (2191 7507). U1, U2, U3, U4 Nollendorfplatz. **Open** *6pm-2am daily (from 8pm in summer).* **No cards.** **Map** *p178 J9. Gay*

A stylish café, lounge and cocktail bar for the fashionable: the front has a 1970s disco feel complete with furry wall; the back lounge offers plush leather seating. It's a good place to kick off an evening, practise some chat-up lines and decide whether or not to go clubbing. It's packed by 11pm on Friday and Saturday.

Mutschmanns

Martin-Luther-Strasse 19 (2191 9640, www.mutschmanns.de). U1, U2, U3, U4 Nollendorfplatz. **Open** *10pm-late Wed, Fri, Sat; 9pm-late Thur.* **Admission** *varies. No cards.* **Map** *p178 H9. Gay*

This well-frequented hardcore bar, with a large and hard darkroom in the basement, is suitable for cruising or just hanging out – albeit with a dress code of leather, rubber or uniform. Rubber Night is the first Saturday of the month.

♥ Neues Ufer

Hauptstrasse 157 (7895 7900, www.neuesufer.de). U7 Kleistpark. **Open** *2pm-2am daily.* **No cards.** **Map** *p178 K11. Mixed*

Established in the early 1970s, this is one of the city's oldest gay cafés. Formerly known as Anderes Ufer ('The Other Side'), it was an old haunt of David Bowie, who used to live just two doors away.

Prinzknecht

Fuggerstrasse 33 (2362 7444, www.prinzknecht.de). U1, U2, U3 Wittenbergplatz. **Open** *3pm-2am Mon, Tue, Thur, Sun; 6pm-2am Wed; 3pm-3am Fri, Sat.* **No cards.** **Map** *p178 H9. Gay*

With a large but underused darkroom out back, this huge, open bar draws in gays from the neighbourhood as well as leathermen and other hardcore customers. The place is somewhat provincial in feel, but nice for a chat and a beer. The crowd moves outside in summer. There's a 2-for-1 happy hour 7-10pm Wednesdays.

Tom's Bar

Motzstrasse 19 (213 4570, www.tomsbar.de). U1, U2, U3, U4 Nollendorfplatz. **Open** *10pm-6am daily.* **No cards.** **Map** *p178 J9. Gay*

Once described by *Der Spiegel* as the climax of the night, Tom's is something of a cruising institution. The front bar is fairly chatty but

In the know
Saunas

The sauna-as-sex-club concept caters almost exclusively to gay men. They're not as popular as they used to be in Berlin and are most frequented after work. Tucked into an off-street courtyard in Kreuzberg (just beyond the queues for Mustafa's revered kebab), **Der Boiler** (5770 7175, www. boiler-berlin.de) is an ultra-modern expanse of saunas, steam rooms, whirlpools, cabins and glory holes, where most of the manhandling takes place in a dark maze. Attracting a hot variety of older and younger men, it's busier and kinkier on evenings and weekends, when it's open all night. There's no real raunchy counterpart for women, but the hammam and sauna at Kreuzberg's **Schokoladenfabrik** (www.schokofabrik.de) has become an unofficial lesbian hangout. Admission to most saunas is upwards of €15, depending on how long you stay.

the closer you get to the steps down to the darkroom, the more intense things become. It's very popular with men of all ages and styles, especially on 2-for-1 Mondays.

Woof

*Fuggerstrasse 37 (2360 7870, www.woof-berlin.com). U1, U2, U3 Wittenbergplatz. **Open** 10pm-late daily. **No cards**. **Map** p178 H9. Gay*

Bears, daddies and leather lovers congregate around the bar or wander the sex rooms out back, especially on happy hour Tuesdays. Wednesdays are called Furry Night, if that's something you're into.

Shops & services

Schöneberg is awash with sex and fetish shops, some of which even come with cruising cabins. If you've got a bit of extra cash to spend on sexy souvenirs, take the U-Bahn to Nollendorfplatz and head for the number of top-quality shops. On Motzstrasse, don't miss **Jaxx** (213 8103, www.thejaxx.de), **Butcherei Lindinger** (2005 1391, www.butcherei.com) and Dutch chain **Mr B** (2199 7704, www.misterb.com). On Fuggerstrasse, **R&Co Berlin** (2196 7400, www.randco.de) offers top-notch leather regalia, as does the made-to-order workshop **Leathers** on Eisenacherstrasse (4427 786, www.leathers.de).

Bruno's

Maassenstrasse 14 (3466 5333, www. brunos.de). U1, U2, U3, U4 Nollendorfplatz.

Open 10am-10pm Mon-Sat. Map p178 J10. Sex shop

A large and rather plush shop with an extensive selection of reading and viewing material, plus cards, calendars, videos, condoms, lube and other paraphernalia.

Prinz Eisenherz

Motzstrasse 23 (313 9936, www. prinz-eisenherz.com). U1, U2, U3, U4 Nollendorfplatz. Open 10am-8pm Mon-Sat. Map p178 J10. Books

One of the finest queer bookshops in Europe, with many titles unavailable in Britain included among its large English-language stock. There's a good art and photography section, plus magazines, postcards and news of book readings and other events. There's a solid section of feminist lit, too.

Clubs & one-nighters
Connection

*Fuggerstrasse 33 (218 1432, www.connection-berlin.com). U1, U2, U3 Wittenbergplatz. **Open** 11pm-6am Fri, Sat. **Admission** €8. **Map** p178 H9. Gay*

A popular weekend club, with DJs playing mainly electronic sounds. If you get bored of the dance floor, you can cruise the vast flesh dungeons of **Connection Garage** (10am-1am Mon-Sat; 2pm-1am Sun) two floors below, which doubles as a fetish shop during the day. After years of being men-only, the club is now open to all, though the darkrooms are still off-limits for women.

Leather, sex & fetish venues

For gay men, Schöneberg is once again where it's at. **Böse Buben** (Sachsendamm 76, www.boesebuben-berlin.de) offers cheap drinks and imaginatively decorated rooms for just about every fetish imaginable. **CDL-Club** (Hohenstaufenstrasse 58, www.cdl-club.de) is new on the scene, with lots of parties throughout the week, including a mandatory mask party. At hardcore **New Action** (Kleist Strasse 35, www.newactionberlin.de), leather, rubber and uniforms rule the roost, and the ever-popular **Scheune** (Motzstrasse 25, www. scheune-berlin.de) is a welcoming place for the well-versed as well as newbies, with a Naked Sex Party every Sunday from 5.30pm. **Ajpnia** (Wartburgstrasse 18, www.ajpnia. de) is frequented by men of all ages, with late-night and after-work parties, as well as their PositHIV-Verkehr, a party by and for HIV-positive men.

Nightlife

Pleasure-seekers, libertines and techno-heads from every corner of the globe come to partake in the city's infamous night scene

Berlin's reputation for decadence and nocturnal high jinks stretches all the way back to the 1920s, when the city's legendary cabaret scene and tolerance of homosexuality made it the destination of choice for Europe's party people. During the Cold War, East Berlin had more liberal licensing laws than London, while the western side of town teemed with nihilistic artists and self-exiled musicians, including David Bowie, Iggy Pop and Nick Cave, who can be seen thrashing his guitar in the classic Berlin flick *Wings of Desire*. In the heady post-Wall years, the West Berlin avant garde collided with party-starved East Berliners to create a DIY rave scene on makeshift dancefloors in abandoned buildings, laying the groundwork for the city's future status as the spiritual home of electronica.

The good news is that Berlin still deserves its reputation as one of the world's best party cities; every taste is catered for here, all night long, in every kind of venue, from desperate dives in temporary locations to swanky premises where mirror balls make the world go round.

Club der Visionaere *p244*

Berlin by night

Berlin's partygoers continue trekking east in search of a good night out. There's a clutch of venues around Ostkreuz in Friedrichshain and more around Kottbusser Tor in Kreuzberg, but two stops east along the U1 to Schlesisches Tor and further east up Köpenicker Strasse is where you'll find most of the action these days.

As for Berlin's most famous club, **Berghain** (*see p243*), there's little new to be said; it's easy enough to find and the best advice is just to dive in and formulate your own opinion of the city's highest-profile nightspot.

One thing remains the same in this sleepless city: techno rules, and electronica in all its forms is still the dominant sound of the city. The capital is synonymous with the genre, which is now reinventing itself (again) as a result of an influx of foreign talent. While electronic beats predominate, you can find any type of music you like, if you look hard enough. Music of black

origin (reggae, hip hop, jazz) isn't as well represented as in London or Paris, reflecting Berlin's more limited racial mix, but other musical styles, long out of fashion in other capitals (punk and emo, for example), steadfastly survive and even thrive in Berlin. But everything's not as rosy as it seems. The club scene is not immune to ever-increasing gentrification, as developers tussle with locals to reclaim venues in Kreuzberg, Friedrichshain and Prenzlauer Berg for more corporate ends. That said, while the gargantuan warehouse techno parties of the 1990s may have faded into mythology, new venues continue to open. And, holding out against the download tide, Berlin still has lots of good record shops, which are useful for finding out what's going on via flyers, posters and word of mouth.

Timings, prices and admission

Berliners don't head to clubs until 1am at the earliest, and it's not unusual to start at a party on Friday night and stumble into bed

Urban Spree concert

❤ Best nights out

Bar jeder Vernunft *p257*
Party like it's 1926 with an evening of dinner and cabaret in an old circus tent.

Berghain *p243*
Experience Europe's best DJs and an anything-goes attitude, if you make it past the doorman.

Buttons at ://about blank *p242*
A fabulously hedonistic queer party with a joyful crowd and plenty of open-air fun.

Clärchen's Ballhaus *p239*
Leave your hipster credentials at the door and dance the night away.

Dr. Pong *p241*
A ping-pong club with a friendly, nostalgic vibe and a competitive streak.

Roses *p231*
Folks from all walks of life come in from the streets for one last drink.

at some point on Sunday afternoon. The real party animals go out during the week too. While this approach is hardcore, the general attitude to clubbing is incredibly laid-back: no dressing up, no planning; Berliners let themselves go with the flow. Admission prices are reasonable, hovering around €10-€15 for big clubs and half that for smaller DJ bars. An increasing number of Berlin clubs operate some sort of door policy. The brutal phrase *Gesichtskontrolle* (face control) means that bouncers get to decide who gets in and who stays out. To increase your chances, there are a few simple rules in the queue. Be as quiet as possible. Don't be obviously off your face. But don't seem too stiff. Don't take pictures. Don't have this guide in your hand. Use English sparingly. Learn the answer to '*Wie viele*?' (How many [people are you])? *Zwei, drei, vier*, and bear in mind that singles and twos have a better chance than sizeable groups. Some clubs don't like people to try too hard; others will turn punters away who haven't made enough effort. Wear whatever you like but bear in mind that Berliners tend not to dress up in a British sense – short skirts and high heels might be better left at home – unless you're in drag of course.

Information

To find out what's on where, pick up a copy of *Zitty* or *Tip*, Berlin's two fortnightly listings magazines, or their English-language monthly equivalent *Exberliner*. Groove (groove.de) and Kaltblut magazine (www.kaltblut-magazine.com) discuss the contemporary music scene; you can check their websites or pick up a paper copy. Other discerning websites include www.iheartberlin.de, www.indieberlin.de and berlinbeat.org.

MITTE

Clubs & late-night bars
Acud
Veteranenstrasse 21 (9835 2613, www.acud. de). U8 Rosenthaler Platz, or S1, S2, S25 Nordbahnhof. **Open** *varies.* **Admission** *varies. No cards.* **Map** *p68 O4.*

A massive complex, containing a cinema, theatre and gallery, operated by a friendly Berlin arts collective. There's also a party floor with a playlist mainly devoted to reggae, breakbeat and drum 'n' bass; the dingy bar is a popular spot for the city's stoners. The cinema programme is interesting, consisting mostly of independent and low-budget films.

There's something going on here most nights of the week, and start times and prices vary accordingly.

❤ Clärchen's Ballhaus
Auguststrasse 24 (282 9295, www.ballhaus. de). S1, S2, S25 Oranienburger Strasse. **Open** *11am-late daily.* **Admission** *€5-€9. No cards.* **Map** *p68 N5.*

In the heart of Mitte, this determinedly un-hip dance hall gives the techno clubs a run for their money in terms of popularity and downright fun. Clärchen's Ballhaus has been frequented by fleet-footed Berliners since it was established by Clara Haberman in 1913. Today, its often cheesy playlists and vintage surroundings attract everyone from students to 75-year-old Ballhaus veterans. It's not unusual to see a geriatric Fred Astaire type teaching a young pink-haired artist how to tango or foxtrot. The Ballhaus has two dance floors: a ground-floor space and the smaller Spiegelsaal (Mirror Salon) upstairs, where huge cracked mirrors, chandeliers, ornate mouldings and candlelight transport guests straight back to the 1920s.

Golden Gate
Schicklerstrasse 4 (5770 4278, www. goldengate-berlin.de). U8, S3, S5, S7, S9 Jannowitzbrücke. **Open** *midnight-late Thur-Sun.* **Admission** *varies. No cards.* **Map** *p68 Q7.*

Once home to a rather hit-and-miss music policy, with the occasional live show, this grimy little club has now settled firmly into a series of all-weekend techno parties. Its location – smack dab in the middle of a motorway – means it has no issue with noise. The Thursday night parties are particularly raucous, with the club carrying on until pretty much Monday afternoon. The atmosphere is extremely relaxed and positive, staying true to the Berlin party ethos of egalitarian fun with no fashion police or posing allowed.

Kaffee Burger & Old CCCP
Torstrasse 60 (no phone, www.kaffeeburger. de). U2 Rosa-Luxemburg-Platz. **Open** *9pm-late daily.* **Admission** *€1-€5. No cards.* **Map** *p68 P5.*

In the know
Photo no-no

Germany has strict privacy laws which prevent photos being taken of private individuals without their express consent. If you are found to be taking photos (even selfies) in a bar or club, you are likely to be asked to leave.

Proudly boasting 200 concerts and 364 parties a year, Kaffee Burger's programme runs the cultural gamut. Early evenings may see readings, lectures, films or live music. Later on, DJs play anything from old-school country to Balkan beats, or even flamboyant Israeli pop at the 'unkosher Jewish night', Meschugge. Adjoining Kaffee Burger is the Russian-themed late bar, **Old CCCP**, with delightfully kitsch décor and lighting that's bright enough to facilitate interaction with strangers. At the weekend, you can bounce between the two for the same cover charge.

KitKatClub

Köpenicker Strasse 76 (no phone, www. kitkatclub.org). U8 Heinrich-Heine-Strasse. **Open** *11pm-late Mon, Fri, Sat.* **Admission** *€10-€15. No cards.* **Map** *p68 Q7.*

This legendary sex and techno club for all is a labyrinthine complex of half a dozen dancefloors, a dubious swimming pool and a grimy dungeon mock-operating room. Saturday nights feature the club's flagship CarneBall Bizarre, with the Afterhour event to follow throughout Sunday. For pure polysexual hedonism, look out for cult party Gegen (http://gegenberlin.com) every two months. Most parties have a fetish dress code – except Electric Mondays – so if you arrive wearing jeans you'll have to leave them in the cloakroom and dance in your knickers.

Tresor

Köpenicker Strasse 70 (no phone, www. tresorberlin.de). U8 Heinrich-Heine-Strasse. **Open** *11pm-late Mon; midnight-late Wed-Sat.* **Admission** *€5-€12. No cards.* **Map** *p68 Q7.*

Berlin's original techno club is housed in what was formerly the main central-heating power station for East Berlin. The colossal location is breathtaking, but only a tiny portion of the vast space is in use; plans to create a huge centre of alternative art and culture have resulted so far in the Ohm performance space next door and large-scale experimental music festivals, such as **Berlin Atonal** (www.berlin-atonal.com). The experience of the basement floor is one you'll not forget; a black hole occasionally

Clärchen's Ballhaus *p239*

punctuated by flashing strobes with some of the loudest, hardest techno it's humanly possible to hear.

Live music

B-Flat

Dircksenstrasse 40 (283 3123, www.b-flat-berlin.de). U8 Weinmeisterstrasse. **Open** *8pm or 9pm-late daily.* **Admission** *free-€13. No cards.* **Map** *p68 P5.*

B-Flat pulls in a decent local guitar hero once in a while, but its strongest nights tend to feature jazz singers. Free Wednesday night jam sessions from 9pm.

Columbiahalle

Columbiadamm 13-21, Tempelhof (6981 7586, www.c-halle.com). U6 Platz der Luftbrücke. **Open** *varies.* **Admission** *varies. No cards.* **Map** *fold-out map N12.*

A roomy venue with a reputation for the best sound in town, Columbiahalle promotes larger acts that haven't made it to blockbuster status, such as Bon Iver or Manu Chao. Drinks are a little expensive, but it's a good-sized place to catch hip-hop superstars such as A$AP Rocky and Snoop Dogg, who would probably be playing stadiums in other cities.

In the know
Music tours

If you have an unquenchable desire to discover the Berlin backdrop to Bowie's *Low/ Heroes* period or to see the bar where Iggy Pop once ended a *Rolling Stone* interview by rolling around on the pavement, the **Fritz Music Tour** (www.musictours-berlin.com) is for you.

PRENZLAUER BERG & MITTE NORTH

Clubs & late-night bars

8MM
Schönhauser Allee 177B (4050 0624, www. 8mmbar.com). U2 Senefelderplatz. **Open** *9pm-late daily.* **No cards.** *Map p116 P4.*

Sometimes the 4/4 techno beat can seem inescapable in Berlin, so head to this one-room dive bar for an alternative. Weekends get raucous with DJs playing a mix of punk and new-wave staples, and the occasional touring band member getting behind the decks for a concert after-party. Drinks are very reasonably priced, making it just the place for your umpteenth nightcap.

♥ Dr. Pong
Eberswalder Strasse 21 (no phone, www. drpong.net). U2 Eberswalder Strasse. **Open** *8pm-late Mon-Sat; 7pm-late Sun.* **No cards.** *Map p116 P3.*

Bring your table-tennis bat (or hire one for a €5 deposit) and prepare for drunken ping-pong carnage. The action doesn't start until around midnight, but then you can expect 30 or so players – some good, some bad – to surround the table in one almighty round-the-world session. There's a bar and, bizarrely, Twiglets for nourishment. Note that the opening hours are unreliable.

Duncker
Dunckerstrasse 64 (445 9509, www. dunckerclub.de). U2 Eberswalder Strasse, or S8, S9, S41, S42 Prenzlauer Allee. **Open** *9pm-late Mon; 10pm-late Thur; 11pm-late Fri, Sat.* **Admission** *€5. No cards. Map p116 Q2.*

Duncker is located, aptly enough, in a neo-Gothic church on a nondescript side street. While the tail end of the week focuses on new wave, dark wave and indie, it's the Dark Monday goth party that is the club's bread and butter. Surprisingly, for a city the size of Berlin, venues catering for our friends in black are few and far between, making this a precious gem for fans of the genre.

Neue Odessa Bar
Torstrasse 89 (0171 839 8991 mobile, www. neueodessabar.de). U8 Rosenthaler Platz. **Open** *7pm-late daily.* **No cards.** *Map p116 O5.*

Acting as the unofficial hub for the hip 'SoTo' set – the area south of Torstrasse – this bar serves a mean cocktail. It's populated by local fashionistas and media-industry expats, who come here for further libations after doing the rounds of nearby gallery openings.

DJs appear at weekends, but it can get very smoky, reflecting the buzz inside. The door staff can appear a bit gruff, however.

Live music

Ausland
Lychener Strasse 60 (447 7008, www. ausland-berlin.de). U2 Eberswalder Strasse. **Open** *varies.* **Admission** *varies. No cards. Map p116 Q2.*

A small bohemian basement staging free jazz, avant-folk and live electronica, as well as films and art installations. Shows usually begin an hour later than the posted time (on principle, apparently). Nights often close with guest DJs, whose musical tastes can get pretty challenging.

Frannz Club
Schönhauser Allee 36 (7262 7930, www. frannz.de). U2 Eberswalder Strasse. **Open** *from 9pm daily.* **Admission** *varies. No cards. Map p116 P3.*

A former GDR youth club, Frannz is a black box with decent sound, pricey drinks and unsmiling doormen. Musically, it's heavy on German acts that don't really translate culturally, though it also favours electro-swing and has, in the past, also booked rockabilly stars such as Wanda Jackson.

Kulturbrauerei
Schönhauser Allee 36 (4435 2170, www. kulturbrauerei.de). U2 Eberswalder Strasse. **Open** *varies.* **Admission** *€5-€30. Map p116 P3.*

With its assortment of venues, outdoor bars and barbecues, this cultural centre housed in an enormous former brewery can resemble a cross between a medieval fairground and a school disco. The two spaces operated by the Kulturbrauerei proper are Maschinehaus and the larger Kesselhaus, where concerts vary from reggae to Frank Zappa cover bands. There's an emphasis on German acts too.

Roadrunner's Paradise
Saarbrückerstrasse 24 (0172 396 4481 mobile, www.roadrunners-paradise.de). U2 Senefelderplatz. **Open** *varies.* **Admission** *€8-€20. No cards. Map p116 P4.*

Navigate your way through to the third courtyard of the former Königstadt brewery and you'll find Roadrunner's tucked away next to a motorcycle repair shop, a suitably greasy location for this butch venue. On offer is a tasty but irregular mixture of live shows and DJ sets, focusing on garage, blues-rock, rockabilly and surf. Alternatively, marvel at the array of 1950s American kitsch while sinking a beer.

FRIEDRICHSHAIN AND LICHTENBERG

Clubs & late-night bars

❤ ://about blank
Markgrafendamm 24C (no phone, http:// aboutparty.net). S5, S7, S8, S9, S41, S42, S75 Ostkreuz. **Open** *midnight-late Thur-Sat.* **Admission** *€5-€15. No cards.* **Map** *p132 V9.*

Particularly famed for its open-air parties, this club near Ostkreuz station is a favourite with the city's more adventurous hedonists – not least for its monthly blowout Buttons (formerly Homopatik).

Kater Blau
Holzmarktstrasse 25 (no phone, www. katerblau.de). S3, S5, S7, S9 Ostbahnhof. **Open** *varies.* **Admission** *€5-€15.* **Map** *p132 R7.*

This is the X-rated part of the expansive, family-friendly Holzmarkt development. With a moored boat, roaring fire at night and many hammock-like structures, the potential for alfresco relaxing is high. At the business end of proceedings, a fine roster of electronic DJs spin away unendingly – sometimes for four days straight. The vibe is more crusty than chic, and increasingly so as the weekend unravels. If you have the stamina (and courage) to last well into Monday afternoon, expect to encounter some of Berlin's strangest creatures.

Monster Ronson's Ichiban Karaoke
Warschauer Strasse 34, (8975 1327, www. karaokemonster.de). U1, S3, S5, S7, S9 Warschauer Strasse. **Open** *7pm-midnight daily.* **Admission** *€3-€5. No cards.* **Map** *p132 T9.*

In 1999, Monster Ronson – aka Ron Rineck – moved to Berlin from Salt Lake City with just $7,000 to his name. His savings dwindled, and he began sleeping in his car. He bought a second-hand karaoke machine and began throwing parties in squat houses all over Europe. Eventually, he saved up enough to open his very own karaoke bar, which is now packed out most nights. Aspiring divas can belt out songs in several different booths, some small and intimate, others with their own stage area.

Paule's Metal Eck
Krossener Strasse 15 (291 1624). U1, S3, S5, S7, S9 Warschauer Strasse. **Open** *7pm-5am Mon-Fri; 3pm-5am Sat, Sun.* **No cards.** **Map** *p132 U8.*

Neither a typical heavy-metal bar nor remotely typical for this area, the Egyptian-themed Eck attracts a young crowd with relentless metal videos, a decent selection of beers, and both pool and table football. Non-working disco balls, overhead lighting in the shape of mummies, and formidable dragon busts deck an interior that's designed half like a gloomy mausoleum, half in pastiche medieval style.

Rosi's
Revaler Strasse 29 (no phone, www. rosis-berlin.de). S5, S7, S8, S9, S41, S42, S75 Ostkreuz. **Open** *11pm-late Thur-Sat.* **Admission** *€2-€7. No cards.* **Map** *p132 U8.*

A typical Berlin club, Rosi's is a tumbledown, DIY affair: all bare bricks and mismatched flea-market furniture. The atmosphere is very relaxed, and the crowd tends to be young and studenty. Live acts are a regular feature; DJs spin mainly electro and rock, and the beer garden is popular on summer nights.

Salon zur Wilden Renate
Alt-Stralau 70 (2504 1426, www.renate. cc). S5, S7, S8, S9, S41, S42, S75 Ostkreuz. **Open** *varies.* **Admission** *varies. No cards.* **Map** *p132 V10.*

This knackered old house was perennially at risk of being torn down and turned into – of course – trendy apartments. Once-sporadic parties follow a regular weekend rhythm these days, usually going till the last man standing. Students and wasted ravers press up against ex-pats from Mitte in the reliably crowded rooms, which are still set up like the flats they once were – complete with the odd bed. On languid summer afternoons, the club hops across the river to an intimate open-air wonderland called Else.

Sisyphos
Hauptstrasse 15 (9836 6839, www. sisyphos-berlin.net). S3 Rummelsburg. **Open** *midnight Fri-10am Mon every other weekend.* **Admission** *€10. No cards.* **Map** *p132 W9.*

You don't make the trek out to Sisyphos just for a snoop and a couple of beers. It's an 'in for a penny, in for a pound' sort of place, where the party begins on Friday and trundles on non-stop until Monday. Vast indoor and outdoor spaces at this former dog-biscuit factory help create a festival-like spirit that's pitch-perfect for sunny weekends. Music ranges from pumping techno inside to more housey tunes out by the 'lake' – more of a scummy pond, really. Crowd-wise, expect it all: fresh-faced student revellers and wizened ravers of a dreadlocked persuasion are among the regulars.

❤ Berghain

Am Wriezener Bahnhof (no phone, www. berghain.de). U1, S3, S5, S7, S9 Warschauer Strasse. **Open** *midnight-late Fri, Sat, Sun.* **Admission** *€10-€14. No cards.* **Map** *p132 S7.*

Easily the city's most famous club – and some would say the best club in the world – Berghain is not just a techno club: it's a way of life for many of the tireless regulars who call it 'church'. Housed within an imposing former power station, it emerged in 2004 from the ashes of its legendary gay predecessor, Ostgut, which had fallen victim to the city's massive infrastructure projects. Even 'non-club' people will be intoxicated by the open atmosphere, liberal attitudes, eccentric characters, the carefully preserved industrial fabric of the building and, of course, the gargantuan sound system. It's open, complete with darkrooms, from Friday midnight until well into Monday morning.

The club's reputation for a difficult and random door policy is not entirely undeserved: doorman Sven (recognisable by his facial tattoos) looms large all night with a seemingly haphazard attitude to who gets in. At peak times on a Saturday night, only a third of the people in the queue will get past him – you'll know you're in if he nods; if he points to his left, hard luck. Don't argue the toss, even if you're feeling brave. We recommend that you be calm, sober and respectful in the queue; it goes without saying that drunken stag dos aren't welcome. Once inside, a zero-tolerance camera ban is enforced – expect to be immediately ejected if you're discovered flaunting the rules. Other than that, you can go wild, safe in the knowledge that nothing you get up to will ever return to haunt you on social media.

Panorama Bar, up a flight of stairs from Berghain, is a smaller dancefloor that plays old-school house and features oversized artworks by Wolfgang Tillmans. Be here when the shutters open just after sunrise for one of the most climactic moments of the weekend.

▶ *Where should you go if you can't get into Berghain (or don't want to risk getting turned away)? For techno, try Tresor (see p240); for electro, try Watergate (see p245) or Ritter Butzke (see p245); and for a grope in the dark, try the KitKatClub (see p240).*

Süss War Gestern

Wühlischstrasse 43. S5, S7, S8, S9, S41, S42, S75 Ostkreuz. **Open** *varies.* **Admission** *varies. No cards.* **Map** *p132 U8.*

With a name meaning 'sweet was yesterday', the 1970s-style décor comes as no surprise. What is a surprise is the free entrance and €2.50 beers. There are three areas for dancing, drinking and hanging out, with different rooms playing different genres of music, from conventional techno to novelty hip hop. Check the website before you go.

YAAM

Schillingbrücke, at Stralauer Platz (615 1354, www.yaam.de). S3, S5, S7, S9 Ostbahnhof. **Open** *varies.* **Admission** *varies. No cards.* **Map** *p132 R8.*

Yet another victim of Berlin's Mediaspree development, YAAM was forcibly evicted from its previous home – but you can't keep a good reggae club down. It quickly found another riverside spot, so it's business as usual for this legendary beach bar and cultural centre. By day, there might be kids playing a laid-back game of volleyball, with a jerk chicken stall on the side. Then, as the light fades, things ease up a notch or two with concerts and parties bouncing to an Afro-Caribbean beat. An ultra-friendly place.

Live music

Astra Kulturhaus

Revaler Strasse 99 (2005 6767, www.astra-berlin.de). U1, S3, S5, S7, S9 Warschauer Strasse. **Open** *varies.* **Admission** *varies.* **Map** *p132 T8.*

Berlin's premier alternative venue, Astra is part of the large RAW Tempel complex on old industrial warehouse grounds that's somewhat reminiscent of Christiania in Copenhagen. Arrive early as it gets crowded, and pillars can mean tricky sightlines. The likes of Bill Callahan, Godspeed You! Black Emperor, Death Cab for Cutie and Damon Albarn have played here.

Kater Blau *p242*

Fritzclub im Postbahnhof

Strasse der Pariser Kommune 8 (698 1280, www.fritzclub.com). S3, S5, S7, S9 Ostbahnhof. **Open** *varies.* **Admission** *€4-€7.50. No cards.* **Map** *p132 S8.*

This restored industrial building is relatively young in comparison to other venues, but its association with Radio Fritz gives it the clout to stage the likes of Arcade Fire, Paloma Faith and Fun Lovin' Criminals, as well as regular indie student parties.

Supamolly

Jessner Strasse 41 (2900 7294, www. supamolly.de). U5, S8, S9, S41, S42, S85 Frankfurter Allee. **Open** *8pm-late Tue-Sun.* **No cards.** **Map** *p132 V8.*

With the few remaining Berlin squats now tourist sites, Supamolly soldiers on as a punk-music venue, bar, cinema and general activist meeting point. You're more likely to encounter itinerant South American musicians these days, although an old-guard of Berlin punks still turns out for the frequent ska and hardcore gigs. It retains its grimy charm, the walls daubed with graffiti and the candlelit bar welcoming all for cheap beer at all hours of the night.

In the know
Queer nightlife

Much of Berlin's nightlife is enthusiastically queer, and the biggest venues (Berghain, KitKat Club, ://about blank) feature large on the LGBT clubbing scene. The atmosphere is generally inclusive and welcoming to anyone who is respectful to the community. However, on some nights, especially increasingly popular 'queer safe space' nights (such as Buttons at ://about blank), straight-presenting individuals may find it more difficult, though not impossible, to get in. For more information, see p224 LGBT.

KREUZBERG & TREPTOW

Barbie Deinhoff's (*see p231*) in Kreuzberg is a bar, alternative art gallery and indie rock venue that embodies the best of Berlin living. And whatever you're into, don't miss the kitsch and brash gay bar, **Roses** (*see p231*).

Clubs & late-night bars

Chalet

Vor dem Schlesischen Tor 3 (6953 6290, www.chalet-berlin.de). U1 Schlesisches Tor. **Open** *midnight-late Tue-Sun.* **Admission** *€10-€12. No cards.* **Map** *p144 T10.*

Chalet was opened by some of the late, great Bar 25 crew – and these guys know a thing or two about getting their groove on. Located in a grand, 150-year-old townhouse, it has multiple levels and rooms to explore, as well as a large luscious garden in which to shoot the breeze when the beats get too much. An altogether stylish and sultry club with a party pretty much every night; more local on weekdays, more touristy at weekends.

Chesters

Glogauerstrasse 2 (no phone, www. chesters-live.de). U1 Görlitzer Bahnhof. **Open** *varies.* **Admission** *€4-€8. No cards.* **Map** *p144 S10.*

It's the eclectic music policy that continues to pull in painfully hip punters to this black-walled bunker of a club. Formerly an indie rock and hip-hop venue, bass-heavy dance genres such as trap and Afro beats have become the order of the day since two New York transplants took control of the booking.

Club der Visionaere

Am Flutgraben (6951 8942, www. clubdervisionaere.com). U1 Schlesisches Tor, or S8, S9, S41, S42 Treptower Park. **Open** *2pm-late Mon-Fri; noon-late Sat, Sun.* **Admission** *€5. No cards.* **Map** *p144 T10.*

One of the first and best, this summer-only canalside club is nestled under an enormous weeping willow. There's a small indoor dancefloor and a rickety open-air area of wooden decking with a large jetty stretching out across the water. You can drop in during the week for a beer, but the place comes to life at the weekend, filling up with an after-hour crowd, happy to chill, drink and dance the day away. Winter parties are now held in the nearby Hoppetosse boat at **Arena Berlin** (Eichenstrasse 4, 533 2030, www.arena-berlin.de).

Farbfernseher

*Skalitzer Strasse 114 (9562 1801, www.farb-fernseher.de). U1 Görlitzer Bahnhof. **Open** 10pm-late Wed-Sat. **Admission** €1-€3. No cards. **Map** p144 Q9.*

Much more than a bar but not quite a club, Farbfernseher hits the mark for the in-betweeners of the Berlin night. Once an old television shop (hence the name, meaning colour TV), it has since become a scenester favourite. Things quickly get hot and heavy on the dancefloor, which is usually marshalled by some rising local talent. Bloke-only groups should expect grief at the door on busier nights.

Gretchen

*Obentrautstrasse 19-21 (2592 2702, www.gretchen-club.de). U1, U6 Hallesches Tor, or U6, U7 Mehringdamm. **Open** varies. **Admission** €8-€15. No cards. **Map** p144 N10.*

Coming straight out of left field, Gretchen hosts an impressive array of nights that aren't afraid of forgoing Berlin's ubiquitous tech-house loops in favour of some trap, dubstep, drum 'n' bass or hip hop. The picturesque vaulted ceilings and intricate columns of this former Prussian stable create a wonderfully incongruous setting for the avant-garde sounds.

Monarch

*Skalitzer Strasse 134 (6165 6003, www.kottimonarch.de). U1, U8 Kottbusser Tor. **Open** 8/9pm-late Tue-Sat. **Map** p144 Q9.*

Finding this bar is part of the fun. It's directly above the Rewe supermarket in an ugly pre-fab; you can see it from the overground platform of the U1 at Kottbusser Tor. To reach it, take the stairs to the right of the supermarket, directly across from the döner shop, and follow the sound of the bass. It's an unpretentious place with regular rock concerts and cheap drinks, and dancing as the night wears on and the booze takes effect.

Prince Charles

*Prinzenstrasse 85F (no phone, www.princecharlesberlin.com). U8 Moritzplatz. **Open** 11pm-late Thur-Sat. **Admission** varies. No cards. **Map** p144 P9.*

Walking down the concrete underpass to the entrance, it feels more like the approach to a car park than a trendy little club. It's situated in a former swimming pool, and the tiled walls and soft lighting create an intimate atmosphere. Artfully dishevelled young things bop along to the house-heavy soundtrack, pausing for a breather outside on the extremely lounge-worthy wooden decking.

Ritter Butzke

*Ritterstrasse 26 (no phone, www.ritterbutzke.de). U8 Moritzplatz. **Open** midnight-late Fri, Sat. **Admission** varies. No cards. **Map** p144 P9.*

This enormous old factory is a party hotspot thanks to its imaginative decor and reliable booking policy; events include 'Wasted Unicorns Summer Party' with AKA AKA and 'Playfulness' with Jake the Rapper. It held illegal parties for years but has now gone legit and even allows its parties to be promoted in listings mags from time to time. It's the antithesis of Berghain, thanks to crowds of locals and amiable bouncers who are occasionally dressed as knights (*Ritter* means 'knight'), but brace yourself for a massive queue if you arrive between 1 and 3.30am.

Watergate

*Falckensteinstrasse 49 (6128 0394, www.water-gate.de). U1 Schlesisches Tor. **Open** midnight-late Wed-Sat. **Admission** varies. No cards. **Map** p144 S9.*

This slick two-level club was a driving force behind the rise of minimal techno in mid 2000s Berlin, as well as the first with a ceiling-mounted responsive LED lighting system, now copied all around the world.

In the know
Buskers

The large number of wannabe musicians in Berlin means that its buskers are more than competent. Popular busking locations include Admiralbrücke, Mauerpark, Görlitzer Park and outside Warschauer Strasse U-Bahn. At the one-day **Fête de la Musique** (www.fetedelamusique.de) in June, amateur musicians are officially allowed to perform in public at sites all over Berlin, and the city becomes one giant jam session.

The Deal with Drugs

Moderation is the key to enjoying a Berlin weekend

Even if you choose not actively to partake, interaction with the city's drug culture is inevitable on a night out. The use of recreational drugs (including amphetamines, MDMA, cocaine, ketamine and cannabis) is illegal but widespread in Berlin. Most bars explicitly forbid drug-taking on their premises, but it is tolerated in some establishments, and some clubs even have designated booths to avoid the otherwise inevitable queues for the toilets.

Despite the prevalence of drug-taking among Berlin's party-goers, over-indulgence is seen as passé, and obviously intoxicated tourists will be met with cold disregard from locals, whose well-practised veneer of cool makes their own drug-taking (almost) undetectable. Berliners have perfected the art of all-weekend partying by developing an informal code of conduct: they don't drink too much alcohol; they only take illicit substances in moderation, and they pause to refuel with well-timed naps, nutritious smoothies,

rejuvenating vitamins and decadent Sunday morning brunches.

If you do choose to indulge, it's worth reiterating that drug use is illegal, and the market is dangerously unregulated. Drug deaths or injuries among tourists in big-name clubs are not uncommon and are notoriously hushed up. Purchase your poison at your peril, as the quality can be highly circumspect; always check you haven't been sold talcum powder or worse, crushed glass. Also be aware of the potency of available drugs. Ecstasy pills, for example, are more concentrated than ever before. Be particularly wary of GHB, which is regarded as a no-go, zero-tolerance drug in Berlin due to its potentially lethal effects when mixed with alcohol and its use as a date-rape drug. It comes in liquid form and can easily be added to drinks. Wherever you go on a night out, take care: watch your drinks, look out for your friends and get a taxi back home at the end of the party.

The downstairs Water Floor is particularly impressive, with its panorama windows looking directly on to the Spree, and a floating deck terrace for watching the sunrise over Kreuzberg. It can feel too touristy at weekends – increasingly populist bookings don't help – but pick the right night, and you'll still feel the original magic.

Live music

Junction Bar
Gneisenaustrasse 18 (694 6602, café 6981 7421, www.junction-bar.de). U6 Gneisenaustrasse. **Open** *Café 5pm-2am Tue-Fri; 2pm-2am Sat, Sun. Bar 8.30pm-late Wed-Sat.* **Admission** *€3-€6. No cards.* **Map** *p144 N10.*

A Kreuzberg landmark that arranges 365 concerts a year of everything from jazz and swing to rock, with DJs keeping the party going into the early hours.

Lido
Cuvrystrasse 7 (6956 6840, tickets 6110 1313, www.lido-berlin.de). U1 Schlesisches Tor. **Open** *varies.* **Admission** *varies. No cards.* **Map** *p144 S9.*

A true Kreuzberg institution, this indie concert venue was a cinema in the 1950s and retains its curved bar and neon signage. Saturday's Karrera Klub has championed guitar-driven music for over a decade, with a live gig followed by DJs playing indie dance

classics. Other live music acts range from the avant-garde (Laibach, Lydia Lunch) to more contemporary bands (Kurt Vile, These New Puritans). Friendly Fires, Taking Back Sunday, The Front Bottoms, We Are Scientists, Shitdisco and The Horrors have all graced the stage in the past.

Passionskirche
Marheinekeplatz 1-2, Kreuzberg (tickets 6959 3624, 6940 1241, www.akanthus. de). U7 Gneisenaustrasse. **Open** *varies.* **Admission** *varies. No cards.* **Map** *p144 O11.*

Folk and world music acts mainly play here, but Beck, Ryan Adams and Marc Almond have also graced the stage of this deconsecrated church. Get there early, as it's one of the few churches in Berlin whose pews regularly overflow.

♥ SO36
Oranienstrasse 190, Kreuzberg (tickets 6110 1313, 6140 1306, www.so36.de). U1, U8 Kottbusser Tor. **Open** *8pm-late daily.* **Admission** *€3-€20. No cards.* **Map** *p144 Q9.*

Still going strong since the punk heyday of the late 1970s, and with no sign of betraying its highly politicised origins, SO36 is suitably scummy inside, with decades of sweat, beer and blood ingrained into the woodwork. While plenty of touring punk and hardcore bands grace the black stage, the venue embraces all sorts of alternative lifestyles; the long-running queer Turkish night, Gayhane (*see p231*) is especially popular.

Wild at Heart

Wiener Strasse 20, Kreuzberg (6107 4701, www.wildatheartberlin.de). U1 Görlitzer Bahnhof. **Open** *8pm-late daily.* **Admission** *€3-€12. No cards.* **Map** *p144 R10.*

Wild at Heart imports artists and DJs from all over Europe to satisfy its enthusiastic, tattooed, rock, punk, rockabilly and ska regulars. It also has a jukebox to help you down one last shot of whiskey at daybreak while you ponder why your shirt is the only one with sleeves.

NEUKÖLLN

Late bars rather than dance clubs characterise the night scene in northern Neukölln; *see p170* and *p174*. For legendary gay club **SchwuZ**, *see p233*.

Clubs & late-night bars

Black Lodge

Sanderstrasse 6 (no phone). U8 Schönleinstrasse. **Open** *8pm-late Tue-Sat.* **No cards.** **Map** *p166 Q10.*

Look for the defunct pub sign 'Mittelpunkt Gaststätte' to discover this Twin Peaks-themed speakeasy complete with hidden back room, trippy red velvet curtains, black and white zig-zag flooring. It serves espresso martinis well into the early hours of the morning.

Griessmuehle

Sonnenallee 221 (no phone, www. griessmuehle.de). S41, S42 Sonnenallee. **Open** *varies.* **Admission** *varies. No cards.* **Map** *p166 U13.*

Abandoned silos, treehouses, bonfires and beaten-up old cars comprise the scenery of this almost derelict club. Needless to say, it's the ideal ramshackle setting for weekend-long, open-air Berlin-style partying, with DJs playing the usual techno. The toilets are perhaps the grimmest in Berlin, which is really saying something.

Loophole Berlin

Boddinstrasse 60 (no phone, www.loophole-berlin.com). U8 Boddinstrasse. **Open** *9pm-5am Mon, Fri, Sat; 7pm-3am Tue-Thur.* **No cards.** **Map** *p166 R12.*

Decadent and trashy in equal measures, this ruin-esque former brothel attracts glitter punks and health goths alike, who flock to

sway to experimental electronic music, down cheap beers and enjoy the laid-back party. A place to come to soak up underground Berlin vibes.

Sameheads

Richardstrasse 10 (7012 1060, www. sameheads.com). U7 Karl-Marx-Strasse. **Open** *6pm-late Tue-Sat.* **Admission** *free-€3. No cards.* **Map** *p166 S13.*

A friendly international hipster enclave that steadfastly refuses to be pigeonholed. What began as an offbeat fashion boutique quickly evolved into a bar and late-night party space. Vintage threads are still on sale in the day, while all manner of antics kick off as the sun goes down. You might stumble upon any or all of the following: comedy open mics, art shows, pub quizzes, film screenings and sweaty raves. It's all masterminded by three British brothers – Nathan, Leo and Harry – aka the Sameheads.

Twin Pigs

Boddinstrasse 57A (no phone, www.facebook. com/twinpigsbar). U7 Rathaus Neukölln, or U8 Boddinstrasse. **Open** *6pm-late Tue-Sun.* **No cards.** **Map** *p166 R12.*

A spacious and cosy bar that's a popular meeting point on a night out thanks to its decent cocktails, craft beer selection and reasonable prices (around €3.50 for a large beer). There are sometimes low-key DJs but never really any dancing – just louder conversations.

Live music

Huxley's Neue Welt

Hasenheide 107-112, Neukölln (780 9980, www.huxleysneuewelt.com). U7, U8 Hermannplatz. **Open** *varies.* **Admission** *varies.* **Map** *p166 Q11.*

This early 20th-century ballroom on the corner of Hasenheide Park is now situated, somewhat incongruously, inside a modern retail park. It has a bit of a Wild West atmosphere and aesthetic, hosting poker championships and tattoo expos when not showcasing gigs by the likes of Elbow and Kasabian.

Werkstatt der Kulturen

Wissmannstrasse 32, Neukölln (609 7700, www.werkstatt-der-kulturen.de). U7, U8 Hermannplatz. **Open** *varies.* **Admission** *varies. No cards.* **Map** *p166 Q12.*

This intimate venue presents traditional ethnic music or local fusions blending jazz, trance or folk elements.

Performing Arts

Berlin's divided history has left the city with a uniquely rich cultural offering

No city in the world can compete with Berlin when it comes to the sheer number of orchestras and opera houses. This cultural richness is a legacy not only of the city's long artistic heritage but also of its Cold War division. East and West Berlin were both awash with state subsidies for cultural institutions, as each side tried to demonstrate the supremacy of its respective ideology. This meant that, after reunification, Berlin had twice as many performing arts venues as other capitals and now boasts enough classical music for two (maybe three) cities. It's not just quantity, but quality too: the Berlin Philharmonic is arguably the world's finest symphony orchestra. The city also has five generously funded multi-stage state theatres, surrounded and supplemented by a huge, thriving fringe theatre scene. And the best thing about this huge amount of accessible culture? Cheap seats are usually available on the day, and there's none of the snootiness apparent in some other European cities.

Staatsballett Berlin *p253*

Komische Oper

Tickets

Tickets are sold at on-site box offices, through venue websites or through ticket agencies (called *Theaterkassen*), though agency commissions can run as high as 17 per cent. Try **www.eventim.de** or **www.ticketonline.de**. At smaller venues, bookings are usually by phone. Almost all venues also offer a walk-up box office (*Abendkasse*) for last-minutes ticket sales an hour before the performance.

Some of the former East Berlin venues remain more affordable than their Western

---

♥ Best for culture vultures

Astor Film Lounge *p220*
Relive the glamour of the silver screen.

Ballhaus Ost *p255*
A versatile performance venue housed in an ex-ballroom.

JazzFest Berlin *p215*
International names play at this first-rate festival.

Komische Oper *p251*
The most daring of Berlin's three major operas.

Maxim Gorki Theater *p255*
Performances as radical as they are entertaining.

Philharmonie *p252*
World-class orchestral music in a sublime setting.

---

counterparts, but the days of dirt-cheap tickets are long gone. Getting seats at the Berlin Phil can still be difficult (although the website is easy to navigate). Standing-room at the top of the Konzerthaus gives a decent view, but before buying cheap seats for the Staatsoper ask how much of the stage you can see. Most venues offer student discounts, but note that many don't accept cards.

CLASSICAL MUSIC & OPERA

Opera companies

The posters on the U-Bahn proclaim Berlin the *Opernhauptstadt* ('opera capital') – and they aren't kidding. Not only does Germany host one-seventh of the world's opera houses, but Berlin alone has three state-subsidised opera houses – the **Deutsche Oper**, the **Staatsoper Unter den Linden** (*see p252*) and the **Komische Oper** – a record not matched even in Italy. These are now incorporated into one foundation, the **Opernstiftung**, but co-ordination of shows isn't fully streamlined, and the summer programme can feel somewhat limited.

For more independent operatic fare, don't neglect the down-at-heel but charming **Neuköllner Oper** (*see p253*) as well as **Novoflot** (www.novoflot.de), **Kiez Oper** (www.kiezoper.com) and **Home Opera** (www.homeopera.net). Expect innovative music and theatre of surprising quality, despite low budgets.

Orchestras

After 15 years garnering accolades under Sir Simon Rattle, the **Berliner Philharmoniker** (*see p252* Philharmonie) is anticipating the arrival of Russian-Austrian conductor Kirill Petrenko in 2019. Petrenko's previous role as general music director at the Komische Oper from 2002 to 2007 may have prepared him for the role, but perhaps not for the extremely high expectations of both fans and critics.

The **Deutsches Symphonie-Orchester Berlin** (www.dso-berlin.de) still receives fairly healthy subsidies and remains one of the finest places in town to hear avant-garde compositions and unusual programmes. Since 2017, it has been under the direction of British-Italian Wunderkind Robin Ticciati.

Groundbreaking 20th-century composers, from Hindemith to Prokofiev and Schönberg to Penderecki, have conducted their own work with the **Rundfunk-Sinfonieorchester Berlin** (www.rsbonline.de). Founded in 1923 to provide programming for the new medium of radio, the orchestra looks set to continue its focus on contemporary work under award-winning conductor Vladimir Jurowski.

Fans of the old masters are still well served by the **Konzerthausorchester Berlin** (www.konzerthausorchester.de), previously known as the Berliner Sinfonie-Orchester. Founded after the building of the Wall as the East's answer to the Berlin Philharmonic, the orchestra has a loyal following that favours a familiar repertoire. The unorthodox Hungarian conductor Ivan Fischer has been principal conductor since 2012 and has introduced some gimmicky policies, such as surprise concerts, encore requests and the *Mittendrin* concerts, where audience members sit within the orchestra. He'll be followed by Christoph Eschenbach, one of Germany's most distinguished conductors, in the 2019/2020 season.

Berlin's chamber orchestras also offer a steady stream of first-rate concerts. A union of two older ensembles formed the **Berlin Opera Chamber Orchestra** (www.berlinoperachamberorchestra.com), which plays opera and contemporary classical music at the Philharmonie. The **Kammerorchester Berlin** (www.kammerorchesterberlin.de) remains popular but predictable, with works ranging from Vivaldi to Mozart and back again. The **Deutsches Kammerorchester Berlin** (www.dko-berlin.de), founded in 1989, has acquired an excellent reputation for working with rising star conductors and soloists, and for offering innovative yet audience-friendly programmes. **Ensemble Mini** (www.minimahler.com), formed by British director Joolz Gale, brings together 20 players who interpret the classics in surprising ways.

▶ *For details of the classical music festivals that pepper the Berlin calendar, see p210* Events.

In the know
ClassicCard

Music-lovers under 30 should consider purchasing the **ClassicCard** (www.classiccard.de): it costs €15, is valid for a year and entitles the holder to excellent seats for a mere €8 for concerts and €10 for opera and ballet. Participating institutions include the Deutsche Oper, Komische Oper, Konzerthaus, Deutsches Symphonie-Orchester Berlin and the Staatsoper Unter den Linden. It can be purchased at these venues and online.

Major venues
Deutsche Oper
Bismarckstrasse 35, Charlottenburg (343 8401, tickets 3438 4343, www.deutscheoperberlin.de). U2 Deutsche Oper. **Box office** *11am-7pm Mon-Sat; 10am-2pm Sun; or online.* **Tickets** *vary.* **Map** *p178 E7.*

With roots dating from 1912, the Deutsche Oper built its present 1,900-seat hall in 1961, just in time to carry the operatic torch for West Berlin during the Wall years. Since reunification it has lost out in profile to the grander Staatsoper. Following the death of former long-time intendant Götz Friedrich in 2000, a revolving door of German opera luminaries has struggled to provide the house with a distinct artistic profile, but it retains a solid reputation for productions of the classics, including by the Staatsballett Berlin. Dietmar Schwarz has been in charge since 2012. Discounted tickets are available half an hour before performances.

❤ Komische Oper
Behrenstrasse 55-57, Mitte (202 600, www.komische-oper-berlin.de). U6 Französische Strasse. **Box office** *Unter den Linden 41 (4799 7400); 11am-7pm Mon-Sat; 1-4pm Sun.* **Tickets** *€12-€79.* **Map** *p68 N7.*

Founded in 1947, the Komische Oper made its reputation by breaking with the old operatic tradition of 'costumed concerts' – singers standing around on stage – and instead emphasising 'opera as theatre', with real acting skill demanded of its young ensemble. It has the smallest budget of the big three and prides itself on contemporary, even controversial, productions and an outreach programme that includes Turkish subtitling. It doesn't shy away from sex and violence either, with a notorious version of Mozart's *Die Entführung aus dem Serail* that used real prostitutes in the cast, who were graphically murdered on stage. Hungarian conductor Henrik Nánási will conclude his tenure at the end of 2018 and is due to be succeeded by Ainārs Rubikis. The Staatsballett Berlin also performs here. Discounted tickets are sold just before performances.

Konzerthaus
Gendarmenmarkt 2, Mitte (2030 92101, www.konzerthaus.de). U6 Französische Strasse. **Box office** *noon-7pm Mon-Sat; noon-4pm Sun.* **Tickets** *€21-€52.* **Map** *p68 N7.*

Formerly the Schauspielhaus am Gendarmenmarkt, this 1821 architectural gem by Schinkel was all but destroyed during the war. Lovingly restored, it reopened in 1984 with three main concert spaces. Organ recitals in the large hall are a treat, played on the massive 5,811-pipe Jehmlich organ. The

🖤 Philharmonie

Herbert-von-Karajan Strasse 1, Tiergarten (2548 8301, www.berliner-philharmoniker. de). U2, S1, S2, S25 Potsdamer Platz. **Box office** *open 3-6pm Mon-Fri; 11 am-2pm Sat, Sun.* **Tickets** *€10-€242.* **Map** *p100 L8.*

Berlin's most famous concert hall, home to the world-renowned Berlin Philharmonic Orchestra, is also its most architecturally daring: a marvellously puckish piece of organic modernism. Designed by Hans Scharoun, the golden building with its distinctive vaulting roof opened in 1963. Its reputation for superb acoustics is accurate, but it does depend on where you sit. Behind the orchestra, the acoustics leave much to be desired, but in front (where seats are much more expensive), the sound is heavenly. The same rules apply in the smaller Kammermusiksaal, which opened in 1987.

The **Berliner Philharmoniker** was founded in 1882 by 54 musicians keen to break away from the penurious Benjamin Bilse, in whose orchestra they played. It has been led by some of the world's greatest conductors, as well as by composers including Peter Tchaikovsky, Edvard Grieg, Richard Strauss and Gustav Mahler. Its greatest fame came under the baton of Herbert von Karajan (1955-89), who was succeeded by Claudio Abbado; since 2002, it's been under the leadership of Sir Simon Rattle. Rattle's tenure attracted younger audiences to the Philharmonie and showcased contemporary composers, such as Thomas Adès and Marc Anthony Turnage. In 2019, the baton will pass to the media-shy Kirill Petrenko, a choice that has been praised in Berlin and in wider classical music circles. Petrenko's relative anonymity and refusal to be interviewed has made him a fascinating enigma for the press, and his arrival is eagerly anticipated.

The Berlin Phil gives about 100 performances in the city during its August to June season, plus 20 to 30 concerts around the world. Some tickets are available at a discount immediately before performances, although it is notoriously difficult to snap one up.

Konzerthausorchester is based here, and the Rundfunk-Sinfonieorchester Berlin and the Staatskapelle Berlin also play here.

Staatsoper Unter den Linden

Unter den Linden 7, Mitte (203 540, tickets 2035 4555, www.staatsoper-berlin.de). U6 Französische Strasse. **Box office** *11am-7pm daily.* **Tickets** *varies.* **Map** *p68 N7.*

After a four-year, €240-million refurbishment that took seven years and €400 million to complete, the Staatsoper reopened on home turf in 2017. Originally founded as Prussia's Royal Court Opera for Frederick the Great in 1742 and designed by Knobelsdorff along the lines of a Greek temple, the building was destroyed in World War II but faithfully rebuilt in 1955. The reopening drew lackluster praise from critics, but its new acoustic-boosting raised ceiling provides optimum conditions for listening to the house orchestra, the Staatskapelle Berlin. Founded in 1570, this is one of the world's finest opera orchestras and has Daniel Barenboim as conductor for life. His presence ensures that performances are of the highest musical quality, even if they have sometimes been overshadowed by peculiar staging. The Staatsballett Berlin also performs here.

Other venues
Akademie der Künste
Pariser Platz 4, Mitte (200 571 000, www. adk.de). U55, S1, S2, S25 Brandenburger Tor. **Box office** *10am-7pm daily.* **Tickets** *€4-€13.* **Map** *p68 M7.*

Founded by Prince Friedrich III in 1696, this is one of the oldest cultural institutions in Berlin. By 1938, the Nazis had forced virtually all its prominent members into exile. It was re-established in West Berlin in 1954 to serve as 'a community of exceptional artists' from around the world. Post-reunification, it moved into a new building at its pre-war address on Pariser Platz, but some events are still held at its Tiergarten address (Hanseatenweg 10). Events include performances of 20th-century compositions, jazz concerts, poetry readings, film screenings and art exhibitions.

Berliner Dom
Am Lustgarten, Mitte (tickets 2026 9136, www.berliner-dom.de). S3, S5, S7, S9 Hackescher Markt. **Box office** *9am-7pm daily.* **Tickets** *vary.* **Map** *p68 O6.*

Berlin's cathedral (*see p77*) holds high-quality concerts, usually of the organ or choral sacred music variety.

Neuköllner Oper
Karl-Marx-Strasse 131-133, Neukölln (6889 0777, www.neukoellneroper. de). U7 Karl-Marx-Strasse. **Box office** *3-7pm Tue-Fri (show days).* **Tickets** *€9-€24.* **Map** *p166 S13.*

No grand opera here, but a constantly changing programme of chamber operas and music-theatre works, much loved by the Neuköllners who come to see lighter, bubblier, cheaper and much less formal works than those offered by Berlin's big three opera houses. Shame about the acoustics, though.

Nikolaisaal Potsdam
Wilhelm-Staab Strasse 10-11, Potsdam (0331 288 8828, www.nikolaisaal.de). S7 Potsdam Hauptbahnhof. **Box office** *11am-6pm Mon-Fri; 11am-2pm Sat.* **Tickets** *€8-€45.*

It's worth a trip out to Potsdam simply for the auditorium: behind a conventional Baroque façade, the white seating and space-age walls of white rubber with protruding ovals are certainly eye-catching, even distracting, but they provide superb acoustics. Expect concerts by the Potsdam Chamber Academy, Brandenburg State Orchestra, Brandenburg Symphony Orchestra and German Film Orchestra Babelsberg, as well as popular music events such as Disney in Concert or an Elvis musical.

St Matthäus Kirche am Kulturforum
Matthäikirchplatz, Tiergarten (tickets 262 1202, www.stiftung-stmatthaeus. de). U2, S1, S2, S25 Potsdamer Platz. **Box office** *11am-6pm Tue-Sun.* **Tickets** *vary. No cards.* **Map** *p100 K8.*

Concerts range from free organ recitals to a chorus of Russian Orthodox monks. Exquisite acoustics.

silent green Kulturquartier
Plantagenstrasse 31 (1208 2210, www. silent-green.net). S41, S42, U6 Wedding. **Open** *performance times vary. Café/ bar 11am-6pm Mon-Fri, 10am-6pm Sat, Sun.* **Map** *p116 K2.*

In 2013, a private group commissioned the transformation of the historic Wedding Crematorium into an independent space for research and experimentation in the arts. The result is fantastic, and for a former crematorium, just spooky enough. A number of arts collectives are headquartered here, and the building's architecture plays a central role: the domed Cupola, once a place for mourning, now hosts concerts.

DANCE

Berlin has a dynamic contemporary dance scene that cultivates fresh ideas while continuing to nurture the strong traditions of German dance theatre. Dance events, including international festivals and co-productions with foreign choreographers, are plentiful, and there's a huge amount of highly experimental work on show, often attracting large audiences.

The **Staatsballett Berlin** (www. staatsballett-berlin.de) performs from September to June at the Deutsche Oper (*see p251*), Komische Oper (*see p251*) and the Staatsoper Unter den Linden (*see p252*), as

Staatsballett Berlin

well as putting on an experimental season at Berghain (*see p243*) called Shut Up and Dance. Sasha Waltz and Johannes Oman will take over as joint artistic directors of the State Ballet in 2019. Waltz (www.sashawaltz.de) is the city's foremost and most famous choreographer. Her pieces, always visually stunning and often heavily dramatic, are performed in the biggest theatres in Europe and Asia but also at **Radialsystem V** (Holzmarktstrasse 33, Friedrichshain, 288 788 588, www.radialsystem.de), a former pumping station by the river.

Other big names in dance are Argentinian choreographer Constanza Macras and her DorkyPark company (www.dorkypark.org), and American choreographer Meg Stuart and her Damaged Goods company (www.damagedgoods.be).

The three-week **Tanz im August** (www.tanzimaugust.de) is one of Europe's leading dance festivals. It shows the most influential and cutting-edge choreography of the season, coupled with workshops for the public and lectures from artists and critics. There's also **Tanztage** (www.sophiensaele.com), held in the first two weeks of January and showcasing work by young local dancers. The **Lucky Trimmer** dance series (www.luckytrimmer.de) in April specialises in short pieces (ten minutes maximum) by established and emerging artists.

For information on upcoming performances, pick up *TanzRaumBerlin* (www.tanzraumberlin.de), a Berlin periodical dedicated to dance.

THEATRE

Berlin's theatre productions are exciting and well attended. The city has five subsidised state theatres – the **Berliner Ensemble**, **Deutsches Theater**, **Maxim Gorki Theater**, **Schaubühne** and **Volksbühne** – supplemented by a multitude of flourishing fringe venues. The blessing and curse of the 'Big Five' is that they run all their productions in an ever-changing, unpredictable repertory system, so, if you want to catch a specific show, check the theatre's website before booking your flights. Conversely, off-scene shows, especially at main venues such as the **HAU** and **Sophiensaele** (*see p256*), tend to have quite short runs, although revivals are not uncommon.

While some performances have English surtitles (most frequently at the Schaubühne), it is equally possible to get a lot out of a show without speaking German, thanks to the frequently astonishing visual aspect of productions. Also, much of the repertoire – especially at the state theatres – includes the same Greek, Shakespeare and Chekhov plays that English audiences are used to, albeit presented with a radically different approach.

Perhaps the most important festival of the year is **Theatertreffen** (*see p213*) at the **Berliner Festspiele** (www.berlinerfestspiele.de), which invites the ten best productions from the whole of Germany to the city, as well as hosting talks on contemporary theatre. Running alongside it is the **Stückemarkt** new plays festival, which presents readings (in German) of the best new national and international scripts. Berliner Festspiele also hosts the international **Foreign Affairs** in October, showcasing unusual international dance, theatre and music. The Schaubühne's **Festival for International New Drama (FIND)** in April provides new works from Germany and abroad.

State theatres

Berliner Ensemble

*Bertolt-Brecht-Platz 1, Mitte (2840 8155,
www.berliner-ensemble.de). U6, S1, S2, S25,
S3, S5, S7, S9 Friedrichstrasse. **Box office**
10am-6.30pm Mon-Sat. **Tickets** €5-€30; €9
reductions. **Map** p68 M6.*

Probably Berlin's most famous theatre, thanks
mainly to its historical association with
Bertolt Brecht. Under current artistic director
Claus Peymann, it is regarded by Germans
as a little too comfortable and touristy, a
place where older, formerly radical directors
go to work. You can still see the late Heiner
Müller's 20-year-old staging of *The Resistable
Rise of Arturo Ui*, along with productions by
Robert Wilson and Peter Stein.

Deutsches Theater

*Schumannstrasse 13A, Mitte (2844 1221,
tickets 2844 1225, www.deutschestheater.
de). U6, S1, S2, S25, S3, S5, S7, S9
Friedrichstrasse. **Box office** 11am-6.30pm
Mon-Sat; 3-6.30pm Sun. **Tickets** €5-€48;
€9 reductions. **Map** p68 M5.*

Of all the theatres in Berlin, the Deutsches
Theater behaves most like a state theatre in
any other German city, offering a *Spielplan* of
new interpretations of works by Goethe and
Schiller alongside Shakespeare, Aeschylus
and a smattering of new plays. Productions
vary enormously, from intensely exciting and
innovative to more stately fare.

♥ Maxim Gorki Theater

*Am Festungsgraben 2, Mitte (2022 1115,
www.gorki.de). U6, S1, S2, S25, S3,
S5, S7, S9 Friedrichstrasse. **Box office**
noon-6.30pm Mon-Sat; 4-6.30pm Sun.
Tickets €10-€30. **Map** p68 N6.*

Shermin Langhoff and Jens Hilje have been
leading the theatre towards ever more socially
inclusive and challenging heights since
they took over the artistic directorship in
2013. Expect new interpretations of classical
and modern dramas, as well as adaptations
from films and novels, with the result that
the atmosphere alone is often enough to
transcend the language barrier.

Schaubühne am Lehniner Platz

*Kurfürstendamm 153, Charlottenburg
(890 023, www.schaubuehne.de).
U7 Adenauerplatz, or S3, S5, S7, S9
Charlottenburg. **Box office** 11am-6.30pm
Mon-Sat; 3-6.30pm Sun. **Tickets** €7-€43; €9
reductions. **Map** p178 D9.*

Of the Big Five, the Schaubühne is most
popular with English audiences and has a
long history of Anglophile collaboration. It
was the theatre that established Brits Mark
Ravenhill and Sarah Kane as Germany's

favourite playwrights. Under artistic director
Thomas Ostermeier, the house style treads a
happy medium between German radicalism
and British realism, which, coupled with
the frequent surtitling of performances in
English, makes it an ideal starting point
for anyone looking for an introduction to
German theatre.

Volksbühne

*Linienstrasse 227, Mitte (2406 5777,
www.volksbuehne-berlin.de). U2 Rosa-
Luxemburg-Platz. **Box office** 11am-7pm
Mon-Sat. **Tickets** €6-€36; €6-€18
reductions. **Map** p68 N8.*

Built in 1914, the Volksbühne is Berlin's most
imposing theatre; its austere exterior was
well suited to the regime of artistic director
Frank Castorf, whose productions seemed
to enrage as much as delight. However, the
appointment of Chris Dercon, former director
of the Tate Modern in London, resulted in
the theatre being occupied by protesters who
worried that it would lose its avant-garde
touch to commercialism and gentrification;
in April 2018, Dercon stepped down. It's not
yet clear how the theatre will proceed, but it
continues to put on 'theatre by the people, for
the people.'

Fringe theatres

Ballhaus Naunynstrasse

*Naunynstrasse 27, Kreuzberg (7545 3725,
www.ballhausnaunynstrasse.de). U1,
U8 Kottbusser Tor. **Box office** 5.30-8pm
Mon-Sat; 4.30-7pm Sun. **Tickets** €14; €8
reductions. No cards. **Map** p144 Q9.*

For the past few years, Ballhaus
Naunynstrasse has been *the* fringe theatre to
visit in Berlin. Located in the largely Turkish
Kreuzkölln district, the company is gaining
a strong reputation for investigating issues
surrounding the immigrant experience and
identity in Germany.

♥ Ballhaus Ost

*Pappelallee 15, Prenzlauer Berg
(4403 9168, www.ballhausost.de). U2
Eberswalderstrasse. **Tickets** €15; €8
reductions. No cards. **Map** p116 P3.*

This somewhat dilapidated ex-ballroom hosts
art, performance art, dance and concerts,
with undiscovered talents performing
alongside more established, internationally
known artists. There's also a lounge and bar
populated by a very cool crowd.

English Theatre Berlin

*Fidicinstrasse 40, Kreuzberg (691 1211,
www.etberlin.de). U6 Platz der Luftbrücke.
Tickets €6-€18. **Map** p144 N11.*

PERFORMING ARTS

English Theatre Berlin

Sophiensaele
*Sophienstrasse 18, Mitte (283
5266, www.sophiensaele.com). U8
Weinmeisterstrasse.* **Tickets** *€15; €10
reductions.* **Map** *p68 O5.*

Hidden on a quiet side road near Hackescher
Markt and set back behind a little courtyard,
Sophiensaele is easy to miss. Here, over four
floors, you're likely to see some of the most
cutting-edge performances in Berlin in some
of the most atmospheric performance spaces
the city has to offer.

Theaterdiscounter
*Klosterstrasse 44, Mitte (2809 3062,
www.theaterdiscounter.de). S1, S2
Oranienburger Strasse.* **Tickets** *€15; €9
reductions.* **Map** *p68 P6.*

Founded in 2003 in an old telegraph office,
this is where an intense group of ten actors
and various directors perform new and
experimental work. It's anti-illusion theatre
with interactive possibilities – very casual
and innovative.

CABARET

Although today's cabaret bears little
resemblance to the classic cabaret of
the Weimar years, there are some great
performers who can re-create an entire
era in one night. Don't confuse cabaret
with *Varieté*: the latter is a circus-like
show, minus the animals but with lots of
dancing girls.

Kabarett is different again: a unique kind
of German entertainment with a strong
following in Berlin; it's basically political
satire sprinkled with songs and sketches,
sometimes intellectual, sometimes crass.
Likely venues include Stachelschweine,
Wühlmäuse or the Mehringhof Theater,
but most of it will be over your head if you
don't have perfect German and a thorough
understanding of local politics.

When it comes to *Travestie* – drag revue
– Berlin has some of the best on offer, from
fabulous to tragic. Venues come in all sizes
and styles, from small and dark to huge
and glittery. For the more progressive and
intelligent drag acts, the BKA Theater is
a safe bet.

Directors Günther Grosser and Bernd
Hoffmeister present a high-quality
programme. Expect house productions,
international guest shows and co-productions
with performers from Berlin's lively
international theatre scene, all in English.
Theater Thikwa, one of Europe's most
renowned companies working with disabled
actors, is also based here.

HAU
*HAU2, Hallesches Ufer 32, Kreuzberg (259
0040, tickets 2590 0427, www.hebbel-am-
ufer.de). U1, U7 Möckernbrücke, or U1, U6
Hallesches Tor.* **Box office** *3-7pm Mon-Sat.*
Tickets *vary.* **Map** *p144 N9.*

Since opening in 2003, HAU – the
amalgamation of the century-old former
Hebbel Theater (HAU1), Theater am
Hallesches Ufer (HAU2) and Theater am Ufer
(HAU3) – has gained an incredible reputation
for hosting Berlin's most innovative and
radical theatre programming, with work by
the likes of Forced Entertainment, Nature
Theater of Oklahoma, Alain Platel, Jerome
Bel and long-standing HAU regulars Gob
Squad and Rimini Protokoll.

Varieté
Chamäleon
*Hackesche Höfe, Rosenthaler Strasse
40-41, Mitte (tickets 400 0590, www.
chamaeleonberlin.de). S3, S5, S7, S9
Hackescher Markt.* **Box office** *noon-6pm
Mon, Sun; noon-8pm Tue-Fri; noon-*

9.30pm Sat. Performances from 6pm daily.
Tickets *€37-€57.* **Map** *p68 O5.*

This beautiful old theatre with a touch of decadence is located in the courtyards of the Hackesche Höfe. The focus is on contemporary circus performances that combine stunning acrobatics with musical theatre.

Friedrichstadtpalast
Friedrichstrasse 107, Mitte (2326 2326, www. palast.berlin). U6, S1, S2, S25, S3, S5, S7, S9 Friedrichstrasse. **Box office** *10am-6.30pm daily.* **Tickets** *€19-€117.* **Map** *p68 N5.*

An East Berlin institution in a building that was originally designed to be the opera house in Damascus, this is the city's biggest revue theatre. Since reunification, it's mainly featured big Vegas-style musical revues – with Vegas-style prices to match. It's usually packed with coachloads of German tourists.

Wintergarten Varieté
Potsdamer Strasse 96, Tiergarten (588 433, www.wintergarten-berlin. de). U1 Kurfürstenstrasse. **Box office** *11am-8pm Mon-Sat; 11.30am-6pm Sun.* **Tickets** *vary.* **Map** *p100 K9.*

Prussia meets Disney with shows that are slick, professional and a little boring. Excellent acrobats and magicians, but some questionable comedy acts.

Cabaret & Revue

❤ Bar jeder Vernunft
Spiegelzelt, Schaperstrasse 24, Wilmersdorf (883 1582, www.bar-jeder-vernunft.de). U3, U9 Spichernstrasse. **Box office** *noon-6.30pm Mon-Fri; 3-5.30pm Sat, Sun. Performances from 7pm daily.* **Tickets** *€12.50-€29.50.* **Map** *p178 G9.*

Some of Berlin's most celebrated entertainers perform in this snazzy circus tent of many mirrors, which takes in shows, comedy, cabaret, literature and theatre. Dinner is an extra €29. It's not the cheapest night out, but it'll be worth it if the place revives its much-lauded production of *Cabaret*.

BKA Theater
Mehringdamm 34, Kreuzberg (202 2007, www.bka-theater.de). U6, U7 Mehringdamm. **Box office** *5-9pm daily.* **Tickets** *€18-€24.* **Map** *p144 N10.*

With a long tradition of taboo-breaking acts, BKA still has some of the weirdest and most progressive performers in town: intelligent drag stand-up, freaky chanteuses, power-lunged divas. There are private tables and arena seats overlooking the stage.

Bar jeder Vernunft

Kleine Nachtrevue
Kurfürstenstrasse 116, Schöneberg (218 8950, www.kleine-nachtrevue.de). U1, U2, U3 Wittenbergplatz. **Box office** *from 8pm Wed-Sat. Performances 9pm Wed-Sat; 11.45pm Fri, Sat.* **Tickets** *€20-€35. No cards.* **Map** *p178 J9.*

Used as a location for many films, this is as close as it gets to real nostalgic German cabaret – intimate, dark, decadent, but very friendly. Shows consist of short song or dance numbers sprinkled with playful nudity and whimsical costumes. Special weekend performances vary from erotic opera to a four-course meal served to songs sung by the male 'reincarnation' of Marlene Dietrich.

Scheinbar
Monumentenstrasse 9, Schöneberg (784 5539, www.scheinbar.de). U7 Kleistpark. Performances 8pm most days. **Tickets** *€8-€11. No cards.* **Map** *p178 L11.*

Experimental, fun-loving cabaret in a tiny club exploding with fresh talent. If you like surprises, try the open-stage nights, where great performers mix with terrible ones, creating a surreal night for all.

Tipi am Kanzleramt
Grosse Querallee, Tiergarten (3906 6550, www.tipi-am-kanzleramt.de). Bus 100, 248. **Box office** *noon-6.30pm Mon-Fri; 3-5.30pm Sat, Sun. Performances 8pm most days.* **Tickets** *€30-€62.* **Map** *p100 K6.*

A circus tent in the Tiergarten, near the Federal Chancellery, hosts cool international performers presenting various comedy, dance and cabaret shows. Fare is similar to Bar jeder Vernunft, except everything's twice the size.

Understand

| History | 260 |
| Architecture | 280 |

DEM DEUTSCHEN VOLKE

Reichstag

History

Occupation, imperialism, republicanism, fascism, communism, division and reunification: Berlin's seen it all

Compared to other European capitals, such as Rome or London, Berlin is just a baby. The area where the city is now was so boggy that nobody bothered to settle there until the 12th century, when German knights under Albert the Bear wrested the swampland from Slavic tribes. The name Berlin is believed to come from the Slav word *birl*, meaning 'swamp'. Berlin and its twin settlement Cölln (on what is now the Museumsinsel) were founded as trading posts on the banks of the River Spree, halfway between the older fortress towns of Spandau and Köpenick. Today, the borough of Mitte embraces Cölln and old Berlin, while Spandau and Köpenick are peripheral suburbs. The town's existence was first recorded in 1237, when Cölln was mentioned in a church document. In the same century, construction began on the Marienkirche and Nikolaikirche, both of which still stand.

Brandenburger Tor

Laying the foundations

The Ascanian family, as Margraves of Brandenburg, ruled over the twin towns and the surrounding region. To encourage trade, they granted special rights to merchants, with the result that Berlin and Cölln – which were officially united in 1307 – emerged as wealthy trading centres linking east and west. Early prosperity ended in 1319 with the death of the last Ascanian ruler, leaving the city at the mercy of robber barons from outlying regions. Yet, despite political upheaval, Berlin's merchants continued their business. In 1359, the city joined the Hanseatic League of free-trading northern European cities.

The threat of invasion remained, however. In the late 14th century, two powerful families, the Dukes of Pomerania and the brutal von Quitzow brothers, vied for control of the city. Salvation came in the guise of Friedrich of Hohenzollern, a southern German nobleman sent by the Holy Roman Emperor in 1411 to bring peace to the region. Initially, Friedrich was well received by the local people. The bells of the Marienkirche were melted down and made into weapons for the fight against the aggressors. Friedrich officially became Margrave and, in 1416, he took the title of Elector of Brandenburg, denoting his right to vote in the election of the Holy Roman Emperor – titular head of the German-speaking states. Gradually, Berlin was transformed from a trading post to a small-sized capital. In 1442, foundations were laid for Berlin Castle and a royal court was established. By 1450, the city's population was 6,000.

With peace and stability came the loss of independent traditions, as Friedrich consolidated power. Disputes rose between the patrician classes and the craftsmen's guilds. Rising social friction culminated in the 'Berlin Indignation' of 1447-48, when the population rose up in rebellion. Friedrich's son, Friedrich II, and his courtiers were locked out of the city, and the castle foundations were flooded; but the uprising soon collapsed, and the Hohenzollerns returned triumphant. Merchants faced new restrictions and the economy suffered.

The Reformation arrived in Berlin and Brandenburg during the reign of Joachim I Nestor (1535-71), the first Elector to embrace Protestantism. He strove to improve Berlin's cultural standing by inviting artists, architects and theologians to the city. In 1538, Caspar Theyss and Konrad Krebbs, two master-builders from Saxony, began work on a Renaissance-style palace. Taking 100 years to complete, it evolved into the bombastic Stadtschloss, which stood on what is now Museumsinsel in the Spree until the East German government demolished it in 1950.

Joachim's studious nature was not reflected in the self-indulgent behaviour of his subjects. Attempts to clamp down on drinking, gambling and loose morals had little effect. Visiting the city, Abbot Trittenheim remarked that 'the people are good, but rough and unpolished; they prefer stuffing themselves to good science.' After stuffing itself with another 6,000 people, Berlin left the 16th century with a population of 12,000.

The outbreak of the Thirty Years War in 1618 dragged Berlin onto the wider political stage. Although initially unaffected by the conflict between Catholic forces loyal to the Holy Roman Empire and the Swedish-backed Protestant armies, the city was eventually caught up in the war, which left the German-speaking states ravaged and divided for two centuries. In 1626, imperial troops occupied Berlin and plundered the city. Trade collapsed, and the city's hinterland was laid waste. Four serious epidemics between 1626 and 1631 killed thousands. By the end of the war, in 1648, Berlin had lost a third of its housing and the population had fallen to less than 6,000.

Painstaking reconstruction was carried out under Friedrich Wilhelm, the 'Great Elector', who succeeded to the post in 1640, but sat out the war in exile. On his return to Berlin, Wilhelm embarked on a policy that linked urban regeneration, economic expansion and solid defence, influenced by Dutch ideas on town planning

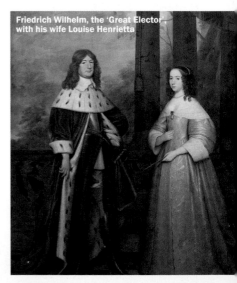

Friedrich Wilhelm, the 'Great Elector', with his wife Louise Henrietta

HISTORY

and architecture. New city fortifications were built and a garrison of 2,000 soldiers was installed, as Friedrich expanded his 'Residenzstadt'. In the centre of town, the Lustgarten was laid out opposite the Stadtschloss. Running west from the palace, the first Lindenallee ('Avenue of Lime Trees' or Unter den Linden) was created.

To revive the city's economy, a sales tax replaced housing and property taxes. With the money raised, three new towns were built – Friedrichswerder, Dorotheenstadt and Friedrichstadt. (Together with Berlin and Cölln, these now form the district of Mitte.) In the 1660s, a canal was constructed linking the Spree and Oder rivers, confirming Berlin as an east–west trading centre.

The common association of Prussia with militarism can broadly be traced back to the efforts of King Friedrich Wilhelm I and his son, Frederick the Great

But Friedrich Wilhelm's most inspired policy was to encourage refugees to settle. First to arrive were over 50 Jewish families from Vienna. In 1672, Huguenot settlers came from France. Both groups brought with them vital new skills. The growing cosmopolitan mix laid the foundations for a flowering of intellectual and artistic life. By the time the Great Elector's son Friedrich III took the throne in 1688, one in five Berliners spoke French. Today, French words still pepper Berlin dialect, among them *boulette* (hamburger) and *étage* (floor). In 1701, Elector Friedrich III had himself crowned Prussian King Friedrich I (not to be confused with the earlier Elector).

The common association of Prussia with militarism can broadly be traced back to the 18th century and the efforts of two men in particular: King Friedrich Wilhelm I (1713-40) and his son Friedrich II (also known as Frederick the Great). Although father and son hated each other and had different sensibilities (Friedrich Wilhelm was boorish and mean, Friedrich II sensitive and philosophical), together they launched Prussia as a major military power and gave Berlin the character of a garrison town.

The obsession with all things military did have some positive effects. The king needed competent soldiers, so he made school compulsory; the army needed doctors, so he set up medical institutes. Berlin's economy also picked up, and skilled immigrants arrived. The result was a population boom – from 60,000 in 1713 to 90,000 in 1740 – and a growth in trade.

Frederick the Great

Frederick the Great (Friedrich II) took Prussia into a series of wars with Austria and Russia (1740-42, 1744-45 and 1756-63; the last known as the Seven Years War) in a bid to win territory in Silesia in the east. Initially, the wars proved disastrous. The Austrians occupied Berlin in 1757, the Russians in 1760. However, thanks to a mixture of good fortune and military genius, Frederick emerged victorious from the Seven Years War.

When not fighting, the king set about forging a modern state apparatus and transforming Berlin and Potsdam. This was achieved partly through conviction – the king was friends with Voltaire and saw himself as an aesthetically minded Enlightenment figure – but it was also a political necessity. He needed to convince enemies and subjects that, even in times of crisis, he was able to afford grand projects. So Unter den Linden was transformed into a grand boulevard. At the palace end, the Forum Fredericianum, designed and constructed by the architect von Knobelsdorff, comprised the Staatsoper, Sankt-Hedwigs-Kathedrale, Prince Heinrich Palace (now housing Humboldt-Universität) and the Staatsbibliotek. Although it was never completed, the Forum is still one of Berlin's main attractions. The Tiergarten was landscaped and a new palace, Schloss Bellevue (now the German president's official residence), built. Frederick also replaced a set of barracks at Gendarmenmarkt with a theatre, now called the Konzerthaus.

To encourage manufacturing and industry, advantageous excise laws were introduced. Businesses such as the KPM (Königliche Porzellan-Manufaktur) porcelain works were nationalised and turned into prestigious and lucrative enterprises. Legal and administrative reforms saw religious freedom enshrined in law and torture abolished. Berlin also became a centre of the Enlightenment. Cultural and intellectual life blossomed around figures such as philosopher Moses Mendelssohn and poet Gottfried Lessing. By the time Frederick died in 1786, Berlin had a population of 150,000 and was the capital of one of Europe's great powers.

Frederick's death marked the end of the Enlightenment in Prussia. His successor,

Friedrich Wilhelm II, was more interested in spending money on classical architecture than wasting time debating the merits of various political philosophies. Censorship was stepped up and the king's extravagance sparked an economic crisis. By 1788, 14,000 Berliners were dependent on state and church aid. The state apparatus crumbled under the weight of greedy administrators. When he died in 1797, Friedrich Wilhelm II left his son with huge debts.

However, the old king's love of classicism gave Berlin its most famous monument: the Brandenburger Tor (Brandenburg Gate). It was built by Karl Gottfried Langhans in 1789, the year of the French Revolution, and modelled on the Propylaea in Athens. Two years later, Johann Schadow added the Quadriga, a sculpture of Victoria riding a chariot drawn by four horses. Originally one of 14 gates, the Brandenburger Tor is now Berlin's geographical and symbolic centre.

If the king did not care for intellect, then the emerging bourgeoisie did. Towards the turn of the century, Berlin became a centre of German Romanticism. Literary salons flourished; they were to remain a feature of the city's cultural life into the middle of the 19th century.

The Napoleonic Wars

In 1806, Berlin came face to face with the effects of revolution in France: following the humiliating defeat of the Prussian forces in the battles of Jena and Auerstadt on 14 October, Napoleon's army headed for Berlin. The king and queen fled to Königsberg, and the garrison was removed from the city. On 27 October, Napoleon and his army marched through the Brandenburger Tor. Once again, Berlin was an occupied city.

Napoleon set about changing the political and administrative structure. He called together 2,000 prominent citizens and told them to elect a new administration, which ran the city until the French troops left in 1808. Napoleon also ordered the expropriation of property belonging to the state, the Hohenzollerns and many aristocratic families. Priceless artworks were removed from palaces and shipped to France. Even the Quadriga was taken from the Brandenburger Tor and sent to Paris. At the same time, the city was hit by crippling war reparations.

When the French left, a group of energetic, reform-minded aristocrats, grouped around Baron vom Stein, moved to modernise the moribund Prussian state. One key reform was the separation of state and civic responsibility, which gave Berlin independence to manage its own affairs.

A new council was elected (though only property owners and the wealthy were entitled to vote). In 1810, the philosopher Wilhelm von Humboldt founded the university. All remaining restrictions on the city's Jews were removed.

Although the French occupied Berlin again in 1812 on the way back from their infamous Russian campaign, this time they were met with stiff resistance. A year later, the Prussian king finally joined the anti-Napoleon coalition, and thousands of Berliners signed up to fight. Napoleon was defeated at nearby Grossbeeren. This, together with a later defeat in the Battle of Leipzig, marked the end of Napoleonic rule in Germany.

In August 1814, General Blücher brought the Quadriga back to Berlin, restoring it to the Brandenburg Gate with one highly symbolic addition: an Iron Cross and a Prussian eagle were added to the staff in Victoria's hand.

The burst of reform was, however, fairly short-lived. Following the Congress of Vienna (1814-15), which established a new political and strategic order for post-Napoleonic Europe, King Friedrich Wilhelm III reneged on promises of constitutional reform. Instead of a greater unity among the German states, a loose alliance came into being; dominated by Austria, the German Confederation was distinctly anti-liberal in its tenor. In Prussia, state power increased. Alongside the normal police, a secret service and a vice squad were established. The police president even had the power to issue directives to the city council. Censorship increased, and the authorities sacked von Humboldt from the university he had created.

With their hopes for change frustrated, the bourgeoisie withdrew to their salons. It's one of the ironies of this time that, although political opposition was quashed, a vibrant cultural movement flourished. Academics such as Hegel and Ranke lectured at the university, enhancing Berlin's reputation as an intellectual centre. The period became known as Biedermeier, after a fictional character embodying bourgeois taste, created by Swabian comic writer Ludwig Eichrodt. Another legacy is the range of neoclassical buildings designed by Schinkel, such as his Altes Museum and the Neue Wache.

For the majority, however, it was a period of frustrated hopes and bitter poverty. Industrialisation swelled the ranks of the working class, so that between 1810 and 1840 the city's population doubled to 400,000. Most of the newcomers lived in conditions that would later lead to riot and revolution.

Revolution & the Iron Chancellor

Prussia was ideally equipped for the industrial age. By the 19th century, it had grown dramatically and boasted one of the greatest abundances of raw materials in Europe. It was the founding of the Borsig Werke in 1837 that established Berlin as the workshop of continental Europe. August Borsig was Berlin's first big industrialist. His factories turned out locomotives for the new railway between Berlin and Potsdam, which opened in 1838. Borsig also left his mark through the establishment of a suburb (Borsigwalde) that still carries his name. The other great pioneering industrialist, Werner Siemens, set up his electrical engineering firm in a house near Anhalter Bahnhof. The Siemens company also created a new suburb, Siemensstadt.

Friedrich Wilhelm IV's accession to the throne in 1840 raised hopes of an end to repression, and, initially, he appeared to share the desire for change. He declared an amnesty for political prisoners, relaxed censorship, sacked the hated justice minister and granted asylum to refugees. Political debate thrived in coffeehouses and wine bars. The university was another focal point for discussion. In the late 1830s, Karl Marx spent a term there, just missing fellow alumnus Otto von Bismarck. In the early 1840s, Friedrich Engels did his military service in Berlin.

The thaw didn't last. It soon became clear that Friedrich Wilhelm IV shared his father's opposition to constitutional reform. Living and working conditions worsened for most Berliners. Rapid industrialisation brought sweatshops, 17-hour days and child labour. This misery was compounded in 1844 by harvest failure, and food riots broke out on Gendarmenmarkt.

Things came to a head in 1848, the year of revolutions. Political meetings were held in beer gardens and the Tiergarten, and demands were made for reform and a unification of German-speaking states. On 18 March, the king finally conceded to allowing a new parliament and vaguely promised other reforms. Later that day, the crowd of 10,000 that gathered to celebrate the victory were set upon by soldiers. Shots were fired and the revolution began. Barricades went up throughout central Berlin and demonstrators fought with police for 14 hours. Finally, the king backed down for a second time. In exchange for the dismantling of barricades, he ordered his troops out of Berlin. Days later, he took part in the funeral service for the 'March Dead' – 183 revolutionaries who had been killed – and promised more freedoms.

Berlin was now ostensibly in the hands of the revolutionaries, and the king seemed to embrace liberalism and nationalism. Prussia, he said, should 'merge into Germany'. But the revolution proved short-lived. When pressed on unification, he merely suggested that the other German states send representatives to the Prussian National Assembly, an offer that was rebuffed. Leading liberals instead convened a German National Assembly in Frankfurt in May 1848, while a new Prussian Assembly met in what is now the Konzerthaus to debate a new constitution. At the end of 1848, reforming fervour took over Berlin.

Winter, however, brought a change of mood. Using continuing street violence as the pretext, the king ordered the National Assembly to be moved to Brandenburg. In November, he brought troops back into Berlin and declared a state of siege. Press freedom was restricted. The Civil Guard and National Assembly were dissolved. On 5 December, the king delivered his final blow by unveiling a new constitution fashioned to his own tastes. Throughout the winter of 1848-49, thousands of liberals were arrested or expelled. A new city constitution, drawn up in 1850, reduced the number of eligible voters to five per cent of the population. The police president became more powerful than the mayor.

An arrogant genius and former diplomat, Bismarck was well able to deal with unruly parliamentarians

By 1857, the king had gone senile. His brother Wilhelm acted as regent until becoming king on Friedrich's death in 1861. Once again, the people's hopes were raised: the new monarch began by appointing liberals to the cabinet. The building of the Rotes Rathaus (Red Town Hall), completed in 1869, gave the city council a headquarters to match the size of the royal palace. But by 1861, the king was locked in a dispute with parliament over proposed army reforms. He wanted to strengthen his control of the armed forces; Parliament refused, so the king went over its members' heads and appointed a new prime minister: Otto von Bismarck.

An arrogant genius and former diplomat, Bismarck was well able to deal with unruly parliamentarians. Using a constitutional loophole to rule against the majority, he quickly pushed through the army reforms. Extra-parliamentary opposition was dealt with in the usual manner:

oppression and censorship. Dissension thus suppressed, Bismarck turned his mind to German unification. Unlike the bourgeois revolutionaries of 1848, who desired a Germany united by popular will and endowed with political reforms, Bismarck strove to bring the states together under the authoritarian dominance of Prussia. His methods involved astute foreign policy and outright aggression.

Wars against Denmark (1864) and Austria (1866) brought post-Napoleonic order to an abrupt end. Prussia was no longer the smallest Great Power, but an initiator of geopolitical change. Austria's defeat confirmed Prussia's primacy among German-speaking states. Victory on the battlefield boosted Bismarck's popularity across Prussia – but not in Berlin itself. He was defeated in his constituency in the 1867 election to the new North German League. This was a Prussian-dominated body, linking the northern states, and a stepping stone towards Germany's overall unification.

Bismarck's third war – against France in 1870 – revealed his scope for intrigue and opportunism. Exploiting a dispute over the Spanish succession, he provoked France into declaring war on Prussia. Citing the North German League and treaties signed with the southern German states, Bismarck brought together a united German army under Prussian leadership. Following the defeat of the French army on 2 September, Bismarck turned a unified military into the basis for a unified nation. The Prussian king would be German emperor: beneath him would be four kings, 18 grand dukes and assorted princes from the German states, which would retain some regional powers.

(This arrangement formed the basis for the modern federal system of regional *Länder*.)

On 18 January 1871, King Wilhelm I of Prussia was proclaimed German Kaiser ('Emperor') in the Hall of Mirrors in Versailles. In just nine years, Bismarck had united Germany and forged an empire that dominated central Europe. The political, economic and social centre of this new creation was Berlin.

Imperial Berlin

The coming of empire threw Berlin into its greatest period of expansion and change. The economic boom (helped by five billion gold francs extracted from France as war reparations) fuelled a wave of speculation. Farmers in Wilmersdorf and Schöneberg became millionaires overnight as they sold off their fields to developers.

During the following decades, Berlin emerged as Europe's most modern metropolis. This period was dubbed the *Gründerzeit* (Foundation Years) and was marked by a move away from traditional Prussian values of thrift and modesty towards the gaudy and bombastic. The mood change manifested itself in monuments and buildings. The Reichstag, the Kaiser-Wilhelm-Gedächtniskirche, the Siegessäule (Victory Column) and the Berliner Dom were all built in this period. Superficially, the Reichstag (designed by Paul Wallot, and completed in 1894) represented a commitment to parliamentary democracy. But, in reality, Germany was still in the grip of conservative, backward-looking forces. The Kaiser's authoritarian powers remained, as demonstrated by the

Kaiser Wilhelm II with his six sons

decision of Wilhelm II to sack Bismarck in 1890 following policy disagreements.

When Bismarck began his premiership in 1861, his offices on Wilhelmstrasse looked over fields. By the time he lost his job, they were in the centre of Europe's most congested city. Economic boom and growing political and social importance attracted hundreds of thousands of new inhabitants. At unification in 1871, 820,000 people lived in Berlin; by 1890 this number had nearly doubled. The working classes were shoehorned into tenements (*Mietskasernen*) that sprouted across the city, particularly in Kreuzberg, Wedding and Prenzlauer Berg. Poorly ventilated and overcrowded, the *Mietskasernen* (many of which still stand) became a breeding ground for unrest.

The Social Democratic Party (Sozialdemokratische Partei Deutschlands, SPD), founded in 1869, quickly became the voice for the have-nots. In the 1877 general election, it won 40 per cent of the Berlin vote. With that was born the left-wing reputation of Rotes Berlin ('Red Berlin') that persists to the present day. In 1878, two assassination attempts on the Kaiser gave Bismarck an excuse to classify socialists as enemies of the state. He introduced restrictive laws to ban the SPD and other progressive parties. The ban lasted until 1890 – the year of Bismarck's sacking – but did not stem support for the SPD. In the 1890 general election, the SPD dominated the vote in Berlin; in 1912, it won more than 70 per cent of the vote, becoming the largest party in the Reichstag.

Kaiser Wilhelm II, famed for his ridiculous moustache, was crowned in 1888, and soon came to personify the new Germany: bombastic, awkward and unpredictable. Like his grandmother, Queen Victoria, he gave his name to an era. Wilhelm's epoch is associated with showy militarism and foreign policy bungles leading to a world war that cost the Kaiser his throne and Germany its stability.

The Wilhelmine years were also notable for the explosive growth of Berlin (the population rose to four million by 1914) and a blossoming of cultural and intellectual life. The Bode-Museum was built in 1904. In 1912, work began on the Pergamonmuseum, while a new opera house was unveiled in Charlottenburg (destroyed in World War II; the Deutsche Oper now stands on the site). Expressionism took off in 1910 and the Kurfürstendamm filled with galleries – Paris was still Europe's art capital, but Berlin was catching up. By Wilhelm's abdication in 1918, Berlin had become a centre of scientific and intellectual development. Six Berlin scientists, including Albert Einstein

and Max Planck, were awarded the Nobel Prize. But by 1914, Europe was armed to the teeth and ready to tear itself apart. In June, the assassination of Archduke Franz Ferdinand provided the excuse.

World War I and the Weimar Republic

No one was prepared for the disaster that followed. Thanks to Bismarck, the Germans had come to expect quick, sweeping victories. The armies on the Western Front settled into their trenches for a war of attrition that would cost over a million German lives. Meanwhile, the civilian population faced austerity. After the 1917 harvest failed, there were outbreaks of famine. Soon, dog and cat meat started to appear on the menu in Berlin restaurants.

The SPD's initial enthusiasm for war evaporated, and in 1916 the party refused to pass the Berlin budget. A year later, members of the party's radical wing broke away to form the Spartacus League. Anti-war feeling was voiced in mass strikes in April 1917 and January 1918. These were brutally suppressed, but, when the Imperial Marines in Kiel mutinied on 2 November 1918, the authorities were no longer able to stop the anti-war movement. The mutiny spread to Berlin, where members of the Guards Regiment came out against the war. On 9 November, the Kaiser was forced into abdication and, later, exile. This date is weirdly layered with significance in German history: it's the anniversary of the establishment of the Weimar Republic (1918), the Kristallnacht pogrom (1938) and the fall of the Wall (1989).

On this day in 1918, Philip Scheidemann, a leading SPD parliamentarian and key proponent of republicanism, broke off his lunch in the second-floor restaurant of the Reichstag. He walked to a window overlooking Königsplatz (now Platz der Republik) where a crowd had massed and declared: 'The old and the rotten have broken down. Long live the new! Long live the German Republic!' At the other end of Unter den Linden, Karl Liebknecht, who co-led the Spartacus League with Rosa Luxemburg, declared Germany a socialist republic from a balcony of the occupied Stadtschloss. Liebknecht and the Spartacists wanted a communist Germany; Scheidemann and the SPD favoured a parliamentary democracy. Between them stood those still loyal to the vanished monarchy. All were prepared to fight; street battles ensued throughout the city. It was in this climate of turmoil and violence that the Weimar Republic was born.

False Economy

Hyperinflation turned the economy – and society – upside down

Of all the disasters that have befallen Berlin, nothing was as mad as the hyperinflation of 1923. It wasn't a sudden catastrophe: the German government had been dallying with inflation for years, funding its war effort by printing bonds. In 1914, a dollar was buying 4.2 German marks; by late 1922, it was buying 7,000. Then the French occupied the Ruhr and things went haywire. By 20 November 1923, the rate was a whopping 4,200,000,000,000 marks to the dollar.

Images from the time are vaguely comic: children using bundles of notes as building blocks; a wheelbarrow of currency for a loaf of bread. At the height of the crisis, over 300 paper mills and 2,000 printing presses worked around the clock to supply the Reichsbank with notes – in denominations of one million, then one billion, then a hundred billion. Some companies paid their employees twice a day, so they could shop at lunch to beat afternoon inflation.

A little hard currency could buy anything – or anyone. Foreign visitors splashed out in an orgy of conspicuous consumption.

Entrepreneurs created whole business empires from ever cheaper marks. And the homes of peasants in nearby villages filled up with Meissen porcelain and fine furniture as Berliners traded valuables for eggs or bread.

People starved as their possessions vanished. The suicide rate shot up, as did infant mortality. Teenagers prostituted themselves after school, often with parental approval. Nothing made sense anymore. And as the fabric of everyday life was seen to unravel, so did people's faith in government. Among the worst hit were those who had most trusted the idea of the German state: the middle-class patriots who had sunk their money into war bonds, only to be paid back in worthless paper. The crisis was eventually brought under control, but the result had been a mass transfer of wealth to a handful of opportunists, big businesses and government. And as a pauperised people wondered who to blame, the hard right had found a cause. Nothing prepared the ground for Hitler better than the literal and moral impoverishment of the inflationary period.

Children playing with banknotes, 1919

Kapp Putsch, March 1920

In March 1920, a right-wing coup was staged in Berlin under the leadership of Wolfgang Kapp, a civil servant from east Prussia. The recently returned government fled the city. For four days Berlin was besieged by roaming Freikorps. Some had taken to adorning their helmets with a new symbol: the *Hakenkreuz* or swastika. Ultimately, a general strike and the army's refusal to join Kapp ended the putsch. But the political and economic chaos in the city remained.

Political assassinations were commonplace, and food shortages led to bouts of famine. Inflation started to escalate (*see opposite* False Economy). There were two main reasons for the precipitate devaluation of the Reichsmark. To pay for the war, the desperate imperial government had resorted to printing more money, a policy continued by the new republican rulers. The burden of reparations also led to an outflow of foreign currency.

In 1923, the French government sent troops into the Ruhr industrial region to take by force reparation goods that the German government said it could no longer afford to pay. The Communists planned an uprising in Berlin for October but lost their nerve.

The Munich Beer Hall Putsch

In November, a young ex-corporal called Adolf Hitler, who led the tiny National Socialist Party (Nationalsozialistische Deutsche Arbeiterpartei, NSDAP or Nazi Party), launched an attempted coup from a Munich beer hall. He called for armed resistance to the French, an end to the 'dictatorship of Versailles' and punishment for those – especially the Jews – who had 'betrayed' Germany at the war's end.

Hitler's first attempt to seize power came to nothing. Instead of marching on Berlin, he went to prison. Inflation was finally brought down with the introduction of a new currency. But the overall decline of moral and social values that had taken place in the five years since 1918 was not so easy to reverse.

Josef Goebbels came to Berlin in 1926 to take charge of the local Nazi Party. On arriving, he noted: 'This city is a melting pot of everything that is evil – prostitution, drinking houses, cinemas, Marxism, Jews, strippers, negroes dancing and all the offshoots of modern art.' The city overtook Paris as Europe's arts and entertainment capital and added its own decadent twist. 'We used to have a first-class army,' mused Klaus Mann, the author of the novel *Mephisto*, '...now we have first-class perversions.'

The revolution in Berlin may have brought peace to the Western Front, where hostilities were ended on 11 November, but in Germany it unleashed political terror and instability. Berlin's new masters, the SPD under Friedrich Ebert, ordered renegade battalions returning from the front (known as the Freikorps) to quash the Spartacists, who launched a concerted bid for power in January 1919.

Within days, the uprising was bloodily suppressed. Liebknecht and Luxemburg were arrested, interrogated in a hotel near the zoo, and then murdered by the Freikorps. A plaque marks the spot on the Liechtenstein Bridge from which Luxemburg's body was dumped into the Landwehrkanal. Four days later, national elections returned the SPD as the largest party: the Social Democrats' victory over the far left was complete. Berlin was deemed too dangerous for parliamentary business, so the government decamped to the provincial town of Weimar, which gave its name to the first German republic.

Germany's new constitution ended up being full of good liberal intentions but riddled with technical flaws, leaving the country wide open to weak coalition government and quasi-dictatorial presidential rule. Another crippling blow was the Versailles Treaty, which set the terms for peace. Reparation payments (set to run until 1988) blew a hole in an already fragile economy. Support for the right-wing nationalist lobby was fuelled by the loss of territories, and restrictions placed on the military led some on the right to claim that Germany's soldiers had been 'stabbed in the back' by Jews and left-wingers.

By 1927, Berlin boasted more than 70 cabarets and nightclubs. While Brecht's *Dreigroschenoper* (*Threepenny Opera*) played at the Theater am Schiffbauerdamm, Dadaists gathered on Tauentzienstrasse at the Romanisches Café (which was later one of the victims of the Allied bombing campaign – the Europa-Center mall now stands on the site). Avant-garde magazines proliferated, focusing on these exciting new forms of art and literature. But the flipside of all the frenetic enjoyment was poverty, substance addiction and seething social tension, reflected in the works of artists such as George Grosz and Otto Dix. In the music halls, Brecht and Weill used a popular medium to ram home points about social injustices.

In architecture and design, the revolutionary ideas of the Bauhaus school in Dessau (it moved to Berlin in 1932 but was closed down by the Nazis a year later) were taking concrete form in projects such as the Shell House on the Landwehrkanal, the Siemensstadt new town and the model-housing project Hufeisensiedlung in Britz. (For more on these, see *p175*.)

The Wall Street Crash and the onset of global depression in 1929 ushered in the brutal end of the Weimar Republic. The fractious coalition governments that had clung to power in the prosperous late 1920s were no match for rocketing unemployment and a surge in support for extremist parties. By the end of 1929, nearly one in four Berliners was out of work. The city's streets became a battleground for clashes between Nazi stormtroopers (the Sturmabteilung, SA), Communists and Social Democrats. Increasingly, the police relied on water cannon, armoured vehicles and guns to quell street fighting. One May Day demonstration left 30 dead and several hundred wounded.

In 1932, the violence in Berlin reached crisis level. In one six-week period, 300 street battles resulted in 70 people dead. In the general election in July, the Nazis took 40 per cent of the general vote, becoming the largest party in the Reichstag. Hermann Göring, one of Hitler's earliest followers and a wounded veteran of the Beer Hall Putsch, was appointed Reichstag president. But the prize of government still eluded the Nazis. In November elections, they lost two million votes across Germany and 37,000 in Berlin, where the Communists emerged as the strongest party. The election was held against the backdrop of a strike by 20,000 transport employees protesting against wage cuts. The strike had been called by the Communists and the Nazis, who vied with each other to capture the mass vote and bring the Weimar Republic

Adolf Hitler with President von Hindenburg, 1933

to an end. Under orders from Moscow, the KPD (Kommunistische Partei Deutschlands, Communist Party) shunned all co-operation with the SPD, ending any possibility of a broad left-wing front.

As Berlin headed into another winter of depression, almost every third person was out of work. A survey recorded that almost half of Berlin's inhabitants were living four to a room, and that a large proportion of the city's housing stock was unfit for human habitation. Berlin topped the European table of suicides.

The new government of General Kurt von Schleicher ruled by presidential decree. Schleicher had promised President von Hindenburg that he could tame the Nazi Party into a coalition. When he failed, his rival Franz von Papen manoeuvred the Nazi leader into power. On 30 January 1933, Adolf Hitler was named chancellor. That evening, the SA staged a torchlight parade through the Brandenburg Gate. Watching from the window of his house, the artist Max Liebermann remarked to his dinner guests: 'I cannot eat as much as I'd like to puke.'

Hitler takes power

Hitler's government was a coalition of Nazis and German nationalists, led by the media magnate Alfred Hugenberg. Together, their votes fell just short of a parliamentary majority, so another election was called for March, while Hitler continued to rule by decree. Weimar's last free election was also its most violent. Open persecution of Communists began. The Nazis banned meetings of the KPD, closed left-wing newspapers and broke up SPD election rallies. On 27 February, a fire broke out in the Reichstag. It was almost certainly started by the Nazis, who used it as an excuse to step up the persecution of opponents. Over 12,000 Communists were arrested. Spelling it out in a speech at the Sportspalast two days before the election, Goebbels said: 'It's not my job to practise justice, instead I have to destroy and exterminate – nothing else.'

The Nazis still didn't achieve an absolute majority (in Berlin they polled 34 per cent), but that didn't matter. With the support of his coalition allies, Hitler passed an Enabling Act that gave him dictatorial powers. By summer, Germany had been declared a one-party state. The paramilitary SS (Schutzstaffel) established itself in Prinz Albrecht Palais, where it was later joined by the secret police, the Gestapo. To the north of Berlin near Oranienburg, the Sachsenhausen concentration camp was set up. Along the Kurfürstendamm, squads of SA stormtroopers would go 'Jew baiting', and on 1 April 1933 the first boycott of Jewish shops began. A month later, Goebbels, who became Minister for Propaganda, organised a book-burning, which took place in the courtyard of the university on Unter den Linden. Books by Jews or writers deemed degenerate or traitors were thrown on to a huge bonfire. The Nazis began to control public life. Party membership became obligatory for doctors, lawyers, professors and journalists. Unemployment was tackled through public works programmes, conscription to an expanding military and by 'encouraging' women to leave the workplace.

During the Night of the Long Knives in July 1934, Hitler settled old scores with opponents within the SA and Nazi Party. At Lichterfelde barracks, officers of the SS shot and killed over 150 SA members. Hitler's predecessor as chancellor, General von Schleicher, was shot with his wife at their Wannsee home. After the death of President von Hindenburg in August, Hitler had himself named Führer ('Leader') and made the armed forces swear an oath of allegiance to him. It had taken the Nazis less than two years to subjugate Germany.

A brief respite came with the Olympic Games in August 1936. To persuade foreign spectators that all was well in the Reich, Goebbels ordered the removal of anti-Semitic slogans from shops. 'Undesirables' were moved out, and the pavement display cases for racist Nazi newspaper *Der Stürmer* (*The Stormtrooper*) were dismantled. The Games, centred on the newly built Olympiastadion, were not such a success for the Nazis. Instead of blond Aryans sweeping the field, Hitler had to watch the African-American Jesse Owens clock up medals and records. The Games did work, however, as a public relations exercise. Foreign visitors left with reports of a strident and healthy nation.

As part of a nationwide campaign to cleanse cultural life of what the Nazis considered *Entartete Kunst* ('degenerate art'), works of modern art were collected and brought together in a touring exhibition designed to show the depth of depravity in contemporary ('Jewish-dominated') culture. But Nazi hopes that these 'degenerate' works would repulse the German people fell flat. When the exhibition arrived at the Zeughaus in early 1938, thousands queued for admission. People loved the paintings. After the exhibition, the artworks were auctioned in Switzerland. Unsold works were burnt in the fire station on Köpenicker Strasse – more than 5,000 were destroyed.

Hitler entrusted young architect Albert Speer with the job of creating a metropolis to 'out-trump Paris and Vienna'

After taking power, Hitler ordered that the lime trees on Unter den Linden be chopped down to give the boulevard a cleaner, more sanitised form – the first step in Nazi urban planning. Hitler's plans for the redesign of Berlin reflected the hatred the Nazis felt for the city. Hitler entrusted young architect Albert Speer with the job of creating a metropolis to 'out-trump Paris and Vienna'. The heart of old Berlin was to be demolished, and its small streets replaced by two highways stretching 37 kilometres (23 miles) from north to south and 50 kilometres (30 miles) from east to west. Each axis would be 90 metres (295 feet) wide. Crowning the northern axis would be a domed Volkshalle ('People's Hall') nearly

Luftwaffe display, 20 April 1939

and violence against Jews, was staged in response to the assassination of a German diplomat in Paris by a young Jewish émigré. Jewish properties across Berlin were stoned, looted and set ablaze. A total of 24 synagogues were set on fire. The Nazis rounded up 12,000 Jews and took them to Sachsenhausen concentration camp.

World War II

Since 1935, Berliners had been taking part in air-raid drills, but it was not until the Sudeten crisis of 1938 that the possibility of war became real. Hitler was able to get his way and persuade France and Britain to let him take over the German-speaking areas of northern Czechoslovakia, but a year later, his plans to repeat the exercise in Poland were met with resistance. Following Germany's invasion of Poland on 1 September 1939, Britain and France declared war on the Reich. Despite the propaganda and early victories, most Berliners were horrified by the war. The first air raids came with the RAF bombing of Pankow and Lichtenberg in early 1940.

In 1941, after the German invasion of the Soviet Union, the 75,000 Jews remaining in Berlin were required to wear a yellow Star of David and the first systematic deportations to concentration camps began. By the end of the war, only 5,000 Jews remained in Berlin. Notorious assembly points for the deportations were Putlitzstrasse in Wedding, Grosse Hamburger Strasse and Rosenstrasse in Mitte. On 20 January 1942, a meeting of the leaders of the various Nazi security organisations at a villa by the Wannsee lake agreed on a 'final solution' to the Jewish question: genocide.

300 metres (1,000 feet) high, with space for 150,000 people. Speer and Hitler also had grand plans for a triumphal arch three times the size of the Arc de Triomphe, and a Führer's Palace 150 times bigger than the one occupied by Bismarck. The new city was to be called Germania.

Little of this was built. The new Chancellery, completed in early 1939, went up in under a year – and was demolished after the war. On the proposed east–west axis, a small section around the Siegessäule was widened for Hitler's 50th birthday in April 1939.

Of the half a million Jews living in Germany in 1933, over a third were in Berlin. For centuries, the Jewish community had played an important role in Berlin's development, especially in financial, artistic and intellectual circles. The Nazis wiped all this out in 12 years of persecution and murder. Arrests followed the boycotts and acts of intimidation. During 1933 and 1934, many of Berlin's Jews fled. Those who stayed were subjected to legislation (the 1935 Nuremberg Laws) that banned Jews from public office, forbade them to marry Aryan Germans and stripped them of citizenship. Jewish cemeteries were desecrated, and the names of Jews chipped off war memorials. Berlin businesses that had been owned by Jews – such as the Ullstein newspaper group and Jonass department store (now the Soho House hotel) – were 'Aryanised'. The Nazis expropriated them or forced owners to sell at absurdly low prices.

On 9 November 1938, Kristallnacht, a wave of 'spontaneous' acts of vandalism

The Battle of Berlin, which the RAF launched in November 1943, reduced much of the city centre to rubble

The turning point in the war came with the surrender at Stalingrad on 31 January 1943. By summer, women and children were being evacuated from Berlin; by the end of 1943, over 700,000 people had fled. The Battle of Berlin, which the RAF launched in November 1943, reduced much of the city centre to rubble. Nearly 5,000 people were killed and around 250,000 made homeless.

On 20 July 1944, a group of officers, civil servants and former trade unionists launched a last-ditch attempt to assassinate Hitler. But Hitler survived the explosion of a bomb placed at his eastern command post in East Prussia by Colonel Count von Stauffenberg.

In early January 1945, the Red Army launched a major offensive that carried on to German soil. On 12 February, the heaviest bombing raid yet on Berlin killed over 23,000 people in little more than an hour. As the Russians moved into Berlin's suburbs, Hitler celebrated his last birthday on 20 April in his bunker behind Wilhelmstrasse. Three days later, Neukölln and Tempelhof fell. By 28 April, Alexanderplatz and Hallesches Tor were in the hands of the Red Army.

The next day, Hitler called his last war conference. He then married his companion Eva Braun and committed suicide with her the day after. As their bodies were being cremated by SS officers, a few streets away a red flag was raised over the Reichstag. The city officially surrendered on 2 May 1945.

When Bertolt Brecht returned to Berlin in 1948, he found 'a pile of rubble next to Potsdam'. Nearly a quarter of all buildings had been destroyed. The human cost of the war was equally startling – around 80,000 Berliners had been killed, not including the thousands of Jews who would not return from the concentration camps. There was no gas or electricity and only the suburbs had running water. Public transport had broken down. In the weeks after capitulation, Red Army soldiers went on a rampage of looting, murder and rape. Thousands of men were transported to labour camps in the Soviet Union. Food supplies were used up and later the harvest failed in the land around the city. Come winter, the few remaining trees in the Tiergarten and other parks were chopped down for firewood.

Clearing the rubble was to take years of dull, painstaking work. The *Trümmerfrauen* ('rubble women') cleared the streets and created literal mountains of junk – such as the Teufelsberg, one of seven hills that now exist as a result. The Soviets stripped factories across Berlin as part of a programme to dismantle German industry and take it back home. As reparation, whole factories were moved to Russia.

Under the terms of the Yalta Agreement, which divided Germany into four zones of control, Berlin was also split into sectors, with the Soviets in the East and the Americans, British and French in the West. A Kommandatura, made up of each army's commander and based in the building of the People's Court in Kleistpark, dealt with the administration of the city. Initially, the administration worked well in getting basics such as public transport back in running order. But tensions between the Soviets and the Western Allies began to rise as civilian government of city affairs returned. In the Eastern sector, a merger of the Communist and Social Democratic parties (both refounded in summer 1945) was pushed to form the Socialist Unity Party (Sozialistische Einheitspartei Deutschlands, SED). In the Western sector, the SPD continued as a separate party. Events came to a head after elections for a new city government in 1946. The SED failed to get more than 20 per cent of the vote, while the SPD won nearly 50 per cent of all votes cast. The Soviets vetoed the appointment of the SPD's mayoral candidate, Ernst Reuter, a committed anti-communist.

Berlin, May 1945

Berlin airlift, March 1949

Berlin Airlift and the Cold War

The situation worsened in spring 1948. In response to the decision by the Western Allies to merge their respective zones in Germany into one administrative entity and introduce a new currency, the Soviets quit the Kommandatura. In late June, all transport links to West Berlin were cut off and Soviet forces began a blockade of the city. Three 'air corridors' linking West Berlin with Western Germany became lifelines as Allied aircraft transported food, coal and industrial components to the beleaguered city.

Within Berlin, the future division of the city began to take permanent shape as city councillors from the West were drummed out of the town hall. They moved to Rathaus Schöneberg in the West. Fresh elections in the Western sector returned Reuter as mayor. The Freie Universität was set up in response to Communist dominance of the Humboldt-Universität in the East.

Having failed to starve West Berlin into submission, the Soviets called off the blockade after 11 months. The Berlin airlift also convinced the Western Allies that they should maintain a presence in Berlin and that their sectors of the city should be linked with the Federal Republic, founded in May 1949. The response from the East was the founding of the DDR (Deutsche Demokratische Republik –

German Democratic Republic, or GDR) on 7 October. With the birth of the 'first Workers' and Peasants' State on German soil', the formal division of Germany into two states was complete.

During the Cold War, Berlin was the focal point for stand-offs between the United States and the Soviet Union. Far from having any control over its own affairs, the city was wholly at the mercy of geopolitical developments. Throughout the 1950s, the 'Berlin Question' remained prominent on the international agenda. Technically, the city was still under Four-Power control, but since the Soviet departure from the Kommandatura and the setting up of the German Democratic Republic with its capital in East Berlin (a breach of the wartime agreement on the future of the city), this counted for little in practice. In principle, the Western Allies adhered to these agreements by retaining ultimate authority in West Berlin, while letting the city integrate into the West German system. Throughout the 1950s, the two halves of Berlin began to develop separately as the political systems in East and West evolved.

In the East, Communist leader Walter Ulbricht set about creating Moscow's most hardline ally in eastern Europe. Work began on a Moscow-style boulevard – called Stalinallee – running east from Alexanderplatz. Industry was nationalised and subjected to rigid central planning. Opposition was kept in check by the new Ministry for State Security: the Stasi.

West Berlin landed the role of 'Last Outpost of the Free World' and, as such, was developed into a showcase. As well as the Marshall Plan, which paid for much of the reconstruction of West Germany, the US poured millions of dollars into West Berlin to maintain it as a counterpoint to communism. The prominence accorded West Berlin was later reflected in the high profile of its politicians (Willy Brandt, for example), who were received abroad by prime ministers and presidents.

Yet despite the emerging divisions, the two halves of the city continued to co-exist in some abnormal fashion. City planners on both sides of the sectoral boundaries initially drew up plans with the whole city in mind. The transport system crossed between East and West, with the underground network being controlled by the West and the S-Bahn by the East. Movement between the sectors (despite 'border' checks) was relatively normal, as Westerners went East to watch a Brecht play or buy cheap books. Easterners travelled West to work, shop or see the latest Hollywood films. The secret services of both sides kept a high presence in the city. Berlin became the espionage capital of the world.

As the effects of US money and the West German 'economic miracle' took hold, West Berlin began to recover. Unemployment dropped from 30 per cent in 1950 to virtually zero by 1961. The labour force also included about 50,000 East Berliners who commuted over the inter-sector borders. In the East, reconstruction was slower. Until the mid 1950s, East Germany paid reparations to the Soviet Union. To begin with, there seemed to be more acts of wilful destruction than positive construction. The old Stadtschloss, slightly damaged by bombing, was blown up in 1950 to make way for a parade ground, which later evolved into a car park.

In 1952, the East Germans sealed off the border with West Germany. The only way out of the 'zone' was now through West Berlin and consequently the number of refugees passing through from the East rose dramatically from 50,000 in 1950 to 300,000 in 1953. Over the decade, one million refugees from the East came through West Berlin.

In June 1953, partly in response to the rapid loss of skilled manpower, the East German government announced a ten per cent increase in working 'norms' – the number of hours and volume of output that workers were required to fulfil each day. In protest, building workers on Stalinallee (now Karl-Marx-Allee) downed tools on 16 June and marched to the government offices on Leipziger Strasse. The government refused to relent, and strikes soon broke out across the city. Crowds stormed Communist Party offices and tore red flags from public buildings. By noon, the government had lost control of the city and it was left to the Red Army to restore order. Soviet tanks rolled into the centre of East Berlin, where they were met by stones thrown by demonstrators. By nightfall the uprising had been crushed. Officially, 23 people died, though other estimates put the figure at over 200.

The 17 June uprising only furthered the wave of emigration. And by the end of the 1950s, it seemed likely that East Germany would cease to function as an industrial state due to the loss of skilled labour. Estimates put the loss to the East German economy through emigration at some 100 billion Deutschmark. Ulbricht increased his demands on Moscow to take action.

In 1958, Soviet leader Nikita Khrushchev tried to bully the Allies into relinquishing West Berlin by calling for an end to military occupation and a 'normalisation of the situation in the capital of the DDR', by which he meant Berlin as a whole. The ultimatum was rejected, and the Allies made clear their commitment to West Berlin. Unwilling to provoke a world war, but needing to prop up his ally, Khrushchev backed down and sanctioned Ulbricht's alternative plan for a solution to the Berlin question.

A tale of two cities

During the early summer of 1961, rumours spread that Ulbricht intended to seal off West Berlin with a barrier or reinforced border. Emigration had reached a high point, as 1,500 East Germans fled to the West each day. However, when in the early hours of 13 August units of the People's Police (assisted by Working Class Combat Groups) began to drag bales of barbed wire across Potsdamer Platz, Berlin and the world were caught by surprise. In a finely planned and executed operation, West Berlin was sealed off within 24 hours. As well as a fence of barbed wire, trenches were dug, the windows of houses straddling the new border were bricked up, and tram and railway lines were interrupted: all this under the watchful eyes of armed guards. Anyone trying to flee to West Berlin risked being shot; in the 28 years the Wall stood, nearly 80 people died trying to escape. Justifying their actions, the East Germans said they had erected an 'Anti-Fascist Protection Rampart' to prevent a world war.

Days later, the construction of a wall began. When it was completed, the concrete part of the 160-kilometre (100-mile) fortification ran to 112 kilometres (70 miles); 37 kilometres (23 miles) of the Wall ran through the city centre. Previously innocuous streets such as Bernauer Strasse (where houses on one side were in the East, on the other in the West) suddenly became the location for one of the world's most deadly borders.

The initial stunned disbelief of Berliners turned into despair as it became clear that (as with the 17 June uprising) the Western Allies could do little more than make a show of strength. President Kennedy dispatched American reinforcements to Berlin and, for a few tense weeks, American and Soviet tanks squared off at Checkpoint Charlie. Vice-President Johnson came to show moral support a week after the Wall was built. Two years later, Kennedy himself arrived and spoke to a crowd of half a million in front of Rathaus Schöneberg. His speech linked the fate of West Berlin with that of the free world and ended with the now famous statement, 'Ich bin ein Berliner!'– which, contrary to popular belief, was correct: doughnuts are known as *Pfannkuchen* in Berlin.

In its early years, the Wall was the scene of many daring escape attempts. People abseiled off buildings, swam across the Spree, waded through sewers or tried to climb over. But as the fortifications were improved with mines, searchlights and guard dogs, and as the guards were given orders to shoot on sight, escape became nearly impossible. By the time the Wall finally fell in 1989, it had been 'updated' four times to render it more or less completely impermeable.

In 1971, the Four Powers met and signed the Quadripartite Agreement, which formally recognised the city's divided status. Border posts (such as Checkpoint Charlie) were introduced and designated to particular categories of visitors – one for foreigners, another for West Germans, and so on.

During the 1960s, with the Wall an infamous and ugly backdrop, the cityscape of modern Berlin (both East and West) began to take shape. On Tauentzienstrasse in the West, the Europa-Center was built, and the bomb-damaged Kaiser-Wilhelm-Gedächtnis-Kirche was given a partner – a new church made up of a glass-clad tower and squat bunker. Hans Scharoun laid out the Kulturforum in Tiergarten as West Berlin's answer to the Museumsinsel complex in the East. The first building to go up was Scharoun's Philharmonie, completed in 1963. Mies van der Rohe's Neue Nationalgalerie was finished in 1968. In the suburbs, work began on concrete mini-towns, Gropiusstadt and Märkisches Viertel. Conceived as solutions to housing shortages, they would develop into alienating ghettos. Alexanderplatz in the East was rebuilt along totalitarian lines, and the Fernsehturm (Television Tower) was finished. The historic core of Berlin was mostly cleared to make way for parks or new office and housing developments. On the eastern outskirts of the city in Marzahn and Hohenschönhausen, work started on soulless mass-scale housing projects.

In 1965, the first sit-down was staged on the Kurfürstendamm by students protesting against low grants and expensive accommodation. This was followed by several student political demonstrations against the state in general and the Vietnam War in particular. The first communes were set up in Kreuzberg, sowing the seeds of a counterculture that would make the district famous. The student protest movement came into violent confrontation with the police in 1967 and 1968. One student, Benno Ohnesorg, was shot dead by police at a demonstration against the Shah of Iran. A year later, the students' leader, Rudi Dutschke, was shot by a right-winger. Demonstrations were held outside the offices of the Springer newspaper group, whose papers were blamed for inciting the shooting. It was out of this movement that the murderous Red Army Faction (also known as the Baader-Meinhof Gang) was to emerge, making headlines in the 1970s with kidnaps and killings.

During the 1960s, with the Wall as an infamous and ugly backdrop, the cityscape of modern Berlin (both East and West) began to take shape

The signing of the Quadripartite Agreement confirmed West Berlin's abnormal status and ushered in an era of decline, as the frisson of Cold War excitement and 1960s rebellion petered out. More than ever, West Berlin depended on huge subsidies from West Germany to keep it going. Development schemes and tax breaks were introduced to encourage businesses to move to the city (Berliners also paid less income tax), but still the economy and population declined. At the same time, there was growth in the number

Die Mauer ist weg!
JEDER darf ab sofort durch!
Deutschland weint vor Freude.
Die ersten sind schon da!
Wir reichen uns die Hände!
B.Z. Berlin ist wieder Berlin!

'The Wall is gone'

of *Gastarbeiter* (guest workers) who arrived from southern Europe and Turkey. Today, there are over 120,000 Turks in the city, largely concentrated in Kreuzberg.

By the late 1970s, Berlin was in a serious malaise. In the West, the city government was discredited by a number of scandals. In East Berlin, where Erich Honecker had succeeded Ulbricht in 1971, a regime that began in a mood of reform became repressive. Some of East Germany's best writers and artists, previously supporters of socialism, emigrated. From its headquarters in Normannenstrasse, the Stasi directed its policy of mass observation and permeated every part of East German society. Between East and West there were squalid exchanges of political prisoners for hard currency. The late '70s and early '80s saw the rise of the squatter movement, which brought violent political protest back on to the streets.

The fall of the Wall and beyond

The arrival of perestroika in the USSR had been ignored by Honecker, who stuck hard to his Stalinist instincts. Protest was strong and only initially beaten back by the police. By the spring of 1989, the East German state was no longer able to withstand the pressure of a population fed up with communism and closed borders. Throughout the summer, thousands fled the city and the country via Hungary, which had opened its borders to the West. Those who stayed began demonstrating for reforms.

By the time Honecker was hosting the celebrations in the Volkskammer (People's Chamber) to mark the 40th anniversary of the GDR on 7 October 1989, crowds were outside, chanting 'Gorby! Gorby!' to register their opposition. Honecker was ousted days later. His successor, Egon Krenz, could do little to stem the tide of opposition. In a bid to defend through attack, he decided to grant the concession East Germans wanted most: freedom to travel.

On 9 November 1989, the gates of the Berlin Wall were opened, just over 28 years after it had been built. As thousands of East Berliners raced through to the sound of popping corks, the end of East Germany and the unification of Berlin and Germany had begun.

With the Wall down, Berlin found itself once again at centre stage. Just as the division of the city defined the split of Europe, so the freedom to move again between East and West marked the dawn of the post-Cold War era. For a year, Berlin was in a state of euphoria. Between November 1989 and October 1990, the city witnessed the collapse of communism and the first free elections (March 1990) in the East for more than 50 years; economic unification, with the swapping of the tinny Ostmark for the Deutschmark (July 1990); and the political merger of East into West, with formal political reunification on 3 October 1990. This was also the year West Germany won its third football World Cup; the team may have come from the West, but in a year characterised by outbursts of popular celebration, East Germans cheered too.

Reunification also brought problems, especially for Berlin, where the two halves of the city now had to be quickly made whole again. While Western infrastructure in the form of roads, telephones and other amenities was in decent working order, in the East it was falling apart. Challenges also came from the collapse of a command economy where jobs were provided regardless of cost or productivity. The Deutschmark put hard currency into the wallets of Easterners, but it also exposed the true state of their economy. Within months, thousands of companies cut jobs or closed down altogether.

Responsibility for restructuring East German industry was placed with the Treuhandanstalt, a state agency that, for a while, was the world's largest industrial holding company. The Treuhand gave high-paid employment to thousands of Western yuppies and put hundreds of thousands of Easterners on the dole. East Germans soon turned on the Treuhand, vilified as the agent of a brutal Western takeover. The situation escalated when Detlev Karsten Rohwedder, a Western industrialist who headed the agency, was assassinated in spring 1991, probably by members of the Red Army Faction. The killing of another state employee, Hanno Klein, an influential city planner, drew attention to another dramatic change brought about by unification: the property boom. In a 1991 parliamentary decision the federal government committed to moving from Bonn to Berlin, provoking a wave of construction and investment to sweep the city.

The giddy excitement of the post-unification years soon gave way to disappointment. The sheer amount of construction work, the scrapping of federal subsidies and tax breaks to West Berlin, rising unemployment and a delay in the arrival of the government all contributed to dampening spirits. In 1994, the last Russian, US, British and French troops left the city; with them went its unique Cold War status. After decades of being different, Berlin was becoming like any other big European capital.

During the 1990s, fast-track gentrification in the East was matched by the decline of West Berlin

The 1990s were characterised by the regeneration of the East. In the course of the decade, the city's centre of gravity shifted towards Mitte. Government and commercial districts were revitalised. On their fringes, especially around Oranienburger Strasse, the Hackesche Höfe and into Prenzlauer Berg, trendy bars, restaurants, galleries and boutiques sprouted in streets that under communism had been grey and crumbling.

Fast-track gentrification in the East was matched by the decline of West Berlin. Upmarket shops and bars began to desert Charlottenburg and Schöneberg. Kreuzberg, once the inelegantly wasted symbol of a defiant West Berlin, degenerated to near slum-like conditions in places, while a new bohemia developed across the Spree in Friedrichshain. Westerners did, however, benefit from the reopening of the Berlin hinterland. Tens of thousands of them swapped the city for greener suburbs in the surrounding state of Brandenburg.

The Berlin Republic

Having spent the best part of a decade doing what it had done so often during its turbulent past – regenerating itself out of the wreckage left by history – Berlin ended the 20th century with a flourish. Many of the big, symbolic construction projects

had already sprouted, including the new Potsdamer Platz and a Reichstag remodelled by Norman Foster. Other major landmarks, such as Daniel Libeskind's Jüdisches Museum and IM Pei's extension to the Deutsches Historisches Museum on Unter den Linden, followed.

The turn of the century also saw Berlin return to its position at the centre of German politics. Parliament, the government and the accompanying baggage of lobbyists and journalists arrived from Bonn. From Chancellor Gerhard Schröder down, everyone sought to mark the transition as the beginning of the 'Berlin Republic' – for which, read: a peaceful, democratic and, above all, self-confident Germany, as opposed to the chaos of the Weimar years or the self-conscious timidity of the Bonn era.

In the early 2000s, Berlin's financial problems – brought on by rocketing demands on expenditure, decline in central government handouts and the collapse of traditional industries – grew steadily worse. Matching this was the ineptitude of the city's political establishment, desperate to hang on to old privileges and unwilling to face up to tough, new choices. This was all encapsulated in the collapse of the Bankgesellschaft Berlin, a bank largely owned by the city, which was felled by a raft of dud and corrupt real-estate loans in the summer of 2001. As well as sparking a further deterioration in the public finances, the scandal brought down the Berlin Senate – a grand coalition of Christian Democrats (Christlich Demokratische Union Deutschlands, CDU) and SPD that had governed the city since 1990. The resulting elections went some way towards a new start. Klaus Wowereit, head of the SPD, broke one of the great post-unification taboos and invited the Party of Democratic Socialism – successor party to East Germany's Communists and winners of half the Eastern vote – into a Social Democrat-led coalition.

At national level, Schröder's second term was far from happy. A brave attempt at welfare reform saw the Chancellor attacked from all sides, including the left of his own SPD. Defeats in regional polls forced Schröder to call an early general election. Schröder entered the bitter campaign trailing his opponent Angela Merkel and the Christian Democrats in the opinion polls but came within a whisker of winning the vote in September. The result was a mess in which both the main parties – CDU and SPD – lost votes, and neither was able to form its preferred coalition. Instead, they were forced into a CDU-led grand coalition with Merkel as Chancellor. As the first woman and first East German to hold the chancellorship, Merkel ensured her place in the history books when she took office in November 2005.

Meanwhile, the final pieces of Berlin's structural reunification puzzle tumbled into place. The following year was to see the colossal new Berlin Hauptbahnhof take a bow as one of Europe's largest stations, while the renovated Olympiastadion would play host to the World Cup Final. Peter Eisenman's grand Denkmal für die ermordeten Juden Europas (Memorial to the Murdered Jews of Europe) was unveiled with the usual whiff of controversy. The hexagon of Leipziger Platz took final shape as the city centre's reception room. And after years of argument, demolition of the Palast der Republik finally began.

The improvement of Germany's international standing was confirmed by the 2006 FIFA World Cup. Berlin was the centrepiece for what was widely judged to be one of the best-organised and – for the fans – most enjoyable competitions in the event's history. Key to the success was the bold decision to welcome all fans – ticket-holders or not – to Germany to take part in the wider experience of the event. It was also the first time that Germans felt comfortable overtly displaying signs of national pride, with flags sprouting up everywhere. Germany may have failed to scoop the cup that year at the Olympiastadion, but their youthful team under Joachim Löw finally clinched it in 2014.

On the political front, the Euro crisis and its ensuing German-led austerity policy demonstrated Merkel's position as the most powerful leader of the trading bloc.

Re-elected in 2009 in coalition with the pro-business FDP, the CDU returned to forming 'grand coalitions' with the SDP in 2013 and 2017, the second time after months of political wrangling and only after all other options had been exhausted.

The 2017 general election saw a significant drop in support for the two traditional 'centre' parties, leaving the right-wing Alternative für Deutschland (AfD) as the largest opposition party in parliament. Even in progressive Berlin, the AfD made surprising gains in several suburbs, a fact that red-faced political commentators blamed on everything from the influx of refugees into the city in 2016 to the pernicious influence of social media.

Long-serving mayor Klaus Wowereit (he of the city's 'poor but sexy' tagline) resigned in 2014 over the Berlin airport debacle, which continues to this day (*see p34*), but his successor, Michael Müller, hails from the same party (SPD) and, since local elections in 2016, has headed a firmly left-of-centre coalition with Die Linke (the Left Party) and the Greens. Many of the biggest issues facing the city government can be traced to Berlin's popularity among disparate groups. For residents expecting to live, work and raise children here, the priorities are improving infrastructure, adding affordable housing stock and increasing the number of school places. For visitors and the tourist industry, the much-delayed opening of the new airport is a key issue. And for those refugees who have come to Berlin since 2016, fleeing war or persecution, the city needs to provide legal recognition, suitable housing and the promise of a better future.

Angela Merkel

Architecture

The city's many styles reflect a complicated history

Following its rapid elevation in the late 19th century to European capital, near obliteration during World War II (from above by the RAF, and on the ground by Soviet forces), and 40 years of straddling the frontline between capitalism and communism, it's hardly surprising that Berlin is a barely coherent mish-mash of architectural styles. But while the German capital lacks the consistency (or immediate beauty) of a Paris or an Edinburgh, it is a curate's egg of great individual buildings, from the Baroque to the Stalinist, from GDR-tastic communist follies to elegant masterpieces of 20th-century modernism, and bravura restorations (often by British architects) of ruined landmarks. A brief lull in the early 2010s, both financial and creative, has done little to slow the city's re-emergence as a cultural and creative metropolis to match its heyday under the Weimar Republic.

Berlin has a long history of architectural development and experimentation. During the 1910s and '20s, the city was home to some of the century's greatest architects and designers, such as Peter Behrens, Bruno Taut, Ludwig Mies van der Rohe and Walter Gropius. But the path to modernism had been launched a century earlier by Karl Friedrich Schinkel, perhaps Berlin's greatest builder.

Bundeskanzleramt *p291*

It wasn't until the late 19th century that Berlin was able to hold its own with grander European capitals, thanks to a construction boom known as the Gründerzeit, triggered by the rapid progress in industry and technology that followed German unification in 1871. The young country was eager for its new capital to achieve the *Weltstadt* (world city) status of Paris or London and so widened its streets and installed large blocks. These followed a rudimentary geometry and were filled in with five-storey *Mietskaserne* (rental barracks) built around linked internal courtyards. The monotony was partially relieved by a few public parks, while later apartment houses gradually became more humane and eventually rather splendid. During the 1920s, this method of development was rejected in favour of Bauhaus-influenced slabs and towers, which were used to fill out the peripheral zones at the edge of the forests. The post-war years saw even more radical departures from the earlier tradition in all sectors of the city.

The post-Wall building boom deposited a new layer, a mixture of contemporary design and historic emulation. The spirit of historic revival even took in the city's most famous landmark, the Wall. Speedily dismantled after 1989, it is now commemorated in public art, from the **Gedenkstätte Berliner Mauer** (*see p125*) at Bernauer Strasse to Frank Thiel's portraits of the last Allied soldiers, suspended above **Checkpoint Charlie** (*see p147*). The former line of the Wall is also marked in places by a cobblestone strip, visible just west of the Brandenburg Gate. But its memory is fading. 'Where was the Wall?' is the first question on many visitors' lips, and the answer is surprisingly nebulous, as the course of the Wall twisted and dog-legged at the most convoluted angles.

Early days

Berlin's long journey to world-city status began in Berlin and Cölln, two Wendish/Slavic settlements on the Spree that were colonised by Germans around 1237 (*see p262*). Among their oldest surviving buildings are the parish churches **Marienkirche** (*see p89*) and **Nikolaikirche** (*see p90*). The latter was rebuilt in the district known as the **Nikolaiviertel**, along with other landmarks such as the 1571 pub Zum Nussbaum and the Baroque **Ephraim-Palais** (*see p88*). The Nikolaiviertel, between Alexanderplatz and the Spree, is the only part of central Berlin to give any idea of how the medieval city might have felt – except it's a kitsch fake, rebuilt by the East

Germans in 1987, just a few decades after they had levelled the original district.

A controversial reconstruction of the massive **Stadtschloss** (1538-1950) – badly damaged in the war, then replaced by the GDR's infamous **Palast der Republik** (itself demolished in 2008) – is scheduled to reopen in late 2019 as a mixed university/museum/exhibition complex (*see p33* Stadtschloss box). The **Schlossbrücke** crossing to Unter den Linden, adorned with sensual figures by Christian Daniel Rauch, and the **Neptunbrunnen** (Neptune Fountain, now relocated south of Marienkirche), modelled on Bernini's Roman fountains, were designed to embellish the original palace.

The Residenzstadt

In 1647, the Great Elector Friedrich Wilhelm II (1640-88) hired Dutch engineers to transform the route to the Tiergarten, the royal hunting forest, into the tree-lined boulevard of Unter den Linden. It led west toward **Schloss Charlottenburg** (*see p187*), built in 1695 as a summer retreat for Queen Sophie-Charlotte. Over the next century, the Elector's *Residenzstadt* expanded to include Berlin and Cölln. Traces of the old stone **Stadtmauer** (city wall) that enclosed them can still be seen on Waisenstrasse in Mitte. Two further districts, Dorotheenstadt (begun 1673) and Friedrichstadt (begun 1688), expanded the street grid north and south of Unter den Linden. Andreas Schlüter built new palace wings for Elector Friedrich Wilhelm III (1688-1713, crowned King Friedrich I of Prussia in 1701) and supervised the building of the **Zeughaus** or armoury (Nering and de Bodt, 1695-1706), now home to the Deutsches Historisches Museum (*see p78*), whose bellicose ornamentation embodies the Prussian love of militarism.

Wilhelm I, the Soldier King (1713-40), imposed conscription and subjugated the town magistrate to the court and military elite. The economy now catered to an army comprising 20 per cent of the population (a fairly constant percentage until 1918). To spur growth in gridded Friedrichstadt – and to quarter his soldiers cheaply – the king forced people to build new houses, mostly in a stripped-down classical style. He permitted one open square, later renamed the **Gendarmenmarkt**, where twin churches had been built in 1701, one of which now houses the Hugenottenmuseum (*see p78*). The square and churches were Baroque-ified with the addition of grandiose porticoes and domed towers in the 1780s.

After the population reached 60,000 in 1710, a new customs wall enclosed four

Berlin's Bunkers

Uncovering relics of the Nazi regime

Next to the railway lines on the Schöneberg–Tempelhof border (General-Pape-Strasse, corner of Dudenstrasse) stands a huge, featureless cylinder of concrete. Built in 1942 as part of the planning for Germania, the Nazi imperial capital that never was, it's a *Grossbelastungskörper* (heavy load testing body) designed to gauge the resilience of Berlin's sandy geology near the site for a proposed triumphal arch. This artless, seldom-noticed lump is the lone physical trace of the north–south axis whose overblown structures were intended to wow the world.

But it's not the only huge hulk of reinforced concrete that the Nazis left behind, and is tiny compared to some of the bunkers, flak towers and air-raid shelters that outlasted the regime they were intended to protect. The question of how to integrate them into the urban landscape has sparked a variety of answers.

Berlin Zoo's flak tower was the biggest bunker in the world when the royal engineers began trying to blow it up in July 1947. One year and 66 tonnes of explosives later, they finally broke the thing open, causing extensive damage to the zoo. It took many further detonations before the foundations were finally cleared in 1969-70.

Given the difficulty of demolition, most of these structures have simply been left where they were. On Pallasstrasse in Schöneberg, an air-raid shelter, formerly part of the otherwise demolished Sportspalast complex, has been used to support one end of an apartment block that bridges the street. After the war,

two enormous concrete towers in what is now **Volkspark Friedrichshain** were blown open, then filled in and covered with rubble from the bombed-out city. Result: the park now has two attractively landscaped hills, and only a few visible segments of balustrade hint at what lies beneath.

A bit more can be seen of a similarly blasted and buried Nazi flak tower in Wedding's **Humboldthain** park. Climbers practise on its north face, several species of bat dwell in its recesses, a viewing platform on the top offers a panorama of the Berlin skyline, and guided tours of the interior are offered by the **Berliner Unterwelten** association (www.berliner-unterwelten.de).

There are two other bunkers you can get inside. Kreuzberg's **Gruselkabinett** is housed in a five-storey concrete hulk and includes an exhibition about the structure itself, which was once an air-raid shelter for the long-destroyed Anhalter Bahnhof. A bunker on the corner of Reinhardtstrasse and Albrechtstrasse in Mitte, previously a not-very-convenient air-raid shelter for Friedrichstrasse station, was repurposed as a techno club in the early 1990s and today houses the fabulous **Sammlung Boros** art collection (see p90).

But of Berlin's most infamous bunker, the one where Hitler spent his frenzied last days, there's no longer any trace – it was demolished in the late 1980s. A sparse information board on Gertrud-Kolmar-Strasse (opposite the junction with An Der Ministeriumsgarten) is all that marks its former location.

Sammlung Boros

Martin-Gropius-Bau

new districts – the Spandauer Vorstadt, Königstadt, Stralauer Vorstadt and Köpenicker Vorstadt; all are now part of Mitte. The 14-kilometre (nine-mile) border remained the city limits until 1860.

Geometric squares later marked three of the 14 city gates in Friedrichstadt. At the square-shaped Pariser Platz, Carl Gotthard Langhans built the **Brandenburger Tor** (*see p71*) in 1789, a triumphal arch later topped by Johan Gottfried Schadow's *Quadriga*. The stately buildings around the square were levelled after World War II but have now largely been rebuilt or replaced, including the **Adlon Kempinski** hotel (Patzschke, Klotz, 1997; *see p298*), on an expanded version of its original site, and the buildings flanking the gate, **Haus Sommer** and **Haus Liebermann** (Kleihues, 1998).

Even with the army, Berlin's population did not reach 100,000 until well into the reign of Frederick the Great (1740-86). Military success inspired him to embellish Berlin and Potsdam; many of the monuments along Unter den Linden stem from his vision of a 'Forum Fredericianum'. Though never completed, the unique ensemble of neoclassical, Baroque and rococo monuments includes the vine-covered **Humboldt-Universität** (Knobelsdorff, Boumann, 1748-53); the **Staatsoper** (Knobelsdorff, Langhans, 1741-43; *see p252*); the **Prinzessinnenpalais** (1733, now the Operncafé) and the **Kronprinzenpalais** (1663, expanded 1732) at Unter den Linden 3.

Set back from the Linden on Bebelplatz are the **Alte Bibliothek** (Unger, 1775-81), part of Humboldt-Universität and reminiscent of the curvy Vienna Hofburg;

and the pantheon-like, copper-domed **Sankt-Hedwigs-Kathedrale** (Legeay and Knobelsdorff, 1747-73; *see p80*). Not long after the Napoleonic occupation, Karl Friedrich Schinkel became Berlin's most revered architect under Prince Friedrich Wilhelm IV. Drawing on classical and Italian precedents, his early stage-sets experimented with perspective, while his inspired urban visions served the cultural

Schinkel's inspired urban visions served the cultural aspirations of an ascendant German state

aspirations of an ascendant German state.

He designed the colonnaded **Altes Museum** (1828; *see p77*), regarded by most architects as his finest work, and the **Neue Wache** (New Guardhouse; 1818; *see p74*), next to the Zeughaus, whose Roman solidity lent itself well to Tessenow's 1931 conversion into a memorial to the dead of World War I. Other Schinkel masterpieces include the **Schauspielhaus** (1817-21, now the Konzerthaus; *see p251*); the neo-Gothic brick **Friedrichswerdersche Kirche** (1830) and the cubic **Schinkel-Pavillon** (1825; *see p187*) at Schloss Charlottenburg.

After his death in 1841, his many disciples continued working. Friedrich August Stüler satisfied the king's desire to complement the Altes Museum with the **Neues Museum**

(1841-59 and 1997-2009; *see p75*), mixing new wrought-iron technology with classical architecture. By 1910, Museumsinsel comprised the neoclassical **Alte Nationalgalerie** (Stüler, 1864; *see p77*), with an open stairway framing an equestrian statue of the king; the triangular **Bode-Museum** (von Ihne, 1904; *see p78*); and the sombre grey **Pergamonmuseum** (Messel and Hoffmann, 1906-09; *see p80*). These are a stark contrast to the neo-Renaissance polychromy of the **Martin-Gropius-Bau** across town (Gropius and Schmieden, 1881; *see p148*).

Era of expansion

As the population boomed after 1865, doubling to 1.5 million by 1890, the city began swallowing up neighbouring towns and villages. Factory complexes and worker housing gradually moved to the outskirts. Many of the new market halls and railway stations used a vernacular brick style with iron trusses, such as **Arminiushalle** at Bremer Strasse 9 in Moabit (Blankenstein, 1892; *see p113*), which is still an indoor food market, and Franz Schwechten's romanesque **Anhalter Bahnhof** (1876-80), now a ruin on Askanischer Platz). Brick was also used for civic buildings, such as the neo-Gothic **Berliner Rathaus** (1861-69; *see p87*), while the orientalism of the gold-roofed **Neue Synagoge** on Oranienburger Strasse (Knoblauch, Stüler, 1859-66; *see p89*) made use of colourful masonry and mosaics.

Restrained historicism gave way to wild eclecticism as the 19th century marched on, in public buildings as well as apartment houses with plain interiors, dark courtyards and overcrowded flats behind decorative façades. This eclectic approach is also reflected in the lavish Gründerzeit villas in the fashionable suburbs to the south-west, especially Dahlem and Grünewald. In these areas, the modest yellow-brick vernacular of Brandenburg was rejected in favour of stone and elaborate stucco.

Foreshadowing a new age of rationality and mechanisation, an attempt at greater stylistic clarity was made after 1900, in spite of the bombast of works such as the new **Berliner Dom** (Raschdorff, 1905; *see p77*) and the **Reichstag** (Wallot, 1894; *see p105*). The Wilhelmine era's paradoxical mix of reformism and conservatism yielded an architecture of *Sachlichkeit* (objectivity) in commercial and public buildings. In some cases, such as Kaufmann's **Hebbel-Theater** (1908, now part of HAU; *see p256*), or the **Hackesche Höfe** (Berndt and Endell, 1906-07; *see p85*), *Sachlichkeit* meant a calmer form of art nouveau (or Jugendstil); elsewhere, it was more sombre, with heavy, compact forms, vertical ribbing and low-hanging mansard roofs. A very sombre example is the stripped-down classicism of Alfred Messel's **Pergamonmuseum**.

The style combined well with Prussian bureaucracy in the civic architecture of Ludwig Hoffmann, city architect from 1896 to 1924. Though he sometimes used other styles for his many schools, courthouses and city halls, his towering **Altes Stadthaus** (1919) on Jüdenstrasse at the corner of Parochialstrasse and the **Rudolf-Virchow-Krankenhaus** (1906) at Augustenburger

Berliner Dom

Siemensstadt

Platz 1 in Wedding (then innovative for its pavilion system) epitomise Wilhelmine architecture.

Prior to the incorporation of Berlin in 1920, many suburbs had full city charters and sported their own town halls, such as the massive **Rathaus Charlottenburg** (1905) on Otto-Suhr-Allee and **Rathaus Neukölln** (1909) at Karl-Marx-Strasse 83-85. Neukölln's Reinhold Kiehl also built the **Karl-Marx-Strasse Passage** (1910, now home of the Neuköllner Oper; *see p253*), and the **Stadtbad Neukölln** (1914; *see p175*), with niches and mosaics evoking a Roman atmosphere. Special care was also given to suburban rail stations, such as the **S-Bahnhof Mexikoplatz** (Hart and Lesser, 1905) in Zehlendorf, set on a garden square with shops and restaurants, and the **U-Bahnhof Dahlem-Dorf**, whose half-timbered style aimed for a countrified look.

Archiectural pioneers

The work of many pioneers brought modern architecture to life in Berlin. One of the most important was Peter Behrens, who reinterpreted the factory with a new monumental language in the façade of the **Turbinenhalle** at Huttenstrasse in Moabit (1909) and several other buildings for AEG. After 1918, the turbulent birth of the Weimar Republic offered a chance for a final aesthetic break with the Wilhelmine style. The humming metropolis gave

birth to a new gothic-industrial style known as Brick Expressionism, used in electricity power stations (HH Müller's 1926 **Abspannwerk**, or transformer station, on the canal in Kreuzberg at the junction of Ohlauerstrasse and Paul-Lincke Ufer), breweries (the original **Berliner Kindl** brewery, now a gay club on Rollbergstrasse, Neukölln) and churches (Fritz Höger's 1932 **Kirche am Hohenzollerndamm**, Hohenzollerndamm 202).

A radical new architecture gave formal expression to long-awaited social and political reforms. The *Neues Bauen* (new buildings) began to exploit the new technologies of glass, steel and concrete, inspired by the early work of Tessenow and Behrens, Dutch modernism, cubism and Russian constructivism. Berlin architects could explore the new functionalism, using clean lines and a machine aesthetic bare of ornament, thanks to post-war housing demand, and a new social democrat administration that put planner Martin Wagner at the helm after 1925.

The city became the pioneer of a new form of social housing. The *Siedlung* (housing estate) was developed within the framework of a 'building exhibition' of experimental prototypes – often collaborations among architects, such as Luckhardt, Gropius, Häring, Salvisberg and the brothers Taut. Standardised sizes kept costs down and amenities such as tenant gardens, schools, public transport and shopping areas were offered when possible. Among the best-known 1920s estates are Bruno Taut's **Hufeisensiedlung** (1927) in Britz (*see p175*), arranged in a horseshoe shape around a communal garden, and **Onkel-Toms-Hütte** (Häring, Taut, 1928-29) on Argentinische Allee, Zehlendorf, which has Salvisberg's linear U-Bahn station at its heart. Most *Siedlungen* were housing only, such as the **Ringsiedlung** on Goebelstrasse in Charlottenburg and **Siemensstadt** (Scharoun et al, 1929-32). Traditional-looking 'counter-proposals' were made by more conservative designers at **Am Fischtal** (Tessenow, Mebes, Emmerich, Schmitthenner et al, 1929) in Zehlendorf.

Larger infrastructure projects and public works were also built by avant-garde architects under Wagner's direction. Among the more interesting are the rounded U-Bahn station at **Krumme Lanke** (Grenander, 1929), the totally rational **Stadtbad Mitte** (1930) on Gartenstrasse; the **Messegelände** (Poelzig, Wagner, 1928) at Messedamm 22, Charlottenburg; the ceramic-tiled **Haus des Rundfunks** (Poelzig, 1930) on Masurenallee, Charlottenburg, and the twin office buildings on the southern corner of **Alexanderplatz** (Behrens, 1932).

Beginning with his expressionist **Einsteinturm** in Babelsberg, Erich Mendelsohn distilled his own brand of modernism, characterised by the rounded forms of the **Universum Cinema** (1928; now the Schaubühne; *see p255*) and the elegant corner solution of the **IG Metall** building (1930) at Alte Jacobstrasse 148, Kreuzberg.

Fascist fantasy

In the effort to remake liberal Berlin in their image, the Nazis banned modernist trademarks such as flat roofs and slender columns in favour of traditional architecture. The Bauhaus was closed down and modern architects fled Berlin as Hitler dreamt of refashioning the city into the fantastical mega-capital 'Germania', designed by Albert Speer. The crowning glory was to be a grand axis with a railway station at its foot and a massive copper dome at its head, some 16 times the size of

Hitler dreamt of refashioning the city into the fantastical mega-capital 'Germania', designed by Albert Speer

St Peter's in Rome. Work was halted by the war, but not before demolition had begun in Tiergarten and Schöneberg.

Speer's fantasy was that Germania would someday leave picturesque ruins. Those ruins came sooner than expected. Up to 90 per cent of the inner city was destroyed by Allied bombing. Mountains of rubble cleared by women survivors rose at the city's edge, such as the **Teufelsberg** (*see p203*) in the West and **Friedrichshain** (*see p132*) in the East. During bombing and reconstruction, many apartment buildings lost their decoration, resulting in the bare plasterwork and blunted lines characteristic of Berlin today.

Fascism also left a less visible legacy of bunker and tunnel landscapes (*see p283* Berlin's Bunkers). The more visible fascist architecture can be recognised by its stripped-down, abstracted classicism, typically in travertine: in the West, **Flughafen Tempelhof** (Sagebiel, 1941; *see p173*) and the **Olympiastadion** (March, 1936; *see p197*); in the East, the marble-halled **Reichsluftfahrtministerium** (Sagebiel, 1936), now the Bundesministerium der Finanzen on Wilhelmstrasse 97, Mitte, and the **Reichsbank** (Wolff, 1938; now the Auswärtiges Amt on Werderscher Markt.

After the war

The **Berlin Wall**, put up in a single night in 1961, introduced a new and cruel reality, and has claim to be the most iconic structure of the 20th century. Very little of the original survives, save for a stretch at Bernauer Strasse (*see p125*), and the East Side Gallery murals (*see p135*). The city's centre of gravity shifted as the Wall cut off the historic centre from the West, suspending the Brandenburger Tor and Potsdamer Platz in no-man's land, while the outer edge followed the 1920 city limits.

Post-war architecture is a mixed bag, ranging from the crisp linear brass of 1950s storefronts to concrete 1970s mega-complexes. Early joint planning efforts led by Hans Scharoun were scrapped, and radical interventions cleared out vast spaces. Among the architectural casualties in the East were Schinkel's Bauakademie and much of Fischerinsel, lost during the clearing of a sequence of wide spaces from Marx-Engels-Platz to Alexanderplatz. In West Berlin, Anhalter Bahnhof was left to stand in ruins and Schloss Charlottenburg narrowly escaped demolition.

Though architects from East and West shared the same modernist education, their work became the tool of opposing ideologies, and housing was the first battlefield. The GDR adapted Russian socialist realism to Prussian culture in projects built with great effort and amazing speed as a national undertaking. First and foremost was **Stalinallee** (1951-54), now Karl-Marx-Allee in Friedrichshain (*see p134*), with its colossal Stalinist twin towers. The Frankfurter Tor segment of its monumental axis was designed by Herman Henselmann, a Bauhaus modernist who briefly agreed to switch styles.

In response, West Berlin called on leading International Style architects including Gropius, Niemeyer, Aalto and Jacobsen to build the **Hansaviertel** (*see p104*). A loose arrangement of inventive blocks and pavilions at the edge of the Tiergarten, it was part of the 1957 Interbau Exhibition for the 'city of tomorrow', which included Le Corbusier's Unité d'Habitation

Though architects from East and West shared the same modernist education, their work became the tool of opposing ideologies

in Charlottenburg (**Corbusierhaus**; *see p196*) just south of Olympiastadion S-Bahn station.

Stylistic differences between East and West diminished in the 1960s and '70s, as new *Siedlungen* were built to even greater dimensions. The **Gropiusstadt** in Britz and **Märkisches Viertel** in Reinickendorf (1963-74) were mirrored in the East by equally massive (if shoddier) prefab housing estates in Marzahn and Hellersdorf.

To replace cultural institutions then cut off from the West, Dahlem became the site of various museums and of the new **Freie Universität** (Candilis Woods Schiedhelm, 1967-79). Scharoun conceived a 'Kulturforum' on the site cleared for Germania, designing two masterful pieces: the **Philharmonie** (1963; *see p252*) and the **Staatsbibliothek** (1976; *see p308*). Other additions were Mies van der Rohe's sleek **Neue Nationalgalerie** (1968; *see p109*) and the **Gemäldegalerie** (Hilmer & Sattler, 1992-98; *see p108*).

In 1967, the US presented Berlin with Hugh Stubbins' **Kongresshalle** in the Tiergarten, now the Haus der Kulturen der Welt (*see p102*), a futuristic work, which embarrassingly required seven years' repair after its roof collapsed in 1980. East German architects brewed their own version of futuristic modernism in the enlarged Alexanderplatz with its **Fernsehturm** (1969; *see p88*); the nearby **Haus des Lehrers** (Henselmann, 1961-64) on Grunerstrasse and Karl-Marx-Allee, with its wonderfully restored frieze; the next-door **Congress Hall** (ICC – as elegant as anything achieved by Oscar Niemeyer in Brasilia), and the impressive cinemas **Kino International** (Kaiser, 1964; *see p222*) and **Kosmos** (Kaiser, 1962) on Karl-Marx-Allee in Friedrichshain. The 1970s even saw a brief burst of Soviet sci-fi architecture, with the bronze glass and brown marble **Czech Embassy** to **the GDR** (Vera & Vladimir Machonin, 1978) at Wilhelmstrasse 44.

Modernist urban renewal gradually gave way to historic preservation after 1970. In the West, largely in response to the squatting movement, the city launched a public-private enterprise within the

Bundeskanzleramt *p291*

Internationale Bauausstellung (IBA – International Architecture Exhibition), to conduct a 'careful renewal' of the *Mietskaserne* and 'critical reconstruction' with infill projects to close the gaps left in areas along the Wall. It is a truly eclectic collection: the irreverent organicism of the prolific Hinrich and Inken Baller at Fraenkelufer in Kreuzberg (1982-84) contrasts sharply with the neo-rationalist work of Peter Eisenman at Kochstrasse 62-63 in Kreuzberg (1988) and of Aldo Rossi at Wilhelmstrasse 36-38, Kreuzberg (1988). A series of projects was also placed along Friedrichstrasse. IBA thus became a proving-ground for contemporary architectural theories.

▶ *For more on the IBA, see Jim Hudson's blog, architectureinberlin.wordpress.com*

In the East, urban renewal slowed to a halt when funds for the construction of new housing ran dry, and, towards the end of the 1970s, inner-city areas again became politically and economically attractive. Most East-bloc preservation focused on run-down 19th-century buildings on a few streets and squares in Prenzlauer Berg. Some infill buildings were also added on Friedrichstrasse in manipulated grids and pastel colours, so that the postmodern theme set up by IBA architects on the street south of Checkpoint Charlie was continued over the Wall. But progress was slow and, when the Wall fell in 1989, many sites still stood half-finished.

Uniting the city

Rejoining East and West became the new challenge, requiring work of every kind, from massive infrastructure to commercial and residential projects. There were two key decisions. The first was to eradicate the Wall's no-man's land zone with projects that would link urban structures on either side. The second was to pursue a 'critical reconstruction' of the old city block structure, using a contemporary interpretation of Prussian scale and order.

The historic areas around Pariser Platz, Friedrichstrasse and Unter den Linden were peppered with empty sites and became a primary focus for this critical reconstruction. The first major commercial project in Friedrichstrasse stuck with the required city scale but took the game rules lightly. The various buildings of the **Friedrichstadt-Passagen** (1996; Friedrichstrasse 66-75, Mitte), despite their subterranean mall link, offer separate approaches. Pei Cobb Freed & Partners' Quartier 206 (*see p76*) is a gaudy confection of architectural devices reminiscent of

Hansaviertel

1920s Berlin, while Jean Nouvel's **Galeries Lafayette** (*see p83*) is a smooth and rounded glass form. Only the third building, **Quartier 205**, by Oswald Mathias Ungers, uses a current German style, with its sandstone solidity and rigorous square grid.

Good examples of the emerging Berliner Architektur, based on the solidity of the past but with modern detailing and expressive use of materials, are to be found in Thomas van den Valentyn and Matthias Dittmann's monumental Quartier 108 (1998; Friedrichstrasse and Leipziger Strasse, Mitte) and in the **Kontorhaus Mitte** (1997; Friedrichstrasse 180-190, Mitte) by Josef Paul Kleihues, Vittorio Magnago Lampugnani, Walther Stepp and Klaus Theo Brenner.

Berliner Architektur is based on the solidity of the past but with modern detailing and expressive use of materials

Deutsches Historisches Museum

On both sides of the city, much historic substance was lost in World War II and the sweeping changes that followed. Today, the rebuilding of the former imperial areas near Unter den Linden, the Museumsinsel and Schlossplatz revolve around a choice between critical reconstruction or straightforward replicas of the past. The Kommandantenhaus, next to the Staatsoper on Unter den Linden, rebuilt by Thomas van den Valentyn as the **Stiftung Bertelsmann** (2004), is an example of the tendency towards historical replication, while David Chipperfield's not-yet-complete **Museumsinsel** is regarded by many as a near-perfect example of past and present working in harmony, especially his breathtakingly elegant restoration of the Neues Museum. The James-Simon-Galerie, designed to act as unified entrance and ticket hall for all the museums on the island, was expected to open at the end of 2018.

With all due respect to Chipperfield's achievements, it's no bad thing that some other designs are decisively and unapologetically contemporary, such as the entrance building to the **Auswärtiges Amt** (Foreign Office, 1999; Werdescher Markt 1) by Thomas Müller and Ivan Reimann, and IM Pei's triangular block for the **Deutsches Historisches Museum** (2003; *see p78*), with its curved foyer and cylindrical stair tower.

Berlin's return to capital city status resulted in the construction of a number of interesting new embassies and consulates in a revived diplomatic quarter. Notable on Tiergartenstrasse are the solid red stone

Indian Embassy by Leon Wohlhage Wernik (2001) and the extension of the existing **Japanese Embassy** by Ryohei Amemiya (2000). There are other intriguing examples around the corner in Klingelhöferstrasse: the monumental, louvre-fronted **Mexican Embassy** by Teodoro Gonzalez de Leon and J Francisco Serrano (2000); and the encircling copper wall of the five **Nordic embassies**, containing work by various Scandinavian architects after a plan by Alfred Berger and Tiina Parkkinen (1999).

Four main sites now link East and West: the area around Potsdamer Platz and Leipziger Platz; the Reichstag and Pariser Platz, reinstated as the historical formal entrance to the city; the government quarter and 'Band des Bundes'; and Berlin Hauptbahnhof. These are mostly stand-alone projects outside the discussion on critical reconstruction; their architecture reflects this in a greater freedom of approach.

Potsdamer Platz (*see p106*) was the first of the four, designed as a new urban area based on the old geometries of Potsdamer Platz and Leipziger Platz. This former swathe of no-man's land was redeveloped not only to forge a link between Leipziger Strasse to the East and the Kulturforum to the West, but also to supply Berlin with a new central focus in an area that was formerly neither one side or the other. **Leipziger Platz** is an enclosed octagonal set-piece, with modern terrace buildings, while Potsdamer Platz is by contrast, once more, an open intersection. Five small quarters now radiate to the south and west, their entrances staked out by major buildings by Hans Kollhoff, Hilmer & Sattler and Albrecht, Helmut Jahn, Renzo Piano and Schweger and Partner (1999-2003). The closed metal and glass block of Helmut Jahn's **Sony Center** (2000) is a singular piece, organised around a lofty central forum with a tented glass and textile roof as its spectacular focus. Offices and apartments look down on to a public space with cinemas, bars, restaurants and the glass-encased remnants of the old Esplanade Hotel.

The **Daimler** (formerly DaimlerChrysler) area on the other side of Potsdamer Strasse is a network of tree-lined streets with squares and pavement cafés. It's also the work of various architects, though Renzo Piano got all the key pieces, notably the **Arkaden** shopping mall, the **Debis headquarters**, and the **Musicaltheater** and **Spielbank** on Marlene-Dietrich-Platz (all 1999), all in a language of terracotta and glass. The quarter's south-west flank facing on to Tilla-Durieux-Park is a rich architectural mix, with Richard Rogers' two buildings of cylinders, blocks and wedges (1998; Linkstrasse) and Arata Isozaki's concoction of ochre and brown stripes topped with a wavy glass penthouse (1998; Linkstrasse). It's often said of the Potsdamer Platz project that 'the world's best architects came – and did their worst buildings'. This is not quite fair, as their original plans were watered down by the city's conservative building commissioner – but it's not far off either.

North of Potsdamer Platz is the **Reichstag** (*see p105*), sitting on the old threshold to the East. It was gutted, remodelled and topped with a new glass dome by Norman Foster in 1999 to bring a degree of public access and transparency to a building with a dark past. Pariser Platz (*see p70*) has since been almost entirely built to its old proportions. Some of the buildings are a pale blend of modern and historic, but there are exceptions, such as the **DG Bank** by Frank Gehry (2000; Pariser Platz 3), with its witty use of a rational façade in front of the spectacular free forms in its internal court, or Christian de Portzamparc's **French Embassy** (2002; Pariser Platz 5), which plays with classical composition but uses contemporary materials. In the opposite corner is the **Akademie der Künste** (Behnisch and Partner; 2005), an exception to its neighbours with a welcoming and open glass façade. Round the corner, Michael Wilford's **British Embassy** (2000; *see p306*) also came to terms with the city's strict planning limitations by raising a conformist punched stone façade, which was then broken open to expose a rich and colourful set of secondary buildings in the

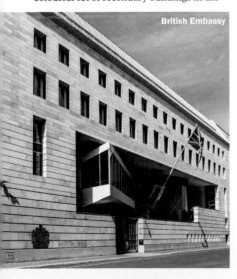

British Embassy

central court. The utterly bland US Embassy, unveiled on 4 July 2008 in the south-west corner, completes the set piece.

The **Band des Bundes**, the linear arrangement of new government buildings north of the Reichstag, is another project linking East and West. The result of a competition won by Axel Schultes and Charlotte Frank, it straddles the Spree and the former border, resembling a paper clip that binds the two halves of the city. The centrepiece is the **Bundeskanzleramt** or Federal Chancellery (2000; Willi-Brandt-Strasse, Tiergarten) flanked by buildings with offices for parliamentary deputies. The arrangement reads like a unity thanks to a common and simple language of concrete and glass.

North of this across the Spree is the central station, **Berlin Hauptbahnhof** (Von Gerkan Marg, 2006; *see p302*), now Europe's largest rail intersection. The 321-metre (1,053-feet) east–west overground platforms are covered by a barrel vault of delicately gridded glass. This is crossed in a north–south direction by a station hall 180 metres (590 feet) long and 40 metres (131 feet) wide, which gives access to the trains on each intersecting level and to the shopping centre. Each side of the station hall is framed by buildings spanning the east–west vault. The building stands as a functional and symbolic link between East and West Germany, and as a hub of the whole European rail network.

The last 20 years have also produced work that has nothing to do with reunification. Daniel Libeskind's **Jüdisches Museum** (1999; *see p149*) in Kreuzberg is a symbolic sculpture in the form of a lightning bolt. Nicholas Grimshaw's **Ludwig-Erhard-Haus** for the stock exchange (1998; *see p181*) breaks with convention by taking the form of a glass and steel armadillo, though a city-required fire wall obscures the structure. Dominique Perrault's **Velodrom** (1997; Paul-Heyse-Strasse 26) sinks into the landscape in the form of a disc and a flat box of glass, concrete and gleaming steel mesh. Sauerbruch and Hutton's striking HQ for the **GSW** (1999; Kochstrasse 22A, Kreuzberg), with its translucent sailed top and colourful and constantly changing façade, shows how singular buildings can take the city's urban quality to the next level. Due to open in 2020, Berlin's next major architectural statement will be the **Axel Springer Campus**. Designed by OMA architects Rem Koolhaas, Chris van Duijn and Katrin Betschinger, the building will take up almost a whole block on Zimmerstrasse, with a series of terraced (and mirrored) floors forming the sides of a 'valley' round an open stage at the centre.

Plan

Accommodation	294
Getting Around	302
Resources A-Z	305
Vocabulary	312
Further Reading	313
Index	315

Accommodation

Berlin is the third most popular European tourist destination after London and Paris but, for now, remains one of the least expensive European cities in which to stay. The average price for a room here is €105 per night, compared to the European-wide average of €131. In other capital cities, it is normal to have to flash your cash in order to secure a half-decent hotel room, but Berlin actually rewards those who splash out a little more. By booking far enough in advance, it's possible to find high-quality affordable accommodation in the most desirable parts of town. And, after a day of graffiti-gazing and educational trips around museums with worrying names (looking at you, Topographie des Terrors), indulging a little with your lodgings may be just the ticket.

There are now so many places to choose from that hoteliers go the extra mile to stand out from the crowd: **Dude** near Heinrich-Heine Strasse has an all-day deli and a high-end steak restaurant; **Nhow** by the river in Friedrichshain attracts music-lovers with two recording studios and Gibson guitars available on room service, and the **Radisson Blu Hotel Berlin** has its own giant aquarium. On the luxury front, the **Adlon Kempinski** and the newer **Das Stue** steal the show, with extremely convenient central locations, but **Soho House** has secured itself an international hipster clientele by applying its studied vintage-chic aesthetic to an old Jewish department store with a swimming pool on the roof.

At the other end of the price spectrum, the city has an abundance of boutique hostels and budget hotels, offering arty DIY interiors at affordable prices: check out the **Circus Hostel** in Rosenthalerplatz and **Lekkerurlaub** in Graefekiez. Or, sleep in a vintage caravan parked in an old vacuum cleaner factory at the **Hüttenpalast** in Neukölln.

Das Stue

In the know
Price categories

Our price categories are based on the hotels' standard prices (not including seasonal offers or discounts) for one night in a double room with en suite shower/bath.

Luxury	above €190
Expensive	€120-€190
Moderate	€70-€120
Budget	under €70

Where to stay

Mitte, the city's historic administrative quarter, is thriving, with an ever-growing number of hotels in all price brackets. The post-Wall charm of one of the city's oldest quarters is popular with those looking for a weekend of gallery-hopping, boutique shopping, third-wave coffee sipping and sightseeing. **Tiergarten** has a few notable hotels dotting the edges of the park, alongside big modern embassies and a complex of cultural institutions. Further west, **Charlottenburg** is the smart end of town, loved by older visitors and fans of KaDeWe, and shunned almost entirely by the young and alternative. Here, five-star luxury hotels sit happily alongside traditional pensions housed in grand 19th-century Gründerzeit townhouses. **Schöneberg** is a very pleasant leafy area, full of cafés, restaurants and shops, but has a dearth of decent hotels. You're better off staying further east in **Kreuzberg**, the former heart of West Berlin's alternative scene, which offers all manner of accommodation options for a variety of visitors, from quietly luxurious hotels by the canal suitable for families and couples, to more lively party hostels around Schlesisches Tor, suitable for clubbers and singles. For all sorts of hip in-comers, **Neukölln** is the place to be in today's Berlin, thanks to its artisan espresso bars, late-night cocktail dens and living-room galleries. The influx of visitors has been met with a huge increase in sub-letting and Airbnb usage – much to the irritation of residents. Across the Spree, **Friedrichshain** hasn't quite become the city's new bohemia, but with decent transport connections, an 'Eastie' alternative feel and varied nightlife, it's a great area to stay in, especially if you're on a tight budget. **Prenzlauer Berg**, by contrast, has a lack of decent hotels, despite the number of daytime visitors it attracts.

In the know
Hotel breakfasts

Most hotels offer a breakfast buffet, which can be as simple as coffee, bread rolls (called *Schrippen* in Berlin), cheese and salami; or the full works, complete with smoked meats, muesli with fruit and yoghurt, and even a glass of sparkling wine. However, if breakfast is *not* included in the room rate, then make the most of Berlin's excellent cafes and eat your brunch elsewhere (*see p192* Berlin brunch).

Apartment Rentals

Suite dreams

Many Berliners rent out their rooms or whole apartments whenever they leave the city, which gives visitors weary of hotels a chance to live like a Berliner. In a city where much of interest lies in the residential areas, apartment rentals make a lot of sense.

The most popular online letting providers are Airbnb and WG-Gesucht. If you are watching your euros and are keen for an authentic Berlin experience, then try **WG-Gesucht** (www.wg-gesucht.de), which usually lists apartments for much the same price as the resident pays: around €20-€50 per night, depending on size and location. Bear in mind, however, that if you rent a room in a shared apartment, you'll be expected to act like a normal housemate, abiding by house rules and learning to navigate up to five different categories of bin for recycling!

Airbnb (www.airbnb.com) is a more straightforward option but is more expensive, though it still works out more affordable than a hotel or hostel with equivalent standards. The average Airbnb price for a double room in Berlin is €55 per night, rising closer to €100 for a small apartment. It's possible to find some gorgeous apartments for even less, if you book well ahead.

It's worth noting that Airbnb has a controversial history in Berlin, with many residents blaming the easy availability of short-term lets for the city's rising rents and housing crisis. In 2016 the city authorities tried to ban short-term letting for most landlords, with a €100,000 fine for transgressors, but the new regulations proved to be as effective as the smoking ban in Berlin bars – that is to say, not at all. In March 2018, the city agreed a compromise: landlords are now permitted to let out their own apartments as much as they want, but second homes can only be let out for 90 days a year, subject to a permit from the local borough. The fine for breaking these new rules is €500,000 – essentially meaning most landlords would have to sell a property to pay the fine.

Serviced apartments are another great alternative to the hotel hustle for families or longer-term visitors. Try **Miniloft Mitte** (Hessische Strasse 5, Mitte, 847 1090, www.miniloft.com), whose modern, airy flats and studios are housed in a renovated apartment building with an award-winning steel/concrete extension designed by the architect-owners. Alternatively, you can stay in an apartment block that was once a KGB listening post: **Lux 11** (Rosa-Luxemburg-Strasse 9-13, Mitte, 936 2800, www.lux-eleven.com) is a stylish, no-nonsense apartment-hotel with an emphasis on well-being and a prime location in Mitte.

Prices and information

Hotels are graded according to an official star rating system – but we haven't followed it in this guide, as the ratings merely reflect room size and amenities, such as lifts or bars, rather than other important factors such as decor, staff or atmosphere. Instead, we've listed our accommodation selections in four price categories (*see 294* In the know).

Many of the larger hotels refuse to publish any rates at all, depending instead on direct booking over the internet (often at a discount), which enables them to vary their prices daily. In addition to the hotels' own websites, check out discount specialists such as www.expedia.com, www.hotels.com and booking.com.

It's wise to reserve in advance whenever possible, especially for weekend stays in Mitte, and always check the cancellation policy before you book. VisitBerlin (2500 2333, www.visitberlin.de) can sort out hotel reservations, tickets for shows and travel arrangements to Berlin.

Note that tourists pay an additional room tax of five per cent per night up to 21 successive days; business travellers are exempt but have to prove they're in Berlin for work.

Nhow

Luxury

Although Berlin's hotels are comparatively cheap, the standards of luxury accommodation in the capital rival any other major European city. The flashy **Ritz-Carlton** (Potsdamer Platz 3, 337 777, www.ritzcarlton.com), elegant **Grand Hyatt** (Marlene-Dietrich-Platz 2, 2553 1234, www.berlin.grand.hyatt.com) and the **Waldorf Astoria** (Hardenbergstrasse 28, Charlottenburg, 814 0000, www.waldorfastoriaberlin.com) all offer the facilities and service expected of these premium chains.

Adlon Kempinski Berlin

Unter den Linden 77, Mitte (226 10, www.hotel-adlon.de). U6 Französische Strasse, or S1, S2, S25 Brandenburger Tor. Map p68 M7.

Not quite the Adlon of yore, which burned down after World War II, this new, more generic luxury version was rebuilt by the Kempinski Group in 1997 on the original site next to the Brandenburg Gate. Apart from a few original features, you're really paying for the prime location and the superlative service: bellboys who pass you a chilled bottle of water when you return from a jog in nearby Tiergarten; as well as dining at Thai concept restaurant Sra Bua by Tim Raue or the extremely formal Lorenz Adlon Esszimmer, which has two Michelin stars. If you want to rent out one of the three bulletproof presidential suites (from where Michael Jackson once dangled his child), it will set you back around €15,000, but you do at least get a 24-hour private butler and limousine for your money.

Hotel de Rome

Behrenstrasse 37, Mitte (460 6090, www.roccofortehotels.com). U6 Französische Strasse. Map p68 N7.

This 19th-century mansion was originally built to house the headquarters of Dresdner Bank, but was transformed into a sumptuous hotel by Rocco Forte in 2006. Despite the intimidating grandeur, the young staff are approachable and friendly. All 146 rooms push the limits of taste, with plenty of polished wood, marble and velvet. The former basement vault houses a pool, spa and fully equipped gym. The lobby restaurant, La Banca, specialises in upscale Mediterranean cuisine with alfresco dining in the summer; cocktails and lighter fare are available at the Rooftop Terrace or the Opera Court, where high tea is served every afternoon.

Mandala

Potsdamer Strasse 3, Tiergarten (590 05 1221, www.themandala.de). U2, S1, S2, S25 Potsdamer Platz. Map p100 L8.

This privately owned addition to the Design Hotels portfolio is, given the address, an oasis of calm, luxury and taste. The 144 rooms and suites, most of which face onto an inner courtyard, are perfectly designed for space and light, decorated in warm white and beige, with comfortable minimalist furnishings and TVs. A sheltered path through the Japanese garden on the fifth floor leads to Facil, an ultra-modern restaurant with two Michelin stars. The Qiu lounge offers lighter fare, and the rooftop spa, windowed from end to end, offers spectacular city views. Reduced rates are available for longer stays.

Patrick Hellmann Schlosshotel

Brahmsstrasse 10, Grunewald, West of the Centre (895 8430, www.schlosshotelberlin.com). S7 Grunewald. Map p197.

Designed down to the dust ruffles by Karl Lagerfeld, this restored 1914 villa on the edge of Grunewald is a luxury escape of which mere mortals can only dream. There are 12 suites and 54 rooms, with elegant marble bathrooms, a limousine and butler service, and well-trained staff to scurry after you. R&R is well-covered too, with a swimming pool, a golf course, tennis courts and two restaurants (with summer dining on the lawn, of course). This is a beautiful place in a beautiful setting, but so exclusive that it might as well be on another planet. It's worth checking the internet for deals, nonetheless.

Sofitel Berlin Gendarmenmarkt

Charlottenstrasse 50-52, Mitte (203 750, www.sofitel.com). U2, U6 Stadtmitte. Map p68 N7.

'Design for the senses' is the motto here. This is a truly lovely hotel, and rooms are often difficult to come by, but it's well worth the fight. So much attention has been paid to the details: from the moment you enter the lobby, with its soothing colour scheme and wonderful lighting, the atmosphere is intimate and elegant. This carries into the rooms, each beautifully styled, with perhaps the best bathrooms in the city. Even the conference rooms are spectacular, and the hotel's 'wellness' area includes plunge pools, a gym and a meditation room. In summer, you can wind down on the sun deck, which perches high above the surrounding rooftops overlooking the splendid domed cathedrals of Gendarmenmarkt.

Das Stue

Drakestrasse 1, Tiergarten (311 7220, www.das-stue.com). S3, S5, S7, S9 Tiergarten. **Map** *p100 H8.*
The hippest member of Berlin's luxury hotel family, Das Stue is located in the 1930s Royal Danish Embassy, restored to its former splendour by Spanish designer Patricia Urquiola. There's a long list of reasons to stay at this Design Hotel, including a pearl-white spa, rooms overlooking the Tiergarten, the original three-storey library, and the Michelin-starred Cinco restaurant (*see p110*), with a menu provided by superstar Catalan chef Paco Pérez. The central location means it's a short walk to most of Berlin's major sights. Some rooms overlook Berlin Zoo, with binoculars provided for close-up views of your four-legged neighbours.

Expensive

Reliable chain choices in this price bracket include **Bristol Berlin** (Kurfürstendamm 27, Charlottenburg, 884 340, www.bristolberlin.com); **Radisson Blu Hotel Berlin** (Karl-Liebknecht-Strasse 3, Mitte, 238 280, www.radissonblu.com/hotel-berlin) and **Sofitel Berlin Kurfürstendamm** (Augsburger Strasse 41, Charlottenburg, 800 9990, www.sofitel.com).

25hours Hotel Bikini Berlin

Budapester Strasse 40, Charlottenburg (120 2210, www.25hours-hotels.com). U2, U9, S3, S5, S7, S9 Zoologischer Garten. **Map** *p178 G8.*

You'll find a 149-room branch of Design Hotels' funky 25hours brand located inside the Bikini Berlin 'concept' shopping mall (*see p180*) that adjoins the Tiergarten. The design is a blend of exposed brick and industrial lighting, softened by plenty of greenery and brightly coloured furnishings. There's great attention to detail, including window-side hammocks, free Mini rental and a fab Middle Eastern restaurant, Neni (*see p183*).

Art Nouveau Berlin

Leibnizstrasse 59, Charlottenburg (327 7440, www.hotelartnouveau.de). U7 Adenauerplatz, or S3, S5, S7, S9 Savignyplatz. **Map** *p178 E9.*
This is one of the most charming small hotels in Berlin. The rooms are decorated with flair, in a mix of Conran-modern and antique furniture, each with an enormous black and white photo hung by the bed. The en suite bathrooms are cleverly integrated into the rooms without disrupting the elegant townhouse architecture. Even the TVs are stylish. The breakfast room has a fridge full of goodies, should you feel peckish in the wee hours, and the staff are sweet.

Dormero Hotel Berlin Ku'damm

Eislebener Strasse 14, Wilmersdorf (214 050, www.dormero.de). U1, U9 Kurfürstendamm, or U3 Augsburger Strasse. **Map** *p178 G9.*
Tucked down a quiet street behind KaDeWe, this hotel offers modern luxury without the stuffiness. Staff are friendly, and the 72 rooms, all done out in a contemporary-elegant style, are warm and relaxing. There's a beautiful Japanese garden in the middle, surrounded by individually decorated salons available for meetings and special occasions. The Quadriga restaurant serves steaks and bistro fare.

Ellington

Nürnberger Strasse 50-55, Charlottenburg (683 150, www.ellington-hotel.com). U1, U2, U3 Wittenbergplatz, or U3 Augsburger Strasse. **Map** *p178 H9.*

This is one of the classiest, most sophisticated joints in Berlin. Hidden within the shell of a landmark art deco dance hall, it combines cool contemporary elegance with warmth and ease. The rooms, mostly white with polished wood accents, are brilliantly simple, with modern free-standing fixtures and half-walls, instilling absolute calm behind the original double windows. The staff are helpful and remarkably cheerful given the daft flat caps they're made to wear. An ambitious menu is served in the Duke restaurant, and there are Sunday jazz brunches in the central courtyard. All this and KaDeWe round the corner… the Duke himself would have been proud.

Garden Boutique Hotel

Invalidenstrasse 122, Mitte (2844 5577, www.honigmond.de). U6 Oranienburger Tor. **Map** *p68 M4.*
Along with its nearby sister Honigmond Boutique Hotel, this 20-room guesthouse is enchanting, and it doesn't cost an arm and a leg. Choose between large bedrooms facing the street, smaller ones overlooking the fish pond and Tuscan-style garden, or spacious apartments on the upper floor. As with all great places, the secret is in the finer detail. The rooms are impeccably styled with polished pine floors, paintings in massive gilt frames, antiques and iron bedsteads. There's also a charming sitting room over-looking the garden. Highly recommended. **Other location** Honigmond Boutique Hotel, Tieckstrasse 11 (284 4550).

Soho House

Torstrasse 1, Mitte (405 0440, www.sohohouseberlin.com). U2 Rosa-Luxemburg-Platz. **Map** *p68 P5.*
The average Berliner has a healthy scepticism for anything 'private' or 'exclusive', so eyebrows were raised when Soho House opened its branch in the German capital in 2010. But even the toughest critic would have to admit that the imposing Bauhaus building and its history deserved a new lease of life; it originally housed a Jewish-owned department store

ACCOMMODATION

before it was taken over, first by the Nazis, then by the Communist regime. These days, Soho House occupies eight floors; in addition to 65 guest rooms, there are 20 apartments and four lofts, plus the excellent Cowshed spa, a library and a cinema. Two floors are given over to the The Store Berlin, Soho House's carefully curated shopping experience (*see p53*), where you'll find Cecconi's restaurant, serving northern Italian cuisine, and The Store Kitchen, which offers lighter fare throughout the day. In the rooms, beautiful old wooden floors and 1920s furniture mix with raw concrete walls. There's a touch of Britishness too, with a kettle and biscuits in each room, all of which combines to create a sense of *Gemütlichkeit* (cosy homeliness). A swim in the rooftop pool overlooking east Berlin rounds off the experience.

Moderate

Other good options include the **Circus Hotel** (*see p301*) and the **Monbijou Hotel** (www. monbijouhotel.com), both in Mitte's Scheunenviertel.

Almodovar Hotel
Boxhagener Strasse 83, Friedrichshain (692 097 080, www.almodovarhotel.com). U5 Samariterstrasse. **Map** *p132 V8.*
This boutique hotel is 'Berlin' through and through: fully vegetarian, with organic products in the rooms and even a complimentary yoga mat. Rooms are bright and spacious, and the penthouse suite even boasts its own sauna – but there's also a spa with ayurvedic treatments that's available to all guests. The lovely rosewood furniture was sustainably made specifically for the hotel.

Art'otel Berlin Mitte
Wallstrasse 70-73, Mitte (240 620, www.artotels.de). U2 Märkisches Museum. **Map** *p68 P7.*
A real gem on the Spree. This delightful hotel is a creative fusion of old and new, combining restored rococo reception rooms with ultra-modern bedrooms

designed by Nalbach & Nalbach. As well as highlighting the artwork of George Baselitz – originals hang in the corridors and all 109 rooms – the hotel's decor has been meticulously thought out to the smallest detail, from the Philippe Starck bathrooms to the Breuer chairs in the conference rooms. Staff are pleasant, and the views from the top suites across Mitte are stunning.

Bleibtreu by Golden Tulip
Bleibtreustrasse 31, Charlottenburg (884 740, www. bleibtreu.com). U1 Uhlandstrasse, or S3, S5, S7, S9 Savignyplatz. **Map** *p178 F9.*
The Bleibtreu is a friendly, smart and cosy establishment popular with the media and fashion crowds. Although on the smaller side, the rooms are very modern and decorated with environmentally sound materials. Private massages are offered, as well as reflexology, making it a wonderful choice for the health-conscious, but good service and plenty of pampering mean it should appeal to anyone.

Dude
Köpenicker Strasse 92, Mitte (411 988 177, www.thedudeberlin.com). U8 Heinrich-Heine-Strasse. **Map** *p68 P7.*
Housed in an elegant 19th-century townhouse, this 27-room boutique hotel was created by an advertising executive to provide a humorous antidote to identikit hotels. There are a number of house rules – including no photography and no large groups – to help foster an atmosphere of anything-goes discretion. The rooms are quite stark, with brass beds offset by block-coloured walls, and there are Molton Brown goodies in the bathroom. Breakfast is served in the all-day deli, and the high-end steak restaurant, The Brooklyn, specialises in rare whiskies and Napa Valley wines.

Hotel Pension Funk
Fasanenstrasse 69, Charlottenburg (882 7193, www. hotel-pensionfunk.de). U1 Uhlandstrasse. **Map** *p178 G9.*

In the area around the Gedächtniskirche, not a lot is left of the charm and glamour that made the Ku'damm the most legendary street of pre-war Berlin. That makes this wonderful pension, which is hidden away on a quiet side street, a real find. The house, built in 1895, used to be home to the Danish silent movie star Asta Nielsen and has been lovingly restored, with elegant dark wood furniture and art deco detailing. The owner has done his best to make the bathrooms match modern standards without destroying the overall feel – one is hidden inside a replica wardrobe – but some fall slightly short of the quality you would expect from a newer hotel. However, the very reasonable prices and spotless surroundings make up for this. And the breakfast, served in the cosy dining room, is as good as anywhere more expensive.

Michelberger
Warschauer Strasse 39-40, Friedrichshain (2977 8590, www. michelbergerhotel.com). U1, S3, S5, S7, S9 Warschauer Strasse. **Map** *p132 T8.*
With its purposefully unfinished look and effortlessly creative vibe, Michelberger might seem like Berlin in a nutshell to some. While the cheaper rooms are characterised by a stylish simplicity reminiscent of a school gym, the pricier rooms have an air of tongue-in-cheek decadence – decked out in gold from floor to ceiling or in the style of a mountain resort – complete with sunken bathtubs and movie projectors. Michelberger might not be as spick and span as other hotels, but it's much more fun. The downside of the convenient location (right across from Warschauer Strasse U-Bahn station) is that some rooms are quite noisy; the quieter ones face the courtyard.

Nhow
Stralauer Allee 3, Friedrichshain (290 2990, www.nhow-hotels.com). U1, S3, S5, S7, S9 Warschauer Strasse. **Map** *p132 T9.*
If you're allergic to pink, you'd be well advised to check in

300

elsewhere. New York designer Karim Rashid opened his eye-popping style and lifestyle hotel in a huge modern building right by the River Spree. Even the elevators are illuminated by different coloured lights, and some are decorated with photos of Rashid and his wife. As you'd expect from a music hotel with its own music manager, all rooms are equipped with iPod docking stations, and if you're in the mood for a spontaneous jam, you can order a Gibson guitar or an electric piano up to your room. More dedicated musicians can make use of the rehearsal rooms and two recording studios, or perform at one of the rooftop gigs and parties. As you can imagine, open mic night here is superb. The river view is beautiful, and the breakfast buffet leaves no wish unfulfilled. There's a pleasant sauna too.

Budget
The Circus Hostel
Weinbergsweg 1A, Mitte (2000 3939, www.circus-berlin.de). U8 Rosenthaler Platz. **Map** *p68 O4.*
Almost the standard by which other hostels should be measured, the Circus is a rarity – simple but stylish, warm and comfortable. And the upper-floor apartments have balconies and lovely views. The laid-back staff can help get discount tickets to almost anything, or give directions to the best bars and clubs, of which there are plenty nearby. The place is deservedly popular and is always full, so be sure to book ahead. The breakfast buffets are bountiful, with an excellent choice of organic granolas, and useful things such as laptops are available to rent, as well as bikes, Segways and even electric motorbikes. There's a quiet bar downstairs which often hosts evening events, such as poetry readings, and offers home brews fresh from the Circus Hostel Brewing Co.

Just across the Platz, the owners also run the moderately priced **Circus Hotel** (Rosenthaler Strasse 1), whose 63 double rooms, each with private bath,

surround a central terraced winter garden and café run by breakfast food maestros Commonground. There are also serviced apartments nearby at Choriner Strasse 84.

Eastern Comfort
Mühlenstrasse 73, Friedrichshain (6676 3806, www.eastern-comfort. com). U1, S3, S5, S7, S9 Warschauer Strasse. **Map** *p132 S9.*
Berlin's 'hostel boat' is moored on the Spree by the East Side Hotel, across the river from Kreuzberg. The rooms – or, rather, cabins – are clean and fairly spacious (considering it's a boat), and all have their own shower and toilet. The four-person room can feel a little cramped, but if you need to get up and stretch there are two common rooms, a lounge and three terraces offering lovely river views. The owners have now done up a second boat, the **Western Comfort**, which is moored across the river on the Kreuzberg bank.

Heart of Gold Hostel Berlin
Johannisstrasse 11, Mitte (2900 3300, www.heartofgold-hostel.de). S1, S2, S25 Oranienburger Strasse. **Map** *p68 N5.*
The prime location aside (it's only 50m from Oranienburger Strasse), this member of the Backpacker Germany Network (www.backpacker-network.de) is loosely themed on Douglas Adams' *The Hitchhiker's Guide to the Galaxy*. Rooms are bright and cheerful, with parquet floors. Lockers are free; individual bathrooms and showers, and a keycard system guarantee security. The laundry is cheap, as are the shots in the bar; and with rentable 'Sens-O-matic' sunglasses and Squornshellous Zeta mattresses to help you recover, what more could a backpacker (or hitchhiker) need? Towels, of course, which are available for free at reception.

Hüttenpalast
Hobrechtstrasse 66, Neukölln (3730 5806, www.huettenpalast. de). U7, U8 Hermannplatz. **Map** *p166 R11.*
The Hüttenpalast (literally 'Cabin Palace') is a large hall that was once the factory floor of an old

vacuum cleaner company. Since 2011, it's been home to eight vintage caravans and three little cabins, each sleeping two people. It's set out like a mini indoor campsite, with separate male and female shower rooms and a tree in the middle. Each morning, guests emerge from their boltholes to discover the tree has borne fruit – well, little bags containing croissants. There's fresh coffee on hand and the streetfront café does an à la carte menu for those with particularly grumbling stomachs. Each caravan is different – Kleine Schwester (Little Sister) is decked out with white wood panelling and matching linen; the Herzensbrecher (Heartbreaker) has a domed metal ceiling; the Schwalbennest (Swallow's Nest) is big enough to squeeze in a table. If you're at all claustrophobic, the cabins, also unique in design and decoration, are slightly larger – and there are also regular loft-style hotel rooms of varying sizes.

Lekkerurlaub
Graefestrasse 89, Kreuzberg (177 257 7568, www.lekkerurlaub.de). U8 Schonleinstrasse. **No cards**. **Map** *p144 Q10.*
This charming bijou B&B is in one of the prettiest and buzziest bits of Kreuzberg, and it feels a little like staying at a chic but welcoming friend's place. Katrin, the host, goes out of her way to make you feel at home. Set on the ground floor of a typical Berlin tenement, the rooms are small but clean. Each room is unique and tastefully decorated, although two of the beds can only be reached by ladder, so avoid these if you're scared of heights. A generous breakfast is served up every morning, and the lovely café serves meals from 9am to 6pm; there are also dozens of bars and restaurants within a two-minute radius.

Getting Around

ARRIVING & LEAVING

By air

The new **Berlin Brandenburg Willy Brandt Airport (BER)** should have opened back in 2012, but current estimates suggest 2020 as the likely date (*see p34* **A Tale of Two Airports**). Until then, Berlin remains served by two airports, **Tegel** and **Schönefeld**, which are likely to cease operation when BER finally opens.

Flughafen Tegel (TXL)

Airport information 6091 1150, www.berlin-airport.de. **Open** *Terminal E 24hrs daily. All other terminals 4am-midnight daily.* **Map** *fold-out map C1.*

More upmarket scheduled flights from the likes of BA and Lufthansa, as well as new routes on discount airlines, use the compact Tegel airport, just 8km (5 miles) north-west of Mitte.

Buses 109 and **X9** (the express version) run via Luisenplatz and the Kurfürstendamm to Zoologischer Garten (also known as Zoo Station, Bahnhof Zoo or just Zoo) in western Berlin. Buses run every 5-15mins, and the journey takes 30-40mins. Tickets cost €2.80 (and can also be used on U-Bahn and S-Bahn services). At Zoo you can connect to anywhere in the city.

From the airport, you can also take bus 109 to Jacob-Kaiser-Platz U-Bahn (U7), or bus 128 to Kurt-Schumacher-Platz U-Bahn (U6), and proceed on the underground from there. One ticket (€2.80) can be used for the combined journey.

The **JetExpressBus TXL** is the direct link to Berlin Hauptbahnhof and Mitte. It runs from Tegel to Alexanderplatz, with useful stops at Beusselstrasse S-Bahn (connects with the Ringbahn),

Berlin Hauptbahnhof (regional and inter-city train services as well as the S-Bahn) and Unter den Linden S-Bahn (north and south trains on the S1 and S2 lines). The service runs every 10 or 20mins, 4.30am-12.30am (5.30am-12.30am at weekends) and takes 30-40mins; a ticket is €2.80.

A **taxi** to anywhere central will cost around €20-€25 and take 20-30mins.

Flughafen Schönefeld (SXF)

Airport information 6091 1150, www.berlin-airport.de. **Open** *24hrs daily.*

The former airport of East Berlin is 18km (11 miles) south-east of the city centre. It's small, and much of the traffic is to eastern Europe and the Middle East. Budget airlines from the UK and Ireland also use it – EasyJet flies in from Bristol, Gatwick, Glasgow, Liverpool, Luton and Manchester; Ryanair from Dublin, East Midlands, Edinburgh and Stansted.

Train is the best means of reaching the city centre. S-Bahn Flughafen Schönefeld is a 5-min walk from the terminal (a free S-Bahn shuttle bus runs every 10mins, 6am-10pm, from outside the terminal; at other times, bus 171 also runs to the station). From here, the **Airport Express regional train** (**RB7 / RB14**) runs to Mitte (25mins to Alexanderplatz), Berlin Hauptbahnhof (30mins) and Zoo (35mins) every half hour from 5am to 11.30pm. You can also take S-Bahn line S9, which runs into the centre every 20mins (40mins to Alexanderplatz, 50mins to Zoo), stopping at all stations along the way. The **S45** line from Schönefeld connects with the Ringbahn, also running every 20mins.

Bus X7, every 10 or 20mins, 4.30am-8pm, runs non-stop

from the airport to Rudow U-Bahn (U7), from where you can connect with the underground. This is a good option if you're staying in Kreuzberg, Neukölln or Schöneberg. When it's not running, bus 171 takes the same route.

Tickets from the airport to the city cost €3.40, and can be used on any combination of bus, U-Bahn, S-Bahn and tram.

A **taxi** to Zoo or Mitte is quite expensive (€30-€35) and takes around 45mins.

By rail

Berlin Hauptbahnhof

0180 699 6633, www.bahn.de. **Map** *p100 L5.*

Berlin's central station is the main point of arrival for all long-distance trains, with the exceptions of night trains from Moscow and Kiev, which usually start and end at Berlin Lichtenberg (S5, S7, S75).

Hauptbahnhof is inconveniently located in a no-man's land north of the government quarter, and is linked to the rest of the city by S-Bahn (S3, S5, S7, S9), and by the U55 underground line that runs to the Bundestag, though parts of this line are often shut for construction work. Eventually, the line will connect to the U5 at Alexanderplatz, via Museumsinsel and Unter den Linden, but not until at least 2019.

By bus

Zentraler Omnibus Bahnhof (ZOB)

Masurenallee 4-6, Charlottenburg (3010 0175, www.zob.berlin). **Open** *24 hrs daily.* **Map** *fold-out map B8.*

Buses arrive in western Berlin at the Central Bus Station, opposite the Funkturm and the ICC. From here, U-Bahn line U2 runs into the city centre. The area around the ZOB is quite barren of cafés, shops or even green spaces to pass the time, so don't arrive for your bus hours in advance.

PUBLIC TRANSPORT

Berlin is served by a comprehensive and interlinked network of buses, trains, trams and ferries. It's efficient and punctual, but not especially cheap.

The completion of the inner-city-encircling Ringbahn in 2002 reconnected the former East and West Berlin transport systems, though it can still sometimes be complicated travelling between eastern and western destinations. But services are usually regular and frequent, timetables can be trusted, and one ticket can be used for two hours on all legs of a journey and all forms of transport.

The Berlin transport authority, the BVG, operates bus, U-Bahn (underground) and tram networks, and a few ferry services on the outlying lakes. The S-Bahn (overground railway) is run by its own authority, but services are integrated within the same three-zone tariff system.

Information

The **BVG** website (www.bvg.de) has a wealth of information (in English) on city transport, and there's usually someone who speaks English at the 24-hour **BVG Call Center** (194 49). The **S-Bahn** has its own website at www.s-bahn-berlin.de.

The Liniennetz, a map of U-Bahn, S-Bahn, bus and tram routes for Berlin and Potsdam, is available free from info centres and ticket offices. It includes a city-centre map. A map of the U- and S-Bahn can also be picked up free at ticket offices or from the grey-uniformed *Zugabfertiger* – passenger-assistance personnel.

Fares & tickets

The bus, tram, U-Bahn, S-Bahn and ferry services operate on an integrated three-zone system. Zone A covers central Berlin, zone B extends out to the edge of the suburbs and zone C stretches into Brandenburg.

The basic single ticket is the €2.80 *Normaltarif* (zones A and B). Unless going to Potsdam or Flughafen Schönefeld, few visitors are likely to travel beyond zone B, making this in effect a flat-fare system.

Apart from the longer-term *Zeitkarten*, tickets for Berlin's public transport system can be bought from the yellow or orange machines at U- or S-Bahn stations, and by some bus stops. These take coins and sometimes notes, give change and have a limited explanation of the ticket system in English. You can often pay by card, but don't count on it (if you do, don't forget to collect your card – infuriatingly, the machines keep the card until all the tickets are printed, making it very easy to forget). An app, FahrInfo Plus, is also available for iOS and Android, which allows you to purchase and carry tickets on your smartphone; details on www.bvg.de/en/travel-information/mobile.

Once you've purchased your ticket, validate it in the small red or yellow box next to the machine, which stamps it with the time and date. (Tickets bought on trams or buses are usually already validated.)

There are no ticket turnstiles at stations, but if an inspector catches you without a valid ticket, you will be fined €60. Ticket inspections are frequent and are conducted while vehicles are moving by pairs of plain-clothes personnel.

Single ticket (Normaltarif)

Single tickets cost €2.80 (€1.70 6-14s) for travel within zones A and B, €3.10 (€2.20) for zones B and C, and €3.40 (€2.50) for all three zones. A ticket allows use of the BVG network for two hours, with as many changes between bus, tram, U-Bahn and

S-Bahn as necessary, travelling in one direction. A four-ticket option (4-Fahrten-Karte) is available for €9.

Short-distance ticket (Kurzstreckentarif)

The *Kurzstreckentarif* (ask for a *Kurzstrecke*) costs €1.70 (€1.30 reductions) and is valid for three U- or S-Bahn stops, or six stops on the tram or bus. No transfers allowed.

Day ticket (Tageskarte)

A *Tageskarte* for zones A and B costs €7 (€4.70 reductions), or €7.70 (€5.30) for all three zones. A day ticket lasts until 3am the morning after validating.

Longer-term tickets (Zeitkarten)

If you're in Berlin for a week, it makes sense to buy a *Sieben-Tage-Karte* ('seven-day ticket') at €30 for zones A and B, or €37.50 for all three zones (no reductions). A stay of a month or more makes it worth buying a *Monatskarte* ('month ticket'), which costs €81 for zones A and B, and €100.50 for all three zones.

▶ For details of tourist discount cards for public transport, sights and attractions, see p64.

U-Bahn

The U-Bahn network consists of ten lines and 170-plus stations. The first trains run shortly after 4am; the last between midnight and 1am, except on Fridays and Saturdays when most trains run all night at 15-min intervals. The direction of travel is indicated by the name of the last stop on the line.

S-Bahn

Especially useful in eastern Berlin, the S-Bahn covers long distances faster than the U-Bahn and is a more efficient means of getting to outlying areas. The Ringbahn, which circles central Berlin, was the final piece of the S-Bahn system to be renovated, though there are still disruptions here and there.

Buses

Berlin has a dense network of 150 bus routes, of which 54 run in the early hours. The day lines run from 4.30am to about 1am the next morning. Enter at the front of the bus and exit in the middle or at the back. The driver sells only individual tickets, but all tickets from machines on the U- or S-Bahn are valid. Most bus stops have clear timetables and route maps.

Trams

There are 21 tram lines (five of which run all night), mainly in the east, though some have been extended a few kilometres into the western half of the city, mostly in Wedding. Hackescher Markt is the site of the main tram terminus. Tickets are available from machines on the trams, at the termini and in U-Bahn stations.

Other rail services

Berlin is also served by the **Regionalbahn** ('regional railway'), which once connected East Berlin with Potsdam via the suburbs and small towns left outside the Wall. Run by **Deutsche Bahn** (www.bahn.de), it still circumnavigates the city. The website has timetable and ticket information in English.

Travelling at night

Berlin has a comprehensive *Nachtliniennetz* ('night-line network') that covers all parts of town, with more than 50 bus and tram routes running every 30mins between 12.30am and 4.30am.

Maps and timetables are available from BVG kiosks at stations, and large maps of the night services are found next to the normal BVG map on station platforms. Ticket prices are the same as during the day. Buses and trams that run at night have an 'N' in front of the number.

On all buses travelling through zones B and C after 8pm, the driver will let you off at any point along the route via the front door.

Truncated versions of U-Bahn lines U1, U2, U3, U5, U6, U7, U8 and U9 run all night on Fridays and Saturdays, with trains every 15mins. The S-Bahn also runs at 30-min intervals.

TAXIS

Berlin taxis are pricey, efficient and numerous. The starting fee is €3.90 and thereafter the fare is €2 per kilometre for the first seven kilometres, and €1.50 per kilometre thereafter. The rate remains the same at night. For short journeys, ask for a *Kurzstrecke* – up to two kilometres for €5, but only available when you've hailed a cab and not from taxi ranks. There is a €1.50 surcharge for payment by credit card; cabs are not obliged to accept credit card payments, so it's wise to have cash on hand.

Taxi stands are numerous, especially in central areas near stations and at major intersections. You can phone for a cab 24 hours daily on 261 026. Most firms can transport people with disabilities but require advance notice. If you want an estate car (station wagon), request a *combi*. As well as normal taxis, **Funk Taxi Berlin** (261 026) operates vans that can carry up to seven people (ask for a *grossraum Taxi*; same rates as for regular taxis) and has two vehicles for people with disabilities.

DRIVING

Despite some congestion, driving in Berlin presents few problems. Visitors from the UK and US should bear in mind that, in the absence of signs or other traffic signals, drivers must yield to traffic from the right, except at crossings marked by a diamond-shaped yellow 'priority' sign. Trams always have right of way. An *Einbahnstrasse* is a one-way street.

Breakdown services

ADAC *Bundesallee 29-30, Wilmersdorf (0180 222 2222). No cards. 24hr assistance for about €65/hr.*

Fuel stations

Aral
Holzmarktstrasse 12, Mitte (2472 0748). Open 24hrs daily. Map p178 Q7.
Kurfürstendamm 128, Wilmersdorf (8909 6972). Open 24hrs daily. Map p178 C10.
Skalitzer Strasse 26, Kreuzberg (6170 2190). Open 24hrs daily. Map p144 Q9.
Sonnenallee 113, Neukölln (681 1313). Open 24hrs daily. Map p166 S12.

Parking

Parking is usually metered in Berlin side streets (residents get an *Anwohnerplakette* pass), but spaces are hard to find. Buy a parking ticket from a nearby machine; if you don't have one, or park illegally, you risk getting your car clamped or towed.

There are long-term car parks at Schönefeld and Tegel airports, and there are many Parkgaragen and Parkhäuser (multi-storey and underground car parks) around the city, open 24 hours, that charge around €2/hr.

Vehicle hire

Car hire is not expensive and all major companies are represented in Berlin, with car hire desks at all the city's airports. Car- and moped-sharing services such as **DriveNow** (www.drive-now.com), **Ubeeqo** (www.ubeeqo.com), **car2go** (www.car2go.com) and **COUP** (www.joincoup.com) are increasingly popular.

CYCLING

See p65 Berlin by bike.

WALKING

Berlin is a good walking city, but it's spread out, and attempting to bridge the gaps between neighbourhoods on foot can mean walking long distances in 'dead zones' surrounded by giant warehouses and not much else. Mitte is pleasant to explore on foot, for example, but if you then want to check out Charlottenburg, you'll need to take a bus or train.

Resources A-Z

Travel Advice

For up-to-date information on travel to a specific country – including the latest on safety and security, health issues, local laws and customs – contact your home country government's department of foreign affairs. Most have websites with useful advice for would-be travellers.

AUSTRALIA
www.smartraveller.gov.au

CANADA
www.voyage.gc.ca

NEW ZEALAND
www.safetravel.govt.nz

REPUBLIC OF IRELAND
foreignaffairs.gov.ie

UK
www.fco.gov.uk/travel

USA
www.state.gov/travel

ACCIDENT & EMERGENCY

Emergency numbers

Ambulance *(Rettungsdienst)* 112
Emergency doctor *(Notarzt)* 112
Fire brigade *(Feuerwehr)* 112
Police *(Polizei)* 110

A&E departments

All hospitals have a 24-hr emergency ward; these are the most central:

Charité Universitätsmedizin *Charitéplatz, Schumannstrasse 20-21, Mitte (45050, www.charite. de). U6 Oranienburger Tor.* **Map** *p68 M6.*

St Hedwig Krankenhaus *Grosse Hamburgerstrasse 5, Mitte (23110, www.alexianer-berlin-hedwigkliniken.de). S5, S7, S75 Hackescher Markt, or S1, S2 Oranienburger Strasse.* **Map** *p68 O5.*

Vivantes Klinikum Am Urban *Dieffenbachstrasse 1, Kreuzberg (13010, www.vivantes.de/kau). U7 Südstern, or bus M41.* **Map** *p144 P10.*

ADDRESSES

In German addresses the house/building number follows the street name (eg Friedrichstrasse 21); numbers sometimes run up one side of the street and back down the other side. *Strasse*

(street) is often abbreviated to '*Str*' and is often appended to the street name rather than written separately. Within buildings: EG means *Erdgeschoss*, the ground floor; 1. OG (*Obergeschoss*) is the 1st floor; VH means *Vorderhaus*, or the front part of the building; HH means *Hinterhaus*, the part of the building off the *Hinterhof*, the 'back courtyard'; SF is *Seitenflügel*, stairs that go off to the side from the *Hinterhof*. In big, industrial complexes, Treppenhaus B, or sometimes just Haus B, would indicate a particular staircase off the courtyard.

AGE RESTRICTIONS

Age of sexual consent 16
Drinking alcohol 16 (beer/wine), 18 (hard liquor)
Driving 18
Smoking 18

ATTITUDE & ETIQUETTE

Be on time for your appointments (but not early) and shake hands when greeting someone you've just met. Germans, in general, and Berliners, in particular, have an undeserved reputation for being 'cold'; in fact, they're just culturally reserved and not particularly interested in small talk. The so-called *Berliner Schnauze* ('Berlin snout') is more than a dialect: it's a sense of humour, a set of mannerisms

and a brash, gruff style of conversation typically used by older Berliners.

If a German invites you ('*Ich lade dich ein.*') for dinner or a drink, it means that they expect to pay. Say a warm thank you and reciprocate later, rather than dancing around the issue, as you might in the US or UK.

CLIMATE

Berlin has a continental climate, which means that it's hot in summer and cold in winter. In Jan and Feb, the city often ices over. Spring begins in late Mar/early Apr. May and June are the most clement months. *See p28 When to Visit.*

CUSTOMS

EU nationals over 17 years of age can import limitless goods for personal use, if bought with tax paid on them at source. For non-EU citizens and for duty-free goods, the following limits apply:

• 200 cigarettes or 50 cigars or 250 grams of tobacco
• 1 litre of spirits (over 22 % by volume) or 2 litres of fortified wine (under 22% by volume)
• 4 litres of non-sparkling wine
• 16 litres of beer
• Other goods to the value of €300 for non-commercial use, up to €430 for air/sea travellers. Travellers should note that the import of meat, meat products, fruit, plants, flowers and protected animals is restricted and/or forbidden.

DISABLED ACCESS

Many but not all U-Bahn and S-Bahn stations have ramps and/or elevators for wheelchair access; the map of the transport network (*see fold-out map*) uses a wheelchair symbol to indicate which ones. Passengers in wheelchairs are required to wait at the front end of the platform to signal to the driver that they need to board; a folding ramp will be supplied. All bus lines and most tram lines are also wheelchair-accessible.

Public buildings and most of the city's hotels have disabled access. However, if you require more specific information about access, contact one of the following organisations:

Beschäftigungswerk des BBV *Weydemeyerstrasse 2A, Mitte (5001 9100, www.bbv-tours-berlin.de). U5 Schillingstrasse.* **Open** *8am-3.30pm Mon-Fri.* **Map** *p68 Q6.* The Berlin Centre for the Disabled provides legal and social advice, together with a transport service and travel information.

Touristik Union International *0511 5678 600, www.tui.com.* The TUI provides information on accommodation and travel in Germany for the disabled.

DRUGS

Berlin is relatively liberal in its attitude towards drugs. In recent years, possession of hash or grass has been effectively decriminalized; anyone caught with an amount under 10g is liable to have the stuff confiscated but can otherwise expect no further retribution. Joint smoking is tolerated in some of Berlin's more youthful bars and cafés – a quick sniff will tell whether you're in one. Anyone caught with small quanitities of hard drugs will net a fine but is unlikely to be incarcerated. For more on drugs and nightlife in Berlin, *see p246*. For **Drogen Notdienst** (emergency drug service), *see opposite*.

ELECTRICITY

Electricity in Germany runs on 230V, the same as British appliances. You will require an adaptor (G to F) to change the shape of the plug. US appliances (120V) require a voltage converter.

EMBASSIES & CONSULATES

Australian Embassy *Wallstrasse 76-79, Mitte (880 0880, www.germany.embassy.gov.au). U2 Märkisches Museum.* **Open** *8.30am-5pm Mon-Fri.* **Map** *p68 P7.*

British Embassy *Wilhelmstrasse 70, Mitte (204 570, www.gov.uk/ government/world/germany). S1, S2, S25 Brandenburger Tor.* **Open** *9.30am-noon Mon, Tue, Thur, Fri.* **Map** *p68 M7.*

Embassy of Canada *Leipziger Platz 17, Mitte (203 120, www.canadainternational.gc.ca/ germany-allemagne). U2, S1, S2, S25 Potsdamer Platz.* **Open** *9am-noon Mon-Fri.* **Map** *p100 M8.*

Embassy of Ireland *Jägerstrasse 51, Mitte (220 720, www.embassyofireland. de). U2, U6 Stadtmitte.* **Open** *9.30am-12.30pm Mon-Fri, by appointment only.* **Map** *p68 N7.*

New Zealand Embassy *Friedrichstrasse 60 (206 210, www.mfat.govt.nz). U2, U6 Stadtmitte.* **Open** *9.30am-1pm, 2-4pm Mon-Fri.* **Map** *p68 N7*

US Embassy *Clayallee 170, Zehlendorf (83050, visa enquiries 032 221 093 243, https:// de.usembassy.gov). U3 Oskar-Helene-Heim.* **Open** *US citizen services phoneline 2-3pm Mon-Thur. Visa enquiries phoneline 8am-8pm Mon-Fri. Adult passport walk-in service 12.30-3pm Mon, Fri.* **Map** *p197.* The main US embassy building is on Pariser Platz, next to the Brandenburg Gate, but consular services still operate out of the original embassy in Zehlendorf.

For all other embassies, see http://embassy.goabroad.com.

HEALTH

EU citizens who hold a **European Health Insurance Card** (EHIC) are entitled to free emergency medical care. Should you fall ill in Berlin, you can take your EHIC to any doctor (*see opposite*) or hospital emergency department (*see p305*) to get treatment. The EHIC doesn't cover all medical costs (dental treatment, for example), so private travel/medical insurance is recommended. In the UK, the EHIC is available by phoning 0300 330 1350 or online at www.ehic.org.uk; you'll need to provide your name, date of birth and national insurance number. **It is unclear whether UK citizens will still be eligible for an EHIC after Brexit in March 2019.** Citizens from non-EU countries should always take out private medical insurance before travelling.

Dentists
The English-language website **AllAboutBerlin** has an updated

Local Weather

Average monthly temperatures and rainfall in Berlin

	High (°C/°F)	Low (°C/°F)	Rainfall (mm/in)
January	2 / 36	-3 / 27	43 / 0.17
February	3 / 37	-2 / 28	38/ 0.15
March	8 / 46	0 / 32	38 / 0.15
April	13 / 55	4 / 39	43 / 0.17
May	18 / 64	8 / 46	56 / 0.22
June	22 / 72	11 / 52	71 / 0.28
July	23 / 73	13 / 55	53 / 0.21
August	23 / 73	12 / 54	66 / 0.26
September	18 / 64	9 / 48	46 / 0.18
October	13 / 55	6 / 43	36 / 0.14
November	7 / 45	2 / 36	51 / 0.20
December	3 / 37	-1 / 30	56 / 0.22

list of English-speaking dentists in the city at allaboutberlin.com/guides/list-of-english-speaking-dentists-in-berlin.

Doctors

The **Ärztlicher Bereitschaftsdienst** (emergency doctor's service, 116 117 specialises in dispatching doctors for house calls. Charges vary according to the treatment required.

The British Embassy (*see opposite*) has a list of English-speaking doctors and dentists, as well as lawyers and interpreters, although you'll find that most German doctors speak some English. Be sure to have either your EHIC or your private insurance documents at hand if seeking treatment. If you do wish to pay privately, just tell the receptionist '*ich möchte selbst bezahlen*' (I want to pay for myself). You'll typically need to have cash on hand; standard visits cost between €20 and €50. The doctors listed below speak excellent English.

HIV/AIDS

Berliner Aids-Hilfe (BAH) *Kurfürstenstrasse 130, Tiergarten (885 6400, advice line 19411, www.berliner-aidshilfe.de). U1, U2, U3, U4 Nollendorfplatz.* **Open** *noon-6pm Mon; noon-2.30pm Wed; noon-3pm Thur, Fri. Advice line noon-10pm Mon-Wed.* **Map** *p100 J9.* Information on all aspects of HIV and AIDS. Free consultations, condoms and lubricant are also provided.

Pharmacies

Prescription and non-prescription drugs (including aspirin) are sold only at pharmacies (*Apotheken*). You can recognise these by a red 'A' outside the front door. A list of the nearest pharmacies open on Sundays and in the evening should be displayed in the window of every pharmacy. A list of emergency pharmacies (*Notdienst-Apotheken*) is available online at www.akberlin.de/notdienst.

HELPLINES

Berliner Krisendiens *(Mitte, Friedrichshain, Kreuzberg, Tiergarten & Wedding 390 6310, Neukölln 390 6390, Charlottenburg & Wilmersdorf 390 6320, Prenzlauer Berg, Weissensee & Pankow 390 6340, Schöneberg, Tempelhof, Steglitz 390 6360, www.berliner-krisendienst.de).* **Open** *24hrs daily.* Help and/or counselling on a range of subjects. The phone lines, organised by district, are staffed 24hrs daily.

Drogen Notdienst *Genthiner Strasse 48 (office 233 240 100, hotline 19237, www.drogennotdienst.org). U1 Kurfürstenstrasse.* **Open** *8.30am-9pm Mon-Fri; 2-9pm Sat, Sun. Phone line 24hrs daily.* **Map** *p100 K9.* At the 'drug emergency service', no appointment is necessary if you're coming in for advice.

Frauenkrisentelefon *615 4243, www.frauenkrisentelefon.de.* **Open** *10am-noon Mon, Thur; 3-5pm Tue; 7-9pm Wed, Fri; 5-7pm Sat, Sun.* Offers advice and information for women, on anything and everything.

ID

By law you are required to carry some form of ID at all times, which, for UK and US citizens, means a passport. If police catch you without one, they may accompany you to wherever you've left it.

INSURANCE

EU nationals are entitled to reciprocal medical care in Germany (*see opposite*). Despite this provision, all foreign visitors are advised to take out private travel insurance to cover a wide range of eventualities from injury to theft. Non-EU citizens should always ensure that they take out comprehensive travel insurance with a reputable company before leaving home; make sure the cover includes medical costs (including repatriation if necessary), luggage, personal belongings and any activities that you wish to pursue while abroad.

LANGUAGE

English is widely spoken in Berlin; in parts of Kreuzberg, Neukölln, Prenzlauer Berg and Mitte, you will also hear French, Spanish, Turkish and Arabic on the streets. But, venture into less 'hip' districts and having a grasp of German becomes more essential. Take the time to learn a few key phrases (*see p312*). *Berlinerisch* can sound a bit harsher than other regional accents. You'll often hear the German '*ich*' ('I') changed to a hard '*ick*', hence the souvenir T-shirts reading '*Ick liebe Berlin*'.

LEFT LUGGAGE

Airports

There is a left-luggage office at Tegel (4101 2315; open 5am-10.30pm daily) and lockers at Schönefeld (in the Multi Parking Garage P4). See p302.

Rail & bus stations

There are left-luggage lockers at Bahnhof Zoo, Friedrichstrasse, Alexanderplatz, Potsdamer Platz, Ostbahnhof, Hauptbahnhof and Zentraler Omnibus Bahnhof (ZOB).

LEGAL HELP

If you get into legal difficulties, contact your embassy (*see opposite*): it can provide you with a list of English-speaking lawyers.

LGBT

See also p224 LGBT.

Help & information

Lesbenberatung *Kulmer Strasse 20A, Schöneberg (215 2000, www.lesbenberatung-berlin.de). U7, S2, S25 Yorckstrasse.* **Open** *2-5pm Mon, Wed, Fri; 10am-4pm Tue; 3-6.30pm Thur.* **Map** *p178 K10.* Counselling in all areas of queer/lesbian life, as well as self-help groups, courses, cultural events and an 'info-café'.

Mann-O-Meter *Bülowstrasse 106, Schöneberg (216 8008, www.mann-o-meter.de). U2, U3, U4 Nollendorfplatz.* **Open** *5-10pm Mon-Fri; 4-8pm Sat.* **Map** *p178 J9.*

Drop-in centre and helpline. Advice about AIDS prevention, jobs, accommodation and gay contacts, plus safer-sex materials. English spoken.

Schwulenberatung
*Niebuhrstrasse 59-60, Charlottenburg (2336 9070, www. schwulenberatungberlin.de). U7 Wilmersdorfer Strasse. **Open** 9am-8pm Mon-Fri. **Map** p178 E8.* Information and counselling about HIV and AIDS, crisis intervention and advice on all aspects of gay life.

LIBRARIES

Berlin has hundreds of *Bibliotheken/Büchereien* (public libraries). Anyone is free to browse, but to borrow books, you need an *Anmeldungsformular* ('certificate of registration'; *see p311*) and a passport.

Staatsbibliothek zu Berlin – Haus Potsdamer Strasse *Potsdamer Strasse 33, Tiergarten (266 433 888, http://staatsbibliothek-berlin. de). U2, S1, S2, S25 Potsdamer Platz. **Open** 9am-9pm Mon-Fri; 10am-7pm Sat. **Map** p100 L8.* Books in English on every subject are available at this branch of the state library.

Staatsbibliothek zu Berlin – Haus Unter den Linden *Dorotheenstrasse 27, Mitte (266 433 888, http:// staatsbibliothek-berlin. de). U6, S1, S2, S3, S5, S7, S9 Friedrichstrasse. **Open** 9am-9pm Mon-Fri; 10am-7pm Sat. **Map** p68 N6.* A smaller range of English books than the branch above, but it's still worth a visit, not least for the café.

LOST/STOLEN PROPERTY

If any of your belongings are stolen while in Berlin, you should go immediately to the police station nearest to where the incident occurred (*see opposite Police*) and report the theft. There you will be required to fill in report forms for insurance purposes. If you can't speak German, an interpreter will be provided free of charge.

If you leave something in a taxi, call the number that's on your receipt (if you remembered to ask for one), and quote the time of your journey, the 4-digit *Konzessions-Nummer* that will be stamped on the receipt, a contact phone number and details of the item you've lost. This information will be passed to the driver, who will call you if your property has been found.

For information about lost or stolen credit cards, *see opposite*.

BVG Fundbüro *Potsdamer Strasse 180, Schöneberg (194 49). U7 Kleistpark. **Open** 9am-6pm Mon, Tue, Thur; 9am-2pm Fri. **Map** p178 K10.* Contact this office if you have any queries about property lost on Berlin's public transport system. If you're robbed on one of their vehicles, you can ask about CCTV footage.

Zentrales Fundbüro *Platz der Luftbrücke 6, Tempelhof (902 773 101). U6 Platz der Luftbrücke. **Open** 9am-2pm Mon, Tue, Fri; 1-6pm Thur. **Map** p166 N12.* Central police lost-property office.

MEDIA

Foreign press

A wide variety of international publications are available at larger railway stations, **Internationale Presse** newsagents and at **Dussmann das KulturKaufhaus** (*see p83*). The monthly *Exberliner* magazine (*see below*) has listings, as well as articles on cultural and political topics in English.

Newspapers

Print media is alive and well in Berlin. As far as dailies go, the **Frankfurter Allgemeine Zeitung** (www.faz.net) is Germany's de facto newspaper of record, with stolid, exhaustive coverage, plus lots of analysis. **Die Welt** (www.welt.de), once a lacklustre mouthpiece of conservative, provincial thinking, has widened its political horizons, though it's still thought of as a yuppy paper. **Handelsblatt** (www.

handelsblatt.com) co-operates with the *Wall Street Journal*'s European offshoot, and **Bild** (www.bild.de) is the flagship tabloid of the Axel Springer group. All offer a modest amount of content in English on their websites.

For local-style Berlin coverage, there's the **Berliner Morgenpost** (www.morgenpost.de) as well as the **Tagesspiegel** (www. tagesspiegel.de) and the **Berliner Zeitung** (www.berliner-zeitung. de). Attempts at English are few are far between, even online.

Far better for English-speakers are **The Local** (www.thelocal. de), which does Berlin-centric news for an expatriate audience (though it newly requires a subscription), as well as the hard-hitting **Deutsche Welle** (www. dw.com) with its large online section of English-only content. **Die Zeit** (www.zeit.de) and **Der Spiegel** (www.spiegel.de) both offer English-speaking readers a good selection of well-translated articles, too.

Listings magazines

Berlin is awash with free listings magazines, notably **[030]** (www.berlin030.de) for music, nightlife, film; **Partysan** (www. partysan.net), a pocket-sized club guide, and their gay counterparts **Siegessaeule** (www.siegessaeule. de) and **Blu** (www.blu.fm). These can be picked up in bars and restaurants. Two newsstand fortnightlies, **Zitty** (www.zitty.de) and the glossier **Tip** (www.tip-berlin.de), come out on alternate weeks. **Exberliner** (www.exberliner. com), Berlin's current English-language monthly, is a lively mix of listings, reviews and commentary, mostly written by youngish American expats.

Radio

Some 29 stations compete for audiences in Berlin, but the two main stations in the city are **Berliner Rundfunk** (91.4) and **r.s.2** (94.3). Commercial stations **104.6 RTL** (104.6) and **Energy 103.4** (103.4) offer standard chart pop spiced with news. **RadioEins** (95.8) is the most adventurous, offering mostly new and old indie music, while **Fritz** (102.6) plays things a little safer. Jazz is round the clock on **Jazz Radio** (106.8). Information-based stations such as **Info Radio** (93.1) are increasing in popularity. The **BBC World Service** (90.2) is available 24hrs a day.

Television

Germany cabled up in the late 1970s, so there is no shortage of channels. But programming revolves around bland, mass-market entertainment, although political talk shows are pervasive and often very good. There are two national public networks, **ARD** and **ZDF**, a handful of no-holds-barred commercial channels and a load of special-interest channels. Channels broadcasting regularly in English include **CNN**, **NBC**, **MTV Europe** and **BBC World**. British or American films on ARD or ZDF are sometimes broadcast with a simultaneous soundtrack in English for stereo-equipped TV sets.

MONEY

One euro (€) is made up of 100 cents. There are 7 banknotes and 8 coins. The notes are: €5 (grey-green), €10 (red), €20 (blue), €50 (orange), €100 (green), €200 (yellow-brown), €500 (purple). The coins (€2, €1, 50 cents, 20 cents, 10 cents, 5 cents, 2 cents, 1 cent) vary in colour, size and thickness.

Compared to the rest of Germany, Berlin (and the East at large) is pretty affordable. It's still possible to eat a good lunch for €5, making Berlin miles cheaper than other Western European capitals, though prices are slowly creeping up. It's by no means difficult to have a major blow-out weekend in Berlin, but with a little effort, it's equally possible to stay here on a reasonable budget. Supermarkets are especially cheap.

ATMs

ATMs are found throughout the centre of Berlin and are the most convenient way of obtaining cash. Most major credit cards are accepted, as well as debit cards that are part of the Cirrus, Plus,

Star or Maestro systems. You will normally be charged a fee for withdrawing cash.

Banks & bureaux de change

Foreign currency and travellers' cheques can be exchanged in most banks. *Wechselstuben* (bureaux de change) are open outside normal banking hours and give better rates than banks, where changing money often involves long queues. The *Wechselstuben* of the Reisebank offer good exchange rates, and can be found at the bigger train stations.

Credit & debit cards

In general, German banking and retail systems are less enthusiastic about credit than their UK or US equivalents, though this is gradually changing. Many Berliners prefer to use cash for most transactions, although larger hotels, shops and restaurants usually accept major credit and debit cards. Contactless payment is virtually unheard of in Berlin for the moment but looks likely to become 'a thing' at younger joints in coming years.

If you want to draw cash on your credit card, some banks will give an advance against Visa and MasterCard cards. However, you may not be able to withdraw less than the equivalent of US$100. A better option is using an ATM.

Lost/stolen cards

If you've lost a credit/debit card, or had one stolen, phone your bank and/or the relevant 24-hr emergency number:

American Express *069 9797 2000.*
Diners Club *069 900 150 135.*
Mastercard *0800 819 1040.*
Visa *0800 811 8440.*

Tax

Non-EU citizens can claim back German value-added tax (*Mehrwertsteuer or MwSt*) on goods purchased in the country, although it's only worth the hassle on sizeable purchases. Ask the shop to provide a Tax-Free Shopping Cheque for the amount of the refund and present this,

with the receipt, at the airport's refund office before checking in.

OPENING HOURS

Most **banks** are open 9am-noon and 1-3pm or 2-6pm Mon-Fri.

Shops can stay open 6am-10pm, except on Sun and hols, though few take full advantage of the fact. Big stores tend to open at 9am and close between 8pm and 10pm. Most smaller shops will close around 6pm. An increasing number of all-purpose neighbourhood 'late shops' (*Späti*) stay open until around midnight. Many Turkish shops are open on Sat afternoons and 1-5pm Sun. Many bakers open to sell cakes 2-4pm Sun.

The opening times of **bars** vary, but many are open during the day, and most stay open until at least 1am, if not through until morning.

Most **post offices** are open 8am-6pm Mon-Fri and 8am-1pm Sat.

POLICE STATIONS

You are unlikely to come into contact with the *Polizei* unless you commit a crime or are the victim of one. There are few patrols or traffic checks.

The central police HQ is at Platz der Luftbrücke 6, Tempelhof (46640); other police stations are listed online at www. berlin.de/polizei/dienststellen/polizei-in-den-bezirken/). Police will be dispatched from the appropriate office if you dial 46640. For emergencies, dial 110.

POSTAL SERVICES

For non-local mail, use the *Andere Richtungen* ('other destinations') slot in postboxes. Letters of up to 20g to anywhere in Germany cost €0.70. For postcards it's €0.45. For anywhere outside Germany, a 20g airmail letter or postcard costs €0.90.

Postamt Friedrichstrasse
*Georgenstrasse 14-18, Mitte (0228 4333 112). U6, S1, S2, S3, S5, S7, S25, S9 Friedrichstrasse. **Open** 6am-10pm Mon-Fri; 8am-10pm Sat, Sun. **Map** p166 N6. This branch inside Friedrichstrasse*

station keeps the longest opening hours of the Berlin offices.

Poste restante

Poste restante facilities are available at the main post offices of each district. Address them to the recipient 'Postlagernd', followed by the address of the post office, or collect them from the counter marked *Postlagernde Sendungen*. Take your passport with you.

PUBLIC HOLIDAYS

On public holidays (*Feiertagen*) it can be difficult to get things done in Berlin. However, most cafés, bars and restaurants stay open – except on Christmas Eve, when almost everything closes.

New Year's Day Neujahr *1 Jan*
Good Friday Karfreitag *Mar/Apr*
Easter Monday Oster Montag *Mar/Apr*
May Day Tag der Arbeit *1 May*
Ascension Day Christi Himmelfahrt *May/June*
Whit Monday Pfingstmontag *May/June*
Day of German Unity Tag der deutschen Einheit *3 Oct*
Christmas Day Erster Weihnachtstag *25 Dec*
Boxing Day Zweiter Weihnachtstag *26 Dec*

RELIGION

More than 60% of today's Berliners have no registered religious affiliation. That said, there are dozens of places of worship scattered throughout the city and sizable communities of Protestant, Roman Catholic and Orthodox Christians, as well as one of the fastest-growing Jewish communities in Europe. Mitte's Neue Synagoge (new synagogue) is an important architectural and religious landmark. There are more than 80 mosques in Berlin catering to the city's significant Muslim population, including Neukölln's Sehitlik Mosque, which can hold up to 1,500 people. Germany's first Buddhist monastery is located in the northern district of Reinickendorf.

SAFETY & SECURITY

In 2018, Berlin's crime rate was on the decline. Most central areas of the city are safe even at night, as long as you use common sense, although pickpockets are not unknown around tourist areas and Alexanderplatz becomes something of a crime hotspot after dark. Visitors who are obviously gay or non-German should avoid the poorer suburbs to the east of the city where right-wing extremism is prevalent. For the police, *see p309*.

SMOKING

Many Berliners smoke, though the habit is in decline. Smoking is banned on public transport, in theatres and many public institutions. Many bars and restaurants have closed-off smoking rooms. Smaller, one-room establishments may allow smoking but must post a sign outside denoting their status as a *Raucherkneipe* (smoker pub). There are no restrictions on smoking at outside tables, which are well used, even in winter.

STUDY

Language classes

Goethe-Institut *Neue Schönhauser Strasse 20, Mitte (259 063, www.goethe.de). U8 Weinmeisterstrasse, or S3, S5, S7, S9 Hackescher Markt.* **Map** *p68 O5.* Although considerably more expensive than most of its competitors, the Goethe-Institut offers the most systematic and intensive language courses in the city with extra-curricular conversation classes, as well as regular cinema, theatre and museum visits.

Tandem *Bötzowstrasse 26, Prenzlauer Berg (441 3003, www.tandem-berlin.de). U2 Eberswalder Strasse.* **Map** *p116 R4.* For a €5 administrative fee, Tandem will put you in touch with German speakers interested in conversation exchange. Formal language classes are also available at €370 a month.

Universities

Freie Universität Berlin FU *Kaiserswerther Strasse 16-18, Dahlem (information 8381, www.fu-berlin.de). U3 Dahlem-Dorf.* **Map** *p197.* Germany's largest university was founded in 1948, after the Humboldt fell under East German control. Centre of the 1969 student movement, the FU was for a long time a hotbed of left-wing dissent but lost much of its prestige to its rival following reunification.

Humboldt-Universität zu Berlin (HUB) *Unter den Linden 6, Mitte (20930, www.hu-berlin.de). U6, S1, S2, S3, S5, S7, S25, S9 Friedrichstrasse.* **Map** *p68 N6.* Humboldt was founded in 1810 by the humanist Willem von Humboldt. Georg Hegel, Arthur Schopenhauer, Albert Einstein, Werner Heisenberg and Max Planck all taught there, and Karl Marx and Heinrich Heine are among the many alumni. The HU entered a dark period in the 1930s, when professors and students joined enthusiastically in the Nazi book-burning on Bebelplatz. After 1945, the university fell into decline under Communism, but since 1989, it has regained much of its former reputation.

Technische Universität Berlin (TU) *Strasse des 17 Juni 135, Charlottenburg (3140, www.tu-berlin.de). U2 Ernst-Reuter-Platz.* **Map** *p178 F7.* The TU began life in 1879 and is strong in chemistry, engineering and architecture. Under the Nazi government it was allocated more funds than any other university in the country. After the war, the TU reopened and expanded to include philosophy, psychology and the social sciences. It is now one of Germany's largest universities. Its **Sprach- und Kulturbörse** (Raum 024, Hardenbergstrasse 36, Charlottenburg, 3147 3224, www.skb.tu-berlin.de) is a language and cultural exchange programme for foreign students at any university in the city.

Universität der Künste Berlin (UdK) *Hardenbergstrasse 33, Charlottenburg (31850, www.*

udk-berlin.de). *U2, U9, S3, S5, S7, S9 Zoologischer Garten.* **Map** *p178 F8.* Formerly the Hochschule der Künste (a name most Berliners still use), this was founded in 1975 to combine the former Colleges of Art, Drama, Music and Printing. The range of subjects has been broadened over the years to include everything from fashion design to experimental film and media.

TELEPHONES

Dialling & codes

All phone numbers in this guide are local Berlin numbers (other than those for Potsdam in the West of the Centre chapter, which begin 0331); if you're dialing from *outside* Berlin, you will need to add the code for the city (030). Numbers beginning 0180 have higher tariffs, and numbers beginning 015, 016 or 017 are for mobile phones.

To phone Berlin from abroad, dial the international access code (00 from the UK, 011 from the US, 0011 from Australia), then 49 (for Germany) and 30 (for Berlin), followed by the local number. To phone another country from Germany, dial 00, then the relevant country code: Australia 61; Canada 1; Ireland 353; New Zealand 64; United Kingdom 44; United States 1. Then, dial the local area code (minus the initial zero) and the local number.

Public phones

Most public phones give you the option of cards or coins, and from Telekom phones (the ones with the magenta 'T') you also can send SMSs. Phonecards can be bought at post offices and newsagents for various sums from €5 to €50.

Operator services

For online directory enquiries, go to www.teleauskunft.de.

International directory enquiries *118 34.*
Operator assistance/German directory enquiries *118 33 (118 37 in English).*
Phone repairs *080 0330 2000.*
Time *0180 4100 100 (automated, in German).*

Mobile phones

Check with your service provider about service provision and roaming charges while you're in Germany, though those with service in the EU should automatically have service in Germany. US mobile phone users should also check their mobile/cell's compatibility with GSM bands. German SIM cards can be purchased easily enough from supermarkets or corner internet shops. (We recommend the latter, as the personnel can help with set-up.) A typical starter pack costs around €15 and comes with an adequate amount of SMS, calls and data, which can be topped up if necessary.

TIME

Germany is on Central European Time, which is 1hr ahead of Greenwich Mean Time. During summer 'daylight saving time', Germany is 2hrs ahead of Greenwich Mean Time, which means, in effect, that Berlin is 1hr ahead of London throughout the year; 6hrs ahead of New York; 9hrs ahead of San Francisco, and 9hrs behind Sydney. Germany uses a 24-hr system. 8am is '8 Uhr' (usually written 8h), noon is '12 Uhr Mittags' or just '12 Uhr', 5pm is '17 Uhr' and midnight is '12 Uhr Mitternachts' or just 'Mitternacht'.

TIPPING

A 10% service charge is included in restaurant bills, but it's common to leave a small tip too. In a taxi, round up the bill to the nearest euro.

TOILETS

Coin-operated, self-cleaning 'City Toilets' are becoming the norm. The toilets in main stations are looked after by an attendant and are pretty clean. Restaurants and cafés have to let you use their toilets by law, and they can't refuse you a glass of water either.

TOURIST INFORMATION

EurAide *DB Reisezentrum, Hauptbahnhof, Tiergarten (www.euraide.de). S5, S7, S75*

Hauptbahnhof. **Open** *Mar, Apr 11am-7pm Mon-Fri. May-July 10am-8pm Mon-Fri. Aug-Oct 10am-7pm Mon-Fri. Nov 11am-6.30pm Mon-Fri. Dec 10am-7.30pm Mon-Fri.* **Map** *p100 L5.* Staff advise on sights, hostels, tours and transport, and sell rail tickets.

VisitBerlin *2500 2323, www.visitberlin.de.* Berlin's official (if private) tourist organisation has information points at Kurfürstendamm 22, Charlottenburg; Brandenburg Gate; Hauptbahnhof (ground floor, Europaplatz exit); Tegel Airport (next to gate 1); and at the base of the TV Tower at Alexanderplatz. All are open daily. The website is comprehensive.

VISAS & IMMIGRATION

A passport valid for 3mths beyond the length of stay is all that is required for UK, EU, US, Canadian and Australian citizens for a stay in Germany of up to 3mths. Citizens of EU countries need only show their ID cards. Citizens of other countries should check with their local German embassy or consulate whether a visa is required well before they plan to travel.

For stays of longer than 3mths, you'll need a residence permit (*Aufenthaltserlaubnis*).

WEIGHTS & MEASURES

Germany uses the metric system for all weights and measures.

WORK

Citizens of the European Union are eligible to work in Berlin without a permit or visa, although a registered address is typically required. All other foreign nationals will require a Working Visa (sponsored by the employer), a Freelance Visa, or a Working Holiday Visa (*see above* Visas & immigration). Those on a Student Visa are allowed to work up to 20hrs per week. Under-the-table work, called *Schwarzarbeit*, is common in small cafés and for menial jobs, but is illegal.

Vocabulary

Pronunciation

• **z** pronounced 'ts'; **w** like English 'v'; **v** like English 'f'; **s** like English 'z', but softer; **r** like a throaty French 'r'; **a** as in father; **e** sometimes as in bed, sometimes as in day; **i** as in seek; **o** as in note; **u** as in loot; **ch** as in Scottish loch; **ä** combination of 'a' and 'e', like 'ai' in paid or like 'e' in set; **ö** combination of 'o' and 'e', as in French 'eu'; **ü** combination of 'u' and 'e', like true; **ai** like pie; **au** like house; **ie** like free; **ee** like hey; **ei** like fine; **eu** like coil.

Useful phrases

Greetings

• **hello/good day** guten Tag; **goodbye** auf Wiedersehen, (informal) tschüss; **good morning** guten Morgen; **good evening** guten Abend; **good night** gute Nacht.

Basic words & requests

• **yes** ja, (emphatic) jawohl; **no** nein, nee; **maybe** vielleicht; **please** bitte; **thank you** danke; **thank you very much** danke schön; **excuse me** entschuldigen Sie mich, bitte; **sorry!** Entschuldigung; **I'm sorry, I don't speak German** Entschuldigung, ich spreche kein Deutsch; **do you speak English?** sprechen Sie Englisch?; **can you please speak more slowly?** können Sie bitte langsamer sprechen?; **my name is...** ich heisse...; **I would like...** ich möchte...; **how much is...?** wie viel kostet...?; **please can I have the bill?** darf ich bitte die Rechnung haben?; **please can I have a receipt?** darf ich bitte eine Quittung haben?; **please can you call me a cab?** können Sie mir bitte ein Taxi rufen?; **open/closed** geöffnet/geschlossen; **with/without** mit/ohne; **cheap/expensive** billig/teuer; **big/small** gross/klein; **help!** Hilfe!

Directions

• **left** links; **right** rechts; **straight ahead** gerade aus; **corner** ecke; **far** weit; **near** nah; **street** die Strasse; **square** der Platz; **city map** der Stadtplan; **entrance/exit** Eingang/Ausgang; **how do I get to...?** wie komme ich nach...?; **how far is it to...?** wie weit ist es nach...?; **where is...?** wo ist...?

Travel

• **arrival/departure** Ankunft/Abfahrt; **airport** der Flughafen; **railway station** der Bahnhof; **ticket** die Fahrkarte, der Fahrschein; **airline ticket** die Flugkarte, der Flugschein; **passport** der Reisepass; **petrol** das Benzin; **lead-free** bleifrei; **traffic** der Verkehr; **underground metro** die U-Bahn; **overground metro** die S-Bahn.

Health & emergencies

• **I feel ill** ich bin krank; **doctor** der Arzt/die Ärztin; **dentist** der Zahnarzt/die Zahnärztin; **pharmacy** die Apotheke; **hospital** das Krankenhaus; **I need a doctor** ich brauche einen Arzt; **please call an ambulance** rufen Sie bitte einen Krankenwagen; **please call the police** rufen Sie bitte die Polizei.

Food & drink

Basics

• **breakfast** Frühstück; **lunch** Mittagessen; **dinner** Abendessen; **snack** Imbiss; **appetiser** Vorspeise; **main course** Hauptgericht; **dessert** Nachspeise; **fried, roasted** gebraten; **boiled** gekocht; **breaded, battered** paniert; **egg, eggs** Ei, Eier; **cheese** Käse; **noodles/pasta** Nudeln/Teigwaren; **sauce** Sosse.

Phrases

• **I'd like to reserve a table for... people** Ich möchte einen Tisch für... Personen reservieren; **I am a vegetarian** Ich bin Vegetarier; **The menu, please** Die Speisekarte, bitte; **We'd/I'd like to order** Wir möchten/Ich möchte bestellen; **The bill, please** Bezahlen, bitte.

Meat (Fleisch)

• **meatball** Boulette; **mince** Hackfleisch; **venison** Hirsch; **chicken** Hähnchen, Huhn, Hühnerfleisch; **rabbit** Kaninchen; **chop** Kotelett; **lamb** Lamm; **liver** Leber; **kidneys** Nieren; **turkey** Pute; **beef** Rindfleisch; **ham** Schinken; **pork** Schweinefleisch; **bacon** Speck; **sausage** Wurst.

Fish (Fisch)

• **eel** Aal; **perch** Barsch; **trout** Forelle; **prawns** Garnelen; **lobster** Hummer; **cod** Kabeljau; **carp** Karpfen; **crab or shrimp** Krabbe; **salmon** Lachs; **haddock** Schellfisch; **tuna** Thunfisch; **squid** Tintenfisch; **clams** Venusmuscheln.

Vegetables (Gemüse) & fruit (Obst)

• **pineapple** Ananas; **apple** Apfel; **pear** Birne; **cauliflower** Blumenkohl; **beans** Bohnen; **green beans** Brechbohnen; **mushrooms** Champignons, Pilze; **green peas** Erbsen; **strawberries** Erdbeeren; **cucumber** Gurke; **raspberries** Himbeeren; **potato** Kartoffel; **cherry** Kirsch; **garlic** Knoblauch; **cabbage** Kohl; **carrots** Möhren/Karotten; **peppers** Paprika; **chips** Pommes; **lettuce** Salat; **asparagus** Spargel; **onions** Zwiebeln.

Numbers

• **0** null; **1** eins; **2** zwei; **3** drei; **4** vier; **5** fünf; **6** sechs; **7** sieben; **8** acht; **9** neun; **10** zehn; **11** elf; **12** zwölf; **13** dreizehn; **14** vierzehn; **15** fünfzehn; **16** sechzehn; **17** siebzehn; **18** achtzehn; **19** neunzehn; **20** zwanzig; **21** einundzwanzig; **22** zweiundzwanzig; **30** dreissig; **40** vierzig; **50** fünfzig; **60** sechzig; **70** siebzig; **80** achtzig; **90** neunzig; **100** hundert; **101** hunderteins; **110** hundertzehn; **200** zweihundert; **201** zweihunderteins; **1,000** tausend; **2,000** zweitausend.

Days & times of day

• **Monday** Montag; **Tuesday** Dienstag; **Wednesday** Mittwoch; **Thursday** Donnerstag; **Friday** Freitag; **Saturday** Samstag, Sonnabend; **Sunday** Sonntag; **morning** Morgen; **noon** Mittag; **afternoon** Nachmittag; **evening** Abend; **night** Nacht; **today** Heute; **yesterday** Gestern; **tomorrow** Morgen.

Further Reading

BOOKS

Fiction

Baum, Vicki *Berlin Hotel* Written in 1944, this pulp thriller anticipates the horror of the collapsing Reich via the story of a German resistance fighter trapped in a hotel with a cast of Nazi bigwigs.

Deighton, Len *Berlin Game, Mexico Set, London Match* Epic espionage trilogy set against an accurate picture of 1980s Berlin.

Döblin, Alfred *Berlin-Alexanderplatz* Devastating expressionist portrait of the inter-war underworld.

Eckhart, Gabriele *Hitchhiking* Short stories viewing East Berlin through the eyes of street cleaners and a female construction worker.

Fallada, Hans *Every Man Dies Alone* Classic tale of a middle-aged couple in wartime Berlin who begin a campaign of resistance to the Third Reich.

Fergusson, Ben *The Spring of Kasper Meier* Post-World War II murder and blackmail that offers one answer to the question: what happened to all of Weimar's gay Berliners?

Harris, Robert *Fatherland* Alternative history and detective novel set in a 1964 Berlin as the Nazis might have built it.

Isherwood, Christopher *Mr Norris Changes Trains, Goodbye to Berlin* Isherwood's two Berlin novels, the basis of the movie Cabaret, offer a sharp picture of the city's slide into Nazism.

Johnson, Uwe *Two Views* Love story across the East–West divide, strong on the mood of Berlin in the late 1950s and early 1960s.

Kaminer, Wladimir *Russian Disco* Bestselling collection of short tales from the Russian émigré and DJ.

Kästner, Erich *Emil and the Detectives* Classic children's book, set mostly around Bahnhof Zoo and Nollendorfplatz.

Kerr, Philip *Berlin Noir* The Bernie Gunther trilogy, about a private detective in Nazi Berlin.

McEwan, Ian *The Innocent* A naive young Englishman is recruited into Cold War plotting with tragi-comic results.

Nabokov, Vladimir *The Gift* Written and set in 1920s Berlin, where an impoverished Russian émigré dreams of writing a book.

Porter, Henry *Brandenburg* Decent fall-of-the-Wall spy thriller, even if the author does get some of the street names wrong.

Regener, Sven *Berlin Blues* Irresponsibility and childhood's end in the bars of late 1980s Kreuzberg.

Vermes, Timur *Look Who's Back* Adolf Hitler wakes up one morning in a patch of Berlin wasteland, the site of the former Führerbunker, to find it's 2011 and life is very different.

Biography & memoir

Anonymous *A Woman in Berlin* Extraordinary diary of a woman fighting to survive at the end of World War II.

Braun, Stuart *City of Exiles* Counter-cultural biography of the rebels, anarchists and free-thinkers who are the source of the city's infamous Berlin Luft.

Funder, Anna *Stasiland* Brutal stories of individuals and the East German state, retold through the author's conversations with friends.

Newton, Helmut *Autobiography* Begins with an absorbing account of growing up Jewish in Weimar Berlin.

Parker, Peter *Isherwood* Vast biography includes a well-researched section on the author's Berlin trouble.

Rimmer, Dave *Once Upon a Time in the East* The collapse of communism seen stoned and from street level.

Schirer, William L *Berlin Diaries* Foreign correspondent in Berlin 1931-41 bears appalled witness to Europe's plunge into Armageddon.

History

Beevor, Antony *Berlin: The Downfall 1945* Bestselling narrative history of the Third Reich's final, desperate collapse.

Friedrich, Otto *Before the Deluge* Vivid portrait of 1920s Berlin, based on interviews with those who survived what followed.

Garton Ash, Timothy *We the People* Instant history of the 1989 revolutions by on-the-spot academic.

Kellerhoff, Sven Felix *The Führer Bunker* The bare facts about Hitler's last refuge and what became of it.

Ladd, Brian *The Ghosts of Berlin: Confronting German History in the Urban Landscape* Erudite and insightful look into the relationship between architecture, urbanism and Berlin's violent political history.

Lawes, James *The Shortest History of Germany* Two millennia of history, brilliantly condensed and radically reinterpreted.

Levenson, Thomas *Einstein in Berlin* Absorbing tale of the historical deal between physicist and city.

Maclean, Rory *Berlin: Imagine a City* A rich history of lives lived in Berlin, real and imagined, from Konrad von Cölln in 1649 to Knut the late, lamented polar bear.

Metzger, Rainer *Berlin in the '20s* A wonderful pictorial record of Berlin's most creative era.

Richie, Alexandra *Faust's Metropolis* The best one-volume history of Berlin.

Taylor, Frederick *The Berlin Wall* Now the definitive history of the notorious border.

BLOGS AND WEBSITES

www.alt-berlin.info Archive of searchable historic Berlin maps, from 1738 to 1989.

www.berlin.de Berlin's official site – run by the tourist board (BTM) – is, inevitably, not its most objective but is nonetheless well written.

www.berlinforallthefamily.com Family-friendly guide to the city aimed at long-stayers but with a helpful activities section.

www.bvg.de Timetable and public transport information for Berlin/Brandenburg, in English/German.

www.dict.leo.org Simply the best English-German online dictionary.

www.iheartberlin.de Berlin's longest running English language blog, an eclectic mix of events listing, restaurant reviews, fashion tips, opinion, party news and more.

www.ostberlin.de Everything you wanted to know about life in the former East Berlin.

www.smb.museum Bilingual site with detailed information on around 20 major Berlin museums.

www.stilinberlin.com Hugely popular food and shopping tips from a Berlin insider.

www.timeout.com/berlin General information and history, plus shop, restaurant, café, bar and hotel reviews, written by residents.

www.tip-berlin.de Zitty's competition (*see below*), with similar functions.

www.exberliner.com Online listings magazine in German only.

www.zitty.de Online listings magazine in German only.

Picture credits

Pages 2 (top), 29, 51, 139, 238 Pascal Feucher/Urban Spree; 2 (bottom), 71, 188 Patryk Kosmider/Shutterstock.com; 3 Alfred Sonsalla/Shutterstock.com; 5 Svetlana Turchenick/Shutterstock.com; 7 katjen/Shutterstock.com; 11 (top), 29 (bottom) S.Borisov/Shutterstock.com; 11 (bottom) Ugis Riba/Shutterstock.com; 12 (top) umut rosa/Shutterstock.com; 12 (bottom), 22 (middle), 105, 135, 237, 258 canadastock/Shutterstock.com; 13 (top) Jule_Berlin/Shutterstock.com; 13 (bottom) pisaphotography/Shutterstock.com; 14 (top), 147 Mauermuseum-Museum Haus am Checkpoint Charlie, Berlin; 14 (middle), 26 (top), 26 (bottom), 28 (top), 37, 42 (bottom), 150, 156 hanohiki/Shutterstock.com; 14 (bottom) © Gedenkstätte Berlin-Hohenschönhausen/Gvoon; 15 (top), 18 (bottom), 25 (top), 31, 54 (top left & right), 55, 57 (bottom), 70, 170, 240, 277 Sophie Blacksell Jones; 15 (bottom) vasi2/Shutterstock.com; 16 (top), 54 (top right) Derek Hudson/The KaDeWe Group; 16 (bottom) Denis Makarenko/Shutterstock.com; 17 (top) Stefan Maria Rother/Stern und Kreisschiffahrt GmbH; 17 (bottom) Geist im Glas; 18 (top) Brian S/Shutterstock.com; 18 (bottom), 35 Cineberg/Shutterstock.com; 20 Ewa Studio/Shutterstock.com; 21 (top) mato/Shutterstock.com; 21 (bottom) Katja Oortman/Lode & Stijn; 22 (top) Silo Coffee Berlin; 22 (bottom), 24 (bottom), 25 (middle), 146 Jo Woolf; 23 (top) fretschi/Shutterstock.com; 23 (middle & bottom) Iko Freese/drama-berlin.de; 24 (top), 115, 284 elxeneize/Shutterstock.com; 25 (bottom) Matthew Dixon/ Shutterstock.com; 27 (top) DARRAY/Shutterstock.com; 27 (middle), 79 © Carola Radke/Museum für Naturkunde Berlin; 27 (bottom) Thomas Rosenthal/Museum für Naturkunde Berlin; 28 (bottom) Frank Middendorf/Shutterstock.com; 29 (top) Elena Krivorotova/Shutterstock.com; 32 (top), 283 360b/Shutterstock.com; 32 (middle) hinterhof/Shutterstock. com; 32 (bottom) 4kclips/Shutterstock.com; 33 Holger Boehm/Shutterstock.com; 34 Christian Heinz/Shutterstock.com; 36 Sergey Kohl/Shutterstock.com; 39, 44, 158 Markthalle Neun; 40 Katz Orange; 41, 294 Courtesy of SO/ Berlin Das Stue; 42 (left) Robert Rieger/Einstein Unter den Linden; 42 (right) Christin Ludwig/Brammibal's Donuts; 43 gkrphoto/ Shutterstock.com; 45 (top) Jules Villbrandt/Benedict; 45 (bottom), 192, 296 Markus Braumann/Benedict; 46, 93 Katy Otto, Courtesy of Princess Cheesecake; 47, 121 Courtesy of Bonanza Roastery; 49 Courtesy of Becketts Kopf; 52 Voo Store; 53 Courtesy of Aura; 54 (bottom) The Fish and the Knife/The KaDeWe Group; 160 Courtesy of Modern Graphics; 56 © mfe Event Coach; 57 (top), 124 (top) FDR Stock/Shutterstock.com; 59 butterflycreationfoto/Shutterstock.com; 61 Matej Kastelic/Shutterstock.com; 65 Armin Staudt/Shutterstock.com; 67 Vitaly Goncharov/Shutterstock.com; 73 tonisalado/ Shutterstock.com; 75, 104, 286, 289, 291 Claudio Divizia/Shutterstock.com; 82, 86 Kiev.Victor/Shutterstock.com; 85 Ralf Gosch/Shutterstock.com; 89 schillermedien/Shutterstock.com; 90 Courtesy of The Corner Berlin; 91 The Circus Hotel; 94 sandraschuk.de; 95 RossHelen/Shutterstock.com; 96 © schmott; 99 ItzaVU/Shutterstock.com; 102, 279 monuierd/ Shutterstock.com; 103, 285 Marila Golovianko/Shutterstock.com; 106 BigRoloImages/Shutterstock.com; 111 Kraft_Stoff/ Shutterstock.com; 113 Vabali Spa Berlin; 118 Sergey Kelin/Shutterstock.com; 120 christianthiel.net/Shutterstock. com; 123 thegoodsamaritan/Shutterstock.com; 124 (middle) elbud/Shutterstock.com; 124 (bottom), 173 katatonia82/ Shutterstock.com; 126 In Green/Shutterstock.com; 127 illpaxphotomatic/Shutterstock.com; 128 philmythen/Shutterstock. com; 131 tichr/Shutterstock.com; 134 Pavel Sepi/Shutterstock.com; 136 Semmick Photo/Shutterstock.com; 138 Nicky Walsh/Big Brobot; 140 Matyas Rehak/Shutterstock.com; 141 Stasimuseum/ASTAK e.V – Photo: John Steer; 143, 175 Anticiclo/Shutterstock.com; 149 (top) J2R/shutterstock.com; 149 (bottom) WorldWide/Shutterstock.com; 152 Simone Hawlisch; 153 Nathan Wright/Another Country; 161 Markus Nass/Arena Berlin; 162 MarinaDa/Shutterstock.com; 165 Uli Herrmann/Wikicommons; 168 Courtesy of Ankerklause; 177 Renata Sedmakova/Shutterstock.com; 182 Monique Wuestenhagen/Story of Berlin; 184 Franz Brueck/Bikini Berlin; 186 Stern und Kreisschiffahrt GmbH; 190 Zoltan Tarlacz/ Shutterstock.com; 195 Weerayoot Yotasing/Shutterstock.com; 196 (top) Tobias Arhelger/Shutterstock.com; 196 (bottom), 199 (bottom) LaMiaFotografia/Shutterstock.com; 198 Jannis Tobias Werner/Shutterstock.com; 199 (top) ebenart/ Shutterstock.com; 202 aldorado/Shutterstock.com; 207 np/Shutterstock.com; 208 vasi2/Shutterstock.com; 208 Sonja Hornung Photograpy; 211 Nicole Kwiatkowski/Shutterstock.com; 212 Lotse/Wikicommons; 214 Wikicommons; 215 ilolab/ Shutterstock.com; 217 Michael von Aichberger/Shutterstock.com; 218 Wikicommons; 219 Denis Makarenko/Shutterstock. com; 225 Cineberg/Shutterstock.com; 226 Montecrux Foto/www.flickr.com/Wikicommons; 228 abackpacker/ Shutterstock.com; 230 Evdoha_spb/Shutterstock.com; 232 Belin Bruisers; 244 Von Dirk Ingo Franke/Wikicommons; 249 Yan Revazov/Staatsballett Berlin; 250 Robert-Recker.de/Komisches Oper; 252 posztos/Shutterstock.com; 254 Fernando Marcos/Staatsballett Berlin; 256 Rodrigo Di Sciasico/English Theatre Berlin; 257 Kathrin Heller/Bar jeder Vernunft; 261, 268 Roger Viollet/Getty Images; 262 Everett - Art/Shutterstock.com; 266, 269, 270, 272, 273 Everett Historical/ Shutterstock.com; 274 Popperfoto/Getty Images; 281 ansharphoto/Shutterstock.com; 288 Sur/Shutterstock.com; 290 Nessa Gnatoush/Shutterstock.com; 293 Electric Egg/Shutterstock.com; 298 NH Hoteles Deutschland.

Index

8MM 241
25hours Hotel Bikini Berlin 299
48 Stunden Neukölln 213
893 Ryotei 182
1900 Café Bistro 182
2006 FIFA World Cup 279
://about blank 242

A

Abgeordnetenhaus von Berlin 146
Abspannwerk 286
accident & emergency 305
Accommodation 294–301
Acne Studios 95
Acud 239
addresses 305
Adlon Kempinski Berlin 284, 298
Admiralspalast 76
age restrictions 305
AIDS/HIV 307
Airbnb 36, 297
airports 34, 302
Ajpnia 235
Akademie der Künste 253, 291
Alaska Bar 233
Alexander Levy 148
Alexanderplatz 84, 86, 287
Alexandrowka 206
Alfilm 218
Alimentari e Vini 159
Alliierten Museum 203
Almodovar Hotel 300
Alte Bibliothek 284
Alte Nationalgalerie 74, 77, 285
Alternative für Deutschland (AfD) 279
Altes Europa 94
Altes Museum 74, 77, 284
Altes Rathaus 205
Altes Stadthaus 285
A Magica 119
Am Fischtal 287
Ampelmännchen 95
Ampelmann Shop 95
Andreas Murkudis 112
Anhalter Bahnhof 285
Ankerklause 166
Anna Blume 119
Anne Frank Zentrum 85, 87
Another Country 152
Anti-Kriegs-Museum 125
Antiquariat Thomas Mertens 193
apartments 297
AquaDom & Sea Life 87
Architecture 280–291
Arirang 183
Arkaden mall 53, 290
Arkonaplatz Flohmarkt 95
Arminiusmarkthalle 113, 285
Aroma 183
Arsenal 220
Art Nouveau Berlin 299
Art'otel Berlin Mitte 300
Asian Film Festival Berlin 220
Astor Film Lounge 220
Astra Kulturhaus 243
ATMs 309
Aufenthaltserlaubnis 311
Aura 171
Ausland 241

Austria Das Original 151
Auswärtiges Amt 290
autumn 29
Axel Springer Campus 291
Azzam 166

B

Baader-Meinhof Gang 276
Babel 119
Babelsberg 204, 207
Babylon 220
Babylon Kreuzberg 221
Backstoltz 207
Badeschiff 161
Baerck 55
Bahnhof Zoo 180
Balikci Ergün 104
Ballhaus Naunynstrasse 255
Ballhaus Ost 255
Band des Bundes 291
banks & currency exchanges 309
Bar 3 94
Barbiche 234
Barbie Deinhoff's 231
Barcomi's 90
Bar jeder Vernunft 257
The Barn 120
Bar Raval 154
bars & pubs 48
  Alexanderplatz & the Scheunenviertel 94
  Bahnhof Zoo & the Ku'damm 184
  East Kreuzberg 158
  Friedrichshain 137
  Köpenick & Around 163
  Kreuzkölln 170
  Moabit 113
  Potsdamer Platz & South of the Tiergarten 111
  Prenzlauer Berg 122
  Schillerkiez & Rixdorf 174
  Schöneberg 193
  South-west Kreuzberg 152
  Unter den Linden & Around 83
  Wedding & Gesundbrunnen 129
  Wilmersdorf 189
Basalt Bar 129
Battle of Berlin 272
Bauhaus 270
Bauhaus Archiv – Museum für Gestaltung 107
Bear City Roller Derby 232
Bearpit Karaoke 124
Bebelplatz 72
Becketts Kopf 122
beer 47
Begine 234
Bei Schlawinchen 158
Benedict 189
Berghain 17, 134, 243
Berlin Airlift 274
Berlinale 16, 218
Berlin Art Week 214
Berlin Brandenburg Willy Brandt Airport 34, 302
Berlin Bruisers 232
Berlin Burger International 168
Berlin CityTourCard 64
Berliner Architektur 289
Berliner Burgerbräu 163
Berliner Dom 77, 253

Berliner Ensemble 255
Berliner Festspiele 254
Berliner Kindl 286
Berliner Märchentage 215
Berliner Philharmoniker 252
Berliner Teufelsberg 203
Berliner Unterwelten 283
Berlin Fashion Week 213
Berlin Hauptbahnhof 291, 302
Berlin Hi-Flyer 148
Berlin Indignation 262
Berlinische Galerie 148
Berlin Marathon 214
Berlin on Bike 65
Berlin Opera Chamber Orchestra 251
Berlin Pass 64
Berlin Philharmonie at the Waldbühne 213
Berlin Today 30–37
Berlin Wall 63, 125, 126, 135, 146, 147, 276, 277, 282, 287
Berlin WelcomeCard 64
Besenkammer 228
Betty F*** 228
B-Flat 240
Biergarten Freiheit Fünfzehn 163
Big Brobot 138
Bikini Berlin 53, 184
Biosphäre 205
Bismarck, Otto von 265
Bite Club 44
BKA Theater 257
Black Lodge 247
Black Style 229
BlainSouthern 112
Bleibtreu by Golden Tulip 300
Blockhaus Nikolskoe 202
blogs 314
boat trips 16, 186
Bode-Museum 78
Der Boiler 235
Bonanza 120
Bonbon Macherei 95
books 313
bookshops 55
Borchardt 81
Borsig, August 265
Böse Buben 235
Botanischer Garten & Botanisches Museum 203
Brammibal's Donuts 42
Brandenburg 204
Brandenburger Tor 11, 70, 71, 284
Brauhaus Spandau 200
breakdown services 304
Brecht, Bertolt 273
Brecht-Weigel-Gedenkstätte 78
Brick Expressionism 286
Briefmarken Weine 137
Brille 54 83
Bristol Berlin 299
British Embassy 291
Britzer Garten 175
BRLO Brauhaus 48
Bröhan-Museum 185
Brot & Butter 183
Brücke der Einheit 202
Brücke-Museum 203
brunch 17, 192

Bruno's 235
Bücherbogen 184
Buchhandlung Walther König 95
Buck and Breck 94
budget travel 24
Bundeskanzleramt 102, 291
bunkers 283
Burgermeister 154
Burgers & Hip Hop 46
buskers 245
bus travel 302, 304
Butcherei Lindinger 235
Butterhandlung 136
Buttons 242

C

cabaret 256
Café am Neuen See 106
Café Aroma 191
Café Berio 234
Café Brick 168
Café Cralle 230
Café Einstein 110
Café Fleury 90
Café Heider 207
Café Melitta Sundström 231
Café Nö! 81
Café Pförtner 127
Café Rix 172
Café Schönbrunn 136
Café Seidenfaden 228
Café Vux 172
cake 47
Il Casolare 154
CDL-Club 235
Chalet 244
Chamäleon 256
Chapel Bar 137
Charité Universitätsmedizin 305
Charlottenburg & Schöneberg 176–193
Checkpoint Charlie 146, 282
Chert Lüdde 154
Chesters 244
Chez Dang 169
Chicago-Williams 90
children 26
Chipperfield, David 290
Christmas markets 215
Christopher Street Day Parade 213
Chutnify 46
Cinco 110
cinemas 220
CineStar IMAX Sony Center 221
The Circus Hostel 301
Circus Hotel 301
City Chicken 169
Civilist 96
Clärchen's Ballhaus 239
classical music 250
ClassicCard 251
Classic Open Air 213
climate 305
Club Culture Houze 233
Club der Visionaere 244
clubs & late-night bars 229, 230, 232, 233, 235, 239, 241, 244, 247
C/O Berlin Amerika Haus 181
CockTail D'Amore 233

cocktails 48, 49
CôCö 91
Cocolo 154
Coda 168
coffee 47
Cold War 274
Cölln 260, 282
Colosseum 221
Columbiahalle 240
Commonground 91
Computerspiele Museum 136
Congress Hall 288
Connection Garage 235
Corbusierhaus 196, 288
Cordobar 94
The Corner Berlin 83
craft beer 48
credit & debit cards 309
CSA 138
cuisine. See food
Curry 36 151
Currywurst 43
Curtain Club 111
customs 305
cycling 18, 65
Czech Embassy 288

D
DAAD Galerie 154
Dahlem 201
Daimler 290
Daimler Contemporary 108
Dalí – Die Ausstellung 108
Daluma 42
dance 253
DasHotel Bar 158
DDR Museum 88
Debis headquarters 290
Deep Neukölln 175
Delphi Filmpalast am Zoo 221
Denkmal für die ermordeten Juden Europas 13, 72, 73
Denkmal für die im Nationalsozialismus verfolgten Homosexuellen 72, 82
dentists 307
Deutsch-Amerikanisches Volksfest 214
Deutsche Bank KunstHalle 78
Deutsche Demokratische Republik (DDR) 274
Deutsche Oper 251
Deutscher Dom 78
Deutsches Currywurst Museum 147
Deutsches Historisches Museum 78, 290
Deutsches Kammerorchester Berlin 251
Deutsches Symphonie-Orchester Berlin 250
Deutsches Technikmuseum Berlin 147
Deutsches Theater 255
Deutschland Pokal-Endspiel 213
Deutsch-Russisches Museum 139
DG Bank 291
Dicke Wirtin 184
Diener Tattersall 184
Dietrich, Marlene 190
disabled travellers 305
discount cards 64
District Mot 91
dive bars 48
D.nik 122
doctors 307
Dollyrocker 138
Domäne Dahlem 203

Dong Xuan Center 141
Dormero Hotel Berlin Ku'damm 299
Double Eye 191
Down Under Berlin 218
do you read me?! 96
Doyum Grillhaus 155
drinking 38, 47
driving 304
Dr Pong 241
Dr To's 169
drugs 246, 306
DSTM 96
Dude 300
Duncker 241
Dussmann das KulturKaufhaus 83
Dutschke, Rudi 148

E
Easter Berlin 227
Eastern Comfort 301
East Side Gallery 15, 135
Eating & Drinking 38–49. See also bars & pubs, restaurants & cafés
Ebert and Weber 56
Eins44 169
Einsteinturm 207, 287
Einstein Unter den Linden 81
Electors of Brandenburg
  Friedrich II 262
  Friedrich III 263
  Friedrich of Hohenzollern 262
  Friedrich Wilhelm 'the Great' 262
  Joachim I Nestor 262
electricity 306
Ellington 299
embassies & consulates 306
emergency numbers 305
Enabling Act 271
Englischer Garten 104
English Theatre Berlin 255
Ensemble Mini 261
Ephraim-Palais 88, 282
Erich Hamann Bittere Schokoladen 189
Ernst 40
L'Escargot 128
Eschenbräu 129
etiquette 49, 305
Europa-Center 180
Europahaus 146
Events 210–215

F
Fahrradstation 65
families 26, 62
Fantasiakulisse 175
Fantasy Film Festival 218
Farbfernseher 245
farmers' market 97, 123, 129, 138, 193
fashion 53
F Bar 129
Fein & Ripp 123
Fernsehturm 88, 288
Festival of Lights 215
festivals. See Events
Fête du la Musique 213
FHXB Friedrichshain-Kreuzberg Museum 154
Ficken 3000 233
Figl 155
Film 216–223
film festivals 218
film Information 217
Filmmuseum Potsdam 205
Filmpark Babelsberg 207
Filmtheater Am Friedrichshain 221

Final Girls Film Festival 220
Final Solution 272
Fischerhütte am Schlachtensee 204
Fischfabrik 120
Five Elephant 156
Flax 229
flea markets 124, 129
Flohmarkt am Boxhagener Platz 138
Flughafen Schönefeld (SXF) 302
Flughafen Tegel (TXL) 302
Flughafen Tempelhof 287
Folsom Europe 227
food 38. See also Eating & Drinking
  fine dining 40
  German 41
  global 44
  shops 56
  street 40
  vegan/vegetarian 42
food blogs 40
The Forsberg 129
Frannz Club 241
Französischer Dom & Hugenottenmuseum 78
Fräulein Frost 169
Freddy Leck sein Waschsalon 113
Frederick the Great 206, 263
Freie Universität 288
French Embassy 291
Friedrichshagen 163
Friedrichshain 132, 287
Friedrichshain & Lichtenberg 130–141
Friedrichstadtpalast 257
Friedrichstadt-Passagen 289
Friedrichstrasse 76
Friedrichswerdersche Kirche 72, 284
Fritzclub im Postbahnhof 244
FSK 221
Fun Factory 96
Funkturm 196
Further Reading 313

G
Galander Kreuzberg 152
Galatea 170
Galerie Eigen Art 86
Galerie Guido W Baudach 112
Galeries Lafayette 83, 289
Gallery Weekend 212
Garage 193
Garcia Kaffeebar 113
Garden Boutique Hotel 299
Garde-Ulanen-Kaserne 206
Gärten der Welt Marzahn 141
Gaslaternen-Freilichtmuseum Berlin 104
Gastarbeiter 277
Gasthaus Lentz 188
Gaston Tapas bar 169
gay venues. See LGBT
Gay Wedding 230
Gedenkstätte Berliner Mauer 125, 282
Gedenkstätte Berlin-Hohenschönhausen 14, 140
Gedenkstätte Deutscher Widerstand 108
Gedenkstätte Haus der Wannsee-Konferenz 202, 203
Gedenkstätte Lindenstrasse 205

Geist im Glas 170
Gemäldegalerie 108, 288
Gendarmenmarkt 76, 282
GentleWomansClub 232
Georg-Kolbe-Museum 196
German Democratic Republic (GDR) 274
Germania 272, 287
Gesundbrunnen 125
Gethsemanekirche 119
Getting Around 302–304
Getting Started 60–65
Das Gift 170
Girlstown 232
Glass 183
Glienicke 202
GMF 229
Goebbels, Josef 269, 271
Golden Gate 239
Goldhahn & Sampson 123
Golgatha 151
Goodies 136
Göring, Hermann 270
Gorki Park 46
Graefekiez 153
Grand Hyatt 298
Green Door 193
Gretchen 245
Griessmuehle 247
Grill Royal 81
Gropiusstadt 288
Grosse Freiheit 114 230
Grosser Müggelsee 163
Gründerzeit 266, 282
Grunewald 201, 227
Grunewaldturm 201
Grüne Woche 215
Gruselkabinett 283
GSW 291
Gugelhof 120

H
Hackesche Höfe 85
Hackesche Höfe Kino 221
Hafen 234
Hako Ramen 136
Hallesches Haus 152
Hamburger Bahnhof – Museum für Gegenwart 112
Hamy Café-Foodstore 156
Hanf Museum 88
Hansaviertel 104, 288
Hard Wax 159
Harry Lehmann 188
Hasir 45
HAU 256
Haus am Checkpoint Charlie 14, 147
Haus der Brandenburgisch-Preussischen Geschichte 205
Haus der Kulturen der Welt 102
Haus des Lehrers 288
Haus des Rundfunks 196, 287
Haus Huth 107
Haus Liebermann 284
Haus Sommer 284
health 306
Heart of Gold Hostel Berlin 301
Heile Welt 234
helplines 307
Henne 156
Hess, Rudolf 200
Himmelreich 230
History 260–279
Hitler, Adolf 269, 270
Hohenzollerns 204
holidays 310
Holocaust Memorial 13, 72, 73
Holy Flat 42

Home Opera 250
Honecker, Erich 277
Hopfen & Malz 129
Hops & Barley 138
Horse Meat Disco 229
Horvath 156
hostels.
    See Accommodation
Hotel de Rome 298
Hotel Pension Funk 300
hotels. See Accommodation
House of Small Wonder 92
Hufeisensiedlung 175, 287
Hugos 110
Humboldt Forum 33, 79
Humboldthain 283
Humboldt-Universität 284
Humboldt, Wilhelm von 264
Hüttenpalast 301
Huxley's Neue Welt 247

I
ID 307
IG Metall 287
ILA Berlin Air Show 212
immigration 36
Imren Grill 169
Indian Embassy 290
inflation 269
Insel der Jugend 161
insurance 307
InterFilm Short Film Festival
    220
International Competition
    (Berlinale) 219
International Conference
    Centre 196
Internationale
    Bauausstellung 289
Internationales Berliner
    Bierfestival 214
Internationales
    Literaturfestival Berlin
    214
International Forum of
    Young Cinema 219
Irrenhouse by Nina Queer
    232
Ishin Mittelstrasse 81
Isla 174
ITB Berlin 212
Itineraries 20–29
Ixthys 191

J
Jan Bouman Haus 206
Japanese Embassy 290
Jaxx 235
JazzFest Berlin 215
Jews in Germany 272
John Muir 158
Jolesch 156
Joseph-Roth-Diele 111
Jüdischer Friedhof 118
Jüdisches Museum 15,
    149, 291
Junction Bar 246

K
KaDeWe 16, 54
Kado 159
KaffeeBar Jenseits des
    Kanals 157
Kaffee Burger & Old CCCP
    239
Kaffee und Kuchen 47
Kaisersaal Café 107
Kaisers of Germany
    Wilhelm I 266
    Wilhelm II 267
Kaiser-Wilhelm-Gedächtnis-
    Kirche 181
Kallasch & Moab Barprojekt
    113
Kammerorchester Berlin

251
Kapp, Wolfgang 269
Karl-Marx-Allee 134
Karl-Marx-Strasse Passage
    286
Karneval der Kulturen 213
Kater Blau 242
Käthe-Kollwitz-Museum
    182
Katz Orange 92
Kellerrestaurant im
    Brecht-Haus 41
Kennedy, John F. 276
K-Fetisch 169
Khrushchev, Nikita 275
Kid Creole 163
Kiez Oper 250
Kim Bar 94
Kin Dee 111
Kings of Prussia
    Friedrich I 263
    Friedrich II 206, 263
    Friedrich Wilhelm I 205,
        263
    Friedrich Wilhelm II 202,
        206, 264
    Friedrich Wilhelm III 202,
        206, 264
    Friedrich Wilhelm IV 265
    Wilhelm I 265, 266
Kino Central 221
Kino International 222, 288
Kirche am
    Hohenzollerndamm 286
Kirschblütenfest 212
KitKatClub 224, 240
Kleine Nachtrevue 257
Kleistpark 191
Klemms 154
Klunkerkranich 174
Kneipen 48
Knoblauchhaus 88
Kollwitzplatz 118
Kollwitzplatz Farmers'
    Market 123
Komische Oper 251
Konditorei Buchwald 106
Kongresshalle 288
König Gallery 146
Konnopke's Imbiss 120
Kontorhaus Mitte 289
Konzerthaus 251
Konzerthausorchester
    Berlin 251
Köpenick & around 163
Körnerpark 172
Kosmos 288
Krasselts 204
Krenz, Egon 277
Kreuzberg 142–160
**Kreuzberg & Treptow
    142–163**
Kreuzkölln 166
Kristallnacht 272
Kronprinzenpalais 284
Krumme Lanke 287
Ku'damm.
    See Kurfürstendamm
Kulturbrauerei 118, 241
Kumru Kuruyemis 160
Kunstgewerbemuseum 109
Künstlerkolonie Berlin 189
Kunst und Trödel Markt 112
Kurfürstendamm 181
KW Institute for
    Contemporary Art 86
KZ Sachsenhausen 128

L
Lab.oratory 230
Labyrinth Kindermuseum
    127
lakes 17, 198
Lakino 220
LaLa Berlin 96
Lange Nacht der Museen

214
language 307
language classes 310
Lavanderia Vecchia 174
Leathers 235
leather, sex & fetish venues
    229, 233, 235
Lebensmittel in Mitte 92
Lebensstern 111
left luggage 307
legal help 307
Legoland Discovery Centre
    109
Leipziger Platz 290
Lekkerurlaub 301
Lenné Dreieck 108
Leopoldplatz Flohmarkt
    129
lesbian venues. See LGBT
Lesbisch-Schwules Stadtfest
    213
LGBT 224–235, 307
libraries 308
Lichtenberg 139
Lido 246
Liebknecht, Karl 33, 267
Liquidrom 152
Lode & Stijn 157
Das Lokal 92
Lon Men's Noodle House
    183
Loophole Berlin 247
lost property 308
L-Tunes 232
Lucky Leek 42, 121
Lucky Trimmer 254
Ludwig-Erhard-Haus 291
Luftwaffenmuseum der
    Bundeswehr Berlin-Gatow
    200
Luise 204
Lunettes Brillenagentur 124
Lutter und Wegner 40
Lux 11 297
Luxemburg, Rosa 267

M
Mabuhay 46
Made in Berlin 96
MaerzMusik - Festival für
    Zeitfragen 212
Mama 170
Mandala 298
Manufactum 184
Marga Schoeller
    Bücherstube 185
Marheineke Markthalle 153
Marienkirche 87, 89, 282
Marietta 229
Marjellchen 183
markets 46, 56
Märkisches Museum 89
Märkisches Viertel 288
Markthalle Neun 160
Marmorpalais 206
Marques Bar 158
Martin-Gropius-Bau 148
Mauerpark 119
Mauerpark Flohmarkt 124
Maxim Gorki Theater 255
Max Und Moritz 157
May Day 212
media 308
Mein Haus am See 94
memorials 82
Merkel, Angela 278
Messe-und
    Ausstellungsgelände 196
Mexican Embassy 290
Michas Bahnhof 193
Michelberger 300
Mies van der Rohe Haus
    141
Mietskaserne 282

Milieuschutz 36
Miniloft Mitte 297
Missing House 85
Mitte 66–97
Moabit 112
Möbel-Olfe 231
Modern Graphics 160
Modulor 160
Mogg 92
Molecule Man 132
Monarch 245
money 309
Monster Ronson's Ichiban
    Karaoke 231, 242
MontRaw 121
Moritz Bar 129
Mo's King of Falafel 157
Motto 160
Moviemento 222
Mr B 235
Mrs Robinson's 121
Müggelsee 199
Müller, Michael 279
Museum Barberini 205
Museum Berggruen 187
Museum der Dinge 154
Museum Europäischer
    Kulturen 203
Museum für Film und
    Fernsehen 109, 182,
    218
Museum für Kommunikation
    80
Museum für Naturkunde 80
Museum in der
    Kulturbrauerei 119
museum passes 74
museums 63. See
    also sights & museums
Museumsdorf Düppel 204
Museumsinsel 74, 290
music
    classical 250
    live 240, 241, 243,
        246, 247
    techno 238
Musicaltheater 290
music tours 240
Musikfest Berlin 214
Musikinstrumentenmuseum
    109
Mustafa's Gemüse Kebap
    151
Mutschmanns 234
Mutzenbacher 136
Mykita 96

N
Napoleonic Wars 264
Nathanja & Heinrich 171
National Socialist Party 269
Naturschutzzentrum
    Ökowerk 201
Nazi Germany 271
neighbourhoods 62
Neni 183
Neptunbrunnen 87, 282
Neue Nationalgalerie 109,
    288
Neue Odessa Bar 241
Neuer Garten 206
Das Neue Schwarz 97
Neues Kranzler-Eck 181
Neues Museum 12, 74,
    75, 284
Neues Off 222
Neues Palais 206
Neues Ufer 234
Neue Synagoge 89, 285
Neue Wache 284
Neukölln 164–175
Neuköllner Oper 253
New Action 235
newspapers 308
Newton Bar 83

Nhow 300
Nightlife 236–247. *See also* LGBT
Night of the Long Knives 271
Nikolaikirche 90, 282
Nikolaikirche (Potsdam) 205
Nikolaikirche (Spandau) 200
Nikolaisaal Potsdam 253
Nikolaiviertel 282
Nil 137
Nobelhart & Schmutzig 150
Nola's am Weinberg 92
Nollendorfplatz 191
Nordic embassies 290
Nordic Embassies Canteen 111
Noto 92
Novoflot 250
Nowkoelln Flowmarkt 171
Nuremberg Laws 272

O
Oberbaumbrücke 132
Odeon 222
Oderquelle 121
Olivia 138
Olivio Pasta Bar 157
Olympiastadion 196, 197, 287
Olympic Games 271
Onkel Philipp's Spielzeugwerkstatt 124
Onkel-Toms-Hütte 287
Oona 97
opening hours 309
    shops 57
opera 250
Osmans Töchter 121
Ostalgie 62
Osteria No.1 151
Osterkonferenz 227
Other Nature 231
outdoor cinemas 221
Overkill 160
Oye Kreuzkölln 171

P
Palast der Republik 33, 282
Panorama 219
Panoramapunkt 110
Papen, Franz von 270
Paris Bar 183
Park Babelsberg 206
Parker Bowles 157
parking 304
Park Sanssouci 206
Passionskirche 246
Pasternak 121
Patrick Hellmann Schlosshotel 298
Paule's Metal Eck 242
Paul Knopf 153
Pauly Saal 40
La Pecora Nera 174
perestroika 277
Performing Arts 248–257
Pergamonmuseum 74, 80
Perle 229
Perspektive Deutsches Kino 219
Pfaueninsel 201, 202
pharmacies 307
Philharmonie 15, 252, 288
Picknweight Concept Store 153
Pizza a Pezzi 169
Playstixx 231
Plötzensee 114
police 309

Porn Film Festival Berlin 220
postal services 309
Potsdam 204
Potsdam Conference 206
Potsdamer Platz 106
Potsdam Museum 205
Prater Biergarten 18, 123
Prenzlauer Berg 118
Prenzlauer Berg & Mitte North 114–129
President Kennedy 191
price codes
    accommodation 294
    restaurants 41
Prince Charles 245
Princess Cheesecake 93
Prinz Eisenherz 235
Prinzessinnengarten 153
Prinzessinnenpalais 284
Prinzknecht 234
property prices 34
Pro QM 97
Prussia 263–266
public holidays 310
public transport 303
pubs 48. *See also* bars & pubs

Q
Quadripartite Agreement 276
Quälgeist 233
Quartier 205 289
Queerclimb 232
Queer Stories 232
Queer Summer Splash 232
Queer Zinefest 232

R
Radialsystem V 254
radio 308
Radisson Blu Hotel Berlin 299
Rathaus Charlottenburg 286
Rathaus Neukölln 286
Rathaus Schöneberg 191
R&Co Berlin 235
The Real Housewives of Neukölln 233
Red Army Faction 276
refugees 35
Reichsbank 287
Reichsluftfahrtministerium 287
Reichstag 10, 102, 105, 291
religion 310
Renger-Patzsch 193
Residenzstadt 282
Resources A-Z 305–321
Restaurant Bierbebau 42
Restaurant Neumann's 113
restaurants & cafés
    Alexanderplatz & the Scheunenviertel 90
    Bahnhof Zoo & the Ku'damm 182
    East Kreuzberg 154
    Friedrichshain 136
    Köpenick & Around 163
    Kreuzkölln 166
    Moabit 113
    North-west Kreuzberg 150
    Potsdam & Babelsberg 207
    Potsdamer Platz & South of the Tiergarten 110
    Prenzlauer Berg 119
    Schillerkiez & Rixdorf 172
    Schloss Charlottenburg & Around 188
    Schöneberg 191

South-west Berlin 204
South-west Kreuzberg 151
Spandau 200
The Tiergarten & the Reichstag 104
Treptow 161
Unter den Linden & around 81
Wedding & Gesundbrunnen 127
Wilmersdorf 189
retro-nova 113
Retrospective 219
reunification 277
Revolver 229
Richard 157
Ringsiedlung 287
Ritter Butzke 245
Ritz-Carlton 298
Rixdorf 172
Roadrunner's Paradise 241
Rogacki 188
Rollberg 222
Roses 231
Rosi's 242
Rotes Rathaus 87
RSVP 97
Rudolf-Virchow-Krankenhaus 285
Rum Trader 189
Rundfunk-Sinfonieorchester Berlin 250
Rundstück Warm 174

S
Sachlichkeit 285
Sachsenhausen concentration camp 271
safety & security 310
Le Saint Amour 170
Saint George's 124
Sale e Tabacchi 150
Salon zur Wilden Renate 242
Sameheads 247
Sammlung Boros 90, 283
Sammlung Hoffman 90
Sammlung Scharf-Gerstenberg 185, 187
Sankt-Hedwigs-Kathedrale 72, 80, 284
Santa Cantina 137
Sasaya 122
saunas 235
S-Bahn 303
S-Bahnhof Mexikoplatz 286
Schaubühne am Lehniner Platz 255
Schauspielhaus 284
Scheidemann, Philip 267
Scheinbar 257
Scheune 235
Scheunenviertel 84
Schillerkiez 172
Schinkel, Karl Friedrich 202, 284
Schinkel-Pavillon 80, 284
Schlachtensee 198
Schleicher, Kurt von 270
Schloss Babelsberg 207
Schlossbrücke 282
Schloss Cecilienhof 206
Schloss Charlottenburg 185, 187, 282
Schloss Charlottenhof 206
Schloss Glienicke 202
Schloss Köpenick 163
Schloss Sanssouci 206
Schneeweiss 137
Schokoladenfabrik 235
Schöneberg 190
Schöneberger Insel 190
Schröder, Gerhard 278
Schwarze Pumpe 122

Schwarzes Café 183
Schwarze Traube 158
Schwarzlicht Minigolf 159
Schwarzwaldstuben 93
Schwules Museum 110
SchwuZ 233
seasons 28
service 46
Shakespeare & Sons 139
Shikgoo 128
Shopping 50–57
shops & services
    Alexanderplatz & the Scheunenviertel 95
    Bahnhof Zoo & the Ku'damm 184
    East Kreuzberg 159
    Friedrichshain 138
    Kreuzkölln 171
    Lichtenberg 141
    Moabit 113
    Potsdamer Platz & South of the Tiergarten 112
    Prenzlauer Berg 122
    Schillerkiez & Rixdorf 175
    Schloss Charlottenburg & Around 188
    Schöneberg 193
    South-west Kreuzberg 152
    Treptow 163
    Wedding & Gesundbrunnen 129
    Wilmersdorf 189
Si An 122
Siedlung 286
Siegessäule 104
Siemensstadt 287
Siemens, Werner 265
sightseeing 60
sights & museums
    Alexanderplatz & the Scheunenviertel 87
    Bahnhof Zoo & the Ku'damm 181
    East Kreuzberg 154
    Friedrichshain 136
    Köpenick & Around 163
    Lichtenberg 139
    Moabit 112
    North-west Kreuzberg 148
    Potsdamer Platz & South of the Tiergarten 107
    Prenzlauer Berg 119
    Schloss Charlottenburg & Around 185
    South-west Berlin 203
    Spandau 200
    The Tiergarten & the Reichstag 104
    Unter Den Linden & Around 77
    Wedding & Gesundbrunnen 125
Westend 196
silent films 218
silent green Kulturquartier 125, 253
Silo Coffee 137
Silver Future 233
Silvester 215
Sing Blackbird 170
Sissi 193
Sisyphos 242
smoking 48, 310
snacks 43
SO36 246
Social Democratic Party (SPD) 267
Sofitel Berlin Gendarmenmarkt 298
Sofitel Berlin Kurfürstendamm 299
Soho House 299
Sonnenallee 166

Sony Center 107, 290
Sophienkirche 85
Sophiensaele 256
Soto 97
south-west Berlin 201
Soviet Memorial
    (Sowjetisches Ehrenmal
    am Treptower Park) 13,
    102, 162
Space Hall 153
Spandau 200
Spartacus League 267
Spätzle & Knödel 137
Speer, Albert 271, 287
Spielbank 290
Spreebogen 102
Spreepark 161
Staatsballett Berlin 253
Staatsbibliothek 288
Staatsoper 72, 284
Staatsoper Unter den
    Linden 252
Stadtbad Mitte 287
Stadtbad Neukölln 175
Stadtmauer 87
Stadtschloss 33, 74, 282
Stagger Lee 193
Stahlrohr 2.0 229
Stalinallee 288
Ständige Vertretung 83
Starstyling 55
Stasi (Ministerium für
    Staatssicherheit) 141
Stasi Museum 141
St Bart's 157
Steiff Galerie 185
St Hedwig Krankenhaus
    305
Stiftung Bertelsmann 290
Stilwerk 185
St Matthäus Kirche am
    Kulturforum 253
Stolpersteine 84
The Store Berlin 53
The Store Kitchen 93
Story of Berlin 182
Strandbad Plötzensee 199
Strandbad Wannsee 198
Strasse des 17 Juni 102,
    103
street art 109
street food 40
Stückemarkt 254
study 310
Das Stue 299
Südblock 231
Supamolly 244
Süss War Gestern 243
swimming 198
Synagoge Rykestrasse 118

T
Tacheles 84
Tadshikische Teestube 93
Tag der deutschen Einheit
    215
Tagesspiegel building 112

Tante Lisbeth 159
Tanz im August 214, 254
Tanztage 254
Tausend 83
tax 309
taxis 304
Teehaus im Englischen
    Garten 106
telephones 311
television 309
Tempelhof Airport 34
Tempelhofer Feld 14,
    34, 173
temperatures 306
Temporary Showroom 125
Teufelsberg 201, 287
Teufelsee 199
Thai Park 189
Theaterdiscounter 256
Theatertreffen Berlin 213
theatre 254
TheLiberate 228
Thirty Years War 262
Tian Fu II 189
Tianfuzius 42
tickets
    film festival 219
    public transport 303
Tier 171
Tiergarten 12, 102, 103
**Tiergarten & Moabit
    98–113**
Tierpark Berlin-
    Friedrichsfelde 141
time 311
Tim Raue 150
Tipi am Kanzleramt 257
tipping 49, 311
toilets 311
Tomasa Villa Kreuzberg 151
Tom's Bar 234
Top 20 10–19
Topographie des Terrors
    148
tourist information 311
tours 64
Trabi Museum 147
trains 302, 303
trams 304
Tränenpalast 81
Transmediale 215, 220
Transnational Queer
    Underground 232
transport 62, 302
    Charlottenburg &
        Schöneberg 180
    Friedrichshain &
        Lichtenberg 134
    Kreuzberg & Treptow 142
    Mitte 70
    Neukölln 168
    Potsdam 194, 204
    Prenzlauer Berg & Mitte
        North 118
    Tiergarten & Moabit 102
    West of the Centre 194
travel advice 305

The Tree 93
Treptow 142, 161
Treptower Park 161, 162
Tresor 240
Treuhandanstalt 277
Triebwerk 233
Trois Minutes sur Mer 93
Turbinenhalle 286
Türkischer Markt 171
Turkish culture 155
Twin Pigs 247

U
U-Bahn 303
Uber 36
Ulbricht, Walter 274
Ultraschall Berlin – Festival
    für Neue Musik 215
universities 310
Universum Cinema 287
Unter den Linden 70
Urban Spree Bookshop &
    Gallery 139

V
Vabali Spa 113
Vagabund Brauerei 48, 129
Les Valseuses 122
vegan & vegetarian
    restaurants 42
vehicle hire 304
Velodrom 291
Veronica Pohle 185
Versailles Treaty 269
Victoria Bar 111
viewpoints 60
Viktoriapark 151
Villa Neukölln 174, 220,
    231, 242, 246, 257
Vin Aqua Vin 171
Viniculture 185
Vintage Berlin 163
Vintage Galore 171
visas & immigration 311
visitor passes 64
Vivantes Klinikum Am Urban
    305
Vocabulary 312
Volksbühne 255
Volkspark Friedrichshain
    283
Volkspark Hasenheide 151
Volkspark Humboldthain
    127
Volt 42
Vöner 137
Voo Store 160

W
Waldhaus an der
    Havelchaussee 204
Wald Königsberger
    Marzipan 188
Waldorf Astoria 298
walking 304
walks 103, 126
Wannsee 201, 227

Watergate 245
weather 306
websites 314
Wedding 125
weekend itinerary 20
weights & measures 311
Weimar Republic 267
Weltrestaurant Markthalle
    158
Werkstatt der Kulturen 247
Westberlin 150
Westend 196
**West of the Centre
    194–207**
WG-Gesucht 297
Whisky & Cigars 97
White Crow Café 161
Wicked Wheels 65
Wild at Heart 247
Wilmersdorf 189
Winterfeldtplatz Market
    193
Wintergarten Varieté 257
Witty's 184
Wohnzimmerbar 122
Wood Wood 97
Woof 235
work 311
Worlds End 55
World War I 267
World War II 272
Wowereit, Klaus 278, 279
Würgeengel 159

X
Xenon 222
Xposed International Queer
    Film Festival 220

Y
YAAM 243
Yalta Agreement 273
Yam Yam 45
Yarok Berlin 94
Young.euro.classic 214

Z
Zeiss-Grossplanetarium
    119
Zentraler Omnibus Bahnhof
    (ZOB) 302
Zentrum für Kunst und
    Urbanistik 112
Zeughaus 282
Zeughaus Kino 222
Zionskirchplatz Farmers'
    Market 97
Zitadelle (Spandau) 200
Zola Pizza 158
zoo 141
Zoologischer Garten &
    Aquarium 110
Zoo Palast 222
Zum Schmutzigen Hobby
    230

Credits

Crimson credits
Text Anna Geary-Meyer, Victoria Gosling, Callie Payne
Layouts Emilie Crabb, Patrick Dawson
Cartography Gail Armstrong

Series Editor Sophie Blacksell Jones
Production Manager Kate Michell
Design Mytton Williams

Chairman David Lester
Managing Director Andy Riddle

Advertising Media Sales House
Marketing Lyndsey Mayhew
Sales Emma Datson

Authors
This edition of *Time Out Berlin* was researched and updated by Anna Geary-Meyer, Victoria Gosling and Callie Payne. Berlin Today was written by Tom Pugh (www.tompughwriter.com); History was written by Frederick Studemann and Tom Pugh; Architecture was written by Michael Lees, Helen Pidd and Tom Pugh.

Acknowledgements
Anna Geary-Meyer would like to thank Verena Spilker from Transnational Queer Underground and Leighton Cheal for their help with the LGBT chapter; Victoria Gosling would like to thank Leighton Cheal, Luke Lalor, Jenna Krumminga, Ulrike Kloss and Michelle Arrouas; Callie Payne would like to thank Kaila Sarah Hier for her help on the Berlinale box. Thanks and acknowledgements are also due to all contributors to previous editions of *Time Out Berlin*, whose work forms the basis for this guide.

Photography credits
Front cover mbbirdy/istock.com
Back cover left Sophie Blacksell Jones; centre left Sophie Blacksell Jones; right ©Markthalle Neun
Inside front cover hanohiki/Shutterstock.com
Pull out map left Santi Rodriguez/Shutterstock.com; centre Matthew Dixon/Shutterstock.com; right www.markopriske.de
Interior Photography credits, *see p314*.

Publishing information
Time Out Berlin City Guide 11th edition

November 2018

ISBN 978 1 780592 64 0
CIP DATA: A catalogue record for this book is available from the British Library

Published by Crimson Publishing
21d Charles Street, Bath, BA1 1HX (01225 584 950, www.crimsonpublishing.co.uk) on behalf of Time Out England.

Distributed by Grantham Book Services
Distributed in the US and Canada by Publishers Group West (1-510-809-3700)

Printed by Replika Press, India.